The Old Testament

The Old Testament
An Introduction to the Hebrew Bible

Stephen L. Harris

Robert L. Platzner

California State University, Sacramento

Boston   Burr Ridge, IL   Dubuque, IA   Madison, WI   New York
San Francisco   St. Louis   Bangkok   Bogotá   Caracas   Kuala Lumpur
Lisbon   London   Madrid   Mexico City   Milan   Montreal   New Delhi
Santiago   Seoul   Singapore   Sydney   Taipei   Toronto

McGraw-Hill Higher Education

A Division of The **McGraw-Hill** *Companies*

5 6 7 8 9 0 FGR/FGR 0 9 8 7 6 5

Library of Congress Cataloging-in-Publication Data

Harris, Stephen L.
   The Old Testament : an introduction to the Hebrew Bible / Stephen L. Harris, Robert L. Platzner.
      p. cm.
   Includes bibliographical references (p.) and index.
   ISBN 0-7674-0980-9
      1. Bible. O.T.—Introductions.   I. Platzner, Robert Leonard.   II. Title.

BS1140.3 .H37 2003
221.6′1—dc21   2002032647

Publisher, Ken King; *sponsoring editor,* Jon-David Hague; *production editor,* Holly Paulsen; *manuscript editor,* Tom Briggs; *design manager,* Sharon Spurlock; *art editor,* Emma Ghiselli; *text designer,* Detta Penna; *cover designer,* Joan Greenfield; *illustrator,* Joan Carol; *photo researcher,* Brian Pecko; *production supervisor,* Richard DeVitto. The text was set in 10/12 Adobe Caslon by G & S Typesetters and printed on acid-free 45# New Era Matte by Quebecor World, Fairfield.

Cover image: Megilla (Scroll of Esther). Illuminated parchment. Italian, 18th century. © Réunion des Musées Nationaux/Art Resource, NY.

Translations from the Bible are from New Revised Standard Version Bible, copyright 1989, Division of Christian Education of the National Council of the Churches of Christ in the United States of America. Used by permission. All rights reserved.

Text and photo credits appear on pages C-1 and C-2, which constitute a continuation of the copyright page.

www.mhhe.com

In memory of Ruby Harris and Dorothy Platzner

Preface

The Old Testament: An Introduction to the Hebrew Bible is designed for beginning students and provides all of the learning aids that these students routinely need and instructors routinely demand. Each book of the Hebrew Bible is discussed in some depth, with careful attention paid to questions of historical context, thematic organization, and literary form. Every effort has been made to expose students to current trends in biblical scholarship and to provide, whenever possible, an overview of major biblical concepts. Such topics as the theological evolution of the concept of God and the formation of biblical Israel are discussed at length and from a variety of perspectives. In addition, students are given an extended view of the apocryphal and pseudepigraphical literature that lies just outside of the historical boundaries of the Jewish canon, as well as a glimpse of those post-biblical forms of Judaism that emerge during the Greco-Roman era.

In discussing the Hebrew Bible — commonly referred to in Jewish tradition by the acronym *Tanak* — this text generally follows the order of the three-part canon that constitutes the basic format of Jewish scriptures: Torah (Pentateuch), Prophets, and Writings. This ancient subdivision of biblical books not only roughly corresponds to the historical pattern of composition but also reflects the theological hierarchy of ancient Judaism, which assigned primary importance to the body of sacred law found within the first five books. Students are also shown the differences in canonical order between the Christian Old Testament and the Hebrew Bible, as well as differences in content between Catholic, Orthodox, Protestant, and Jewish editions of the Bible. Furthermore, in presenting those historical and cultural developments in the ancient Near East that influence the history of biblical Israel, this text carefully traces the time lines of intersecting civilizations, offering an expanded historical perspective on events and personalities within biblical literature that are seen from a narrower, more ethnocentric, point of view.

To deepen the student's appreciation and understanding of the Hebrew Bible, a number of different pedagogical aids are provided in this text including maps, architectural diagrams, photographs of relevant historical sites and archaeological discoveries, informational boxes, chronologies, and charts. In addition, each chapter begins with a concise summary of "Key Topics/Themes" and concludes with review questions, topics for further discussion, key terms and concepts, and a brief list of recommended readings. Within each chapter, major terms and concepts are **boldfaced,** while related blocks of information are organized under topic headings that make the content of each reading more accessible to the first-time student. A general glossary is provided to facilitate the student's assimilation of unfamiliar terms and ideas, and a selected bibliography of valuable resource works is also included. In sum, this is a reader-friendly text that both invites and challenges the novice student to undertake a serious, focused, contextualized study of biblical literature within an academic setting.

Acknowledgments   Among those who have helped make this text a reality, we would particularly like to thank the following reviewers whose practical advice helped to shape and reshape this text from its beginnings:

S. Daniel Breslauer, University of Kansas

Camilla Burns, Loyola University of Chicago

Robert Cate, Oklahoma State University

Sister M. Felicity Dorsett, University of
   St. Francis

Rodney K. Duke, Appalachian State University

Carl D. Evans, University of South Carolina

Paul Flesher, University of Wyoming

Stan Harstine, Baylor University

John Phillips, Springfield College in Illinois

Allen Podet, Buffalo State College

Linda Schearing, Gonzaga University

John K. Simmons, Western Illinois University

We would also like to express our gratitude to publisher Ken King and sponsoring editor Jon-David Hague, as well as to Holly Paulsen, our production editor, and Tom Briggs, our manuscript editor.

Contents

PART II   THE BIBLICAL WORLD: CULTURE AND RELIGION   31

Chapter 3   *The Ancient Near East*
The Environment That Produced the Bible   *31*

Chapter 4   *The God of Israel*
An Evolving Portrait   *60*

Chapter 7

In the Beginning
The Book of Genesis   *106*

Chapter 8

Freedom and Responsibility
The Book of Exodus   *125*

Chapter 9

Regulating the Divine-Human Bond
The Books of Leviticus and Numbers   143

Chapter 10

A Mosaic Legacy
The Book of Deuteronomy   153

Chapter 18   The Assyrian Crisis

Isaiah of Jerusalem, Micah, Zephaniah, and Nahum   230

Chapter 19   The Babylonian Threat

The Books of Jeremiah, Habakkuk, and Obadiah   241

Boxes, Tables, and Illustrations

Illustrations

CHAPTER 1

The Hebrew Bible

A Composite Portrait of God and the Divine-Human Relationship

---

Key Topics/Themes The first section of the Christian Bible, the Old Testament, is a library of ancient Israel's sacred literature. Written in the Hebrew language (hence the name *Hebrew Bible*), it is commonly referred to in Hebrew as the *Tanak,* an acronym based on the first letter of each of its three major divisions: Torah (Law, or Divine Instruction); Nevi'im (Prophets); and Kethuvim (Writings). The three-part Tanak explores the relationship between God and Israel, his chosen people, with whom he concludes a series of covenants, including divine promises for a homeland and other blessings. Revealing himself to Moses as a God of liberation who rescues his enslaved people from Egypt, the Deity also manifests himself as a mysterious, even paradoxical, figure. A guiding presence in the books of the Torah, he becomes increasingly remote, even absent, in latter parts of the Tanak.

Sacred to two global religions, Judaism and Christianity, the Old Testament continues to shape the lives of more than 2 billion people, approximately one-third of the world's population. The composite portrayal of God it presents — Creator, Lawgiver, Warrior, Judge, and Savior — and the ethical standards it imposes on human behavior permeate almost every aspect of Western civilization. From assumptions about life's ultimate purpose to speculations about a future Day of Judgment and universal peace, most Westerners — even when unaware they are doing so — commonly express ideas articulated in the Old Testament. Compiled during a span of more than 1000 years, this collection of ancient Hebrew writings is not a single work but a multivolume anthology of law, poetry, prophecy, and historical narrative that reflects a great diversity of thought and religious experience.

The Old Testament and the Hebrew Bible

The Old Testament forms the first section of the Christian Bible, the second part of which is the New Testament, a collection of twenty-seven books that the early Christian community added to the older Jewish Scriptures. (**Scripture** refers to a body of writings that a religious group considers sacred and authoritative in determining the group's beliefs and practices.) Created by and for the Jewish community of faith, out of which the early Christian movement grew, the Old Testament is more accurately known as the **Hebrew Bible,** an anthology of sacred texts in the Hebrew language (with some later books written in a related tongue, **Aramaic**).

Although the Hebrew Bible, the official Scripture of Judaism, is commonly regarded as synonymous with the Old Testament, there are some significant differences between them. Most Protestant editions of the Old Testament contain the same books as the Hebrew Bible, albeit in a slightly different order. Catholic and Greek Orthodox versions, however, include about a dozen books or parts of books that early Jewish editors excluded from the Hebrew Bible. These additional books, known as the **Apocrypha,** were generally composed later than those in the Hebrew Scriptures and were incorporated in a Greek edition of the Hebrew Bible known as the **Septuagint.** (For a discussion of individual books of the Apocrypha, such as Tobit, Judith, and the Wisdom of Solomon, see Chapter 29.)

During the first centuries c.e.,* the Christian church adopted the Septuagint edition of the Hebrew Bible as its Scripture, calling it the Old Testament to distinguish it from the New Testament collection. After the Protestant Reformation in the sixteenth century c.e., Protestant Bibles typically relegated the apocryphal books to a separate unit between the Old and New Testaments. By the early nineteenth century, most Protestant Bibles deleted the Apocrypha altogether (Table 1.1). In some recent English Protestant translations, however, such as the Revised English Bible and the New Revised Standard Version (NRSV), the edition used in this text, the apocryphal writings have been restored.

---

*c.e. refers to the "common era," a religiously neutral term many scholars use instead of the traditional a.d. (*anno domini,* Latin for "in the year of the Lord"). b.c.e. means "before the common era" and corresponds to b.c., "before Christ."

THE THREE-PART HEBREW BIBLE (TANAK)

Most editions of the Old Testament, both Catholic and Protestant, divide the biblical documents into four major sections, grouping books together according to their literary category, regardless of their original function or date of composition. The four-part Christian Old Testament begins with the **Pentateuch** (a term meaning "five scrolls," the first five books of the Bible: Genesis, Exodus, Leviticus, Numbers, and Deuteronomy); continues with a long list of historical books, from Joshua to Ezra and Nehemiah (or to 1 and 2 Maccabees in Catholic bibles); is followed by works of Wisdom and poetry, such as Job, Proverbs, and Psalms; and concludes with anthologies of speeches ascribed to individual prophets, such as Isaiah, Jeremiah, Amos, and Malachi (the last book in both Protestant and Catholic editions). In contrast, the Jewish Bible, the Tanak, follows a three-part division — Torah (Law), Nevi'im (Prophets), and Kethuvim (Writings) — that more accurately reflects the chronological order in which the books were first written and subsequently added to the **canon,** the official list of documents that a religious community regards as authoritative and binding. The authors of this textbook believe that the most helpful and effective way to study the Hebrew Bible is to observe the traditional arrangement of its contents made by ancient Jewish editors.

THE TANAK

During the last centuries b.c.e. and first century c.e., Jewish scholars completed the long process of compiling and editing their sacred literature to form the present three-part Hebrew Bible. Taken as a whole, the Hebrew Bible's three major divisions form a complex exploration of God's ongoing relationship with **Israel,** the ancient Near Eastern people to whom he accorded a special revelation (Box 1.1). The first part, consisting of the five scrolls of the Pentateuch, is called the **Torah,** which means "teaching" or "instruction." Because **Moses** is the principal figure in four books of the Torah

Table 1.1   Order of Books in the Old Testament (Tanak)

Hebrew Bible (Masoretic Text)	Greek Septuagint Bible	Roman Catholic and Greek Orthodox Old Testament	Protestant Old Testament
I. Torah (Pentateuch)	*Pentateuch*	*Pentateuch*	*Pentateuch*
Genesis	Genesis	Genesis	Genesis
Exodus	Exodus	Exodus	Exodus
Leviticus	Leviticus	Leviticus	Leviticus
Numbers	Numbers	Numbers	Numbers
Deuteronomy	Deuteronomy	Deuteronomy	Deuteronomy
II. Nevi'im (Prophets)			
(Former Prophets)	*Historical Books*	*Historical Books*	*Historical Books*
Joshua	Joshua	Josue (Joshua)	Joshua
Judges	Judges	Judges	Judges
	Ruth	Ruth	Ruth
1–2 Samuel	1–2 Regnorum (1–2 Samuel)	1–2 Kings (1–2 Samuel)	1–2 Samuel
1–2 Kings	3–4 Regnorum (1–2 Kings)	3–4 Kings (1–2 Kings)	1–2 Kings
	1–2 Paralipomenon (1–2 Chronicles)	1–2 Paralipomenon (1–2 Chronicles)	1–2 Chronicles
	1 Esdras	1–2 Esdras (Ezra-Nehemiah)	Ezra Nehemiah
	2 Esdras (Ezra-Nehemiah)		
	Esther	Tobias (Tobit)*	Esther
	Judith	Judith*	
	Tobit	Esther (with additions)	
	1–4 Maccabees	1–2 Maccabees*	
	Poetry and Wisdom	*Poetry and Wisdom*	*Poetry and Wisdom*
	Psalms	Job	Job
	Odes	Psalms	Psalms
	Proverbs	Proverbs	Proverbs
	Ecclesiastes	Ecclesiastes	Ecclesiastes
	Song of Songs Job	Canticle of Canticles (Song of Songs)	Song of Songs
	Wisdom of Solomon	Wisdom of Solomon*	
	Sirach (Ecclesiasticus) Psalms of Solomon	Ecclesiasticus* (Wisdom of Jesus ben Sirach)	

(continued)

Table 1.1 *(continued)*

Hebrew Bible (Masoretic Text)	Greek Septuagint Bible	Roman Catholic and Greek Orthodox Old Testament	Protestant Old Testament
(Latter Prophets)	*Prophetic Books*	*Prophetic Books*	*Prophetic Books*
Isaiah		Isaias (Isaiah)	Isaiah
Jeremiah		Jeremias (Jeremiah)	Jeremiah
		Lamentations	Lamentations
		Baruch (including the epistle of Jeremias)*	
Ezekiel		Ezechiel (Ezekiel)	Ezekiel
		Daniel (with additions: Prayer of Azariah and Song of the Three Young Men,* Susanna,* Bel and the Dragon*)	Daniel
Book of the Twelve			
Hosea		Osee (Hosea)	Hosea
Amos		Joel	Joel
Micah		Amos	Amos
Joel		Abidas (Obadiah)	Obadiah
Obadiah		Jonas (Jonah)	Jonah
Jonah		Micheas (Micah)	Micah
Nahum		Nahum	Nahum
Habakkuk		Habucuc (Habakkuk)	Habakkuk
Zephaniah		Sophonias (Zephaniah)	Zephaniah
Haggai		Aggeus (Haggai)	Haggai
Zechariah		Zacharias (Zechariah)	Zechariah
Malachi		Malachias (Malachi)	Malachi
III. Kethuvim (Writings)	Isaiah		
Psalms	Jeremiah		
Job	Baruch		
Proverbs	Lamentations		
Ruth	Epistle of Jeremiah		
Song of Songs	Ezekiel		
Ecclesiastes	Susanna		
Lamentations	Daniel		
Esther	Bel and the Dragon		
Daniel			
Ezra-Nehemiah			
1–2 Chronicles			

*Not in Jewish or most Protestant Bibles; considered deuterocanonical in Catholic and Orthodox Old Testaments.

BOX 1.1
Multiple Meanings of the Name "Israel"

In the Hebrew Bible, the name *Israel* has several meanings. As used by many biblical writers, it denotes collectively the descendants of Jacob (whose name was changed to Israel), the people bound to YHWH (Yahweh) in a special covenant relationship. It also refers historically to three different but related political entities: (1) the twelve-tribe United Kingdom of Israel under kings Saul, David, and Solomon (c. 1020–922 B.C.E.); (2) the northern ten-tribe kingdom that formed after Solomon's death (922 B.C.E.) and that was destroyed by Assyria two centuries later (many biblical writers also refer to the northern kingdom as **Ephraim,** the name of its most important tribe); and (3) YHWH's covenant people generally,

even after Assyria's destruction of Israel in 722–721 B.C.E.

Following the northern tribes' secession from the United Kingdom in 922 B.C.E., the smaller southern state of **Judah** continued to be ruled by King David's successors and is commonly still alluded to figuratively as Israel, in the sense of being YHWH's covenant community—a practice observed in this text. Dominated successively by the empires of Babylon, Persia, Greece, and Rome, the inhabitants of Judah, or **Judeans,** eventually became known as **Jews,** a term that also included persons of Judean descent who were dispersed from the home country in the **Diaspora** (scattering abroad).

(Exodus–Deuteronomy), the person through whom God conveys his legal precepts and other instructions, the Torah is also known as the "Mosaic Law" or "Books of Moses" (see Chapter 5).

The Hebrew Bible's second part, the **Nevi'im** (Prophets), is divided into two subsections. The first consists of narratives relating Israel's historical experience, from its **conquest of Canaan,** the homeland God had promised to the Israelites, to its loss of that land when the Near Eastern empire of Babylon destroyed Israel's capital, **Jerusalem,** and took its ruling classes captive. Recounted in the books of Joshua, Judges, Samuel, and Kings, this narrative section covers the period from about 1250 B.C.E. to 587 B.C.E., the latter date marking a crucial turning point in Israel's history. (Figure 1.1 shows Israel's location between the ancient empires of Babylon and Egypt.) After the Babylonian destruction of Jerusalem and final overthrow of its kings in 587 B.C.E., the people of Israel never again enjoyed full political independence. (The single exception, a short-lived autonomy in the late second and early first centuries B.C.E., is discussed in Chapters 28 and 29.)

The second subsection of the Nevi'im is devoted to collections of **oracles** (pronouncements believed to be divinely inspired) of Israel's prophets. The prophetic books feature three "major" prophets— Isaiah, Jeremiah and Ezekiel—and twelve "minor" prophets including Amos, Hosea, Micah, Jonah, and Malachi. Most of the prophetic oracles relate to specific political crises in Israel's history, such as the threat from Assyria, an aggressive military power during the eighth and seventh centuries B.C.E., and the Babylonian invasion of the early sixth century B.C.E. (see Chapters 18–20). As arranged in the Hebrew Bible, the prophetic works immediately follow the historical narratives, illustrating the issues, such as Israel's breaking its pledge to worship God alone, that, according to many biblical authors, ultimately led to the nation's defeat by the empires of Assyria and Babylon.

The third division, the **Kethuvim** (Writings), contains the most diverse material, including volumes of poetry, such as Psalms, Song of Songs, and Lamentations; short stories, such as Ruth and Esther; historical narratives, such as Ezra and Nehemiah (which describe Jewish life after the people's

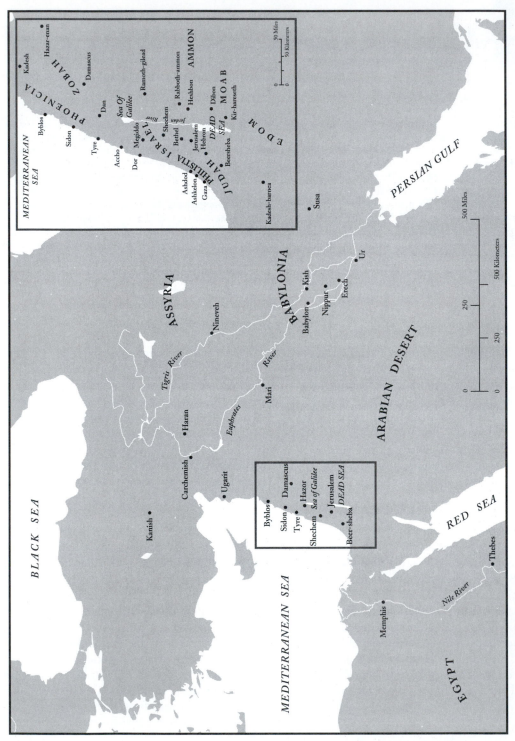

Figure 1.1 Map of Israel and the Ancient Near East Located between the major powers of Mesopotamia (Assyria and Babylon) and Egypt, the kingdom of Israel was repeatedly devastated by the military invasions of its stronger neighbors, events that loom large in the biblical narratives. The inset shows Israel as it appeared between about 921 and 721 B.C.E., when it was divided into the southern kingdom of Judah and the northern kingdom of Israel. The northern state of Israel ceased to exist when the Assyrians destroyed it in 721 B.C.E. The smaller state of Judah, with its capital at Jerusalem, however, was partly restored about fifty years after the Babylonians destroyed it in 587 B.C.E.

BOX 1.2
Tanak—The Three-Part Hebrew Bible

A comparatively recent term for the Jewish Scriptures, Tanak (also spelled Tanakh) is an acronym composed of the first letters of the three major divisions of the Hebrew Bible. Vowel sounds are inserted between the consonants.

T Torah (the five books of Mosaic instruction): Genesis, Exodus, Leviticus, Numbers, Deuteronomy

N Nevi'im (Prophets)

- The Former Prophets (Deuteronomistic History): Joshua, Judges, 1 and 2 Samuel, and 1 and 2 Kings
- The Latter Prophets (compiled in the prophets' names): Isaiah, Jeremiah, Ezekiel, and the Scroll of the Twelve (Hosea, Amos, Micah, Joel, etc.)

K Kethuvim (Writings)

- Psalms
- Job, Proverbs (Wisdom books)
- Festival scrolls: Ruth, Song of Songs, Ecclesiastes, Lamentations, Esther

- Daniel (an apocalypse)
- Ezra-Nehemiah, 1 and 2 Chronicles (historical narratives)

In the traditional arrangement of books in the Hebrew Bible, the Prophets are placed next to the historical narratives of Joshua through 2 Kings, juxtaposing the prophetic warnings about Israel's misconduct with the story of Israel's political rise and fall. Because 2 Kings ends with the overthrow of the Davidic dynasty and the people's exile to Babylon, it is appropriate to link historical events with the message of the prophets, the large majority of whom were active during or immediately after the period of the monarchy. The third section, the Kethuvim, contains works mostly composed after the exile, including reinterpretations of Israel's history, material focusing on the community's formal worship, and speculations about the nature of Wisdom and God's plans for the world.

return from Babylon) and 1 and 2 Chronicles (which repeat much of the material in 1 and 2 Kings); books of Wisdom, such as Proverbs, Job, and Ecclesiastes; and an **apocalypse,** the Book of Daniel (which contains visions of the rise and fall of Near Eastern empires and God's future triumph over the foreign powers oppressing Israel).

Whereas Christians commonly refer to the Hebrew Bible as the Old Testament (contrasting the Mosaic dispensation with that of Jesus in the Gospels), Jews refer to it as the **Tanak,** an acronym derived from the initial consonants of the Bible's three parts: Torah, Nevi'im, and Kethuvim (Box 1.2). In general, this textbook will follow the order of books in the Hebrew Bible (Tanak), discussing first the Pentateuch and then the historical books, the individual prophets, and the miscellaneous writings. We will also examine some of the later documents that

Jewish scholars did not accept into the Tanak but that were included in the Septuagint edition of the Jewish Scriptures. Widely used in the early Christian community, these works of the Apocrypha are regarded by the Catholic and Orthodox churches as composing a **deuterocanon**—belonging to a second or later canon—and incorporated among the historical, Wisdom, or poetic books in their editions of the Old Testament (see Table 1.1 and Chapter 29).

AN OVERVIEW OF THE TANAK'S STRUCTURE AND SOME UNIFYING THEMES

The Torah's Promises and Delayed Fulfillment
The general organization of the three-part Hebrew Bible (Tanak) reflects some important aspects of its meaning. Each major division of the Tanak,

as arranged by the editors responsible for its final contents, opens and/or closes with a statement about God's repeated promises to make Israel a mighty nation with a secure homeland. By examining what happens at the beginning and ending of each of the Tanak's three principal divisions, we begin to recognize the editorial perspective that largely controls its overall message. After a brief survey of human origins (Chs. 1–11), Genesis begins Israel's story with God's sudden appearance to **Abraham,** regarded as Israel's preeminent ancestor, unconditionally promising him many descendants, the divine presence, universal blessings, and the territory of Canaan, which Abraham's progeny will possess "forever" (Gen. 12:1–3; 15:1–21; 17:1–27; 22:15–18). The remainder of Genesis contains reiterations of the divine promises to **Isaac** and **Jacob** (respectively, Abraham's son and grandson), as well as descriptions of the obstacles that delay their fulfillment. Illustrating the theme of promises deferred, Genesis concludes with Jacob's twelve sons, progenitors of the twelve tribes of Israel, settled in Egypt, far from the land that God had vowed to give them (Gen. 49:1–50:26).

In Exodus, the second book of the Torah, God summons Moses to lead the Israelite tribes, now enslaved to Egypt's ruler, the pharaoh, out of bondage. After rescuing his people from pursuing Egyptian armies on the shores of a chaotic sea, God guides them to Mount **Sinai** (also called **Horeb** in some passages), where he delivers the Ten Commandments and approximately 600 additional statutes that the Israelites promise to obey. Much of the Torah, from Exodus 20 through all of Leviticus to Numbers 10, is a detailed enumeration of God's instructions, ethical and ritual, to Israel. Deuteronomy, the final Torah book, presents a revised version of the divine teaching in the form of three Mosaic speeches. It ends with the ancestral promises about to be realized: Abraham's descendants, the populous tribes of Israel, are poised to enter Canaan. Their leader, Moses, is permitted to glimpse the Promised Land from afar but is not allowed to share his people's inheritance (Deut. 34:1–8). That Moses dies before he can experience the realization of Israel's national hopes further emphasizes the pervasive theme of divine promise and deferred fulfillment that significantly shapes the Hebrew Bible's structure.

The Prophets: The Land Gained and Lost The second part of the Hebrew Bible—the Nevi'im (Prophets)—opens with a long prose narrative, the books of Joshua through 2 Kings, recounting Israel's historical rise and fall (c. 1250–562 B.C.E.). In the Book of Joshua, Moses' successor, Joshua, conducts a lightning-fast military conquest of Canaan, which gives Abraham's progeny (almost) full possession of that territory (Josh. 1:1–24:33). After Judges recounts the Israelite tribes' failure to unite against common enemies, the books of Samuel and 1 Kings describe the successful rise of Israel as a united people, culminating in the establishment of a powerful Israelite monarchy under King **David** and his son **Solomon** (1 Sam. 8:1 through 1 Kings 2:46). Echoing his pact with Abraham, whose descendants were to include a line of kings, God vows that David's royal heirs will rule over Israel "forever" (2 Sam. 7:11–17; but see 1 Kings 8:25–26 for a revised version of the divine oath). Israel's national story ends disastrously, however, with 2 Kings reporting Babylon's overthrow of the Davidic monarchy and destruction of Jerusalem, including the Temple where God had placed his "name" (2 Kings 24:1–25:30). Although the narrative concludes with a hopeful incident—a Davidic prince is released from a Babylonian prison in 562 B.C.E.—the monarchy that God had sworn to protect was never restored. The biblical story that had begun optimistically with the Deity's promises to Israel's ancestors thus ends tragically, with everything—land, nationhood, monarchy, and center of worship—utterly lost. As we shall see, the shock of this national trauma in 587 B.C.E. had a profound effect on Israel's view of its relationship with God, significantly influencing the way in which authors of the Hebrew Bible interpreted Israel's historical experience (see Chapters 19–23). Although many exiles eventually returned from Babylon to their homeland, this restoration was only partial, leaving postexilic writers to ponder the question of why their God no longer seemed to act on their behalf.

Whereas the historical books of the Nevi'im (Prophets) tell how Israel acquired Canaan and then lost it, the second portion of this Tanak division is an anthology of books named for various prophets, most of whom were active during the Davidic monarchy (c. 1000–587 B.C.E.). This subsection begins with the Book of Isaiah, a prophet who advised Davidic kings when invading Assyrian armies seized most of Israel's northern territory (eighth century B.C.E.). In the second prophetic book, Jeremiah advises Jerusalem's rulers as they faced imminent destruction by Babylon. The third book, Ezekiel, addresses the Israelite community exiled in Babylon and anticipates a national rebirth and reconciliation with God. These three collections of prophetic oracles, as well as the books of the minor prophets, are characterized by two overriding themes: warnings of divine judgment for violating God's commands, and promises of future blessings for obeying them. While threats of punishment for wrongdoing seem to dominate many prophets' messages, assurances of divine mercy and pledges of Israel's ultimate restoration help to balance the gloomier pronouncements. Although the prophets are primarily concerned with Israel's fate, they also include visions of a gloriously renewed creation benefiting all peoples, a "new heavens and a new earth" that bring universal peace and harmony (Isa. 65:17; cf. 2:2–4). The prophetic section closes with the brief oracles of Malachi, named for the messenger who cautions Israel to behave righteously, lest God afflict "the land" with yet another curse (Mal. 4:4–5). (For discussions of individual prophetic books, see Chapters 16–21.)

The Postexilic Readjustment The third great division of the Hebrew Bible, the Kethuvim (Writings), opens with the Book of Psalms, devotional poetry sung during services at the rebuilt Jerusalem Temple, the religious and geographical center of the Jewish community that had returned from exile in Babylon. Containing a great variety of literary genres, this collection includes historical narratives

(Ezra-Nehemiah and 1 and 2 Chronicles), passionate love poems (Song of Solomon), short stories (Ruth and Esther), apocalyptic visions (Daniel), and books of both practical and speculative Wisdom (Proverbs, Job, and Ecclesiastes). This section (and thus the entire Hebrew Bible) closes with 1 and 2 Chronicles, which retells the story of the Davidic monarchy from a postexilic perspective. By according 2 Chronicles the important end position — literally the last word of Israel's Scriptures — Jewish editors violated the chronological sequence of the historical narratives contained in this section; events narrated in Ezra and Nehemiah occur considerably *after* those reported in Chronicles. Whereas the Hebrew Bible begins in Genesis with God acting alone to create the universe, it concludes in 2 Chronicles with the actions of a human king, **Cyrus the Great,** emperor of Persia, who orders the rebuilding of the Jerusalem Temple and the return of Jewish exiles to their home territory, the land that God had long ago promised Abraham's descendants (2 Chron. 36:22–23).

Although events recounted in Chronicles are followed chronologically by those in Ezra and Nehemiah, which describe conditions under Cyrus's successors in the partly restored Jerusalem community, the Tanak's final editors chose to place Chronicles's statement highlighting Cyrus's invitation to all Jews to support God's worship in their homeland as the climactic summation of Israel's historical experience. (Cyrus's crucial role in Israel's history is indicated by his identification as God's "messiah" [anointed one] in the oracles of a prophet known as Second Isaiah [Isa. 45:1–4].) Cyrus's reestablishment of a worshiping community — the culmination of a narrative sequence that opened with the creation — is not accomplished by military aggression, as was Joshua's invasion of Canaan. Instead, Cyrus, who pursued a policy of encouraging local religions throughout his vast empire, uses his imperial might to reassemble Israel peacefully. Henceforth, human leaders, acting as God's instruments for historical change, become the guarantors of Israel's future possession of its homeland (see Chapters 22–27). (Box 1.3 contains a summary of some representative literary genres in the Hebrew Bible).

BOX 1.3
Some Representative Literary Genres in the Hebrew Bible

A library of ancient Israelite literature, the Hebrew Bible (Tanak) contains a remarkable variety of literary genres composed over a period of more than 1000 years. Scholars believe that ancient hymns celebrating Israel's military victories (late second millennium B.C.E.) are among the oldest documents incorporated into the biblical text; mystical visions of future history, such as those found in Daniel, are thought to be among the last written (c. 165 B.C.E.). Scholars disagree on the dates of composition for most of the examples given below.

GENRE	REPRESENTATIVE EXAMPLE
Battle/victory hymns	"Song of the Sea" (Exod. 15:1–18), "Song of Deborah" (Judg. 5:1–31)
Fable	"Jotham's Fable of Kingship" (Judg. 9:8–15)
Historical narrative	Prose epic of Israel's origins: from the call of Abraham to the Israelites' arrival at Mount Sinai/Horeb (Gen. 12:1–Exod. 19:25); from the formulation of the Mosaic Covenant to the forty-year wandering in the wilderness (Exod. 24:1–18; 32:1–34:35; Num. 10:11–26:4; 31:1–36:13); from the conquest of Canaan to the fall of Jerusalem to Babylon (Josh. 1:1–2; Kings 25:30).
Divine commands and statutes	The Ten Commandments (Exod. 20:1–17; Deut. 5:6–21); the Book of the Covenant (legal regulations) (Exod. 20:22–23:33); collections of divine decrees and ordinances (Exod. 35:1–40:33; Lev. 1:1–27:34; Num. 1:1–10:10; Deut. 4:44–30:20)
Genealogies	Tables of descent: from Adam to Noah (Gen. 5:1–32); from Noah to Abraham (Gen 10:1–32; 11:10–27); sons of Jacob (Israel) (Gen. 35:22–26; 46:8–27; cf. Exod. 1:1–5); from Adam to the family of Saul, first king of a united Israel (1 Chron. 1:1–9:35); list of returnees from the Babylonian exile (Ezra 2:1–63; Neh. 7:6–63)
Short stories	Prose tale of a Moabite ancestress of King David (Ruth 1:1–4:22); nationalistic tale of a heroic queen (Esther 1:1–10:3).
Wisdom books	Collection of practical advice (Prov. 1:1–31:31); poetic drama questioning divine justice (Job 1:1–42:8); skeptical meditations on life's futility (Eccles. 1:1–12:14)
Devotional poetry	Anthology of lyrics sung at Temple services, including songs of praise, bitter complaints, and appeals for help (Pss. 1:1–150:6).
Erotic poetry	Compilation of passionate lyrics celebrating physical love (Song of Songs 1:1–8:14)
Prophetic oracles	Collections of warnings and promises, commonly in poetry, by Israel's prophets (Isa. 1:1–66:24; Hos. 1:1–14:9; Mic. 1:1–7:20; Joel 1:1–3:21, etc.)
Apocalypse (a revelation or unveiling of the spirit world and/or future events)	Mystical visions, in highly symbolic language, of God's long-term plans for Israel and the world (Dan. 2:1–45; 7:1–12:13)

The God of the Hebrew Bible and His Troubled Relationship with Israel

The Hebrew Bible's diverse contents are at least partly unified by two overarching themes: a complex portrait of God, drawn from a variety of sources, and an equally complex account of God's partnership with Israel. According to Deuteronomy, God selected Israel "out of all the peoples on earth to be his people, his treasured possession" (Deut. 7:6; cf. Deut. 7:7–9; 10:14; 14:2). Although ancient Israel understood itself to enjoy a uniquely favored position in God's plan for humankind — and the means by which "all the families of the earth" will eventually "be blessed" (Gen. 12:3) — the Hebrew Bible depicts God's relationship with Israel as deeply conflicted. The same warrior God who invisibly accompanies the Israelites into battle and accords military victory (as in Josh. and 2 Sam.) will also turn on them with equal ferocity, inflicting defeat and humiliation when they prove disobedient. A champion of strict justice, Israel's God is as ready to punish his own people for misbehavior as he is their enemies. Although some passages portray God as "Lord of all the earth," as concerned about Egypt and other foreign nations as he is about Israel (cf. Isa. 19:19–24; Amos 9:7), most of the Hebrew Bible presents world events exclusively from Israel's perspective. To many readers, however, Israel's story serves as a template or paradigm of God's relationship with all people, a model of divine-human interaction in which a single righteous Deity guides humanity toward a renewed creation in which peace and justice prevail (cf. Isa. 2, 11, 40–45).

For some authors of the Hebrew Bible, God is not only ultimate reality but also the sole guarantor of meaning in human life. In depicting the almost infinitely varied ways in which God relates to the people of Israel, both individually and collectively, and the equally varied ways in which Israel responds to God, biblical writers produce a cumulative record of religious experience — from humble submission to the divine will to angry accusations of divine injustice — that encompasses a wide range of divine-human interaction. The prophet Hosea (eighth century B.C.E.) compares the God–Israel bond to that of a troubled marriage, in which a loving husband (God) suffers the pangs of unrequited love, grieved by his faithless wife (Israel), who prefers other partners (foreign gods) (Hos. 1–3). In another simile, the same prophet likens God to a devoted father abandoned by his beloved son (Hos. 11:1–12).

The Covenant: A Divine-Human Bond

Although the bonds between parent and child or husband and wife are commonly used to illustrate God's special relationship with Israel, in most of the Hebrew Bible, God's preferred means of establishing alliances is through a **covenant** (Hebrew, *berith*). A common sociopolitical concept in the ancient Near East, covenant means "agreement," "pact," "vow," "promise," "treaty," or even "contract." Covenants may consist of mutual agreements or pacts between individuals, formal treaties between political states, or divine promises made to benefit a favored party, such as God's vow to multiply Abraham's progeny. The first two parts of the Hebrew Bible (Torah and Nevi'im) are largely structured around four covenants concluded between God and selected partners or recipients, each named after the person for or through whom the covenant is negotiated — Noah (Gen. 9:1–17), Abraham (Gen. 12:1–3; 15:1–21; 17:1–27; 22:15–18), Moses (Exod. 34:1–32), and David (2 Sam. 7:11–17; 23:1–5). In each case, God voluntarily initiates the covenant arrangement and sets its terms, unilaterally imposing a binding relationship on the human participants.

Unlike the other three, which deal exclusively with Israel, God's first covenant — a mixture of ethical commands and ecological principles — is made with all humankind. Immediately after the great Flood, God categorically promises Noah that he will never again destroy (almost all) humanity (Gen. 8:21), at least by flooding or drowning them (Gen. 9:11–15), a vow he reminds himself to keep by following rainstorms with rainbows. In the **Noachan Covenant,** God encompasses all forms of life as equally sacred, emphasizing the interrelatedness of humans, animals, birds, and the earth itself. A bond "between God and every living creature," this covenant is universal and "everlasting" (Gen. 9:1–17)

In contrast to the universality of the pact with Noah, the **Abrahamic Covenant** embodies God's oath to a single individual and his descendants. Fundamental to Israel's understanding of its special relationship to God, the covenant with Abraham entails a series of promises in which God swears to fashion Abraham's progeny into a mighty nation, to create from them a line of kings, to give them the land of Canaan in perpetuity, and to cause "all nations of the earth [to] gain blessings for themselves" (cf. Gen. 12:1–3; 15:1–21; 17:1–27; and 22:15–18). Descended from Abraham's son Isaac and grandson Jacob, Israel saw itself as the heir of God's promises to this ancestor, whom Genesis portrays as a model of faith and obedience. Israel's possession of Canaan, its homeland, is thus viewed as a divine right, a unilateral land grant from the Deity.

Whereas the Abrahamic Covenant largely consists of divine promises made without specific conditions imposed on the covenant bearer, the covenant formulated through Moses at Mount Sinai/Horeb is explicitly *conditional* on the people's voluntary compliance with a large body of legal requirements. At Sinai, the Deity announces that he is a "jealous God" who will not share Israel's allegiance with any rival power; his first demand on the Israelites is that they must worship him exclusively (Exod. 20). The **Mosaic Covenant,** named for its human mediator, involves pledges from both God and Israel and makes clear that the people's future welfare depends entirely on their collective obedience. *If* the people keep their promise to obey all the approximately 600 laws and statutes promulgated at Sinai, *then* God will be their champion, fight their battles, give them material prosperity, and guarantee their permanent possession of Canaan.

Conversely, if the Israelites fail to honor God alone — rejecting all other deities — he will abandon them to their enemies. Thus, in describing the origin of Israel's relationship with God, the biblical authors establish the terms by which they will narrate and interpret Israel's later history. Israel's historical experience — its military victories and political success under leaders such as King David — result from adherence to Mosaic principles, just as its eventual fate — defeat by Babylon and loss of the promised homeland — are the consequences of its failure in covenant obedience. Editors of the long historical narrative that begins in Genesis and extends through 2 Kings (often called Israel's national epic) foreshadow Israel's tragic destiny by inserting dire warnings of the divine curses that will befall Israel for its disloyalty to God (see Lev. 26; Deut. 27–28; cf. 2 Kings 24). (For a more detailed discussion of the covenant concept, including the political model in which God acts as great king or *suzerain* and Israel as dependent vassal, see Chapter 8.)

The fourth and final major biblical covenant, the **Davidic Covenant** — God's unequivocal promise to keep royal heirs of King David on Israel's throne forever (2 Sam. 7:11–17; Ps. 89:19–37) — resembles the Abrahamic Covenant in being entirely unconditional. The contrast between God's unequivocal vows to Abraham for Israel's permanent possession of its land and to David for an "everlasting" dynasty, on the one hand, and the highly conditional nature of the Mosaic Covenant, on the other, generates considerable tension in the Hebrew Bible. When, as 2 Kings records, Israel's history culminated in national disaster, the destruction of its holy city and Temple, and the final overthrow of the Davidic kings, some biblical authors wrestled with the painful disparity between God's pledges and the historical reality of Israel's humiliation and suffering (Ps. 44, 89).

Diverse Portraits of God

The Hebrew Bible's portrayals of God — which profoundly influenced the concepts of divinity later depicted in the Christian New Testament and the Islamic Qur'an (Koran) — are extremely diverse. Authors of different biblical writings not only present God in a wide variety of roles and images, ranging from warrior and executioner to tender parent and gracious husband, but also show the Deity engaged in an astonishing array of paradoxical actions. God (in Hebrew, **El** [singular] or **Elohim** [plural]) first appears in the opening chapters of Genesis, where, by the power of his word alone, he creates the universe, transforming a dark, watery chaos into an orderly **cosmos** (harmonious system) in which life can flourish. A few chapters later, however, God is "sorry" that he created humanity and abruptly returns the world to its primordial state of turbulent sea, drowning the entire human race except for a single family. The tension between God's will to create and to destroy, to bless and to curse, established in the first eight chapters of Genesis, suggests his ambivalent relationship with humankind. Demanding that the rational creatures whom he fashioned as "images" and "likenesses" of himself offer total obedience, God manifests a distinctly humanlike disappointment and anger when humans fail to submit to his authority. Balanced against his righteous determination to punish disobedience, however, is the Deity's *hesed* (a Hebrew word meaning "steadfast love") toward those who honor him. Far from the emotionally aloof center of cosmic reason posited by some philosophers, the God of the Hebrew Bible is a multifaceted personality capable of strong passion, a being who loves and hates, who saves his favorites and exterminates his enemies. He eventually became known as the only God.

Moses' Encounter with YHWH, the God of Liberation

The character of Israel's God is largely established in the first two books of the Torah — Genesis and Exodus — where he appears to humans more frequently than in any other part of the Hebrew Bible. Known as a **theophany** (Greek, a "manifestation of God"), this series of divine appearances illustrates the Deity's close communication with humanity. Throughout Genesis, God holds conversations with almost every major figure, from Adam and Eve, the first human couple, to Abraham and members of

his extended family, including his wife (Sarah), concubine (Hagar), and daughter-in-law (Rebekah). In most of these divine-human encounters, God manifests himself to issue specific commands, punish disobedience, or formulate covenant promises. It is not until Exodus, however, that he explicitly discloses his personal identity and long-term goals. According to Exodus 3, God suddenly appears to Moses, at that time a refugee from Egypt living in the Sinai desert, and orders him to confront Egypt's ruler, Pharaoh, with an astounding message: Pharaoh must set his Israelite slaves free. In one of the most momentous encounters with God presented in the Hebrew Bible, Moses and the Deity—who speaks from a burning bush—engage in a long dialogue that expresses the dual themes of God's mysterious nature and his direct involvement in human lives (Exod. 3:1–4:23). He commands Moses to bring the Israelites from Egypt to Horeb, the "mountain of GOD," the desert peak on which their conversation takes place (the exact location of Sinai/Horeb is unknown). Like other deities in the ancient Near East, Israel's God was commonly associated with a sacred mountain, an earthly representation of the cosmic heights on which he invisibly dwelt.

REVELATION OF THE DIVINE NAME

When the voice emanating from fire first addresses Moses, he identifies himself as "the God of your father, the God of Abraham, the God of Isaac, and the God of Jacob," the chief ancestors of the Israelite tribes (Exod. 3:6). The Deity's reference to long-dead forebears elicits an immediate objection from Moses: Who is this God (*Elohim*)? (In Hebrew, *Elohim*, the plural form of *El*, is a generic term for divine beings and may apply to any number of ancient Near Eastern deities [see Chapter 4].) If the Israelites ask which deity promises to liberate them, they will demand to know "his name" (Exod. 3:13). God's reply constitutes one of the most important passages in the Hebrew Bible, a revelation (or subtle concealment) of God's personal name:

> I AM who I AM. . . . Thus you shall say to the Israelites, "I AM has sent me to you." . . . The

LORD [YHWH], the GOD of your ancestors, the GOD of Abraham, the GOD of Isaac, the GOD of Jacob has sent me to you: This is my name forever, and this my title for all generations. (Exod. 3:14–15)

Although most English translations blandly render the divine name as "the LORD," this practice obscures the essential significance of God's self-disclosure to Moses. In the ancient world, personal names had real meaning: When Israel's God confides his name to Moses, he simultaneously discloses much about his nature and purpose. Occurring almost 7000 times in the Hebrew Bible, the divine name is represented by four consonants, which are transliterated into English as **YHWH** and designated by the Greek term **Tetragrammaton** (literally, "four letters"). According to one widely accepted theory, the name YHWH derives from the Hebrew verb "to be" or "to cause to be" (create), as God explains to Moses when he states, "I AM who I AM" (or, in another rendering, "I Shall Be What I Shall Be"). God is here speaking in the first person; in the third-person singular, the phrase becomes "Yahweh" ("He Is"). The meaning of YHWH's name is thus closely tied to the Hebrew Bible's view of God as the Lord of history, the eternal Being who not only has long-range plans for his people but also takes decisive action to bring them into existence.

Composed in the Hebrew language (hence the name Hebrew Bible), the biblical text is written almost entirely in consonants; readers must supply the vowel sounds, including those of the divine name. Although we do not know exactly how the four consonants were pronounced, many scholars agree that YHWH may be vocalized as "Yahweh," as it is rendered in some modern translations, such as the Anchor Bible and the New Jerusalem Bible. Late in biblical history, reverence for God's name and anxiety about profaning it through unworthy usage prompted Jewish religious authorities to substitute **Adonai** (Hebrew, "Lord") when reading aloud passages containing the Tetragrammaton. Eventually, the name came to be pronounced publicly but once a year, by Israel's High Priest on the Day of Atonement. For centuries, Christian Bible translators followed the Jewish custom of substituting "Lord" or "God" wherever the divine name occurred. Most modern English editions, including the King James Bible (Authorized Version), the New Revised Standard Version, and the Revised English Bible, indicate the sacred name by printing GOD or LORD with initial capital and small capitals where YHWH appears in the Hebrew manuscript. In this book, which quotes primarily from the New Revised Standard Version, the authors use YHWH (which may be pronounced "Yahweh") to represent the divine name.

While confiding his personal name and commissioning Moses to lead Israel from Egyptian bondage, YHWH displays an astonishing flexibility and resourcefulness in persuading a very reluctant Moses to represent him. To each of Moses' numerous objections, God responds with pragmatic solutions, promising to equip him with magical powers, to instruct him on what to say at Pharaoh's court, and even to provide his inarticulate agent with an eloquent mouthpiece, Moses' older brother **Aaron** (Exod. 4:1–16). In thus negotiating with Moses, ingeniously finding effective ways to overcome human inadequacy and uncooperativeness, YHWH manifests one of the major qualities that characterize the Hebrew Bible's complex portrayals of God — divine **immanence** (presence in human life). As an immanent Being, God intimately communicates with humans, operating within the realm of material reality and remaining accessible to the human mind and consciousness. In Genesis and Exodus, divine immanence takes several forms, ranging from direct appearances (God shares meals with Abraham in Genesis 18 and with Israel's leaders in Exodus 24:9–10) to inspired dreams and visitations from angels (supernatural messengers).

Although most of the theophanies to Israel's ancestors are described as peaceful and benign, after Exodus 19, when YHWH assembles Israel's tribes at the foot of Mount Sinai/Horeb, the Deity suddenly becomes less accessible — even dangerous. Veiled in storm clouds and surrounded by thunderbolts, YHWH erects barriers of terror, threatening to destroy any Israelite who trespasses on his sacred mountain and reminding his worshipers of the enormous gulf between divinity and humanity (Exod. 19:9–23). In revealing his majesty and power, YHWH demonstrates that he belongs to the *numinous*—a frightening, mysterious, and unpredictable spiritual force that may or may not prove beneficent to humans.

The awe-inspiring and unapproachable nature of divinity described at the Sinai theophany—which paradoxically is also the occasion for formalizing YHWH's covenant partnership with Israel—suggests God's **transcendence,** his absolute independence of both the human and natural worlds. Unlike other ancient Near Eastern gods, who were typically identified with natural phenomena such as storm and rain or with psychological states such as love and desire, YHWH is usually portrayed as infinitely surpassing the limits of physical nature, undefinable by any aspect of the material universe. Although different biblical concepts of God emphasize different divine attributes, one of the Tanak's controlling principles is that no image can be made of Israel's God—he cannot be represented (and thus limited) by any concrete form (Exod. 20:3–6; cf. Deut. 5:8–10). Insisting on God's transcendence, the author of 1 Kings depicts Solomon as contrasting the inadequacy of the Temple he built to house YHWH's "name" with the Deity's infinite majesty: "Even heaven and the highest heaven cannot contain [God], much less this house that I have built" (1 Kings 8:27–30). Free of finite constraints, the divine mind is infinitely superior to earthbound humans. Declaring that YHWH differs qualitatively from humans, Second Isaiah represents YHWH as saying,

> For as the heavens are higher than the earth,
> so are my ways higher than your ways
> and my thoughts than your thoughts. (Isa. 55:9)

The Disappearance of God

Increasing emphasis on God's supernatural majesty and transcendence during Israel's later history may help account for another significant biblical theme—the gradual disappearance of God from

the Tanak. Shortly before Moses' death, forty years after his initial encounter with God, YHWH tells his prophet that sometime in the future "I shall hide my face from them [Israel] . . . ; let me see what their end will be" (Deut. 32:20). The progressive "hiddenness" of God in the later books of the Hebrew Bible—he does not appear at all in many books of the Kethuvim   contrasts markedly with his many appearances in the books of the Torah. As scholars such as Richard E. Friedman have pointed out, in the course of the biblical narrative, direct encounters with YHWH virtually cease. As God withdraws from the earthly scene, some of the qualities and functions formerly assigned to God alone are gradually assumed by selected human figures. While maintaining the huge chasm that separates the Deity from his mortal creation, some later biblical writers show human beings eventually taking on the responsibility for the divine plan. Whereas the Hebrew Bible begins with God alone creating the universe (Gen. 1–2) and then directly acting to create Israel through the exodus from Egypt, it concludes with accounts in which human figures, ostensibly acting on their own initiative, take charge of historical events. Books recounting Israel's history after its return from the Babylonian exile, such as Ezra-Nehemiah and Esther, include no theophanies and no accounts of direct divine intervention. The final book of the Hebrew Bible, 2 Chronicles, shows a human leader, Cyrus the Great of Persia, restoring the exiles to their homeland, reenacting the role of national savior that YHWH had played in the Exodus. (Table 1.2 summarizes key events described in the Hebrew Bible.) Although God presumably remains invisibly in charge of events, the movement from divine to human agency in the unfolding of history constitutes a distinctive shift in the divine-human relationship (see Chapters 22 and 27).

QUESTIONS FOR REVIEW

1. What is the Old Testament? Explain its relationship to the Hebrew Bible (Jewish Scriptures). Why do some editions of the Old Testament, primarily Catholic and Orthodox versions, contain books

Table 1.2 Some Crucial Events Described in the Hebrew Bible and Where to Find Them

APPROXIMATE DATE B.C.E.	EVENT	BIBLICAL REFERENCE
	Creation of universe	
	First creation account	Genesis 1:1–2:4a
	Second creation account	Genesis 2:4b–2:25
	Global Flood	Genesis 6:5–8:22
	YHWH's vow to make Abraham a "great nation" and give his descendants the land of Canaan	Genesis 12:1–3; 15:1–21; 17:1–27; 22:15–18
	Migration of Jacob's (Israel's) twelve sons from Canaan to Egypt	Genesis 45:16–50:26
1250	YHWH's commissioning of Moses and the Exodus of Israel's twelve tribes from Egypt to Sinai/Horeb	Exodus 1:1–19:25
	Deliverance of YHWH's instructions and institution of the Mosaic Covenant at Sinai/Horeb	Exodus 20:1–Numbers 10:11
	Revised (Deuteronomic) version of the Torah and the death of Moses in Moab	Deuteronomy 1:1–34:12
1200	Settlement of Israelite tribes in Canaan and ratification of covenant with YHWH	Joshua 1:1–24:33
1200–1020	Period of political disunity under judges	Judges 1:1–21:25
1020	Establishment of Davidic dynasty in Israel	2 Samuel 2:1–23:7
950	Construction of Solomon's Temple in Jerusalem	1 Kings 6:1–8:66
922	Division of Israel into northern kingdom of Israel and southern kingdom of Judah	1 Kings 11:9–12:33
722–721	Assyria's destruction of the northern kingdom of Israel	2 Kings 17:1–41
622	King Josiah's religious reforms and centralization of Judah's worship at the Jerusalem Temple	2 Kings 22–23
587	Babylon's destruction of Judah and demolition of the Jerusalem Temple, ending the Davidic dynasty	2 Kings 25:1–29
539	Cyrus the Great's conquest of Babylon and release of Judean captives	2 Chronicles 36:20–23; Ezra 1:1–4
515	Construction of the Second Temple in Jerusalem	Ezra 3:1–6:22

not included in the Hebrew Bible? What are these additional books called?

2. What do B.C.E. and C.E. mean? How do they correspond to the conventional B.C. and A.D.?

3. What does the term *Tanak* stand for? List the Tanak's three major divisions, and describe the order of contents in these three distinct parts.

4. How does concern for the homeland God promised to Abraham's descendants help to shape the structure of the Tanak (Hebrew Bible)? What was ancient Israel, and what special relationship did God establish with the Israelites? How does the national epic of Israel—Genesis through 2 Kings—begin and end? What crucial event changed the course of Israel's history in 587 B.C.E.?

5. Define *covenant (berith)* as used in the Hebrew Bible. Describe each of the four covenants made with Noah, Abraham, Moses, and David. Which are unconditional? Which covenant explicitly depends on

the fidelity of the human partner? How does the covenant principle define the relationship between God and Israel?

6. In spite of its diversity in literary form and theological content, what two overarching themes help to unify the Hebrew Bible as a whole?

7. Define *theophany.* In what books of the Hebrew Bible do most theophanies occur? Explain what happened between God and Moses at the burning bush. What information about his personal name and saving intentions for Israel does God reveal to Moses? Explain the significance of the divine name YHWH.

8. Define the terms *immanence* and *transcendence,* and explain how they apply to different biblical portrayals of God. What is meant by the statement that God eventually "disappears" from the biblical text? Would this gradual disappearance be true for the Christian Old Testament as well as the Tanak?

QUESTIONS FOR REFLECTION AND DISCUSSION

1. Although the Hebrew Bible focuses largely on the partnership between God and his chosen people, Israel, it also contains indications that God is concerned about all of humanity. In what ways are these universal concerns expressed in the covenants with Noah and with Abraham? Why is a study of history — the gradual unfolding of God's relationship with Israel over time and under ever-changing circumstances — important to understanding the Hebrew Bible? How can Israel's story serve as a paradigm or model of the ongoing interaction between God and humankind in general? What principles operating in the YHWH–Israel relationship also apply to the Deity's interaction with other peoples?

2. From this brief introductory survey of some diverse portrayals of God in the Hebrew Bible (thought to derive from different traditions and from different historical periods), what attributes of YHWH do you think have most influenced your own ideas about God? Explain the concepts of divine immanence and transcendence, and give a biblical example of each quality. How can God be both a pure Spirit unencumbered by the physical universe and also a covenant-making Deity who closely communicates with earthbound individuals?

TERMS AND CONCEPTS TO REMEMBER

Aaron
Abraham, Isaac, and Jacob
Abrahamic Covenant, promises of
Adonai
apocalypse
Apocrypha/differences in content between Jewish Scriptures and Catholic and Orthodox Old Testaments
Aramaic
canon/deuterocanon
C.E./B.C.E.
Conquest of Canaan
cosmos
covenant *(berith)*
Cyrus the Great of Persia
David and Solomon
Davidic Covenant, promises of
Diaspora
El, Elohim
Ephraim
Hebrew Bible/Old Testament
immanence
Israel
Jerusalem
Jew
Judah
Judea
Mosaic Covenant, conditional terms of
Moses
Mount Sinai/Horeb
Noachan Covenant, terms of
oracles
Pentateuch
Scripture
Septuagint
theophany
Three-part Tanak: Torah/Nevi'im/Kethuvim
transcendence
YHWH/Tetragrammaton

RECOMMENDED READING

Alter, Robert, and Kermode, Frank, eds. *The Literary Guide to the Bible,* repr. ed. Cambridge, Mass.: Harvard University Press, 1990. A collection of informative essays analyzing books of both the Hebrew Bible and the New Testament.

Birch, Bruce; Brueggemann, Walter; Fretheim, Terence E. and Petersen, David L. *A Theological Introduction to the Old Testament.* Nashville, Tenn.: Abingdon Press, 1999. Thoughtful and clearly written analyses of evolving theological ideas presented in the Hebrew Bible.

Bright, John. *A History of Israel* (Westminster Aids to the Study of Scriptures), 4th ed. Louisville, Ky.: Westminster/John Knox Press, 2000. A standard reference on the historical development of ancient Israel, emphasizing both archaeological and biblical evidence.

Friedman, Richard Eliott. *The Hidden Face of God.* San Francisco: HarperSanFrancisco, 1995. A stimulating investigation of the progressive disappearance of God from the text of the Hebrew Bible.

Gabel, John B.; Wheeler, Charles B.; and York, Anthony D. *The Bible as Literature: An Introduction,* 3rd ed. New York: Oxford University Press, 1996. An excellent survey of biblical literary genres and themes for the beginning student.

Levenson, Jon D. *Sinai and Zion: An Entry into the Jewish Bible.* San Francisco: HarperSanFrancisco, 1985. Relatively brief, but packed with insights into the two major components of biblical thought, the sometimes conflicting traditions associated with the Mosaic revelation at Sinai/Horeb and the royal covenant theology associated with the Jerusalem Temple cult.

Miller, Patrick D. *The Religion of Ancient Israel.* Louisville, Ky.: Westminster/John Knox Press, 2000. An important study of key aspects of ancient Israelite beliefs and practices, including evolving concepts of God.

Niditch, Susan. *Ancient Israelite Religion.* New York: Oxford University Press, 1997. A good introductory survey of some major topics and themes in Israel's religious beliefs.

Shanks, Hershel, ed. *Ancient Israel: A Short History from Abraham to the Roman Destruction of the Temple,* rev. ed. Washington, D.C.: Biblical Archaeology Society, 1999. A collection of accessible essays on the major periods of Israelite history.

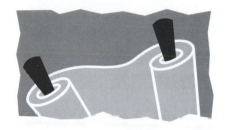

CHAPTER 2

The Process of Formation

The Transmission, Canonization, and Translation of the Hebrew Bible

Key Topics / Themes With no original texts by the Tanak's authors or editors surviving, scholars must rely on copies of the Hebrew Bible made many centuries after the works were first composed. Before the Dead Sea Scrolls were discovered beginning in 1947, the oldest biblical texts were the series of manuscripts produced by medieval Jewish scholars, known as the *masoretes* (literally, "transmitters"). This Masoretic Text (MT), produced from the ninth through the early eleventh centuries C.E., is the edition on which most translations are based. Dating from about 250 B.C.E. to the first century C.E., some of the Dead Sea Scrolls, mostly in fragmental form, are almost 1000 years older than the standard Masoretic Text and contain numerous variations from the MT. The Septuagint (abbreviated LXX), the first major translation of the Hebrew Bible into another language, was a Greek version of the Hebrew text begun in Alexandria, Egypt, about 250 B.C.E. By the end of the first century C.E., Jewish scholars had affirmed the contents of the three-part Tanak, recognizing a canon of authoritative books. In the early fifth century C.E., a Christian scholar, Jerome, translated both the Tanak and the New Testament into Latin — the Vulgate — but another millennium passed before the entire Bible was made available in modern languages.

Transmitting the Biblical Texts

From ancient Hebrew battle songs chanted aloud after Israel's military victories during the early first millennium B.C.E. to a bound and printed volume in English used in today's synagogues, churches, and universities, the story of the Hebrew Bible's transmission is long and complex. Our knowledge of the Tanak's formation and transmission is severely limited by the fact that not a single scrap of any biblical writer's original composition has survived. Many centuries separate the time in which the older parts of the Hebrew Bible were written from that in which the earliest extant copies were made. The great chronological gap between a given book's date of composition and the oldest version we have of it is significant because it is during a document's earliest stages of copying and transmission, before it acquires the status of recognized scripture, that the text is most fluid, subject to editorial additions, deletions, and other changes.

Ideally, one might think that, once a particular book had been completed, a single master copy would be made and that all subsequent copies would faithfully reproduce it. In practice, however, in the earliest stages of transmission, many ancient scribes apparently also acted as editors, adding explanatory phrases or otherwise modifying the text to reflect the covenant community's ever-changing circumstances (Figure 2.1). Many editorial changes were minor, mere errors in copying, but others produced notable differences in content. Some manuscripts of Isaiah and Jeremiah, for example, are much shorter

Figure 2.1 The facial expression on this statuette of an ancient Egyptian scribe reveals the intelligence and consciousness of power characteristic of the literate professional class that controlled the preservation and interpretation of Egypt's history. In common with its Near Eastern neighbors, Israel developed a scribal class associated with the royal court that played a major role in creating the Bible.

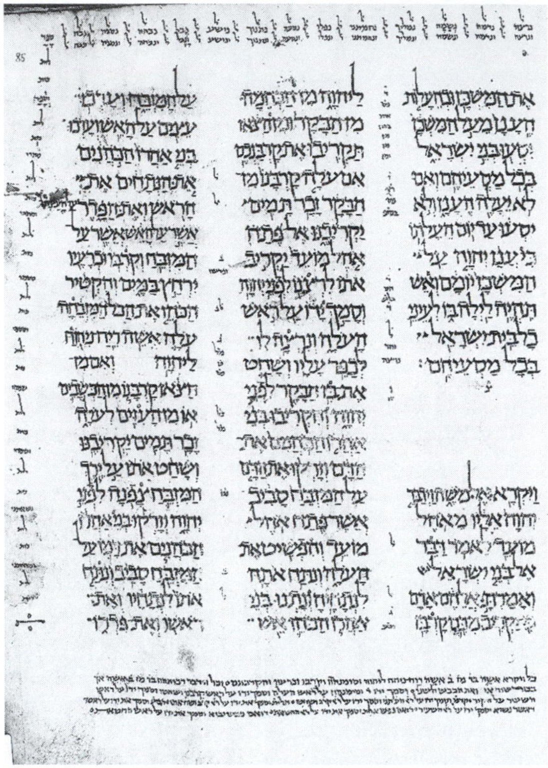

Figure 2.2 This page from the Book of Leviticus belongs to one of the oldest copies of the Hebrew Torah, the Masoretic (traditional) Text, dating from the mid-ninth century C.E.

than what came to be accepted as the standard version.

Because neither the author's original text nor copies made soon after a book first appeared survive, it is impossible to determine the full extent to which later copies differ from the writer's original version. By carefully studying the received biblical texts, however, scholars have been able to detect clear evidence that ancient editors freely reworked many parts of the Hebrew Bible before they attained their present canonical form. Close examination of the **Deuteronomistic History (DH)**—Deuteronomy and the sequence of narrative books from Joshua through 2 Kings that adopts Deuteronomy's distinctive view of history—indicates

that these documents underwent extensive revision after the Babylonian exile (see Chapters 11–15).

Most contemporary editions of the Hebrew Bible/Old Testament rely primarily on the **Masoretic Text (MT),** which takes its name from *Masorah* (Hebrew, "transmission"), a term referring to a school of medieval Jewish scholars known as the **masoretes** who, during the ninth and tenth centuries C.E., produced a series of Tanak manuscripts (Figure 2.2). Two representatives of the Masoretic tradition, the Aleppo Codex and the Leningrad Codex, are among the most important manuscripts. Noted for their scrupulous care in copying each letter of the text, the masoretes also added vowel sounds and accent marks to the consonantal Hebrew script. Their work, including marginal notes, remains an invaluable resource for modern translators.

Until about fifty years ago, most scholars assumed that the MT represented a single authoritative textual tradition going back to biblical times. Attempts to look beyond the MT to earlier phases of the text's transmission were unsuccessful. Beginning in 1947, however, the situation changed dramatically. A series of manuscript discoveries near the Dead Sea (an area now controlled by the modern state of Israel) unexpectedly provided scholars with copies of biblical manuscripts up to 1000 years older than the MT. Known collectively as the **Dead Sea Scrolls,** two groups of manuscript discoveries were particularly important: those found in eleven caves near Qumran, dating from about 250 B.C.E. to 68 C.E., and a group of slightly younger texts recovered from sites bordering the Dead Sea south of Qumran.

These two manuscript collections effectively illuminate a landmark change in the Hebrew Bible's textual development. Many of the almost 200 biblical scrolls found near Qumran, most in a highly fragmentary condition, showed significant differences from the Masoretic Text, including variations not only in wording but also in content, with some containing sentences and even whole paragraphs absent in the medieval texts. Other Qumran manuscripts lacked whole passages found in the MT. One version of the Book of Jeremiah, for example, was considerably shorter than the MT edition, and one collection of the Psalms included lyrics not found in the MT. In contrast, the somewhat younger manuscripts recovered south of Qumran, written during the late first and early second centuries C.E., showed a striking agreement with the medieval MT. The relative uniformity of this second group of manuscripts indicates that, at some point after the first Roman destruction of Jerusalem in 70 C.E., Jewish scribes succeeded in producing a relatively standardized edition of the biblical text, the forerunner of the medieval MT. A few more recent Bible translations, such as the New Revised Standard Version, have taken advantage of these manuscript finds to correct earlier renderings of the Hebrew text. (The complete extant Dead Sea texts of canonical books, as well as some apocryphal documents, are available in an English translation, *The Dead Sea Scrolls Bible;* see Martin Abegg, Jr., et al. in "Recommended Reading.")

The Canon of the Hebrew Bible

In producing a text that included only a limited number of books, Jewish scholars of the late first century C.E. also contributed to the formation of the biblical canon. **Canon** derives from the Greek term for a "straight stick by which something is ruled or measured"; it refers here to a list of books, distinguished from all others, that a religious community holds as uniquely authoritative in defining and teaching its essential beliefs. Considering the great diversity of religious literature contained among the Dead Sea Scrolls—and manuscripts discovered at **Masada,** a Jewish mountaintop stronghold that Roman armies destroyed in 73 C.E.—the canon or list of Israel's sacred books was not yet fully determined at the time of the first Jewish revolt (66–73 C.E.). Along with books from the Torah, Prophets, and Writings, archaeologists investigating the Qumran caves and Masada found manuscripts of such works as 1 Enoch and the apocryphal Wisdom of Jesus Son of Sirach (also called Ecclesiasticus), neither of which was ultimately included in the Tanak. (See the discussion of deuterocanonical and noncanonical books in Chapters 29 and 30.)

The process of defining the Hebrew Bible canon, like the composition and redaction of the various books eventually included in it, was a long and gradual one. At no time did a religious council or other authority decree what the covenant community was to accept as canonical. The Hebrew Bible grew by slow degrees, its contents intermittently expanding to incorporate new documents as Israel's writers, over many generations, recorded and interpreted their nation's political and spiritual experiences.

After the Babylonian exile, Israel's legal and prophetic writings grew ever more venerable and were quoted, debated, and read publicly at national festivals until familiarity with their teaching and their recognized place in the formation of the Jewish faith made them, by use and habit, part of Israel's sacred books. Perhaps as early as the fourth century B.C.E., when Persian administrators actively encouraged the publication of Judea's religious laws, Mosaic legal traditions were reshaped into the five books of Torah and proclaimed as binding on all Jews (Neh. 8; Ezra 7). This collection, the Pentateuch, was the first part of the Hebrew Bible to achieve canonical status.

Although not all scholars agree, many believe that the second main division of the Tanak, the Prophets (Nevi'im) was generally accepted by about 200 B.C.E., at least by some influential groups within the Jewish community. The earliest reference to all three parts of the Tanak as authoritative occurs in the preface to the Wisdom of Jesus Son of Sirach (Ecclesiasticus), in which the author's grandson and translator mentions "the Law [Torah] and the Prophets [Nevi'im] and the other books of our ancestors." Written in Egypt about 132 B.C.E., the preface's allusion to the "other" ancestral books refers to the Tanak's third division, the Writings (Kethuvim), a miscellaneous anthology of postexilic literature that was the last written and the last to be canonized. Although some of the Writings, such as the Psalms, had been used in Judah's worship for generations, this part of the Scripture may have remained open-ended well into the first centuries C.E., with some Jewish groups, such as those living in Egypt, accepting books that ultimately were not included in the Tanak. It was apparently not until after the Romans had destroyed the Temple in Jerusalem (70 C.E.) that the Jewish community began to set a precise limit on the number of books composing the Writings. Then the challenge facing rabbinical scholars was not as much what to accept, considering the large number of religious volumes available, as what to omit.

Following the Roman destruction of the Jewish state, a group of distinguished **rabbis** (Hebrew, "teacher") assembled at the coastal town of **Jamnia (Yavneh)** to consolidate and unify postwar Judaism.

The **Academy of Jamnia** (Yavneh), founded about 90 C.E., was once thought to have formally closed the canon, deciding exactly which books constituted genuine Scripture. Scholars now believe, however, that no such conclusive action was taken, although the rabbis did debate the merits of certain books, such as Ezekiel, which seems to contradict the Mosaic Torah; Ecclesiastes, which displays a skeptical attitude toward conventional piety; and the Song of Songs, which celebrates erotic love. Even these seemingly questionable books, perhaps because they were traditionally ascribed to King Solomon, were accorded scriptural status. Defining the precise limits of the Writings, however, may have been a function of the rabbis' creating a standard biblical text—prototype of the later Masoretic Text—produced during the tumultuous period between the two uprisings against Rome (66–73 C.E. and 132–135 C.E.).

Writing late in the first century, the Jewish historian **Flavius Josephus** (c. 37–100 C.E.) seems to assume the existence of an established canon. In the work *Against Apion*, Josephus defends his Jewish tradition against Greco-Roman criticism, emphasizing the limited number of its sacred books:

> For we [the Jews] have not an innumerable multitude of books among us, disagreeing from and contradicting one another [as the Greeks have] but only *twenty-two books*, which contain the records of all past times; which are justly believed to be divine; and of them five belong to Moses, which contain his laws and the traditions of the origin of mankind till his death. . . . the prophets, who were after Moses, wrote down what was done in their times in thirteen books. The remaining four books contain hymns to God and precepts for the conduct of human life. ("Against Apion," Bk. 1.8)

Josephus's reference to a total of twenty-two volumes of Scripture probably corresponds to the twenty-four books into which the Tanak's present contents are divided. (Ruth was commonly added to the Book of Judges, and Lamentations to Jeremiah.) Although the Protestant Old Testament has exactly the same books as the Tanak, it counts the twelve minor prophets individually and breaks the books of Samuel, Kings, and Chronicles into two parts each, making a total of thirty-nine. As noted in Chapter 1, Catholic and Orthodox Bibles, which include the apocryphal books, feature a longer Old Testament.

The Translation of the Hebrew Bible

Events leading to the first major translation of the Hebrew Bible began in the 330s B.C.E. when **Alexander the Great** led his Greek-speaking armies through the ancient Near East, conquering the Persian Empire and incorporating its vast territories into a new Greek-speaking dominion (Figure 2.3). Although Alexander died before realizing his presumed ideal of welding his conquests into a viable political unit, his successors established several long-lasting kingdoms that fostered Greek language, literature, and religion throughout the eastern Mediterranean region. Egypt, ruled by descendants of Alexander's general Ptolemy, then contained a large community of Diaspora Jews in its major port city, Alexandria. About 250 B.C.E., during the reign of Ptolemy II (ruled 285–246 B.C.E.), Jewish scholars in Alexandria undertook the task of translating the Hebrew Bible into Greek, beginning with the Torah (Figure 2.4). According to a legend preserved in the noncanonical Letter of Aristeas, seventy-two scholars from Jerusalem, working in pairs, labored seventy-two days to produce a definitive Greek edition of the Tanak. Known as the **Septuagint** (abbreviated **LXX,** popularly called the "work of the seventy"), this rendering of the Hebrew and Aramaic texts into *koinē*, the "common" Greek spoken by Alexander's soldiers and others, became widely used in Greek-speaking Jewish communities of the Diaspora. (Box 2.1 lists common abbreviations associated with the Bible.) Eventually adopted by the early Christian community, it is this Greek edition of the Hebrew Bible from which most New Testament writers quote.

Figure 2.3   Bust of Alexander the Great Although he managed to conquer most of the known world before his death at age thirty-two, Alexander's dream of unifying East and West under a single government was never achieved.

Although the Letter of Aristeas presents the Septuagint as a source of sweeping agreement among seventy-two Jerusalem scholars, six from each Israelite tribe, contemporary scholars find the account implausible. Aristeas's claim that Ptolemy II authorized a Greek translation of the Torah to place in Alexandria's famous library may be accurate (Ptolemy was an avid collector of books), but the rest of the Hebrew Bible was not rendered into Greek until much later. The process of translation that began with the Pentateuch continued over many generations, with the Prophets and Writings

Figure 2.4 Copies of the Mosaic Torah are kept in every Jewish temple or synagogue. This elegant manuscript is approximately one-third the size of the standard Torah scroll.

gradually added to the Greek collection. The Septuagint apparently remained open-ended well into the first centuries C.E., with some editions containing a number of books—the Apocrypha—that rabbis did not include in the Tanak.

In his preface to the Wisdom of Jesus Son of Sirach, the author's grandson bemoans the enormous difficulty translators face in trying to express the exact meaning of a text in a different language. Despite his "diligent labor in translating," he states, readers with a knowledge of biblical Hebrew may find that he has "rendered some phrases imperfectly."

> For what was originally expressed in Hebrew does not have exactly the same sense when translated into another language. Not only this book [Ecclesiasticus], but even the Law [Torah] itself, the Prophecies, and the rest of the books differ not a little when read in the original. (Ecclus. prologue)

Even the best-equipped modern translators can experience the same kind of frustration that beset Sirach's grandson when attempting to render a Hebrew or Aramaic text in contemporary English. Some Bible translators try to give the most literal translation possible, sometimes with almost unintelligible results; others seek to find approximate English equivalents of the original phrasing.

Whereas the Septuagint was designed for a Greek-speaking Jewish audience living in a world created by Alexander's conquests (see Chapter 3), other translations were undertaken for Aramaic-speaking Jews during the postexilic era. Known as Targums, these Aramaic translations or paraphrases of the biblical texts include a manuscript of Job found at Qumran. Most extant Targums, however, date from the later Roman and medieval periods. Although parts of the Hebrew Bible/Old Testament had been translated into Latin in the early centuries C.E., the first major translation of the entire Bible for a specifically Christian audience was that by Jerome, one of the leading scholars of the later Roman Empire. During the late fourth century C.E., the bishop of Rome commissioned Jerome to produce a work known as the **Vulgate,** a Latin translation in the "vulgar," or common,

BOX 2.1
Abbreviations of Books of the Bible, in Alphabetical Order

THE HEBREW BIBLE
(Tanak or Old Testament)

Amos	Amos
1 Chron.	1 Chronicles
2 Chron.	2 Chronicles
Dan.	Daniel
Deut.	Deuteronomy
Eccles.	Ecclesiastes
Esther	Esther
Exod.	Exodus
Ezek.	Ezekiel
Ezra	Ezra
Gen.	Genesis
Hab.	Habakkuk
Hag.	Haggai
Hos.	Hosea
Isa.	Isaiah
Jer.	Jeremiah
Job	Job
Joel	Joel
Jonah	Jonah
Josh.	Joshua
Judg.	Judges
1 Kings	1 Kings
2 Kings	2 Kings
Lam.	Lamentations
Lev.	Leviticus
Mal.	Malachi
Mic.	Micah
Nah.	Nahum
Neh.	Nehemiah
Num.	Numbers
Obad.	Obadiah
Prov.	Proverbs
Ps. (pl., Pss.)	Psalms
Ruth	Ruth
1 Sam.	1 Samuel
2 Sam.	2 Samuel

Song	Song of Songs
Zech.	Zechariah
Zeph.	Zephaniah

DEUTEROCANONICAL (Apocryphal) BOOKS

Add. to Dan.	Additions to Daniel
Add. to Esther	Additions to Esther
Bar.	Baruch (includes Letter of Jeremiah)
Ecclus.	Ecclesiasticus (Wisdom of Jesus ben Sirach)
1 Esd.	1 Esdras
2 Esd.	2 Esdras
Jth.	Judith
1 Macc.	1 Maccabees
2 Macc.	2 Maccabees
Tob.	Tobit
Wisd. of Sol.	Wisdom of Solomon

OTHER ABBREVIATIONS

B.C.E.	Before the common era; dates correspond to dates B.C.
C.E.	Common era; dates correspond to dates A.D.
JB	The Jerusalem Bible
KJV	The King James Version of the Bible, also called the Authorized Version (AV)
NAB	The New American Bible
NEB	The New English Bible
NIV	The New International Version of the Bible
NJB	The New Jerusalem Bible
NKJV	The New King James Version of the Bible
NRSV	The New Revised Standard Version of the Bible
NT	The New Testament
OT	The Old Testament
RSV	The Revised Standard Version of the Bible
SV	The Scholars Version of the Bible

tongue of the Western church. Working directly from Hebrew and Greek manuscripts between about 385 and 405 C.E., Jerome created a landmark edition that became the official Bible of the Catholic Church. Following the collapse of the western Roman Empire in the late fifth century C.E., literacy rapidly declined. Accordingly, no other major translation of the Bible was published for nearly 1000 years. Prior to the Protestant Reformation in the early sixteenth century, most translators merely rendered Jerome's Latin into some modern European languages (Figure 2.5). Not until the 1500s were translations again made directly from the Hebrew and Aramaic texts.

The Bible in English

EARLY ENGLISH TRANSLATIONS

Although none of his work has survived, the first person credited with translating the Bible into his native English was the Venerable Bede, a Benedictine monk and historian of Anglo-Saxon England. In the 730s C.E., Bede rendered part of the Latin Vulgate into Old English. During the tenth and eleventh centuries, a few other biblical books, such as the Psalms, also appeared in English, but an English version of the entire Christian Old Testament was not available until the fourteenth century. To make Scripture more accessible to the British public, John Wycliffe, an English priest, translated both the Old and New Testaments, completing the project around 1384. Fearing the effect that the Bible's availability in English might have on the untutored populace, however, the church in 1408 condemned Wycliffe's version and forbade any future translations.

Two historical events ensured that the Bible would find a large reading public in English. The first was Johannes Gutenberg's invention of movable type in 1455, a revolutionary advance in technology that made it possible to print books relatively quickly, rather than having to copy them laboriously by hand. The second was a strong religious move-

ment known as the Protestant Reformation, begun in Germany in 1517. In that year, a German monk named Martin Luther vigorously protested practices within the Catholic Church and promoted a widespread study of Scripture. Luther's German translation of the Bible (1522–1534) was the first version in a modern European language based not on Jerome's Vulgate but directly on the Hebrew text.

The first English translator to work directly from Hebrew and Greek manuscripts was William Tyndale; under the threat of church persecution, he fled to Germany, where his translation of the New Testament was published in 1525 (revised 1534). Official hostility to his work prevented him from completing his translation of the Old Testament, and, in 1535, he was betrayed, tried for heresy, and burned at the stake.

Although the Anglican Church under Henry VIII forbade the reading of Wycliffe's or Tyndale's translations, it nevertheless permitted free distribution of the first printed English Bible — the Coverdale Bible (1535), which relied heavily on Tyndale's work. Matthew's Bible (1537), containing additional sections of Tyndale's Old Testament, was revised by Coverdale, and the result was called the Great Bible (1539). The Bishop's Bible (1568) was a revision of the Great Bible, and the King James Version was commissioned as a scholarly revision of the Bishop's Bible. The Geneva Bible (1560), which English Puritans had produced in Switzerland, also significantly influenced the King James Bible.

THE KING JAMES BIBLE (AUTHORIZED VERSION)

By far the most popular English Bible of all time, the King James translation was authorized by James 1, son of Mary, Queen of Scots, who appointed fifty-four scholars to compile a new version of the Bishop's Bible for official use in the Anglican Church. After seven years' labor, during which the oldest manuscripts then available were diligently consulted, the king's scholars produced in 1611 the Authorized or King James Version.

Figure 2.5 This exquisitely decorated page from Genesis in the Hebrew Bible was produced in Provence, probably Avignon, in about 1422.

Despite the beauties of its rhythmic prose, the King James Version has serious drawbacks as a text for studying the Hebrew Bible. The very poetic qualities that contribute to its linguistic elegance — the archaic phrasing and rhetorical style — tend to obscure the explicit meaning of the text for many readers. Translated by scholars who grew up on the then-contemporary poetry of Edmund Spenser and William Shakespeare, the King James text presents real problems of comprehensibility to the average American student. Readers who have difficulty with *Hamlet* or *Macbeth* cannot expect to follow the sometimes convoluted sentence structure and Renaissance vocabulary of this government-authorized translation. In addition, the seventeenth-century translators did not have access to many of the best manuscripts now available to modern scholars, making some of their renditions less accurate than more recent versions.

SOME MODERN ENGLISH AND AMERICAN TRANSLATIONS

Realizing that language changes over time and that words lose their original meanings and take on new connotations, Bible scholars have repeatedly updated and reedited the King James text. The first Revised Version of the King James was published in England between 1881 and 1885; a slightly modified text of this edition, the American Standard Revised Version, was issued in 1901. Drawing on the (then) latest studies in textual criticism and linguistics, the Revised Standard Version (RSV) appeared between 1946 and 1952. Because modern scholarship continues to advance through the discovery of ancient biblical manuscripts, such as the Dead Sea Scrolls, and in the understanding of ancient Near Eastern languages, an updated edition, the New Revised Standard Version (NRSV), with the Apocrypha, was published in 1991. Unless otherwise indicated, this textbook uses the NRSV for all quotations from the Tanak.

Other important translations of the Hebrew Bible include that of the Jewish Publication Society (1985), the New Jerusalem Bible (NJB) (1989), which transliterates several Hebrew names for God — notably the personal name *Yahweh* and the title *El Shaddai* — into the English text; the Revised English Bible (REB) (1989); the New American Bible (NAB) (1970) and the New International Version (NIV) (1978). All of these translations — Jewish, Protestant, and Catholic — incorporate the benefits of expert scholarship that draws on interdisciplinary fields of linguistic, historical, and literary studies. Except for the Jewish Publication Society's Tanakh and the NIV, an evangelical Protestant work, all of these new translations include the Apocrypha, books that reflect the evolution of religious ideas in Judaism during the centuries immediately preceding the rise of Christianity.

Scholarly translations of individual parts of the Hebrew Bible, such as the Pentateuch, or of individual biblical volumes are also available. A work that successfully captures the flavor of the Hebrew idiom is *The Five Books of Moses* by Edward Fox. Although Fox's edition contains only the books of the Torah, its extraordinarily vivid rendering of the Hebrew text rewards careful reading. The multivolume Doubleday Anchor Bible is an excellent study aid. A cooperative effort by Jewish, Catholic, and Protestant scholars, each volume in the series is the work of an individual translator, who provides extensive interpretive commentary.

QUESTIONS FOR REVIEW

1. What are some of the problems confronting scholars attempting to reconstruct an accurate text of the Hebrew Bible? What difficulties arise when there is a large chronological gap between the time of a book's composition and that of the oldest surviving copies of the work?

2. What is the Masoretic Text (MT)? When was it produced? What relationship does it have to modern editions of the Hebrew Bible/Old Testament?

3. What are the Dead Sea Scrolls? When were they discovered, and why are they important in helping to reconstruct the biblical texts?

4. Define the term *canon.* How was the canon of the three major divisions of the Hebrew Bible established?

5. Define the term *rabbi,* and describe the work of the rabbis at the Academy of Jamnia (Yavneh). To what historical events were the rabbis at Jamnia responding, and what was their role in helping to establish a standard text for the Tanak?

6. Describe the historical circumstances that led to the first Greek edition of the Hebrew Bible — the Septuagint (LXX). According to legend, how was this landmark translation made? What are some of the difficulties in translating a Hebrew document into another language?

7. Describe the work of Jerome in producing a new Latin translation of the Bible, the Vulgate.

8. What revolutionary events of the late fifteenth and sixteenth centuries contributed to the translating of the Bible into modern languages? What role did Martin Luther play?

9. Who were John Wycliffe and William Tyndale? What were their contributions to creating a Bible in English? Did contemporary authorities endorse their work?

10. What is the King James Bible (Authorized Version), and under what circumstances was it produced? Why are many later translations more reliable than the King James? List some important contemporary English editions of the Bible, such as the New Revised Standard Version used in this textbook.

QUESTIONS FOR REFLECTION AND DISCUSSION

1. Why is the gap between the earliest extant copies of the Hebrew Bible and their time of composition significant? How can we be sure that surviving manuscripts accurately represent the work of their authors? What commonly happens to a document during the long process of copying, editing, and transmitting the text?

2. What role does a group's ongoing familiarity with and use of a text play in its acceptance into the canon? Why are some books included in the Hebrew Bible and others rejected? Why do you think that the Jewish community rejected the apocryphal books of the Septuagint? Why did the Christian community endorse them? Do you think that future generations will add more books to the Old Testament canon? Explain your answer.

3. What are some of the features you look for in a contemporary English edition of the Bible? Which editions do you think are reliable translations from the original Hebrew and Aramaic? Without studying the ancient languages, how can we make a judgment? Do we rely on pastoral advice, church authority, or scholarly consensus?

TERMS AND CONCEPTS TO REMEMBER

Academy of Jamnia (Yavneh)	Jamnia (Yavneh)
	koinē
Alexander the Great	Masada
canon	masoretes
Dead Sea Scrolls	Masoretic Text (MT)
Deuteronomistic History (DH)	rabbi
	Septuagint (LXX)
English translations	Vulgate
Flavius Josephus	

RECOMMENDED READING

Abegg, Martin, Jr.; Flint, Peter; and Ulrich, Eugene; eds. *The Dead Sea Scrolls Bible.* San Francisco: HarperSanFrancisco, 1999. Translates into contemporary English all manuscript fragments of canonical books of the Hebrew Bible, plus 1 Enoch and ben Sirach.

Barr, James. *Holy Scripture: Canon, Authority, Criticism.* Louisville, Ky.: Westminster, 1983.

Bruce, F. F. *History of the Bible in English,* 3rd ed. New York: Oxford University Press, 1978. A concise history and critical evaluation of all major English translations from Anglo-Saxon times to the late twentieth century.

Gneuse, Robert. *The Authority of the Bible: Theories of Inspiration, Revelation, and the Canon of Scripture.* New York: Paulist Press, 1985. A brief but thoughtful review of the scriptural canon and its religious authority.

Fox, Everett, ed. *The Five Books of Moses.* The Schocken Bible, Vol. 1. New York: Schocken Books, 1995. The first part of the Tanak in unusually vivid prose.

Fredricks, E. S., ed. *The Bible and Bibles in America.* Louisville, Ky.: John Knox, 1988.

Friedman, Richard E. *The Hidden Book in the Bible: The Discovery of the First Prose Masterpiece.* San Francisco: HarperSanFrancisco, 1998. Includes a full translation of an early narrative (the J document) that editors later wove into the present biblical text.

Jewish Publication Society. *Tanakh: The Holy Scriptures.* Philadelphia: Jewish Publication Society, 1985. An authoritative English translation for the Jewish community.

Josephus, Flavius. "Against Apion." In *Complete Works*, pp. 607–638. Translated by William Winston. Grand Rapids, Mich.: Kregel, 1960. Contains Josephus's description of the Hebrew Bible's contents (Bk. 1, sec. 8).

Leiman, Sid Z. *The Canon and Masorah of the Hebrew Bible: An Introductory Reader.* New York: KTAV, 1974.

Lewis, Jack P. *The English Bible from KJV to NIV: A History and Evaluation.* Grand Rapids, Mich.: Baker Book House, 1982. A scholarly review of major English translations from the King James Version to the New International Version.

Metzger, Bruce M., and Murphy, Roland E., eds. *The New Oxford Annotated Bible: New Revised Standard Version.* New York: Oxford University Press, 1991. Includes both Testaments and the Apocrypha.

The Revised English Bible with the Apocrypha. Oxford and Cambridge: Oxford University Press, Cambridge University Press, 1989. A clear, readable translation utilizing recent scholarly research.

Rost, Leonard. *Judaism Outside the Hebrew Canon: An Introduction to the Documents.* Nashville, Tenn.: Abingdon Press, 1976. Surveys the Apocrypha and other books not included in the Tanak.

Sanders, James. *From Sacred Story to Sacred Text: Canon in Paradigm.* Minneapolis: Fortress Press, 1986. An influential study.

————. *Torah and Canon.* Minneapolis: Fortress Press, 1972. A standard reference.

Tucker, Gene M.; Petersen, David L.; and Wilson, Robert R.; eds. *Canon, Theology, and Old Testament Interpretation.* Minneapolis: Fortress Press, 1988.

von Campenhausen, Hans. *The Formation of the Christian Bible.* Translated by J. A. Baker. Philadelphia: Fortress Press, 1972.

Wegner, Paul D. *The Journey from Texts to Translations: The Origin and Development of the Bible.* Grand Rapids, Mich.: Baker Book House, 2000. A readable investigation of the Bible's literary evolution.

Wurthwein, Ernst. *The Text of the Old Testament.* Translated by E. F. Rhodes. Grand Rapids, Mich.: Eerdsmans, 1979.

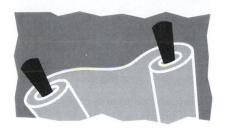

CHAPTER 3

The Ancient Near East

The Environment That Produced the Bible

Key Topics/Themes Archaeological evidence indicates that humans have inhabited the Near East for tens of thousands of years. Sites of prehistoric villages, small towns, and other settlements abound from central Anatolia (modern Turkey), to Syria, to Mesopotamia (modern Iraq). It was not until about 3200 B.C.E., however, that the first large urban centers were established. Originating in southern Mesopotamia, the first urban civilization (Sumer) produced a written literature about the gods, the creation of the world, and the afterlife that significantly influenced the biblical worldview. Whereas Sumerian and later Babylonian city-states typically remained relatively small and autonomous, the Egyptians created the first unified national state in the mid-third millennium B.C.E. For most of its history, Israel, located geographically between powerful empires in Egypt and Mesopotamia, was dominated politically by a succession of Egyptian, Assyrian, Babylonian, Persian, and Greek invaders. Events recounted in the Hebrew Bible are set almost entirely in this ancient Near Eastern context. (Table 3.1 shows a chronology of major events in biblical and general history.)

A Prologue to the Biblical World

For many thousands of years before Israel came into existence, the **Fertile Crescent**—a strip of arable land curving from the head of the Persian Gulf nothwestward to Syria and then southward through Canaan into Egypt—was studded with tiny villages and other settlements (Figure 3.1). At **Jericho,** famous for its walls that reputedly tumbled before the blast of Joshua's trumpets, archaeologists have discovered evidence of human habitation dating back to 9000 B.C.E. Lying six miles west of the Jordan River, north of the Dead Sea, Jericho is the world's oldest known walled town. Archaeological excavations have uncovered the ruins of a circular stone tower thirty feet high, as well as plastered, painted skulls with eyes made from seashells. Like other figurines from the Stone Age, these reconstructions of human faces probably had a religious meaning that is now impossible to know (see Figure 3.2 for some Sumerian examples).

Repeatedly abandoned and then resettled, perhaps because of invasions or fluctuations in the climate, Jericho's ruins now form a high mound of rubble called a **tel.** Composed of numerous layers of debris, each representing a different period of settlement, tels mark the sites of ancient cities throughout the Near East.

Only recently discovered, another important site, called Ain Ghazal (Arabic, the "spring of the gazelle"), is located northeast of modern Amman,

Table 3.1   Some Major Events in the History of Biblical and Other World Religions

Approximate Date	Event	Biblical Reference
15,000 B.C.E.	Elaborate cave paintings are created at Lascaux, France; rituals of magic and religion evolve.	
10,000 B.C.E.	Pleistocene (Ice Age) glaciers retreat; Stone Age settlements are built in Canaan.	
9000 B.C.E.	The first permanent settlement occurs at Jericho.	
7000–5600 B.C.E.	Catal Huyuk, a town in south-central Turkey, is the apparent center of fertility cult, goddess worship.	
6000 B.C.E.	Neolithic pottery and figurines are crafted at Jericho.	
3500 B.C.E.	The wheel is invented in Mesopotamia; trade, commerce, and the communication of ideas expand.	
	I. Early Bronze Age (c. 3400–2100 B.C.E.)	
3300 B.C.E.	Sumerian city-states form; cuneiform writing is invented; ancient Mesopotamian traditions about creation and divine-human relationships develop; temples are built to honor gods.	
3000 B.C.E.	The first nation-state forms in Egypt; traditions of creation and divine justice evolve.	
2500 B.C.E.	The Egyptian pyramids are built (First through Third dynasties); a powerful priestly class develops; rituals are encoded to ensure a happy afterlife.	
2500 B.C.E.	Pre-Hindu civilization flourishes in the Indus Valley.	
2330 B.C.E.	Sargon I conquers Mesopotamian city-states and creates the first empire; Sargon supports the worship of Sin, the Akkadian moon god, for whom Mount Sinai is named.	
	II. Middle Bronze Age (2100–1550 B.C.E.)	
2000–1450 B.C.E.	Minoan civilization flourishes on Crete; worship of goddess figures develops.	
1850–1700 B.C.E.	Nomadic Hebrews roam the Fertile Crescent in the age of biblical patriarchs.	Genesis 12–50
1700 B.C.E.	Hammurabi of Babylon produces a law code endorsed by the sun god Shamash, protector of justice.	
	III. Late Bronze Age (1550–1200 B.C.E.)	
1500 B.C.E.	Compilation of Vedic literature begins in India; Stonehenge is built in England.	
1350 B.C.E.	Akhenaton orders the worship of one god, the sun, which briefly establishes the world's first monolatry.	
1250 B.C.E.	Moses leads Israelite slaves from Egypt and establishes the worship of YHWH at Mount Sinai (formerly sacred to the moon god Sin).	Exodus 13–34
1250–1200 B.C.E.	Mycenaean Greeks besiege Troy in northwestern Turkey, the source event of Homer's *Iliad* and *Odyssey* (written eighth century B.C.E.).	

Table 3.1 (continued)

Approximate Date	Event	Biblical Reference
	IV. Iron Age (c. 1200 B.C.E.)	
1200 B.C.E.	Israelite tribes settle in Canaan; Yahwism competes with the worship of Baal and Asherah.	Joshua 1–24; Judges 1–21
1000 B.C.E.	David becomes king of united Israel.	2 Samuel 2–21
950 B.C.E.	Solomon builds YHWH's Temple in Jerusalem; a Yahwist writer later composes the earliest account of Israel's history (J document).	1 Kings 3–11
922 B.C.E.	Israel splits into rival kingdoms of Judah (south) and Israel (north).	2 Kings 12–13
860–840 B.C.E.	The prophets Elijah and Elisha denounce Canaanite influences and promote Yahwism alone.	1 Kings 17–22; 2 Kings 9
850–750 B.C.E.	The Greek poets Homer and Hesiod describe forms, qualities, and functions of the Greek gods.	
750 B.C.E.	The prophets Amos and Hosea are active in Israel; a northern Israelite storyteller compiles an account of Israelite history (E document).	Amos 1–9; Hosea 1–14
721 B.C.E.	Assyrian armies destroy the northern ten-tribe nation of Israel; the prophet Isaiah is active in Judah.	2 Kings 17–20; Isaiah 36–37; 2 Chronicles 32–34
621 B.C.E.	An early edition of Deuteronomy is discovered in Solomon's Temple; King Josiah's reforms centralize Yahwism in Jerusalem.	2 Kings 22–23
604 B.C.E.	Lao Tzu, founder of Taoism, is born.	
600 B.C.E.	The prophet Zoroaster, founder of the dualistic religion Zoroastrianism, which becomes Persia's state religion, is born; in Judah, the prophet Jeremiah advocates submission to Babylonian dominion.	Jeremiah 1–26
587 B.C.E.	The Babylonians under Nebuchadnezzar destroy Jerusalem, ending the royal Davidic dynasty.	2 Kings 24; Psalms 74, 89
587–538 B.C.E.	Babylonian captivity begins the Jewish Diaspora; in Babylon, Jewish priests begin the final process of compiling the Torah and revising the Deuteronomistic History.	
563–483 B.C.E.	In India, Siddhartha Gautama experiences mystical enlightenment, becoming the Buddha.	
551–479 B.C.E.	In China, Master Kung (Confucius) enunciates a religious philosophy that becomes the basis of the Chinese educational system.	
539 B.C.E. and after	After Cyrus the Great conquers Babylon in 539 B.C.E., the Jewish upper classes return to Jerusalem; the postexilic prophets Haggai and Zechariah urge the rebuilding of the Temple.	Ezra 1–6; Haggai 2
538–330 B.C.E.	Persia rules Judah; the influence of Zoroastrianism promotes a belief in cosmic dualism and angelology.	
515 B.C.E.	A new sanctuary is completed on the site of Solomon's Temple.	
500–400 B.C.E.	The great Hindu epics *Ramayana* and *Mahabharata* are composed.	
445 B.C.E.	Ezra brings an edition of the Torah from Babylon and promulgates reforms in Jerusalem.	Nehemiah 8

(continued)

Table 3.1   *(continued)*

APPROXIMATE DATE	EVENT	BIBLICAL REFERENCE
336–323 B.C.E.	Alexander the Great conquers most of the known world, bringing Greek culture and ideas to the ancient Near East.	1 Maccabees 1
167–164 B.C.E.	The Greek-Syrian king Antiochus IV attempts to eradicate Judaism; the Maccabean Revolt begins; the Book of Daniel, adapting Zoroastrian dualism to Yahwism, predicts the final conflict between cosmic Good and Evil.	2 Maccabees 4; Daniel 1–12
142–63 B.C.E.	Hasmonean (Maccabean) kings rule Judah.	1 Maccabees
63 B.C.E.	Pompey makes Judea part of the Roman Empire.	
27–30 C.E.	Jesus of Nazareth preaches Torah reforms and is executed by the Roman governor Pontius Pilate.	
30 C.E.	The first Christian community is formed in Jerusalem.	
35–62 C.E.	Paul, a Diaspora Jew who converted to Christianity, founds a series of non-Jewish Christian churches in Syria, Asia Minor, and Greece.	
66–73 C.E.	The Jews revolt against Rome.	
66–70 C.E.	The first narrative of Jesus' life, the Gospel of Mark, is written.	
70 C.E.	Roman armies destroy Jerusalem and its Temple.	
80–90 C.E.	The Gospels of Matthew and Luke are written.	
90 C.E.	The Rabbinical Council at Jamnia leads the reconstruction of Judaism after the Roman destruction of the Jewish state.	
200 C.E.	The Mishnah, the first part of the Talmud, is compiled.	
313 C.E.	The Roman emperor Constantine issues the Edict of Milan, making Christianity a legally recognized religion.	
500 C.E.	Compilation of the Talmud is complete.	
570–632 C.E.	The Prophet Mohammed writes the *Qur'an* and founds the religion of Islam.	
632–750 C.E.	Islam spreads rapidly through the Near East and into North Africa, Spain, and France.	

Jordan, near the Zarqa River (the biblical Jabbok). Established about 7200 B.C.E., Ain Ghazal was inhabited continuously for about 2000 years. At its height, the town covered thirty acres, about ten times the size of contemporaneous Jericho. Like Jericho, this site offers persuasive evidence that the region was inhabited for many millennia before Israel's forebears appeared on the scene.

The contours of the biblical world are broadly outlined by the journeys of Abraham, whom Genesis depicts as the primary ancestor of Israel. According to Genesis, Abraham was born in Ur, one of the oldest cities of southern Mesopotamia, later moving to **Haran** in Syria. Following a divine summons, he and his family subsequently traveled from northwest Mesopotamia through Canaan to Egypt and back again, their itinerary encompassing virtually the entire geographical region in which the biblical drama is staged. The tradition placing Israel's ultimate origins in Mesopotamia is significant, for much of the Hebrew Bible reflects Mesopotamian views about the nature and structure of the cosmos and the interrelationship of gods and mortals. Centuries of political domination by Mesopotamian powers such as Assyria and Babylon climaxed in 587 B.C.E. when the covenant people were exiled in

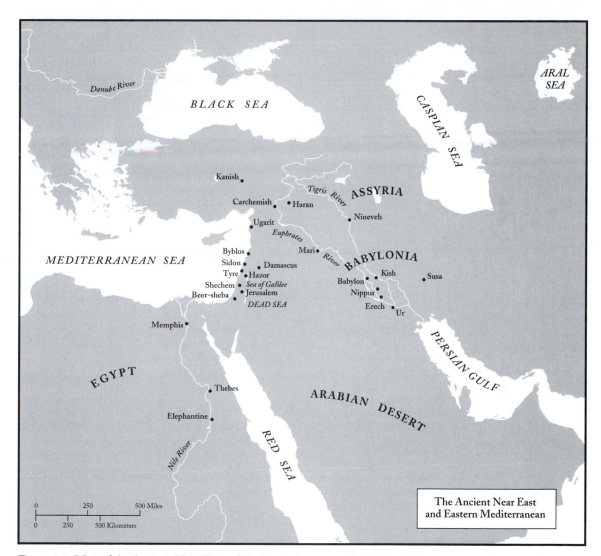

Figure 3.1 Map of the Ancient Near East   The Fertile Crescent, which extends from the head of the Persian Gulf northwestward through Syria and then southwestward through Canaan into Egypt, was the location of the world's oldest urban civilizations. In Genesis, the itinerary of Abraham's travels — from Ur on the southern Euphrates River to Haran in northern Mesopotamia and thence into Canaan and Egypt — marks the boundaries of the biblical world.

Figure 3.2 In the 1920s, archaeologists found remarkable works of art in the royal tombs of Ur's Third Dynasty (c. 2060–1950 B.C.E.), including this Standard of Ur, a decorative mosaic of inlaid shell and lapis lazuli. The bottom scene depicts men and animals carrying goods, perhaps from a military victory that the seated figures (top level) are celebrating. Note the musician entertaining the banqueteers (top right).

Babylon. Prolonged exposure to Babylonian cultural traditions, scholars believe, resulted in a strong Mesopotamian flavoring to many biblical narratives, including the first eleven chapters of Genesis (see Chapter 7).

Mesopotamia: Site of the World's First Urban Civilization

Mesopotamia— the "land between the rivers"— is the name the Greeks assigned to a region at the head of the Persian Gulf in what is now southern Iraq. In this flat, swampy area near the mouths of the **Tigris** and **Euphrates** rivers, the world's first urban civilization was born. Shortly after 3500 B.C.E., a people called the **Sumerians** founded the earliest cities, such as **Ur,** Abraham's birthplace, and **Uruk,** home to **Gilgamesh,** the first hero of Western literature (Figure 3.3). A remarkably innovative people, the Sumerians constructed elaborate irrigation systems, erected monumental temples to their gods, and devised the first law codes to protect property and foster social order. By inventing the wheel (fourth millennium B.C.E.), they facilitated travel, trade, and economic prosperity. At an early

date, Sumerian merchants exported goods to Egypt, which was simultaneously evolving a highly sophisticated civilization in northeast Africa.

About 3200 B.C.E., the Sumerians devised a system of writing — known as **cuneiform**— that used wedge-shaped symbols inscribed with a metal stylus on clay tablets. When dried or baked, these inscribed tablets proved almost indestructible, surviving to the present in the tens of thousands (Figure 3.4). Although cuneiform was invented primarily to record tax lists, inventories, and various business transactions, it was also used to record topics ranging from magical formulas to mythical tales of gods and heroes. Some cuneiform literature anticipates themes found in the Hebrew Bible, including traditions about the world's creation from a watery chaos and a devastating prehistoric flood.

Sumer's lasting contributions to subsequent cultures range from the fields of religion and literature to those of mathematics and architecture (Figure 3.5). Fashioning a numerical system based on sixty, symbol of the sky god **Anu,** head of their pantheon, the Sumerians introduced the practices of dividing the hour into sixty minutes and the circle into 360 degrees. Although less well known today than Egypt's pyramids, Sumerian building enterprises were no less impressive. Because the alluvial plain they occupied lacked the granite and limestone

Figure 3.3 The wealth and elegance of Ur's Third Dynasty are reflected in this splendid gold headdress found in Lady PuAbi's tomb, which Sir Leonard Woolley excavated in the 1920s.

Figure 3.4 One of the oldest — and most durable — documents of world history, this clay prism records a cuneiform list of Sumerian kings "from the time that kingship was lowered [to human society] from heaven." Probably derived from a Sumerian original composed about 2100 B.C.E., the purpose of this compilation was to demonstrate that the gods selected one city — Uruk, Ur, or another — to rule successively over its Mesopotamian neighbors. These citations of the lengths of each king's reign anticipate the genealogies of Genesis and the Israelite dynastic records of Kings and Chronicles.

used by Egyptian builders, the Sumerians mass-produced clay bricks, typically baked and glazed, with which they constructed massive walls around their cities, which also featured large temple complexes honoring the city's patron deity. Their most distinctive architectural form was the **ziggurat,** a towering, multitiered edifice that typically dominated the city's skyline (Figure 3.6). At the top level stood a chapel or shrine believed to house the divinity, such as Anu, to whom the building was dedicated. With broad staircases connecting its several levels, the ziggurat functioned like the spire of a Christian cathedral, a visible link symbolically connecting humans on earth with invisible deities inhabiting the sky.

The importance of the ziggurat, and the sacred urban site on which it stood, is expressed in Mesopotamian place names. *Babylon,* which eventually became the region's greatest city, means the "gate of the god," indicating its status as the holy place of **Marduk,** creator of the universe and king of the gods. The significance of Marduk's Babylonian ziggurat is also suggested by its name, *Etemenanki,* which translates as the "house that is the foundation of heaven and earth."

When Jacob, Abraham's grandson, dreams of a vast ramp or "ladder" by which supernatural beings

Figure 3.5 Fashioned of limestone, this Sumerian figurine dates from about 2500 B.C.E. The shaved head and long, flounced tunic were typical Sumerian styles of dress.

ascend to or descend from heaven, his vision conveys the ziggurat's religious function, providing a sacred zone at which the divine and human realms intersect. Setting up a stone pillar to commemorate his glimpse of the spirit world, Jacob exclaims that Bethel, the "House of GOD" where he slept and communicated with YHWH, is nothing less than the "gate of heaven" (Gen. 28:10–19), his personal Babylon. Jacob's perception of the ziggurat's transcendent purpose reveals a more plausible understanding of Mesopotamian religion than the equally famous story of the Tower of Babel in Genesis 11. In the **Babel** episode, the author represents humanity's prideful attempt to erect a structure high

enough to "reach heaven" as an offense against YHWH. Accordingly, YHWH thwarts human ambition by overthrowing the ziggurat, scattering its builders abroad, and confusing their language. Although this tale explains why earth's inhabitants are divided by both geographical distance and language barriers, some commentators believe that it distorts the Mesopotamians' reasons for constructing their sacred towers.

The Akkadian Invasion and the Formation of the First Empire

About 2500 B.C.E., Sumer was invaded by a Semitic people known as the **Akkadians.** Assimilating the older Sumerian culture, including its cuneiform script, which they adapted to transcribe their own language, the Akkadians established the world's first empire. **Sargon I** of Akkad (ruled c. 2334–2279 B.C.E.), rose from obscurity to become the earliest ruler to forge a union of previously independent city-states. After conquering Ur, he appointed his daughter as high priestess of the Akkadian moon god **Sin.** For the next 1800 years, Mesopotamian rulers followed Sargon's lead by appointing their daughters to officiate at the moon god's temple. According to many scholars, Sinai, the mountain where Moses encountered YHWH, takes its name from Sin, the Akkadian lunar deity.

Sargon's most celebrated successor, his grandson **Naram-Sin,** proclaimed himself "king of the four quarters of the earth," indicating that he may have extended his rule over most of Mesopotamia (Figure 3.7). Among Naram-Sin's many exploits was his destruction of **Ebla,** a major city in northern Syria. In 1975, archaeologists excavating Ebla's royal archives uncovered an extensive library written in cuneiform. Dating to the twenty-third century B.C.E., Ebla's collection of hymns, proverbs, myths, and rituals offers a fascinating glimpse into a sophisticated northwest Mesopotamian culture that flourished several centuries before Abraham. Shortly after Ebla's discovery, a few scholars made

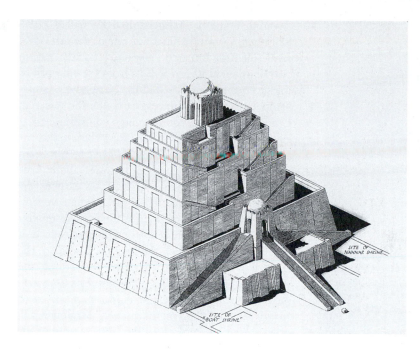

Figure 3.6 The Sumerians built the world's first skyscrapers, towers of sunbaked bricks known as ziggurats. In this artist's reconstruction of the ancient ziggurat at Ur, the chapel to Nanna, god of the moon, crowns the temple structure. These artificial mountains served as pedestals to which heavenly beings could descend to earth, treading the sacred stairways linking the human and divine worlds. Jacob's dream at Bethel (Gen. 28:2–11) envisions a similar "gateway to heaven."

sweeping claims about its supposed connection to the Hebrew Bible. One proposed that Ebla's pantheon included a god named Ya, an abbreviated form of Yahweh, and that a king called Ebrum may have been a forefather of Abraham. The majority of scholars, however, have since rejected such assertions as premature and unverifiable. Although further study is necessary before Ebla's possible relevance to biblical traditions is understood, some early findings may be significant. One personal name appearing in the documents—*Ishra-il*—seems too similar to *Israel* to be merely coincidental. Genesis states that Jacob had his name changed to *Israel* after wrestling with a mysterious nocturnal visitor at Peniel. The Ebla text suggests, however, that the name existed long before it was bestowed on the progenitor of Israel's twelve tribes.

After dominating Mesopotamia for two centuries, Sargon's empire fell to a new invader, the **Amorites** (or "Westerners"), who swept through many parts of the Fertile Crescent. Merely raiding and looting in some areas, the Amorites settled in others, building new towns in northern and western Canaan. They also founded or greatly expanded two important city-states in Mesopotamia—**Mari** on the middle Euphrates and **Babylon** on the river's southern segment. Located near the modern border of Syria and Iraq, the Mari site has yielded more than 20,000 clay tablets approximately 4000 years old. Some of these cuneiform texts contain information about Bronze Age social customs that provides valuable background for the Genesis stories about Abraham, Isaac, and Jacob. A similar literary find at Nuzi on the upper Tigris River illuminates legal and marital practices of the mid-second millennium B.C.E., a period shortly after the traditional dates for the patriarchal age. Despite alleged parallels to the domestic arrangements of Abraham and Sarah or of Jacob and his family, however, continued study of the Nuzi tablets suggests that the social mores they reflect are not those in the Genesis narratives. Although archaeologists can uncover material remains of vanished civilizations presumably contemporaneous with biblical characters and events, they have not been able to verify the historicity of Israel's ancestors.

Figure 3.7 In this stele commemorating a victory of Naram-Sin, grandson of the Akkadian empire-builder Sargon I, the king ascends a mountain whose peak reaches into heaven, while his enemies are crushed beneath his feet. During Naram-Sin's thirty-seven-year reign in the twenty-third century B.C.E., the Akkadian Empire reached its height.

The *Epic of Gilgamesh*

In addition to innumerable legal and commercial documents, archaeologists have also discovered important works of Mesopotamian literature that contain many similarities to passages in the Hebrew Bible. During the mid-nineteenth century C.E., archaeologists uncovered the cuneiform library of the

Assyrian emperor **Ashurbanipal IV** (ruled 668–627 B.C.E.). Ashurbanipal was one of the last powerful rulers of imperial **Assyria,** a warlike nation that dominated the Near East from the eleventh to the seventh centuries B.C.E. In the ruins of Ashurbanipal's palace at **Nineveh,** capital of the Assyrian Empire, excavators found a large collection of ancient literary documents, including the most complete extant copy of the *Epic of Gilgamesh.* Although the Sumerians had composed stories about Gilgamesh, a legendary ruler of Uruk, as early as the second millennium B.C.E., the Akkadian version found in Ashurbanipal's royal library has greater significance to biblical scholars. On the eleventh of twelve tablets on which the poem is inscribed, the Akkadian scribes who translated and edited the work inserted into the hero's adventures a long narrative about a global deluge. Apparently borrowed from a separate flood myth featuring **Atrahasis,** another Akkadian hero, the Gilgamesh version of the deluge contains remarkably close parallels to the account in Genesis 6–8, in which YHWH drowns almost all the world's population (an abridged translation of the Gilgamesh flood story appears in Box 3.1). Discovery of the Gilgamesh flood story made scholars aware, for the first time, that the Genesis authors had drawn on an older Mesopotamian tradition in composing the biblical text. Widely disseminated throughout the ancient Near East, tablets containing all or parts of the epic have been found in innumerable ancient libraries, including one at the Hittite capital in central Asia Minor. Gilgamesh's adventures were read even in Israel; a fragment was recovered at Megiddo in lower Galilee, and the hero is mentioned by name in the Dead Sea Scrolls, documents dating from about 200 B.C.E. to 68 C.E.

Gilgamesh's story has two distinct parts. In the first, he strongly bonds with a wild man, Enkidu, whom the gods created out of clay to be his life-partner. After the two friends slay monsters—such as the fiery Humbaba and the ferocious "bull of heaven," a personification of drought and earthquake—Gilgamesh commits a grave offense by rejecting the sexual advances of **Ishtar,** patron goddess of his city, Uruk. After Ishtar persuades the heavenly

BOX 3.1
Excerpts from the Mesopotamian Flood Story in the Gilgamesh Epic

Living on a floodplain bordering the Euphrates and Tigris rivers, the ancient inhabitants of Mesopotamia repeatedly experienced severe floods, some of which destroyed early centers of civilization. Two Mesopotamian poems, the epics of Gilgamesh and Atrahasis, render ancient flood traditions in terms of a single catastrophic event that wipes out all of humanity—except for a single patriarch who survives by building an ark. In the Sumero-Babylonian *Epic of Gilgamesh*, the title hero, seeking everlasting life, visits his ancestor Utnapishtim, the only man to survive the global deluge. Utnapishtim tells Gilgamesh that long ago, when the gods, led by Enlil, deity of storm and wind, determined to drown all humanity, Ea, the kindly god of wisdom, warned Utnapishtim of the coming disaster. Like the biblical Noah, Utnapishtim is ordered to construct a wooden ark, stock it with supplies, and take aboard animals and birds.

> Utnapishtim spoke to him, to Gilgamesh,
> Let me reveal to you a closely guarded matter,
>   Gilgamesh,
> And let me tell you the secret of the gods.
> Shuruppak is a city that you yourself know,
> Situated [on the bank of] the Euphrates.
> That city was already old when the gods within it
> Decided that the great gods should make a flood.
> There was Anu their father,
> Warrior Ellil their counsellor . . .
> Far-sighted Ea swore the oath (of secrecy) with
>   them,
> So he repeated their speech to a reed hut,
> "Reed hut, reed hut, brick wall, brick wall,
> Listen, reed hut, and pay attention, brick wall.
> (This is the message:)
> Man of Shuruppak, son of Ubara-Tutu,
> Dismantle your house, build a boat.
> Leave possessions, search out living things.
> Reject chattels and save lives!
> Put aboard the seed of all living things, into
>   the boat.
> The boat that you are to build
> Shall have her dimensions in proportion,
> Her width and length shall be in harmony,
> Roof her like the Apsu."
> I realized and spoke to my master Ea,
> "I have paid attention to the words that you spoke
>   in this way,
> My master, and I shall act upon them.
> But how can I explain myself to the city, the men
>   and the elders?"

> Ea made his voice heard and spoke,
> He said to me, his servant,
> "You shall speak to them thus:
> "I think that Ellil [Enlil] has rejected me,
> And so I cannot stay in your city,
> And I cannot set foot on Ellil's land again.
> I must go down to the Apsu and stay with my
>   master Ea . . ."
> I put on board the boat all my kith and kin.
> Put on board cattle from open country, wild beasts
>   from open country, all kinds of craftsmen.
> Shamash had fixed the hour:
> In the morning cakes/"darkness",
> In the evening a rain of wheat/"heaviness"
> (I) shall shower down:
> Enter into the boat and shut your door!"
> That hour arrived;
> In the morning cakes/"darkness," in the evening a
>   rain of wheat/"heaviness" showered down.
> I saw the shape of the storm,
> The storm was terrifying to see.
> I went aboard the boat and closed the door.
> To seal the boat I handed over the (floating) palace
>   with her cargo to Puzur-Amurru the boatman. . . .
> [Storm gods bring the Flood, returning the world to
>   a dark watery chaos.]
> Everything light turned to darkness.
> On the first day the tempest [rose up],
> Blew swiftly and [brought (?) the flood-weapon],
> Like a battle force [the destructive *kašušu*-weapon]
>   passed over [the people]
> No man could see his fellow,
> Nor could people be distinguished from the sky.
> Even the gods were afraid of the flood-weapon.
> They withdrew; they went up to the heaven of Anu.
> The gods cowered, like dogs crouched by an outside
>   wall.
> Ishtar screamed like a woman giving birth;
> The Mistress of the Gods, sweet of voice, was
>   wailing,
> "Has that time really returned to clay,
> Because I spoke evil in the gods' assembly?
> How could I have spoken such evil in the gods'
>   assembly?
> I should have (?) ordered a battle to destroy my
>   people;
> I myself gave birth (to them), they are my own
>   people,
> Yet they fill the sea like fish spawn!"
> The gods of the Anunnaki were weeping with her.
> The gods, humbled, sat there weeping.

(continued)

BOX 3.1 *(continued)*

Their lips were closed and covered with scab.
For six days and [seven (?)] nights
The wind blew, flood and tempest overwhelmed
  the land;
When the seventh day arrived the tempest, flood and
  onslaught
Which had struggled like a woman in labour, blew
  themselves out (?).
The sea became calm, the *imhullu*-wind grew quiet,
  the flood held back.
I looked at the weather; silence reigned,
For all mankind had returned to clay.
The flood-plain was flat as a roof.
I opened a porthole and light fell on my cheeks.
I bent down, then sat. I wept.
My tears ran down my cheeks.
I looked for banks, for limits to the sea.
Areas of land were emerging everywhere (?).
The boat had come to rest on Mount Nimush.
The mountain Nimush held the boat fast and did not
  let it budge. . . .
When the seventh day arrived,
I put out and released a dove.
The dove went; it came back,
For no perching place was visible to it, and it turned
  round.
I put out and released a swallow.
The swallow went; it came back,
For no perching place was visible to it, and it turned
  round.

I put out and released a raven.
The raven went, and saw the waters receding.
And it ate, preened (?), lifted its tail and did not turn
  round.
Then I put (everything?) out to the four winds, and I
  made a sacrifice. . . .
The gods smelt the fragrance,
The gods smelt the pleasant fragrance,
The gods like flies gathered over the sacrifice.
As soon as the Mistress of the Gods arrived
She raised the great flies which Anu had made to
  please her:
"Behold, O gods, I shall never forget (the significance
  of) my lapis lazuli necklace,
I shall remember these times, and I shall never
  forget."
[As in Genesis, the rainbow (Ishtar's jeweled neck-
  lace) serves to remind the gods of the conse-
  quences of their destructive impulses.]

(To compare the Genesis version of the Flood story,
see Box 5.1.)

Reprinted from *Myths of Mesopotamia: Creation, the Flood,
Gilgamesh, and Others*, edited and translated with an introduction and notes by Stephanie Dalley (Oxford World Clas-
sics, 1998). © Stephanie Dalley, 1989. Reprinted by permission of Oxford University Press.

council to punish Gilgamesh by afflicting Enkidu with a fatal disease, Gilgamesh, overwhelmed by grief and terrified by his first personal encounter with death, experiences a crisis that changes his life. He determines, through sheer strength of will, to find a way to escape human mortality.

In the epic's second part, Gilgamesh leaves Uruk and embarks on a long, dangerous quest to find ever-lasting life. Abandoning the known world, he crosses the "waters of death" and journeys through a region of total darkness to find the remote is-land dwelling of his ancestor, **Utnapishtim.** Like the later figure of Noah, Utnapishtim is the only man to have survived the great flood; he is also the only one to whom the gods have granted immortal-ity. After enduring many hardships, Gilgamesh ar-rives exhausted at Utnapishtim's "faraway" paradise. Scoffing at his descendant's ambition to live forever,

Utnapishtim reminds Gilgamesh that his host's pos-session of eternal life stems from unique, unrepeat-able circumstances: being selected by the wise divin-ity **Ea** to build an ark, take aboard pairs of animals, and thus survive a watery cataclysm that annihilates the rest of humanity (see Box 3.1). In pity at Gil-gamesh's despair, Utnapishtim's wife persuades her husband to reveal that a plant capable of miracu-lously restoring youth grows at the bottom of the sea. After risking his life to obtain the rejuvenating plant, Gilgamesh begins his perilous return to Uruk, only to have the plant stolen from him and eaten by a snake. The serpent is thus able to shed its skin, ap-parently renewing its life, whereas mortal humans tragically lack the ability to recapture lost youth.

On his journey to Utnapishtim's, Gilgamesh meets Siduri, a wise barmaid and minor goddess, who tells him that he will never find the everlasting life he seeks, reminding him that the gods reserve it exclusively for themselves. Instead of wearing himself out trying to be a god, she says, he must accept the ordinary consolations of humanity's mortal state:

> As for you, Gilgamesh, fill your belly with good things; day and night, night and day, dance and be merry, feast and rejoice. Let your clothes be fresh, bathe yourself in water, cherish the little child that holds your hand, and make your wife happy in your embrace; for this too is the lot of man.

Siduri's advice is echoed almost exactly in the Book of Ecclesiastes, where the author deplores the unacceptable fact that all human effort ends in death. Life's only comfort lies in the enjoyment of commonplace pleasures that God concedes to mortals:

> Go, eat your bread with joy and drink your wine with a glad heart; for what you do God has approved beforehand. Wear white [the garment of festivity] all the time, do not stint your head of oil. Spend your life with the woman you love, through all the fleeting days of the life God has given you under the sun. (Eccles. 9:7–9, Jerusalem Bible)

Ecclesiastes' emphasis on human mortality reflects the Bible's general agreement with ancient Mesopotamian beliefs about the gods' prerogatives: Humans do not share their immortality. In Genesis 3, YHWH posts a cherub wielding a fiery sword to keep the first humans from eating of the "tree of life" that grows in Eden, the "garden of GOD." Humanity is barred from tasting the tree's fruit, lest they imitate divinity and "live forever" (Gen. 3:22–24).

The Law Code of Hammurabi

The city of Babylon, which plays a pivotal role in biblical history, first achieved prominence when the Amorites founded a dynasty there. In the reign of **Hammurabi** (also spelled Hammurapi), sixth king of the Amorite line, the city became the center of a new Mesopotamian empire. Uniting all Mesopotamian city-states under his rule, Hammurabi created a broad dominion that rivaled that of Sargon I. Because of the enormous difficulties in establishing a definitive chronology for events in the remote past, historians do not agree on Hammurabi's dates. Many scholars place his forty-two-year reign between 1792 and 1750 B.C.E., but another widely accepted chronology gives his dates as 1728–1686 B.C.E. An effective general and capable administrator, Hammurabi is best remembered for a code of law published late in his reign. Divided into 282 separate units by modern scholars, the **Code of Hammurabi** is inscribed on a solid **stele** of black diorite nearly eight feet tall (Figure 3.8). Originally erected for public reading in the Babylonian city of Sippar, the block was later carried off by Elamites to Susa, where archaeologists found it more than 3000 years later. At the top of the diorite column, a sculptor carved a bas-relief portrait of Hammurabi receiving the laws from the sun god **Shamash,** exactly as Moses is later represented as receiving the Torah from YHWH at Mount Sinai (Figure 3.9).

Hammurabi's laws are expressed in the same literary structure and, in some instances, have the same content as Mosaic decrees. Both the Hammurabic and Mosaic legal formats employ the casuistic form: If such and such happens, then such and such will be the punishment. Part of the Mosaic legislation is also codified in a manner resembling the older Babylonian model, as in the section of Exodus known as the Book of the Covenant (Exod. 20:22–23, 33; 24:7). Babylonian, Egyptian, and Israelite traditions commonly reflect similar concepts of justice, including protection of society's poor and powerless members. Both the Hammurabic and Mosaic laws refer specifically to "widows and orphans" as representing a class of people who need to be shielded from exploitation.

Hammurabi declares that his purpose is to "promote the welfare of the people, . . . to cause justice to prevail in the land, to destroy the wicked and the evil, that the strong might not oppress the weak." As in earlier Mesopotamian law codes, however, Hammurabi's system did not offer equal protection to people belonging to different classes. In general, the nobility fared far better than the social classes

Figure 3.8 The legacy of Babylon's first important king, the stele of Hammurabi — a basalt slab nearly eight feet tall — records an ancient Sumero-Babylonian legal code that contains statutes resembling laws found in the Mosaic Torah. Erected in the eighteenth century B.C.E., it reflects legal principles common to ancient Mesopotamia, the original home of the Israelite ancestors.

beneath them: Whereas an aristocrat was allowed to pay a fine for manslaughter, a slave was automatically condemned to death. Merely injuring a person who stood higher in the social hierarchy brought more severe penalties than did murdering a slave.

Both Mesopotamian and Mosaic laws levied the death penalty for numerous offenses, and both allowed physical mutilation of the condemned. Under Hammurabi, if a nobleman injured a social equal, he was to suffer an equivalent maiming:

> If a seignior [nobleman] has destroyed the eye of a member of the aristocracy, they shall destroy his eye.
>   If he has broken another seignior's bone, they shall break his bone. . . .
>   If a seignior has knocked out the tooth of a seignior of his own rank, they shall knock out his own tooth. (Code of Hammurabi, secs. 196, 197, 200)

Using the same examples found in Hammurabi's code, the Mosaic Torah perpetuated the ancient Near Eastern demand for exact retaliation:

> If a man injures his neighbor, what he has done must be done to him: broken limb for broken limb, eye for eye, tooth for tooth. As the injury inflicted, so must the injury be suffered. (Lev. 24:19–20)

Judges and executioners are to "show no pity" (Deut. 19:21) in enforcing the biblical *lex talionis,* the law of retaliation. This principle of inflicting precisely the same kind of injury that had been inflicted on a victim was central to the Israelite sense of justice. Biblical writers considered the *lex talionis* so important that they proclaimed it in three of the five books of Torah (Exod. 21:23–25; Lev. 24:19–21; Deut. 19:21).

Figure 3.9 In the ancient Near East, law codes — which kings and other leaders imposed on their people — were commonly ascribed to the nation's gods. In this scene from the top of the stele of Hammurabi, Hammurabi receives legal commands from the enthroned sun god Shamash, just as Moses is represented as receiving Torah laws from YHWH 500 years later.

While making similar distinctions between persons of different social rank, the Mosaic code introduced a more humane element: A master who injured his slave had to set that slave free:

> When a man strikes the eye of his slave, male or female, and destroys the use of it, he must give him his freedom to compensate for the eye. If he knocks out the tooth of his slave, male or female, he must give him freedom to compensate for the tooth. (Exod. 21:26–27)

Although slaves were regarded as physical property throughout the ancient Near East, the biblical provision was innovative in recognizing slaves' humanity and granting the right to freedom in compensation for injury.

Egypt: The First National State

The name **Egypt** derives from *Aiguptos,* the Greek version of *Hut-Ptah,* the "Temple of Ptah," the term by which the Egyptians identified their country. The "temple," or holy dwelling place, of Ptah, the Egyptian creator god, was the strip of fertile land bordering the Nile River. Beyond this narrow cultivated zone, watered by annual inundations of the Nile, stretched vast, inhospitable deserts that effectively isolated Egypt from its neighbors. Whereas the broad plains of Mesopotamia were easily — and frequently — invaded by foreign armies, Egypt's unique geographical features allowed it to develop independently of most foreign influences. Bordered on the east and west by arid wastes and on the south by a rugged terrain through which the Nile flowed in impassable cataracts, ancient Egypt enjoyed an uninterrupted period of stability and nation building.

FROM KINGDOM TO EMPIRE

Beginning as a coalition of small political districts called *nomes,* Egypt first evolved into two distinct kingdoms, known as Upper Egypt and Lower Egypt. About 3100 B.C.E., the two kingdoms were

In both the Mosaic and Hammurabic codes, the *lex talionis* served to limit the degree of vengeance to which a wronged party was legally entitled: Injured persons could not take an aggressor's life but could only inflict wounds precisely equivalent to those they received. Both codes agreed, however, that upper-class offenders could escape physical punishment by paying for injuries inflicted on social inferiors. According to Babylonian law, a nobleman who blinded or knocked out the tooth of a commoner had to pay a fine; if he seriously harmed another nobleman's slave, he had to pay one-half of the slave's value (Hammurabi, secs. 199, 201, etc.).

merged under the rule of Narmer, king of Upper (southern) Egypt. From this point on, Egyptian pharaohs wore a headdress combining the white crown of Upper Egypt with the red crown of Lower Egypt.

Historians divide subsequent ancient Egyptian history into three major periods: (1) the Old Kingdom, or Pyramid Age (Third to Sixth Pharaonic Dynasties, c. 2686–2160 B.C.E.); (2) the Middle Kingdom, or Feudal Age (the Eleventh and Twelfth Dynasties, c. 2030–1720 B.C.E.); and (3) the New Kingdom, or Empire (the Eighteenth to Twentieth Dynasties, c. 1570–1075 B.C.E.) Under the Empire, New Kingdom pharaohs such as Thutmose I extended Egypt's dominion northeastward into Canaan. About 1490 B.C.E., Egyptian forces defeated a coalition of more than one hundred rulers of Syrian and Canaanite city-states at the Battle of **Megiddo,** a site that in later history marked several decisive Israelite defeats. (Apparently regarded as of crucial significance in biblical history, sixteen centuries later Megiddo lent its name —*Har-Megiddo* [Armageddon]— to identify the place where cosmic Good and Evil would fight their ultimate battle [Rev. 16:16].) Until near the end of the New Kingdom, Egypt maintained a line of military fortresses in Canaan, guarding against unwanted incursions from Mesopotamia or Asia Minor.

The Later New Kingdom, however, witnessed a gradual decline in power, as Egypt was plagued by internal divisions, economic difficulties, and foreign aggression. During the Late Dynastic Period (Twenty-first to Thirty-first Dynasties, eleventh to fourth centuries B.C.E.), Egypt was invaded by both Assyria and Persia. The end of native Egyptian rule arrived with Alexander the Great in 332 B.C.E. A dynasty founded by Alexander's successor, Ptolemy I, lasted for 300 years, eclipsed only when Rome incorporated Egypt into its empire in 30 B.C.E.

EGYPT'S ENDURING LEGACY

The Egyptian system of writing in pictorial characters —**hieroglyphics**— developed about the same time as, or shortly after, the invention of cuneiform script in Mesopotamia. The Egyptians also made spectacular advances in mathematics and astronomy, devising a calendar based on the solar year of 365 days. This calendar featured twelve months of thirty days each, to which five festival days were added to round out the year. The familiar practice of dividing the day into twenty-four hours and beginning a new day at midnight is also a legacy from ancient Egypt.

Egypt's numerous gifts to the modern world include the science of geometry. Devising methods to compute the areas and volumes of abstract geometric forms, Egyptian architects applied these skills to build the world's first large-scale structures in stone. An edifice of massive grandeur, the multitiered Step Pyramid was constructed for King Zoser (Djoser) about 2650 B.C.E. Erected shortly afterward, the enormous pyramids at Giza still tower hundreds of feet above the Nile valley, the sole survivors of the ancient world's Seven Wonders.

Egypt's great pyramids and colossal sphinx at al-Jizah were already many centuries old when Abraham's grandson Jacob and eleven of his sons, driven by famine in Canaan, sought refuge in the prosperous Nile region. Because the Nile supplied Egypt's extensive irrigation system even in many drought years when crops in neighboring areas failed, Ptah's land attracted many nomadic peoples hoping to secure Egyptian grain. According to Genesis, Israel's ancestors — the tribes of Jacob (Israel) — were among many who settled temporarily in the delta region.

One popular theory holds that Semitic nomads were welcome in Egypt at the time Israelite tribes entered because Egypt was then ruled by foreigners known as the **Hyksos.** Although native Egyptian control of the country was rarely surrendered, in the seventeenth century B.C.E. the Semitic Hyksos infiltrated the population, eventually usurping Pharaoh's throne. In 1560 B.C.E., an Egyptian revolt expelled the Hyksos rulers and established the Eighteenth Dynasty (see Chapter 9). This native royal line included some of Egypt's most famous rulers, including Queen Hatshepsut, the great military strategist Thutmose III, and Amenhotep IV.

Amenhotep IV, who changed his name to **Akhenaton** (ruled 1364–1347 B.C.E.), scandalized the Egyptian priesthood by ordering that only a single deity, the sun god **Aton,** be universally acknowledged. Whereas some historians believe that Akhenaton established the world's first monotheism, many think that his cult of Aton was really an example of **monolatry**—worship of a single god while conceding the existence of other deities. Although Akhenaton's religious experiment was brief—his youthful successor, Tutankhamen, revoked his reforms—it may have set a precedent that indirectly influenced Moses' concept of YHWH's "jealousy." The revolutionary belief that a single god could require his devotees to honor no other gods is the cornerstone of the Mosaic religion.

Correspondence preserved in the ruined archives of Tel el Amarna, the site to which Akhenaton moved his capital, gives a vivid picture of Egypt during the dominion of Aton. The **Amarna Age,** the period of Akhenaton's reign, and the exclusive cult of the sun were largely forgotten by 1306 B.C.E., when Rameses I founded a new royal dynasty, the nineteenth. Under Rameses II (ruled 1290–1224 B.C.E.), the Egyptian Empire reached its zenith in prosperity and prestige. Many historians believe that **Rameses II,** a vigorous—and vainglorious—leader was the pharaoh of the Exodus (Figure 3.10). Rameses made a habit of recording his military defeats, as well as his genuine victories, as complete triumphs. If a band of Hebrew slaves did escape from Egypt during his long reign, it is not surprising that court scribes did not see fit to mention it.

The earliest known reference to Israel as a distinct people appears on a victory inscription of **Merneptah,** Rameses II's son and successor (Figure 3.11). Merneptah boasts of his conquests in Canaan, claiming to have laid Israel waste, indicating that the Israelites were already established in Canaan shortly after 1220 B.C.E., the approximate time of Merneptah's campaign. (Box 3.2 reviews non-Israelite inscriptions referring to Israel or Judah.)

One of the most important finds of modern archaeology is the justly famous **Rosetta Stone,** a

Figure 3.10 This granite statue of Rameses II (1290–1224 B.C.E.) only hints at the Egyptian ruler's enormous power. Appearing deceptively mild, Rameses wears the distinctive royal headdress and holds the scepter symbolizing his absolute control of the state. Many historians believe that Rameses II was the unnamed pharaoh of the Exodus.

large, flat slab of basalt inscribed with the same message in three different scripts—Greek, hieroglyphic, and demotic. In the 1820s, a French scholar, Jean-François Champollion, deciphered the inscriptions and thereby discovered the key to reading Egyptian hieroglyphics. Champollion's breakthrough allowed scholars for the first time to

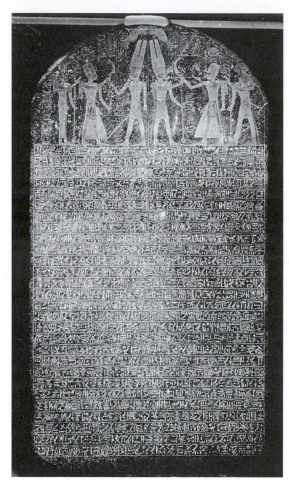

Figure 3.11 The stele of Merneptah (c. 1224–1211 B.C.E.), son of and successor to Rameses II, contains the first extrabiblical reference to Israel's existence. Advertising his victories over various Canaanite states, Merneptah claims that he has so devastated Israel that its "seed [offspring] is not," a conventional military boast. A double figure of the god Amon appears at top center, with Pharaoh Merneptah (also in double representation) standing on either side of the deity.

understand previously inaccessible works of Egyptian literature. Scholars have since translated many Egyptian documents related to the biblical text, finding several parallels to the Book of Proverbs, Job, and other examples of wisdom writing (see Chapter 25).

Egyptian-Israelite Affinities

Many similarities and affinities exist between ancient Egyptian and Israelite cultures. For example, Moses' name, like those of many subsequent Israelite priests, is Egyptian. His name is derived from the Egyptian verb *msw* (to be born) or the noun *mesu* (child, son). The same root appears in such Egyptian names as Thutmose and Ahmose.

Some scholars believe that Egyptian ethical and religious motifs, such as the concept of **Maat**—which combined justice, truth, right thought, and conduct—helped shape ancient Israel's view of divine righteousness. Another possible connection between the Egyptian and Israelite religions appears in the way in which the two peoples housed their gods. In Egypt, statues of the gods—visible symbols of the divinity's invisible presence—were hidden away in windowless sanctuaries. Because the statues were protected from public gaze by massive stone walls, the gods' holiness was enhanced by elements of secrecy and mystery. Only official priests and Pharaoh himself were allowed into the inner room that contained the deity's sacred image. In Israel, King Solomon built a similar kind of temple to house the Ark of the Covenant, on which YHWH's *kavod* (glory) was enthroned. In some biblical writers' judgment, however, Solomon allied himself too closely with Egypt, marrying the pharaoh's daughter and erecting shrines to the gods of his many foreign wives in the Temple precincts (1 Kings 9:16–18, 21; 11:1–8). Even after Solomon's time, Temple rituals continued to resemble those of Egypt: Only the hereditary high priest was permitted to enter the sanctuary's innermost chamber, the Holy of Holies that sheltered YHWH's unseen

BOX 3.2
Some Non-Israelite Inscriptions Referring to Israel or Judah

Although characters such as Abraham and Moses and events such as the Exodus from Egypt loom large in the Hebrew Bible, we have no extrabiblical confirmation of their historical reality. The earliest extrabiblical reference to Israel's existence—Pharaoh Merneptah's inscription commemorating Egyptian victories in Canaan—dates to the late thirteenth century B.C.E. After Merneptah's inscription, which indicates that Israel was then an identifiable people, there is a gap of several centuries before another inscription mentions Israel. It is not until the ninth century B.C.E. that an imperfectly preserved inscription found at Tel Dan seems to allude to the "house of David," as does a stele erected by Mesha, king of **Moab** (ruled c. 849–820 B.C.E.), a small state bordering Israel. For the entire time span from the Exodus through the conquest of Canaan, the period of the judges, and the rise of the kingdom of David, the archaeological record is largely silent. Because we have only the biblical account of Israel's growth into a powerful political state in the tenth century B.C.E., a few scholars question the historicity of the Davidic kingdom, regarding it as a postexilic glorification of Israel's distant past. While

acknowledging the theological bias of biblical historians, however, the majority of scholars still accept the historicity of a united kingdom under David and Solomon.

Although relatively sparse, we have more extrabiblical data for the period of the divided kingdom, when Israel and Judah were separate nations. Omri, one of Israel's most militarily successful rulers, is mentioned in several ninth- and eighth-century B.C.E. inscriptions, including those of Mesha and the Assyrian emperors Tiglath-pileser III and Sargon II. Assyrian archives also refer to several other Israelite kings, most of whom paid heavy tribute to their Assyrian overlords, including Jehu, Menahem, Pekah, and Hoshea.

Assyria also forced the tiny southern kingdom of Judah to pay over a large part of its income. Royal annals record that kings Uzziah, Ahaz, and Hezekiah poured money into Assyrian coffers. Following Assyria's decline, the Babylonian ruler Nebuchadnezzar conquered Judah, imprisoning one of Judah's last kings, Jehoiachin, in Babylon, where scribes kept a careful record of his rations.

---

presence. (Box 3.3 offers an account of possible links between Egyptian myths and biblical concepts of creation.)

The Egyptian Afterlife

Until relatively late in its history, the Israelite community did not adopt one of the Egyptian religion's central tenets: the expectation of a joyous afterlife. A firm conviction that the next world offered rewards for good behavior inspired the Egyptians' famous practice of embalming their beloved dead and placing them in richly decorated tombs. Whereas Egyptian, Greek, and other ancient cultures exhibited a strong interest in the afterlife, it was not until the second century B.C.E. that apocalyptic visionaries, such as the authors of Daniel and 1 Enoch, began to express hope in future resurrection similar to that of the Egyptian religion.

The apocalyptic concept of postmortem judgment, which the Egyptian faith had honored for millennia, was eventually passed on from Judaism to Christianity. The Christian Apocalypse (Revelation) pictures cosmic judgment, in which names are read from a "book of life," in terms echoing ancient Egyptian beliefs (Rev. 20). Egyptian artworks depicting **Osiris,** god of the dead, weighing the deceased's heart on a scale balanced by the feather of truth, anticipate Judeo-Christian doctrines about the afterlife and final judgment (see Rev. 20).

Perhaps Egypt's most lasting contribution to biblical religion was the ritual practice of **circumcision**—the surgical removal of the foreskin (prepuce) from the penis. Circumcision was a physically

BOX 3.3
Egyptian Myths Anticipating Biblical Concepts of Creation

In Mesopotamian, Egyptian, and Hebrew traditions, water is the primal substance out of which the universe developed. Ancient **cosmogonies** (stories about the birth or origin of the cosmos) typically pictured major elements composing the world — earth, sky, atmosphere — as gods, a means by which thinkers in a prescientific age could denote the superhuman forces that fashioned and sustained the universe. Thus, the Babylonian *Enuma Elish* depicts the precreation waste of limitless water as the deities Apsu (sweet, or potable, water) and Tiamat (saltwater). Similarly, the Egyptian creation account associated with Heliopolis (meaning "City of the Sun") postulates a primordial expanse of water, called Nu, that had to be separated and divided during the process of forming the world. According to the Heliopolis account, the sun god Aton arose out of Nu, standing on a primeval mound, a prototype of the inhabitable earth, surrounded by a vast watery chaos.

Aton, who in his divine being encompassed the totality of everything that exists, became the source of all other gods, the first two of whom he spewed forth in his semen. Producing Shu and Tefnut (thought to signify air and moisture, respectively) from his body, Aton initiated the proliferation of divine life that included Geb (the male principle, earth) and Nut (the female principle, sky). His progeny also included the gods who symbolized the divinely ordained structure of Egyptian society: Osiris, lord of the Underworld; his consort Isis, symbolizing the royal throne; Seth, Osiris's destructive brother, a personification of chaos; Nephthys, sister of Isis and wife of Seth; and Horus, son of Osiris and Isis, who represented the power of the reigning pharaoh.

Although Aton, the supreme creator god who embodies the life-giving energy of the sun, presides over an ordered harmonious system (the cosmos), the Egyptians apparently feared an eventual return of the original watery chaos. In Egyptian **cosmology** (a philosophical view of the universe's nature and purpose), even after creation the primal waters continued to surround the world, separated from it by the vault of the sky (Nut) and confined to subterranean regions by the overlying earth (Geb). The Egyptian notion of waters gathered above the atmosphere and below the earth is essentially that presented in Genesis 1, where Elohim (God) "divided the waters above the vault [sky, or "firmament"] from the waters under the vault" (Gen. 1:6–7). When God brings the Flood, he simply releases the primal waters stored above the vault by activating the "sluices of heaven" (openings in the sky's broad dome) and by causing the "springs of the great deep [water-filled abyss beneath the earth]" to break through to the surface (Gen. 7:11–12). (See also Exodus 20:4, which refers to the "waters beneath the earth," the underground remnant of primeval sea on which the dry land is precariously balanced.) Interestingly, the Egyptians had no tradition of a global deluge, perhaps because they received very little rain and anticipated the annual inundations of the Nile as a natural blessing that ensured the fertility of their fields.

Another Egyptian account, devised by the priests of Ptah at Memphis during the thirteenth century B.C.E., offers a creation by divine thought and speech, a concept employed not only in Genesis 1 but also in the Gospel of John. Ptah, after whom the nation of Egypt (the "Temple of Ptah") is named, was promoted by the Memphis priests as superior to all other deities, including Aton, the sun god. According to a late version of the myth, inscribed on stone by order of Pharaoh Shabaka about 700 B.C.E., Ptah gave birth to all things, including the gods, by his "heart" and "tongue." Because many ancient languages, including biblical Hebrew, which has few abstract terms, used the word for heart to designate "mind" or "consciousness," Ptah created by thinking the universe into existence, fashioning it by the power of his word. When Ptah conceived an idea of something, he then pronounced its identity, causing it to be — a process that Elohim also follows in Genesis 1.

distinguishing mark on all Israelite males. According to the Greek historian Herodotus, this originally Egyptian practice spread to a few other nations, whereas the majority of men "leave their private parts as nature made them" (*The Histories,* Bk. 2, 37; cf. Josh. 5:2–6 and Jer. 9:25–26). In ancient Israel (and in modern Judaism), all male infants, when eight days old, routinely had the foreskin amputated (Gen. 17:12; Lev. 12:3; Luke 1:59; Phil. 3:5). This ancient Egyptian rite, in fact, is interpreted as the indelible "sign" of God's covenant with Abraham and all his descendants: "My Covenant shall be marked on your bodies as a Covenant in perpetuity" (Gen. 17:9–14).

Israel and Its Neighbors

CANAAN AND ISRAEL

Located strategically between the great powers of Egypt and Mesopotamia, Israel and its Canaanite neighbors shared both a common culture and a vulnerability to foreign invasion (Figure 3.12). Excavations at the ancient Canaanite settlement of **Ugarit** (now the modern city of **Ras Shamra** in Syria) uncovered a library of cuneiform texts that, like the *Epic of Gilgamesh* and the *Enuma Elish,* anticipate ideas that appeared later in the Hebrew Bible. Composed in a hitherto unknown Semitic language that, when deciphered, showed affinities with biblical Hebrew, the Ugaritic texts provide a major source of information about Canaanite religion, including tales about conflicts between the gods and natural forces. Dating from about 1600 to 1400 B.C.E., these documents reveal that the chief Canaanite god, **El**—the general Semitic name for deity—was thought of in much the same way as early Israelite concepts of YHWH (see Chapter 4). Called "Father of Years," "Compassionate," and "Father of Humankind," El is also referred to in epithets suggesting that he is the world creator and source of the watery abyss that precedes creation in Genesis 1:1.

Although Israel's religious leaders staunchly resisted any compromise with El's son **Baal,** the Canaanite god of storm, rain, and fecundity, many scholars believe that qualities and attributes of El were assimilated into the biblical portrait of YHWH. As they settled in Canaan, the Israelites gradually took over many older Canaanite shrines and sanctuaries, such as those at Bethel, Shechem, and Salem (Jerusalem). Comparative study of Canaanite and biblical literature indicates that the Israelites also adopted some Canaanite hymns, poems, and religious titles and applied them to YHWH's worship.

ISRAEL AND THE NEAR EASTERN POWERS

Although it was too small and its period of national unity too brief for Israel to play a dominant role in international politics, Israel's religious legacy accords it a significant place in Near Eastern history. A brief survey of Israel's story, including its conflicts with the empires of Egypt and Mesopotamia, is a necessary prerequisite to understanding the biblical account. According to the books of Samuel and Kings, the Israelite kingdom that David and Solomon built—extending from the borders of Egypt northward to the Euphrates River—was at first militarily successful, temporarily subjugating several smaller neighboring states, such as Moab, Ammon, and Edom. Little archaeological evidence of Solomon's reputed wealth has been uncovered, leading some historians to doubt the historicity of the biblical account. Nevertheless, most scholars believe that a united Israelite kingdom in the tenth century B.C.E. may have been successful politically, if only because the major powers of Mesopotamia and Egypt were then politically weak.

THE DIVIDED KINGDOM AND THE ASSYRIANS

After Solomon's death in 922 B.C.E., the larger portion of his kingdom broke away to form the northern kingdom of Israel, with the much smaller territory of Judah still ruled by Davidic kings.

Figure 3.12   Map of Canaan, the Land promised to Abraham's Descendants The map shows the areas occupied by Judah and Samaria after the fall of the northern kingdom of Israel in the late eighth century B.C.E.

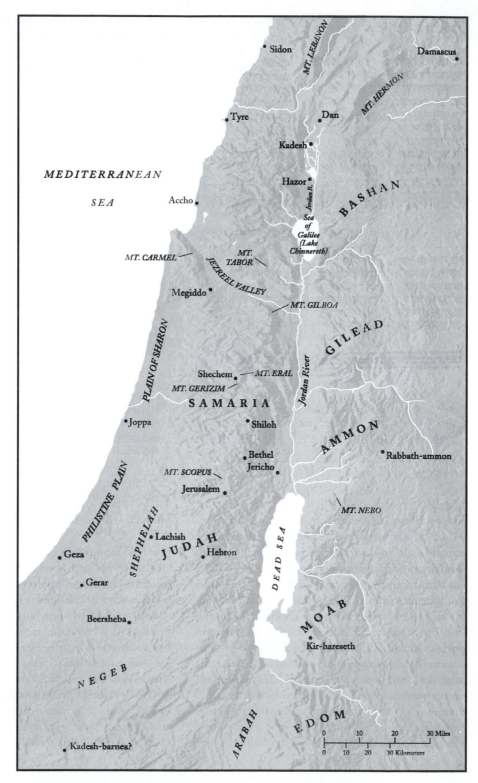

According to an influential critical theory known as the **documentary hypothesis,** at some time during the period of the divided monarchy, oral traditions celebrating Israel's ancestors and the Davidic dynasty were first compiled into a continuous narrative. Called the **Yahwist** because he (or she) consistently uses the divine name YHWH, this anonymous writer is widely credited with composing an account that became the narrative framework for the Torah. (For a discussion of theories about the Torah's authorship, see Chapter 5.)

In the ninth century B.C.E., the **Assyrians,** a Mesopotamian people named for **Assur,** their god of war, began a series of conquests that created perhaps the most feared of all ancient Near Eastern empires. Efficiently organized and ruthlessly aggressive, Assyrian armies terrorized the Near East with their iron war chariots and seemingly invincible cavalry. Walled cities that refused to surrender were mercilessly sacked and burned, with their inhabitants enslaved and deported to distant parts of the empire. Prisoners were routinely tortured, flayed alive, and otherwise hideously mutilated—an effective means of discouraging resistance.

By the eighth century B.C.E., the kingdoms of both Israel and Judah were essentially vassals of the Assyrian emperor, who extorted vast sums of tribute, impoverishing both states. During this troubled epoch, ancestral tales of northern Israel began to coalesce in a (possibly oral) narrative that provided a second major source of the Torah. Known as the **Elohist,** the narrator regularly uses Elohim as the preferred name for God. About the same time, the prophets Amos and Hosea were active in the northern region, castigating the ruling classes for their exploitation of the poor and for adulterating YHWH's cult with that of Baal. When Israel revolted against Assyrian oppression, **Sargon II** laid siege to the Israelite capital, **Samaria,** destroying it in 722–721 B.C.E. and deporting the urban upper classes. According to 2 Kings, the Assyrians settled foreigners in Israel's former territory who mixed with the remaining Israelites and adopted the worship of YHWH. Their descendants, who came to be known as **Samaritans,** were harshly condemned for maintaining YHWH's sanctuary near the ancient site of Shechem, denounced by southern writers as an illicit rival to the Jerusalem Temple. Some Israelite refugees, fleeing from the Assyrians, apparently settled in Judah, bringing with them Elohist traditions, which Judean scribes substantially revised, combining them with and subordinating them to the Yahwist's older account. This blending of sources produced a composite literary narrative known as **JE,** an epic celebration of Israel's past relationship with YHWH.

Another Assyrian emperor, **Sennacherib,** invaded Judah and destroyed most of its fortified cities, although he failed to capture Jerusalem. The apparently miraculous deliverance of Judah's holy city appeared to confirm that the Davidic kings who ruled there would be protected by YHWH's presence in the national sanctuary. During the Assyrian crisis, the prophet Isaiah urged King Hezekiah not to make foreign alliances against the invaders but to rely solely on YHWH's salvation. (The contemporary prophet **Micah,** however, predicted the eventual destruction of Jerusalem for its inhabitants' misdeeds [cf. Mic. 3:9–12; 4:9–10].) For a time, Jerusalem escaped the fate of Samaria, but its rulers had to pay a humiliating tribute to keep the Assyrians at bay (2 Kings 18:13–16).

As the seventh century B.C.E. drew to a close, Assyria's growing weakness brought rapid change to the Near East. Taking advantage of Assyrian decline, the Judean king **Josiah** (ruled 640–609 B.C.E.) expanded Judah's territory, reconquering part of Israel's former land and enacting major religious reforms that revived Mosaic traditions, including a national celebration of the Passover. Josiah also banned sacrifice at any shrine except the Jerusalem Temple, a prohibition found only in one "book of the law," Deuteronomy. Scholars believe that the Deuteronomy scroll, "found" during Temple repairs, was probably composed during or shortly before Josiah's religious revival and served as the scriptural authority for his actions. Incorporating a variety of older oral and written sources, including royal archives, the first edition of the Deuteronomistic History, encompassing Joshua through

2 Kings, was also written at this time. After Judah's fall to Babylon, however, it was significantly reedited to provide a theological explanation for the debacle.

When Nineveh, the Assyrian capital, fell in 612 B.C.E. to a coalition of Babylonians and Medes (an ancient Iranian people), a general sense of relief must have swept through the Near East. The brief oracles of Nahum reflect Judah's rejoicing at the prospect of a world freed from Assyrian violence (see Chapter 18). Judah's respite from foreign domination was short-lived, however. In 609 B.C.E., the Egyptian pharaoh Necho invaded Judah and killed Josiah at Megiddo, also ending the revitalization of Judah's worship. Then, in 605 B.C.E., Necho faced Babylon's **Nebuchadnezzar** at the epochal Battle of **Carchemish,** a city in Syria; Necho's defeat decisively ended Egypt's role as an international power, leaving Babylon as the Near East's new master.

The Fall of Jerusalem and the Babylonian Exile

Reduced to vassalage under the Neo-Babylonian Empire, Judah rebelled in 587 B.C.E., resulting in the sacking of Jerusalem by Nebuchadnezzar and the deportation of its upper classes to Babylon. Among the exiles was the priest-prophet **Ezekiel** (see Chapter 20). More than a century earlier, Isaiah had assured King Hezekiah that YHWH would not permit the Assyrians to desecrate the city where he had placed his name (2 Kings 19:32–34). In contrast, during Judah's Babylonian crisis, both Ezekiel and **Jeremiah** preached a strikingly different message: Neither YHWH's presence in the Temple nor his promise to maintain the Davidic dynasty would save Judah. Jeremiah urged **Zedekiah,** the last Davidic king, to submit to Babylon as YHWH's rod of correction. When Zedekiah's advisors, hoping for aid from Egypt, persuaded the king to rebel in 587 B.C.E., Nebuchadnezzar promptly marched on Jerusalem, capturing and demolishing

it along with Solomon's Temple. A large part of the population was removed to Babylon, with only the poor left behind.

The period of the **Babylonian exile** (587–538 B.C.E.) and the centuries immediately following, when **Persia** replaced Babylon as ruler of the Near East, were the most productive era in terms of biblical composition. Scholars believe that much of the Hebrew Bible, including the Torah and the historical books (Joshua through 2 Kings), as well as the collections ascribed to various prophets, was throughly revised and reedited during the late sixth, fifth, and fourth centuries B.C.E. The composite (JE) epic of Israel's origins, along with Deuteronomy and the Deuteronomistic History, were partly rewritten from the perspective of Judah's catastrophic defeat by Babylon. Without king, country, or sanctuary, the Jewish exiles in Babylon pondered the national disaster that had robbed them of all the divine promises made to Abraham and David. In its final edition, the Torah thus does not end as one would expect, with Israel's possession of Canaan. Instead, it concludes with Moses' ultimate disappointment — seeing the Promised Land from afar and then dying before he can enter it. The divine promises remain in effect, but their fulfillment lies in the indefinite future.

Taken as a whole, the long historical account of Abraham's heirs, beginning in Genesis and extending through 2 Kings, ends on a similarly disquieting note, with the covenant people still not possessing the land, but only remembering it from their distant captivity in Babylon. At that low point in their history, it may have seemed as if God had entirely abandoned his people. During the exile and its aftermath, Judean writers produced varied works that dramatized their nation's misfortunes, including the Book of Job, in which a righteous man reexamines traditional concepts of God's character and divine justice. As Job, after almost unbearable suffering, is finally returned to divine favor, so Israel could hope for restoration.

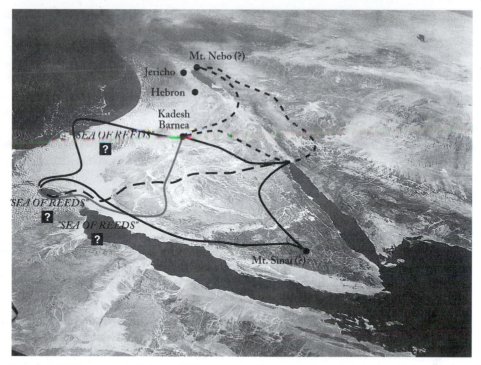

Figure 3.13 Photographed from a U.S. spacecraft, this view of the southeastern corner of the Mediterranean shows southern Palestine (top left) and the Sinai desert (center). The Gulf of Suez lies below the Sinai peninsula and the Gulf of ʿAqaba above it. The long, troughlike depression extending northward from Aqabah holds the Dead Sea, Jordan Valley, and the Sea of Galilee. Shown are possible routes of the Exodus.

The Return from Babylon and the Dominance of Persia

After Judah's former leaders had passed almost half a century in exile, a new prophet, Second Isaiah, proclaimed to his fellow Judeans that YHWH had forgiven them and would soon stage a new Exodus, returning them to the Promised Land (Isa. 40–55). (Figure 3.13 shows the region of the traditional Exodus.) In 539 B.C.E., the ruler of Persia, **Cyrus the Great,** captured Babylon. A year later, as part of a general policy to earn the loyalty of Babylon's former subjects, Cyrus permitted the exiles to return to the ruins of Jerusalem and restore the worship of

their God. Many Judean exiles, however, remained in Mesopotamia, where they continued to compile and edit legal and prophetic documents that eventually became part of the Hebrew Bible.

Although the Persians did not permit a reestablishment of the Davidic monarchy, they did endorse the rebuilding of YHWH's Jerusalem Temple, which was rededicated in about 515 B.C.E. The approximately six centuries following this reconstruction are known as the **Second Temple period,** during which the territory surrounding Jerusalem — henceforth known as **Judea**— was dominated by a series of foreign powers, including Persia, Greece, and Rome. Much of the Bible's third main division, the Kethuvim (Writings), was composed during the time of Persian rule, including the later historical books of 1 and 2 Chronicles, Ezra, and Nehemiah, which bring the postexilic story of the covenant people to the fourth century B.C.E. Although it contains some older material, the collection of Psalms, which is commonly designated as a songbook for the Second Temple, was probably also compiled during the Persian era, as was an anthology of practical wisdom, the Book of Proverbs. Although it shows the Jews fighting for their survival against some hostile Persian administrators, the Book of Esther suggests a generally benevolent treatment of the covenant people by Persia's rulers.

Alexander's Conquests and the Hellenistic Era

The biblical world changed swiftly and pervasively with the conquests of **Alexander the Great,** whose armies swept through the Persian Empire in the late fourth century B.C.E. Building a vast empire that stretched from Greece eastward to western India and as far south as Egypt, Alexander (ruled 336–323 B.C.E.) actively promoted **Hellenism**— the adoption of Greek language, literature, social customs, and ethical values — throughout the eastern Mediterranean region. Alexander's policies, perpetuated by his successors, created a new international culture known as **Hellenistic.** A fusion of classical Greek (Hellenic) civilization with Near Eastern cultures, the Hellenistic synthesis produced a creative flowering of Greek and Oriental motifs in art, architecture, philosophy, science, literature, and religion. Arbitrarily dated as beginning with Alexander's death in 323 B.C.E., the Hellenistic period chronologically overlaps the period of Roman expansion and continues into the early centuries C.E.

Along with a new form of the Greek language, the *koinē* spoken by Alexander's soldiers, Hellenistic culture introduced new ways of thought and expression into the eastern Mediterranean world. It also produced, among educated classes at least, a more open worldview in which Hellenistic peoples saw themselves as citizens not merely of a particular city-state (*polis*) but of the world (*cosmos*) as a whole. This *cosmopolitan* outlook helped break down barriers between different traditions, allowing an integration of Greek with other ethnic customs, a widespread process by which even the Palestinian Jewish community became partly Hellenized, adopting Greek styles of education, dress, behavior, and other social practices. *Koinē* became so widely spoken that Jews living in Alexandria, Egypt's largest city, found it necessary to translate the Hebrew Bible into *koinē* Greek, beginning about 250 B.C.E. This Greek translation, the Septuagint (see Chapter 2), was not only the edition used by many Jews living in the **Diaspora** (those "scattered" beyond the Jewish homeland) but also the one adopted by the early Christian community, which wrote its own scriptures, the New Testament, in *koinē* Greek.

Following Alexander's death at Babylon (a city he planned to rebuild), his far-flung empire was divided among his most powerful generals, including **Ptolemy,** who took Egypt as his portion, and **Seleucus,** who ruled over Syria, which then also encompassed the territory of Mesopotamia. The tiny region of Judea initially was under Ptolemaic control, but, after 199 B.C.E., it was ruled by the Seleucid dynasty. When the Seleucid king **Antiochus IV** (ruled 175–163 B.C.E.) attempted to unify the ethnically diverse peoples of his kingdom by forcibly imposing Hellenization, the **Maccabees,** a band of Torah-observant Jews, resisted violently. They waged guerilla warfare against Antiochus's troops until the Syrian forces were eventually driven from Judea in 142 B.C.E. Two deuterocanonical histories, 1 and 2 Maccabees, vividly dramatize Antiochus's persecutions of the **hasidim**—Jews loyal to their national religion — and the Maccabean Revolt that followed. Most scholars believe that the Book of Daniel, with its mystical visions of Gentile empires rising and falling according to a divinely predestined plan and its promise that those who died faithful to their Torah obligations would be resurrected to future life, was composed during this exceptionally turbulent period (see Chapter 28).

Whereas the books of Daniel and Maccabees reject Jewish adoption of Greek or other foreign customs, the deuterocanonical Wisdom of Solomon offers an innovative assimilation of Greek ideas into the biblical tradition. Writing in Greek during the first century B.C.E., the author of this pseudonymous wisdom book accepts a variety of Greek philosophical notions, including the supreme value of cultivating ethical virtues and a belief in the soul's innate immortality and its preexistence before descending to earth to inhabit a human body. At the same time that he integrates Hellenic and Hebraic concepts, the writer also provides an extended denunciation of idolatry, making the common but erroneous assumption that non-Jews actually worshiped a god's physical image rather than the idea of divinity that it represented.

The Roman Occupation of Judea

As Rome, which had dominated the western Mediterranean basin since the third century B.C.E., expanded eastward, it gradually absorbed the Hellenistic kingdoms of Macedonia, Syria, and Egypt. Roman troops, led by **Pompey,** occupied Judea in 63 B.C., bringing to an end the briefly independent Jewish kingdom that the Maccabees' descendants, the **Hasmoneans,** had ruled from 142 to 63 B.C.E. In 40 B.C.E., the Roman Senate appointed **Herod I,** an Idumean (Edomite) prince whose family had converted to Judaism, as king of Judea. Extremely unpopular with his prospective subjects, Herod had to take Jerusalem by force and thereafter ruled with a strange mixture of political cunning and open brutality. Almost 130 years after the Roman legions arrived in Judea, the Jews rebelled against Roman rule (66–73 C.E.). Whereas Jewish fighters under the Maccabees eventually had succeeded in expelling Seleucid occupation forces and gaining political autonomy, the revolt against Rome ended tragically. Roman armies led by **Titus,** son of the emperor **Vespasian** (ruled 69–79 C.E.), captured and destroyed Jerusalem (70 C.E.), massacring tens of thousands of Jews and demolishing the great Temple that Herod had lavishly rebuilt. In the aftermath of this disaster, which effectively ended the Jewish state, a more united form of Judaism arose, led by rabbis who reinterpreted Torah regulations for the Jewish community's radically changed circumstances. (For further discussion of Hellenistic culture, the Maccabean uprising, and the conflict with Rome, see Chapters 28 and 31.)

QUESTIONS FOR REVIEW

1. Define the Fertile Crescent and the region of Mesopotamia. What are some of ancient Sumer's contributions to civilization, in addition to the invention of cuneiform and the religious function of the ziggurat?

2. Who were the Akkadians and Amorites? What political innovation did Sargon I introduce?

3. Summarize the story of Gilgamesh and its relationship to later biblical traditions. How does the flood account in Gilgamesh anticipate that in Genesis 6–8?

4. Enumerate some of the parallels between Hammurabi's legal code and some regulations and statutes found in the Mosaic Covenant. How do you explain the resemblance between Mesopotamian and biblical law?

5. From what god is the name *Egypt* derived? Describe some of the achievements of this first nation-state. What religious innovations did Akhenaton promote? What is the importance of the Merneptah stele?

6. What discoveries were made at Ugarit (Ras Shamra), and what do they reveal about El, head of the Canaanite pantheon? Who was Baal?

7. After the kingdom of Israel under David and Solomon split into two kingdoms—Israel in the north and Judah in the south—how were they affected by the rise of Assyria?

8. Who was Josiah, and what reforms did he bring to Judah? After the fall of Assyria, what new power dominated the Near East? What happened to Jerusalem and its upper classes under Nebuchadnezzar?

9. How did the policies of Cyrus the Great affect Judean exiles in Babylon? What new political power now ruled the Near East, including Judea?

10. Who was Alexander the Great, and what was his role in Hellenizing the Near East, including Judea? How did a descendant of one of Alexander's

successors, Antiochus IV, attempt to destroy Judaism? What role did the Maccabees play in liberating their country?

11. How did Judea come under Roman rule, and what resulted when the Jews revolted against Rome in 66–73 C.E.?

QUESTIONS FOR REFLECTION AND DISCUSSION

1. As many historians have observed, ancient Israel—which produced the Hebrew Bible—did not exist in a cultural vacuum, but assimilated and transformed many of the ideas and practices of older Near Eastern civilizations. Describe some of the customs and religious concepts from ancient Egypt and Mesopotamia that, reinterpreted according to the Israelite faith in YHWH, became part of the Hebrew Bible/ Old Testament. How did biblical writers transform old traditions about a great flood to express their belief in a righteous God? What similarities can you see between Ptah's creation of the universe and the account of creation in Genesis 1? Why did Egyptian, Mesopotamian, and Israelite views of creation all postulate the existence of a primal watery abyss?

2. Ancient Israel's geographic location between the mighty empires of Egypt and Mesopotamia virtually ensured its repeated domination by superior military forces. Rather than view their history as the result of a vulnerable position and the realities of international aggression, however, most biblical writers interpreted Israel's rise and fall as a consequence of its failure to worship YHWH alone. How do you interpret Judah's destruction by Babylon (587 B.C.E.) and again by Rome (70 C.E.)? Why did YHWH not protect his covenant people from their enemies?

TERMS AND CONCEPTS TO REMEMBER

Akhenaton
Akkadians
Alexander the Great
Amarna Age
Amorites
Antiochus IV
Anu
Ashurbanipal IV
Assur
Assyria

Assyrians
Aton
Atrahasis
Baal
Babel
Babylon
Babylonian exile
Carchemish, Battle of
circumcision
Code of Hammurabi

cosmogony
cosmology
cuneiform
Cyrus the Great
Diaspora
documentary hypothesis
Ea
Ebla
Egypt
El
Elohist
Ezekiel
Fertile Crescent
Gilgamesh
Hammurabi
Haran (in Syria)
hasidim
Hasmoneans
Hellenism/Hellenistic
Herod I
hieroglyphics
Hyksos
Ishtar
JE
Jeremiah
Jericho
Josiah
Judea
lex talionis
Maat
Maccabees
Marduk
Mari
Megiddo
Merneptah

Mesopotamia
Micah
Moab
monolatry
Naram-Sin
Nebuchadnezzar
Nineveh
Osiris
Persia
Pompey
Ptolemy
Rameses II
Rosetta Stone
Samaria/Samaritans
Sargon I
Sargon II
Second Temple period
Seleucis
Sennacherib
Shamash
Sin
stele
Sumerians
tel
Tigris and Euphrates
    rivers
Titus
Ugarit (Ras Shamra)
Ur
Uruk
Utnapishtim
Vespasian
Yahwist
Zedekiah
ziggurat

RECOMMENDED READING

Baines, J., and Malek, J. *Atlas of Ancient Egypt.* New York: Facts on File, 1980.

Coogan, Michael D. *The Oxford History of the Biblical World.* New York: Oxford University Press, 1998. Provides the latest archaeological and historical background for each period of Israelite development, from the patriarchal to the Greco-Roman epoch.

———. *Stories from Ancient Canaan.* Philadelphia: Westminster Press, 1978. A paperback collection of Canaanite myths and their biblical parallels.

Cross, Frank M., ed. *Canaanite Myth and Hebrew Epic, Essays in the History of the Religion of Israel.* Cambridge, Mass.: Harvard University Press, 1973.

Dalley, Stephanie. *Myths from Mesopotamia: Creation, the Flood, Gilgamesh, and Others.* New York: Oxford University Press, 1989.

Damrosch, David. *The Narrative Covenant: Transformations of Genre in the Growth of Biblical Literature.* San Francisco: Harper & Row, 1987.

Foster, Benjamin R. *From Distant Days: Myths, Tales, and Poetry of Ancient Mesopotamia.* Bethesda, Md.: CDL Press, 1995.

Foster, John L. *Hymns, Prayers, and Songs: An Anthology of Ancient Egyptian Lyric Poetry.* Atlanta: Scholars Press, 1995.

Gordon, Cyrus, and Rendsburg, Gary A. *The Bible and the Ancient Near East,* 4th ed. New York: Norton, 1997.

Gray, John. *Near Eastern Mythology.* New York: Peter Bedrick Books, 1982.

Hallo, William W., ed. *The Context of Scripture.* Vol. 1, *Canonical Compositions from the Biblical World.* Leiden, The Netherlands: Brill, 1997. The first in a series of volumes on ancient Near Eastern literature.

Harris, Roberta L. *The World of the Bible.* London: Thames & Hudson, 1995. An illustrated survey of biblical history and archaeology.

Heidel, Alexander. *The Gilgamesh Epic and Old Testament Parallels.* Chicago: University of Chicago Press, 1949.

Hobson, Christine. *The World of the Pharaohs: A Complete Guide to Ancient Egypt.* New York: Thames & Hudson, 1987.

Ions, Veronica. *Egyptian Mythology.* New York: Peter Bedrick Books, 1982.

Jacobson, Thorkild. *The Treasures of Darkness: A History of Mesopotamian Religion.* New Haven, Conn.: Yale University Press, 1976.

Kramer, Samuel N. *Cradle of Civilization.* New York: Time-Life Books, 1967.

———. *History Begins at Sumer.* New York: Doubleday/Anchor Books, 1959.

———. *The Sumerians.* Chicago: University of Chicago Press, 1963.

Kuhrt, Amelie. *The Ancient Near East, c. 3000–330 B.C.* New York: Routledge, 1996. A comprehensive and authoritative study.

Maier, John, ed. *Gilgamesh: A Reader.* Wauconda, Ill.: Bolchazy-Carducci, 1997. A collection of informative scholarly essays on the background and interpretation of the Gilgamesh epic.

Matthews, Victor H., and Benjamin, Don C. *Old Testament Parallels: Documents from the Ancient Near East,* rev. ed. New York: Paulist Press, 1997.

Murnane, William J. *Texts from the Amarna Period in Egypt.* Atlanta: Scholars Press, 1995.

O'Connor, David. *A Short History of Ancient Egypt.* Pittsburgh: Carnegie Museum of Natural History, 1990.

Parker, Simon B. "The Ancient Near Eastern Literary Background of the Old Testament." In *The New Interpreter's Bible,* Vol. 1, pp. 228–243. Nashville, Tenn.: Abingdon Press, 1994. An authoritative and readable overview.

———. *Stories in Scripture and Inscriptions: Comparative Studies on Narratives in Northwest Semitic Inscriptions and the Hebrew Bible.* New York: Oxford University Press, 1997.

———. *Ugaritic Narrative Poetry.* Atlanta: Scholars Press, 1997. Shows parallels between Canaanite and biblical views of divinity.

Pritchard, James B., ed. *The Ancient Near East: An Anthology of Texts and Pictures.* Princeton, N.J.: Princeton University Press, 1965. A less expensive work containing excerpts from the preceding book and *Ancient Near Eastern Texts.*

———. *Ancient Near Eastern Texts Relating to the Old Testament,* 3rd ed., supp. Princeton, N.J.: Princeton University Press, 1969. Translations of relevant Egyptian, Babylonian, Canaanite, and other ancient literatures — the standard work.

———. *The Ancient Near East in Pictures Relating to the Old Testament.* Princeton, N.J.: Princeton University Press, 1965. A companion volume to *Ancient Near Eastern Texts.*

Redford, Donald B. *Egypt, Canaan, and Israel in Ancient Times.* Princeton, N.J.: Princeton University Press, 1992. A recent scholarly study of the first civilizations in North Africa and western Asia.

Roaf, Michael. *Cultural Atlas of Mesopotamia and the Ancient Near East.* New York and Oxford: Facts on File, 1990.

Roth, Martha T. *Law Collections from Mesopotamia and Asia Minor.* Atlanta: Scholars Press, 1997.

Sandars, N. K. *The Epic of Gilgamesh.* Baltimore: Penguin Books, 1972. A freely translated version of the *Epic of Gilgamesh* with a scholarly introduction.

———. *Poems of Heaven and Hell from Ancient Mesopotamia.* New York and London: Penguin Books, 1971.

Sasson, Jack M., ed. *Civilizations of the Ancient Near East,* 4 vols. New York: Simon & Schuster/Macmillan, 1995. A compendium of scholarly essays on historical, cultural, and religious aspects of ancient Near Eastern life, many of which relate to the Hebrew Bible.

Wilson, John A. *The Culture of Ancient Egypt.* Chicago: University of Chicago Press, 1963.

Wolkstein, Diane, and Kramer, S. N. *Inanna: Queen of Heaven and Earth. Her Stories and Hymns from Sumer.* New York: Harper & Row, 1983.

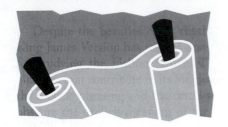

CHAPTER 4

The God of Israel

An Evolving Portrait

Key Topics/Themes Although Israel ultimately proclaimed that YHWH alone was God, the biblical concept of Deity, evolving slowly over time, incorporated many different cultural sources to create a composite portrait of divinity. Historically, biblical writers appear to have appropriated traditions about El, head of the Canaanite pantheon, as well as other Near Eastern deities. Some scholars believe that YHWH, the personal name of Israel's divine patron, may have originated among the Kenites, a people of Midian with whom Moses was closely allied. A champion of cosmic justice who jealously demands exclusive devotion, YHWH is variously portrayed as warrior, king, judge, holy Being, and loving partner.*

Hear, O Israel: The LORD [YHWH] is our GOD, the LORD alone. You shall love the LORD with all your heart, and all your soul, and all your might. (Deut. 6:4)

This famous command in Deuteronomy, known as the **Shema** (Hebrew, "hear" or "listen"), is the essential expression of Israel's faith, a passionate commitment to a single God, YHWH. Like the Shema, the first of the Ten Commandments enjoins Israel to worship YHWH exclusively, to "have no other gods before [him]" (Exod. 20:3; cf. Deut. 5:7). Neither of these Torah demands for total loyalty to YHWH, however, denies that divine rivals to Israel's God may exist.

Although some Tanak writers, such as the anonymous poet whom scholars call Second Isaiah,

eventually created a genuine monotheism (see Chapter 20), unmistakable traces of polytheism in the Hebrew Bible indicate that, at least in its earlier stages, the Israelite religion was not monotheistic but henotheistic. **Henotheism**—allegiance to one god while conceding that others also exist—characterizes numerous biblical passages scattered throughout the canon. In Moses' song celebrating YHWH's miraculous deliverance of his people at a chaotic sea, the poet asks,

Who is like you, O LORD [YHWH], *among the gods?* (Exod. 15:11, emphasis added)

Israel's God is "incomparable" in his justice and saving power, but he is not the only deity in the universe. In Israel's eyes, he is simply superior to the others: "For the LORD is a great GOD, and a great king above all gods" (Ps. 95:3); he is "exalted far above all gods" (Ps. 97:9).

On its long path to formulating the world's first ethical monotheism, Israel not only conceived of its God as one among many but also borrowed titles

---

*Before undertaking this discussion of the historical origins of the complex, and even contradictory, nature of the biblical God, it is helpful to read the presentations of God's character in Genesis 1–35; Exodus 1–20, 24, and 32–34; Numbers 11–14; and Deuteronomy 1–9 and 28–34.

and attributes of foreign gods that were subsequently applied to the Israelite Deity. The biblical portrait of God — to whom Tanak authors assign an astonishing variety of roles and functions — is thus a creative synthesis that draws on many different sources.

Portrayals of the Deity

An important clue to some of the diverse elements that contributed to the Bible's composite portrayal of the Deity appears in the multiplicity of names and titles given him in the Hebrew text. Many English translations, however, tend to obscure the biblical texts' distinctions between divine names. Although occasionally employing such titles as "the Holy One of Israel," English Bibles commonly use only a few terms to designate the Deity — "God," "the Lord," "LORD" or "GOD," and, less frequently, "the Almighty." Such uniform use of "Lord" or "LORD GOD" disguises and misrepresents the variety of terms that the authors of the Tanak evoked to express their vision of divinity. The presence of these different names is significant, offering important insights into the historical evolution of Israel's ideas about the Deity and suggesting that the origin of Israel's God is as complex, and in some ways as mysterious, as the historical origins of Israel itself (see Chapter 12).

ELOHIM

Several biblical books, notably Genesis, Exodus, Psalms, and Job, employ a particularly large number of terms to identify God. The first chapter of Genesis uses the generic name **Elohim,** the plural form of El, denoting "gods" or "divine powers." Depending on its literary context, the plural *Elohim* is translated as either "gods" (when referring to non-Israelite deities) or "God" (a capitalized singular when alluding to the biblical Deity). In Genesis 1, for example, *Elohim* takes a singular verb, reflecting the writer's intent to focus on the uniqueness of

Israel's God. The most common biblical term for God, the plural *Elohim* may have been used even by strictly monotheistic writers as a grammatical device to emphasize God's supreme excellence and majesty.

THE CANAANITE EL

The singular form, **El,** is the common word for "divine being" in several ancient Near Eastern languages, including Hebrew and Canaanite, the language of **Canaan,** the region in which the Israelite religion developed. As a proper noun, El is the name of the chief god of the Canaanite **pantheon,** the roster of a community's officially recognized gods. Regarded as a divine king who presided over a heavenly assembly of other gods, El was worshiped throughout Canaan and Syria both before and after the establishment of Israel in Canaan. At a very early stage of the Israelite religion, it appears that the Canaanite El was also acknowledged as Israel's patron deity, with whom YHWH, the God of the Covenant, was later identified.

According to Genesis 33:20, *"El-Elohe-Israel"* —"El [is the] God of Israel." The crucial importance of El in the evolution of biblical religion is clearly evident in Israel's name, which is a compound of El, meaning either "May El [God] contend" or "May El [God] rule." (For two different versions of God bestowing the name *Israel* on the patriarch Jacob, see Genesis 32:25–32 and 35:9–15.)

In the late 1920s, archaeologists excavating at **Ugarit** (Ras Shamra) discovered an extensive Canaanite library, which included several texts preserving myths about El. Featured prominently in Ugaritic traditions from the fifteenth century B.C.E.—such as the myths of Aqhat, Keret, and Sahar and Salim—El was viewed as the world's creator and the divine authority responsible for cosmic order. As the divine sovereign who ruled over both the celestial assembly and earthly political systems, El had a special relationship to the human king, who was called "son of El [God]." Known as the "Father of Years" and revered for his merciful

Figure 4.1   The El Stele from Ugarit Scholars believe that the seated figure receiving homage represents the sky god El, head of the Canaanite pantheon and father of Baal, god of storm and earth's fertility. Whereas biblical writers consistently denounce Baal, they say nothing against El, who was widely worshiped as a celestial guarantor of justice throughout Syria and Canaan and was apparently identified with the Israelite YHWH early in the development of the biblical concept of God. According to Genesis 33:20, "El [is the] God of Israel," a statement emphasizing Israel's prehistoric bond to El.

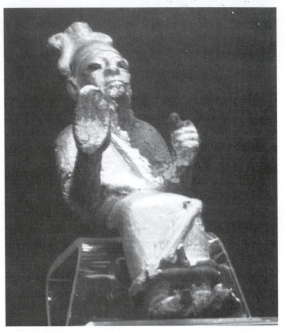

Figure 4.2 This statuette of bronze covered with gold depicts El, who was regarded as an embodiment of divine wisdom and compassion, qualities also ascribed to YHWH.

nature, El is depicted in Canaanite art as a dignified old man with a long beard and seated on a throne (Figure 4.1). This image of an aged divinity, serene and benevolent, may have influenced one of the Bible's best-known descriptions of God as the white-haired "Ancient of Days" in the Book of Daniel (7:9–14) (Figure 4.2).

The theory that the Canaanite El (a name occurring about 200 times in the Tanak) was assimilated into the biblical concept of God at an early date is reinforced by the fact that no biblical writer says a negative word about El. Despite the fact that El had altars and sanctuaries throughout the region,

Israel's religious leaders apparently did not regard him as a threat. The opposite is true of El's son, **Baal,** the Canaanite god of storm and fertility (Figure 4.3). In book after book, Israelite prophets vehemently denounce the worship of Baal, who is consistently condemned as the chief rival of YHWH. Baal and his female consort **Asherah** (Athirat, in Ugaritic) appear frequently as almost irresistibly attractive evils who lead Israel away from its covenant obligation to worship YHWH alone (Figure 4.4). The prophets' total silence about Baal's parent indicates that, by the time the prophetic literature was officially compiled, El had already merged with the figure of YHWH, who assimilated many of the older Canaanite creator deity's qualities into his character.

In many biblical passages, El appears as part of a formulaic phrase, such as *El Shaddai, El Olam,* or *El Elyon,* or with other epithets that designate his spe-

Figure 4.3 This relief shows a storm god standing on a bull pedestal, as well as a depiction of the sacred tree. Symbols of male strength and virility, figures of bulls were commonly used in art to symbolize a divine being, who was imagined as invisibly present, standing on the bull's back. Whereas Mosaic Law prohibited making images of YHWH (Exod. 20:1–4), some Israelite leaders used bull statues or "golden calves" to represent Israel's God (1 Kings 12; cf. Exod. 32).

cial attributes. In Genesis, which preserves traditions about Israel's ancestors Abraham, Isaac, and Jacob wandering through the land of Canaan, the authors candidly lay out the evolutionary process by which some of El's traits were gradually assumed by YHWH. When Abraham's Egyptian concubine, Hagar, unexpectedly receives YHWH's promise that she will be blessed with countless descendants, she spontaneously identifies the unknown divine speaker as *El Roi*, the "God of Seeing," realizing that she has "seen the one who sees me" (Gen. 16:7–14). At the Canaanite sanctuary of **Salem** (thought to be the future site of Jerusalem), Abraham is shown explicitly appropriating one of El's exalted titles, *El Elyon*, the "God Most High," for his family deity, YHWH (Gen. 14:17–23). At Beersheba, another Canaanite site, Abraham venerates *El Olam*, the "Everlasting God," whom he commemorates by planting a tamarisk tree (Gen. 21:33). When Jacob dreams of a stairway to heaven, he names his God-haunted resting place *Bethel*, the "House of El," a site that played an important part in Israel's later worship.

According to one tradition incorporated into the Book of Exodus, before the time of Moses the ancestral God was known to the Israelites only as **El Shaddai** (Exod. 6:2–3), a phrase usually translated as "God Almighty" although many scholars believe that it means "God of the Mountain." The biblical

Deity, like many other gods of Mesopotamia, Canaan, and Greece, was thought to dwell invisibly on a heavenly mountain, a cosmic peak such as that represented by the Greek Mount Olympus, celestial home of Zeus and the other Olympian gods. Exodus repeatedly refers to the "mountain of GOD"—which is given two names, Sinai and Horeb—the place where God commissions Moses, where he identifies himself as *both* El Shaddai and YHWH (cf. Exod. 3 and 6), and where he later communicates the Torah to his people (Exod. 19, 24, 34). (After Solomon's Temple was built on Mount Zion in Jerusalem, the sacred hill was seen as the earthly counterpart of YHWH's heavenly abode [see Jon Levenson in "Recommended Reading"].)

YHWH: Leader of the Divine Council

Some of the Hebrew Bible's oldest poetry depicts Israel's God as a member of the divine council, a heavenly assembly of divine beings. A belief that the gods who govern the cosmos regularly met to discuss their policies and formulate their plans for humankind permeates ancient Near Eastern

Figure 4.4 A source of enormous controversy since its discovery in the late twentieth century, an inscription on this ancient pottery shard apparently identifies the two figures at the left as "Yahweh and his Asherah." Scholars disagree as to whether "Asherah" refers to YHWH's female consort or to a geographical place or shrine where the Deity was worshiped. In one interpretation of the drawing, the anthropomorphic YHWH figure wears a bull mask (see Figure 4.3) and the figure next to him is actually a female partner wearing a cow mask; this "Asherah" thus allegedly resembles depictions of Hathor, the Egyptian cow-goddess. If YHWH originally had a divine mate, like all other sky gods of the ancient Near East, biblical editors rigorously purged this element from his official biography.

thought. Apparently modeled on the practice of kings and emperors holding conferences with high-ranking advisors, the concept of a celestial assembly plays a prominent role not only in Canaanite myth but also in such Mesopotamian works as the *Enuma Elish* creation story and the epics of Atrahasis and Gilgamesh. In the *Enuma Elish*, the Babylonian

gods, threatened by Tiamat's aggression, meet to bestow supreme power on Marduk, acclaiming the young warrior-god their champion against the dragon of chaos. In Gilgamesh, the gods hold council after the flood to lament their destructive excesses; they also assemble to discuss ways to punish Gilgamesh for rejecting Ishtar's sexual advances. In the Atrahasis epic, they similarly confer after the great deluge, exploring less extreme options — such as plague, famine, and the assaults of wild beasts — for limiting human population growth (see Stephanie Dalley in "Recommended Reading").

In biblical parallels to these Near Eastern divine assemblies, Israel's God is distinguished from other deities by his ethical character, particularly his concern for humanity's poor and downtrodden. According to Psalm 82, God implicitly contrasts his passion for justice with the other gods' misguided support of social and economic oppression:

> GOD has taken his place in the divine council,
> in the midst of the gods he holds judgment:
> "How long will you [the other gods] judge
>   unjustly
> and show partiality to the wicked?
> Give justice to the weak and the orphan;
> maintain the right of the lowly and the destitute.
> Rescue the weak and needy;
> deliver them from the hand of the wicked."
> (Ps. 82:1–4)

Because his fellow divinities lack the biblical God's insight and compassion, "they have neither knowledge nor understanding," causing them to blunder about "in darkness," undermining the "foundations" of justice on which the universe is based (Ps. 82:5). Without the capacity for ethical growth, the rival deities are doomed to extinction, a prediction that forms the poem's climax:

> I say, "You are gods, children of the Most High
>   [Elyon], all of you;
> nevertheless, you shall die like mortals, and fall
>   like any prince." (Ps. 82:7)

The notion that a god can die may startle contemporary readers, but in the ancient world, defeated gods could indeed cease to exist. After Marduk overthrows Tiamat's divine consort, Kingu, he slays his fallen opponent, later appointing Ea (Marduk's father) to fashion humankind out of Kingu's clotted blood. And after killing Tiamat, Marduk dismembers her corpse, utilizing part of her body to make the earth and the remainder to shape the vault of heaven.

Echoing traditions of El's heavenly court and Canaanite polytheism, Psalm 89 also portrays YHWH as a member of the "assembly of holy ones" who is characterized by his unique "faithfulness":

> For who in the skies can be compared to the
> LORD [YHWH]?
> Who among the heavenly beings is like the LORD,
> a GOD feared in the council of the holy ones,
> great and awesome above all that are around him?
> (Ps. 89:6–7)

Empowered by his great wisdom and ethical superiority, YHWH is eventually seen as reigning supreme over other council members, known collectively as the "sons of the gods" (*bene ha elohim*). Ultimately reduced to a dependent status as YHWH's vassals and servants, the "sons of the gods" become YHWH's divine courtiers, running errands and conveying orders to human recipients. It is presumably these subjugated divine beings whom Elohim addresses at creation when he proposes, "let us make humankind in our image, according to our likeness" (Gen. 1:26). God's associates in creation are also identified as the "morning stars" and "heavenly beings" who joyfully acclaim the universe's formation (Job 38:7). In the second creation account, YHWH similarly evokes his supernatural retinue, observing that because "the man has become like one of us"—acquired godlike knowledge by eating of the forbidden tree—the mortal human must be evicted from paradise before he becomes fully divine by also ingesting from the "tree of life" (Gen. 3:22). YHWH therefore posts **cherubim**—hybrid creatures with the combined physical characteristics of humans, animals, and birds—to keep humanity from returning to its garden home, making inaccessible the earthly source of immortality.

Although biblical writers rarely allude to YHWH's hidden activities in heaven, three Tanak authors briefly lift the veil separating the spiritual realm from our material world, showing YHWH holding court in heaven. In 1 Kings 22, the narrator portrays YHWH seated on his throne and surrounded by "all the host of heaven"—the divine courtiers and soldiers who constitute his invisible armies. YHWH's objective in calling this assembly is to fashion a strategy by which Ahab, king of Israel, can be lured into fighting a battle in which he will be killed. After the council members offer contradictory suggestions, one "spirit" volunteers to perform the deception:

> "How?" the LORD [YHWH] asked him. He replied, "I will go and be a lying spirit in the mouth of his prophets." Then the LORD said, "You are to entice him, and you shall succeed; go out and do it." (1 Kings 22:19–22)

In this brief glimpse of YHWH's ordinarily invisible manipulation of human actions, the writer depicts the Deity using devious means to effect his purpose, sending a "lying spirit" to inspire Ahab's court prophets with false assurances of victory and thus leading the unsuspecting king to his death.

A similar instance involving YHWH's use of his courtiers' negative qualities implicitly lies behind the story in which one of God's supernatural agents afflicts **Saul,** Israel's first king, with madness. Having resolved to overthrow the man he had previously selected as king, YHWH dispatches an "evil spirit" to torment Saul, intensifying his emotional instability and subverting his ability to reign effectively. Because he has decided to replace Saul with young David, YHWH arranges to bring David to prominence at Saul's court, where the youth's musical skills prove indispensable in calming Saul's mind:

> And whenever the evil spirit from GOD came upon Saul, David took the lyre and played it with his hand, and Saul would be relieved and feel better, and the evil spirit would depart from him" (1 Sam. 16:23)

Given some of the heavenly courtiers' willingness to lie, deceive, or torment, albeit on his own orders, it is not surprising that YHWH is reluctant to trust them:

> Even in his servants he puts no trust,
> and his angels he charges with error. (Job 4:18)

The prophet Zechariah offers a second portrayal of the heavenly court in session, envisioning YHWH as rendering judgment between two opposing members of his retinue. One figure, the "Satan," acts as YHWH's prosecuting attorney whose function is to detect and expose humanity's errors, accusing them to the heavenly king. (In the Hebrew Bible, the "Satan," which means "obstacle" or "adversary," is only humanity's enemy, not God's; Tanak writers do not grant him the cosmic authority he assumes in the New Testament.) In Zechariah's account, YHWH ignores his prosecutor's recommendation and decides in favor of the accused, Joshua the High Priest, whose case is represented by the second heavenly figure, an angel. Representing the covenant community on earth, Joshua is symbolically absolved of wrongdoing, his "filthy" garments exchanged for clean raiment. YHWH's **angel**—a term meaning "messenger"—who had defended Joshua against Satan's accusations, accordingly restores the priest to divine favor (Zech. 3:1–10).

The Book of Job describes two parallel meetings of the heavenly council. In the first, YHWH summons all the "sons of the gods" before his throne, among whom is the "Satan." As in Zechariah's account, the "Satan" is primarily a functionary, a regular member of the divine court whose job, like that of the secret police of an ancient Near Eastern emperor, involves his patrolling the earth to ferret out potentially disloyal subjects. Serving as the appointed officer through whom YHWH identifies and punishes human misconduct, the "Satan" introduces his deep distrust of humanity into the celestial proceedings. Apparently aware of his servant's cynicism, YHWH brings Job, a person of exemplary righteousness, to his prosecutor's attention. Satan promptly accuses Job, and by implication all other mortals, of worshiping God for selfish reasons, seeking the protection from harm and the material rewards that the Deity accords his favorites. For unknown reasons, YHWH accepts Satan's challenge, stripping Job of all he holds dear, including his children, health, reputation, and confidence in God's justice (Job 1–2; see Chapter 25 and Box 25.1).

The authors of Samuel, Kings, and Job unveil deliberations of the divine council to portray God in seeming collusion with a "lying spirit," an "evil spirit," and the "Satan" to accomplish his goals. Other biblical passages indicate that some members of the heavenly assembly also assisted God in his governance of the world. According to an old poem incorporated into Deuteronomy, when the "Most High [Elyon]" first assigned nations and peoples "according to the number of the gods," giving each deity a particular group to rule, YHWH, who is here probably distinct from the "Most High," received Israel as his "portion" or "allotted share" (Deut. 32:8–9). This ancient tradition apparently lies behind the Book of Daniel's portrayal of different heavenly beings directing the activities of different nations. In Daniel, the only canonical book in the Hebrew Bible to provide names for individual angels, Gabriel, a conveyer of visions, informs Daniel that each of the empires that successively dominates the ancient Near East is ruled by a spirit prince and that Israel's supernatural patron and protector is Michael, an archangel (Dan. 10:4–21; cf. Dan. 12:1).

YHWH's Geographical Associations

Whereas El was well known throughout ancient Canaan and Syria long before Israel became a nation, YHWH seems to have been much less widely recognized. When Moses appears before Pharaoh to demand Israel's release from bondage, the Egyptian ruler implies that he has never heard of the Israelite God or at least does not regard him as a power to be reckoned with. "Who is Yahweh?"

Pharaoh demands, "that I should listen to him and let Israel go? I know nothing of Yahweh" (Exod. 5:2–3, Jerusalem Bible). Indeed, YHWH explicitly states that one of his primary reasons for staging all the spectacular "signs and wonders" involved in liberating Israel from Egyptian control is to enhance his public reputation. He instructs Moses to inform Pharaoh that YHWH could easily have wiped Egypt from the face of the earth but allowed Pharaoh to remain "to show [him] my power, and to make my name resound through all the earth" (Exod. 9:15–16).

Later, in the Sinai wilderness, when YHWH angrily threatens to exterminate a faithless Israel, Moses dissuades him, pointing out that YHWH must realize that the international community will regard Israel's destruction as evidence of YHWH's insufficient power: "Now, if you kill this people [Israel] all at one time, then the nations who have heard about you [because of the plagues on Egypt] will say it is because the LORD was *not able* to bring this people into the land he swore to give them" (Num. 14:15–16, emphasis added). Accepting Moses' argument, YHWH determines that only the adult generation that left Egypt shall die; those under twenty will survive to enter Canaan.

THE ROLE OF JETHRO AND THE KENITES

In Exodus, both accounts describing God's revelation of his personal name agree that the Deity did not reveal himself as YHWH until he did so to Moses at the burning thorn bush (cf. Exod. 3:1–16; 6:2–13). How, then, did Moses experience a theophany in which El Shaddai was identified with a previously unknown divinity named YHWH? According to some scholars, the origins of YHWH's worship are to be found in the culture of ancient **Midian,** a region east of the Gulf of 'Aqaba in northwestern Arabia (Figure 4.5). An early tradition integrated into the Exodus narrative places the "mountain of GOD," where Moses first encountered YHWH, in or near Midian. Two different sources integrated into the Exodus narrative concur that after Moses fled from Egypt he came under the protection of a "priest of Midian," called **Jethro** in Elo-

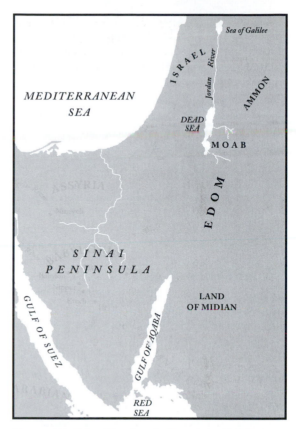

Figure 4.5 Map Showing the Location of Midian
The geographical region associated with Midian was the northwestern corner of the Arabian Peninsula, east of the Gulf of 'Aqaba and south of Edom. According to an ancient tradition now embedded in the Exodus narrative, Moses first encounters YHWH while working for his father-in-law Jethro (also called Ruel), a "priest of Midian." Some scholars believe that the "mountain of GOD" ("Sinai" in one literary strand and "Horeb" in another) was located in Midian rather than on the Sinai Peninsula. In this view, YHWH was originally the god worshiped by Midianites and later identified with El, head of the Canaanite pantheon (cf. Exod. 3:13–15; 6:2–4).

hist passages and **Ruel** in the Yahwist account (see Chapter 5). Not only does Jethro/Ruel take Moses under his wing and give the fugitive his daughter **Zipporah** as a wife, he later presides over communal meals with YHWH and acts as Moses' advisor in organizing Israel's judicial system. Although easy to overlook in the Torah's emphasis on Moses, Jethro's importance is evident at several crucial points in the story of Moses' relationship with YHWH. It is while tending Jethro's flocks on Horeb/Sinai, God's sacred mountain, that Moses receives the revelation of the divine name, YHWH. Immediately after that first theophany — and before carrying out YHWH's orders to return to Egypt — Moses goes to Jethro to request permission to leave Midian (Exod. 4:18).

As Moses leads the people from Egypt back to the Midianite "mountain of GOD" for a second theophany — at which YHWH's legal instructions for Israel will be disclosed — Jethro reappears in the narrative, his activities filling an entire chapter (Exod. 18). Again, Jethro's importance is highlighted, with Moses showing deference to his father-in-law by going out of the camp to meet him, bowing down before him, and personally bringing him up to date on Israel's escape from Egypt. Jethro's response to YHWH's humiliation of Pharaoh serves to confirm that YHWH's goal in publicizing his "name" among the nations has been accomplished: "Now I know that the LORD [YHWH] is *greater than all the gods* because he delivered the people from the Egyptians" (Exod. 18:11, emphasis added; cf. Exod. 9:15–16). Even though Aaron, Israel's official High Priest, is present on this occasion, Jethro takes precedence over Aaron by presiding over the priestly rituals, offering sacrifices "in the presence of GOD" (Exod. 18:12). Moses then carries out Jethro's detailed instructions for establishing a hierarchy of magistrates to settle the people's legal disputes. In his last recorded service to Israel, Jethro is shown guiding Moses and the Ark of the Covenant as they leave the "mountain of GOD," where YHWH had revealed his Torah, to begin the long wilderness journey to Canaan (Num. 10:29–32).

The old traditions that associate Jethro and Midianite territory with YHWH's sacred mountain and the commissioning of Moses are reenforced by some of Israel's earliest poetry. An archaic war hymn in Judges states that YHWH traveled to Canaan, Israel's Promised Land, from regions south and east of Israel:

> LORD [YHWH], when you went out from Seir,
> when you marched from the region of Edom,
>   the earth trembled,
>   and the heavens poured,
> the clouds indeed poured water.
> The mountains quaked before the LORD, the
>   One of Sinai,
> before the LORD, the God of Israel (Judg. 5:4–5)

Ancient verses appended to Deuteronomy agree that

> The LORD [YHWH] came from Sinai,
>   and dawned upon Seir upon us;
> he shone forth from Mount Paran.
> With him were myriads of holy ones
>   at his right, a host of his own. (Deut. 33:2)

Another reference, from the prophet Habakkuk, gives the same locale for YHWH's mountain abode:

> GOD came from Teman,
>   the Holy One from Mount Paran.
> His glory covered the heavens,
>   and the earth was full of his praise . . .
> He stopped and shook the earth;
>   he looked and made the nations tremble.
> The eternal mountains were shattered;
>   along his ancient pathways
>   the everlasting hills sank low.
> I saw the tents of Cushan under affliction;
>   the tent-curtains of the land of Midian
>   trembled. (Hab. 3:3–7)

Because these early traditions concur that YHWH and his geographical homeland were to be found in Seir, Edom, Teman, Cushan, and Midian, all of which are located in the northwest Arabian Peninsula — Midian territory — some scholars argue that Yahwism originated there.

Jethro, the priest to whom even Moses and Aaron deferred, belonged to a subgroup of the Midianites known as the **Kenites,** famous for their skill in metal craft. The theory that the Mosaic cult of YHWH originated in this branch of the Midianites is known as the **Kenite hypothesis.** First proposed about a century ago, this hypothesis has recently been revived and revised by such scholars as Frank M. Cross (see "Recommended Reading"). Although many scholars find the Kenite proposal suggestive, it has won only limited acceptance. Proponents of the theory point out, however, that the passages showing Jethro and the Midianites in a favorable light must belong to an early tradition. By the time Israel was fully settled in Canaan, the Midianites had become political enemies (see Judg. 6–8), and later Israelite writers are unlikely to have composed narratives in which the authority of a Midianite religious leader is recognized by both Moses and Aaron. Recent archaeological discoveries in northern Arabia indicate the presence of Midianites there before 1100 B.C.E. Egyptian inscriptions of the period refer to this group by the general term *Shasu;* a list by Pharaoh Amenhotep III mentions the "land of the Shasu: *S'rr,*" which probably designates Seir. Another list cites the "land of the Shasu: *Yhw3,*" an apparent reference to Yahweh (see Michael Coogan in "Recommended Reading").

Roles and Characteristics of the Biblical God

GOD AS CREATOR AND DESTROYER

Whatever the geographical origins of YHWH, the diverse Near Eastern sources blended together in the biblical portrayal of God are reflected in the Deity's multifaceted character. The Hebrew Bible begins its composite portrait with a narrative (probably composed during the late sixth or fifth century B.C.E.) celebrating his creative might. In Genesis 1, Elohim first appears as the originator of light, methodically transforming the sterile darkness of primal chaos into a life-filled cosmos in which light and dark alternate. Surveying his completed work, Elohim pronounces the harmonious world order he has fashioned, including its human reflections of his divinity, "very good" (Gen. 1:31). Only six chapters later, however, YHWH reverses Elohim's opti-

mistic evaluation of humanity: "And the LORD was sorry that he had made humankind on the earth, and it grieved him to his heart. So the LORD said, 'I will blot out from the earth the human beings I have created — people together with animals and creeping things and birds of the air, for I am sorry that I have made them'" (Gen. 6:6–8). Repelled by humankind's "wickedness," YHWH then drowns all of earth's creatures, both human and animal, except for the few that he preserves in Noah's Ark.

The Hebrew Bible's first eight chapters, in which God first creates life and then exterminates it, establish a tension between the Deity's creative and destructive tendencies that characterizes his behavior throughout the Tanak. Although capable of mercy and compassion, the biblical Deity possesses so lofty an ethical sense that he rarely tolerates anything less than total adherence to his exacting standards. In the Torah worldview, human misconduct inevitably invites divine retribution, often of a spectacularly violent nature, as when YHWH incinerates entire cities with fire from heaven (Gen. 19), slays all of Egypt's first-born sons (Exod. 14), or sends epidemics to wipe out tens of thousands of his own people (Num. 14, 16; cf. 2 Sam. 24).

The seeming paradox of God as both Creator and Destroyer of life stems in part from conflicting traditions about the gods that Israel inherited from older Near Eastern cultures. In the myths from ancient Mesopotamia, different gods played different roles in stories about creation and a prehistoric flood. In the *Enuma Elish,* one god — Marduk — subdues the forces of chaos and creates the world from Tiamat's body, after which he delegates the task of creating humankind to his father Ea, the god of wisdom. Another tradition, found in the Atrahasis epic, states that a mother goddess, Nintu-Mami, is the divine potter who shapes humans out of clay. In Mesopotamian tradition, however, none of these creator gods is responsible for destroying humanity in a global deluge. According to the Gilgamesh epic, it is Enlil, the ill-tempered god of storm and wind, who persuades the divine assembly to drown all humanity. A friend to humanity, the compassionate Ea subverts Enlil's destructive plan by secretly warning the man Utnapishtim of the imminent disaster and instructing him to build an ark in which his family, as well as representative animals, reptiles, and birds, will be saved. The ancient polytheistic version of the Flood story, in which two opposing deities, Enlil and Ea, take opposite roles of destroyer and savior, thus makes reasonably good sense. When the Genesis writers revised and adapted the Mesopotamian traditions to fit their emerging monotheism, however, they assigned the actions of three different deities—Marduk, Enlil, and Ea—to a single divinity, YHWH/Elohim. As the author of Joshua observes, Israel's forebears were familiar with Mesopotamian gods and their worship (24:14); during their captivity in Babylon, Israelite leaders become equally well acquainted with Babylonian traditions, including stories of creation and the Flood. (Compare the Gilgamesh deluge story [Box 3.1] with that in Genesis [Box 5.1].)

As a result of this merging of formerly separate divine personalities, the biblical God manifests seemingly contradictory qualities and is consequently represented as having to change his mind about his own creative work, feeling "sorry" that he had made a flawed humanity (see also Exodus 32:14 for another incident in which "the LORD changed his mind"). In Genesis 6–8, which weaves together two originally independent deluge accounts (see Box 5.1), God takes over both Enlil's role as violent destroyer and Ea's as savior of Noah, his three sons, and their wives—survivors who will repopulate the post-Flood world. In monotheism—which ascribes all things to one Deity—light and dark, mercy and judgment, peace and violence, life and death necessarily must have a single divine source (see Isa. 45).

Although the biblical God may have assumed some of the conflicting traits of older Near Eastern deities that contribute to his somewhat paradoxical character, he also manifests qualities that radically distinguish him from other ancient gods. YHWH is unique in his inflexible demand to be worshiped exclusively. Although all the major gods of polytheism expected suitable recognition and respect, they

did not ask people to honor *them alone.* YHWH, however, describes himself as a "jealous GOD," roused to fury whenever anyone in the covenant community prays or sacrifices to any of the innumerable other deities whom the Israelites are said to have worshiped along with YHWH. (See Judges 10:6 for a partial list of Near Eastern nations whose gods [*elohim*] the Israelites also revered.) In addition to refusing to share Israel's allegiance with other divine beings, YHWH also forbids any artistic representation of himself or of his material creation (Exod. 20:3–6; see Chapter 8 for an apparent exception to this rule: golden images of the cherubim that guard the Ark of the Covenant).

In perhaps his most fundamental self-description, YHWH outlines both the kindness and severity inherent in his character. Alone with Moses atop Mount Sinai/Horeb, YHWH permits Moses to observe his back (to see his face is prohibited) while striding before his servant and reciting,

> The LORD [YHWH], the LORD, a god merciful and gracious, slow to anger, and abounding in steadfast love and faithfulness, keeping steadfast love for the thousandth generation, forgiving iniquity and transgression and sin, yet by no means clearing the guilty, but visiting the iniquity of the parents upon the children and the children's children, to the third and the fourth generation. (Exod. 34:5–7)

YHWH thus informs Moses of the conflicting qualities, simultaneously beneficent and dangerous, that he will express in his relationship with Israel. Although he is gracious, merciful, loving, and patient, his perfect righteousness demands that human wrongdoing be punished. YHWH's resolve to chastise any generation of Israel for the sins of its ancestors is an expression of his divine sovereignty—a function of his omnipotence and absolute freedom. It is this unlimited sovereignty that allows him to employ any means he wishes to accomplish his goals. He is not subject to human standards of fairness or ethical responsibility, as in his "hardening" of Pharaoh's "heart" or his use of "evil" or "lying" spirits to manipulate disobedient humans.

In time, YHWH modifies the Torah principle of penalizing the entire covenant community for errors committed by previous generations. During the Babylonian exile (sixth century B.C.E.), he declares to the prophet Ezekiel that henceforth the Israelites will not be made to suffer for their predecessors' misconduct. Having punished Israel so thoroughly that it was virtually annihilated, YHWH states that in the future he will deal with each new generation separately; those persons who faithfully keep Torah regulations will not be punished for the sins of either their ancestors or their descendants (Ezek. 18).

GOD AS WARRIOR

At different periods of its history, Israel emphasized different traits and functions of its God. Because of limited space, we will discuss only a few of the biblical God's many specific roles: warrior, holy Being, king, Lord of history, loving partner, and ultimate reality. Although both Canaanite and Israelite tradition generally depict El as a pacific figure, YHWH appears to have emerged in Israel's consciousness first as a divine warrior, the powerful conqueror of Egypt's Pharaoh and the battle captain who led Israel's forces into Canaan. Long before priestly writers made their God the universal Creator, Israelite poets sang of YHWH's prowess on the battlefield, praising him as *Yahweh Sabaoth.* Commonly translated "LORD of Hosts," this phrase actually refers to YHWH as cosmic general, commander of invisible armies that he unleashes against Israel's Canaanite enemies (Josh. 5:13–15).

In most ancient societies, the earliest literature takes the form of oral poetry, such as war hymns commemorating a people's victories. Most scholars believe that some of the oldest passages in the Bible are based on archaic military songs that were composed and transmitted orally for centuries before they were crystallized in writing. Some of these songs were apparently collected in an anthology (now lost) known as the Book of Jashar, or the Book of the Just, which is cited in the canonical Joshua. A verse quoted from Jashar contains the famous command for sun and moon to "stand still over Gibeon," evoking nature's cooperation so that Israelite troops can take advantage of extended daylight to slaughter their opponents (Josh. 10:13).

A similar poetic volume, the Book of the Wars of YHWH, is quoted in Numbers 21, in which YHWH supplies Israel's invading armies with fresh well water, enabling them to sweep like a "fire" over Sihon, an Amorite king who refuses to allow Israelite tribes to pass through his territory (Num. 21:15, 18, 28–30). Other ancient war poetry, incorporated into the Book of Judges, appears in the Song of Deborah, who extols the woman Jael for murdering Sisera, a Canaanite leader who took refuge in her tent. Deborah's poem applies to YHWH's fierce advance from Edom (Seir) some of the same images of violent storms that Canaanite poetry uses to describe Baal as warrior (Judg. 5:4–5).

YHWH's greatest military achievement is his defeat of the Egyptian army, which he drowns in a turbulent sea, a miraculous victory celebrated in the Song of Moses:

> I will sing to the LORD [YHWH], for he has triumphed gloriously;
> horse and rider he has thrown into the sea. . . .
> *The LORD is a warrior;*
> The LORD [YHWH] is his name. (Exod. 15:1, 3, emphasis added)

By briefly reviving the primal watery chaos that preceded creation (Gen. 1:1) to engulf his enemies, YHWH decisively answers Pharaoh's earlier question "Who is the LORD [YHWH] that I should heed him . . . ?" (Exod. 5:2).

When the Israelites are about to invade Canaan, YHWH, or his agent, appears to assure their leader, Joshua, that his people enjoy the support of divine battalions. Joshua sees a mysterious figure who grasps a "naked sword" and who identifies himself as the "commander of the army of the LORD," guaranteeing that an obedient Israel is invincible. Centuries later, YHWH's importance as warrior is again emphasized when young David, Israel's future king, tells the giant Goliath that "Yahweh is the lord of the battle" (1 Sam. 17:47, Jerusalem Bible). As late as the sixth century B.C.E., Second Isaiah, who envisions YHWH leading his people on a "new exodus" out of Babylon, describes God as a mighty warrior (Isa. 42:13; cf. Isa. 45:1–6, 13).

GOD AS HOLY BEING

Whereas Israel's oldest conceptions of YHWH may have presented him primarily as warrior, his supreme holiness is also a vital part of the composite biblical portrait. To the priestly writers who composed the elaborate instructions for ritual worship found in parts of Exodus, Leviticus, Numbers, and Ezekiel, their God was absolutely holy—set apart from ordinary life and approachable only through elaborate ceremonies that he himself prescribed. The vast gulf between the holy, ineffable God and ordinary Israelites could be bridged only through the ministrations of Israel's hereditary priests, who mediated between worshiper and Deity. After David's son Solomon centralized Israel's worship by building a new royal sanctuary in Jerusalem, officially delegated priests presided over the numerous animal sacrifices believed necessary to atone for sin and reconcile God and his people (see Chapter 9).

While in the Jerusalem Temple (c. 742 B.C.E.), the prophet Isaiah experiences a vision of the heavenly reality that the earthly sanctuary represents: Suddenly transported into the divine presence, the prophet sees the "LORD [YHWH] sitting on a throne, high and lofty, and the hem of his robe [fills] the temple" (Isa. 6:1). God is surrounded by tens of thousands of celestial beings called *seraphim* (singular, *seraph*), all chanting "Holy, holy, holy is the LORD of hosts." Mentioned only in this passage, the **seraphim**'s principal function is to praise YHWH. Possessing three pairs of wings, the seraphim use one set for flying, one for covering their eyes (shielding them from the glare of God's blinding radiance), and one for covering their "feet," perhaps a euphemism for genitals (Isa. 6:1–8). Because the Hebrew word *seraph* appears several times associated with the serpents that attacked the Israelites in the wilderness (Num. 21:8; Deut. 8:15;

Isa. 14:29; 30:6), many scholars believe that it refers to "fiery serpents." As the cherubim displayed the nonhuman features of birds and animals, so the seraphim may have been serpentine in form and radiated flame, a common symbol of divinity. Common in Egyptian art, flying serpents are shown guarding the throne of Pharaoh. Archaeologists have unearthed scarab seals featuring winged serpents from approximately the time of Isaiah (cf. 2 Kings 18:4).

GOD AS KING

As Isaiah's vision indicates, one of the Tanak's fundamental assumptions is that YHWH invisibly reigned over Israel as king (Deut. 33:5; Judg. 8:23; Isa. 43:15). Several psalms also hail Israel's God as ruler of all nations (Pss. 22:28; 47:2, 7–8). A group of poems, known as the "Enthronement Psalms" (Pss. 93, 95–99), emphasize his universal sovereignty, as well as his future intention to subdue all peoples (Pss. 96:13; 98:9; see Chapter 24). As heaven's king, YHWH establishes a special relationship with Israel's royal family, authorizing the institution of monarchy and guaranteeing that David's heirs will rule over Israel "forever" (2 Sam. 7:8–17; 23:5; Ps. 89:19–37). When Davidic kings are crowned, YHWH adopts them as "sons," echoing El's paternal relationship to Canaanite rulers (Pss. 2, 110). Because of the close bond between YHWH and the Davidic dynasty, the authors of Chronicles can refer to the Davidic throne as God's "kingdom" (1 Chron. 17:14; 28:5; 29:11). As cosmic sovereign who administers earthly societies through kingly representatives, YHWH, in some respects, resembles the idealized monarch of a Near Eastern empire—powerful and scrupulously just, but jealous of his supreme authority and easily provoked to punish insubordination.

GOD AS LORD OF HISTORY

The author-editors of Israel's national epic, the long prose narrative contained in Genesis through 2 Kings, present YHWH as the Lord of history, the all-powerful director of human events who determines the fate of both Israel and its neighboring states. For some later writers, YHWH also writes the script of global history. In Daniel, he is shown overseeing the succession of ancient Near Eastern powers, from Babylon and Persia to Greece and the Hellenistic kingdoms. In this role, YHWH is also cosmic Judge, the Being on whose will all persons and nations depend for justice. As the prophet Amos states, it was commonly believed that the biblical God controlled everything that happened, from Israel's military victories and defeats to great natural disasters (Amos 3:3–8).

GOD AS LOVING PARTNER

While emphasizing YHWH's firm control of history, many of Israel's prophets also proclaimed his almost infinite capacity to love. Balancing the fear-inspiring aspects of divine power and holiness with divine *hesed*—which can be translated as "steadfast love" or "loyal affection"—several prophets designate this quality as one of God's most distinguishing characteristics. To illustrate God's passionate attachment to Israel, Hosea compares the Deity to a loving husband whose wife (Israel) is faithless and ungrateful. Hosea also uses the metaphor of a doting father, whose rebellious son, like an adulterous wife, could legally be condemned to death (Lev. 20:10; Deut. 21:18–21; 22:22). Although God's justice prompts him to execute Israel for its crimes, Hosea states that his *hesed* leads him to "recoil" from so harsh a judgment. He cannot bring himself to abandon "Ephraim" (a northern tribe standing for all Israel) to its enemies:

> When Israel was a child, I loved him,
>   and out of Egypt I called my son.
> The more I called them, the more they went
>   from me;
> they kept sacrificing to the Baals,
>   and offering incense to idols.
> Yet it was I who taught Ephraim to walk,
> I took them up in my arms;
> but they did not know that I healed them. . . .
> How can I give you up, Ephraim?
>   How can I hand you over, O Israel? . . .
> [God cannot bear to destroy his beloved.]

> My heart recoils within me;
>   my compassion grows warm and tender.
> I will not execute my fierce anger;
>   I will not again destroy Ephraim;
> for I am GOD and no mortal;
>   the Holy One in your midst,
>   and I will not come in wrath.
>   (Hos. 11:1–3, 8–9)

Providing a rare glimpse into God's thought processes—an inner debate between conflicting emotions, righteous anger and "tender" compassion—Hosea shows God's *hesed* winning out over his wrath. For he is "GOD," and not a fallible "mortal" who must behave according to merely human standards of retributive justice.

Because God loves Israel, he asks for Israel's love in return. Alone among the gods of antiquity, YHWH asks his people not only to worship him exclusively but also to offer him unconditional love. The Shema's demand that Israelites love YHWH with all their hearts and souls, unparalleled in ancient religion, implies that Israel's God, as Hosea declared, feels a similar emotion for them (Deut. 6:4).

GOD AS ULTIMATE REALITY

Perhaps the most powerful declarations of God's unrivaled might and majesty occur in the pronouncements of Second Isaiah (Isa. 40–55). One of the greatest poets in the Hebrew Bible, Second Isaiah is an uncompromising monotheist who explicitly states that YHWH alone is God, the incomparable Being whose will is irresistible both on earth and in heaven. Categorically rejecting the existence of other divinities, the poet states that YHWH is the source of all things, including both good and evil:

> I am the LORD [YHWH], and there is no other.
> I form light and create darkness,
> I make weal [good fortune] and create woe
>   [calamity];
> I the Lord do all these things. (Isa. 45:6–7)

In making YHWH not only supreme, as other Tanak writers did in asserting his superiority to other members of the divine assembly, but also the

BOX 4.1
Anthropomorphism, Patriarchy, and the Gender of God

Although numerous Bible writers insist on God's **transcendence**—his absolute freedom from earthly or other material limitations—others portray the Deity in anthropomorphic language. **Anthropomorphism**—ascribing human shape, form, and emotion to a divinity—characterizes most ancient religions, in which artists typically portrayed gods as idealized human beings, larger and enormously more powerful. Rare in passages by priestly or wisdom authors, anthropomorphism is relatively common in the Tanak's narrative and prophetic literature. In Genesis and Exodus, God is endowed with human characteristics and behaviors: He strolls through Eden to enjoy a cooling breeze (Gen. 3:8); he appears to Abraham in the guise of a traveler enjoying a meal (Gen. 18–19); he inscribes stone tablets with his "finger" (Deut. 9:10); he permits Moses to observe his "back" while shielding his "face" from view (Exod. 33:22–23); he even allows seventy Israelite leaders to look directly at him as if he were an object of physical sight (Exod. 24:9–11). In the Prophets and Psalms, writers make innumerable references to the divine anatomy, citing such appendages or features as his "feet," "hands," "mouth," or "nostrils" (characteristically dilated in anger). Daniel provides what has become perhaps the most enduring popular image: God as the "Ancient One," with the "hair of his head like pure wool," and wearing "clothes white as snow" (Dan. 7:9). Although traditional interpreters regard these anthropomorphic features as literary metaphors, we cannot be certain that ancient poets consciously saw them as mere figures of speech.

The Genesis assertion that God fashioned humanity as an "image" and "likeness" of himself has invited considerable speculation about the nature of the divine-human affinity. Although the traditional Judeo-Christian interpretation denies that Genesis implies a physical resemblance between God and humans, some biblical writers suggests a spiritual, psychological, or even political "likeness." Psalm 8, for example, states that YHWH made "human beings" only "a little lower than God" and "crowned them with glory and honor," putting "all things under their feet" (Ps. 8:4–6). Mirroring God's sovereignty on an earthly level, humans, in their role as caretakers of creation, rank close to God himself when exercising wise governance of the terrestrial environment.

---

single universal Deity, Second Isaiah articulates an important new dimension in Israelite thought. When viewed as the sole source of everything that happens—light and dark, good and bad—the biblical God ultimately becomes even more problematic, his universal omnipotence raising ethical and theological issues with which Israel's wisdom teachers would stage a long and creative struggle (see Chapter 25).

The biblical account of Israel's historical partnership with YHWH—the central subject of the Tanak—features many memorable human figures, from Abraham and Sarah to Ruth and David. No matter how vividly realized, however, human actors in the biblical drama are always secondary to God, who is not only the object of Israel's worship but also the Hebrew Bible's undisputed protagonist. What human participants do, what they achieve by war, conquest, or any other means—all is explicitly ascribed to YHWH's actions. In the Exodus story, for example, Moses, his brother Aaron, his sister Miriam, and even Pharaoh are merely instruments that YHWH maneuvers to achieve his long-term historical goals. Although biblical writers address only a limited segment of human history in one small part of the world, they nonetheless establish an enduring pattern of the divine-human relationship that remains the standard for both Judaism and Christianity. (Box 4.1 discusses the Deity's affinity with humankind.)

QUESTIONS FOR REVIEW

1. What does the Shema ask of Israel?

2. Define *monotheism* and *henotheism*. Judging by references to YHWH and "other gods" in the biblical texts, was ancient Israel always fully monotheistic?

To many modern readers, one of biblical anthropomorphism's most troubling aspects is its consistent association of God with traditional male roles and its use of masculine pronouns when alluding to the Deity. Although a few writers evoke maternal images in describing YHWH (Isa. 49:15), most portray God in decidedly masculine terms: he is a warrior, king, judge, or executioner who intimidates and dominates because of his enormous strength. He is also imagined in familial terms, as a father who laments the waywardness of his children (Hos. 11) or a husband who agonizes over the infidelity of his treacherous wife (Hos. 1–2). Because the power to control nature and intervene in human affairs is a prerequisite of divinity in almost every culture — and because ancient societies typically emphasized masculine values and attitudes — it is perhaps historically inevitable that Israel's God is regularly portrayed in masculine terms. Like most of its Near Eastern neighbors, ancient Israel was a **patriarchy,** a social organization marked by the supremacy of the father in a clan or family, a sociopolitical arrangement in which male leadership and standards constitute the prevailing norm and in which women and children are generally subject to patriarchal control.

While espousing patriarchal values, however, the Genesis authors also suggest that God transcends common notions of gender: He creates *both* males and females "in his image" (Gen. 1:27). According to some commentators, this passage implies that the Creator is androgynous, encompassing both masculine and feminine qualities in the divine nature. It also reminds us that the Deity belongs to the numinous — a category of supernatural power that transcends the material realm of mortal life. Infinitely mysterious and ultimately unknowable, God by definition represents forces beyond human ability to emulate or comprehend. Although given anthropomorphic traits, the biblical Deity embodies a mode of existence profoundly different from that of humanity.

Given the historical fact that both the Hebrew Bible and the New Testament were written by and for members of a thoroughly patriarchal society, today's readers may view the anthropomorphic and gender-biased portraits of the Deity as culture-bound. While respecting the integrity of the ancient texts in which God is invariably "he" — and the simple linguistic fact that the Hebrew language has no word for "it" — many contemporary believers, in both synagogue and church, acknowledge that the ineffable Being whom biblical authors seek to communicate cannot be contained in finite human categories, including those of gender. (See also Box 8.3, "Was God 'Seen' at Mount Sinai?")

3. Who was El to the Canaanites? How was El identified with Israel's divine patron, YHWH? What qualities do they have in common? How does the name *Israel* incorporate the concept of El?

4. What was the divine council in ancient Near Eastern religious thought, and how did YHWH come to dominate it? What were the attributes that distinguished him from other deities?

5. Who were the cherubim and seraphim? What are angels? What roles do they play in the divine court?

6. Define and explain the Kenite hypothesis. Why do many historians think that the worship of YHWH originated in Midian? How does the Exodus account link Jethro, priest of Midian, with Moses?

7. Describe the different roles that different biblical authors ascribe to YHWH. How did Israel envision YHWH both as world sovereign and as Israel's special patron?

8. What anthropomorphic qualities do you find in biblical portrayals of God?

QUESTION FOR REFLECTION AND DISCUSSION

Ancient Mesopotamian poets could explain the contradictory actions of divine beings by subscribing to the notion that the god who created the world (Marduk) was not the same god who subsequently drowned almost all humanity in a global deluge (Enlil). In adapting these traditions to Israel's faith in YHWH, biblical authors combined both the creative and the destructive aspects of divinity in a single God, one who creates out of beneficence and annihilates out of righteous indignation when his human creation behaves badly. This concept of a Deity who is both gracious and violently punitive — the consequence of melding two different divine functions into one — has dominated the monotheistic religions for more than two millennia. Are divine benevolence (God as loving partner) and divine brutality (God as warrior) really compatible?

TERMS AND CONCEPTS TO REMEMBER

angel	God's chief attributes
anthropomorphism	henotheism
Baal and Asherah	Jethro
Canaan	Kenites/Kenite
cherubim	hypothesis
divine council	Midian
El, Elohim	pantheon
El Shaddai	patriarchy
God as divine warrior	Ruel
God as holy Being	Salem
God as king	Saul
God as Lord of history	seraphim
God as loving partner	Shema
God as synthesis of Near	transcendence
Eastern deities	Ugarit (Ras Shamra)
God as ultimate reality	Zipporah

RECOMMENDED READING

Albright, William F. *Yahweh and the Gods of Canaan: A Historical Analysis of Two Contrasting Faiths.* New York: Doubleday/Anchor Books, 1969. A pioneering study of Israelite religion evolving in its ancient Canaanite context.

Anderson, Gary A. "Introduction to Israelite Religion." In *The New Interpreter's Bible.* Vol. 1, pp. 272–283. Nashville, Tenn.: Abingdon Press, 1994. A scholarly survey of the historical evolution of Israel's God concept.

Brueggemann, Walter. *Theology of the Old Testament: Testimony, Dispute, Advocacy.* Minneapolis: Fortress Press, 1997. A thorough and highly sophisticated study of the Hebrew Bible's paradoxical portrayal of God.

Coogan, Michael D., ed. *The Oxford History of the Biblical World.* New York: Oxford University Press, 1998. Includes discussion of the Kenite hypothesis, which traces the origins of Yahwism to ancient Midian.

Cross, Frank Moore. *Canaanite Myth and Hebrew Epic: Essays in the History of the Religion of Israel.* An authoritative examination of parallels between Canaanite religion and the biblical concept of God. Cambridge, Mass.: Harvard University Press, 1973. (paperback reprint, 1997).

———. *From Epic to Canon: History and Literature in Ancient Israel.* Baltimore: Johns Hopkins University Press, 1998. A collection of essays on Near Eastern cultural influences on Israelite religion.

Dalley, Stephanie. *Myths from Mesopotamia: Creation, the Flood, Gilgamesh, and Others.* New York: Oxford University Press, 1989. Includes the *Enuma Elish* and Atrahasis flood story.

Friedman, Richard E. *The Hidden Face of God.* San Francisco: HarperSanFrancisco, 1995. Traces the apparent gradual disappearance of God from the biblical text, following the arrangement of books in the Tanak.

Frymer-Kensky, Tikva. *In the Wake of the Goddesses: Women, Culture, and the Biblical Transformation of Pagan Myth.* New York: Fawcett Columbine, 1992. A brilliant analysis of the cultural processes by which biblical authors eliminated or transformed ancient concepts of feminine divinity.

Gerstenberger, Erhard S. *Yahweh the Patriarch: Ancient Images of God and Feminist Theology.* Minneapolis: Fortress Press, 1986. Argues that YHWH originally had a female consort, Asherah, who was later purged from the postexilic cult.

Good, Robert M. "Asherah," "Baal," and "El." In P. J. Achtemeier, ed., *The HarperCollins Bible Dictionary,* pp. 82–83, 94–95, 275–276. San Francisco: HarperSanFrancisco, 1996. Gives concise descriptions of three major gods in the Canaanite pantheon.

Lang, Bernhard. *The Hebrew God: Portrait of an Ancient Deity.* New Haven, Conn.: Yale University Press, 2002. Describes five chief roles of the Israelite God, placing YHWH in his ancient Near Eastern context.

Levenson, Jon D. *Sinai and Zion: An Entry into the Jewish Bible.* San Francisco: HarperSanFrancisco, 1985. Includes discussion of Israelite henotheism.

Miles, Jack. *God: A Biography.* New York: Knopf, 1995. Analyzes the Israelite God as he appears as a literary character in the Hebrew Bible (Tanak).

Miller, Patrick D. *The Religion of Ancient Israel.* Louisville, Ky.: Westminster/John Knox Press, 2000. Analyzes the growth of Israel's God concept, emphasizing parallels to other ancient Near Eastern views of divinity.

Niditch, Susan. *Ancient Israelite Religion.* New York: Oxford University Press, 1997. Places Israel's evolving concepts of God in their historical, sociological, and archaeological contexts.

Parker, Simon B. *Ugaritic Narrative Poetry.* Atlanta: Scholars Press, 1997. Shows important parallels between Canaanite literature and biblical descriptions of God.

Rabinowitz, Jacob. *The Faces of God: Canaanite Mythology as Hebrew Theology.* Woodstock, Conn.: Spring Publications, 1998. Explores the influences of Canaanite myth on biblical concepts of God, particularly the relationship of El to YHWH.

Rose, Martin. "Names of God in the OT." In D. N. Freedman, ed., *The Anchor Bible Dictionary,* Vol. 4, pp. 1001–1011. New York: Doubleday, 1992. An excellent essay with which to begin a study of the biblical God.

Smith, Mark S. *The Early History of God: Yahweh and the Other Deities in Ancient Israel.* San Francisco: Harper & Row, 1990. An indispensable study.

————. *The Origins of Biblical Monotheism: Israel's Polytheistic Background and the Ugaritic Texts.* New York: Oxford University Press, 2001. Places the emergence of Israelite monotheism in the context of Ugaritic beliefs about divinity.

————. *Untold Stories: The Bible and Ugaritic Stories in the Twentieth Century.* Peabody, Mass.: Hendrickson, 2001. Traces the course of Ugaritic scholarship and its implications for biblical studies.

Terrien, Samuel. *The Elusive Presence: The Heart of Biblical Theology.* San Francisco: Harper & Row, 1978. A perceptive study of the biblical concept of God.

Thompson, Henry O. "Yahweh." In D. N. Freedman, ed., *The Anchor Bible Dictionary,* Vol. 6, pp. 1011–1012. New York: Doubleday, 1992. Discusses the significance of the personal name of God, YHWH.

CHAPTER 5

Who Wrote the "Books of Moses"?

Key Topics/Themes According to a large majority of biblical scholars, the Tanak's first five books (the Pentateuch) are not the work of a single author, such as Moses but the product of a long process of composition, revision, and editing by different writers and redactors (editors) spanning many different periods of Israel's history. Although some scholars recently have proposed alternative theories, most still accept some form of the documentary hypothesis, which holds that the Pentateuch is a composite work incorporating at least four different literary and/or oral strands. The four sources, known as J, E, D, and P, were eventually combined by postexilic redactors to create the Pentateuch we have today.

Because they contain the Torah — teachings about Israel's origins and its legal obligations to God — the Bible's first five books (Pentateuch) are of crucial importance to many believers. In some views, the question of authorship — traditionally ascribed to Moses — is virtually inseparable from the Pentateuch's validity as Scripture. Until about 250 years ago, most Westerners, both Jewish and Christian, uncritically assumed that Moses had written all five books (presumably excepting the account of his own death, which closes Deuteronomy, the fifth book of the Torah). Since the Enlightenment, however, when new methods of scientific analysis began to challenge all traditional claims to authority, including those made by the world's religions, theo-ries about the composition and authorship of the Pentateuch have changed radically.

Traditional Views of Authorship

The ancient tradition that Moses composed the Pentateuch is based partly on several passages in Exodus, Numbers, and Deuteronomy in which YHWH orders Moses to write down some of God's specific instructions. According to Exodus 17:14, YHWH tells Moses to "write [about the defeat of Amalek, a local king] as a reminder in a book." After receiving from YHWH a list of legal ordinances

(Exod. 21–23), known as the **Book of the Cove-nant,** Moses "wrote down all the words of the LORD" (Exod. 24:4); he also commits to writing the ritual laws revealed in Exodus (34:27–28) and Israel's travel itinerary during its long journey from Egypt through the Sinai wilderness (Num. 33:2). In all of these texts, Moses is depicted as recording only specific events and particular legal codes, not the whole Pentateuch.

In Deuteronomy, however, Moses is pictured as compiling the entire law code contained in that book (Deut. 31:9), as well as lyrics to a "song" he taught Israel (Deut. 31:19, 22). According to Deuteronomy, he was responsible for the "words of this law [Torah] to the very end" (Deut. 31:24), composing "this book of the law," which he then entrusts to Israel's priests for safekeeping (Deut. 31:9, 24–26). Most scholars believe that this legal work is the same "book of the law [Torah]" found during repairs on the Jerusalem Temple during the late seventh century B.C.E., more than 600 years after the period when Moses supposedly lived (2 Kings 22:8–23:3). The validation of sweeping religious reforms by King **Josiah** (ruled 640–609 B.C.E.), this early edition of Deuteronomy (probably consisting of Chs. 12–26) was subsequently expanded to become the fifth book of the Pentateuch. In time, not only the legal code embedded in Deuteronomy but all of Israel's sacred laws contained in the Pentateuch were ascribed to Mosaic authorship, imbuing them with that leader's stature and authority.

Problems with Mosaic Authorship

In contrast to traditional views of Mosaic authorship, virtually all contemporary scholars are convinced that, in its present form, the Pentateuch could not have derived from Moses. Careful scrutiny of the text offers compelling evidence that the Bible's first five books are not the work of a single author but are the product of multiple authors and editors laboring over many centuries.

Even casual readers commonly notice numerous repetitions, contradictions, and discrepancies that point to the composite nature of the Pentateuch. If Moses is the presumed author, why is he always referred to in the third person, as an author writing *about* him would do? If Moses is truly "very humble, more so than anyone else on the face of the earth," as Numbers 12:3 describes him, would he plausibly make such an immodest evaluation of his personal humility? Readers also note Deuteronomy's many repetitions of the phrase "until this day," a clear indication that the writer was looking back from his time to that of a distant past (Deut. 3:14; 34:6; etc.).

Deuteronomy's account of Moses' death might be seen as a postscript by a later hand, were it not written in exactly the same style as that of the rest of the book—and in language virtually identical to that in the historical books (Joshua–2 Kings) that follow (see Chapters 10 and 11). Frequent anachronisms—the placing of persons or events out of their proper chronological order—also indicate post-Mosaic authorship. Many statements in Genesis, such as "At that time Canaanites were in the land" (Gen. 12:6; 13:7), refer to an epoch centuries after Moses' time, when the original inhabitants of Canaan had been expelled or assimilated by the Israelite population. References to territories east of the Jordan River as lying "beyond the Jordan" presuppose a vantage point on the west side of the river, but Israel's tribes did not occupy this western region until long after Moses' era (Gen. 50:10; cf. Num. 21:1). Other anachronisms, such as the Genesis list of Edom's kings who ruled "before any king reigned over the Israelites" (Gen. 36:31), demonstrate that the author lived at some time after Israel's monarchy had been established, centuries after Moses' day.

Even when studying the Pentateuch for the first time, readers are commonly struck by the great number of duplications—passages in which the same story, or a close variant, is told a second time, sometimes with the same characters and other times with different characters involved. The phenomenon of duplication, present throughout both narrative and legal sections of the Pentateuch, begins with two different versions of creation. In Genesis 1, which has a lofty, majestic style, Elohim (God) creates all life forms, beginning with plants and animals and culminating with human beings, male and female, made simultaneously in his own image. Beginning in Genesis 2, which has a more vivid, earthy style, it is "YHWH Elohim" (Yahweh God) who fashions the first man and, only after creating a series of animals — none of which proves a suitable mate for the human male — models the first woman from the man's rib. Whereas biblical editors sometimes placed two different accounts of the same event side-by-side, as they did with Genesis's two distinct creation stories, at other times they interwove two originally separate narratives. In Genesis 6–8, editors combined two stories of a global deluge — Noah's Flood — that can easily be disentangled to produce two parallel flood stories that are fully complete in themselves (Box 5.1).

A story that illustrated a particular theme — the irresistible beauty of some Israelite women and the threat this attraction posed to fulfillment of God's vow to multiply Abraham's descendants — was apparently particularly popular with biblical writers, who include in Genesis three variations of the same tale. While traveling in Egypt, Abraham fears that Pharaoh will kill him in order to possess Abraham's wife, Sarah, whom he accordingly passes off as his sister. After Pharaoh places Sarah in his harem, compensating her "brother" with lavish gifts of livestock, YHWH afflicts Egypt's royal household with plagues (foreshadowing the ten plagues visited on a later pharaoh). Chastened, Pharaoh returns Sarah to her husband, reproaching Abraham for having deceived him (Gen. 12:10–20). Seemingly unmindful of Pharaoh's just criticism, in Genesis 20, Abraham again represents Sarah as his sister, this time to Abimelech, a Canaanite king. Again, God is angry, appearing to Abimelech in a dream and threatening to kill him for appropriating Abraham's wife. As in the previous version, Abraham receives a rich reward in cattle and slaves for having deceived a foreign ruler (Gen. 20:1–18). In yet another variation on this theme, it is Isaac, son of Abraham, who deceives Abimelech — now identified as a "Philistine" ruler — by misrepresenting his

wife, Rebekah, as his sister. Although Abimelech reprimands Isaac for lying about his relationship with Rebekah, Isaac is richly rewarded by God, who makes him a rich man (Gen. 26:1–14).

Genesis also includes two different versions of Jacob's encounter with God in which his name is changed to Israel, identifying him as the progenitor of the twelve Israelite tribes. In the first, Jacob wrestles all night at Peniel with a mysterious figure whom he later identifies as God and who confers the name change (Gen. 32:22–32). In the second, which occurs not at Peniel but at Bethel, the Deity calls himself *El Shaddai*—"GOD Almighty" or "GOD of the (Cosmic) Mountain"— and again announces that Jacob will henceforth be called Israel (Gen. 35:9–15). Similarly, Genesis records two contradictory accounts of Joseph's descent into Egypt. In one, his brothers sell him to Ishmaelites, who take him to Egypt (Gen. 37:25–27); in the other, Midianites pull him out of a dry well into which his jealous brothers have thrown him, and it is they who sell him to the Ishmaelites (Gen. 37:21–25, 28–30).

As in the deluge story, the Exodus account of the Israelites crossing a chaotic sea is a blend of two (or three) once-separate traditions that now appear as a single narrative (Exod. 14–15; see Chapter 8). Exodus also includes two distinct versions of YHWH's revelation to Moses of his sacred name. Three chapters after God's extended conversation with Moses at the burning bush, in which he identifies himself as the "GOD [Elohim] of your fathers" whose previously hidden name is YHWH (Exod. 3:1–4:17), he again appears to Moses, as if for the first time. In this second version of the commissioning of Moses, YHWH states that he was formerly known to Israel's ancestors not as Elohim, as Exodus 3:6 states, but as El Shaddai:

> I am the LORD [YHWH]. I appeared to Abraham, Isaac, and Jacob as God Almighty [El Shaddai], but by my name "The LORD [YHWH]" I did not make myself known to them. (Exod. 6:3)

The Deity's unequivocal declaration that he had not revealed his personal name, YHWH, before confiding it to Moses contrasts strikingly with

BOX 5.1
Two Versions of the Flood Story

The present text of Genesis relating the story of a universal deluge combines two Flood accounts, attributed, respectively, to the Yahwist writer (J) and the priestly writer (P). Each of the two accounts stands alone as a complete and independent narrative in this translation from the Jerusalem Bible.

THE FLOOD — GENESIS 6:5–8:22

(Priestly text in **boldface** capitals, J text in regular type)

Genesis 6

5　And Yahweh saw that the evil of humans was great in the earth, and all the inclination of the thoughts of their heart was only evil all the day.

6　And Yahweh regretted that he had made humans in the earth, and he was grieved to his heart.

7　And Yahweh said, "I shall wipe out the humans which I have created from the face of the earth, from human to beast to creeping thing to bird of the heavens, for I regret that I have made them."

8　But Noah found favor in Yahweh's eyes.

9　**THESE ARE THE GENERATIONS OF NOAH: NOAH WAS A RIGHTEOUS MAN, PERFECT IN HIS GENERATIONS. NOAH WALKED WITH GOD.**

10　**AND NOAH SIRED THREE SONS: SHEM, HAM, AND JAPHETH.**

11　**AND THE EARTH WAS CORRUPTED BEFORE GOD, AND THE EARTH WAS FILLED WITH VIOLENCE.**

12　**AND GOD SAW THE EARTH, AND HERE IT WAS CORRUPTED, FOR ALL FLESH HAD CORRUPTED ITS WAY ON THE EARTH.**

13　**AND GOD SAID TO NOAH, "THE END OF ALL FLESH HAS COME BEFORE ME, FOR THE EARTH IS FILLED WITH VIOLENCE BECAUSE OF THEM, AND HERE I AM GOING TO DESTROY THEM WITH THE EARTH.**

14　**MAKE YOURSELF AN ARK OF GOPHER WOOD, MAKE ROOMS WITH THE ARK, AND PITCH IT OUTSIDE AND INSIDE WITH PITCH.**

15　**AND THIS IS HOW YOU SHALL MAKE IT: THREE HUNDRED CUBITS THE LENGTH OF THE ARK, FIFTY CUBITS ITS WIDTH, AND THIRTY CUBITS ITS HEIGHT.**

16　**YOU SHALL MAKE A WINDOW FOR THE ARK, AND YOU SHALL FINISH IT TO A CUBIT FROM THE TOP, AND YOU SHALL MAKE AN ENTRANCE TO THE ARK IN ITS SIDE. YOU SHALL MAKE LOWER, SECOND, AND THIRD STORIES FOR IT.**

17　**AND HERE I AM BRINGING THE FLOOD, WATER OVER THE EARTH, TO DESTROY ALL FLESH IN WHICH IS THE BREATH OF LIFE FROM UNDER THE HEAVENS. EVERYTHING WHICH IS ON THE LAND WILL DIE.**

18　**AND I SHALL ESTABLISH MY COVENANT WITH YOU. AND YOU SHALL COME TO THE ARK, YOU AND YOUR SONS AND YOUR WIFE AND YOUR SONS' WIVES WITH YOU.**

19　**AND OF ALL THE LIVING, OF ALL FLESH, YOU SHALL BRING TWO TO THE ARK TO KEEP ALIVE WITH YOU, THEY SHALL BE MALE AND FEMALE.**

20　**OF THE BIRDS ACCORDING TO THEIR KIND, AND OF THE BEASTS ACCORDING TO THEIR KIND, AND OF ALL THE CREEPING THINGS OF THE EARTH ACCORDING TO THEIR KIND, TWO OF EACH WILL COME TO YOU TO KEEP ALIVE.**

21　**AND YOU, TAKE FOR YOURSELF OF ALL FOOD WHICH WILL BE EATEN AND GATHER IT TO YOU, AND IT WILL BE FOR YOU AND FOR THEM FOR FOOD."**

22　**AND NOAH DID ACCORDING TO ALL THAT GOD COMMANDED HIM — SO HE DID.**

Genesis 7

1　And Yahweh said to Noah, "Come, you and all your household, to the ark, for I have seen you as righteous before me in this generation.

2　Of all the clean beasts, take yourself seven pairs, man and his woman; and of the beasts which are not clean, two, man and his woman.

3　Also of the birds of the heavens seven pairs, male and female, to keep alive seed on the face of the earth.

4　For in seven more days I shall rain on the earth forty days and forty nights, and I shall wipe out all the substance that I have made from upon the face of the earth."

5　And Noah did according to all that Yahweh had commanded him.

6　**AND NOAH WAS SIX HUNDRED YEARS OLD, AND THE FLOOD WAS ON THE EARTH.**

7 And Noah and his sons and his wife and his sons' wives with him came to the ark from before the waters of the flood.

8 OF THE CLEAN BEASTS AND OF THE BEASTS WHICH WERE NOT CLEAN, AND OF THE BIRDS AND OF ALL THOSE WHICH CREEP UPON THE EARTH,

9 TWO OF EACH CAME TO NOAH TO THE ARK, MALE AND FEMALE, AS GOD HAD COMMANDED NOAH.

10 And seven days later the waters of the flood were on the earth.

11 IN THE SIX HUNDREDTH YEAR OF NOAH'S LIFE, IN THE SECOND MONTH, IN THE SEVENTEENTH DAY OF THE MONTH, ON THIS DAY ALL THE FOUNTAINS OF THE GREAT DEEP WERE BROKEN UP, AND THE WINDOWS OF THE HEAVENS WERE OPENED.

12 And there was rain on the earth, forty days and forty nights.

13 IN THIS VERY DAY, NOAH AND SHEM, HAM, AND JAPHETH, THE SONS OF NOAH, AND NOAH'S WIFE AND HIS SONS' THREE WIVES WITH THEM CAME TO THE ARK.

14 THEY AND ALL THE LIVING THINGS ACCORDING TO THEIR KIND, AND ALL THE BEASTS ACCORDING TO THEIR KIND, AND ALL THE CREEPING THINGS THAT CREEP ON THE EARTH ACCORDING TO THEIR KIND, AND ALL THE BIRDS ACCORDING TO THEIR KIND, AND EVERY WINGED BIRD.

15 AND THEY CAME TO NOAH TO THE ARK, TWO OF EACH, OF ALL FLESH IN WHICH IS THE BREATH OF LIFE.

16 AND THOSE WHICH CAME WERE MALE AND FEMALE, SOME OF ALL FLESH CAME, AS GOD HAD COMMANDED HIM. And Yahweh closed it for him.

17 And the flood was on the earth for forty days and forty nights, and the waters multiplied and raised the ark, and it was lifted from the earth.

18 And the waters grew strong and multiplied greatly on the earth, and the ark went on the surface of the waters.

19 And the waters grew very very strong on the earth, and they covered all the high mountains that are under all the heavens.

20 Fifteen cubits above, the waters grew stronger, and they covered the mountains.

21 AND ALL FLESH, THOSE THAT CREEP ON THE EARTH, THE BIRDS, THE BEASTS, AND THE WILD ANIMALS, AND ALL THE SWARMING THINGS THAT SWARM ON THE EARTH, AND ALL THE HUMANS EXPIRED.

22 Everything that had the breathing spirit of life in its nostrils, everything that was on the dry ground, died.

23 And he wiped out all the substance that was on the face of the earth, from human to beast, to creeping thing, and to bird of the heavens, and they were wiped out from the earth, and only Noah and those who were with him In the ark were left.

24 AND THE WATERS GREW STRONG ON THE EARTH A HUNDRED FIFTY DAYS.

Genesis 8

1 AND GOD REMEMBERED NOAH AND ALL THE LIVING, AND ALL THE BEASTS THAT WERE WITH HIM IN THE ARK, AND GOD PASSED A WIND OVER THE EARTH, AND THE WATERS WERE DECREASED.

2 AND THE FOUNTAINS OF THE DEEP AND THE WINDOWS OF THE HEAVENS WERE SHUT, and the rain was restrained from the heavens.

3 And the waters receded from the earth continually, AND THE WATERS WERE ABATED AT THE END OF A HUNDRED FIFTY DAYS.

4 AND THE ARK RESTED, IN THE SEVENTH MONTH, IN THE SEVENTEENTH DAY OF THE MONTH, ON THE MOUNTAINS OF ARARAT.

5 AND THE WATERS CONTINUED RECEDING UNTIL THE TENTH MONTH; IN THE TENTH MONTH, ON THE FIRST OF THE MONTH, THE TOPS OF THE MOUNTAINS APPEARED.

6 And it was at the end of forty days, and Noah opened the window of the ark which he had made.

7 AND HE SENT OUT A RAVEN, AND IT WENT BACK AND FORTH UNTIL THE WATERS DRIED UP FROM THE EARTH.

8 And he sent out a dove from him to see whether the waters had eased from the face of the earth.

9 And the dove did not find a resting place for its foot, and it returned to him to the ark, for waters were on the face of the earth, and he put out his hand and took it and brought it to him to the ark.

10 And he waited seven more days, and he again sent out a dove from the ark.

11 And the dove came to him at evening time, and here was an olive leaf torn off in its mouth, and Noah knew that the waters had eased from the earth.

12 And he waited seven more days, and he sent out a dove, and it did not return to him ever again.

(continued)

BOX 5.1 *(continued)*

13 AND IT WAS IN THE SIX HUNDRED AND FIRST YEAR, IN THE FIRST MONTH, ON THE FIRST OF THE MONTH, THE WATERS DRIED FROM THE EARTH. And Noah turned back the covering of the ark and looked, and here the face of the earth had dried.

14 AND IN THE SECOND MONTH, ON THE TWENTY-SEVENTH DAY OF THE MONTH, THE EARTH DRIED UP.

15 AND GOD SPOKE TO NOAH, SAYING,

16 "GO OUT FROM THE ARK, YOU AND YOUR WIFE AND YOUR SONS' WIVES WITH YOU.

17 ALL THE LIVING THINGS THAT ARE WITH YOU, OF ALL FLESH, OF THE BIRDS, AND OF THE BEASTS, AND OF ALL THE CREEPING THINGS THAT CREEP ON THE EARTH, THAT GO OUT WITH YOU, SHALL SWARM IN THE EARTH AND BE FRUITFUL AND MULTIPLY IN THE EARTH."

18 AND NOAH AND HIS SONS AND HIS WIFE AND HIS SONS' WIVES WENT OUT.

19 ALL THE LIVING THINGS, ALL THE CREEPING THINGS AND ALL THE BIRDS, ALL THAT CREEP ON THE EARTH, BY THEIR FAMILIES, THEY WENT OUT OF THE ARK.

20 And Noah built an altar to Yahweh, and he took some of each of the clean beasts and of each of the clean birds, and he offered sacrifices on the altar.

21 And Yahweh smelled the pleasant smell, and Yahweh said to his heart, "I shall not again curse the ground on man's account, for the inclination of the human heart is evil from their youth, and I shall not again strike all the living as I have done.

22 All the rest of the days of the earth, seed and harvest, and cold and heat, and summer and winter, and day and night shall not cease."

Reprinted with the permission of Simon & Schuster from *Who Wrote the Bible?* by Richard Friedman. Copyright © 1987 by Richard Friedman.

another tradition in the Pentateuch that YHWH's name was known and used long before the Flood. Beginning in Genesis 2:4b, where "the LORD GOD [YHWH Elohim] made the earth and the heavens," one literary strand identifies God as YHWH throughout the Pentateuch. According to this contributor to the composite biblical story, "people began to invoke the name of the LORD [YHWH]" during the time of Enosh, grandson of Adam, the first man (Gen. 4:26). These conflicting claims about when YHWH first disclosed his name offer important clues to the different sources and authorship of the Pentateuch.

Some Scholarly Methods Used in Analyzing the Biblical Text

HISTORICAL CRITICISM

For almost three centuries, an international community of biblical scholars has closely examined the text of the Pentateuch, analyzing its many duplica-

tions and inconsistencies, and has proposed several theories to explain them. Seeking to understand the complex process by which the Pentateuch evolved into its present form, scholars developed a variety of methods and techniques for studying the biblical text. A diverse body of scholars — including historians, archaeologists, anthropologists, linguists, sociologists, theologians, and literary critics — pursued a wide range of goals in their research. In general, scholarly approaches can be divided into two broad categories: historical and literary. (Some literary, or rhetorical, approaches to the Pentateuch are discussed in Chapter 6.)

In this discussion, we will focus on **historical criticism,** which involves the examination of documents, such as the narratives in Genesis, Exodus, or the books of Kings, that purport to record historical events, a methodology that attempts to illuminate the historical setting in which the books were originally written, as well as the differing circumstances in which they were later revised. Historical criticism investigates such matters as the time and place of a book's composition; its sources, authorship, and editorial history; the audience for whom it was originally intended; and the social, political, and religious forces that may have influenced the authors' or editors' views of their subject. Using standards of evidence similar to those for testing a scientific hypothesis, historical critics examine a given account according to several criteria, including factual accuracy, logical plausibility, and authorial objectivity. In investigating the reliability of the Exodus account of Israel's origins, for example, historical critics look for extrabiblical evidence, such as archaeological discoveries, that may confirm the book's claims about Israel's presence in Egypt, the plagues that decimated Egypt's population, or the drowning of Pharaoh's army. Despite the wealth of Egyptian records, however, no evidence verifying any of these events has yet been produced, creating a problem for scholars hoping to clarify the relation of the biblical text to actual history.

Whenever possible, scholars compare the biblical version of events with archaeological data — ancient inscriptions, texts from Near Eastern archives, and artifacts from excavations at sites mentioned in the Bible. In the case of Joshua, which depicts Israel's rapid conquest of Canaan, archaeological evidence does not, in many instances, support the biblical claims (see Chapter 12). The general lack of nonbiblical data to substantiate either the Exodus or the Conquest causes many scholars to doubt their historicity. Biblical writers seem less concerned with recording precisely what occurred than with presenting a *theological* interpretation of Israel's past, an account that functions primarily to illustrate the ideological nature of the covenant people's relationship with YHWH. As a group, ancient Near Eastern writers of historical narrative did not have the same goals as modern historians; they wrote chiefly to convey ideas about the social or religious *meaning* of their nations' historical experience, not to compile a dispassionate record of the "facts."

In scrutinizing the Torah, scholars discovered that, in many cases, the long narrative sections are made up of many small units — individual stories, folktales, genealogies, war hymns, battle accounts, biographical sketches — that are self-contained entities only loosely related to the surrounding text. Many scholars believe that the individual unit, called a **pericope,** had an independent existence before editors incorporated it into a continuous narrative. According to this theory, pericopes are the building blocks out of which the present biblical text, from Genesis to 2 Chronicles, is constructed.

FORM CRITICISM

An important technique employed by historical critics, **form criticism** looks behind the written version of a pericope to discover the older oral form in which it circulated before being fixed in writing. The form critic tries to ascertain the *Sitz-im-Leben* (German for "life setting"), the social and historical circumstances in which an individual pericope, such as Abraham's near-sacrifice of Isaac or Jacob's dream of a celestial staircase, originated. Oral traditions about the Moses–Sinai covenant probably were recited annually at various covenant renewal ceremonies at local shrines, such as those at Bethel, Shechem, or Jerusalem, gathering new meanings and adding interpretations as Israel's political and religious situation changed over the years. Most scholars believe that many generations passed before these oral recitations crystallized in written form.

REDACTION CRITICISM

Whereas form criticism concentrates on the stages of development that orally transmitted traditions undergo before they are committed to writing, **redaction criticism** emphasizes the role of the individual biblical author. Redaction critics point out that the author-**redactor** (-editor) does not slavishly copy sources but instead typically revises them, weaving together and shaping older documents and oral lore to achieve a specific theological purpose. This method's emphasis on the author's distinctive role in assembling, rearranging, and reinterpreting older material highlights the importance of individual authorial contributions to inherited traditions. The priestly writers who made extensive additions to older stories about Moses and the Sinai covenant, for example, succeeded in largely transforming their sources and, in many cases, giving them a distinctively priestly perspective.

The Documentary Hypothesis: Four Sources of the Pentateuch

Closely related to form criticism, **source criticism** endeavors to isolate and identify the different sources, both oral and written, that redactors incorporate into a written document. In terms of the compositional history of the Pentateuch, source criticism has proven enormously influential, providing a comprehensive theory that many scholars think best accounts for the duplications, contradictions, and other discrepancies found in the "Books of Moses." Known as the **documentary hypothesis,** this theory holds that the Pentateuch can be best understood by recognizing its composite nature. Although a minority of scholars has recently challenged it, the documentary hypothesis remains the standard model in Pentateuchal studies and serves as the point of departure even for those who disagree with it.

According to this theory, the Torah is a literary patchwork in which at least four originally separate sources—dating from four different periods of Israelite history—have been stitched together to form the present text. The interweaving of four once-independent strands explains both the repetitions and the discrepancies in the present text.

J, THE YAHWIST SOURCE

According to the documentary hypothesis, the earliest source is called **J** because its author typically uses the name Yahweh (German, *Jahweh*) for God. The **Yahwist** writer, also known as J, is the first to compose a continuous narrative of Israel's origins. J's work incorporates ancient **oral traditions** about Israel's prehistory and tales of the ancestral fathers and mothers. Designating God as YHWH from the outset of his account, J opens his narrative with the second creation story (Gen. 2:4b–25) and the parable of Adam and Eve's loss of Eden (Gen. 3:1–24), as well as one version of the flood story (see Box 5.1). Emphasizing the indispensable role of women such as Sarah, Rebekah, Leah, and Rachel in the saga of Israel's ancestors, J recounts the wan-

derings of the patriarchs, their descent into Egypt, and their rescue from Egyptian bondage by YHWH, who guides them to Mount Sinai, where he reveals his Torah. Although some scholars believe that J's narrative—distinctive portions of which are embedded in Genesis, Exodus, and Numbers—originally extended into the story of the conquest of Canaan and the establishment of the Davidic monarchy as recounted in Joshua, Judges, and 1 and 2 Samuel, many scholars find it difficult to determine exactly where J's narrative ends. Some have proposed that J's contribution to the biblical story includes the **Court History,** an account of David's rise to power as king of Israel, that forms the basis for most of 2 Samuel and 1 Kings 1–2. (See Richard E. Friedman in "Recommended Reading.")

Although most scholars recognize the existence of the J strand in the Pentateuch, controversy rages over the time of its composition. According to the classic version of the documentary hypothesis, J's narrative was produced, at least in part, as a justification for or validation of the Davidic monarchy (established c. 1000 B.C.E.) After Davidic rulers had transformed Israel's formerly competing tribes into a fragile political unity—with both kings and priests recently centered at the new capital of Jerusalem—the Yahwist writer composed a literary affirmation of the new order, perhaps in the late tenth century B.C.E. (see Box 14.1). The J narrative, from the call of Abraham to the conquest of Canaan and the rise of the Davidic kings, presumably functioned as a foundation document illustrating that Israel's social, political, and religious institutions were the outworking of YHWH's historical purpose.

Certainly, the J material woven into the Torah focuses on **Judah,** the name of both the tribe to which David belonged and the southern territory over which he and his heirs ruled. To emphasize the importance of Judah in Israel's past, J associates many of the patriarchs with geographical sites that are also significant to Judah's royal dynasty. Thus, in J's account, Abraham dwells in Hebron or Mamre (Gen. 13:18; 18:1), the location of Judah's first capital city, where David's reign was first acclaimed

(2 Sam. 2–5), and the hometown of Zadok, who served as High Priest under David and Solomon (2 Sam. 8:17; cf. 1 Kings 1:32–45). J's description of the boundaries of the land that YHWH promised to Abraham's progeny (Gen. 15:18) corresponds to the political frontiers of the Davidic kingdom (cf. 1 Kings 4:21). By contrast, J gives a negative account of **Shechem** (Gen. 34), which in the late tenth century B.C.E. had become the capital of anti-Judean northern tribes that had seceded from the Davidic monarchy after Solomon's death. Because J emphasizes Judah's central role in Israel's story, he is regarded as a native of Judah, perhaps a member of the royal court living at Jerusalem, giving J's literary symbol a double meaning.

Whereas the standard documentary view holds that the Yahwist author wrote during the period of the monarchy, a few critics have recently argued that the Yahwist account is a relatively late work, composed some time *after* the Babylonian destruction of Judah brought the Davidic monarchy to an end. In this revisionist theory, the Tanak's first four books (Genesis–Numbers), were compiled by post-exilic writers as a preface to Deuteronomy (see Rolf Rendtorff, John Van Seeters, and R. N. Whybray in "Recommended Reading").

E, THE ELOHIST SOURCE

According to the documentary hypothesis, the Pentateuch's second oldest narrative strand (which some scholars think was oral rather than written) is that identified as **E,** the **Elohist** tradition, so named because this source characteristically uses Elohim rather than YHWH as the preferred term for God. Of the four hypothetical Pentateuchal sources, E is the least well preserved, although extended Elohist passages have been identified in Genesis and Exodus. According to the sequence of events postulated by the documentary hypothesis, after Israel's twelve tribes had split into the two rival kingdoms of Judah and Israel (following 921 B.C.E.), a writer in the northern kingdom of Israel produced a second narrative of his people's origins, or at least a collection of individual stories about Abraham, Isaac, Jacob, Esau, Joseph, and Moses. Perhaps consciously de-

signed as a corrective to J's Judah-oriented account, the Elohist material focuses on traditions associated with the northern part of Israel. E does not review early human history as J had done, beginning instead with tales of Abraham and his descendants. As Martin Noth has observed, E survives in the Pentateuch only as disconnected fragments, preserving very few traditions that are not duplicated in other sources. Within Genesis, E contributes mainly to stories of sibling conflict, such as the rivalry between Jacob and Esau, as well as that between Joseph and his brothers. In Exodus, E provides accounts of Jethro, Moses' father-in-law; the revelation of YHWH's name to Moses; and Israel's encounter with God on his sacred mountain. The large majority of E material parallels narratives from J and other contributors, adding traditions, including Abraham's near-sacrifice of his son Isaac, to the end of the Abraham cycle (Gen. 20–22), as well as variant material to the Jacob–Esau and Joseph cycles.

Although some scholars view E as primarily supplemental oral material added to enrich J's narrative, E introduces some important differences in the biblical tradition. Whereas J specifies Mount Sinai as the sacred locale of YHWH's revelation of the Torah to Israel, E calls it Horeb. J refers to the inhabitants of Palestine as Canaanites, whereas E labels them Amorites. J names Moses' father-in-law as Ruel or Hobab, whereas E knows him as Jethro, priest of Midian.

According to J, people worshiped YHWH almost from the beginning of human history (Gen. 4:26), but E states that YHWH kept his name secret until Moses' time (Exod. 3:15). Whereas J's portrait of God is strongly anthropomorphic, E paints a somewhat more abstract and remote Deity. J describes YHWH strolling through Eden to enjoy a cooling breeze, dining with Abraham under the oaks of Mamre, personally wrestling with Jacob, and appearing directly to Moses. Elohist material tends to present God as transcendent, typically employing an angelic go-between when speaking to Abraham or Moses. Recounting Jacob's dream at Bethel, E depicts the invisible link between heaven and earth with the image of a celestial stairway trod by divine beings (Gen. 28:10–19). Whereas J sets many of the ancestral tales in Judah's territory, E prefers geographical sites connected with the northern tribes, the most prominent of which was **Ephraim,** thus also giving E's symbol a twofold significance.

Because the E strand survives only in fragmental form, many scholars doubt that it originated as a continuous narrative or that it was ever a separate written document. Some critics argue that E merely represents variations on ancient Israel's vast storehouse of oral traditions, which redactors added to expand on J's story of Israel's formation.

THE JE EPIC

Elohist material, whether oral or written, may have been integrated into J's account after 721 B.C.E., when the northern kingdom of Israel fell to the Assyrians. Israelite refugees fleeing south into Judah may have brought Elohist traditions with them to Jerusalem, where they eventually were incorporated into the Yahwist's narrative. If E was indeed a written source, it is not surprising that the unknown Judean scribe or editor who combined it with J rigorously subordinated E material to J's narrative framework, breaking it up into short fragments that supplemented the Yahwist document. The resultant composite work, the **JE** epic, inevitably contained innumerable conflicts and repetitions, such as the three similar incidents in which a patriarch's wife is represented as his sister when desired by a foreign ruler (cf. Gen. 12:10–20; 20:1–18; 26:6–11). The JE redactor skillfully dovetailed these redundant passages, retaining even contradictory accounts as equally venerable.

D, THE DEUTERONOMIST SOURCE

The third principal source of the Pentateuch is known as **D, the Deuteronomist.** Scholarly opinion is sharply divided over the extent to which the Deuteronomist's influence is present in the five Torah books. Some critics believe that, whereas J and E passages appear throughout Genesis, Exo-

dus, and Numbers, D's work is largely confined to the Book of Deuteronomy. Conversely, a growing number of scholars regard D as the dominant influence in the Pentateuch, with some maintaining that the core of Deuteronomy (12–26) may be the oldest part of the Torah, to which JE material was later added as an extended introduction. At the least, some scholars have recently identified a large number of Deuteronomy-influenced passages that were interpolated into the JE narratives of Genesis, Exodus, and Numbers.

While differing about the relative ages and literary relationship of JE and D, most scholars agree that Deuteronomy, or at least its central section, was the "book of the law [Torah]," discovered in 621 B.C.E. during repairs on the Jerusalem Temple. Discovery of this allegedly Mosaic document helped fuel or validate a major reform of Israelite religion initiated by King Josiah, who zealously followed Deuteronomy's injunction to centralize Judah's worship "at the place [YHWH] will choose . . . to set his name there and give it a home" (Deut. 12:4–6). Acting on Deuteronomy's declaration that YHWH would accept sacrifices only at the "place" designated—assumed to be Jerusalem—Josiah systematically destroyed all other altars and shrines, including those at Bethel and other sanctuaries associated with the Genesis patriarchs (2 Kings 22:3–23:25; cf. 2 Chron. 34–35). Josiah's other reforms, such as the celebration of a national Passover feast, also echo policies advocated in Deuteronomy.

Deuteronomy's insistence that Israel's national welfare was conditional on the people's loyalty to YHWH and their allegiance to Torah requirements shaped the way in which subsequent writers presented Israel's story. The prose narratives that follow Deuteronomy—Joshua through 2 Kings—relate Israel's historical experience almost entirely in terms of Deuteronomic theory. Because these books are so thoroughly permeated by Deuteronomy's equation of disobedience with national failure, this sequence is called the **Deuteronomistic History (DH).** (In this text, the adjective *Deuteronomic* refers to the Book of Deuteronomy and the philosophy of history it promotes. In contrast, the term *Deuteronomistic* refers to material pertaining to the historical narratives, Joshua through Kings. [See Chapter 11 for a more detailed discussion on this topic.])

In its major themes and theological viewpoint, Deuteronomy belongs with the Deuteronomistic narratives that follow it and that promote exactly the same philosophy of history. Originally, it probably stood at the head of the series of books—Joshua, Judges, 1 and 2 Samuel, and 1 and 2 Kings—that together form a cohesive literary unit. In editing the Hebrew Bible, however, redactors separated Deuteronomy from the narratives that are largely shaped by its ideas and placed it as the fifth book of the Torah. The Pentateuch thus concludes with Moses' warnings about the painful consequences of covenant breaking.

P, THE PRIESTLY SOURCE

The fourth and final contribution to the Torah, according to the documentary hypothesis, was the work of **priestly** writers who lived during and after the Babylonian exile (from 587 to perhaps as late as the fourth century B.C.E.). Given the scholarly designation of **P**, this component of the Pentateuch represents the concerns of a postexilic school of priestly redactors who labored to collect, preserve, and edit Israel's religious heritage. The P school assembled several originally separate legal codes, encompassing hundreds of laws, statutes, and ordinances, and inserted them at various points in the JE epic of old Israel. Extensively revising the older material, the priestly editors compiled the vast body of legal material that extends from Exodus 35, through Leviticus, to Numbers 10. Although the priestly contribution emphasizes rituals, purity laws, genealogies, and the minutiae of cult sacrifice, it also includes significant additions to the JE narrative. In addition to interpolating a priestly version of the Abrahamic Covenant (Gen. 17), P scribes wove their tradition of the Flood story into that of J, producing a considerably expanded (and self-contradictory) version of a global deluge (see Box

5.1). They also added another creation account (Gen. 1) and the narrative of Moses' death (Deut. 34), thus giving the Pentateuch its crucial opening and closing passages and determining its final shape and structure.

P's version of creation, which serves as a preface to the entire Hebrew Bible, emphasizes the kinds of distinctions and divisions that characterize the separations of pure and impure in Leviticus. Culminating in Elohim's establishment of the first Sabbath, P's creation account provides cosmic validation of that priest-regulated institution. P gives exhaustively detailed instructions for building Israel's portable shrine, the **Tabernacle,** a dwelling place for God that is rendered in terms similar to those that describe the creation (Exod. 25–31, 35–40). The elaborate machinery of the sacrificial cult, including animal offerings to expiate sin and guilt—also under priestly jurisdiction—occupies much of Leviticus. (Table 5.1 summarizes the documentary hypothesis).

Some Recent Modifications of the Documentary Hypothesis

For more than a hundred years, most biblical scholars have endorsed some form of the documentary hypothesis, making it the dominant model in studies of the Pentateuch's origins. It has never been without its critics, however. Like any theory, the documentary hypothesis is useful only as long as it can successfully account for all the available facts, such as the repetitions, anachronisms, and innumerable inconsistencies found in the Torah. Although no scholarly consensus has thus far emerged, some recent critics have proposed alternate models, rejecting the classical assumption that the Tanak's initial five books represent the compilation of four originally independent sources—J, E, D, and P.

Some critics argue that P was not originally a separate document; instead, P material is a series

Table 5.1 *The Documentary Hypothesis: Four Sources of the Pentateuch*

Source	Characteristics
J (Yahwist)	Uses the personal name *Yahweh* for God
	Has an anthropomorphic portrayal of Deity
	Features a vivid, concrete style and a dramatic storyline, beginning with creation (Gen. 2:4b) and extending at least to the conclusion of the Mosaic Covenant at Sinai
	Has a strong orientation toward traditions of Judah, setting many patriarchal tales in that region
E (Elohist)	Uses the generic plural *Elohim* for God
	Features a style less picturesque and a view of the Deity less anthropomorphic than J's
	Begins the narrative with Abraham and concludes with the Israelites at the "mountain of GOD," which E calls Horeb
	Has a strong orientation toward the northern kingdom of Israel (Ephraim), where most patriarchal stories are set
D (Deuteronomist)	Emphasizes the conditional nature of the Mosaic Covenant and interprets Israel's military/political defeats as a direct result of the people's failure to worship YHWH wholeheartedly
	Features a more elaborate rhetorical style than J or E
	Reflects policies of Josiah's religious reforms (c. 621 B.C.E.)
	Insists that only one central sanctuary is acceptable to YHWH
	Has a strong influence on the writing of Joshua to 2 Kings, the Deuteronomistic History (DH)
P (Priestly)	Focuses on priestly interests, particularly legalistic and ritual aspects of Israel's religion
	Features a precise, pedantic style, meticulously listing genealogies, censuses, dates, and instructions for the cult
	Is thought to have been added to the older JE epic during and after the Babylonian exile (following 587 B.C.E.)
	Has a strong affinity with concepts expressed by the exilic prophet Ezekiel

of unconnected interpolations that postexilic redactors inserted into the older narratives. Some scholars view P as representing a long succession of priestly editors who, over a century or two, gradually reshaped Israel's ancient and sometimes conflicting traditions into a semblance of literary unity. By binding an expanded and edited version of Deuteronomy to the JE (Yahwist-Elohist) account, into which they had inserted their distinctive legal instructions, the P school eventually created the five-part Torah we have today.

Other scholars contend that the various strands of tradition woven into the Pentateuch do not derive from older written texts, such as J or E, but are based primarily on oral traditions about Israel's national **cult** (formal system of worship), particularly oral recitations of allegiance to YHWH, such as the statements preserved in Deuteronomy 6 and 26 and Joshua 24 (cf. Deut. 6:20–25; 26:5–9; Josh. 24:2–13). Before Josiah's reforms centralized worship at Jerusalem late in the seventh century B.C.E., public reiterations of the laws, rituals, and ancient lore associated with Moses or tribal ancestors were performed at many different shrines and religious centers scattered throughout Israelite territory. At seasonal festivals, Israel's various clans and/or tribes would assemble at one of their local holy places, such as those at Bethel, Shechem, Kadesh-barnea, Shiloh, or Jerusalem, where they would renew their covenant vows to YHWH. Evolving differences between individual tribal stories recounted at these different sanctuaries may have contributed to the different strata of thought or theological viewpoints found in the Torah.

According to this theory, the Torah rituals and narratives were compiled from diverse blocks of previously independent oral (and perhaps some written) material at a relatively late date, perhaps the fifth century B.C.E., or even later. The current trend among scholars who reject the documentary hypothesis is to date the Torah's composition to long after the Babylonian exile, when Persian administrative patronage mandated an official formulation of the Judean religious heritage (cf. Ezra 7:1, 11–26; 8:1; see Chapter 23) A few advocates of this view have recently proposed that the first four Pentateuchal books, Genesis through Numbers, are largely the work of a single author-editor who, during the late fifth or fourth century B.C.E., first incorporated Israel's extremely diverse oral traditions into a continuous narrative. This late composition was then added to the previously existing Deuteronomy to complete the Pentateuch. Because the scribal editors or redactors who gave the Pentateuch its final form most likely belonged to a priestly group living under Persian rule, it is not surprising that they validated their work by ascribing all the legal material they incorporated into their revised text to the authority of Moses. Thus, laws developed during the time of the monarchy and after the exile, as well as liturgical practices of the **Second Temple period** (after about 515 B.C.E., when the Jerusalem sanctuary was rebuilt), were made part of the Mosaic revelation at Sinai, ensuring that Israel's entire legacy of law and tradition served to express the bond between YHWH and his people. (For these and other recent scholarly theories about the making of the Pentateuch, see Arthur Quinn and Isaac Kikawada, Rolf Rendtorff, and R. N. Whybray in "Recommended Reading.")

At the beginning of the twenty-first century, the question of the Torah's authorship and date of composition remains unresolved. Although many scholars accept some form of the documentary hypothesis, which is still taught at many universities and seminaries, there is no broad scholarly consensus. Scholars rightly emphasize the enormous complexity of the process that culminated in the Hebrew Bible's first five books, noting that each of the individual sources amalgamated into the Pentateuch — whether written or oral — had its own long evolution before being integrated into the present text.

While recognizing that many repetitions, contradictions, and other incongruities of the Pentateuch can be explained most effectively by the biblical writers' and editors' use of diverse sources, the authors of this textbook will focus on the Pentateuch's final narrative form, exploring the significance of its major themes, characters, and events. So skillfully did the Tanak's redactors accomplish their task that the stories they wove together — from the wanderings of Abraham to the divine revelation at Sinai — continue to fascinate. (Students who wish to review a clear summary of the evidence for multiple sources in the Torah will find Richard E. Friedman's thoughtful works, such as *Who Wrote the Bible?* and his article "Torah (Pentateuch)," in *The Anchor Bible Dictionary,* a great help. *Sources of the Pentateuch* by Antony Campbell and Mark O'Brien is also a major resource; see "Recommended Reading.")

QUESTIONS FOR REVIEW

1. According to tradition, who was the author of the Pentateuch (the first five books of the Hebrew Bible)? What aspects of the biblical text have caused scholars to doubt Mosaic authorship?

2. Describe some methods that scholars have devised to examine the biblical text, including historical, form, and redaction criticism.

3. Explain the documentary hypothesis and its view of the Pentateuch as a composite document in which four distinct oral and/or literary sources are combined. Identify the four main sources, giving their names and chief characteristics.

4. State the theory of history spelled out in Deuteronomy and its influence on the composition of the historical narratives in Joshua through 2 Kings, the Deuteronomistic History.

5. When, and under what circumstances, do scholars believe that the Pentateuch underwent its final compilation and editing?

6. Outline some of the objections that some recent scholars have to the documentary hypothesis. According to these critics, how and when did the Pentateuch come into existence?

QUESTIONS FOR REFLECTION AND DISCUSSION

1. If scholars are correct that the Pentateuch is a composite work that evolved slowly over time, added to and reshaped according to Israel's changing historical circumstances, how does that knowledge affect your view of the work's authenticity and religious authority? Does the Pentateuch need to have come from Moses' pen in order to have ethical and religious value? Explain your answer.

2. If the present form of the Pentateuch represents many generations of Israelite thought about the nature of God and the divine-human relationship, how, then, does it contribute to our understanding of Israel's religious development in the ancient world? Instead of being viewed as a static work embodying only one moment (Moses' lifetime) in the flow of humanity's spiritual evolution, is the Pentateuch more valuable viewed as a witness to the progressive steps toward God that Israel made over a long and eventful journey through time?

TERMS AND CONCEPTS TO REMEMBER

alternatives to
   documentary
   hypothesis
Book of the Covenant
Court History
cult
D (Deuteronomist)
Deuteronomistic
   History (DH)
documentary hypothesis
E (Elohist)
Ephraim
form criticism
historical criticism
J (Yahwist)
JE epic

Josiah
Judah
oral tradition
P (priestly source)
pericope
problems with
   traditional authorship
redaction criticism
redactor
Second Temple period
Shechem
Sitz-im-Leben
source criticism
Tabernacle
traditional authorship of
   Pentateuch

RECOMMENDED READING

Blenkinsopp, Joseph. "Introduction to the Pentateuch." In *The New Interpreter's Bible*, Vol. 1, pp. 305–318. Nashville, Tenn.: Abingdon Press, 1994. A good survey of scholarly work on the Torah's multiple sources and themes.

Bright, John. *A History of Israel,* rev. ed. Louisville, Ky.: Westminster/John Knox Press, 2002. An update of a standard work that covers Israelite history to 70 C.E.

Campbell, Anthony F., and O'Brien, Mark A. *Sources of the Pentateuch: Texts, Introductions, Annotations.* Minneapolis: Fortress Press, 1993. Prints the priestly, Yahwist, and Elohist texts separately.

Crusemann, Frank. *The Torah: Theology and Social History of Old Testament Law.* Translated by Allan W. Mahnke. Minneapolis: Fortress Press, 1996. An exhaustive scholarly analysis of the historical, cultural, and literary development of the Pentateuch.

Ellis, Peter. *The Yahwist: The Bible's First Theologian.* Notre Dame, Ind.: Fides, 1968. An insightful study of the J document, thought to be the earliest literary strand in the Torah.

Friedman, Richard E. *Commentary on the Torah with a New English Translation.* San Francisco: HarperSanFrancisco, 2001. An interpretive analysis by a leading scholar.

————. *The Hidden Book in the Bible: The Discovery of the First Prose Masterpiece.* San Francisco: HarperSanFrancisco, 1998. Contains the author's translation of the entire J narrative, which he believes extends through the books of Joshua, Judges, Samuel, and 1 Kings 1–2.

————. "Torah (Pentateuch)." In D. N. Freedman, ed., *The Anchor Bible Dictionary*, Vol. 6, pp. 605–622. New York: Doubleday, 1992. Provides a lucid and well-reasoned presentation of evidence supporting the documentary hypothesis.

————. *Who Wrote the Bible?* New York and San Francisco: Harper & Row, 1987. An excellent introduction to scholarly speculations about authorship of the Hebrew Bible.

Jenks, Alan W. "Elohist." In D. N. Freedman, ed., *The Anchor Bible Dictionary*, Vol. 2, pp. 478–482. New York: Doubleday, 1992. A description of the Elohist writer's characteristics.

Milgrom, Jacob. "Priestly ('P') Source." In D. N. Freedman, ed., *The Anchor Bible Dictionary*, Vol. 5, pp. 454–461. New York: Doubleday, 1992. Summarizes literary and theological characteristics of the priestly school.

Nicholson, Ernest. *The Pentateuch in the Twentieth Century: The Legacy of Julius Wellhausen.* Oxford: Clarendon Press, 1998. A thorough examination of recent criticism of the documentary hypothesis and an able defense of the standard model.

Noth, Martin. *A History of Pentateuchal Traditions.* Translated by B. W. Anderson. Englewood Cliffs, N.J.: Prentice-Hall, 1972. An influential study of literary sources in the Pentateuch.

Pury, Albert de, "Yahwist ('J') Source." In D. N. Freedman, ed., *The Anchor Bible Dictionary*, Vol. 6, pp. 1013–1020. New York: Doubleday, 1992. Reviews the literary style and theological viewpoint of the Yahwist (J) author.

Quinn, Arthur, and Kikawada, Isaac. *Before Abraham Was: The Unity of Genesis 1–11.* Harrison, N.Y.: Ignatius Press, 1989. Argues for a single author of the primeval history.

Rendtorff, Rolf. *The Problem of the Process of the Transmission of the Pentateuch.* Sheffield, England: JSOT Press, 1990. Argues that the Deuteronomistic school compiled the Torah and denies the existence of earlier written sources, such as J or E.

Tigay, Jeffrey. "The Evolution of the Pentateuchal Narratives in the Light of the Evolution of the Gilgamesh Epic." In Jeffrey Tigay, ed., *Empirical Models for Biblical Criticism.* Philadelphia: University of Pennsylvania Press, 1985. Compares the literary evolution of the Sumero-Babylonian epic to the growth of the Pentateuch.

Van Seters, John. *Abraham in History and Tradition.* New Haven, Conn.: Yale University Press, 1975.

———. *In Search of History: Historiography in the Ancient World and the Origins of Biblical History.* New Haven, Conn.: Yale University Press, 1983. Argues that the Pentateuch was composed significantly after the Babylonian exile.

———. *Prologue to History: The Yahwist as Historian in Genesis.* Louisville, Ky: Westminster/John Knox Press, 1992. Regards the Yahwist strand as directed to a postexilic document.

Whybray, R. N. *The Making of the Pentateuch: A Methodological Study.* Sheffield, England: JSOT Press, 1987. Views the Torah as a postexilic document.

CHAPTER 6

The Five Books of Torah (Divine Instruction)

Key Topics/Themes Depicting human history as a progressive revelation of the divine will, the Torah emphasizes both the promises of future benefits that YHWH makes to Israel's ancestors — Abraham, Isaac, and Jacob — and the obligation laid upon these patriarchs' descendants — the Israelites — to worship YHWH exclusively and obey all his laws. Both an unprecedented blessing and a challenge, YHWH's commands regulating both ethical behavior and ritual worship define Israel's historical purpose as a source of universal blessing. Containing a diverse mixture of narrative,

genealogy, poetry, law, folklore, and myth, the first five books of the Tanak are too complex in both literary origin and content to be reduced to a single unified viewpoint. The great variety of materials and religious perspectives incorporated into the Torah, however, are at least partly unified by an emphasis on YHWH's covenant relationship with his people and the recurrent theme of divine promises that are only partially fulfilled. In its final form, the Torah addresses the questions and concerns of a community of exiles hoping to repossess the land God had vowed to give Abraham's progeny.

The Torah: An Overview

The first division of the three-part Hebrew Bible, the Torah opens with an account of God's creation of the world and early interaction with humanity as a whole (Gen. 1–11) but quickly shifts emphasis to focus on the creation of Israel. Beginning with the call of Abraham in Genesis 12, the five books of the Torah tell the story of Israel's origins and its transformation from a band of slaves into a "holy nation" dedicated to the service of YHWH. Virtually all events in Israel's story, including its escape from Egyptian bondage and miraculous deliverance next to a chaotic sea, are merely a prelude to the grand culmination—YHWH's theophany at Mount Sinai/Horeb. The heart and soul of Torah

(law, or divine instruction) lie in the vast body of laws, statutes, and precepts that YHWH transmits through Moses to the Israelites, prescribing a way of life that qualitatively distinguishes them from all other peoples. Even though the series of divine promises repeated throughout Genesis are only partly realized at the conclusion of Deuteronomy, God's instruction to Israel is by then complete, a divinely authorized legacy to guide all future generations of Abraham's descendants.

Near the end of Deuteronomy, Israel is asked to choose between fidelity to YHWH, which will bring abundant life and prosperity to the nation, and the worship of other gods, which will inevitably bring suffering and death (Deut. 27–30). Israel's response to YHWH's challenge determines its subsequent history: the Deuteronomistic narratives

(Joshua–2 Kings) that follow the Torah illustrate the disastrous consequences of breaking the Sinai agreement.

ORAL AND WRITTEN TRADITIONS

Behind the written Torah lie countless generations of oral tradition during which stories of YHWH's saving acts were transmitted only by word of mouth. As Moses admonishes the people,

> Remember the days of old,
> consider the years long past;
> ask your father and he will inform you;
> your elders, and they will tell you. (Deut. 32:7)

Although scholars do not agree on when Israel's tales of "years long past" were finally preserved in writing, many believe that the first continuous narrative that ultimately became part of the Hebrew Bible was composed by the Yahwist (J), a writer from the southern kingdom of Judah (see Chapter 5). Extending from creation through the escape from Egypt and the encounter with YHWH at Sinai, the Yahwist narrative also may have included an account of the conquest of Canaan and the allotment of the land to various tribes, a development now contained in the Tanak's sixth book, Joshua. If J's story of Israel's beginnings encompassed the settlement in Canaan, the original edition of the Torah, supplemented by Elohistic traditions from the north, was a **Hexateuch,** a six-book sequence that moved logically from YHWH's promises to fulfillment under Joshua's leadership. (For a readable English edition of J's supposed narrative, see Richard Friedman, *The Hidden Book in the Bible,* in "Recommended Reading.")

According to the documentary hypothesis, the combined Yahwist-Elohist (JE) epic of Israelite origins was further expanded by priestly additions after the exile, with the JEP material ultimately being grafted onto Deuteronomy, which had a separate compositional history (see Chapters 5 and 10). As noted in Chapter 5, a few contemporary scholars who reject the documentary hypothesis argue that an early form of Deuteronomy was the first

part of Torah written and that the books that now precede it, Genesis through Numbers, were composed long after the exile as a kind of extended preface to Deuteronomy (see John Van Seters and R. N. Whybray in "Recommended Reading"). In this view, Deuteronomic material comprises the original core of the Pentateuch (Greek, "five books"), and Genesis through Numbers form a later **Tetrateuch** (Greek, "four books"), perhaps compiled by a single author-editor in the postexilic community.

Despite wide scholarly disagreements about the dating and order of composition of various parts of the Torah, virtually all scholars recognize that the present work is an amalgamation of multiple sources, its complex literary history betrayed by the many duplications, contradictions, and other discrepancies. The current debate centers on how much — if any — of the Torah's sources existed as written documents before the exile (587–538 B.C.E.). Although it seems clear that extensive editing of both the Pentateuch and other biblical books took place following the exile, a large number of scholars offer persuasive evidence that Israel had produced many documents about its ongoing relationship with YHWH long before the fall to Babylon (see works by Anthony Campbell and Mark O'Brien, Richard Friedman, and Ernest Nicholson in "Recommended Reading").

Major Themes of the Pentateuch

While recognizing the value of source criticism in discussing many passages in the Pentateuch, this book will focus on the present form of the text. Despite its multiple authorship and long history of editorial additions and revisions, the final version of the Pentateuch presents some recurring themes that provide some degree of coherence. Although they worked with diverse materials dating from different periods in Israel's history, the Pentateuch's final editors carefully arranged their various sources to highlight the historical development of YHWH's unique partnership with Israel. Two themes in particular help to unify the Pentateuch's rich compendium of ancestral tradition, genealogy, law and poetry: YHWH's unsolicited promises to Abraham, Isaac, and Jacob, and YHWH's ongoing relationship with these patriarchs' descendants, the Israelites. The divine promises (grouped together in Genesis 12–50) and YHWH's binding demands upon his people (specified in the Torah's extensive legal requirements) shape not only the Pentateuch's general structure but also the Deuteronomistic History that follows (see Chapters 11–15). Poised between the promises on the one hand and the fearful necessity of consistently obeying all of YHWH's exacting commands on the other, the covenant community struggles to find its way between the opposite poles of hope and retribution. Encompassing both the divine promise of blessing and the threat of future loss, the Torah story prepares readers for the account of Israel's bittersweet historical experience that lies ahead.

POTENTIAL BLESSING AND CURSING

The curses Deuteronomy specifies for a disobedient Israel—reflecting the redactors' awareness of Israel's fall to Assyria (721 B.C.E.) and Judah's exile in Babylon (after 587 B.C.E.)—provide a counterpoint to the promised blessings (Deut. 28; cf. Lev. 26). Throughout the Pentateuch and Deuteronomistic History, the author-editors depict two opposing forces at work in human history: God's positive intentions for an obedient humanity, and a negative human rebelliousness that subverts the divine will. The conflict between YHWH's plan for his human creation and humankind's resistance to it begins with the first human couple's disobedience in Eden (Gen. 3) and dominates the Primeval History (Gen. 1–11; see Chapter 7). Human ingratitude for divine blessings persists in Israel's story, particularly the people's complaints about Moses' leadership and their flagrant disloyalty to the God who rescued them from Egyptian slavery. In Exodus and Numbers, the Israelites—apparently unmindful of the benefits of freedom and nationhood that YHWH confers on them—break virtually every commandment, violating the terms of their covenant bond at

the very moment of its inception (Exod. 32; cf. Num. 14). The Torah's description of Israel's wanton behavior at Sinai/Horeb, in fact, sets the tone for the deeply troubled relationship between YHWH and his people narrated in Judges through 2 Kings, as well in as the prophetic books.

In emphasizing Israel's repeated violation of its covenant obligations, the Torah narrative highlights the flaws in the Israelite community that will eventually result in its suffering the curses of national defeat, exile, and extreme suffering that YHWH had enunciated as the inevitable consequences of disobedience. Viewing their past from the perspective of exile, the Torah editors also envision a restoration of the divine-human relationship, expressed in a return to the land promised Abraham's descendants (Deut. 30). In predicting Israel's future restoration, in fact, God makes perhaps his most astonishing promise: He will give the Israelites the ability to trust and worship him alone, effecting an inner change that enables the people to love him with all their "hearts . . . and souls" (Deut. 30:4–6).

Before examining the Torah's depiction of the partnership between YHWH and Israel, we will consider the vows that YHWH makes to Israel's ancestors. (For a more complete discussion of covenant themes, see the works by David Clines and John Scullion in "Recommended Reading.") The divine promises, all contained in Genesis, may be divided into six components: YHWH swears to give Abraham and/or his grandson Jacob (1) a son, (2) descendants, (3) his presence, (4) land, (5) blessing, and (6) covenant. Although the partial fulfillment of these vows serves to tie together the patriarchal stories of Genesis with some of the later Torah narratives, as well as the historical books that follow, it is important to remember that not all versions of the divine promises contain all six of the provisions. Because each source now embedded in the Torah had its own tradition of the divine oaths, no two of them are precisely alike.

A Son and Descendants   The promise of a son occurs alone in Genesis 18, but it is usually linked with the more general promise of the patriarchs' descendants, which are to be as innumerable as the "stars of heaven" or the "sands of the sea." Abraham will become the father of a "multitude of nations" (including Israel through Isaac and, according to another tradition, the Arab peoples through Ishmael), as well as a line of kings (the royal dynasty founded by David many centuries later). In Genesis, which is deeply concerned with issues of fertility and reproduction, the divine guarantee of progeny is countered by repeated threats to its fulfillment, expressed in the theme of the "barren wife" (for most of their lives, Abraham's wife, Sarah, and Jacob's wife, Rachel, are unable to bear children) and in YHWH's own demand that Abraham sacrifice his son Isaac, the sole heir through whom YHWH's promises were to be accomplished.

An interesting variation of the son motif appears in Torah stories about God's favoring younger sons. Although the principle of *primogeniture* (the practice of giving the right of inheritance to the eldest son) was common in the ancient Near East, several narratives feature the triumph of a younger son over his older brothers. This pattern is established early in Genesis when God accepts Abel's worship while rejecting that of his older brother Cain (Gen. 4:1–16). Abraham's firstborn son Ishmael is superseded by Isaac, just as Esau is displaced by his younger twin Jacob (Gen. 21, 27). Later, Jacob confers his primary blessing on Judah, his fourth-born son, repudiating Reuben, his firstborn (Gen. 49). Joseph is preferred over his ten older brothers, anticipating David's precedence over his seven older siblings (1 Sam. 16) and Solomon's inheritance of Israel's throne, displacing his older fraternal rival (1 Kings 1–2). Some scholars think that the Torah's oft-repeated exaltation of younger men above their brothers was a device to help justify Solomon's kingship, an ascension that involved the killing of David's oldest son and presumed heir. Even if these stories (mostly found in J and the Court History) were intended to offer literary precedents for Solomon's actions, they may also provide a clue to the time of their composition (see Box 14.2).

Divine Presence   YHWH's pledge to be an invisible companion to his chosen worshipers figures most prominently in the Jacob story, in which God states that he will accompany Jacob on his many journeys (Gen. 26:3, 24; 28:15; 31:3). The theme of divine presence reappears as a major feature of YHWH's intimate relationship with Moses (Exod. 3–4) and is also the force that guides and protects Israel on its perilous trek through the Sinai wilderness. Demonstrating the crucial importance of housing the divine presence in Israel's midst, detailed instructions for constructing the Tabernacle and Ark of the Covenant take up almost eleven chapters in Exodus (Exod. 25–31, 35–40). Interestingly, it is David who later installs the ark in Jerusalem, which he captures from a Canaanite tribe to make his capital, and it is David with whom the divine presence is said to figure most prominently (2 Sam. 5:1–8:18). David's heir, Solomon (perhaps the youngest of his many sons), is granted the privilege of building YHWH's Temple in Jerusalem, the sanctuary at which God places his sacred "name," emblem of the divine presence (1 Kings 8; cf. Deut. 12).

Land   The theme of descendants and nationhood is closely linked to the promise of land, the territory of Canaan that YHWH swears to give Abraham and his offspring (Gen. 12:1–8; 13:14–17; 15:7–21). This pledge is reiterated to Jacob and his sons (Gen. 26:3–4; 28:4; 35:12; 50:24) but is fulfilled only in the united kingdom of David and Solomon (1 Kings 4:21). The entire narrative sequence of Genesis through 2 Kings, in fact, is largely a theological claim for Israel's divinely granted right to wrest the land from its native inhabitants, the Canaanites, balanced by a theological argument explaining why Israel ultimately forfeited its possession of the land. Deuteronomy's recitation of Israel's religious and moral failings provides the rationale for the people's loss of their national heritage (Deut. 28–30; Lev. 26).

Universal Blessing   Whereas the promise of land relates specifically to Israel's identity as a national state, YHWH's assurance of blessing to Abraham and his descendants has a more universal application. At the outset of his personal relationship with Abraham, YHWH offers assurances that not only

Abraham's heirs but "all the tribes [families] of the earth will bless themselves by you" (Gen. 12:3). The theme of a divine blessing that will ultimately encompass all peoples emphasizes the importance of Israel's mission as conveyer of YHWH's favor to humankind (Gen. 18:18; 22:18; 26:3–4; 28:14).

Covenant   As explained in Chapter 1, God's preferred means of defining his special relationship with Israel is through initiating a series of covenants contracting him to remain Israel's patron Deity forever. Whereas God's pledge to Noah (Gen. 9) is made with all humankind, the various covenants with Abraham (Gen. 12, 15, 17, 22) relate exclusively to the chosen people. In Genesis 17, a priestly composition that brings together almost all the elements of the divine promises, God links together the assurance of countless descendants, divine presence, land, kingship, and blessing, combining all these elements in a "Covenant in perpetuity, to be your GOD and the GOD of your descendants after you" (17:4–10). In making this covenant (*berit*), a term repeated thirteen times in twenty-two verses, God emphasizes that he solemnly binds himself to Abraham's progeny not only in the present but also in the future, perpetuating the God–Israel association for all time to come (see Chapter 7).

PARTIAL FULFILLMENT OF THE VOWS

Different aspects of the Genesis promises are highlighted in the next four Torah books. In Exodus, the promise that Abraham would have multitudinous descendants is already partially fulfilled, with Egypt's ruler becoming alarmed at the Israelites' unprecedented fecundity. Exodus also extensively elaborates the theme of covenant, giving it a radical new twist. Whereas Genesis presents all God's promises as unilateral—voluntary pledges on the Deity's part that require few reciprocal obligations from the human recipients—Exodus makes God's vow to protect Israel explicitly dependent on the people's obedience to the entire body of legal instruction given at Mount Sinai/Horeb. Underscoring the theme of YHWH's presence, manifested visibly in a "pillar of cloud" by day and a "pillar of fire" by night, Exodus also makes provision for later generations' ongoing communion with God through construction of the Tabernacle, in which YHWH's "glory" is enshrined (Exod. 40:34–36; see Chapter 8).

The Book of Leviticus, which prescribes regulations for Israelite behavior that will render the chosen people ritually pure in approaching YHWH, further develops the themes of divine presence and Israel's special partnership with the Lord. Demanding that Israel must be as holy as its God (Lev. 11:44), Leviticus articulates a sacred ethic that grounds human interaction in a conception of the Deity's nature (see Chapter 9).

Numbers, emphasizing both the numerical increase of Abraham's progeny and their lack of gratitude to the Deity who delivered them from Egyptian slavery, also recounts the Israelites' preparations for laying siege to the land of Canaan. The determination to enter the Promised Land further resounds through Deuteronomy, which stipulates YHWH's specific requirements for a successful invasion of Canaan, as well as dire warnings about the consequences of Israel's failure to adhere to Deuteronomic law. Moses' admonition makes clear that the covenant community's actual possession of the land and growth to true nationhood depend entirely on the people's living up to YHWH's exacting standards (see Chapter 10).

The Complex Nature of YHWH's Bond to Israel

At the close of Deuteronomy, Moses is said to have composed a song that includes a tradition about how YHWH came to be Israel's God. Evoking images of the heavenly council at which all the gods assemble to administer earthly affairs, Moses states that when the "Most High [Elyon]," head of the Canaanite pantheon, assigned the various nations their patron deities—"according to the number of the gods"—YHWH's "portion" and "allotted share" was Israel (Deut. 32:8–9). Israel's assignment to

YHWH proves to be a difficult match for both parties, partly because YHWH's ethical character differs so radically from that of the other gods (see Chapter 4).

In addition to his justice and compassion, YHWH has other character traits that set him apart from the gods of Egypt, Canaan, and Mesopotamia. After guiding Israel to Sinai/Horeb and binding the people to him in a covenant of mutual loyalty, he reveals an attitude toward human worship that differs sharply from that of other divinities. The need for absolute commitment to him alone is an intrinsic component of the divine personality, "because the LORD [YHWH], whose name is Jealous, is a jealous God" (Exod. 34:14). In the symbolic marriage between YHWH and Israel, absolute monogamy is essential; serving "gods . . . whom he had not allotted to them," worshiping other members of the divine council, will destroy the partnership (Deut. 29:26; cf. Hos. 1–3).

In the Torah narratives, YHWH's graciousness in liberating the Israelites from slavery and nurturing them as they journey through the wilderness is contrasted with his impatience and anger when the people repeatedly fail to show gratitude for his generosity. At the very moment when YHWH is conveying his commandments to Moses atop Mount Sinai/Horeb, the people below hold a riotous celebration worshiping the notorious "golden calf," a flagrant breach of loyalty that brings YHWH close to severing the covenant relationship altogether (Exod. 32). (For the significance of the calf/bull figure as a symbol of YHWH's power, see Chapter 4, especially Figures 4.3 and 4.4, and Figure 8.5)

From their infidelity at Sinai through their forty-year wandering in the desert, the Israelites are characterized by their grumbling, complaints, and apparent inability to worship YHWH with the single-mindedness he requires. Although YHWH leads them to oases of fresh water, feeds them with **manna** (a grainlike substance described as falling daily from heaven), sends flocks of birds to supply them with meat, and keeps their clothes from wearing out, the people respond only with "murmuring" and rebellion against Moses. When they reach the borders of the Promised Land and dispatch spies to investigate its inhabitants' potential resistance to their invasion, they listen only to the negative reports, demonstrating a total lack of faith in YHWH's power to grant them military victory. In Numbers, their defeatist attitude contrasts markedly with Moses' praise of YHWH as an invincible "warrior" after his triumph at the chaotic sea (Num. 14; cf. Exod. 15). Instead of increasing their devotion, the Israelites' forty years of companionship with YHWH has a paradoxical result: The closeness and accessibility of God seems to diminish the people's capacity to revere him.

Despite YHWH's daily presence, manifest in formations of cloud and in fire, during Israel's wilderness journey, the partnership between God and the people repeatedly threatens to unravel. Whereas YHWH alternates between solicitous concern and destructive anger, the people's response fluctuates between fear of the divine presence and an odd collective amnesia that seems to keep them from realizing the significance of YHWH's saving deeds in Egypt and at the tumultuous sea. Near the end of Deuteronomy, as the people make their final approach to Canaan's frontier, Moses concisely summarizes the Torah's portrait of the divine-human relationship. In this estimate, YHWH the "Rock" is without fault whereas the human partner is deeply flawed:

> The Rock, his work is perfect, and all his ways
> are just.
> A faithful GOD, without deceit, just and upright
> is he;
> yet his degenerate children have dealt falsely
> with him,
> a perverse and crooked generation.
> Do you thus repay the LORD, O foolish and
> senseless people? (Deut. 32:4–6)

In thus depicting the unequal union between the perfect YHWH and a morally defective Israel, the Torah unequivocally pins the responsibility for the quality of Israel's future—prosperity or adversity—on the people themselves. In the account of Israel's historical experience in Canaan that ensues, the nation's sufferings derive not from YHWH's unwillingness or inability to protect his people, but from his righteous anger at their faith-lessness, which eventually incites him to abandon his people to their political enemies.

Some Literary Forms in the Pentateuch

Although the Torah is primarily regarded as sacred teaching, a theologically oriented account of YHWH's unique relationship with Israel over space and time, it is also a composite document encompassing several distinct categories of literature. Among the literary forms it contains are narrative, genealogy, etiology (a subgenre of narrative), itinerary, and cult legend, as well as legal codes.

NARRATIVES

Much of the Torah is devoted to YHWH's laws and ordinances, but stories are an equally important component. Genesis, most of Exodus, and much of Numbers consist of **narrative**— an account of characters and events arranged in sequential order to illustrate a major theme or concept. Following a generally chronological development — from the creation of the world to the creation of Israel — the Torah contains all the elements typical of a story. These include setting (from Mesopotamia, to Canaan, to Egypt), character (from Adam and Eve, to Abraham and Sarah, to Moses, Aaron, and Miriam), conflict (from the sibling rivalry of Cain and Abel to YHWH's ambivalent relationship with Israel), and plot (with the promises to Abraham advancing through a series of loosely connected incidents until their partial culmination in the formation of Israel, a step-by-step unfolding of the Deity's long-range historical plan).

Overlap Among Narratives   Although editors divided the Torah into five individual books, each occupying a separate scroll, there is considerable overlap among them, with narratives and legal material carrying over from one volume to the next. The first continuous narrative unit, Genesis 1:1 to Exodus 19:3, moves from God's creation of the universe to his assembling of the Israelites at the foot of Mount Sinai/Horeb. This narrative sequence includes a large chronological gap between the descent of Jacob's sons into Egypt, which concludes Genesis, and the description of their descendants' Egyptian bondage, which opens Exodus; nevertheless, the entire Genesis-Exodus account functions as a coherent literary whole. From the call of Abraham in Genesis 12 to his progeny's arrival at Sinai/Horeb, the extended narrative functions as a prelude to the Torah's climactic event — the giving of YHWH's law and the formalizing of the covenant with Israel.

The second major segment of the Pentateuch, Exodus 19:4 through Numbers 10:10, subordinates narrative to large blocks of ethical, ritual, and legal material defining the terms of YHWH's contract with Israel. Beginning in Exodus 19, narrative movement comes to an almost complete halt as YHWH issues orders to prepare the people ritually for his appearance among them; in Exodus 20, he personally delivers the Ten Commandments to a terrified people. The rest of Exodus, all of Leviticus, and much of Numbers are largely devoted to the enumeration of more than 600 laws, ordinances, statutes, and rituals that make up the covenant alliance. Relatively short fragments of narrative are interspersed among several lawgiving episodes — notably, Exodus 24, which describes the formal ratification of the Mosaic Covenant, and Exodus 32–34, which relates the Israelites' violation of the covenant in the golden calf incident and YHWH's graciousness in renewing the pact. Anchored at a single location, Sinai/Horeb, this Torah section temporally occupies almost a year; it begins with the ritually purified Israelites vowing to obey YHWH's laws (most of which they have not yet heard) and ends with their leaving the "mountain of God" to head toward Canaan.

The third part of Torah, also a mixture of narrative and legal instruction (Num. 10:10–Deut. 34:12), covers Israel's forty-year journey through the desert, where YHWH continues to deliver still more laws at the Tabernacle. It closes on the plains of Moab, near the borders of Canaan, where Moses gives three farewell speeches recounting Israel's adventures with YHWH up to that moment and issuing an extensive revised edition of the law (Deut. 1:1–33). After prophesying Israel's future exile, Moses dies and is buried at an unknown location, the last event recorded in the Torah (Deut. 34).

The Narrative Voices   As in other surviving ancient Near Eastern literature, such as the *Epic of Gilgamesh* and the *Enuma Elish,* the Torah has a narrator, the unidentified person who tells the story. In fact, as a result of its multiple sources, the Torah has multiple narrative voices, each of which assumes absolute knowledge of the subject related. Speaking in the third person, the narrators presume to report the precise events of creation, a global flood, the origins of different national and ethnic groups, and other events of the remote past. Like the different poets who contributed to the composition of the *Epic of Gilgamesh,* the Torah authors commonly advance the narrative through dialogue, recounting long conversations between two characters even when no third party was present to witness the exchange. Examples include the debates between YHWH and Abraham over the ethical issue of YHWH's destroying Sodom (Gen. 18) and between Moses and YHWH over the Deity's proposal to exterminate Israel (Exod. 32; Num. 14).

As many Near Eastern texts demonstrate, it was common literary practice for ancient writers to create speeches for both long-dead heroes and their gods, such as Gilgamesh's dialogue with his divine patron Shamash in the bejeweled "garden of the gods." Torah writers thus present much of YHWH's self-revelation on Sinai/Horeb through private conversations with Moses (Exod. 3, 24, 32–34). Other Tanak authors compose scenes set entirely in heaven, at which divine beings speak among themselves, such as the portrayal of YHWH's celestial court in Job (Job 1–2; cf. 1 Kings 22:18–28 and Zech. 3). The custom of fashioning dialogue for gods, prevalent in Mesopotamian and Egyptian literature, is well illustrated in Homer's *Iliad* and *Odyssey,* epic poems perhaps contemporaneous with some Torah sources, in which Zeus and his fellow Olympians meet in council to discuss their plans for humankind.

Biblical Transformations of Myth   Although the Torah, definitively edited by monotheistic redactors during and after the Babylonian exile, contains no extended myths comparable to those in the Homeric epics, it does contain a number of mythological motifs. From the Greek word *mythos* (something uttered, a story), **myth** refers to traditional narratives about gods and heroes, typically involving stories of creation and/or origins of religious and social customs. Mythic language and imagery occur in such biblical passages as the angels' descent from heaven to mate with mortal women, producing a race of heroes and giants (Gen. 6). The notion that great men of the prehistoric era inherited their superhuman qualities from a divine parent permeates both Mesopotamian and Greek mythology; while including a brief allusion to the tradition, however, the Genesis narrator carefully avoids any description of the heroes' mythic exploits. Whereas Genesis provides only a cursory reference, the noncanonical Book of 1 Enoch offers an elaborate account of the fate of Genesis's "fallen" angels, who also taught humankind the arts and technologies of civilization (see Chapter 30). Such mythical creatures as Rahab, Behemoth, and Leviathan, primordial dragons of chaos, also figure prominently in biblical imagery. (See the discussion of Job 40:15–41:26 in Chapter 25. For references to the mythological concept of a divine council, see Chapter 4.)

GENEALOGIES

The use of **genealogies,** a literary genre, to bind together individual narrative units and provide continuity, is largely a priestly contribution to the Pentateuch. Whereas the Yahwist writer in Genesis creatively interweaves brief genealogies with narrative, the priestly school inserts them into the narrative as relatively large blocks of material, using a rigid formula that lists a patriarch's age at the time he fathered his first son, the number of years he lived after his firstborn, his age at the time of death, and the fact that "he died" (see Gen. 5). Reenforcing the importance of male offspring, the priestly genealogies trace an unbroken line of descent from Adam to Abraham. A variation of the genealogical lists occurs in Genesis 49, where Jacob, in the form of prophecy, pronounces moral judgments on his twelve sons. Another extensive genealogy occupies the opening chapters of Numbers, along with lists of priestly functions.

ETIOLOGIES

Some Torah passages take the form of **etiologies**—a particular kind of narrative that explains the cause or origin of some natural phenomenon, social custom, or religious ritual. Genesis features several etiological anecdotes, such as the folktale in which Lot's wife is changed into a pillar of salt, presumably to account for the unusual salt formations bordering the Dead Sea. The story of Jacob's wrestling with a mysterious nocturnal visitor is also given an etiological emphasis, according to which the Israelites do not eat part of an animal's hip "because [the wrestler] had struck Jacob in the socket of the hip on the sciatic nerve" (Gen. 32:25–33). Interestingly, this prohibition against consuming this part of an animal's anatomy does not appear in any of the Torah's several law codes.

In a broad sense, the divine speeches in which El Shaddai or YHWH promises Canaan to Abraham's descendants function as etiologies, asserting that Israel's political claim to the territory originates in divine action. By placing the promises for land early in Israel's prehistory—centuries before Israelite tribes actually occupied Canaan—the Genesis authors show that Israel's right to possess the area was part of God's plan from the beginning. Genesis also explains why Israel became a sovereign state relatively late in Near Eastern history: Although nationhood was its preordained birthright, it was God's pleasure to delay implementation of his promise.

ITINERARIES

A literary category that characterizes nomadic societies, the **itinerary**—accounts of a people's movements from one geographical area to another—may represent one of the Torah's oldest strata. The Genesis account of Abraham's migration from Mesopotamia to Canaan traces a route marked by conventions of the genre, noting the place of departure, the destination, and specific place names (such as oases or campsites) along the way, as well as other geographical features. Related to the itinerary genre, the journey motif dominates much of the Torah action. Abraham, Jacob, Joseph, Moses, and the people of Israel are almost constantly on the move, traveling to or from the Promised Land. While Exodus recounts the Israelites' journey from Egypt to meet YHWH at Sinai/Horeb, Numbers underscores their subsequent forty-year trek through an arid wilderness. The metaphor of homeless wanderers ever seeking a permanent resting place dominates the Torah story of Israel's early life.

CULT LEGENDS

Many tales of the patriarchs dramatize their religious experiences at a particular site, such as Bethel, Hebron, or Shechem, which later became important centers of Israelite worship. Known as **cult legends** because they serve to validate centers of worship, these stories may also have etiological purposes, explaining when and how the place became sacred through its association with one of Israel's ancestors. After Jacob has his visionary dream of ascending and descending divinities at Luz, he changes its name to Bethel—"House of God"—erecting a stone monument there to commemorate his experience (Gen. 28:10–19). A second version of Jacob's naming Bethel (and of God's changing Jacob's name to Israel) appears in Genesis 35, where Jacob again erects a stone monument. The ancient Canaanite sanctuary at Shechem, where Israel's tribes later held covenant renewal ceremonies, had a similar cult legend. At Shechem, Jacob buys property and erects an altar, which he calls "El, God of Israel" (Gen. 33:18–20).

MULTIPLE PURPOSES FOR THE GENRES

The Torah's mixture of different literary genres, in which narrative and legal instruction figure most prominently, suggests not only its multiple sources but also its multiple purposes. From the poetic creation account in Genesis 1 to Moses' "song" deploring the Israelites' misconduct in Deuteronomy 32, the five Torah books utilize both storytelling and legal instruction to illustrate the complex nature of the divine-human relationship. In preserving ancient traditions about Israel's bond to YHWH, narrative demonstrates how God interacts with such characters as Abraham, Jacob, and Moses. These leaders, who "listen" attentively to God's voice, provide later readers with models for maintaining a dynamic bond with Israel's Deity.

Whereas the narratives of Genesis, Exodus, and Numbers focus on divine intervention and human response, the Torah's extensive legal codes present the means by which YHWH wishes to regulate human life and worship. In its final form, the Torah incorporates at least five originally separate bodies of law in addition to the Decalogue (Ten Commandments). Scholars believe that these formerly distinct codes derive from different groups within Israelite society, with their inclusion in the Torah probably representing a compromise among the competing claims of rival priesthoods (Aaronic and Levite), as well as from groups deeply influenced by the prophetic tradition (see Box 10.2). During the final process of editing the Torah, both the legal and the narrative legacies treasured by discrete social groups were ultimately combined to provide Israel with its most authoritative guide.

The Audience for the Pentateuch

If we knew at what particular historical periods the various parts of the Pentateuch were composed, and under what circumstances it received its final form, we could in not only better trace the evolution of Israel's religion but also better understand its pre-sumed intent and meaning. When, for example, did the Genesis promises of land, nationhood, and a line of kings originate? Some scholars think that YHWH's promises, probably in oral form, first served the interests of the Israelite tribes who occupied Canaan, providing a divinely mandated right to drive out the native inhabitants and take over the region. Other scholars argue that the promises derive from the later monarchy, a premise supported by the close verbal parallels between YHWH's covenant with Abraham and his similarly unconditional pact with King David (cf. Gen. 12, 15, 17, 22; 2 Sam. 7; see Box 14.2). In this view, the promises may already have been incorporated into the Yahwist's (J's) account, perhaps as early as the late ninth or eighth century B.C.E. A small number of scholars, however, date the first four books, the Tetrateuch, long after the end of the Davidic monarchy, during the Persian or even Hellenistic period (see Chapter 5).

Whether the Pentateuch was composed entirely after the exile and primarily from oral traditions, as a few recent critics speculate, or whether it was simply revised and reedited from previously existing written sources, as the documentary hypothesis proposes, in its final form it was addressed to a community of exiles. The Genesis stories of wandering families, journeying rootlessly from Mesopotamia to Canaan to Egypt, would strike a responsive chord among exiles whom the Babylonians had driven to these very locations. The theme of divine promises made to the peripatetic ancestors—yet to be fulfilled, and then only partially, at some unspecified future time—spoke directly to the exiles' homelessness and anxieties about the future. Like Abraham, Sarah, Jacob, Rachel, and Joseph and his eleven brothers, these expatriates longed to possess assurance of a secure homeland from an unimpeachable source, the ancestral God. Exiles could also closely identify with the Exodus story of miraculous deliverance from foreign bondage, particularly when a prophet of the exile, Second Isaiah, compared repatriation from Babylon to a new exodus, evoking ancient tradition to envision a glorious future (Isa. 40–55).

As finally redacted, the Pentateuch assures YHWH's people that, true to his covenant with Abraham, God will take them under his protective wing, providing not only the blessings of prosperity and protection from enemies but also divine instruction that gives meaning to life. In these assurances, the completed Pentateuch embodies the ultimate goals of Israel's collective aspirations. It is not the hope of a posthumous reward—the Mosaic teachings do not even mention the idea of immortality or a future life in heaven—but the hope for a fulfilling life in the here and now, in a material world that God had pronounced "very good" (Gen. 1:31), a divine evaluation of creation that Israel fully endorsed. Israel's goal of an abundant earthly life proves hauntingly elusive, however, as foreshadowed by the Pentateuch's highly inconclusive ending. In Deuteronomy's final chapter, most of the promises are still unrealized; the covenant people are still outside the land of promise; their national leader, Moses, is dead; and their future prospects are profoundly uncertain. Such was the covenant people's situation in exile, when priestly editors shaped the Pentateuch into a form that gave its audience both a privileged identity and a lasting purpose.

QUESTIONS FOR REVIEW

1. Define the terms *Pentateuch*, *Hexateuch*, and *Tetrateuch*, and list the books they include.

2. Describe some of the major themes in the Pentateuch and their function in helping to bind together the diverse materials in the Tanak's first five books. How do the divine promises serve to provide a unifying element in the long narratives extending from Genesis to 2 Kings?

3. The Pentateuch consists of both story and law. In what ways are these two different literary genres related? How does Israel's response to YHWH's ethical and legal commands at Sinai/Horeb shape the narrative sections?

4. Define *myth*, and explain its function in illustrating the divine-human relationship.

5. Define the term *cult legends*, and explain their function in validating or justifying a particular center of worship in Canaan. How do traditions that Israel's ancestors worshiped El/YHWH at a given shrine or that they erected monuments testifying to a theophany at a particular locale serve to explain how that site became regarded as a suitable place of worship or sacrifice for later generations of Israelites?

6. Describe the probable audience for the Pentateuch. How do its narratives relate to a group in exile? Does the tradition that Abraham's family originated in Mesopotamia and that Jacob's sons settled in Egypt have any bearing on the circumstances of people exiled far from their homeland?

QUESTIONS FOR REFLECTION AND DISCUSSION

1. Why does the Pentateuch conclude with few of the promises made to Abraham fulfilled? Why does Moses, the leading figure of four books of the Pentateuch, die before reaching the Promised Land? Why do Israel's most sacred documents not include a narrative about the Israelites taking control of Canaan? What historical circumstances at the time the Pentateuch was finally redacted may have influenced its present form and content?

2. How well do you think that the Pentateuchal theme of divine promises indefinitely deferred serves to enhance or strengthen the divine-human bond? Explain your answer.

TERMS AND CONCEPTS TO REMEMBER

cult legends
etiology
genealogy
Hexateuch
itinerary
literary forms in
  the Pentateuch
manna

myth
narrative
original audience for the
  Pentateuch
promises to Abraham
Tetrateuch
YHWH's relationship
  to Israel

RECOMMENDED READING

Alter, Robert. *The Art of Biblical Narrative.* New York: Basic Books, 1982. An influential study of the literary components of biblical narratives.

Anderson, Gary A. "Introduction to Israelite Religion." In *The New Interpreter's Bible*, Vol. 1, pp. 272–283.

Nashville, Tenn.: Abingdon Press, 1994. An informative survey of important ideas in biblical religion.

Blenkinsopp, Joseph. "Introduction to the Pentateuch." In *The New Interpreter's Bible,* Vol. 1, pp. 305–318. Nashville, Tenn.: Abingdon Press, 1994. A good source for beginning students.

———. *The Pentateuch: An Introduction to the First Five Books of the Bible.* New York: Doubleday, 1992.

Birch, Bruce C.; Brueggemann, Walter; Fretheim, Terence E.; and Peterson, David L. *A Theological Introduction to the Old Testament.* Nashville, Tenn.: Abingdon Press, 1999. Includes cogent discussions of the Pentateuch, including historical-critical and literary analyses, by leading biblical scholars.

Brueggemann, Walter. *Theology of the Old Testament.* Minneapolis: Fortress Press, 1997. One of the most important works in biblical theology, focusing on the complex character of God.

Campbell, Anthony F., and O'Brien, Mark A. *Sources of the Pentateuch: Texts, Introductions, Annotations.* Minneapolis: Fortress Press, 1993. Identifies passages ascribed to the J, E, and P sources, and prints them as separate blocks of material.

Clines, David J. A. *The Theme of the Pentateuch,* 2nd ed. Supplement Series 10. Sheffield, England: JSOT Press, 1997. Discusses literary themes that unify diverse Torah narratives.

Dorsey, David A. *The Literary Structure of the Old Testament: A Commentary on Genesis-Malachi.* Grand Rapids, Mich.: Baker Books, 1999. Detailed analysis of thematic continuities, organization, and literary units in each book of the Hebrew Bible.

Fox, Everett. *The Five Books of Moses.* The Schocken Bible, Vol. 1. New York: Schocken Books, 1995. A fresh new translation that includes helpful interpretative commentary.

Fretheim, Terence E. *The Pentateuch.* Nashville, Tenn.: Abingdon, 1996. A concise discussion of unifying themes and theological motifs in the five books of Torah.

Friedman, Richard E. *Commentary on the Torah with a New English Translation.* San Francisco: HarperSanFrancisco, 2001. A scholarly but readable analysis of the five books of the Torah.

———. *The Hidden Book in the Bible: The Discovery of the First Prose Masterpiece.* San Francisco: HarperSanFrancisco, 1998. Identifies J's once independent account, now embedded in the Torah and Deuteronomistic History, and translates it as a continuous narrative.

Gabel, John B., and Wheeler, Charles B. *The Bible as Literature: An Introduction,* 3rd ed. New York: Oxford University Press, 1996. Examines major literary elements of the biblical text.

Nicholson, Ernest. *The Pentateuch in the Twentieth Century: The Legacy of Julius Wellhausen.* Oxford: Clarendon Press, 1998. A detailed critique of recent attacks on the documentary hypothesis and a thoughtful defense of the classic theory.

Schwartz, Regina M., ed. *The Book and the Text: The Bible and Literary Theory.* London: Blackwell, 1990.

Scullion, John J. "Genesis, the Narrative of." In D. N. Freedman, ed., *The Anchor Bible Dictionary,* Vol. 2, pp. 941–962. New York: Doubleday, 1992. Examines major themes and literary categories in Genesis.

Van Seters, John. *In Search of History: Historiography in the Ancient World and the Origins of Biblical History.* New Haven, Conn.: Yale University Press, 1983. Argues for the postexilic origin of the Pentateuch.

Whybray, R. N. *The Making of the Pentateuch: A Methodological Study.* Sheffield, England: JSOT Press, 1987. Rejects the documentary hypothesis and views the Torah as a postexilic creation.

CHAPTER 7

In the Beginning

The Book of Genesis

Key Topics/Themes Opening with a priestly narrative extolling God's creative majesty and an etiological tale dramatizing humanity's alienation from its Creator, Genesis introduces themes that will dominate most of the Hebrew Bible. In the Primeval History (Chs. 1–11), the first of three parts into which the book is divided, the Deity manifests a profound ambivalence toward his flawed human creation. After expelling the first humans from their paradise home, YHWH/Elohim almost completely annihilates humankind in a global deluge. Then he permanently divides the population by erecting language barriers between peoples and scattering them over the face of the earth. In the second section, however—the cycle of ancestral stories (Chs. 12–36)—the divine-human relationship improves as the narrative focuses on God's series of promises to a specific group, the family of Abraham, Isaac, and Jacob, the progenitors of Israel. In the third section, the story of Joseph (Chs. 37–50), God utilizes the rivalry among brothers to further his purpose of making Abraham's descendants a source of universal blessing. Genesis concludes with the chosen people still few in number and settled in Egypt, far from their promised homeland.

As the first book of the Torah, Genesis serves as a prologue to the story of Israel's formation narrated in the remaining four volumes of the Pentateuch. By identifying YHWH/Elohim, the God of Israel, as the creator of the universe, the Torah narrator not only places Israel's history in a cosmic context but also introduces God as the Tanak's true protagonist, the principal actor in the biblical drama. The Genesis portrayal of the Deity, drawn from a variety of ancient sources, establishes a concept of God that prevails throughout the Hebrew Bible and continues to inform the theology of the world's monotheistic faiths.

Although in Genesis 1 God initially appears as a transcendent, distant Being who speaks the world into existence, in Genesis 2 he is shown as immanent, first stooping to mold the first human out of clay, and later frequently descending to earth and communicating with his chosen favorites. Both creator of the world and master of human history, the biblical God operates directly, through visible materializations to human companions, and indirectly, behind the scenes, to implement his plans for Israel. By the end of Genesis, he has maneuvered Israel's ancestors into Egypt, where Joseph foretells the next major event in the biblical epic, the Israelites' flight from Egypt and eventual possession of the Promised Land (Gen. 50:24–25).

The composite nature of Genesis becomes evident from a careful reading of the first three chapters, which present two very different versions of creation and human origins. Differences in style, vocabulary, and theology indicate that the first account is a priestly composition (Gen. 1:1–2:4a) but that the second (Gen. 2:4b–3:24) is the work of the Yahwist (J). Using the Deity's personal name, YHWH, from the outset, the Yahwist provides the main story line for most of the book. Elohistic (E)

Table 7.1   Some Sources Used in Genesis

According to the documentary hypothesis, the text of Genesis is a literary patchwork woven from at least three originally distinct sources, known as J (the Yahwist), E (the Elohist), and P (the priestly), plus additions from redactors who compiled the once-separate traditions into a literary whole. Some representative passages that scholars assign to the three different sources are listed below.

Topic	Yahwist (J)	Elohist (E)	Priestly (P)
Creation	2:4b–25	—	1:1–2:3
Garden of Eden	3:1–24	—	—
Cain and Abel	4:1–26	—	—
Adam's genealogy	—	—	5:1b–28, 30–32
Flood	(See Box 5.1 for parallel accounts by J and P)		
Tower of Babel	11:1–9	—	
Divine promises to Abraham	12:1–4a; 15:1–21	22:16b–19	17:1–27
Hagar and Ishmael	16:1–2, 4–14	21:8–21	16:3, 15–16
Promised son	18:1–33	—	—
Sodom and Gomorrah	19:1–28, 30–38	—	19:29
Binding of Isaac	—	22:1–10	—
Isaac and Rebekah	24:1–67	—	25:20
Jacob and Esau	25:11b, 21–34; 27:1–45	—	26:34–35; 27:46; 28:1–9
Jacob and God at Bethel	28:10–11a, 13–16, 19	28:11b–12, 17–18, 20–22	—
Jacob, Leah, and Rachel	29:1–30	—	—
Jacob and Dinah	34:1–31	33:8–20	—
Joseph and his brothers	37:2b, 3b, 5–11, 19–20, 23, 25b–27, 28b, 31–35	37:3a, 4, 12–18, 21–22, 24, 25a, 28a, 29, 36	37:1
Judah and Tamar	38:1–30	—	—
Joseph and Potiphar's wife	39:1–23	—	—
Joseph's dream interpretations in prison	—	40:1–23	—

As this sampling of theoretical sources indicates, the Yahwist commonly emphasizes the role of women in the unfolding of Israel's prehistory, composing passages in which Eve, Sarah, Hagar, Rebekah, Tamar, and Potiphar's wife figure prominently. Whereas the Yahwist typically evokes Yahweh's immanence in dealing with humanity, the Elohist tends to stress Elohim's use of intermediaries — angels, dreams, and visions — in relating divine communications.

material, which survives only in fragments integrated into J's continuous narrative, first appears in the cycle of stories about Abraham, most prominently in Genesis 20–22 (Table 7.1).

Next to the Yahwist, the priestly school (P) makes the largest contribution to Genesis. In addition to the first creation account, the priestly source includes its own version of the flood story, which later editors intricately interwove with the Yahwist's older deluge narrative (see Box 5.1). P is also responsible for the longest description of the Abrahamic Covenant (Gen. 17) and the episode in which Abraham purchases a burial cave, the only parcel of the Promised Land he is ever to own. For many readers, perhaps the most noticeable P sections are the genealogies — long lists of names that trace the descent of a person, family, or ethnic group from a given ancestor. Although readers often skip these elaborate family trees, their presence helps to tie together the various narrative segments in Genesis and impose a schematic order on the book's diverse contents. With the same concern for orderly sequence that characterizes P's creation story, the genealogies present human history in a highly symmetrical format, listing ten generations between Adam and Noah (Gen. 5) and ten generations between Noah and Abraham (Gen. 11). For P, the proliferation of humanity, in obedience to a divine command (Gen. 1:28; cf. Gen. 9:1) can be expressed in an orderly pattern.

The Primeval History

CREATION: THE PRIESTLY ACCOUNT

Whereas most of the Pentateuch concentrates on YHWH's special relationship with Israel, Genesis begins with accounts of creation and human origins, giving a universal perspective to the narratives about Israel's ancestors that follow. In the priestly story (Gen. 1:1–2:4a), Elohim transforms a dark, watery chaos into the **cosmos,** an orderly system characterized by predictability and harmony. Although some theologians interpret Genesis 1 as depicting creation *ex nihilo*—"out of nothing"—the Hebrew text does not unequivocally support that view. Elohim does not bring forth the cosmos out of emptiness, but uses preexisting raw material— a boundless, formless abyss of water—to fashion the universe. The Jewish Publication Society thus translates the Bible's opening lines: "When GOD [Elohim] began to create the heaven and the earth—the earth being unformed and void, with darkness over the deep [*tehom*] and the wind from GOD sweeping over the waters. . . ." The English term "the deep" translates the Hebrew *tehom*, which refers to the ancient Near Eastern concept of an undifferentiated sea that existed before divine action brought the world into being (Box 7.1). Working with this primordial substance, Elohim employs a

six-step process by which the primal chaotic ocean is illuminated, divided, and shaped into a structured environment that will support life.

Highly methodical, the priestly source arranges the creative week into two sets of three related actions. On day 1, Elohim creates light (the illuminating opposite of primal darkness, sterility, and death, and thus a basic expression of the divine nature) and then separates light from darkness, initiating the regular alternation of day and night that governs human existence. On day 2, he creates the "dome" or vault of heaven (Hebrew, *rakiah,* sometimes translated as "firmament"), a cosmic arch that divides the primal waters above the domed sky from those below, making room for subsequent life to flourish. On day 3, he separates dry land from the surrounding sea, providing an environment for the terrestrial animals that are created on day six (Table 7.2).

In the second three-day unit, Elohim creates birds, fish, and animals to inhabit the three regions—air, sea, and earth—he previously separated and shaped from the primal watery element. The sky "dome" formed on day 2 becomes the structure into which God fits astronomical bodies, the "lights" of sun, moon, and stars. Although sun and moon were commonly worshiped as divinities in the Near East, P does not even name them, stating that they exist only to "rule" or regulate the seasons, allowing humans to devise calendars. P's reluctance to name these "lights" may stem from the fact that the Hebrew word for sun, *shemesh,* is virtually identical to the name *Shamash,* the Babylonian solar deity.

On day 5, Elohim generates creatures to swim through the lower sea and fly through the sky vault that had been separated from each other on day 2. Days 3 and 6 also correspond: The dry land and plants created on day 3 provide a sustaining environment for the animals and humans formed on day 6.

The creation of humanity, male and female together, *both* in the divine "likeness" and "image," marks the climax of the priestly narrative. Immediately following his creative labors, which he pronounces "very good," God "rests." God's day of

BOX 7.1
Some Ancient Near Eastern Parallels to Genesis

THE PRIMACY OF WATER

In assuming that a formless body of water preceded creation, the priestly writer of Genesis 1 echoes ideas prevalent throughout the ancient Near East. According to the Egyptian creation account associated with Heliopolis—"City of the Sun"—the primal element was an infinite expanse of water, called Nu, that had to be separated and divided during the process of forming the world. In the Heliopolian tradition, the sun god Aton arose out of Nu, standing on a primeval mound, a prototype of the earth's future landmasses, surrounded by an endless ocean. From that vantage point, Aton then created the inhabitable world. (For another Egyptian creation account, in which the god Ptah, like Elohim, speaks the universe into existence, see Box 3.3.)

THE *ENUMA ELISH*

In Mesopotamia, the native land of Israel's forebears and the place where many biblical author-editors spent a long exile, literary antecedents to the Genesis creation story abound. P's vision of precreation as a dark, amorphous, windswept body of water is also the assumption of the *Enuma Elish*, a Mesopotamian creation epic dating from about the twelfth century B.C.E. A celebration of Marduk (head of the Babylonian pantheon) as world-creator, the *Enuma Elish* was recited annually at public festivals, some of which may have been observed by exiles from Judah. The Mesopotamian poem resembles Genesis in beginning with a description of the primal chaos, an abyss of undifferentiated waters, from which several generations of gods progressively emerge. Both Genesis 1 and the *Enuma Elish* show creation occurring in six distinct stages—the six generations of Babylonian gods corresponding to Genesis's six creative days. In both works, the creative process culminates in the appearance of humans.

The differences between the biblical and the Mesopotamian versions of creation, however, are more important than their similarities. The Genesis authors omit all references to ancient myths about the cosmic conflict that preceded creation, battles in which Marduk defeats older generations of gods to reign supreme; Genesis retains only Elohim's brief invitation to the divine council to fashion humans "in our image, according to our likeness" (Gen. 1:26). Excluding the old mythology of violent warfare, Genesis depicts an omnipotent God, facing no opposition and creating solely by the power of his word. In stating the purpose of human creation, the two accounts are also strikingly different. In the *Enuma Elish,* Marduk shapes humanity from the blood of Kingu, a slain god, so that the victorious gods can be relieved of work; humans exist only to build and maintain the gods' altars and temples, where they burn animal sacrifices to keep their divine masters well nourished. In Genesis 1, humans are formed as the pinnacle of creation and given godlike dominion over it (Gen. 1:26–29). Carrying out the divine mandate to multiply and to administer the earthly sphere, they become partners in God's ongoing plan for the world. This priestly view of human preeminence is summarized most forcefully in Psalm 8:5, which states that humanity has been created only "a little lower than GOD," and "crowned with glory and honor." (In contrast, the Yahwist account retains an element of the old Mesopotamian tradition, stating that YHWH installed the first human in a garden "to till it and keep it" (Gen. 2:15), assigning him the task of maintaining the Deity's property.

Although purged almost entirely from Genesis, echoes of conflict mythologies are evident in other parts of the Hebrew Bible. In Psalm 89, YHWH bisects **Rahab,** the primal dragon of chaos, as Marduk split the monster Tiamat, using the two parts of her body to make the physical earth and vault (firmament) of heaven. YHWH's primordial battle with chaos to create the present world order also resounds through Psalm 74, which recounts a series of heroic acts by which YHWH divided the ancient sea, crushed the sea dragon, and then established the cosmic order of alternating night and day—a sequence that roughly parallels events in both Genesis and the *Enuma Elish.* (See also references to the "Sea," "Dragon," "Rahab," "Leviathan," and "fleeing serpent" in Isaiah 51:1 and Job 7:12; 26:1–14; and 40–41; these are discussed in Chapter 25.)

Table 7.2   Parallels of Habitat and Inhabitant

In Genesis 1, the priestly writer divides Elohim's creative work into six distinct stages, or "days." In this carefully arranged scheme, the element, region, or environment created on days 2 and 3 provide the place or sphere of existence for the objects or creatures created on days 4–6.

Day	Region or Habitat	Day	Inhabitant
1	Light (day and night)	—	—
2	"Dome" of sky (a)	4	Astronomical "lights"
	separated from sea (b)	5	Birds and sea creatures
3 (a)	Dry land	6 (a)	Land animals
3 (b)	Vegetation	6 (b)	Humanity

postcreation repose is later cited as a divine precedent for Israel's observing the **Sabbath,** the seventh day of the week, in which all work ceases (cf. Exod. 20:8–11). Note, however, that Deuteronomy's version of this commandment gives a different rationale for the Sabbath, declaring it an opportunity to remember Israel's escape from forced labor in Egypt (Deut. 5:12–15). (Figure 7.1 shows one version of the ancient biblical view of the universe.)

CREATION: THE YAHWIST VERSION

Whereas the P source depicts an elevated, transcendent, and highly structured view of creation, the Yahwist (J) narrative brings creative events down to earth, portraying an anthropomorphic YHWH and a humanity (Hebrew, *adam*) composed of dust (*adamah*). P's creation emerges from an oceanic abyss, but J's precreation environment is a rainless, empty desert that YHWH irrigates with subterranean waters (Gen. 2:5–6).

J also gives a different order to creation. Whereas P states that Elohim creates men and women simultaneously, at the end of a long sequence, J shows YHWH fashioning the first man *before* animals, trees, or the first woman are created. Whereas P's humanity is imprinted with the divine image, J's is shaped of ordinary clay, which is then animated by YHWH's "breath." After designing the human creature (*adam*), a mortal duality of earth and divine energy, YHWH then plants a garden "in Eden," where he causes vegetation to grow, including a tree

of life and a tree of knowledge. (The term *adam* here means "humankind"; **Adam** is not used as the first man's personal name until later in the narrative.)

Only after placing the human alone in Eden, as gardener and caretaker, does YHWH apparently notice that total solitude is "not good" for him. Resolving to "make him a helper as his partner," YHWH then proceeds to create a variety of animals and birds, bringing them to *adam* to name. As if expecting *adam* to select a mate from this menagerie, YHWH parades all his nonhuman species past the mortal, who can find no suitable companion among them. Perceiving that *adam* is qualitatively different from the other creatures he has made, YHWH then puts *adam* to sleep, removes part of his body (the famous rib), and uses it to fashion the first woman. The woman's appearance—she is not called **Eve** until Genesis 3:20—inspires the first poetry: *adam* rejoices that she is "bone of my bones and flesh of my flesh" (Gen. 2:23). The affinity between the pair is expressed in the poem's wordplay on *ish* (Hebrew, man) and *ishah* (woman). Unlike the animal species, she is his true kin, an appropriate partner. (For Laban's use of the same poetic phrase to describe his blood kinship to Jacob, see Genesis 29:14.)

ADAM, EVE, AND THE SERPENT

In J's tale of human origins and humanity's loss of paradise, the writer introduces one of the staples of global folklore: a talking animal (The only other

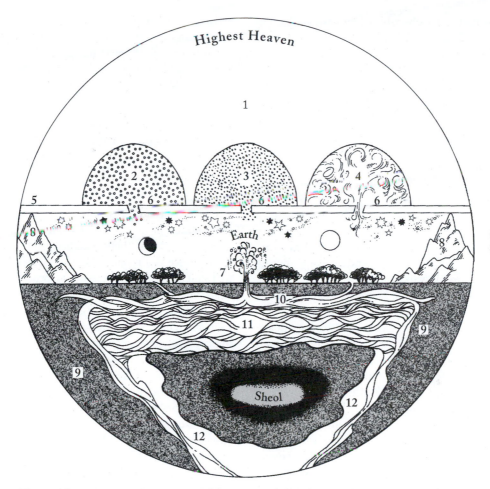

Figure 7.1 The artist's re-creation of the ancient biblical view of the universe shows (1 and 11) the waters above and below the earth; (2, 3, and 4) chambers or storehouses of hail, rain, and snow; (5 and 6) the firmament with its openings or sluices; (7) fountains of the deep; (8) the mountain pillars on which the firmament rests; (9) the pillars of the earth; (10) the navel of the earth; and (12) the watery abyss. Sheol, abode of the dead, is the dark cavern at the center of the lower hemisphere.

speaking animal in the Hebrew Bible appears in the story of Balaam's donkey [Num. 22–24]; see Chapter 9.) Although the Genesis serpent is generally interpreted negatively and commonly identified with Satan, neither J nor any other Tanak writer does so. In the Yahwist's fable, the serpent is not called "evil," but merely "subtle" or "crafty," possessing a skeptical intelligence that questions the way God runs things. It knows what God knows — that eating forbidden fruit will impart knowledge of

"good and evil," giving humans a godlike perspective (Gen. 3:1–7). In fact, YHWH confirms that the prohibited fruit has magically transformed humans into "one of us [beings of the heavenly council]," which prompts him to keep the pair from acquiring another prerogative of divinity, immortality. To prevent their eating from the "tree of life" and liv-ing "forever," YHWH evicts Adam and Eve from Eden, putting this source of divinity permanently out of reach. The way back to their garden home is barred by **cherubim,** who wield flaming swords (3:22–24; see Chapter 4). Common figures in Mesopotamian art, the cherubim typically guard the entrances to temples and royal palaces; in Exodus 25–31, YHWH orders that images of them be placed on either side of the Ark of the Covenant, symbolizing his celestial throne and its guardians (see Chapter 8).

J states that the effects of human disobedience—the deliberate breaking of God's command—are immediate and deeply painful. Losing their former innocence, Adam and Eve suddenly realize that they are naked, perhaps implying a hitherto unknown sense of sexual shame. Like naive children, they attempt to hide from YHWH, who, not yet informed of their misconduct, soon appears for his customary walk through the garden. Once he becomes aware of their betrayal, YHWH's judgment is swift and severe: The "crafty" serpent who pointed out that they could acquire divine knowledge is stripped of its limbs and reduced to an object of human fear (Gen. 3:5, 14–15). YHWH condemns the woman to pain in childbirth and to domination by her husband—a reflection of women's subordination to men in J's patriarchal society, but not part of the original divine plan. For the man, YHWH blights the soil, consigning males to the exhausting labor that peasant farmers experience in trying to wrest a living from arid Near Eastern fields, a harsh condition also absent from the Deity's original intentions.

The cost of knowledge without divine permission or guidance also includes a frightening consciousness of human mortality, and YHWH reminds the pair that they must return to the soil from which they were formed. As the serpent had observed, they do not die in the same "day" that they disobeyed—Adam lives on for nearly 1000 years—but the huge gulf between mortal humanity and immortal divinity is clearly drawn. Although Israel's neighbors, particularly the civilizations of Egypt and Greece, developed elaborate traditions about the human soul and its posthumous rewards or punishments, the Hebrew Bible has little to say on the subject. It is not until the last-written part of the Tanak—the Book of Daniel—appears in the

second century B.C.E. that a biblical writer explicitly introduces ideas about a future life, envisioning not an immortality of spirit but a resurrection of the physical body (Dan. 12:1–3; see Box 25.1 and Chapter 28).

THE CONSEQUENCES OF HUMAN DISOBEDIENCE

Cain and Abel Despite the severity of his judgment, J's Deity is capable of surprising tenderness and concern for the humans who failed to trust his governance. Before driving Adam and Eve out of their garden home, YHWH makes clothes of animal skins to cover their nakedness. After the exile, his presence abides with the couple, enabling them to fulfill the earlier mandate of procreation: Eve bears the world's first child, **Cain,** "with the help of the LORD" (Gen. 4:2). Even while bearing sons and daughters, Adam and Eve soon learn the inescapable consequences of their disobedience, which injects an element of lethal violence into the human predicament.

Introducing a theme of rivalry between brothers that disrupts family relationships throughout the Genesis narrative (and resurfaces in stories about King David's sons in 2 Samuel), J shows Cain bitterly envious of his younger brother **Abel.** When YHWH prefers the animal sacrifices of Abel, a shepherd, to the grain offerings of Cain, a farmer, Cain reacts against this divine favoritism by killing Abel. Despite the seriousness of the crime—the first taking of a human life—YHWH treats Cain with leniency, imprinting him with a special "mark" that prevents other people (of unexplained origin) from punishing the murderer (Gen. 4:13–16). Once the shedding of human blood has begun, however, humanity's condition deteriorates rapidly. J's list of Cain's descendants culminates in **Lamech,** who savagely boasts that he avenges every wrong "seventy-sevenfold" (4:17–24), establishing a culture of violence that eventually leads to humanity's destruction.

The Flood and the Covenant with Noah In the Genesis account of a global flood, God's response to human "wickedness" includes a profound sorrow. Observing that human mentality had degenerated to the extent that every thought "was only evil continually," YHWH is "grieved . . . to his heart" (Gen. 6:5–6). Now "sorry that he had made humankind," YHWH resolves to wipe his failed experiment from the face of the earth. In P's version of the deluge, God brings back the chaotic sea that he divided and tamed in Genesis 1, opening the "windows of the heavens" to release waters stored above the sky "dome" and causing subterranean "fountains of the great deep [primal abyss]" to "burst forth" (6:11). Drawing on Mesopotamian lore concerning a prehistoric deluge (compare Box 3.3 and Box 5.1), both J and P reproduce elements from the Atrahasis and Gilgamesh traditions, including a divine decision to spare a single human family. Like the Babylonian Utnapishtim, Noah is instructed to build an ark and stock it with all kinds of birds and animals. Unlike his violent contemporaries, Noah has "walked with GOD" (6:9; cf. 5:22), which results in his preservation, along with that of his wife, his three sons, Ham, Shem, and Japheth, and their wives.

Emphasizing that in God's purpose even global catastrophe involves a creative and saving element, Genesis 9 presents the post-Flood world as a new beginning for humanity. After repeating the command to "be fruitful" and repopulate the earth (9:7; cf. 1:28), God institutes the first of four biblical covenants. The covenant with Noah and his descendants is universal, encompassing the entire world population. Described as "everlasting," it includes a declaration of the sacredness of life, both human and animal, and a divine promise never again to drown the earth (9:1–11). Like the later agreements made through Abraham and Moses, the pact with Noah has a "sign"—the rainbow as a visible symbol of God's reconciliation with humankind.

The Primeval History concludes by tracing the genealogies of Noah's sons, **Ham, Shem,** and **Japheth,** who represent the three principal branches of the human family known to the ancient Hebrews (Gen. 10–11). From Shem come the Semitic peoples, among them the Babylonians, Assyrians, Arabs, and Israelites. Ham was the **eponymous** (name-giving) ancestor of the Egyptians and their (then) political dependents, including the Canaanites, while Japheth was the supposed progenitor of the Aegean Sea peoples, including the Greeks.

The Tower of Babel   Amid the lengthy genealogies—sometimes called the "table of nations"—editors inserted J's story of the Tower of Babel. An etiological account explaining the great diversity of languages spoken in different geographical areas, the story contains themes of human ambition and divine retribution that initially appeared in J's narrative about the expulsion from Eden. When humanity, united in language and purpose, attempts to build a tower "with its top in the heavens" and thus "make a name for [themselves]," YHWH realizes that "nothing that [humans] propose to do now will be impossible for them." Accordingly, he overthrows the tower, "confuses" their speech so that they can no longer understand each other, and scatters a linguistically divided humanity throughout the earth (Gen. 11:1–9). Deeply distrustful of human culture, particularly when concentrated in cities, J regards the Babel incident as exemplifying an attitude the Greeks called *hubris*—a pride that offends the gods.

Stories of Israel's Ancestors

After surveying the human race as a whole, the Genesis account narrows to focus on the ancestors of a single nation, Israel. The remainder of Genesis (Chs. 12–50) is devoted to relating the stories of Abraham and Sarah, progenitors of the future Israel, and their colorful descendants through four turbulent generations. Opening with God's call to Abraham in **Haran,** a major city in northwestern Mesopotamia, the action then shifts all over the map of the Fertile Crescent, ending with Abraham's great-grandchildren — Joseph and his eleven brothers, eponymous founders of the **Twelve Tribes of Israel**— settled in Egypt. The journeys of Abraham and his progeny, in fact, outline the geographical contours of the biblical world, from the valley of the Euphrates to that of the Nile (see Figure 3.1). In their wandering between the two Near Eastern centers of political power, Mesopotamia in the north and Egypt in the south, the patriarchal families also anticipate the later historical movements of the Israelite people.

The story of Abraham (Gen. 12–25) introduces a positive new phase in the divine-human partnership. In the Primeval History, God's relationship with humanity as a whole was largely adversarial, culminating in global destruction. By Genesis 12, however, YHWH is apparently resigned to the inevitability of human wrongdoing (8:21–22) and prepared to display great flexibility in anticipating and circumventing the results of human frailty. In dealing with selected individuals — the patriarchs and their strife-torn families — the Deity utilizes even such undesirable human qualities as jealousy, greed, and deviousness to accomplish his purpose. Even Abraham, the biblical model of righteous obedience, the foundation on which Israel's claim to God's continuing favor is largely based, shows weaknesses that require divine mediation. Not once but twice Abraham lies about his relationship to Sarah, who is both his half-sister and his wife, allowing her to be taken into a foreign ruler's harem. On another occasion, apparently for the sake of domestic peace, he meekly permits Sarah to expel his concubine, **Hagar,** and their son, **Ishmael,** endangering the lives of both mother and child. In each case, YHWH saves the situation, rescuing Sarah before she is compromised, preserving Hagar and Ishmael, and even making the unvalued son the father of twelve populous tribes (16:1–16; cf. 25:12–18).

In Genesis's second narrative cycle (Chs. 25–36), God is equally resourceful in managing the sibling rivalry between **Esau** and **Jacob,** twin sons of **Isaac** and **Rebekah,** to realize his goals. Drawing on the flawed personalities of both brothers — Jacob's calculating self-interest and Esau's crass indifference to his heritage — to achieve the desired outcome, God ensures that the Abrahamic promise is transmitted according to his long-range plan. Perhaps Genesis's most notable example of God's transforming potentially lethal domestic strife into an occasion for fulfilling the divine will occurs in the third narrative cycle (Chs. 37–50), stories involving Joseph and his envious brothers.

The biblical narrator typically expresses God's interaction with humanity by describing a **theophany** — a visible or otherwise perceptible appearance of the Deity to human beings. In Genesis, God appears more frequently to more individuals, and over a longer span of time, than in any other book of the Hebrew Bible. After the Primeval History, however, divine communication changes significantly in both content and purpose. Whereas before the Flood, God's conversations with such figures as Adam, Eve, Cain, and Noah usually involve prohibitions, condemnations, or warnings, after the Flood his speeches mostly take the form of vows and promises. Providing thematic coherence to the diverse ancestral tales, the divine promises to Abraham and his heirs — for multitudinous descendants, land, blessing, the divine presence, and a special covenant partnership — help to unify the entire Pentateuch (see Chapter 6).

The Story of Abraham and Sarah

According to Joshua 24, neither Abraham nor his father Terah was originally a worshiper of YHWH. As natives of Ur, one of Mesopotamia's oldest cities, they naturally "served other gods" (Josh. 24:2; cf. Gen. 11:26–31). YHWH's reason for uniquely honoring Abraham, the product of a polytheistic society, is not explicitly stated, but this can be partly inferred from Abraham's behavior. In Genesis 12, when YHWH suddenly breaks into Abraham's consciousness, ordering him to abandon his home in Haran, where Terah had settled his family, and journey to an unspecified destination, Abraham immediately complies. Throughout the narrative, whenever God speaks, Abraham *listens,* in the biblical sense of the verb — paying full attention to the divine summons and responding obediently. With an extraordinary capacity for listening to and translating divine commands into action, Abraham displays an exemplary trust in his God.

As Genesis 15 expresses it, Abraham "believed" YHWH's promises, "and the LORD reckoned it to him as righteousness" (15:6).

In Genesis 14, Abraham takes on the unexpected role of warrior, rescuing his nephew **Lot,** son of his uncle Haran, from a coalition of Canaanite kings. After defeating the kings, he pays ten percent of his captured booty to **Melchizedek,** the king-priest of **Salem,** a Canaanite sanctuary thought to be the future site of Jerusalem (Gen. 14:18–22).

THE ABRAHAMIC COVENANT

When YHWH next appears to Abraham, God conducts a mysterious nocturnal ritual, in which he passes between the two halves of a slaughtered animal, ratifying the covenant with his friend (Gen. 15:1–18). The Abrahamic Covenant, four different versions of which are included in Genesis (12:2–3; 15:1–21; 17:1–22; 22:15–18), is a solemn contractual agreement by which YHWH pledges to make Abraham the progenitor of nations (particularly Israel), to give his innumerable descendants the entire territory of Canaan, and to be their God forever. The version outlined in Genesis 15 specifies the Promised Land's boundaries, which are to extend from the valley of the "great river" Euphrates to that of the Nile (15:18), and from northwest Mesopotamia to the northeast border of Egypt. Because Israel's territory did not extend that far until the reigns of David and Solomon—and then only briefly—scholars believe that this form of the promise can be dated no earlier than the period of the monarchy, many centuries after Abraham's time (cf. 1 Kings 4:21). YHWH's confiding to Abraham that his promised descendants will spend 400 years as slaves in Egypt (Gen. 5:12–14) also connects the ancestral stories to later events and places them in historical perspective.

Torah and History As many biblical scholars have pointed out, Torah authors characteristically are less interested in recording precise historical fact than in creating stories that convey a sense of God's participation in human lives. Thus, they typically evoke legendary figures and events from the past to teach lessons about the divine-human relationship that are edifying to audiences of their own time. By projecting religious insights gained from the historical experience of a later era into narratives celebrating Israel's distant ancestors, biblical storytellers emphasize the temporal and ethical continuity of divine-human interaction.

A good example of retrojecting later religious observances into the ancestral past appears in the priestly version of the Abrahamic Covenant. In Genesis 17, YHWH is shown introducing a ritual requirement for Abraham and all his male offspring, **circumcision**—surgical removal of the foreskin of the penis. As a physical "sign" of an Israelite's Abrahamic descent (17:11), P regards circumcision as so important that he anachronistically ascribes it to the patriarchal epoch. Although incorporated into the Mosaic law (Lev. 12:1–5; cf. Exod. 12:44, 48), the ritual was probably not widely observed until much later in Israel's history, as indicated by conflicting traditions about its origin. Although presumably descended from Abraham, Moses apparently is unaware that YHWH requires circumcision, a lapse for which YHWH threatens to kill him (Exod. 4:22–24). Although this puzzling episode may have served an etiological purpose, highlighting the need for all Israelite males to be circumcised, another tradition, preserved in Joshua 5, provides a different account of Israelites' initiating the circumcision ritual. Before invading Canaan, Joshua orders his troops to submit to mass circumcision (5:2–7), a practice with which they were apparently unfamiliar.

Abraham's Sons At age eighty-six, eleven years after first receiving YHWH's sworn oath to give him a son, Abraham finally has a child, Ishmael—not by his wife, Sarah, but by Hagar, Sarah's slave. Another thirteen years pass, and Abraham is ninety-nine before YHWH appears again, this time under the oak trees of Mamre (Gen. 18:1), where Abraham is informed that within a year he and his wife will have a son. Overhearing the prophecy, Sarah laughs—both she and Abraham are long past the age of procreation (18:1–15).

From the Genesis narrator's viewpoint, however, it is precisely *because* the couple has grown too old to reproduce that the divinely planned moment finally arrives. By the next year, Sarah and Abraham indeed have an heir of their "own flesh and blood"—Isaac, whose name (literally, "laughter") echoes his mother's mirth at hearing an "impossible" prediction.

Narrative Difficulties and a Divine-Human Debate

Although scholars attribute most of Chapter 18 to the Yahwist, the narrative seems to combine conflicting traditions about the nature of YHWH's visit at Mamre. Whereas Genesis 18:1 states that YHWH appears (cf. 18:13–14, 22), the next verse says that Abraham merely saw "three men" (18:2), whom he addresses in the singular as "my LORD" (18:3), but who are later referred to in the plural as "they" (18:5; cf. 18:22; 19:1). The apparent confusion of pronouns may result from J's wish to depict the mysterious nature of the divine presence, with Abraham seeing three humans (and Sarah but one? [cf. 18:10]). After the forecast of Isaac's imminent birth, however, "two men" depart for Sodom, and it is clear that Abraham now speaks directly to YHWH, who remains behind to announce that, having heard rumors of their wickedness, he is on his way to inspect personally the cities of **Sodom** and Gomorrah. Perceiving YHWH's intention to destroy the cities, Abraham questions God's justice in annihilating whole populations: "Shall not the Judge of all the earth do what is just?" Submitting to his covenant partner's courteous but persistent questioning, YHWH finally declares that he will not destroy the cities if even ten righteous people can be found in them (18:16–35). In the end, YHWH incinerates five cities located near the Dead Sea, but only after rescuing Abraham's nephew Lot and his two daughters.

In some views, YHWH's wrath toward Sodom was ignited by its residents' homosexuality. Genesis 19, however, describes an attempted gang rape of two male visitors, not the sexual activity of mutually consenting adults. In contrast to Abraham's generous hospitality, the men of Sodom violently assault strangers, whom Near Eastern custom dictated should be welcomed and protected. When alluding to Sodom's notoriety, later biblical authors do not mention sexual misconduct, emphasizing instead the city's failure to help the "poor and needy" and its deplorable lack of hospitality. (See Ezekiel's comparison of Sodom and Judah [Ezek. 16:48–58].)

National Etiologies

Before fire from heaven consumes Sodom and its sister cities, YHWH, out of regard for Abraham, rescues Lot and his two daughters. Like Noah after an even greater cataclysm, Lot becomes drunk, and—his wife having been changed into a pillar of salt—commits incest with his two daughters. The sons of this illicit union are the eponymous ancestors of **Moab** and **Ammon,** two small states that bordered ancient Israel. Commonly presenting a single individual as the progenitor of an entire people or nation, the Genesis authors claim that Jacob's brother Esau literally "is Edom" (36:1). Similarly, Jacob is identified as Israel (32:28; 35:10), and his twelve sons are depicted as identical with the later twelve tribes that traditionally composed the kingdom of Israel (29:31; 30:24; 35:16–20; 49:16). In these legendary etiologies, Israel receives its name from God as a validation of its chosen status, whereas neighboring countries such as Ammon and Moab are the products of unspeakable sin. Meanwhile, Edom, Israel's cultural "twin," derives its name from one whom God rejects as covenant bearer.

The Binding of Isaac

Whereas most of God's direct communication with Abraham takes the form of assured blessings, God's abrupt order to give him Isaac as a human sacrifice is a startling contrast. Up to this point, the narrative has been moving slowly toward Abraham's goal of fathering his own son and heir, the promised child that YHWH himself now threatens to destroy in an episode (from the Elohist) known as the "binding of Isaac" (Gen. 22). Abraham's willingness to kill Isaac without pleading for the boy as he did for Sodom and his silence in the face of this horrific demand have long troubled Bible readers (Box 7.2). With his knife raised to cut his son's throat, Abraham is stopped by

BOX 7.2
YHWH and Child Sacrifice

Although the Genesis narrator interprets God's demand for human sacrifice as a mere test of Abraham's exemplary obedience, the episode raises many troubling issues, about both the ethical nature of the biblical God and the character of ancient Israelite religion. According to the second Torah book, Exodus, all of Israel's firstborn sons belong to YHWH, as do the firstborn of "flocks and herds" (22:29–30). Although Torah regulations permit Israelites to "redeem" their sons by offering an animal substitute (34:20), there are hints that YHWH did not always discourage child sacrifice. In Judges, Jephthah is possessed by the "spirit of the LORD" when he resolves that, if YHWH will grant him military victory, he will make a "burnt offering" of the first person he meets after the battle. Ironically, the first to greet Jephthah upon his triumphal return home — for YHWH has given him success — is his daughter, who then undergoes a rite of mourning for her unfulfilled life. The Judges author presents Jephthah's vow to sacrifice a human being as if it were not unusual (11:29–40), perhaps because the early Israelites, to some extent, shared the practice with their immediate neighbors, the Canaanites. When the prophet Micah (eighth century B.C.E.) rhetorically asked, "Shall I give my first-born for my transgression, the fruit of my body for the sin of my soul?" he evidently expected that at least some in his audience would respond in the affirmative (6:6).

How effective the offering of a royal child could be at a time of national crisis is illustrated in a story about Mesha, king of Moab (ninth century B.C.E.). When Israelite armies besiege Mesha's fortified city, the king, in desperation, brings out his firstborn son, the heir to his throne, and sacrifices him on the city wall, in full view of the attackers. The result of Mesha's act, presumably a last-ditch appeal for help to the Moabite god **Chemosh,** is the instant withdrawal of Israelite troops, thus delivering the Moabites from their enemies. The biblical text in this passage has apparently been edited, making what supposedly happened strangely ambiguous: We are told only that, after Mesha offered his son, "great wrath came upon Israel" (2 Kings 3:26–27). The text does not indicate whether the "wrath" was that of YHWH or Chemosh. The Israelites' failure to capture Mesha's stronghold is particularly notable because this episode immediately follows the prophet Elisha's prediction that YHWH will "hand Moab over to you [Israel]," allowing it to "conquer every fortified town" (2 Kings 3:18–19)— a prophecy ostensibly thwarted by Mesha's resorting to a supreme act of faith: child sacrifice.

The Hebrew Bible's severest condemnation of child sacrifice occurs in the Book of Jeremiah (early sixth century B.C.E.), where the prophet denies that Yahweh ever ordered— or even considered— such atrocities (19:5–6). Jeremiah's contemporary, the priest-prophet Ezekiel, however, contends that Yahweh did indeed legislate child sacrifice— but as a bad law that he would then punish the Israelites for observing:

> "Moreover I gave them statutes that were not good and ordinances by which they could not live. I defiled them through their very gifts, *in their offering up all their first-born,* in order that I might horrify them, so that they might know that I am the LORD [YHWH.]" (Ezek. 20:25–26, emphasis added)

According to Ezekiel, YHWH's command to offer firstborn sons as if they were animals (an allusion to Exodus 22:30?) is "not good," a snare that leads Israel astray. Perhaps the prophet implies that the recipients of YHWH's Torah should have had the ethical vision to discern between what was potentially good or evil in it, rejecting the latter even when a law purported to derive from God.

In his recognition that YHWH would prefer to accept a ram instead of Isaac — obeying the second voice, which spared human life, rather than the first, which ordered him to kill — Abraham proved decisively that he possessed the saving power of spiritual discernment. Noting that YHWH's command to offer Isaac for sacrifice was unworthy, some later **rabbis** (Jewish teachers) suggested that it was not God but the Satan (the negative aspect of divinity) who tempted Abraham to commit an abomination (cf. Job 1–2). (See Jon D. Levenson, *The Death and Resurrection of the Beloved Son: The Transformation of Child Sacrifice in Judaism and Christianity* [New Haven, Conn.: Yale University Press, 1993].)

Figure 7.2 A treasure from the Royal Cemetery of Ur, this ornamental goat stands on its hind legs, leaning against a golden plant. Probably a fertility icon, the goat has horns and eyes of lapis lazuli, with face, horns, and legs of wood overlaid with gold. Originally thought to represent the ram caught in the thornbush, scholars now doubt this.

the intervention of an angel, who directs him to spare Isaac and offer instead a ram caught in a nearby thornbush (Figure 7.2). Gratified by Abraham's remarkable display of obedience, YHWH (in a J fragment?) then reaffirms his covenant vows, reiterating the promise made during his first appearance to Abraham ten chapters earlier—that his covenant partner will be the source of universal blessing (22:15–18; cf. 12:3).

"An old man and full of years," Abraham dies at age 175 and is buried near Sarah's grave in Canaan (Gen. 25:7–11). Ever sensitive to the divine presence, Abraham is the biblical model of supreme self-surrender, embodying an exemplary willingness to submit every part of his life to the divine will. He also embodies the paradox inherent in the divine-human relationship: Divine favor invariably encompasses suffering as well as blessing. With most of God's promises to be realized only in the distant future, he receives the only form of posthumous reward recognized in the Torah—vicarious survival through progeny and a reputation so "great . . . that [he] will be a blessing" to all (12:2).

The Story of Jacob and His Family

ISAAC AND REBEKAH

After devoting a dozen chapters to Abraham and Sarah, Genesis passes briefly over the career of Isaac, who emerges as an essentially passive figure. In his most memorable postures, Isaac is shown as either a hapless youth stretched out on a sacrificial altar (Ch. 22) or an aged man lying prone on his bed (Ch. 27), the victim of a deceitful conspiracy by his wife and younger son. (Although Isaac, old and feeble, appears near death in Genesis 27, he does not actually die until decades later, when he is allegedly 180 [35:27–29]; the Genesis narratives do not always follow a linear movement.) Isaac's wife Rebekah, a far more decisive character, first appears in Genesis 24 when Abraham's servant returns to the patriarch's Mesopotamian homeland to find Isaac a mate from among Abraham's kinfolk. In offering water from a well to Abraham's travel-weary emissary, Rebekah manifests the hospitality that marks admirable behavior. Then, as if recognizing a divinely presented opportunity, she courageously volunteers to wed a stranger and cast her lot in a strange land. After marrying Isaac and giving birth to twin sons, Esau (the firstborn) and Jacob, she plays a major part in shaping Israel's destiny. Privately informed that YHWH prefers the younger son (who is also her personal favorite), she not only initiates the plot to deceive Isaac into blessing Jacob rather than Esau, but also arranges for Jacob to escape his brother's vengeance by sending him from Canaan to her relatives in Mesopotamia. Considering Rebekah's assertiveness, it is not surprising that her husband has no other wives or concubines, making Isaac the only truly monogamous patriarch.

JACOB

A spiritual cousin of the quick-witted Greek hero Odysseus (Ulysses), Jacob is sometimes regarded as primarily a trickster. His function in the biblical narrative, however, is far more complex than that dismissive label implies, for Jacob's strengths and weaknesses, and his dynamic relationship to God, serve as a paradigm for the character of Israel, the nation named after him. In the totality of his story, which extends from prenatal struggles with Esau in Rebekah's womb (Gen. 25:21–28) to deathbed evaluations of his twelve sons more than a century later (Ch. 49), Jacob undergoes a variety of powerful, life-changing experiences. As a young man, he shrewdly exploits his older brother's demand for instant gratification, persuading Esau to sell him his birthright for a pot of stew (25:29–31). He then completes the theft of Esau's inheritance, his legal right as firstborn, by appropriating his brother's identity, lying to his nearly blind father and deceiving Isaac into conferring the paternal blessing on him (Ch. 27).

After Rebekah learns that Esau plans to kill his usurping brother and she sends Jacob fleeing northward to Mesopotamia, YHWH begins a series of encounters with the fugitive that culminates in his bestowing a significant new identity on Jacob. The first theophany occurs at Luz, where Jacob stops overnight on his way to Haran. Sleeping outdoors with a stone for his pillow, he dreams of a "ladder," a ramp reaching from earth to heaven, on which angels ascend and descend—as Mesopotamian deities were thought to tread invisibly the ceremonial stairway of a Babylonian ziggurat. YHWH also appears in the dream and restates the familiar promise to Abraham, adding a vow that he will accompany Jacob on his journey. On awakening, Jacob behaves in characteristic fashion, combining reverence for the divine presence with a pragmatic concern for his personal welfare. Although impressed by the sanctity of the place, which he re-

names **Bethel** (literally, the "house of El") (Gen. 28:10–22), Jacob is unwilling to commit himself to YHWH on the basis of a mere dream, however awe-inspiring. After anointing a stone pillar with oil to commemorate his unexpected contact with divinity, Jacob boldly adds his own terms to the covenant promises YHWH had just enunciated: "*If* GOD will be with me and will keep me [safe] . . . and will give me bread to eat and clothing to wear, . . . so that I come again to my father's house in peace, *then* the LORD [YHWH] shall be my GOD. . . ." Casting his covenant stipulations in the same "if . . . then" formula typical of the later Mosaic law, Jacob informs the Deity that allegiance to him will depend on how effectively divine promises are translated into the realities of food and security (28:18–22).

THE THEOPHANY AT PENIEL (PENUEL)

Despite conflict with his uncle **Laban,** whose daughters **Leah** and **Rachel** he marries, Jacob's twenty-year sojourn in Mesopotamia is productive in almost every sense. Not only does he acquire great wealth in the form of sheep, goats, and cattle, he also fathers eleven sons (some by his wives' maids) and a daughter, **Dinah.** (A twelfth son, Benjamin, is later born to Rachel.) Traveling back to Canaan to meet his estranged brother, Jacob has a second nocturnal theophany, this time at Peniel by the river Jabbok, a tributary of the Jordan. Alone in the dark and terrified of the next day's reunion with Esau, whose vengeance he has good reason to fear, Jacob suddenly finds himself attacked by an unknown "man." Wrestling all night, the two opponents are so evenly matched that neither can defeat the other. Only in the predawn light does Jacob recognize his mysterious assailant's identity, suddenly realizing that "I have seen GOD face to face" (Gen. 32:30). Although a variant account of Jacob's encounter refers to his opponent as an "angel" (Hos. 12:4), one of the traditions incorporated into this passage implies that Jacob's adversary is God himself. If so, the Deity apparently assumes human form (and therefore has only limited human strength) for this physical struggle with

Jacob. When Jacob refuses to release him, the divine attacker bestows both blessing and a name change — henceforth, Jacob is Israel, the one who has "striven with GOD and with humans, and [has] prevailed." Instead of being Jacob (meaning "Supplanter" [cf. Gen. 25:26; 27:36]), the trickster who stole Esau's legal rights, he is now Israel, signaling a new identity as one who effectively struggles with both God and mortals — and survives. Although modern scholars think that *Israel* probably means "GOD [El] rules," the Genesis writer's interpretation is highly appropriate to the biblical portrayal of Israel as a nation locked in a complex (and sometimes adversarial) relationship with God. Memorializing the encounter, Jacob renames the site Peniel (Penuel), which means the "Face of El [God]" (32:22–32).

After his reconciliation with Esau (Gen. 33), Jacob makes another pilgrimage to Bethel, where God again appears, this time identifying himself as El Shaddai and renewing his covenant vow, adding that Jacob's descendants will include kings (35:1–14). In this second (probably Elohist) version of Jacob's name change to Israel, Jacob again sets up a stone pillar, again anoints it, and again changes the site's name from Luz to Bethel (Ch. 35; cf. Ch. 32). Although in Chapter 37 the narrative shifts from Jacob's adventures to concentrate on the conflict among his sons, Jacob once more takes center stage near the end of Genesis, when the dying patriarch offers an extensive catalogue of "blessings" (including some curses and severe condemnations) for each of his twelve male offspring (Ch. 49). After his death, he is buried near Abraham's grave in Canaan.

The Story of Joseph and His Brothers

Although the final section of Genesis (Chs. 37–50) focuses on the story of **Joseph**, the book's editors title it "the story of the family of Jacob" (37:2). This editorial emphasis on Jacob/Israel's family as a group highlights the narrative's larger purpose, the transition from God's relationship with individual ancestors, such as Abraham and Jacob, to the Deity's evolving partnership with a whole people. As the nucleus of a future nation, Jacob's twelve sons, with their wives and children, now form a corporate body, a development illustrated in Chapter 49, where Jacob describes each of his sons as distinctive tribal entities. "All these [Jacob's sons]," the narrator points out, "are the twelve tribes of Israel" (49:28). In moving from tales about individual family units to the portrayal of a much larger ethnic coalition, Genesis prepares readers for the emergence of Israelite nationhood described in the next book of the Torah, Exodus.

The dramatic account of Joseph's rise from kidnap victim, slave, and prisoner to a powerful position at the Egyptian royal court — the subject of Chs. 37–50 — is thus set in the larger context of God's plans for Israelite nationhood. Although Joseph's personal story occupies the narrative foreground, God operates unobtrusively behind the scenes, using Joseph as his instrument who will ultimately reconcile Jacob's quarreling sons, forging them into a united people. In this section, God makes only one appearance, and not to Joseph but to Jacob, in a "night vision" (46:2–4; cf. 48:3–4). Instead of direct theophanies, Joseph receives only dreams — and a divinely granted ability to interpret them.

Whereas the tales of Abraham, Isaac, and Jacob are highly episodic — consisting of loosely connected narrative units bound together only by repeated divine promises and travel itineraries — the Joseph story forms a coherent literary whole. (Chapter 38, an interpolated episode in which Tamar poses as a prostitute to claim her legal right to a child from Jacob's son **Judah,** is one of the few major digressions.) Often called a short story or novella, the self-contained Joseph section has a unified plot in which the consequences of fraternal strife lead to a climactic reversal of the brothers' initial status, with Joseph transformed from helpless victim into imperial vizier, and his bullying brothers into humble suppliants. As a longer and more structured narrative than those found earlier in Genesis, the Joseph saga resembles other short stories found in the Hebrew Bible, such as Ruth and Esther. Like the major characters in Esther and the title hero of Daniel, Joseph is an essentially solitary member of the covenant community living in a foreign land, where he succeeds spectacularly because, as the narrator points out, "GOD is with him."

In the opening scenes of conflict between the brothers, reminiscent of that between Cain and Abel or Jacob and Esau, Joseph is introduced as Jacob's favorite son. Decked out in his father's gift of an elaborate garment, he antagonizes his siblings by telling them two dreams that foreshadow his future greatness. In the first dream, his ten older brothers bow low before him, honoring his superiority; in the second, even the sun, moon, and stars (his two parents and their other children) do obeisance. Only seventeen years old, Joseph foresees future glory for himself but is woefully insensitive to the feelings of his older brothers.

The JE text describing the brothers' conspiracy to punish Joseph's youthful arrogance combines two conflicting versions of the tale. In the Elohist source, the eldest brother, Reuben (representing a northern tribe), persuades the others not to kill Joseph but merely to throw him into a dry well, where passing Midianites extricate him and take him to Egypt. In the Yahwist account, Judah (representing the most prominent southern tribe) intercedes for Joseph, suggesting that he not be harmed but be sold as a slave to a caravan of Ishmaelites, who then transport him to Egypt.

As a result of editors' bringing together two different literary strands, Joseph is twice sold into Egyptian slavery, first by E's Midianites (Gen. 37:36) and then by J's Ishmaelites (39:1–2). In both versions, his Egyptian buyer and new master is **Potiphar,** an important official at Pharaoh's court. At this point, the biblical tradition apparently draws on an ancient Egyptian tale about a virtuous young man who resists the attempt of his brother's wife to seduce him and who, after many misadventures, subsequently rises to become Egypt's crown prince (see James Pritchard's "The Tale of Two Brothers"

in "Recommended Reading"). Although he rejects the sexual advances of Potiphar's wife, Joseph—like the hero of the Egyptian legend—is falsely accused of betraying his master and is thrown into prison.

Even in disgrace, Joseph benefits from YHWH's "steadfast love," receiving special favor from the chief jailer, who places the Hebrew in charge of the other prisoners. Joseph's ability to interpret the dreams of two of Pharaoh's imprisoned courtiers eventually leads to his being released from jail and brought to Pharaoh's court, where he also practices the art of divination (foretelling future events). His fortune is made when he correctly relates that Pharaoh's two dreams about seven starving cows eating seven fat cows are prophetic—seven years of abundant crops will be followed by a severe, prolonged famine. Emphasizing that this foreknowledge is possible only because God chooses to reveal his intentions, Joseph is appointed Pharaoh's chief administrator. During the years of prosperity, Joseph governs Egypt shrewdly, filling its warehouses with surplus grain. When famine strikes, he controls the food supply, exchanging grain and seed for the people's money, livestock, and land, all of which then become Pharaoh's property. By famine's end, the Egyptian population—excepting the priestly class, which retains its economic autonomy—has been reduced to mere "slaves," landless tenants working for Pharaoh, who is now Egypt's sole landowner (Chs. 41, 47).

The artistry with which Joseph's story is told appears in the use of a recurring motif—changes of clothing, each of which marks a significant stage in his growth from obscure Hebrew shepherd to Egypt's political savior. In his first appearance, Joseph wears the symbol of his father's indulgence, a robe traditionally called a "coat of many colors" (or a striped tunic), which his malicious brothers strip from him before casting him into a pit and reporting him dead (37:3–4, 23–35). Joseph's clothing is again violently torn from his body in the encounter with Potiphar's wife, and, falsely accused of attempted rape, he is again plunged into the "pit" of Pharaoh's dungeon (39:6–20). In the third change of clothing, the previous equation of loss of raiment with loss of status is reversed: Pharaoh publically exalts Joseph, placing him "over all the land of Egypt," dressing him in "garments of fine linen," and adorning him with a gold signet ring and gold chain, visible symbols that he now outranks every Egyptian except Pharaoh himself (41:39–46).

Just as famine drove Abraham from Canaan to Egypt (12:10), so Jacob's ten oldest sons migrate from Canaan to the Nile region, seeking grain. (Jacob's twelfth son, Benjamin, stays home with his father.) There, the brothers fall into Joseph's power, fulfilling Joseph's adolescent dream of being exalted above his older siblings (Chs. 42–45; cf. 37:2–11). Only after putting his brothers, now needy and dependant, through prolonged anxiety and humiliation does Joseph—with impressive self-dramatization—reveal his identity, graciously forgiving them the wrongs they have done him. Although the Joseph story reaches its climax in the brothers' recognition that Egypt's preeminent governor is none other than their formerly despised sibling, the ultimate purpose of the Genesis narrative is not realized until Jacob is also brought into Egypt and the entire family is settled in the eastern Nile delta. The "story of the family of Jacob" (37:2), riven by conflict and crisis that threatens to disrupt the Abrahamic lineage, at last achieves a peaceful resolution, with the previously divided group reunited and welcomed by Pharaoh as alien residents in Egypt (Ch. 50).

In a final speech to his brothers, Joseph tells them that, although they "intended to do harm," God "intended it for good" (50:20), seizing on human weakness, such as the brothers' murderous jealousy, and converting its consequences (Joseph's abduction to Egypt) into an opportunity to benefit both Israelites and Egyptians. By Genesis's conclusion, the vow that YHWH makes during his first appearance to Abraham (12:1–3)—that all earth's families will find blessing through Abraham's progeny—is already being fulfilled. Joseph's deathbed request that his bones eventually be taken for reburial in Canaan also points toward future developments in the divine plan, indicating that Israel's Egyptian sojourn will be only an extended detour

in the long pilgrimage toward the Promised Land (50:24–26; cf. Exod 13:19).

QUESTIONS FOR REVIEW

1. What literary sources do scholars believe were incorporated into the Book of Genesis? In what specific ways—including the sequence of events—do the two creation accounts differ? How do the two flood stories differ, and in what respects are they similar?

2. What significance do scholars find in the use of different divine names—such as Elohim, YHWH, and El—in the Genesis text?

3. Describe the content of the Abrahamic Covenant. In this pact, what specific advantages does God promise for Abraham's descendants? What aspects of the promises are fulfilled in Genesis? Which parts of the covenant remain unfulfilled at the end of the book?

4. Why does God ask Abraham to sacrifice his son Isaac? Why does Abraham obey the command for human sacrifice? What ethical issues are involved in this episode?

5. Describe the roles of the Genesis matriarchs, such as Sarah, Hagar, Rebekah, Leah, and Rachel. How do their stories compare with those of Lot's wife and daughters, Jacob's daughter Dinah, and Potiphar's wife?

6. Paint a verbal portrait of Jacob. Why is he sometimes called a trickster? How does God relate to him in unusual ways, including sending him dreams and wrestling with him during a night visitation? How does he become the progenitor of the twelve tribes of Israel?

7. Summarize the story of Joseph and his brothers. In what ways does Joseph's personal biography relate to the divine will in bringing Jacob's family to Egypt? Why does the author emphasize Joseph's importance to Egypt's ruler?

QUESTIONS FOR REFLECTION AND DISCUSSION

1. Why does God banish the first human couple from Paradise? What reason does he give? Why does God "regret" that he created humanity, and why, starting in Genesis 12, does he apparently become somewhat reconciled to human misbehavior, undertaking a

new approach to dealing with humanity? Why does the biblical tradition portray a Deity who is both Creator and Destroyer?

2. Egyptian, Mesopotamian, and Israelite creation stories all presume that the cosmos began with a universal sea, the primal element out of which various creator deities fashioned the present cosmos. How do these ancient Near Eastern traditions about world origins differ from the concepts of modern science? How do the presuppositions and methodologies of contemporary science and traditional religion differ? Given the fact that biblical writers, completely unaware of modern discoveries in physics, astronomy, geology, paleontology, and anthropology, composed Genesis 1 and 2 as testimonies of faith in the creative power of Israel's God, should we regard their work as literally factual? Could God have employed the force of biological evolution as his creative tool? Give your reasons—and concrete evidence—for supporting one side or the other on this issue.

3. Discuss the conversations that characters in Genesis have with the Deity. How do these dialogues express some of Genesis's main themes? Given that ancient Near Eastern and Greek writers routinely depicted gods conversing among themselves at divine councils and/or with humans, how should we view these biblical discourses?

TERMS AND CONCEPTS TO REMEMBER

Adam	Joseph
Ammon	Judah
Bethel	Laban
Cain and Abel	Lamech
Chemosh	Leah
cherubim	Lot
cosmos	Melchizedek
circumcision	Moab
Dinah	Potiphar
Esau	rabbi
Eve	Rachel
Hagar	Rahab
Ham, Shem, and	Rebekah
Japheth	Sabbath
Haran	Salem
Isaac	Sodom
Ishmael	theophany
Jacob	Twelve Tribes of Israel

RECOMMENDED READING

Alter, Robert. *Genesis.* New York: Norton, 1996. A fresh translation and commentary.

Anderson, Bernhard W. *Creation Versus Chaos: The Reinterpretation of Mythical Symbolism in the Bible.* New York: Association Press, 1967.

———, ed. *Creation in the Old Testament.* Philadelphia: Fortress Press, 1984.

Bailey, Lloyd R. *Genesis, Creation, and Creationism.* Mahwah, N.J.: Paulist Press, 1991. Examines the claims of fundamentalist creationists.

Clines, David J. A. *The Theme of the Pentateuch,* 2nd ed. Supplement Series 10. Sheffield, England: JSOT Press, 1997. Discusses literary themes that unify diverse Torah narratives.

Coats, George W. *Genesis.* Grand Rapids, Mich.: Eerdmans, 1983.

Ellis, Peter. *The Yahwist: The Bible's First Theologian.* Notre Dame, Ind.: Fides, 1968.

Fox, Everett, ed. *The Five Books of Moses.* The Schocken Bible, Vol. 1. New York: Schocken Books, 1995. A superb translation that captures the flavor of the original Hebrew.

Fretheim, Terence E. "The Book of Genesis." In *The New Interpreter's Bible,* Vol. 1, pp. 321–674. Nashville, Tenn.: Abingdon Press, 1994. Contains extensive scholarly commentary on the Genesis text.

Fukkelman, J. P. *Narrative Art in Genesis: Specimens of Stylistic and Structural Analysis.* Assen, Netherlands: Van Gorcum, 1975.

Hendel, Ronald S. "Genesis, Book of." In D. N. Freedman, ed., *The Anchor Bible Dictionary,* Vol. 2, pp. 933–941. New York: Doubleday, 1992.

Jeansonne, Sharon P. *The Women of Genesis: From Sarah to Potiphar's Wife.* Minneapolis: Fortress Press, 1990.

Kikawada, Isaac M. "Primeval History." In D. N. Freedman, ed., *The Anchor Bible Dictionary,* Vol. 5, pp. 461–466. New York: Doubleday, 1992. Examines Genesis 1–11, placing biblical narrative in the context of Near Eastern creation and flood myths.

Levenson, Jon D. *Creation and the Persistence of Evil: The Jewish Drama of Divine Omnipotence.* San Francisco: Harper & Row, 1988.

Niditch, Susan. *Chaos to Cosmos: Studies in Biblical Patterns of Creation.* Chico, Calif.: Scholars Press, 1985.

Pagels, Elaine. *Adam, Eve, and the Serpent.* New York: Random House, 1988. Critically examines the historical-political origins of the Christian doctrine of original sin.

Pritchard, James B., ed. *Ancient Near Eastern Texts Relating to the Old Testament,* 3rd ed. Princeton, N.J.: Princeton University Press, 1969. Contains "The Story of Two Brothers," which an Israelite author adapted for the Joseph story in Genesis.

Sailhamer, John H. *The Pentateuch as Narrative: A Biblical-Theological Commentary.* Library of Biblical Interpretation. Grand Rapids, Mich.: Zondervan, 1992. Examines the literary continuity of Torah stories.

Sarna, Nahum M. *Understanding Genesis.* New York: Schocken Books, 1970.

Scullion, John J. "Genesis, The Narrative of." In D. N. Freedman, ed., *The Anchor Bible Dictionary,* Vol. 2, pp. 941–962. New York: Doubleday, 1992.

Speiser, E. A., ed. *Genesis.* Anchor Bible. Garden City, N.Y.: Doubleday, 1964. A scholarly translation with extensive notes.

Trible, Phyllis. *God and the Rhetoric of Sexuality.* Philadelphia: Fortress Press, 1978. A close examination of Genesis 2–3 and other relevant biblical texts.

von Rad, Gerhard. *Genesis.* Philadelphia: Westminster Press, 1972. A standard work.

Westermann, Claus. *Genesis 1–11.* Minneapolis: Augsburg, 1984.

———. *Genesis 12–36.* Minneapolis: Augsburg, 1985.

———. *Genesis 37–50.* Minneapolis: Augsburg, 1986.

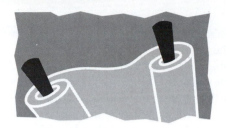

CHAPTER 8

Freedom and Responsibility

The Book of Exodus

Key Topics/Themes In Exodus, God's promises to Abraham for multitudinous descendants, the divine presence, blessings, and a special relationship begin to be fulfilled. The families of Jacob and his twelve sons — numbering only seventy members — who had settled in Egypt at the conclusion of Genesis have, after many generations, become a populous community and a perceived threat to Egypt's ruler. After a long silence, YHWH at last "remembers" his vow to Abraham and commissions Moses to lead the Israelites from Egyptian oppression to freedom as the "people of GOD." Divided into two main sections, the deliverance from Egypt and journey to Sinai/Horeb (Chs. 1–18) and the revelation of God's law at Sinai (Chs. 19–40), Exodus balances its initial theme of liberation from human tyranny with its later emphasis on Israel's ethical and legal responsibilities to its divine liberator. In the Torah (instruction) that he communicates through Moses at Sinai, YHWH introduces an entirely new dimension into his relationship with Abraham's progeny: Israel henceforth must adhere to a vast body of legal and ritual regulations if it is to benefit from YHWH's patronage, its strict obedience a condition of divine favor. Major components of Exodus include the story of Moses (Chs. 2–6); YHWH's war against Pharaoh and the institution of the Passover (Chs. 7–13); the miraculous sea crossing and desert journey to Sinai/Horeb (Chs. 14–18); the Sinai theophany, golden calf episode, and ratification of the Mosaic Covenant (Chs. 19–24, 32–34); and instructions for the Tabernacle cult (Chs. 25–31, 35–40).

With the possible exception of Deuteronomy, Exodus expresses the core of Israelite faith more than any other book in the Hebrew Bible. In this dramatic account of Israel's escape from Egyptian bondage and sudden emergence as a society ruled directly by God — a **theocracy** — Exodus explicitly defines the nature of YHWH's relationship to his chosen people. The narrative traces the Israelites' journey from the rigidly structured nation of Egypt, where Pharaoh reigns as a god-king, to an uninhabited desert, where YHWH reveals that he alone is Israel's ruler. Descending to the summit of Mount Sinai/Horeb like a lightning bolt from heaven, YHWH discloses to an awestruck people that he has rescued them from Pharaoh's control and given them freedom for one purpose: to worship and obey him. Unlike the Abrahamic Covenant, which makes few specific demands on the human partner, the pact that YHWH concludes with Israel at Sinai is bilateral — the people must swear to observe a large body of law or he will reject them. Although the Mosaic Torah regulates a variety of Israel's activities—including formal worship, sacrifice, civil order, some property rights, and slavery—it does not govern every aspect of life in the covenant community (there are laws regulating divorce, for example, but none covering marriage). Despite its omissions, the Torah serves effectively to define the ethical and religious bonds linking Israel to its divine protector. Because observance of the *mitzvot* (Hebrew, "divine commandments") is designed to permeate and shape many aspects of the Israelites' daily existence, it functions as a constant reminder of their obligation to YHWH.

Israel in Egypt

While in Egypt, the Israelites became so numerous "that the land was filled with them" (Exod. 1:7), creating a population boom of foreign immigrants that alarmed Egyptian authorities and resulted in the Israelites' enslavement. The blessings of fecundity, so prominent in Genesis's alternating tales of barrenness and childbearing, inadvertently brought Israel into conflict with a new Egyptian dynasty, a pharaoh "who did not know Joseph [and his contribution to Egyptian well-being]" (1:8). Although the narrative states that Israel's sojourn in Egypt lasted 430 years (12:40), other passages imply that it was much shorter (only four generations according to 5:16–20), a time span that many historians regard as more plausible.

PROBLEMS OF HISTORICITY

To date, historians and archaeologists have not been able to verify any of the events described in Exodus. No known Egyptian records refer to the plagues that allegedly devastated Egypt, the flight of Hebrew slaves, or the drowning of an Egyptian army. Nor do Egypt's many surviving archives mention the biblical Moses (who bears an Egyptian name) or the contest between his deity, YHWH, and Pharaoh, who was believed to embody Horus, a form of the sun god. The earliest Egyptian reference to Israel's existence, Pharaoh Merneptah's victory stele, dates from the late thirteenth century B.C.E., when the Israelites were already settled in Canaan (see Chapter 3).

The fact that Exodus does not name either the pharaoh who oppressed Israel or the one whom Moses confronted creates a problem in dating the events it relates. Although the lack of references to specific historical figures increases the difficulty in establishing a reliable historical context for the Exodus, many scholars believe that the most probable setting for the story was Egypt's Nineteenth Dynasty (c. 1306–1200 B.C.E.) (Figure 8.1). Historians favor this period because the radical changes in Egyptian political leadership that preceded the Eighteenth and Nineteenth dynasties provide a plausible background to events described in Exodus 1, particularly the shift in governmental attitude toward the Hebrews (a term commonly used for the Israelites before their establishment in Canaan). Although, for most of its long history, Egypt was ruled by native kings, the succession of Egyptian pharaohs was interrupted between about 1750 and 1550 B.C.E. when non-Egyptian rulers dominated northern Egypt. Known as the **Hyksos** (an Egyptian term for "foreign princes"), this Semitic group is thought to have infiltrated Egypt from Syria and/or Canaan, roughly the same region in which the Israelite ancestors had lived. It was probably a Hyksos pharaoh who, sharing many of the same social customs as the Hebrews, welcomed Joseph and his family to Egypt. Resentful of these foreign rulers, however, native Egyptian leaders drove the Hyksos out of Egypt about 1550 B.C.E., reestablishing Egyptian control of the state and (probably) adopting a hostile policy toward the remaining immigrants from Canaan. If this reconstruction of events is correct, the pharaoh who enslaved the Israelites was probably Seti (Sesthos) I (c. 1305–1290 B.C.E.) and Moses' royal antagonist was **Rameses II** (c. 1290–1224 B.C.E.) (Figure 8.2).

NEUES REICH
Dyn.XVIII.

THEBEN
aus einem Grabe von Abd el Qurna.

Figure 8.1   This Egyptian tomb painting depicts slaves making bricks for the building enterprises of an Eighteenth Dynasty pharaoh. Although the work pictured is almost identical to that ascribed to Hebrew slaves in the Book of Exodus, archaeologists — despite Egypt's wealth of extant inscriptions, archival records, and other artifacts — have been unable to find any physical evidence corroborating the Hebrews' presence there.

LITERARY SOURCES

Although some scholars argue that the Tetrateuch (first four books of the Pentateuch) was composed, perhaps by a single author, well after the exile, many scholars believe that the documentary hypothesis still best explains the internal contradictions in and the diverse nature of the material found in Exodus (Table 8.1). As in Genesis, the disparate strands of the Yahwist, the Elohist, the priestly school, and, as some scholars now propose, the Deuteronomist, are intricately interwoven. According to most scholarly analyses of the text, the Yahwist (J) supplies the main narrative, supplemented by excerpts from the Elohist source (E). The JE account apparently was reworked by both the Deuteronomist (the version of the Ten Commandments in Exodus 20 seems to be based on the commandments listed in Deuteronomy 5) and the postexilic priestly school, which added considerable genealogical, legal, and ritual material, including the Tabernacle instructions in Chapters 25–31 and 35–40 (see also Box 10.2). Priestly editors also made numerous additions to the JE narrative, heightening the miraculous element of Israel's deliverance and providing a second

version of Moses' reception of the divine name (6:3–13). (For an informed discussion of specific passages by J, E, D, or P, see Anthony Campbell and Mark O'Brien in "Recommended Reading"; see also Ernest Nicholson.)

Moses and YHWH

No figure looms larger in Israel's story than Moses, the man whom tradition credits with founding the Yahwist faith. Moses' agency both in forming the Israelite nation and in transmitting YHWH's Torah to the covenant people is regarded as so crucial that later writers who contributed to the different literary strands in Exodus portray him in a dazzling variety of roles — lawgiver, prophet, judge, and even military leader. Like the Deity, Moses is made to fulfill almost every function that biblical authors regard as important to their society. Described as initially reluctant to take on the tasks that YHWH assigns him (Exod. 4:10–17), Moses becomes not only God's chief instrument in creating Israel but

Figure 8.2   The temple of Amon at Karnak, Egypt, has 134 gigantic columns bearing hieroglyphic inscriptions, one of which records Pharaoh Shiskak's invasion of Palestine (c. 918 B.C.E.). The massive structure was probably completed during the reign of Rameses II (c. 1290–1224 B.C.E.).

Moses' role, this exceedingly meek man (Num. 12:3) with a debilitating speech impediment (Exod. 4:10–11) acts as a "god for pharaoh" (Exod. 7:1), a human vehicle for conveying divine power.

YHWH'S PREEMINENT SERVANT

In any ancient Near Eastern tradition other than that of Israel, Moses undoubtedly would be accorded superhuman status, made another Sargon or Gilgamesh — a glorious hero whose exploits elevate him to semidivinity. As the man who successfully defies Egypt's tyrant, releases raging waters to drown pursuing armies, and leads his people through a dangerous wilderness to freedom and nationhood, Moses is without peer: "Never again," states Deuteronomy, "has there arisen a prophet in Israel like Moses, whom the LORD knew face to face" (Deut. 34:10). While affirming Moses' unparalleled contribution to forging Israel's bond with YHWH, however, the Torah writers are careful to subordinate him to the God he serves. Rather than a hero in his own right, Moses is always YHWH's obedient spokesman. The priestly authors who prepared the final edition of the Torah took pains to explain why YHWH did not allow his devoted servant to enter the Promised Land. "Because you did not trust in me, to show my holiness before the eyes of the Israelites," YHWH tells Moses and Aaron, "therefore you shall not bring this assembly into the land that I have given them" (Num. 20:12). Although Moses' fatal error is not specified, some commentators assume that it is the lawgiver's failure to give YHWH full credit when he causes water to gush from a rock (Num. 20:10). Considering Moses' self-sacrificing commitment to YHWH and his people — including his refusal to accept YHWH's offer to make the family of Moses, and not Israel, his chosen nation (Num. 14:12) — God's verdict may seem unduly harsh. For the Torah writers, however, Moses is both a model of humble service *and* a demonstration that even the greatest of human beings cannot measure up to YHWH's standard of perfect righteousness.

also his intimate confidant, speaking with YHWH "face to face, as one speaks to a friend" (Exod. 33:11; cf. Deut. 34:10–11). Whereas YHWH may commune indirectly with others by vision or dream, with Moses he "speaks plainly and not in riddles," even permitting him to see "the form of the LORD" (Num. 12:8). So lofty is Moses' reputation as a legislator that all of Israel's laws, even those that clearly date from much later periods, are assigned Mosaic origins and thus given his unimpeachable authority. As YHWH himself describes

Table 8.1 Sources in Exodus

As in Genesis and Numbers, repetitions and discrepancies in the Exodus text can best be explained in terms of the biblical redactors' use of formerly separate documents (including oral traditions) when composing the story of Israel's escape from Egyptian slavery. The narrative flow is repeatedly interrupted by redactors' interpolation of extensive blocks of legal and ritual materials. Some representative examples of J (Yahwist), E (Elohist), and P (priestly) passages follow.

TOPIC	J (YAHWIST)	E (ELOHIST)	P (PRIESTLY)
Bondage of Hebrews	—	1:8–12	1:13–14
Killing of Hebrew infants	1:22	1:15–21	—
Moses' early life	2:1–23a	—	—
Revelation of divine name	3:1–8, 16–22; 4:1–31	3:9–15	6:2–25 (cf. 7:1–9)
Plagues on Egypt	5:1–6:1; 7:14–29; 8:1–28; 9:1–7, 13–34; 10:1–29; 11:1–9	—	7:10–13; 9:8–12
Passover and death of firstborn	12:21–23	12:34–39; 13:1–16	12:1–20, 40–49
Deliverance at sea	14:5–7, 10b, 13–14, 19b, 20b, 21b, 24, 27b, 30–31; 15:1–18	13:17–19; 14:11–12, 19a, 20a, 25a; 15:20–21	13:21–22; 14:1–4, 8, 9b, 10a, 10c, 15–18, 21a, 21c, 22–23, 26–27a, 28–29
Jethro's role	—	18:1–27	
Theophany at Sinai/Horeb	19:10–25; 24:1–18; 34:1–13	19:2–9; 20:18–21 — 33:12–23	19:21 — —
Ten Commandments	—	20:1–17	Editorial revisions
Ritual commandments	34:14–28	—	—
Covenant code	—	20:22–23:33	—
Golden calf	—	32:1–33:11	—
Tabernacle instructions	—	—	25:1–31:11
Tabernacle construction	—	—	35:1–40:38

MOSES' INFANCY

Most scholars recognize that the Torah combines too many strands of tradition to permit an accurate recovery of the "historical Moses." The problem of Moses' historicity is compounded by the presence of legend and folklore embedded in his story. According to Exodus 1–2, Moses is born under Pharaoh's decree that all Hebrew boys must be drowned, a fate he escapes when his mother secretly sets him adrift on the Nile in a watertight cradle. A childless daughter of Pharaoh—a princess who apparently does not fear to disobey her father's edict—finds the boy and raises him as her own, a rescue from a near-death experience that characterizes many myths about the infancy of future heroes (Box 8.1). Given an Egyptian name derived from the same root as pharaohs Thutmose and Ahmose, Moses becomes familiar with the royal court, presumably an advantage when he later appears before Pharaoh to demand Israel's release.

THE FLIGHT FROM EGYPT TO MIDIAN

The incident that prompts the first of two major transitions in Moses' life foreshadows an important motif in the Pentateuch—his fellow Israelites'

BOX 8.1
Parallels to the Infancy Story of Moses

Tales involving an infant who narrowly escapes death and later becomes a national hero are common in mythology. In Greek myth, numerous future heroes are abandoned and/or almost killed in their early youth: The newborn Perseus is imprisoned in a chest with his mother and thrown into the sea, only to be rescued and live to avenge the wrongs done him; the baby Heracles (Hercules), who will grow up to earn glory by slaying monsters and redressing injustice, is almost strangled in his cradle by snakes; the infant Oedipus, who later becomes king of Thebes, is left out on a lonely hillside to be devoured by wild animals; even the young Dionysus, a future Olympian god, is torn to pieces by the Titans before his father Zeus, king of the gods, resurrects him to immortality. In Roman mythology, perhaps the most famous endangered children are the twins Romulus and Remus, the future founders of Rome, who as babies are cast out and then adopted and nursed by a she-wolf.

In Near Eastern lore, the closest parallel to Moses' story is the Akkadian tale about **Sargon I,** who, like the endangered Hebrew child, is cast adrift on a great river. After Sargon's mother places him in a pitch-sealed basket to float down the Euphrates River, he is rescued not by a princess but by an ordinary gardener, who subsequently raises the boy as his own. From such humble origins, Sargon rises to displace the Sumerian monarch Ur-Zababa as the ruler of Kish and to found the first Mesopotamian empire. By adding this element of deliverance to J's story of Moses, a later redactor emphasizes the specialness of Moses' role, a variation on another biblical theme of the "barren wife" who, after many childless years, unexpectedly bears a son chosen to become a leader of his people, such as Isaac, Jacob, Joseph, Samson, or Samuel—most of whom are selected before birth to serve the divine purpose.

failure to value Moses' leadership. The day after killing an Egyptian whom he found beating a Hebrew, Moses returns to the same location, where two Hebrews are now fighting. When Moses rebukes the aggressor for striking his fellow Israelite, implying that the oppressed Hebrews should support each other, the assailant shows no gratitude for Moses' attempt to defend or make peace among his people. Instead, the bully frightens Moses by alluding to the murder of the Egyptian, an offense that could bring the death penalty.

Moses flees from Egypt and then settles in **Midian,** a desert region south of Edom, where he lives as a shepherd and marries the daughter of a local priest, named **Jethro** in E's account and **Ruel** in J's version. (See Chapter 4 for a discussion of the Kenite hypothesis and the possible Midianite origin of Yahwism.) It is while tending sheep on the "mountain of GOD" in Midianite territory that

Moses experiences the second great transition in his life course.

Two Revelations of the Divine Name

Although they derive from separate sources, Exodus's two accounts of the revelation of the divine name (Chs. 3 and 6) have similar purposes: to demonstrate that El, Elohim, or El Shaddai, forms of the Deity worshiped by Israel's distant ancestors, and YHWH, the divinity who speaks to Moses, are the same God. In his version of Israel's past, the Yahwist writer has already made this crucial identification, retrojecting YHWH's worship as far back as the pre-Flood era and asserting that people had evoked the name YHWH almost from the beginning of human history (Gen. 4:26). In contrast, the Elohist and priestly writers believe that the divine name, YHWH, was not known until God revealed it to Moses (Exod. 3:13–15; 6:2–4). Both Exodus 3 (E) and Exodus 6 (P), therefore, make a special point of insisting that El, the ancient Canaanite deity, and YHWH, Israel's divine patron, are one and the same.

THE FIRST THEOPHANY

The first revelation of God's personal name occurs at a burning bush on Sinai/Horeb. Climbing the sacred mountain to investigate the phenomenon of a shrub that flames without being consumed, Moses unexpectedly encounters God, who announces that he is the same deity who made promises to Moses' remote ancestors, vows that for centuries had gone unfulfilled. A voice from the midst of fire — the transforming element that symbolizes divinity — orders Moses to remove his sandals, for he treads on ground made holy by the divine presence. Identified as the Elohim of Abraham, Isaac, and Jacob, the voice employs a series of verbs expressing God's movement from heaven to earth, from transcendence to immanence, to initiate a series of events that will culminate in Israel's historical redemption. From above, he has "observed" his people's misery, "heard their cry," and "come down" (to earth) in order to "deliver them from the Egyptians" and "bring them" to their own land (Exod. 3:7–8). After dealing with only a few individuals in Genesis, followed by a centuries-long (apparent) absence, YHWH is suddenly about to act, not only to fulfill ancient vows, but also, for the first time, to intervene on the world stage of national politics. He proposes to crush one powerful nation-state in order to create another, a "holy nation," dedicated to his service. The revelation of the divine name serves both to identify YHWH with various manifestations of the ancestral El and to disclose God's future plans for both Israel and other "nations" who will speak of his saving actions (Exod. 3: 1–16; cf. Exod. 32:11–14; Num. 14:19–21). (For further

discussion of the significance of the divine name, see Chapters 1 and 4.)

THE SECOND THEOPHANY

Whereas E (and perhaps some D) material underlies YHWH's self-disclosure in Exodus 3–4, a second revelation of the divine name comes from the priestly source. In P's version of YHWH's initial appearance to Moses, the Deity states,

> I am Yahweh. To Abraham and Isaac and Jacob I appeared as El Shaddai. I did not make myself known to them by my name Yahweh. . . . (Exod. 6:1–8, Jerusalem Bible)

Like the author(s) of Exodus 3, the priestly writer also insists that El Shaddai, known from ancient times, is really YHWH. Although associated with a specific geographical locale — the "mountain of GOD" near Midian — YHWH has no earthly limitations on his power: He will accompany Moses to Egypt, where his presence will humble Pharaoh, and thence to Canaan, where he will lead Israel's armies in a successful invasion.

YHWH'S ATTACK ON MOSES

Immediately following the first account of Moses' call, Torah redactors insert a narrative fragment that seems strangely incongruous with the surrounding material, a brief incident recounting YHWH's attempt to kill the man whom he has just authorized to represent him before Pharaoh. Reminiscent of the mysterious figure that wrestled all night with Jacob (Gen. 32:24–31), YHWH stages a nocturnal assault on Moses, who is saved only when his wife Zipporah seizes a sharp flint, circumcises their son, and touches her husband's "feet" (a euphemism for genitals) with the bloody foreskin (4:24–26). By smearing her son's blood on his father's male organ, Zipporah performed a symbolic fulfillment of YHWH's circumcision requirement (hitherto unknown?), thereby averting God's wrath. (For a discussion on the conflicting biblical traditions about when circumcision was introduced among the Israelites, see the section on Genesis 17 in Chapter 7.)

By including this brief but disturbing incident, the narrator not only foreshadows Moses' ultimate failure to please YHWH entirely but also shows how dangerous a relationship with the Deity can be. In the previous narrative unit, God's instructions to Moses at the burning bush, YHWH has already declared his lethal intentions toward Egypt; the passage closes with YHWH's announcement that, even before sending Moses to Egypt, he has already decided to kill Pharaoh's firstborn son (Exod. 4:23). Because the Deity does not hesitate to exercise his absolute power over life and death, close proximity to God, such as Israel will soon experience, entails enormous risk. Embodying power so great that at times he seems unable to restrain it, YHWH repeatedly will threaten to "break out" against his own people, "consuming" them in his rage (19:24; 33:3–5; cf. 2 Sam. 6:6–9).

YHWH's War Against Pharaoh

THE TEN PLAGUES

The Hebrews in Egypt at first openly doubt Moses' authority to lead them, a response that anticipates their future complaints and rebellions in the wilderness. Pharaoh also refuses to recognize the authority of either Moses or his God, declaring that he knows nothing of YHWH. As he informed Moses at the burning bush, YHWH is prepared to deal with Pharaoh's stubbornness, inflicting a sequence of plagues calculated to break Egyptian resistance to his will. Beginning with a bloody pollution of the Nile and other Egyptian waters, the plagues gradually increase in severity. Swarms of frogs, then mosquitoes, and then gadflies afflict the Egyptians, demonstrating YHWH's control of nature. Pharaoh begs Moses to end the plagues, promising to free Is-

rael, but then treacherously reneges on his word after the pests disappear.

The narrator attributes Pharaoh's obstinacy to YHWH, who resolves to "harden" Pharaoh's heart even before the ruler has an opportunity to make up his own mind (Exod. 4:21–23; cf. 7:3; 10:1, 20, 27; 14:8), thus forcing him to "sin" in refusing to let Israel go. God's apparent interference with Pharaoh's free will may distress contemporary readers, but in the Exodus tradition, his resistance was necessary to the Deity's purpose. Pharaoh *had* to be uncooperative in order for YHWH's power to be revealed (9:15–16; 10:1–2). If Egypt had meekly submitted to Moses' request, there would have been no awesome plagues, no "signs and wonders" demonstrating the supremacy of Israel's God. In biblical portrayals, the Deity is characteristically shown as focused on his public reputation, maneuvering people and events to maximize general awareness of his universal sovereignty (cf. Exod. 9:15–16).

As Pharaoh consistently refuses to acknowledge the God of his slaves, the plagues increase in deadliness. From diseases of livestock, to devastating storms, to invasions of locusts, Egypt experiences the wrath of YHWH. In the ninth plague, darkness shrouds the entire land except where the Hebrews live, a frightening return to the primal darkness that engulfed the earth before God created light. In comparing the Yahwist and priestly accounts of the calamities inflicted on Egypt, scholars have discovered that, whereas the Yahwist recognizes only eight plagues, the priestly school added two others — the infestation of gnats (Exod. 8:16–19) and the affliction of boils on humans and animals (9:8–12) — making up the familiar ten. A separate tradition preserved in Psalm 105 reports only seven plagues and presents them in a different order (105:26–38; cf. Ps. 78:43–51).

DEATH OF THE FIRSTBORN

In Genesis, God utilized natural forces to punish disobedience, exterminating most of humanity in a flood and consuming all the inhabitants of five cities in fire (Gen. 6–8, 19). For the climactic act of divine destruction in Exodus, however, YHWH employs a supernatural agent, the Angel of Death (a lethal aspect of the Deity), and does not indiscriminately kill the entire affected population. An example of retributive justice — "eye for eye" and "life for life" (see Box 10.1) — YHWH's choice of Egyptian victims is a grimly ironic response to an earlier pharaoh's policy of killing newborn Hebrew males (Exod. 1:15–22).

According to Exodus 12:29, YHWH himself carries out the death sentences, "from the firstborn of Pharaoh who sat on his throne to the firstborn of the prisoner who was in the dungeon." Today's readers may blanch at divine executions that include persons, such as the children of Pharaoh's prisoners, who had nothing to do with their ruler's policies, but the narrator is concerned with the *thoroughness* of YHWH's action, which encompasses all classes of Egyptian society. No one, guilty or innocent, is allowed to escape the divine judgment on the group to which he belongs.

THE PASSOVER

To make sure that the Angel of Death distinguishes between Egyptian and Israelite households and spares the latter, the Israelites are told to sacrifice a goat or lamb and to smear the blood on their doorposts, prompting the divine executioner to "pass over" their dwellings. According to the priestly account in Exodus 12, the feast of **Passover** was initiated during the Hebrews' last night in Egypt when, shadowed by the dread angel's wings, they gathered safely inside blood-marked houses to eat unleavened bread, bitter herbs, and the sacrificed lamb. In this section, the eating of unleavened bread is explained in terms of the haste with which the Israelites had to flee — they had no time to allow yeast to leaven the bread. A major annual observance in both ancient Israel and modern Judaism, the Passover ceremony is described in several Torah passages (Lev. 23:5–8; Num. 28:16–25). Whereas Exodus depicts Passover as a private family meal, with neither altar nor officiating priest,

Deuteronomy transforms it into a public national festival: According to the Deuteronomic code, all Israelites must leave their homes and travel to Jerusalem to observe Passover (16:1–8), an ordinance reflecting King Josiah's late-seventh-century B.C.E. centralization of YHWH's cult at his royal capital (2 Kings 23).

Although Exodus links the feast of unleavened bread with the ritual slaying of a young goat or lamb, many historians believe that these two rites originated separately and were later combined by priestly editors. The annual spring sacrifice of a year-old specimen from the flocks was probably developed from a pastoral (shepherds') fertility ceremony, and the practice of consuming unleavened bread from a prehistoric festival celebrating the wheat harvest (cf. Exod. 5:1; 23:14–17; 34:18–25). Besides the Passover celebration, the tenth plague is also associated with the enriching of the former slaves: The terrified Egyptians urge the Israelites to leave, showering them with "jewelry of silver and gold," the "spoils" of Egypt that are the first material signs of the promised blessings to come (12:33–36).

The Escape from Egypt

DELIVERANCE AT THE *YAM SUF*

For the ultimate demonstration of YHWH's might, Pharaoh is prompted to lead his army in pursuit of the Israelites. Trapped between Egyptian charioteers and an unpassable sea, the Israelites seem doomed to an ignominious return to slavery. At this crucial moment, however, YHWH intervenes to deliver his people in an act that forever after would be remembered as the pivotal event in the story of Israel's salvation. The two chief sources of the present text, the Yahwist and the priestly, agree on the miraculous character of Israel's deliverance but present distinctly different versions of what happened. According to J's tradition, the Israelites remained quietly on the shore while YHWH employed a strong east wind that blew "all night," driving back the sea and leaving its bed dry. In the morning, after the wind has presumably died down and the waters have flowed back to their normal depth, YHWH causes the Egyptian troops to panic and dash headlong into the sea, so that "the Lord tossed the Egyptians into the sea" (Exod. 14:13–14, 24, 25b, 27). In J's account, only the Egyptians enter the sea; the Israelites merely "keep still" and watch their former oppressors drown. J's story roughly approximates the version preserved in the "Song of Moses," an ancient poem that praises YHWH as triumphant warrior: "Horse and rider he has thrown into the sea . . . Pharaoh's chariots and his army, he cast into the sea" (15:1, 4).

The priestly additions to J's narrative greatly intensify the miraculous element. Here, when Moses stretches out his hand, the sea literally parts, enabling the Israelites to walk across the seafloor between two standing walls of water, one on their right and one on their left. When Moses raises his hand a second time, the walls of water collapse: "The waters returned and covered the chariots and the chariot drivers, the entire army of Pharaoh that had followed them into the sea" (Exod. 14:15–18; 21–23, 28).

A fragment from another tradition, perhaps the Elohist, suggests a more mundane turn of events, noting that YHWH "clogged [the Egyptians'] chariot wheels so that they turned with difficulty"; when the Egyptians realize that Israel's God is successfully opposing them, they lose courage and give up their pursuit (Exod. 14:25). Although all traditions evoke a spectacularly well-timed rescue from Egyptian pursuers, the numerous discrepancies are almost impossible to reconcile.

THE YAM SUF

In Hebrew, the location of Israel's dramatic sea rescue is called *yam suf,* which the Septuagint translates as the "Red Sea," a custom followed by the Vulgate and most English editions of the Hebrew Bible. With few sites mentioned in the Exodus narrative positively identified, neither the route the Israelites took from Egypt nor the body of water they encountered is known. If there is any historical basis to the Exodus tradition, the *yam suf* is unlikely to be the main channel of the Red Sea, which is an enormous rift valley, flooded by the Arabian Ocean, a geological spreading center along which the continents of Africa and Asia are slowly pulling apart. Even if its waters were supernaturally divided to form a dry pathway, crossing its bed would require descending into, and then ascending from, a chasm deeper and more precipitous than Arizona's Grand Canyon.

Because *suf* commonly means "reed," as it does in the story of the infant Moses being discovered among reeds of the Nile (Exod. 2:3–5), the Jerusalem Bible renders the phrase as "Reed Sea" or "Sea of Reeds," indicating that the body of water may have been a large marsh or lake, perhaps the swampy region north of the Gulf of Suez. Other suggestions for the geographical location of the *yam suf* include Lake Sirbonis (Lake Bardawil) and a southern extension of the present Lake Menzaleh. In the absence of any hard evidence identifying the Israelites' itinerary from Egypt to the Sinai wilderness, scholars have suggested several possible routes. One plausible reconstruction of Israel's path across the Sinai Peninsula in shown in Figure 8.3; an alternate route, favored by some early Jewish and Arabic traditions, places the "mountain of God," the goal of the Israelites' exodus from Egypt, near Edom or Midian, desert regions southeast of Canaan (see Chapter 4).

The Yahwist's concluding summation of the sea episode highlights its theological meaning: Annihilation of the Egyptian army inspires Israel's growing confidence in YHWH. For the first time, the people unanimously acknowledge both YHWH's saving power and the importance of Moses: "Israel saw the great work that the Lord did against the Egyptians. So the people feared the Lord and believed in the Lord and in his servant Moses" (Exod. 14:31). Whatever the actual historical events underlying the *yam suf* tradition, biblical writers consistently used it for the dual purpose of

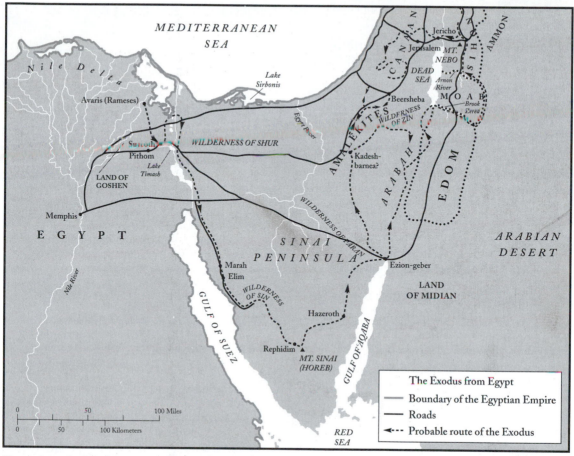

Figure 8.3   A plausible reconstruction of the Israelites' path across the Sinai Peninsula, from Egypt to the Promised Land. Although this map places Sinai/Horeb on the southern Sinai Peninsula, many historians believe that the sacred mountain was located in Midian, home of the priest Jethro, Moses' father-in-law.

testifying to YHWH's redemptive acts and to the origin of Israel's faith.

The Theophany at Sinai/Horeb

THE COVENANT WITH YHWH

In Exodus 19, the long narrative that began with the call of Abraham (Gen. 12) reaches its culmination. As Abraham's descendants, allegedly numbering 600,000 men, plus women and children (Exod. 12:37), assemble at the foot of Mount Sinai/Horeb, the literary character of the Pentateuch undergoes a marked change. Instead of narrative, which makes up most of Genesis 1:1 through Exodus 19, the Torah henceforth consists primarily of specification of the terms of the covenant between YHWH and Israel. Several important narrative passages appear, particularly Exodus 24 and 32–34, but the entire central section of the Pentateuch—Exodus 20:1 to Numbers 10—is devoted to the enumeration of YHWH's detailed requirements for his people, who are to be a "priestly kingdom and a

BOX 8.2
The Mosaic Covenant

The central expression of YHWH's partnership with Israel, the **Mosaic Covenant** consists of two unequal parts: the lengthy enumeration of God's ethical and legal requirements, encompassing all the laws in Exodus, Leviticus, Numbers, and Deuteronomy; and the people's brief collective pledge to obey them all. Many scholars believe that the Mosaic agreement was at least partly modeled on a treaty form common in ancient Near Eastern political alliances, the *suzerain treaty*. In such agreements, the suzerain — or great king — agreed to aid or protect a less powerful vassal, who in turn pledged an oath of loyalty to his overlord. In the treaty concluded at Mount Sinai/Horeb, the sovereign YHWH dictates the terms of the agreement, to which the inferior party, Israel, must agree. A study of Near Eastern treaties from the first millennium B.C.E., particularly Hittite and Assyrian examples, shows that they typically included the following provisions:

1. A preamble
2. An account of historical circumstances leading to the treaty
3. Stipulations and requirements

4. Arrangements for public reading of the text and its safekeeping in a shrine
5. A list of divine witnesses to the treaty
6. A vivid catalogue of blessings for abiding by its terms and curses for violating them

All of these provisions occur in the Torah, although they are found in widely scattered fragments throughout the biblical text.

After YHWH arrives at Sinai/Horeb to conclude his treaty with Israel, he speaks directly to the people, reducing the traditional preamble and historical recapitulation to a brief statement identifying himself as suzerain and giving the reason for his vassals' submission to him: "I am the LORD [YHWH] your God, who brought you out of the land of Egypt, out of the house of slavery" (Exod. 20:1–2). In fact, YHWH's terse statement summarizes the entire Exodus narrative up to that point, with the Torah story of Israel's deliverance from Egyptian bondage functioning as an elaborate preamble to the Sinai treaty making.

Only one small part of YHWH's covenant requirements — the Ten Commandments and the Book

---

holy nation" (Exod. 19:6) (Box 8.2). The people remain camped at the "mountain of GOD" for more than a year while YHWH's teaching (*torah*, with a small *t*) is transmitted in discrete stages through Moses (Exod. 19:1; Num. 10:11) (Figure 8.4).

THE TEN COMMANDMENTS

God's instructions for Israel, the observance of which will identify the nation as truly his people, open with the famous **Ten Commandments**. Also called the **Decalogue** (literally, "ten words"), this part of the Torah has the distinction of being the only passage in the Hebrew Bible reportedly written by YHWH himself and spoken directly to the people (Exod. 20:1; 24:12). Israel's obligation is, first, to worship YHWH alone and, second, to

make no images of him. Although the narrative commonly portrays him anthropomorphically (in human form), the ineffable Deity cannot be represented in any material way (Box 8.3). Attempts to liken God to "anything" that lives in the three-tier universe — "in heaven above, . . . on the earth beneath, or in the waters under the earth [subterranean remnants of the precreation sea]" — are denounced as "idolatry" and expressly forbidden (20:4–6). Nor is YHWH's personal name to be invoked unworthily, as in false oaths or for magical purposes. (In the ancient world, knowledge of a deity's "hidden" or self-defining name was thought to give persons the ability to exert magical control.)

As Genesis 2:2–3 presents God's rest day — the **Sabbath** — as divinely instituted, so the Decalogue insists that Israel scrupulously observe the week's of the Covenant (Exod. 20–23)—is given before Israel's ratification of the treaty takes place. In Exodus 24, the Israelites are pictured as unanimously accepting their covenant obligations, "with one voice," swearing to abide by all of YHWH's demands (Exod. 24:3). Moses then performs a binding ritual, slaughtering sacrificial animals and casting part of the blood on an altar representing YHWH, thus sealing the treaty. After Moses reads from the Book of the Covenant and the people again vow to uphold all its provisions, he sprinkles the Israelites with the rest of the sacrificial blood, thereby confirming the people's commitment to the divine suzerain.

Although Moses calls on no divine witnesses to the covenant, the twelve stone pillars he sets up to represent the twelve tribes of Israel (Exod. 24:4) may have served that function. When Moses' successor, Joshua, conducts a similar covenant ritual, he erects a memorial stone that "has heard all the words of the LORD" spoken to the Israelites and will be a "witness" against them if they default (Josh. 24:27). In Deuteronomy, Moses calls on "heaven and earth" to testify against Israel if the people break their vows, invoking the whole cosmos as a sign of the seriousness of Israel's promise (Deut. 30:19). Observing the custom of recording and safeguarding Near Eastern treaties, both Moses and Joshua are shown preparing written documents that are then deposited in a shrine (Exod. 24:27; Josh. 24:25–26).

The blessings that will accrue from keeping the covenant and the curses that will result from violating it are enumerated in Deuteronomy 28–30 and Leviticus 26. Echoing similar benefits promised for loyalty or penalties decreed for treachery contained in Near Eastern treaties, YHWH's threat to trap covenant breakers in a harsh world in which the heavens are like "brass" and the earth is like "iron" (Deut. 28:23; Lev. 26:19) is almost identical to the metallic imagery of curses listed in a treaty that Esar-haddon, king of Assyria, concluded in 677 B.C.E.

Whereas some Torah commands—such as YHWH's insistence on being worshiped exclusively and his prohibition against making images of him—are unparalleled in antiquity, other covenant regulations resemble those found in many Near Eastern legal codes. **Policy law** (also called **apodictic law**), such as the Ten Commandments, with their imperative absolutes ordering the people not to kill, steal, or bear false witness, is unusual in form, but the ethical principles expressed are commonly recognized in non-Israelite cultures. In contrast, **legal procedures** (also known as **case law**), with its typical formula "if such and such is the case, then such and such must be done," characterizes many Near Eastern laws. The "if . . . then" pattern appears throughout the famous Code of Hammurabi (c. 1690 B.C.E.) and typifies many legal procedures outlined in the Torah (Exod. 20:22–23:5; Lev. 1–7; 12–15; etc.).

seventh day as a memorial, remembering that after completing his six-day creation Elohim desisted from labor. All levels of Israelite society, including women, children, and slaves, are to be regularly granted this respite from work (Exod. 20:8–10; cf. Gen. 2:2–3). The tenth commandment, not to "covet" or persist in desiring what is not rightfully one's own, goes beyond outward behavior to urge the people to reject feelings of envy that may lead not only to chronic discontent but also to harmful action. The remaining commandments—to honor one's parents and refrain from antisocial acts such as murder, theft, adultery, and perjury—are paralleled in the legislation of other Near Eastern societies. Israel's resolve to recognize only one God, who permits no image of his divinity, however, is unique in the ancient world.

The collection of statutes and ordinances that follows the Decalogue (Exod. 20:18–23:33) is known as the Book of the Covenant. Although the laws in this section presuppose a settled agrarian existence in Canaan, they may be among the oldest legislation in the Pentateuch. After the Decalogue's revolutionary commitment to worshiping a single God and total rejection of images, however, this section's laws validating and regulating human slavery may come as a shock. Considering that the Torah narratives have just recounted Israel's liberation from bondage, it may seem inconsistent that YHWH's law provides for Israelites to enslave their fellow citizens. Accepting the widespread practice of selling people to pay off debt, the Book of the Covenant reflects the social norms of antiquity, safeguarding the rights of property owners

Figure 8.4 This rugged peak in the Sinai desert is the traditional site at which YHWH communicated the Torah to Moses. Known as Mount Sinai in J's account, it is called Horeb in the E and D traditions. Although much of the Torah's action takes place in Sinai's shadow, where the Israelites camp for more than a year (Exod. 19:2–Num. 10:12), archaeologists have been unable to find any physical evidence of the tribes' sojourn there — or at any other peak in the region. Many scholars think that Sinai/Horeb is to be found in Midian.

(21:1–11; cf. Deut. 15:12–18). Because neither the Hebrew Bible nor the New Testament condemns the owning, buying, or selling of human beings, many Western slaveholders later argued that the biblical Deity condoned the institution of slavery, a position bitterly contested before, during (and even after) the American Civil War.

THE GOLDEN CALF

The Exodus narrative, interrupted by a long block of priestly material (Chs. 25–31), resumes in Chapter 32. While Moses spends forty days atop Sinai, listening to YHWH's exhaustive instructions for the Tabernacle and receiving the Decalogue that God's "finger" has inscribed on two stone tablets, the people urge Aaron, Moses' brother and Israel's High Priest, to create a golden calf, which they immediately identify as the "gods [plural] . . . who brought [them] out of Egypt" (32:1–6). Informing Moses that he has observed the Israelites' lapse into idolatry and that he plans to wipe them out, YHWH offers to replace Israel with Moses and his family. After persuading YHWH to "change his mind" for the sake of his reputation among the Egyptians, Moses descends from the mountain, smashes the two tablets God inscribed (32:7–20), and calls on the Levites (members of his own tribe)

to slaughter the golden calf worshipers. Again climbing Sinai (he makes at least eight ascents in the Exodus narrative) to confer with God, Moses inscribes a second set of tablets, symbolizing YHWH's reconciliation with a presumably repentant Israel (Chs. 33–34).

The golden calf episode, which most scholars believe is a later addition to the JE narrative, seems to reflect events in Israelite history that occurred long after Moses' time. The idolators' cry, "These are your gods, O Israel, that brought you . . . [from] Egypt," corresponds almost word for word with a phrase in 1 Kings, where King Jeroboam sets up two "golden calves" as objects of worship and credits them with Israel's escape from slavery (cf. Exod. 32:4, 7; 1 Kings 12:28). By inserting a story about Israel abandoning YHWH at Sinai to honor a **golden calf,** the Exodus redactors make the point that such acts not only violate the covenant with God but also will trigger divine wrath leading to national disaster, a lesson well known to the book's postexilic audience.

Although both Exodus and Kings portray "calf worship" as disloyalty to YHWH, most scholars believe that it was not really an abandonment of Yahwism. Archaeological finds, including the El texts from Ugarit, indicate that Near Eastern gods commonly were envisioned as standing invisibly on

BOX 8.3
Was God "Seen" at Mount Sinai?

The interweaving of multiple literary sources in the Exodus account of YHWH's appearances on Mount Sinai/Horeb has resulted in the incorporation of radically contrasting ideas about the Deity's physical visibility. According to Exodus 33:20, God informs Moses that he is forbidden to see God's "face," because "no one shall see me and live." A few verses earlier, however, we are told that YHWH "used to speak to Moses face to face, as one speaks to a friend" (33:11). Postulating an abstract, ineffable, and transcendent Deity, traditional religion usually emphasizes the first statement: Mortals cannot survive an unmediated experience of divinity. The anthropomorphic concept of a deity who can be visible to human eyes, which is also embraced by the canonical text, is typically denied or explained away.

The God who insists that his face not be seen remains essentially hidden during the disclosure of his "glory" to Moses. Placing Moses in a rocky cleft and shielding him with his "hand," YHWH projects his "goodness" as if it were a separate entity traversing the mountaintop. When God finally moves the hand obstructing Moses' vision, it is only to allow the prophet a glimpse of his "back," which is not described. This account of the Sinai theophany is paradoxically almost as much a concealment as a revelation, serving to deepen the divine mystery (Exod. 33:17–25).

In contrast, a different tradition embedded in Exodus indicates that mortals could look directly at God and survive. In Exodus 24, Moses, Aaron, and seventy Israelite "elders" climb Sinai to enjoy a meal with God, an event that may have been based on the ancient Near Eastern custom of holding banquets to commemorate a powerful tribal chief's acceptance of lesser clans into a status of kinship. According to this passage, Moses and the elders "saw the GOD of Israel," who did not strike down his guests but permitted them to "eat and drink" as they "beheld" their divine host (24:9–11). Remaining firmly in the flesh, they consume material food even while basking in the divine presence, as a group repeating the experience of Abraham, who apparently dined with God under the oak trees near Hebron (Gen. 18).

The Torah's inclusion of both anthropomorphic imagery in which God may be visible to human eyes (as J and other traditions say he was to Abraham, Jacob, and Moses) and its seemingly contradictory proclamation that Israel's God does not appear in physical form conveys both the transcendence and immanence of the biblical Deity. The mystery of a unknowable Spirit who can create the universe and also stoop to break bread with his mortal creation is maintained.

the backs of calves, bulls, or other powerful animals (Figure 8.5). The calf figures were merely pedestals for the divine presence.

THE TABERNACLE

Much of the remainder of Exodus is devoted to detailed provisions for providing YHWH with a shelter as he accompanies the Israelites on the long journey to Canaan. By far the longest Torah passages concerning a single topic, Exodus 25–31 enumerates YHWH's instructions for building the **Tabernacle**—the portable tent-shrine that he will

symbolically inhabit—while Exodus 35–40 records its actual construction. Skilled artisans undertake the project from the inside out, first building the **Ark of the Covenant,** a rectangular chest, plated in gold leaf, on which YHWH's "glory" will rest. The golden statues of cherubim, token representations of the supernatural courtiers that surround God's heavenly throne, are placed at each end of the ark. Their wings extended, they shelter the *kapporeth,* or ark cover (later called the "mercy seat"), the place where the Deity is invisibly enthroned and from which he will henceforth issue his commands to Moses (Ch. 37; cf. Ch. 25). After

Figure 8.5   Hadad, Syrian god of storm, strides atop a bull in this basaltic stele. Grasping lightning bolts in each hand, Hadad invisibly rides an animal symbolizing power and terror. Because Canaanite artists commonly show El, father of the gods, also standing on a bull, many scholars believe that the notorious golden calf that Moses' brother Aaron manufactured and the two calf sculptures that Jeroboam set up in Israel were not intended as rivals to YHWH, but only as pedestals on which the Deity could be invisibly enthroned (Exod. 32:1–35; 2 Kings 12:26–33).

fashioning symbols of the divine council, the craftsmen then construct the other appurtenances of YHWH's cult, including a golden candelabrum, an altar, and numerous utensils used in killing, skinning, and burning sacrificial animals. Exodus reaches its climactic moment when YHWH, shrouded in cloud, enters the completed Tabernacle, filling it with his "glory." Stipulating that Israel will not take a single step toward its promised destination unless the "cloud" lifts from YHWH's tent-shrine as a sign that the day's travels are to begin, Exodus concludes with an affirmation that the covenant people are at last being led directly by God himself. "For the cloud of the LORD was on the tabernacle by day, and the fire was in the cloud by night, before the eyes of all the house of Israel at each stage of their journey" (40:38). For the first time since he strolled through Eden, YHWH will again dwell intimately with mortals, assuming the challenge of shaping Israel in his image.

QUESTIONS FOR REVIEW

1. According to Exodus, how did the descendants of Abraham and Jacob (Israel) become enslaved in Egypt? Explain how Egyptian governmental policy toward Semitic immigrants may have been influenced by the historical expulsion of the Hyksos.

2. Granting the historicity of the Exodus tradition, why do many historians think that Rameses II may have been the pharaoh whom Moses confronted?

3. Describe the role of Moses in rescuing the Israelites from Egyptian slavery. How did Moses come to live in Midian and associate with Jethro/Ruel?

4. Analyze the two different accounts in which the divine name is revealed to Moses (cf. Exod. 3–4 and 6). Why does there seem to be some doubt that the El/Elohim worshiped by Israel's distant ancestors is the same deity who discloses himself to Moses? How do the two disclosure accounts link El with YHWH?

5. Describe the plagues that YHWH inflicts on Egypt, including the deaths of the firstborn and its connection with the Israelite Passover observance.

6. What is the *yam suf,* and what deliverance of his people did YHWH stage there? In what different ways do two different source traditions describe the event?

7. Summarize the pact between YHWH and Israel made at Sinai/Horeb. List the Ten Commandments (Decalogue) and describe some of the other laws contained in the Book of the Covenant. How is the Mosaic Covenant formalized?

8. Explain the significance of the golden calf episode. How does the people's disloyalty affect YHWH? What does the Deity propose to Moses, and how does Moses dissuade YHWH from his wish to destroy Israel?

9. Explain the function of the Tabernacle and the Ark of the Covenant it contained. Why was this portable shrine also called the "tent of meeting"?

QUESTIONS FOR REFLECTION AND DISCUSSION

1. How does the Mosaic Covenant differ from the earlier covenants made through Noah and Abraham? How does YHWH's "jealousy"—his demand for exclusive worship—affect the terms of the covenant? When Israel erects the golden calf, why does YHWH so quickly decide to exterminate the entire people whom he has just rescued from Egypt? How does Moses persuade God to change his mind—and what does this sequence of events reveal about the characters of both Israel and YHWH?

2. Why do the writer-redactors of Exodus portray YHWH as "like a devouring fire" (Exod. 24:17–18), so dangerously violent that he repeatedly threatens to "break out" against the Israelites and consume them? How does the Deity's "jealous" wrath, manifested at the very outset of the covenant partnership with Israel, foreshadow Israel's later history, particularly its eventual destruction by Assyria and Babylon?

TERMS AND CONCEPTS TO REMEMBER

Ark of the Covenant
golden calf
historical evidence for the Exodus
Hyksos
Jethro/Ruel
Legal procedures, or case law
literary sources of Exodus
Midian
Mosaic Covenant and suzerain treaty
Passover

plagues on Egypt
policy law, or apodictic law
Rameses II
Sabbath
Sargon I
Tabernacle
Ten Commandments (Decalogue)
theocracy
theophany at Sinai/Horeb
yam suf

RECOMMENDED READING

Albertz, Rainier. *A History of Israelite Religion in the Old Testament Period.* Vol. 1, *From the Beginning to the End of the Monarchy.* Louisville, Ky.: Westminster/John Knox Press, 1994. Includes a detailed analysis of the historical and social contexts for the composition and redaction of Exodus.

Brueggemann, Walter. "The Book of Exodus." In *The New Interpreter's Bible,* Vol. 1, pp. 677–981. Nashville, Tenn.: Abingdon Press, 1994. Contains extensive scholarly commentary on the Exodus text.

Campbell, Antony F., and O'Brien, Mark A. *Sources of the Pentateuch: Texts, Introductions, Annotations.* Minneapolis: Fortress Press, 1993. Includes an identification of different sources of Exodus—primarily J, E, and P—and prints each source as a separate document.

Childs, Brevard S. *The Book of Exodus.* Philadelphia: Westminster Press, 1974. A standard commentary.

Clifford, Richard J. "Exodus." In R. E. Brown et al., eds., *The New Jerome Biblical Commentary,* 2nd ed., pp. 44–60. Englewood Cliffs, N.J.: Prentice-Hall, 1990.

Coogan, Michael D., ed. *The Oxford History of the Biblical World.* New York: Oxford University Press, 1998. Discusses the Kenite hypothesis and possible Midianite origins of Yahwism.

Cross, Frank Moore. *Canaanite Myth and Hebrew Epic: Essays in the History of the Religion of Israel.* Cambridge, Mass. Harvard University Press, 1973. A major scholar's investigation of the historical origins of ancient Israelite beliefs.

———. *From Epic to Canon: History and Literature in Ancient Israel.* Baltimore: Johns Hopkins University Press, 1998. Essays on Near Eastern influences on

Israelite religion, including the concept of the covenant relationship between YHWH and Israel.

Crüsemann, Frank. *The Torah: Theology and Social History
of Old Testament Law.* Minneapolis: Fortress Press,
1996. An exhaustive analysis of the historical and literary development of the biblical text.

de Vaux, Roland. *The Early History of Israel.* Translated
by D. Smith. Philadelphia: Westminster Press, 1978.
Analyzes the Exodus and Sinai traditions.

Hoffmeier, James K. *Israel in Egypt: The Evidence for the
Authenticity of the Exodus Tradition.* New York: Oxford University Press, 1999. Argues for a nucleus of
historical fact behind the tradition.

Kitchen, K. A. "Exodus, The." In D. N. Freedman, ed.,
The Anchor Bible Dictionary, Vol. 2, pp. 700–708.
New York: Doubleday, 1992.

Mendenhall, George E. "Covenant." In G. A. Buttrick,
ed., *The Interpreter's Dictionary of the Bible,* Vol. 2,
pp. 714–723. New York and Nashville, Tenn.:
Abingdon Press, 1962. A concise, insightful summary
of the biblical concept of covenant relationships.

———. *Law and Covenant in Israel and the Ancient
Near East.* Pittsburgh: Biblical Colloquium, 1955. An
influential study of correspondences between ancient
treaty documents and the growth of Israel's covenant
tradition.

Noth, Martin. *Exodus.* Philadelphia: Westminster Press,
1962.

Sarna, Nahum M. "Exodus, Book of." In D. N. Freedman, ed., *The Anchor Bible Dictionary,* Vol. 2, pp. 689–
700. New York: Doubleday, 1992.

———. *Understanding Exodus.* New York: Schocken
Books, 1987.

CHAPTER 9

Regulating the Divine-Human Bond

The Books of Leviticus and Numbers

Key Topics/Themes Though dissimilar in terms of literary format and focus, the books of Leviticus and Numbers carry forward, each in its own way, the unfolding story of Israel's emergence as a "kingdom of priests," summoned to serve YHWH as the covenant people. In Leviticus, covenant obligations assume a legislative and ceremonial form, as Israel and its priestly class are bound to divine service through a network of ritualized behaviors, often centering on the desert Tabernacle (and, later, Solomon's Temple). In Numbers, the covenant relationship is presented in narrative form, as Israel struggles both with God and with itself before committing to the rigors of the holy life and, subsequently, of holy war. And whereas Leviticus conceives of the covenant as a largely static, ahistorical system of sanctifications, Numbers presents it as a dynamic sequence of spiritual crises through which Israel purges itself of its internal contradictions. Leviticus gives a glimpse of an ideal Israel, dedicated to the forms and seasons of divine worship; Numbers traces Israel's real-life struggle to maintain its faith in its leaders and in the God who has only recently liberated it from slavery.

The Book of Leviticus

The Book of Leviticus is not only the shortest book of the Pentateuch but in many ways the most distinctive. In Hebrew, Leviticus is referred to simply as *Vayikrah* (meaning "He [God] called"—the opening word of that text), but its name in English is derived from both the Greek and Latin translations of the Hebrew Bible. Clearly, the editors of the Septuagint and the Vulgate, respectively, thought of this book as an instructional manual for priests, a view shared by ancient rabbis and modern readers alike. Scholars who are committed to the documentary hypothesis normally attribute the sacred legislation found in Leviticus to the priestly source in the belief that P was most likely responsible for codifying and preserving laws and customs related to the Tabernacle and to priestly duties.

Ironically, the Levites for whom this book is named are referred to in only one passage (Lev. 25:32–34), but because every member of the priestly caste was presumably a member of the Levite tribe, the term can be used inclusively in this context. The book itself is divided into twelve sections, which may reflect the enduring importance of the tribal structure of early Israelite society. Though it has traditionally been seen as the legislative "heart" of the Torah, Leviticus is, in fact, a rather diverse collection of laws regulating such things as diet, sexual relations, sacred festivals, and private and public morality.

THE PRACTICE OF HOLINESS

With Leviticus, the narrative of the Exodus comes to a virtual halt. Except for brief narrative segments dealing with the punishment of those who violate the protocols of worship and sacrifice (such as the death of Aaron's sons, **Nadab** and **Abihu** in 10:1–7), Leviticus consists of laws governing the sanctity of both the Tabernacle and of everyday life, and, for the first time, the practical implications of the earlier declaration at Sinai/Horeb that Israel is to become a "kingdom of priests, a holy nation" (Exod. 19:6) begin to be revealed. Not only are priests officiating at the Tabernacle expected to be in a state of ritual purity while offering sacrifices to God, but ordinary Israelites are expected to observe purity laws that affect what they eat and wear, who and what they come in contact with, and whom they can have sexual relations with. For Leviticus, "holiness" is both a physical state and a set of moral behaviors; even more important, it is an attribute of the Deity himself:

> You are to make yourselves holy and keep yourselves holy, because I am holy. (Lev. 11:44)

To enter the condition of holiness, therefore, is to imitate God through a multilevel process of sanctifications. Holding this entire process together is one very basic distinction, common to all taboo systems worldwide—the distinction between the sacred and the profane. To enter or remain within the domain of the sacred, one must avoid actions, substances, and relationships designated within that system as profane. In Leviticus, this binary system is presented first as a distinction between the "holy" and the "common" (in Hebrew, *kodesh* and *chol,* respectively) and then as a parallel distinction between the "clean" and the "unclean" (in Hebrew, *tahor* and *tameh,* respectively) (10:10). It is important, however, to recognize that these terms seldom refer to the presence or absence of what we would think of today as physical defects or biological impurities. Something or someone—to be holy, or ritually pure—must be literally set apart from the rest of life, a distinction that can be applied equally to time or space and to persons or things. Functionally, the unclean is anything that cannot be brought into or consumed within the precincts of the Tabernacle (and later the Temple) or worn by a priest officiating within the Tabernacle. And when that principle is applied to nonritual modes of behavior

in the form of group morality, we see for the first time how the idea of Israel as a "holy nation" can be realized in everyday conduct and nonceremonial behaviors.

TRANSGRESSION AND SACRIFICE

The idea of sanctity takes its most obvious and direct form in the first seven chapters of Leviticus, where the proper procedures for offering animal sacrifices in the Tabernacle are described in considerable detail. One expressed motive for bringing animal sacrifices to the Tabernacle was the desire to make expiation for some accidental or inadvertent action that resulted in the violation of a divine commandment, such as unknowingly eating a forbidden food. Willful violations of a commandment, of course, could not be expiated through ritual means alone; in such cases, restitution or even severe punishment was mandated (see Lev. 6:2–5). Furthermore, the entire system of symbolic offerings presupposed an attitude of contrition on the part of the person bringing a sacrifice. Some of the animals brought for this purpose were completely consumed by fire, but other sacrifices (the grain offerings and shared offerings, for example) were partly consumed as food by both priests and ordinary people.

It is important to note, however, that nowhere does the Pentateuch express the idea that YHWH himself must be fed. At most, a vestige of this familiar Mesopotamian idea—that deities are pleased or even nourished by the smell of human food—is retained in the image of God smelling the "pleasing odor" of Noah's sacrifice after the Flood (Gen. 8:21), and those very words are used repeatedly in Leviticus to describe divine acceptance of a burnt offering. In fact, if anyone actually partakes of some portion of a sacrifice, it will be not YHWH but rather Aaron and his sons, whose consumption of a grain offering, for example, represents the consummating act of the process of ritual atonement (Lev. 14–18).

On a very different level, the sacrificial system can be seen as a symbolic means of restoring order to a world disrupted by human perversity and negligence while also serving as a vehicle for the expression of gratitude to the Deity for the bounty of nature. Though the Latter Prophets often attacked both the Temple hierarchy and the public perception of the sacrificial system (see, for example, Amos 5: 21–24; Isa. 1:11–17; Jer. 7:1–15), in the normative view, animal sacrifice remained a divinely legitimated way of communication and propitiation between Israel and YHWH. It was only with the destruction of the Second Temple in 70 C.E. that prayer alone came to be seen as the appropriate — and, pragmatically, the only available — means of human dialogue with God.

ISRAEL'S PURITY LAWS

Having described the elaborate process of installing the **Aaronite** priests in the Tabernacle (Lev. 8–10), the focus then shifts to the sanctity of laypeople in their everyday lives, and, in Leviticus 11–15, the author lays out a series of ritual protocols through which clean and unclean foods and practices can be distinguished from one another. Some of these routines may have been motivated by a concern for protecting a population from contamination — as in the regulations governing the quarantining of persons suspected of having leprosy or some other malignant skin disease (Ch. 13) — but most do not turn on any question of personal or public hygiene at all. Camels are forbidden as food, not because they are likely to be carriers of infectious disease, but because they do not have split hooves (11:4), and for no other stated reason. Similarly, Israelites are forbidden to weave wool and linen together into a single fabric or to sow a field with two different kinds of seed (19:19), but not because of any presumptive calamity that might follow from either practice.

The priestly worldview demands that boundaries between the pure and the impure be drawn clearly, so that any Israelite can know, at any given moment, which domain he or she is in. To be in a state of holiness, as the root meaning of the Hebrew word for "holy" (*kodesh*) implies, is to be kept "apart from" those things that have no sacred value. Because it is not possible to reside perpetually within the circle of sanctity, even if one is a priest, ceremonial means must then be provided for distancing oneself from impurity, if only briefly. This differentiation of ritual domains is particularly clear where essential biological functions are concerned. Both men and women can become ritually unclean from the discharges that their bodies naturally produce (for men, the discharge is semen; for women, it is menstrual blood). Such "impurity," even though it extends beyond the body to anything the "impure" man or woman might touch, does not imply that sexual relations or menstruation are morally objectionable or physically abnormal but rather that both lie outside the realm of the ritually pure. The same rule applies to a woman in childbirth, where even more blood flows than during menstruation, thus necessitating an even longer period of "recovery" before she can renew ordinary human contact and, more important, approach the Tabernacle (Lev. 12:6–8). With the birth of a daughter, this problematic state is enhanced twofold (12:5), as the mother must then "expiate" both her own impurity and that of the newborn — a situation that does not present itself with the birth of a son. Blood can, of course, be used in purification ceremonies within the Tabernacle itself (9:8–18), but its status or function changes when it is associated with either menstruation or food consumption.

RITUALS OF ATONEMENT

In Leviticus 16, the focus shifts once again from the sanctity of individuals to the sanctity of the community as a whole, with the ceremony of the **scapegoat.** The term *scapegoat* — which has come to mean any innocent person who suffers for the actions of others — is not actually used in this chapter, and early translators of the Hebrew text were simply paraphrasing the language used to describe this ceremony. In its origins, the scapegoat ritual may have involved homage in the form of the sacrifice of a young goat to a desert demon or deity known as **Azazel.** In Chapter 16, however, this ceremony is transformed into a "riddance rite" through which the guilt of the entire Israelite community can be transferred to the scapegoat, who is then sent off to the wilderness (or to Azazel, which, in this context, may be either the personal name of a supernatural being or a place name) to die. To reinforce the idea that this ceremony is, in fact, an act of communal expiation, the Levitical author then links the scapegoat to the **Day of Atonement (Yom Kippur),** even though a later description of this holy day (23:27–32) makes no mention of this rite. The object of this ritual, like that of so many of the expiation rites of Leviticus, is to enable the Israelites to achieve reconciliation with God through the externalizing mechanism of a symbolic act. A much fuller expression of this idea can be found in the Book of Isaiah, where the prophet describes a "Suffering Servant" (52:13–53:12) who wins forgiveness for his people through an act of symbolic substitution (see Chapter 20 on Second Isaiah).

THE HOLINESS CODE

With Leviticus 17–26, the presentation of sanctity laws moves to another and generally higher level. These chapters are commonly referred to as the **Holiness Code,** and in Chapter 19, the author makes a conscious effort to model his presentation after the Ten Commandments:

> You shall be holy, because I, the LORD your GOD, am holy. You shall revere, every man of you, his mother and his father. You shall keep my sabbaths. I am the LORD your GOD. Do not resort to idols. (Lev. 19:2–4)

By expanding conditionally each of the apodictic statutes that constitutes the original Decalogue, the author extends the scope of moral responsibility and compassion, commanding not only obedience to God's will but also love of one's neighbor, even if one's neighbor happens to be a resident alien (19:34). In the context of this new priestly *torah*, it is no longer enough simply to abstain from theft; one must go further and ensure a greater measure of social justice by not withholding a workingman's wages till the following morning (19:13). Similarly, it is no longer permissible to even feel hatred of another, let alone express it or plot revenge (19:17–18). A "holy" community, then, is one in which un-

spoken rancor and open malice are replaced with candor and understanding love. Such concern for just, amicable relations among men and women is remarkably close, in its emphasis on conscientiousness and moral intent, to the Deuteronomic school of thought, and the argument for viewing Leviticus as a postexilic composition—and therefore possibly influenced by the Deuteronomic tradition—is strengthened by such resemblances.

It is important to note, however, that nowhere in these chapters does the Levitical author attempt to create a hierarchy of sacred obligations. Thus, in the very same passage that admonishes the Israelites to observe strict justice and avoid nourishing hatreds, we also find a reminder to abstain from eating meat that has any blood in it or from shaving the edge of one's beard (19:26–28). Whether intentionally or not, the Levitical code fails to differentiate between moral duties and ritual requirements, and in this respect, it is no different from Babylonian or Hittite law codes of an earlier period. The later prophetic view of the priority of ethical duties over ceremonial performance (cf. Mic. 6:6–8) represents a striking departure from this priestly tradition.

One segment of the Holiness Code, however, where ritual and moral concerns more nearly converge involves the establishment of a sacred calendar (Lev. 23, 25). Each of the "appointed seasons" that constitutes this calendar is thought of as a kind of sabbath (indeed, Chapter 23 begins with a reference to observance of the Sabbath), characterized by the cessation of work and the presentation of sacrificial offerings. The number of such occasions has clearly multiplied (cf. Exod. 23:14–19) from three to five, and the ceremonies have become more elaborate. But what is even more remarkable is the addition to the calendar of a cycle of septennial "sabbaths," a cycle of seven sabbatical years culminating in the **Jubilee.** Once more, Leviticus expands on an earlier tradition (Exod. 23:10–11) by creating a more radical and comprehensive version of earlier sabbatical legislation, requiring not only an agricultural hiatus in which the land is neither tilled nor systematically harvested but also a return of property to its "original" owners. Behind this new provision, apparently, are two concerns: the permanent loss of property by the clan or tribal unit that once claimed it, and the growing impoverishment of a significant segment of the Israelite population. And, once again, as in Deuteronomy, the Israelites are strongly urged to deal generously with their indentured kinfolk in the hope of breaking the cycle of poverty and destitution (Lev. 25:35–44). The principle of compassion is repeatedly invoked and given precedence over the principle of acquired wealth and social status; although Leviticus never envisions a classless society, the bitter inequities that social class differences can create are mitigated by the commandment that "no one shall rule over the other with harshness" (25:49).

LEVITICUS AND DEUTERONOMISTIC HISTORY

The Book of Leviticus concludes with a series of promises and warnings, and a brief discourse on vows and tithes (Chs. 26–27). Those who see Leviticus as a relatively late composition — that is, as a work written and/or redacted after the Babylonian exile — are careful to point out the close parallels between the covenant stipulations in Leviticus 26 and in Deuteronomy 28–30. Thus, if Leviticus is an echo rather than an anticipation of the Deuteronomic view of the blessings and curses that will descend on Israel in return for its obedience or disobedience to the covenant, then the conclusion of this book represents a double attempt to bring Leviticus's view of Israel's sacred vocation into line with both history and Deuteronomistic historiography. If the tragedy of exile has already befallen Israel, then it becomes necessary for the Levitical author to explain why the system of sacred observances has failed to protect God's "kingdom of priests" from collective disaster. And, as in the prophetic literature, this is accomplished by projecting "in advance" the punishment that has already overtaken the nation:

> I will scatter you among the heathen, and I will pursue you with the naked sword; your land shall be desolate . . . [and] all the time that it lies desolate, while you are in exile in the land of your ene-

mies, your land shall enjoy its sabbaths to the full. (Lev. 26: 33–34)

Both the irony and the implied moral reproach implicit in this "predictive" statement would have struck a postexilic audience as a tragically appropriate judgment of Israel's history of lost opportunities. The very commandments to social justice and divine service that Israel neglected during its tenure in the land would now be observed in absentia, and not by the people, but by the land itself.

Of course, exile is not the last word, and as in the prophetic and Deuteronomic traditions, the renewal of the covenant and the return to the land are held out to Israel as more than merely remote possibilities, contingent on repentance. If those scholars who place the redaction of Leviticus in the time of Ezekiel (or even later) are correct, then the imminent prospect of the return of the exiled community and the rebuilding of the Temple would necessitate the retrieval of as much ancient tradition surrounding both Temple and Tabernacle as the collective memory and contemporary imagination would permit. The writing and redaction of Leviticus could then be seen as part of the prerestoration efforts of Levites like Ezra to prepare for the reestablishment of the Temple priesthood (cf. Ezek. 44:10–31) in the fifth and sixth centuries B.C.E. and the implementation of ancient purity laws in a more rigorous and self-conscious way (see Chapter 23).

The Book of Numbers

With the Book of Numbers, the narrative of the Exodus resumes and, with it, a renewed account of the failure of the Israelite community to remain steadfast, in either its obedience to God or its commitment to Moses and Aaron. Commentators often refer to this book as the "book of rebellions," and, at several junctures in this narrative, it seems as if the emergent nation of Israel is about to unravel and the Exodus itself to fail. The problematic character of this book can be seen in its structure as much as in its content, and scholars have long noted its heterogeneous appearance. Narrative, legislative, and genealogical materials are indiscriminately intermingled, with no apparent purpose. This patchwork arrangement has been attributed to its diverse sources, chiefly the P source for sacred law and some combination of the J and E sources for the Exodus narrative. Time certainly flows unevenly in Numbers, where forty years of wandering are telescoped into a single verse (33:37), and the passage of the Israelites from slavery to possession of their ancestral land clearly is of more archetypal than strictly historical interest.

ISRAEL IN THE DESERT

The first four chapters of Numbers consist of precisely that: numbers or, rather, census figures broken down by tribe and by clan. These census figures appear, at first glance, to be highly implausible (the total number of men of military age is given as 603,550 [Num. 1:46]). Scholars have suggested two alternative interpretations of the data that might make them a little more credible: We are looking at census figures from a much later period, or the word for "thousand" (Hebrew, *elef*) should be understood to designate a military unit of no more than 10 men, thus reducing the total number to 6000-odd men-at-arms. However we interpret these figures, perhaps the most striking fact of all is the exclusion of the Levites from this census and their emergence as a separate priestly caste whose exclusive function is to serve as both guards and officiants at the Tabernacle under the leadership of Aaron and his sons. In contrast to the earlier, seemingly egalitarian, declaration at Sinai/Horeb that all Israelites were to constitute a "kingdom of priests" (Exod. 19:6), Numbers now assigns to the Levites the unique role of communal surrogates. They alone will have direct access to the Tabernacle and, by implication, to God.

Having established the preeminence of the Levite clans within the sacred domain, Numbers goes on to relate a further redistribution of authority within the Israelite community (Ch. 11). The occasion is a by-now familiar complaint that the diet of **manna** (provided miraculously by God in Exodus 16:14–15) is too restrictive; the grumbling Israelites recall fondly their diet of fish, cucumbers, and watermelons while they were in Egypt. Moses' response to this exhibition of collective softness and ingratitude is to complain to God that the burden of leadership is too great for him to bear. In so doing, he demonstrates some of the same weakness of purpose his people have just exhibited. God's reaction to this double rebellion is to "take back" a portion of the prophetic spirit that he had earlier conferred on Moses alone, transfer it to seventy tribal elders, and then punish the remainder of the people with a plague. This slightly confusing account of divine intervention in Israel's internal squabbles may well represent, scholars tell us, a conflation of two once-separate narratives. Whatever its origins, this story serves as a paradigm for subsequent accounts of popular discontent and swift retribution from God.

Moses' leadership during this period of the Exodus is portrayed as increasingly problematic, and even his own brother and sister (Aaron and Miriam) question his authority and criticize his decision to marry a Cushite wife (presumably Zipporah, who is identified in Exodus as a **Midianite**). God reaffirms Moses' unique role as intermediary—"with him I speak face to face, openly and not in riddles" (Num. 12:8)—and even punishes Miriam with a leprosy-like condition (she later dies in **Kadesh-barnea;** Figure 9.1). But that is not enough to deter a member of the Levite tribe, **Korah,** from mounting an even more serious challenge to Moses' spiritual authority. Korah's rebellion has, at first glance, an air of plausibility about it, in that it echoes the egalitarian rhetoric of an earlier covenant ideal: "Every member of the community is holy and the Lord is among them all" (16:3). That he is joined by two Reubenites in his rebellion suggests both a political and a religious repudiation of the exclusivity of Moses' position and of the theocratic elite he and Aaron embody. The Korah narrative may well be, as contemporary scholarship supposes, two independent versions of the same story joined together. But this composite tale of mass insurrection against charismatic leadership

Figure 9.1 Kadesh-barnea is an oasis located in the north-eastern part of the Sinai Peninsula. Referred to several times in the Penta-teuch, it served as an important campsite for the Israelites during the Exodus wanderings. According to a Pentateuchal tradition, Moses' sister Miriam was buried there (Num. 20:1).

raises unsettling questions about one of the corner-stone institutions of Israelite culture. By the time of the early monarchy, political and prophetic authority have already begun to dissociate from each other, and, before long, the prophets will become either independent of or antagonistic to the "anointed" king — a development foreshadowed in Samuel's opposition to Saul (see Chapter 14).

Even more unsettling, and more damaging to Israel's immediate fortunes, is the misadventure of the "spies" (Num. 13). Representing each of the twelve tribes, the spies are sent into southern Canaan to reconnoiter in obvious preparation for an invasion, but their subsequent report reveals just how unprepared even the warrior class is for the battle that awaits them. The conclusion they reach — "we are not able to go up against this people, for they are stronger than we" (13:31) — is as much an expression of distrust of divine promises of certain conquest and repatriation as it is a blow to Moses' credibility. Clearly, the generation of Israelites that left Egypt is not ready, spiritually or psychologically, to

enter and possess the land "flowing with milk and honey." Only **Caleb** and **Joshua** (earlier identified as Moses' loyal assistant) have sufficient faith and courage to urge an immediate invasion of Canaan, and they alone of this generation will survive the subsequent forty years of wandering in the wilderness of Sinai. Though it is not apparent at first, Israel is about to experience a dramatic collective *peripeteia*, a reversal of perspective, as a new generation arises — one that has never known slavery.

Nevertheless, for all Israel's complaints and weaknesses, by Numbers 21 their fortunes have begun to mend, and the Exodus narrative has once again begun to move forward. One of the sources from which the narrative material in this chapter has been drawn is actually mentioned by name — the "Book of the Wars of the LORD" (21:14) — and briefly quoted from. The author-redactor of this passage may have wished to corroborate his own account of this war story by alluding to another, presumably widely known, collection of poetic sagas dealing with the Exodus. Whatever his motives, the reference provides an unexpected window onto the compositional process. This "lost" book of the Bible may well represent only a fraction of the unnamed sources, oral as well as written, to which the authors of the Pentateuch had recourse. And what emerges from this composite "history" of Israel's passage through neighboring kingdoms is a pattern of military engagement and triumph that marks a dramatic reversal of Israel's prior conduct. No longer a ragtag band of irresolute and disheartened ex-slaves, they are now able to overcome the very peoples — Edomites, Moabites, and Amorites — whom Israel's kings will later subdue (see, for example, 2 Sam. 8:1–14).

BALAAM'S BLESSING

The **Balaam** narrative that follows (Num. 22–24), the longest independent narrative segment in Numbers, reveals how and why Israel's fortunes have changed for the better now that the period of wandering is past. Balaam has been summoned by Balak, king of Moab, to curse the Israelites in the name of their god, which presupposes that Balaam has, in fact, some prophetic access to YHWH. What follows, however, is a confusing, spliced-together version of two originally divergent accounts of Balaam's response to Balak. In the first version (23:7–21), Balaam agrees to accompany the second delegation from Balak only after God has told him, explicitly, to go and "do only what I tell you." The second version (23:22–35) portrays God as angered by Balaam's decision to comply with Balak's request, and, so, before Balaam is allowed to proceed, he must be taught a humiliating lesson. This narrative sequence features one of the few genuine fables in biblical literature, featuring a talking donkey that, ironically, has better sight than her fortune-telling master. When the animal speaks to him, Balaam never exhibits the slightest surprise (one never does in a true fable) and willingly accepts reproof from the mouth of his beast when he, too, for the first time, sees the angel standing in his path with a drawn sword. Once again, Balaam is instructed to proceed and speak only those words that God permits him.

The three oracular speeches that follow are poems of praise — "how goodly are your tents, O Jacob" (Num. 24:5) — and virtual celebrations of the covenant relationship. It is little wonder, therefore, that Balak feels cheated and parts in anger from Balaam. More intriguing, however, than this slightly comic denouement is an allusion to a mysterious redemptive figure whom Balaam envisions in the distant future:

> I see him, but not now;
> I behold him, but not near:
> a star shall come forth out of Jacob,
> a comet arise from Israel.
> He shall smite the squadrons of Moab,
> and beat down all the sons of strife.
> (Num. 24:17)

Scholars commonly assume that this unnamed figure is King David and view this passage as a type of prophecy after the fact describing David's conquest of Israel's neighbors. The intrusion of what appears, therefore, to be material from the post-Davidic period provides one possible clue to the redactional character of this entire episode. As a predictive — or, at the very least, symbolic — utterance, Balaam's speech foretells not only Israel's imminent victory over the Moabites but also the triumphant history of the Davidic monarchy. In this way, it validates the claims of that dynastic line to "divine" legitimacy. (See Chapter 14 for a discussion of the Royal Covenant.)

But just as the revelation at Sinai/Horeb was followed by the incident of the golden calf, so Balaam's hymns of praise to Israel's integrity are followed almost immediately by one more act of rebellion and disloyalty, the incident of Baal-peor (Num. 25). Baal was one of the principal gods of the Canaanite peoples, and the worship of Baal was sufficiently popular throughout Israel for prophets of a much later period to warn the Israelites of dire consequences of paying homage to him rather than to YHWH. In this incident, however, there are two correlated acts of disobedience to God — intermarriage (with either Moabite or Midianite women) and apostasy — the implication being that one leads inevitably to the other. Indeed, the plague, which

YHWH characteristically visits upon the Israelites in response to these twin acts of sacrilege, ceases only after Phinehas, Aaron's grandson, drives a spear through the entrails of both an Israelite man and the Midianite woman he has taken into his family (25:6–8). Why the Midianites—who were earlier, in the time of Jethro (see Exod. 18), depicted in a positive light—have suddenly become a threat to Israel's survival is never explained. Nor is it clear why (apart from an obvious conflation of sources) the Midianites are lumped together with the Moabites, or why marriage with a Midianite warrants a death penalty. To this point in the Pentateuch, attitudes toward **exogamy** (marriage outside of one's community) have been ambivalent or simply contradictory. Thus it should come as something of a surprise to readers to learn that the marriage of an Israelite man to a Midianite woman was done in "open defiance of Moses and all the community of Israel" (Num. 25:6). After all, had not Moses himself earlier married a Midianite (or Cushite) woman? When Aaron and Miriam rebuke him for having done so (Ch. 12), God vindicates Moses and punishes his siblings. Moreover, if intermarriage under any conditions was unacceptable to God, then Moses' provision for sparing the lives of Midianite virgins (who are then eligible to enter Israelite-harems) becomes completely illogical. Though this double attitude toward exogamy persisted throughout biblical history, as texts as diverse as the books of Ezra and Ruth suggest, the question of intermarriage remained largely unresolved well into the post-exilic period.

NUMBERS' CONCEPTION OF GOD

Perhaps the most problematic issue in Numbers, however, is that of the divine nature itself. In this text, as much as in any other, we are confronted by the problem of **anthropomorphism.** The biblical image of God, as noted previously, runs the gamut from the austere, transcendent Creator of Genesis 1 to the rather humanized and fully embodied YHWH of Exodus 33, and this spectrum of images is evident in Numbers as well. Upon learning of Israel's cowardice and unfaithfulness (Num.

13), God's first response is to threaten to exterminate the Israelites altogether, sparing only Moses and his descendants. Happily, Moses dissuades the Deity from this course of action by reminding him (as he had earlier in Exodus 32:11–12) that the surrounding peoples are likely to attribute his action to an inability to make good on his covenant promises. In effect, Moses is appealing to YHWH's vanity or, at least, to his sense of his growing reputation. As it turns out, God's eagerness to annihilate the Midianites is even keener than his desire for vengeance against faithless Israel, and contemporary readers have a particularly difficult time accepting a God concept that entails extreme violence and intolerance. We would do well to remember, however, that Israel's worship of YHWH is often juxtaposed with its homage to Baal and other Canaanite deities. Therefore it is hardly astonishing to find in relatively early traditions an image of divinity that is neither ethically exalted nor stripped of its mythological associations. Moreover, Israel's varied perceptions of its Deity are intertwined with its equally varied perceptions of the covenant relationship and its own "manifest destiny." Just as these latter concepts evolve over time, so does its understanding of God.

QUESTIONS FOR REVIEW

1. How does the Book of Leviticus distinguish between the clean and the unclean? Is there any ethical counterpart to this distinction in the Holiness Code?

2. What is the purpose of the scapegoat ritual in Leviticus 16, and what connection does this ceremony have with the Day of Atonement?

3. How did the Jubilee legislation overturn existing property rights and economic relationships?

4. What significance do you assign to the forty years of Israel's wandering in the desert? Did the passing of an entire generation bring about a collective change in Israel's fighting spirit and in its dedication to the covenant?

5. Why does Balak, king of Moab, hire Balaam to curse the Israelites? Is there a presumption here that Balaam—a Canaanite seer—can, in fact, communicate with Israel's God?

6. Why is it necessary for YHWH to constantly reaffirm Moses' authority? Aren't all of the Israelites part of the "kingdom of priests" and therefore equal in God's eyes?

QUESTIONS FOR REFLECTION AND DISCUSSION

1. Consider the binary nature of taboo systems like the one in Leviticus. Is it possible (or even desirable) to separate all persons, objects and actions into categories like clean/unclean or holy/common?

2. How does a system of animal sacrifices make it easier for a penitent Israelite to seek reconciliation with God? Isn't prayer sufficient?

3. What is the connection between rebellion against Moses' leadership and rebellion against God? Is prophetic authority in Israel so uncertain that, even within a relatively brief period of time, the people's loyalty to either YHWH or his prophets is always in question?

4. Why does Aaron seem strangely immune to punishment, even though he is implicated in the incident of the golden calf and guilty of undermining Moses' authority? Miriam, after all, is punished severely for her part in their sibling revolt against Moses, but Aaron escapes with nothing more than a divine scolding. Can it be that Aaron's role as High Priest — and therefore as progenitor of the entire priestly line — places him beyond serious censure in the eyes of the Pentateuchal writers?

TERMS AND CONCEPTS TO REMEMBER

Aaronite	Caleb
Abihu	*chol*
anthropomorphism	Day of Atonement
Azazel	(Yom Kippur)
Balaam	exogamy

Holiness Code	manna
Joshua	Midianites
Jubilee	Nadab
Kadesh-barnea	scapegoat
kodesh	*tahor*
Korah	*tameh*

RECOMMENDED READING

Ackerman, James. "Numbers." In Robert Alter and Frank Kemode, eds., *The Literary Guide to the Bible.* Cambridge, Mass.: Harvard University Press, 1987.

Alt, Albrecht. "The Origins of Israelite Law." In *Essays in Old Testament History and Religion,* pp. 79–132. Translated by R. A. Wilson. New York: Doubleday, 1967.

Douglas, Mary. *Leviticus as Literature.* Oxford: Oxford University Press, 1999.

———. *Purity and Danger.* London: Thames & Hudson, 1966.

Dozeman, Thomas B. "The Book of Numbers." In *The New Interpreter's Bible,* Vol. 2, pp. 1–268. Nashville, Tenn.: Abingdon Press, 1998.

Hallo, William. "Numbers and Ancient Near Eastern Literature." In W. Gunther Plaut, ed., *The Torah: A Modern Commentary.* New York: Doubleday, 1981.

Kaiser, Walter C. "The Book of Leviticus." In *The New Interpreter's Bible,* Vol. 1, pp. 983–1191. Nashville, Tenn.: Abingdon Presss, 1994.

Levine, Baruch. *In the Presence of the Lord.* Leiden: Brill, 1974.

Maccoby, Hyam. *Ritual and Morality.* Cambridge: Cambridge University Press, 1999.

Milgrom, Jacob. *Cult and Conscience.* Leiden: Brill, 1976.

———. "Numbers, Book of." In D. N. Freedman, ed., *The Anchor Bible Dictionary,* Vol. 4, pp. 1146–1155. New York: Doubleday, 1992.

Noth, Martin. *Leviticus.* Philadelphia: Westminster Press, 1975.

———. *Numbers.* Philadelphia: Westminster Press, 1968.

CHAPTER 10

A Mosaic Legacy
The Book of Deuteronomy

Key Topics/Themes The fifth canonical book of the Hebrew Bible, and the final segment of the Pentateuch, is known in English as Deuteronomy, a name that reflects the designation of this book in the Septuagint. Greek-speaking Jews of the Hellenistic period referred to this book as the *Deuteronomion,* or "Second Law," a title based on their interpretation of the instructions Moses gave the Israelites when he told them to "prepare a copy of this Torah" (Deut. 17:18), understanding "Torah" to mean all of the laws of the four books that precede Deuteronomy. But, in fact, Deuteronomy is much more than a repetition of earlier teachings and traditions: It is, at heart, a *revision* of earlier law codes and a rethinking of earlier theological principles. As such, it represents a departure from, rather than a summation of, the traditions of the Tetrateuch (Genesis through Numbers). Recently, some scholars have suggested that Deuteronomy may well have been the starting point for postexilic redactors engaged in the construction of the Pentateuch, providing a framework for the JEP narratives that precede it. This is not a widely held view, however, and most still view Deuteronomy as the final retrospective link in the compositional chain that brought the Torah into being.

The Deuteronomic View of History

It is important to note that the Book of Deuteronomy looks forward as well as backward, anticipating the major themes of the historical writings that follow it. Collectively, the books from Joshua to Kings are commonly referred to as the **Deuteronomistic History,** for the simple reason that each of these books, in its own way, embodies one central historical thesis that we first encounter in the pages of Deuteronomy:

> If you will only obey the LORD your GOD, by diligently observing all his commandments that I am commanding you today, the LORD your GOD will set you high above the nations of the earth; . . . But if you will not obey the LORD . . . then all of these curses shall come upon you and overtake you: . . .
>
> The LORD will cause you to be defeated before your enemies, . . . You shall become an object of horror to all the kingdoms of the earth. (Deut. 28:1, 15, 25)

As the prologue to the Deuteronomistic History, the Book of Deuteronomy provides the interpretive framework for the narrative histories that follow, demonstrating in advance the inevitable and tragic consequences that will befall Israel for its unfaithfulness to YHWH. For the authors of both Deuteronomy and the Deuteronomistic History, the only measure of Israel's success—and the only guarantee of its continued existence—is obedience to God and commitment to the covenant and its laws. Yet that is the one thing that Israel and its leaders finally prove incapable of.

BOX 10.1
The Torah's Three Versions of the Law of Retaliation

A legal principle widely known in Mesopotamia long before the time of Moses, the *lex talionis* (law of retaliation) appears prominently in three books of the Torah. In the section of Exodus known as the Book of the Covenant, the *lex talionis* is applied to cases of physical assault, where it specifies penalties levied against masters who beat, maim, or kill slaves and against men whose fighting injures a pregnant woman, causing her to miscarry. If a mistreated slave dies under a master's blows, the owner must be punished. However, if the slave survives "a day or two, there is no punishment, for the slave is the owner's property" (Exod. 21:20–21). In the case of quarreling men whose violence causes a pregnant woman to lose her child, the aggressor must pay her master or husband an appropriate sum of money; if the woman dies, however, the *lex talionis* is enforced: "you shall give life for life, eye for eye, tooth for tooth . . . burn for burn, wound for wound, stripe for stripe" (21:22–25).

Whereas Exodus evokes the law of retaliation to punish those who cause physical harm, Deuteronomy employs it as an instrument of poetic justice — the wrong one person tries to inflict on another is instead visited on him. According to Deuteronomy, if a man testifies falsely against another Israelite, the magistrates must "do to the false witness just as the false witness had meant to do to the other," making the liar's punishment an example to others who might be tempted to commit perjury in court (19:15–21).

In Leviticus, which contains the Torah's third version of the *lex talionis,* infliction of physical injuries must be repaid strictly in kind: "fracture for fracture, eye for eye, tooth for tooth; the injury inflicted is the injury to be suffered" (24:19–20). Whereas persons who kill another's animal must make restitution for its value, those who commit homicide must die (24:21–22). It is not known if Israelite officials regularly enforced the principle of exact retaliation — condemning persons who accidentally damaged another's eye to undergo state-administered mutilation — but the ancient Near Eastern law did serve to shield offenders from being put to death for causing nonfatal injuries.

As the final act in the Exodus drama, however, Deuteronomy offers us a highly dramatic, almost theatrical, setting for the presentation of this thesis and of the revisionist legal code that accompanies it. Moses assembles the people of Israel on the plains of Moab for the last time to deliver a series of three farewell addresses (1:6–4:40; see also Chs. 5–23, 29, and 30). Moses knows that he will soon die, without seeing the land of the patriarchs that God commanded Israel to return to and occupy. This is his last opportunity to offer guidance to the people he has led through the desert, and he prefaces his final speeches with a brief recapitulation of the Exodus and of Israel's principal conflicts with itself and with God. By focusing on the many struggles that have characterized God's relationship with Israel in the desert, Moses is preparing the Israelites for the even greater struggle that awaits them: the conquest of Canaan under the leadership of Joshua. And by insisting that nothing may be added to or taken away from the "statutes and ordinances" he has incorporated into this text (4:2), the author of Deuteronomy is attempting to bring historical closure to the very process of revising earlier law codes he is engaged in. (Box 10.1 discusses the *lex talionis,* a legal principle that appears prominently in three books of the Torah.)

JOSIAH'S REIGN AND THE DISCOVERY OF THE BOOK OF THE LAW

Biblical historians agree that Deuteronomy is a literary work of distinctive style and theological outlook, and many scholars believe that the Book of the Law (literally, "book of instruction," or *sefer ha-torah* in Hebrew), reportedly found in the Temple during the late-seventh-century-B.C.E. reign of King Josiah (2 Kings 22:3–10), is none other than the Book of Deuteronomy — or at least some significant portion of that book. Josiah is so clearly impressed by the dire warnings in this newly discovered book that it is tempting to imagine him reading Deuteronomy 28 with growing anxiety over its increasingly terrifying predictions of national disaster. Josiah's determination to reform Israel's religious life suggests that, if Deuteronomy was not actually written or even edited in the seventh century B.C.E., then, at the very least, its major themes began to enter the consciousness of some of Israel's leading religious personalities, including the prophet Jeremiah. Certainly, Josiah's decision to destroy altars and shrines located throughout Judah and to focus the nation's cultic observances on the Temple in Jerusalem suggests the direct influence of Deuteronomy 12:14, with its insistence on the centralization of worship at one (unnamed) shrine.

For all its influence on the southern kingdom of Judah, however, it is now presumed that some of the traditions that found their way into Deuteronomy had their origins in the northern kingdom of Israel. After the Assyrian invasion and destruction of that kingdom in 721 B.C.E., northern priests and scribes probably fled south, bringing with them a collective memory of covenant renewal ceremonies, like those enacted by Joshua at the northern shrine of Shechem, which then merged with southern covenant ceremonies centered in Jerusalem (cf. Deut. 27, Josh. 24). Josiah's reformist agenda would then have provided the ideal climate for the editing and promulgation (if not the actual composition) of the Book of Deuteronomy as we know it. At this point in the process of composition/redaction, presumably, a specifically Judean perspective was introduced into the evolving text of Deuteronomy. Certainly, a southern audience would have found the idea of total triumph over its enemies — and those include its Canaanite neighbors (see Deut. 11:24) — and a systematic refocusing of national religious life on Jerusalem particularly appealing in the wake of Assyria's near-destruction of Judah during the reign of Hezekiah.

However Deuteronomy may have come into existence, its author-redactor — whom we can refer to for convenience's sake as the **Deuteronomist** — was determined to bring Moses before readers in a more vivid and memorable way than ever before. Suddenly, the man of few words becomes a speech maker of extraordinary eloquence, determined to his last breath to hammer home the central themes of covenant theology and Israel's history as the Deuteronomistic school understood that history. For the Deuteronomist, Israel's relationship to God is based on reciprocal love and on a profound and unchanging commitment to fulfill the Ten Commandments that God imparted to Israel at Sinai/Horeb. This relationship is similar to that of a powerful king and his vassals who have sworn "fealty" or absolute loyalty to him; indeed, in both language and structure, Deuteronomy often resembles a diplomatic treaty between a great and a lesser power. The difference here, of course, is that the "king" is the Creator of the universe, and Deuteronomy is unambiguous in its assertion of monotheism: "This day, then, be sure and take to heart that the LORD is GOD in heaven above and on earth below; there is no other" (4:39). In its emphasis on sincerity and conscientiousness in the service of this one God, Deuteronomy sets a higher, more rigorous standard of covenant loyalty, with even greater penalties for dereliction of duty than earlier Pentateuchal texts had imagined.

MOSES' FIRST TWO SPEECHES

Structurally, the Book of Deuteronomy consists of one short speech (1:1–4:44) in which Moses reviews the history of the Exodus and its significance, and a second, much longer, discourse (Chs. 5–26, 28) in which Moses lays out expanded versions of the Decalogue and of statutes found elsewhere in the Pentateuch (Box 10.2). Many of the changes that are introduced in this core segment of Deuteronomy reflect a heightened sense of moral urgency and of devotion to YHWH. Following this second speech is what amounts to a coda consisting of two chapters in which Moses binds the people

BOX 10.2
Different Legal Codes Embedded in the Pentateuch

Although Mosaic commandments, statutes, and ordinances are commonly regarded as a single body of law, the Pentateuch actually contains several different legal codes. Because each code appears separate and distinct from the other codes, scholars believe that each one originated independently among different groups at different times in Israel's history. These discrete legal documents may have been combined during and after the Babylonian exile (late sixth and fifth centuries B.C.E.) when the covenant community was part of the Persian Empire. According to the Book of Ezra, Persian administrators ordered the exiles who had returned to Jerusalem to govern the partly restored community by producing a compilation of Israel's legal traditions that would become the official law of the land. Conformity to a single sacred legal corpus derived from the Mosaic heritage was enforced by imperial Persian authority: "All who will not obey the Law [*torah*] of your God and the law of the king [Persian emperor] let judgment be strictly executed on them, whether for death or for banishment or for confiscation of their goods or for imprisonment" (Ezra 7:26). The Persian threat of financial loss or capital punishment for those not practicing the divinely (and governmentally) sanctioned *torah* was a strong inducement for scribes to

produce and the people to accept a definitive edition of Israel's legal code. Whatever the time and place of its origin, all legislation now contained in the Pentateuch was ultimately assigned to Moses and thus given his prestige and authority. The discrete legal corpora finally incorporated into the Pentateuch included at least the following six sources, listed according to the order in which they appear in the biblical text:

1. The Decalogue, the Ten "Words" or Commandments (Exod. 20:1–17; cf. Deut. 5:6–21)

2. The Book of the Covenant, the Elohist's revision of an ancient legal code (Exod. 20:18–23:33)

3. The Ritual Decalogue, the Yahwist's compendium of henotheistic and cultic requirements (Exod. 34:11–26)

4. The Priestly Code, formal liturgies and sacrificial rituals (Lev. 1–16; Num. 1–10; cf. the Tabernacle cult [Exod. 25–31; 35:40])

5. The Holiness Code, rituals separating and distinguishing Israel from surrounding peoples (Lev. 17–26)

6. The Deuteronomic Code, the core of canonical Deuteronomy, introduced during the reign of Josiah (late seventh century B.C.E.) (Deut. 12–26)

and their tribal leaders to an oath of loyalty to YHWH, complete with warnings of collective disaster if Israel turns aside from God and reassurances of divine compassion and national restoration if Israel turns back to the Deity it has betrayed and abandoned. Finally, there are two miscellaneous poems attributed to Moses — the Song of Moses in Chapter 32 and the Blessing of Moses in Chapter 33 — and a concluding account of Moses' death that elevates him to the rank of foremost prophet in Israel: "There has never yet risen in Israel a prophet like Moses, whom the Lord knew face to face" (34:10), a view that does not appear to be shared by other, later, biblical writers. Overall, there is a marked tendency toward revisionism in each of the

major segments of this book, a tendency that may well echo the themes of the Josianic reformation.

SLAVES AND OTHER MARGINALIZED GROUPS

The most obvious changes that the Deuteronomist seeks to accomplish involve laws whose prior language and even intent have undergone a perceptible, and even radical, transformation. Consider, for example, laws affecting slavery. In Exodus 21:2–11, the Covenant Code differentiates between the treatment accorded male and female slaves, allowing male slaves to go free after six years of indentured service while retaining female slaves who have had sexual relations with their master or his sons. In Deuteronomy 15:12–17, the female slaves receive the same grant of freedom accorded their male counterparts. Even more important, Deuteronomy cautions against setting a slave free with no means of support:

> But when you set him free, do not let him go empty-handed. Give to him lavishly from your flock, from your threshing-floor and from your wine-press. Be generous to him because the LORD your GOD has blessed you. . . . Remember that you were slaves in Egypt and the LORD your GOD redeemed you. (Deut. 15:13–15)

The purpose of such legislation, clearly, is to break the cycle of poverty that leads the poor to seek slavery as an alternative to starvation. An even more dramatic shift in the Deuteronomic perception and treatment of slaves, however, occurs in Chapter 23:15–16, where the Israelites are told (in contradistinction to prevailing Mesopotamian law) that they are *not* to surrender runaway slaves to their masters, and, in fact, that the slaves should be allowed to settle wherever they wish. No such provision exists anywhere else in the Pentateuch, and one can only wonder what would have happened if a general slave uprising had led to a mass flight of slaves seeking refuge in a different tribal territory. Still, no provision for a general manumission of slaves is to be found in Deuteronomy, and the "right of escape" that this statute provides is nowhere reconciled with the older and more general right to "own" slaves and/or indentured servants.

Other marginalized segments of the population also receive renewed attention from the Deuteronomist, including widows, orphans, and resident aliens. Several times in the course of explaining the terms of a particular statute, the Deuteronomist has Moses remind his audience that kindness toward the most vulnerable in their society is a sign of obedience to God's will (see, for example, 25:17–18). Nor is it enough, the Deuteronomist insists, simply to conform outwardly to a divine commandment: For the covenant to be truly fulfilled, the "heart and soul" must be engaged in the service of the Deity. Nowhere is this ideal more eloquently stated than in the often-quoted passage known in Hebrew as the **Shema:**

> Hear o Israel, the LORD is our GOD, one LORD, and you must love the LORD your GOD with all your heart and soul and strength. These commandments which I give you today are to be kept in your heart; you shall repeat them to your sons, and speak of them indoors and out of doors, when you lie down and when you rise. Bind them as a sign on the hand and wear them as a phylactery on the forehead; write them on the door-posts of your houses and on your gates. (Deut. 6:4–9)

In time, this exhortation would become one of the central prayers in the synagogue liturgy, and by Jesus' time, it was so familiar a passage that he could quote verse 5 with every expectation that his audience would know exactly which portion of Deuteronomy he was alluding to (see Matt. 22:36).

COVENANT RENEWAL AND NATIONAL RESTORATION

The idea that YHWH can only really be obeyed by internalizing the precepts of the Torah and by the constant application of the mind and will in his service can be found throughout Deuteronomy—especially in those passages in which the Israelites are told to circumcise the "foreskin" of their hearts (10:16) or are reminded that they are not to "live by bread alone" but are to nourish themselves through "every word that comes from the mouth of the Lord" (8:3). Such heightening of covenant awareness and obligation, of course, carries with it a higher level of anxiety lest the covenant relationship be broken. The Deuteronomic view of history that emerges from this book places responsibility for the shattering of that relationship, and for all of the calamities that follow from it, on the shoulders of the Israelites. In Chapters 28–30, the Israelites are told repeatedly that they have a choice between obedience to YHWH or disobedience; obedience leads to success in life and longevity in the land, whereas disobedience leads to collective disaster and exile. And if the Book of Deuteronomy is, as most scholars assume, a seventh-century work whose author-redactor could not help but reflect on the fall of the northern kingdom of Israel in 721 B.C.E., then the so-called Deuteronomic view is a retrospective interpretation of Israel's political demise, sustained by the conviction that the cause of Israel's downfall lies with Israel alone. Once again, the Deuteronomist employs ancient Near Eastern treaty language to convey the idea that Israel's contract with YHWH has been broken unilaterally: God was faithful to his promises, but Israel was not.

However, the Deuteronomist is just as convinced that, though YHWH is clearly prepared to punish the Israelites for their crimes and their apostasies, he is also willing to forgive them if they approach him with a contrite heart:

> . . . if you turn back to him and obey him heart and soul in all that I command you this day, then the LORD your GOD will show you compassion and restore your fortunes. He will gather you again from the countries to which he has scattered you. Even though he were to banish you to the four corners of the world, the LORD your GOD will gather you from there, from there he will fetch you home. (Deut. 30:2–4)

For prophets of the late seventh and sixth centuries, this idea of national restoration and covenant renewal was not only an expedient consolation for a community of exiles but also a logical corollary of the belief that YHWH is a God whose capacity for forgiveness is at least as great as his need to punish (see Ezek. 36:22–28). It is hardly surprising, then, to find these same sentiments expressed in a contemporary text like Deuteronomy. To reinforce this lesson, and to underscore the belief that YHWH is indeed the Lord of history, the Deuteronomist presents two seemingly contradictory theses, each linked to God's dual nature:

> It was not because you were more numerous than any other people that the LORD set his heart on you and chose you. . . . It was because the LORD loved you and kept the oath that he swore to your ancestors, that the LORD has brought you out with a mighty hand and redeemed you from slavery. . . . Know therefore that the LORD your GOD is GOD, the faithful GOD who maintains covenant loyalty with those who love him and keep his commandments, to a thousand generations, and who

repays in their own person those who reject him. (Deut. 7:7–10)

This "theology of grace," as it is sometimes called, thus presents the covenant as an unearned gift, bestowed upon a possibly undeserving but nevertheless obligated Israel, from whom the Promised Land can be taken just as swiftly as it was given, and to whom it can yet be given back again.

A MORE TRANSCENDENT DEITY

The Deuteronomist's view of God is no less innovative than his view of the covenant. In sharp contrast to earlier Pentateuchal traditions, particularly those associated with the J source, YHWH is deliberately spoken of as an incorporeal deity who cannot be seen. Twice, during his recounting of the experiences at Horeb/Sinai, Moses insists that the Israelites saw nothing: "When the LORD spoke to you from the fire you heard a voice speaking, but you saw no figure; there was only a voice" (4:12), which then becomes a rationale for banning all physical representations of the divine. Israel's distinctiveness among the nations is to be defined, then, not only by its festivals and its dietary code but, more important, by its anti-iconographic mode of worship. It has been suggested that, more than any other Pentateuchal writer, the Deuteronomist is determined to "demystify" earlier views of YHWH and his relationship to the Tabernacle by insisting that God's "dwelling place" (Hebrew, *mishkan*) is simply the place where his "name" resides (see Deut. 12:11). As for the ark, it becomes simply a receptacle for the Ten Commandments, and no mention is made of the Deity hovering over its lid or cover. This "name theology," as it has been called, finds even fuller expression in 1 Kings 8, where Solomon dedicates his new Temple to YHWH with the explicit assurance that no human structure could possibly "hold" God when "even heaven and the highest heaven cannot contain you" (8:27).

In the light of this more transcendent (and nonanthropomorphic) conception of the Deity, the cultic dimension of Israelite worship undergoes a similar transformation in Deuteronomy. No longer do we read of the "pleasing odor" of animal sacrifice — a persistent image in the priestly tradition (Lev. 1:9, 13, 17) — nor do we encounter even the barest suggestion that YHWH somehow needs the sacrifices that Israel was commanded to offer him. Instead, it is the poor who must be fed, and along with the resident aliens, they have become as much the beneficiaries of the tithing system as the Levites once were (Deut. 14:28–29; 26:12–13).

WAR AND CONQUEST

The Deuteronomist's view of war and conquest is just as idiosyncratic as his view of the Deity, and potentially contradictory as well. In contrast to the more sweeping and merciless order of battle in Numbers 31:17 — where the Israelites are instructed by an indignant Moses to "kill every male dependant and . . . every woman who has had intercourse with a man" — Deuteronomy 20:10–20 commands the Israelites to make an offer of peace before laying siege to a city, as long as that city is not nearby. The passage goes on to make provisions for sparing not only women and children but even trees that are not needed for war materials. In the very next chapter, a similar degree of compassion is extended to enemy women taken captive during a battle, and the Israelites are, once again, enjoined to respect the humanity of their opponents (21:10–14). At the same time, the older (and, for modern readers, the more appalling) concept of **herem** — that is, of total destruction of everything associated with one's enemy — is invoked, albeit focused this time on the seven "nations" that bordered on or interacted with Israel (7:1–6). The coexistence of these totally conflicting guidelines for holy war was destined to create confusion for later generations (cf. Josh. 9:3–27) and testifies, once again, to the composite nature of the legislation found in the Deuteronomic Code.

PROPHECY

No less perplexing, is the Deuteronomist's position on prophecy, and the means by which any prophetic claimant can be judged authentic or untrue. Deu-teronomy offers two "tests" by which any prophetic utterances can be verified: a pragmatic test and a dogmatic test. The latter can be found in Chapter 13, where the people are told to disregard a "prophetic" prediction — *even if it comes true* — when the clear intent of the "prophet" is to inspire the people to worship other gods. What matters, then, is not the prophet's prognosticative talents but the religious content of his message. In Chapter 18, however, the Deuteronomist brings back the older, divinatory view of prophecy by insisting that the final test of a prophet's credibility is the accuracy of his predictions: "When the word spoken by the prophet in the name of the LORD is not fulfilled and does not come true, it is not a word spoken by the LORD" (18:22). But whichever standard of prophetic trustworthiness the Israelites finally adopt, they are at the same time assured that "the LORD your GOD will raise up a prophet from among you like myself" (18:15). Prophecy itself, in short, will continue to be one of the defining institutions of Israelite religious culture, the Deuteronomist insists, even after Moses, the greatest of prophets, has departed the scene — though anxiety over the reliability of individual prophets will also continue well beyond the period of the Exodus.

THE DEATH OF MOSES

Moses' departure from the scene is almost as sudden and mysterious as his entrance, and the narrator's inability to locate Moses' burial place ensures that, like the prophet Elijah, his death will be viewed by later generations as partly inexplicable and so potentially supernatural. Certainly, no natural cause is given for Moses' death. Quite the contrary: We are told that, although he was 120 years old, "his sight was unimpaired and his vigor had not abated" (Deut. 34:7). It was left to later generations of commentators to speculate that Moses was prevented from crossing the Jordan as a punishment for his presumptuous behavior — drawing water from a rock without first acknowledging the power acting through him — at Meribah (Num. 20:2–13). But, whatever the reason, there are few images in the Pentateuch more poignant than that of Israel's greatest prophet glimpsing only from a distance the Promised Land that he will never set foot on.

Before his death, Moses is given the opportunity to bless the tribes and, in a sense, to foretell their future destinies, just like the patriarch Jacob in Genesis 49. The differences between these two respective "testaments," however, are both glaring and instructive. In Genesis, two tribes clearly dominate the rest and so receive the lion's share of Jacob's blessing: Judah and Joseph. In addition, we find Jacob cursing Simeon and Levi for their warlike behavior and predicting their demise (Gen. 49:5–7). Deuteronomy 33 lays out a very different scenario with the elevation of Levi to priestly status and the disappearance of Simeon altogether. Perhaps the most remarkable shift in this tribal hierarchy is the diminution of Judah, whose precarious situation is barely alluded to in Moses' prayerful wish that YHWH help defend Judah in its struggle with its "adversaries" (Deut. 33:7). The variable tribal fortunes to which these two overlapping yet discordant traditions attest, as well as the uncertain destiny of the emergent nation of Israel, will become the focal point of the next segment of the Tanak, the Prophets (Nevi'im).

QUESTIONS FOR REVIEW

1. In what ways is Deuteronomy different from the other books of the Pentateuch? How does the term *revisionist* help us to define this difference?

2. How does the discovery of a scroll (or "book of instruction") during the seventh-century-B.C.E. reign of Josiah, as related in 2 Kings 22:3–10, connect to the writing of Deuteronomy?

3. What is the Deuteronomic view of history? What, according to this thesis, are the ultimate consequences of covenant breaking for Israel?

QUESTIONS FOR REFLECTION AND DISCUSSION

1. How useful is the Deuteronomic view of history as an explanation of Israel's failures and triumphs? Why don't modern historians employ a similar historical logic to account for the rise and fall of nations and empires?

2. Why is Moses kept, at the last, from entering the Promised Land? Hasn't he served God faithfully enough to deserve more than a glimpse of the land he has struggled so hard to regain?

TERMS AND CONCEPTS TO REMEMBER

Deuteronomic view of history
Deuteronomist
Deuteronomistic History

herem
lex talionis
"name theology"
Shema

RECOMMENDED READING

Friedman, Richard E. *Who Wrote the Bible?* New York: Harper & Row, 1987.

McKenzie, Steven L. "Deuteronomistic History." In D. N. Freedman, ed., *The Anchor Bible Dictionary*, Vol. 2, pp. 160–168. New York: Doubleday, 1992.

Nicholson, E. W. *Deuteronomy and Tradition.* Philadelphia: Fortress Press, 1967.

Weinfeld, M. *Deuteronomy and the Deuteronomic School.* Oxford: Oxford University Press, 1972.

CHAPTER 11

Introduction to the Deuteronomistic History

Key Topics/Themes The second major section of the Hebrew Bible, the Prophets (Hebrew, *Nevi'im*), is divided traditionally into two parts: the Former Prophets, consisting of the historical narratives from Joshua through 2 Kings, and the Latter Prophets, consisting of four books of prophetic narrative and proclamation—Isaiah, Jeremiah, Ezekiel, and the Book of the Twelve. The rationale for referring to this entire collection as the "Prophets" seems to derive from the view that all of Israel's history is to be understood in the light of prophetic *torah*—namely, that whatever happened to Israel, from the conquest of Canaan in the late thirteenth century B.C.E. to the Babylonian conquest and the destruction of the kingdom of Judah in the sixth century B.C.E., was a direct consequence of Israel's covenant with YHWH and its repeated violations of that covenant. So understood, Israel's history becomes something more than the story of the rise and fall of a relatively short-lived and politically insignificant monarchy. Both the Former and the Latter Prophets proclaim a theological interpretation of historical data according to which the judgment of God can finally be seen to prevail over Israel's obstinacy and disloyalty. This convergence of history and prophecy is what gives this segment of the Tanak its internal coherence and allows us to view its diverse writings through a single interpretive framework.

The Deuteronomistic Theory of History

Over the past half-century, biblical scholars have come to refer to the books of the Former Prophets as the **Deuteronomistic History (DH).** The use of this term reflects one basic assumption—namely, that embedded in the historical narratives of Joshua through 2 Kings is an argumentative thesis that comes directly out of the Book of Deuteronomy. According to this thesis (as noted in the analysis of Deuteronomy in Chapter 10), the fate of Israel and its kings is ultimately contingent on faithfulness to the covenant and observance of covenant obligations. Like a treaty established between a powerful king and a vassal, Israel is bound by the commitments made on its behalf by its remote ancestors (the Patriarchs) and by Moses, its greatest leader and lawgiver. As long as Israel adheres to the terms of that commitment, it will prosper; but the moment it turns against YHWH or toward other (usually Canaanite) deities, it brings on itself a series of deserved punishments, culminating in destruction

BOX 11.1
Major Events in the Deuteronomistic History (Joshua–2 Kings)

In creating a distinctive literary blend of theology and history intended to illustrate the principles enunciated in the Book of Deuteronomy, the author-editors of the Deuteronomistic History present the following six developments as crucial in YHWH's difficult partnership with Israel.

1. Joshua: the **conquest of Canaan** (c. 1200 B.C.E.). Obedient to YHWH's commands, the tribes of Israel succeed in conquering most of the land promised to Abraham's progeny.

2. Judges: the period of the **judges** (c. 1200–1040 B.C.E.). Unlike the idealized portrayal of the conquest given in Joshua, Judges shows a disunited and politically chaotic group of tribes struggling to maintain a toehold in Canaan. Emphasizing that Israel's obedience to YHWH brings military victory and disobedience only failure, a series of individualistic judges (spirit-directed leaders) remain intermittently at war with their Canaanite neighbors.

3. 1 and 2 Samuel and 1 Kings 1–11: the united monarchy (c. 1040–922 B.C.E.). Philistine aggression leads to Israel's political unification under a single ruler, first **Saul** and then **David,** who is succeeded by his son **Solomon.** YHWH vows to keep David's heirs on Israel's throne "forever."

4. 1 Kings 12–2 Kings 17: the divided kingdom (922–721 B.C.E.). After Solomon's death, the ten northern tribes secede to form the northern kingdom of Israel, while the smaller southern kingdom of Judah remains loyal to the Davidic dynasty. Kings' parallel account of rulers in the two kingdoms ends with Assyria's destruction of Samaria, Israel's capital (721 B.C.E.). With Israel reduced to a vassal state by Assyria, Judah now stands alone.

5. 2 Kings: Josiah's reforms. Portrayed as the ruler most devoted to YHWH since David, King **Josiah** (640–609 B.C.E.) takes advantage of Assyria's decline to conduct a thorough reform of Judah's cult, centering all worship at the Jerusalem Temple, an innovation supported by the discovery of a "lost" book of *torah* (Deuteronomy). Despite his covenant loyalty, Josiah is killed by the invading Pharaoh Necho.

6. 2 Kings: Judah's fall to Babylon. After Josiah's death and Zedekiah's rebellion, the Babylonian ruler, Nebuchadnezzar, destroys Jerusalem, razes Solomon's Temple, and exiles Judah's upper classes to Babylon (587 B.C.E.).

---

and exile. Chapters 28–30 of Deuteronomy lay out this scenario in painful detail, no doubt reflecting the sense of collective shame and abandonment felt by the first generation of Israelite exiles living in Babylon after 587 B.C.E. By projecting the belief that they had only themselves to blame for the loss of their nation back to the era of their beginnings as a nation, Judahites in exile (or, more precisely, priestly authors and redactors) were able to impose on their recent and even on their more remote history a single, consistent view of their catastrophe — its causes and its consequences. (Box 11.1 summarizes major events in the DH.)

Two Editions of the Deuteronomistic History

Though scholars differ widely over who might have written and/or redacted the Deuteronomistic History — with some favoring a single author (like Jeremiah or his secretary, Baruch) and others preferring to speak of a school or circle of priestly writers — most are in agreement that the process by which this history was put together proceeded through at least two stages. The earliest version of the DH seems to have been composed during the

Figure 11.1   This portion of the so-called Temple Scroll spells out some of the rights and obligations of Israel's monarchy. Other parts of the scroll describe in detail the kings' responsibilities with regard to military and judicial issues and marriage. The Temple Scroll is believed to be either the Book of Deuteronomy or some portion thereof.

reign of Josiah (640–609 B.C.E.) to accompany (and presumably validate) the reforms undertaken by the king. Clearly, the Deuteronomistic author saw in Josiah the very model of a righteous king who had committed himself to YHWH "with all his heart, with all his soul, and with all his might" (2 Kings 23:25). He even insists that there has never been a king quite like him in Judah. Such high praise, and in language that explicitly echoes the Book of Deuteronomy, suggests a direct connection between the reformist agenda of the Josianic monarchy and the composition of the DH as its virtual manifesto, if only because of its largely negative view of the kings who precede and follow Josiah. Furthermore, the discovery of a scroll in the Temple that scholars now believe to be either the Book of Deuteronomy or some portion thereof serves to reinforce the belief that the period of Josiah's rule over Judah was the era in which the DH (which derives its fundamental assumptions from Deuteronomy) was composed (Figure 11.1).

By selecting those traditions that best conformed to his interpretation of history, the Deuteronomist (or the Deuteronomic school) was able to subdivide the history of Israel into essentially four distinct periods: the era of Moses and the Exodus, the time of the conquest of Canaan, the period of the judges, and the history of the monarchy. This schematization of Israel's past allowed the Deuteronomist to review the history of Israel's covenant relation in precise Deuteronomic terms. What emerges from this overview is a picture of Israel's response to YHWH that is at once linear and cyclical in nature. Seen in long perspective, Israel moves almost inexorably toward its collective tragedy as king after king displays indifference toward or contempt for the *torah* of YHWH, whether revealed at Sinai/Horeb to Moses or through a succession of prophets from Samuel to Malachi.

This downhill slide toward **apostasy** and immorality, however, is interrupted periodically by the appearance of a judge or a king who is obedient to

Figure 11.2 Like many cities throughout Canaan, Lachish was attacked repeatedly by invading armies. This Assyrian bas-relief from the royal palace at Nineveh realistically portrays the armies of Sennacherib laying siege to Lachish (701 B.C.E.). Although Lachish, along with forty-six other Judean towns, was totally demolished (2 Kings 23:18), Jerusalem miraculously survived the Assyrian invasion. Note the assault ramp built against Lachish's gates and the civilian inhabitants fleeing by a side exit (right), while three naked captives are impaled on pointed wooden stakes (lower center).

YHWH's will and who leads Israel toward repentance and a temporary reprieve from the effects of divine judgment. King David, in spite of his checkered past, becomes the archetype of such a leader, for, as long as David is true to YHWH's teachings, David and Israel prosper, conquering their enemies and moving closer to the ideal of a holy nation that YHWH has summoned them to become. Later, **Hezekiah** embodies many of the same virtues as David, purging Judah of its Canaanite religious symbols and practices (2 Kings 18) and placing his trust in YHWH and his appointed prophet, Isaiah. Hezekiah's devotion is sufficient to avert the disaster of an Assyrian invasion—which has already destroyed the northern kingdom—but the kings who follow Hezekiah are just as corrupt as their predecessors (and their counterparts in the northern kingdom); YHWH's hand is stayed, but only for a time (Figure 11.2).

Josiah's appearance on the scene, then, occurs at the end of a long sequence of royal failures, from Jeroboam through Manasseh, and from the northern kingdom of Israel to the southern kingdom of Judah. Furthermore, Josiah's early death (609 B.C.E.) in battle and the reversal of his policy of religious reform and renewal under the reign of Jehoiakim made necessary a revision of the earlier version of the DH. It was no longer possible to ar-

gue that the nation of Judah had at last found a descendant of David who would lead it back to a relationship of trust in and obedience to YHWH. From the perspective of a postexilic historian, it must have seemed that Israel's fate was sealed from the moment Josiah's movement to restore the covenant failed. And just as David once provided the archetype of royal devotion to YHWH, so Manasseh (Josiah's grandfather) became a prototype of the wicked king whose cruelty to his people and whose disloyalty to YHWH finally brought down irrevocable judgment on Judah:

> Surely this [the Babylonian Conquest] came upon Judah at the command of the LORD, to remove them out of his sight, for the sins of Manasseh, and for all that he had committed, and also for the innocent blood that he had shed; for he filled Jerusalem with innocent blood, and the LORD was not willing to pardon. (2 Kings 24:3–4)

This second, and more inclusive, version of the DH attributes an essentially tragic arc to Israel's history. Even though the very last entry in 2 Kings records the release of Jehoiachin from his Babylonian prison (2 Kings 25:27–28) in 562 B.C.E., the royal court and a significant portion of the Judahite priesthood and ruling class remain in exile, and the prophetic promise of restoration—both to the land of Judah and to God's favor — remains unfulfilled. Sixth-century-B.C.E. prophets like Ezekiel and Jeremiah did, in fact, provide a visionary sequel to this history, ultimately predicting not only a return of the Judahites to their land but a profound spiritual renewal as well, a new covenant of devotion and trust to replace the shattered covenant relationship with which the Deuteronomists conclude this history (see Jer. 31:31–36; Ezek. 37).

Kings, Priests, and Prophets

Because the final version of the Deuteronomistic History had to be embedded in a postexilic interpretive structure, a select number of themes dominates this narrative, themes that reflect an essentially critical view of two of Israel's central institutions: the monarchy and the priesthood. From its very inception, the monarchy is viewed with suspicion by the prophet-judge Samuel, whose warnings of a tyranny that will inevitably envelop the royal throne are borne out in almost every generation:

> These will be the ways of the king who will rule over you: he will take your sons and appoint them to his chariots and to be his horsemen, and to run before his chariots; and he will appoint for himself commanders of thousands and commanders of fifties, and some to plow his ground and to reap his harvest, and to make his implements of war and the equipment of his chariots. . . . He will take the best of your fields and vineyards and olive orchards and give them to his courtiers. . . . He will take one-tenth of your flocks, and you shall be his slaves. (1 Sam. 10–17; cf. Deut. 17:14–20)

This portrait of a despot-king could, of course, be Solomon in his later years (as some have suggested), or Rehoboam, or Ahab, or Manasseh, but it remains a type-figure that points to the essential corruptibility of the office itself. That personalities as gifted and as astute as David and Solomon could end their respective reigns under a cloud of personal guilt and apostasy suggests that there is something in the nature of royal power that turns heads and

hearts away from God. And even though 2 Samuel contains an account of a Royal Covenant, specific to the Davidic line, according to which the king of Israel enters into a singular and protective relation with God (2 Sam. 7:12–17), there is nothing in the cumulative history of the twin monarchies, north and south, that suggests a father–son bond between YHWH and the occupant of either throne. Quite the contrary, and repeated references in the books of Kings to monarchs who "did what was evil in the sight of YHWH"— most of them northern kings who promote foreign cults (see 1 Kings 12:25–33)— make clear that, for the Deuteronomists, the king is both a source and a microcosm of Israel's apostasies; as the king sins, so sin the people.

However, the corruption of the throne is matched by the arrogance and spiritual incompetence of the priesthood. Throughout the DH, priests and Levites are portrayed with remarkable consistency as generally deficient in both integrity and insight. **Eli,** for example, the officiating priest at the sanctuary at Shiloh in the opening chapters of 1 Samuel, epitomizes much that is wrong with the priestly class in his obtuseness and irresponsibility. When the grieving, childless Hannah prays with quiet fervor at the Tabernacle, Eli mistakenly assumes that she is drunk and bitterly scolds her, only to realize, a moment later, how wrong his judgment was. In an even more dramatic reversal scene, a "man of GOD" appears before Eli to denounce the corruption of Eli's sons and to predict their deaths, only to have that prophecy reaffirmed by the child Samuel, who places the blame for the sons' misbehavior directly on Eli himself (1 Sam. 12–14). Though Eli appears to accept this judgment against his house with an unusual degree of calm, when this prophecy is finally fulfilled, he falls off his chair in apparent shock and breaks his neck (1 Sam 4:17–18). This grotesque end for a weak and ineffectual leader provides one measure of how irrelevant to the spiritual welfare of Israel the priesthood finally becomes.

Even greater, however, is the moral failure of succeeding generations of priests in the eyes of the Latter Prophets, who continue the trajectory of the Deuteronomists' critique of the priesthood and who find both the Temple and those who worship there lacking in piety and remorse:

> Its priests have done violence to my teaching and have profaned my holy things; they have made no distinction between the holy and the common, neither have they taught the difference between the clean and the unclean, and they have disregarded my sabbaths, so that I am profaned among them. Its officials within it are like wolves tearing the prey, shedding blood, destroying lives to get dishonest gain. (Ezek. 22:26–27)

Because the priesthood does not serve as a counterweight to the sins of Israel's kings, the prophets have to bring the full scope of covenant faithlessness before the king and the people. Thus, it is Nathan alone who is able to confront David with the fact of his adultery with Bathsheba and his subsequent murder of Uriah (2 Sam. 12:1–14). For the Deuteronomists, it is the "true" prophet alone who constitutes the moral center of Israel's existence and who is often the only one in his generation to foresee the tragic consequences of Israel's betrayal of YHWH.

In the figure of Elijah, for example, we find the prototype of the Deuteronomic prophet whose mantic powers — he can foretell the coming of rain (1 Kings 18:41–45) and revive a seemingly dead child (1 Kings 17:17–24) — are more than matched by his moral indignation. He is precisely what Ahab describes him as being: the "troubler of Israel." As the nation's conscience (and YHWH's advocate), it is left to him to indict Ahab and Jezebel for their crimes and to challenge the people to abandon their local deities. For all Elijah's courage and steadfastness, however, neither he, nor his disciple Elisha, nor any of the Latter Prophets who follow them can stay Israel from its course of spiritual and political self-destruction. The DH invests the prophetic class with a retrospective stature that it does not appear to have possessed in reality, but it cannot disguise the fact of the prophets' collective failure to turn the kings of Israel and Judah from their moral or political folly or the common people from their apostasies.

The Sources of the History

Whether one regards the Deuteronomistic History as the work of a single postexilic author or of a school of author-redactors, this history clearly draws its data from a number of diverse sources:

- Stories related to the ark and its history (1 Sam. 2:12–17, 22–25; 4:1–7:1)
- A narrative cycle relating to Saul (1 Sam. 9:1–10:16; 10:27–11:15; 13:2–7, 15–23; 14:1–46)
- An apologetic account of David's rise to power (1 Sam. 18–20)
- A **Court History** relating stories from David's court and Solomon's accession to power (2 Sam. 9–1; 2 Kings 2)
- Oral traditions surrounding the prophets Elijah and Elisha (1 Kings 17–2 Kings 9)
- Royal archives containing accounts of the kings of Judah and Israel (1 Chron. 29:29–30)

In addition to these principal sources, allusions are made to the Book of Jashar (Josh. 10:13; 2 Sam. 1:18)—a collection of narrative poems whose stories run parallel to those from the conquest and early monarchy periods—and archival material the Deuteronomists evidently chose not to use directly. These titles are merely listed for us: the Book of the Acts of Solomon (1 Kings 11:41); the Book of the Annals of the Kings of Judah (1 Kings 14:29); and the Book of the Annals of the Kings of Israel (1 Kings 14:19–20).

On a more speculative level, one biblical scholar has argued recently that much of the narrative material found in the DH represents the work of the Yahwist (J) author whose accounts of the patriarchs and the Exodus constitute one of the major literary strands of the Pentateuch. According to this view, both a consistent historical perspective and vocabulary permeate large segments of Joshua through the early chapters of Kings, and this "hidden" narrative can be understood only as a part of an unfolding epic whose subject is the evolution of Israel from family to nation, culminating in the establishment of the Davidic monarchy and its triumph under Solomon. Though this thesis, admittedly, has few adherents, it does emphasize what all contemporary biblical scholars now recognize is the core placement of the DH within the Tanak and its function as the necessary framework for the prophetic writings that follow it.

QUESTIONS FOR REVIEW

1. The term *Former Prophets* refers to what portion of the Hebrew Bible? What kinds of books are found among the Former Prophets?

2. Why do biblical scholars use the term *Deuteronomistic History* to refer to the books from Joshua to Kings? What interpretation of Israel's history do these books offer?

QUESTIONS FOR REFLECTION AND DISCUSSION

1. Why is the prevailing view of the monarchy in the Deuteronomistic History so negative? After all, not all of Israel's kings were worshipers of Baal, and some of its more distinguished kings — such as David, Solomon, and Josiah — appear to have been quite committed to the service of YHWH and are believed to have written some of Israel's sacred literature.

2. Why would postexilic readers of the Deuteronomistic History have derived a sense of both historical closure and promise from reading these books? Wouldn't the Deuteronomic view of history have left them in a state of total depression, having found in their own sinfulness the cause of Israel's downfall?

TERMS AND CONCEPTS TO REMEMBER

apostasy	Hezekiah
conquest of Canaan	Josiah
Court History	judges
Deuteronomistic	David
History (DH)	Saul
Eli	Solomon

RECOMMENDED READING

Doorly, William J. *Obsession with Justice: The Story of the Deuteronomists.* New York: Paulist Press, 1994.

Friedman, Richard E. *The Hidden Book in the Bible.* London: Profile Books, 1999.

———. *Who Wrote the Bible?* New York: Harper & Row, 1987.

McKenzie, Steven L. "Deuteronomistic History." In D. N. Freedman, ed., *The Anchor Bible Dictionary,* Vol. 2, pp. 160–168. New York: Doubleday, 1992.

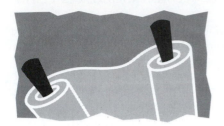

CHAPTER 12

The Origins of Israel
The Book of Joshua

Key Topics/Themes No topic related to the Hebrew Bible has been more hotly debated than the admittedly speculative origins of the Israelites and their culture. The Book of Genesis, of course, is clear on the subject of Israel's ancestry, tracing its beginnings back to the patriarchs Abraham, Isaac, and Jacob, and deriving its collective name from the divinely bestowed "covenant" name of the last of those patriarchs (*Yisra-El*, "one who struggles with El"). Crucial to Israel's self-understanding, and to the biblical portrait of who the Israelites really were, is the conviction that, however nomadic the life habits of their remote ancestors, the people of Israel (who only rarely referred to themselves as "Hebrews") were the rightful possessors of the land of Canaan and that their conquest of Canaanite territories during the early Iron Age was, in their view, a *reconquest* after a long period of slavery in Egypt (Figure 12.1).

The Historical Origins of Ancient Israel

In many ways, Israel's destiny was shaped by its geography. Situated on a land bridge between Mesopotamia, Asia Minor, and Africa, Israel saw its territory overrun by armies of the far more powerful civilizations that surrounded it and found itself swallowed up by a succession of mighty empires: the Assyrian, the Babylonian, the Medo-Persian, the Macedonian Greek, and, finally, the Roman. Had Israel been placed anywhere else, far from the crossroads of international commerce and imperialism, it might have escaped the devastation and exile that was its fate. Two major highways traversed Israelite territory: the "way of the sea" (Isa. 8:23), which extends north along the Mediterranean coastline through Megiddo and Hazor to Damascus, and the "King's Highway" (Num. 21:22), which branches off toward Mesopotamia. These were the principal routes followed by both armies and caravans, and the mountainous terrain of much of the land of Israel and Transjordan made it impossible to travel long distances by any other network of roads.

THE GEOGRAPHY OF PALESTINE

This comparatively narrow strip of land (approximately 150 miles long and 70 miles wide) is referred to in the Hebrew Bible as the "land of YHWH," the "land of Israel," and the "good land," but most often as the "land of Canaan" or the "land of the Canaanites." Greek geographers assigned the name **Palestine** to the entire country—naming it after the Philistines who occupied the Mediterranean coast at about the same time as the Israelites settled inland—and it is the Greek name that is commonly used to describe the region. Viewed topographically,

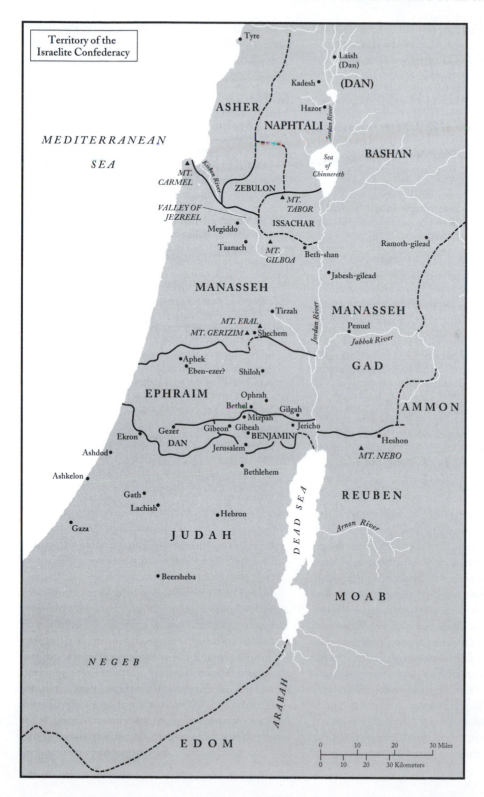

Figure 12.1 Map of the Israelite Confederacy
Traditionally, Israelite territory extended from Dan (Laish) to Beersheba in the south.

Territory of the Israelite Confederacy

Tyre

Laish (Dan)

Kadesh

ASHER

(DAN)

Hazor

NAPHTALI

MEDITERRANEAN SEA

Sea of Chinnereth

BASHAN

Jordan River

MT. CARMEL

Kishon River

ZEBULON

MT. TABOR

VALLEY OF JEZREEL

ISSACHAR

Megiddo

MT. GILBOA

Ramoth-gilead

Taanach

Beth-shan

Jabesh-gilead

MANASSEH

Tirzah

MANASSEH

MT. EBAL

Penuel

MT. GERIZIM   Shechem

Jabbok River

Aphek

Eben-ezer?

Shiloh

GAD

EPHRAIM

Ophrah

Bethel

Gilgah

AMMON

Mizpah

Gezer

Gibeon   Gibeah   Jericho

Ekron

DAN

BENJAMIN

Heshon

Ashdod

Jerusalem

MT. NEBO

Ashkelon

Bethlehem

Gath

REUBEN

Lachish

DEAD SEA

Gaza

Hebron

Arnon River

JUDAH

Beersheba

MOAB

NEGEB

ARABAH

EDOM

0   10   20   30 Miles

0   10   20   30 Kilometers

Palestine is divided into four rather distinct regions, each with its own climate and geological peculiarities. Moving from west to east, the first region one encounters is the coastal plain, a narrow strip of land between 20 and 30 miles wide. This is the part of Palestine that most travelers would have seen as they passed along the coastal highway between Mesopotamia and Egypt. The next region consists of low foothills, referred to in the south as the Shephelah. This hilly range is broken in the north by the plain of Megiddo, and, together with the valley of Jezreel to the east, it forms a greenbelt of arable land. These uplands can rise to a height of over 3000 feet and then drop steeply as one moves eastward into the next geographical zone, a rift valley that runs the length of the entire region. It is within this geological fault zone that one finds the Jordan River, which rises in the Sea of Galilee in the north and flows 65 miles southward to the Dead Sea, a huge saltwater lake that lies 1290 feet below sea level — the lowest point on the earth's surface. The fourth and final region, referred to as Transjordan, is a mountainous area with deep canyons and steeply ascending plateaus.

The varied geography of this region had several consequences for the people who occupied it. Differences in rainfall and arability of land meant that only certain areas were suitable for farming or for grazing; a large cities were located mainly in the central hill country. Viewed from a cultural and political perspective, however, the most important division of this territory was the north-south, which became formalized in 922 B.C.E. after the once-united kingdom of David and Solomon split into two rival kingdoms, Israel in the north, and Judah in the south. Tensions between these two Israelite kingdoms continued until the destruction of the northern kingdom at the hands of the Assyrians in 721 B.C.E., at which point some portion of the northern population fled south while the rest were either deported or scattered to neighboring regions or were killed in the fighting that preceded the fall of the northern kingdom. From a southern perspective, the kings of the north, and the religious practices they encouraged, represented "evil in the sight of YHWH," and their destruction was seen as

fit punishment for repeatedly flouting the will of God — a judgment that was, of course, later applied to the kingdom of Judah as well. Seen from a non-Deuteronomic (and certainly more secular) point of view, the survival of the two kingdoms as independent political entities was bound to be short-lived, given the fact that, whatever their moral or religious character, both lay in the path of advancing and more powerful armies.

THE COVENANT LAND

The geography and even the human history of the land, however, are only a part of the story, for biblical writers had another, often idealized and explicitly theological, view of the land of Canaan/Israel that transcended questions of climate, topography, and natural resources:

> For the LORD your GOD is bringing you into a good land, a land with flowing streams, . . . a land of wheat and barley, of vines and fig trees and pomegranates, a land of olive trees and honey, a land where you may eat bread without scarcity, where you will lack nothing, a land whose stones are iron and from whose hills you may mine copper. You shall eat your fill and bless the LORD your GOD for the good land that he has given you. . . .
>
> Do not say to yourself, "My power and the might of my own hand have gotten me this wealth." But remember the LORD your GOD, for it is he who gives you power to get wealth, so that he may confirm his covenant that he swore to your ancestors, as he is doing today. If you do forget the LORD your GOD and follow other gods to serve and worship them, I solemnly warn you today that you shall surely perish. Like the nations that the LORD is destroying before you, so shall you perish, because you would not obey the voice of the LORD your GOD. (Deut 8:7–20)

Fundamental to the biblical understanding of the relationship of Israel to the land it occupied was the belief that the land, with all its goodness, was a "gift" from YHWH that, like the covenant of which it was a part, was given on condition of service and loyalty. The Hebrew term most often used to define the nature of this gift is *nahalah*, meaning either "portion" or "inheritance." Whichever specific meaning one assigns to this word, it clearly presupposes that Canaan was not "won" by the Israelites through feats of arms but, rather, given to them as an act of generosity by YHWH and in remembrance of the loyalty of the patriarchs. What follows from this conviction was the often-repeated assumption that Israel would continue to reside upon the land "flowing with milk and honey" only as long as YHWH permitted it, and whatever entitlement the Israelites imagined they had to this land, it could easily be taken away by the very God who had bestowed this territory upon them in the first place.

Expressions of this belief vary. In Leviticus 25, for example, where the laws governing the Sabbatical and Jubilee years are explained, YHWH is quoted as saying, "The land shall not be sold in perpetuity, for the land is mine; with me you are but aliens and tenants" (25:23). Deuteronomy 28 elaborates on this thesis even more ominously by threatening dispossession and exile from the land as just punishment for Israel's breaking of the covenant; Israel has no "right" to the land if YHWH will not ratify that right, and the Israelites' betrayal of him certainly nullifies any earlier promises made to them at Sinai/Horeb. The prophets echo this Deuteronomic perspective, arguing, quite consistently, that if YHWH can "summon" the Israelites out of captivity in Egypt, settling them securely in their own land, then he can just as surely send them back again as punishment:

> When Israel was a child, I
>   loved him,
> and out of Egypt I called my son.
> The more I called them,
>   the more they went from me;
> they kept sacrificing to the Baals,
>   and offering incense to idols . . .
> They shall return to the land of
>   Egypt,
>   and Assyria shall be their king,
> because they have refused to
>   return to me. (Hos. 11:1–5)

Possession of the land, like nationhood itself, is therefore contingent (as are all things) upon divine judgment. Given the generally tragic course of Is-

rael's history, its loss of both land and nationhood can be understood by biblical writers only in conformity with the inexorable logic of the Deuteronomistic History.

Yet, for all of Israel's uncertain tenure in the land, both the divine promise and the human expectation of restoration to that land — in spite of exile and military defeat — remain recurrent themes of prophetic literature. From Amos through Malachi, Israel is assured that YHWH will not entirely abandon them, that their exile will not last forever, and that, at the very least, a "remnant" of the Diaspora will return to a rebuilt and spiritually restored Judah. In what is perhaps one of the most poignant and evocative prophetic images of return, Jeremiah compares the land of Israel to the matriarch Rachel, longing for the return of her exiled "children":

> A voice is heard in Ramah,
>   lamentation and bitter weeping.
> Rachel is weeping for her children;
>   she refuses to be comforted for
>   her children,
>   because they are no more.
> Thus says the LORD:
> Keep your voice from weeping,
>   and your eyes from tears; . . .
>   they shall come back from the
>   land of the enemy;
>   there is hope for your future,
>   says the LORD:
> your children shall come back to
>   their own country. (Jer. 31:15–17)

What is sometimes called the "territorial dimension" of the covenant — the belief that Israel's attachment to the land is as enduring as God's love — is the theological assumption that stands behind this passage and many others like it. It may appear contradictory for any prophet to argue, on the one hand, that Israel has no entitlement or "right of possession" to the land and that, in fact, it will be driven from its land on account of its sins, while, on the other, to proclaim that Judah will inevitably be restored. But this is precisely the core of the prophetic message with respect to the exile and all that follows from it. What we are witnessing here is the emergence of an essentially *dialectical* view of

Israel's covenant relationship to both YHWH and to that portion of the Fertile Crescent that he set aside for his "kingdom of priests." Like any dialectic, it is an argument that attempts to juxtapose (and perhaps reconcile) two apparently opposing points of view. The dialectic of land theology, then, is simply one expression of the persistent biblical belief that the covenant itself is, at heart, a relationship of unconditional (and therefore redemptive) love, amid all the uncertainties of history and the predictable catastrophes of national life.

Given Israel's comparatively brief history as a nation, and its often complex and dialectical view of both its past and its future in Palestine, it is hardly surprising, then, that modern Near Eastern scholarship has raised some troubling questions regarding the authenticity of the "constructed" history and the extent to which contemporary archaeology and social science can verify Israel's historical claims to land and nationhood. In fact, biblical authors provide claims that seem to rest entirely on theological presuppositions.

The Israelites and Their Land

BIBLICAL VERSUS SCHOLARLY ACCOUNTS

From time to time, biblical writers offer an alternative scenario of Israel's origins that is strikingly different from the "official" account found in the books of Exodus through Joshua. Ezekiel, for example, chides the Israelites in God's name and describes them as a nation of multinational foundlings:

> Canaan is the land of your ancestry and there you were born; an Amorite was your father and a Hittite your mother. . . . Then I came by and saw you kicking helplessly in your own blood; I spoke to you, there in your blood, and bade you live. (Ezek. 16:3–6)

Even the Deuteronomist, while rehearsing the Exodus story (in what appears to be a liturgical formula), still refers to Israel's ancestors as "homeless Arameans" (Deut. 26:5) — evoking an image of unsettled nomadism that is at odds with the Genesis

account of a more sedentary pattern of territorial occupation. But numerous biblical texts make reference to Israel's kinship connection to the Edomites (going back to the time of Jacob and Esau [Gen. 25:27–34]), suggesting a largely unacknowledged history of close and enduring relationships (as well as conflicts) with a people indigenous to this territory. None of these variant traditions, of course, is compatible with the Exodus/conquest story.

Over the past generation, biblical archaeologists and social historians have placed less and less credence in the scriptural account of Israel's return from Egypt and its resettlement of the land once supposedly promised to Abraham and his descendants. Scholars have repeatedly noted the striking similarities between the material culture of the Israelites (for example, their domestic architecture and pottery) and that of their Canaanite neighbors, as well as shared linguistic and religious traditions. And many scholars have come to the conclusion that the idea of Israel, prior to the establishment of the Davidic monarchy, was just that: an *idea* — or, more precisely, an ideological construct designed to legitimate the dynastic and territorial claims of later Israelite kings. It should not surprise us, then, to read that the people of Israel continued to worship an array of Canaanite deities right up to the last stages of the Babylonian conquest of Judah. The so-called Israelites were, it is argued, really Canaanites by another name, or at the least, so assimilated to Canaanite culture that it is virtually impossible now to distinguish an Israelite settlement from a Canaanite village or to separate the Israelite worship of YHWH from the cult of Baal (see Chapter 13). Any sharp separation of the Israelites from the society and culture of their Canaanite neighbors — based on the adversarial relationship that biblical literature records — is thus a form of postexilic revisionism rather than authentic history.

RIVAL THEORIES OF ISRAEL'S ORIGINS

To date, three distinct and often competing perspectives on the history of early Israel have emerged, each offering an interpretation of archaeological and literary data that differs markedly from the biblical account:

- The conquest model
- The peaceful infiltration model
- The social revolution model

The first of these models (or historical reconstructions of Israel's beginnings) is the most conservative, in that it argues for a residue of authentic historical memory in the biblical narratives of the Exodus and the conquest. After all, it is argued, archaeologists have found extensive evidence of destruction at such late–Bronze Age cities as Hazor, Bethel, and Lachish; why not assume, then, that this devastation was directly linked to an Israelite invasion of Canaan sometime during the late thirteenth or early twelfth century B.C.E.? Even if the conquest of Jericho cannot be confirmed, and Egyptian literature makes no mention of the sudden departure of hundreds of thousands of former slaves, something like the Exodus and the conquest could conceivably have occurred on a much smaller scale. As for the conquest narrative, confirmation of at least an Israelite military presence in Canaan can be found in the Merneptah stele, or victory stone (1209 B.C.E.), where Israel is referred to by name, although identified as a people rather than as a city-state. Surely that alone is sufficient proof of Israel's cultural and political distinctness, if only in the eyes of Egyptian authorities (see Chapter 3). Of course, what the Merneptah stele cannot account for is Israel's supposed departure from Egypt sometime earlier.

Advocates of the peaceful infiltration model (sometimes referred to as the immigration model) posit a very different scenario. Why, they ask, would a successful invasion of Canaan by Israelite forces lead, shortly thereafter, to an Israelite retreat to the highlands, away from the more fertile lowlands and from the major cities the Bible claims they overran? Suppose nothing like the conquest of Canaan ever took place, and instead, diverse nonindigenous peoples (some of whom may well have come from Egypt) gradually migrated to this territory. This would explain why Israelite pottery looks so much like Canaanite pottery and why the Israelites read-

ily adopted Canaanite words like *El* and *Elohim* to describe their deity; these are just so many signs of acculturation and assimilation.

This account of Israel's gradual assimilation to Canaanite culture and politics not only explains the enduring popularity of Canaanite gods like Baal and Asherah among the Israelite masses but also helps to explain Israel's extraordinary disunity during the period of the judges, as well as the deep ambivalence toward the monarchy among its tribal leaders. After all, why would a loose alliance of miscellaneous peoples want a strong centralized leadership? And if the people we call Israel had any connection to the outlaw nomads the Egyptians called the *shasu*—some of whom settled in Canaan—then the Exodus/conquest story may have some remote and mythologically transformed relation to the wanderings and plunderings of this outcast community.

The social revolution (or revolt) model represents the most radical departure from the biblical account and the most controversial of the three theories. This theory proposes that we not only set aside the biblical version of Israel's origins but also invert it and attempt to trace Israel's emergence as a nation in the course of the early Iron Age solely in relation to the internal dynamics of Canaanite society. For supporters of this position, the Israelites (or "proto-Israelites," to be more precise) were actually a composite of various indigenous Canaanite peoples who shared a common alienation from the feudal aristocracy that governed Canaan during a period of declining Egyptian influence. Some of these Canaanite revolutionaries are referred to in the Amarna letters as *Hapiru*, whom the Egyptians saw merely as bandits (and sometimes employed as mercenaries), but who may well have constituted a class of rebellious city-dwellers and peasant farmers who attacked several Canaanite cities from within as well as without. Exactly why this aggregate of Canaanite dissidents would have wanted to identify themselves collectively as former Egyptian slaves, worshiping YHWH, a nonindigenous deity, is far from clear. But this theory does at least offer a plausible explanation for later Israelite antimonarchism: The very idea of monarchy was anathema to the populist, egalitarian revolutionaries who dominated this community of breakaway Canaanites (cf. 1 Sam. 8:10–18). As for marked similarities between Canaanite and Israelite material culture, what else would one expect from a community that was historically and ethnically Canaanite? Moreover, the rapid decline of Egyptian control over Canaan following the death of Rameses III in 1153 B.C.E. would certainly have made it easier for a peasant uprising to succeed, particularly if the catalyst for that revolt was the development of a new religious cult, the cult of YHWH.

At present, none of these models provides a complete and consistent explanation for the often-fragmentary material evidence that contemporary archaeology has unearthed, and, as a consequence, each of these models entails a great deal of sheer conjecture. Even today, relatively little is known about Canaanite demographics, such as the ethnic/cultural composition of peoples within Canaan, or about the movements of these people within or outside this territory. Nor is it possible to speak with absolute conviction about Israel's relation to either the Midianites, nomadic traders and shepherds, or the Sea Peoples, who invaded the region from the west beginning in the thirteen century B.C.E. If recent archaeological speculations are correct, then the tribe of Dan may well represent an offshoot of Philistine culture, thus presenting us with an even more complex (and composite) picture of emergent Israelite society. Two large questions, then, concerning Israel's origins remain partly unanswered: Why and how did those communities that later called themselves the *bene yisrael* come to embrace a complex blend of nomadism and liberation? and When did they decide to commit themselves (however half-heartedly) to the worship of a singular deity whose most sacred site is located somewhere in the Sinai Peninsula? If, as the social revolution theory asserts, the Israelites were actually a subset of Canaanite society, then what could have motivated them to identify themselves as former slaves or to serve a god as foreign, as demanding, and as elusive as YHWH, when Baal and Asherah were still, evidently, held in awe by the "Israelite" masses? However inadequate the conquest model must seem when viewed against a backdrop of early–Iron Age archaeology and social history, it still explains, with remarkable simplicity, how and why the Israelites insisted on seeing themselves as a people who dwelt apart. What the conquest model cannot provide, however, is the equivalent of footprints in the sand.

The Book of Joshua

In the canonical order of the Hebrew Bible, the Book of Joshua is the sixth book, coming immediately after the Book of Deuteronomy and continuing the story of the Exodus after the death of Moses. From the perspective of contemporary biblical scholarship, however, it makes more sense to view Joshua as the first book of a larger literary unit commonly referred to as the Deuteronomistic History (DH). This "history," described at length in the previous chapter, tells the story of Israel's emergence as a nation and its ultimate destruction. Underlying this history is one fairly simple thesis: Israel's fate and its covenant with God are one and the same. As long as Israel upholds the covenant, it prospers and its enemies are defeated; the moment it abandons the covenant, however, its downfall becomes inevitable. All of the historians whose books make up the DH appear to have embraced this view — as do virtually all of the prophets — and the classic statement of this thesis is to be found, naturally, in Deuteronomy:

> If you forget the LORD your GOD and adhere to other gods, worshipping them and bowing down to them, I give you a solemn warning this day that you will certainly be destroyed. You will be destroyed because of your disobedience to the LORD your GOD, as surely as were the nations whom the LORD destroyed at your coming. (Deut. 8:19–20)

The Book of Joshua stresses the positive dimension of Israel's relation to YHWH by demonstrating in battle after battle how obedience to the divine will ensures fulfillment of the very promises made earlier to both the patriarchs and to Moses: promises of nationhood and of secure settlement in the "land flowing with milk and honey."

THE CONQUEST OF CANAAN AS COVENANT FULFILLMENT

It should not surprise us, then, to find a persistent emphasis on Israel's responsiveness to divine imperatives in Joshua. Indeed, from the very first page of this book, the author presents God in dialogue with Joshua, assuring him that, if he is "resolute" in his devotion to the *torah* of Moses, every promise made to him will be fulfilled. What follows, then, is a series of conquest narratives in which God's initial promise to Joshua ("every place where you set your foot is yours" [Josh. 1:3]) is realized step-by-step. Whatever the historical reality behind Israel's invasion of Canaanite territory may have been, the author of Joshua has no doubt that the conquest was both swift and divinely ordained:

> Thus the LORD gave Israel all the land which he had sworn to give their forefathers; they occupied it and settled in it. The LORD gave them security on every side as he had sworn to their forefathers. Of all their enemies not a man could withstand them; the LORD delivered all their enemies into their hands. (Josh. 21:43–44)

There are, of course, a few exceptions to this general rule — the city of Jerusalem, for example, remains in Canaanite hands (Josh. 15:63) — but the overall impression one gets from Joshua (in sharp contrast to the Book of Judges) is that the invasion of Canaan proceeded more or less smoothly and that, by the end of this campaign, practically all of the tribes and their constituent clans had established themselves in a defensible territory. When Israel fails, at first, to overrun a region or conquer a particular town (see Josh. 7, the battle for 'Ai), it does so only because it has temporarily lapsed into a condition of disobedience and has, for a time, forfeited the right to divine protection.

THE CONQUEST AND HOLY WAR

The extent to which God is prepared to go in support of the Israelite army is illustrated by two of the best-known conquest stories: the destruction of **Jericho** and the defeat of the Amorites at **Gibeon** (Figure 12.2). At Jericho, the Israelites do not have

Figure 12.2   The world's "oldest walled town," Jericho was first occupied by prehistoric settlers about 9000 B.C.E. The round tower, twenty-five feet high, dates from the earliest Neolithic (New Stone Age) period (8000–7000 B.C.E.). Erosion has removed most of Jericho's remains from the late Bronze Age period, the time of Israel's invasion of Canaan described in the Book of Joshua (c. 1200 B.C.E.).

to lay siege to the city walls. Instead, seven priests march in front of the Ark of the Covenant, making a circuit of the city on seven successive days, blowing ram's horns as they march. On the seventh day, this ceremony is repeated seven times, culminating in a collective shout by the men of the Israelite army, whereupon the walls of Jericho collapse (Josh. 6:2–20). In an even more extravagantly supernatural way, the battle for Gibeon is won when Joshua commands the sun and moon to "stand still" (10:12–13) until Israelite forces have had enough time to pursue and annihilate their enemies. That "the LORD fought for Israel" (10:14) is evident not only from the completeness of the victory but also from the fact that "not a man of the Israelites suffered so much as a scratch on his tongue" (10:21).

As in the Exodus account of Israel's defeat of the Amalekites (Exod. 17:8–16), divine intercession or the supernatural empowerment of a leader, or both, are the indispensable elements of military victory. Such is the concept of "holy war" that Israel and its neighbors evidently embraced, and however repugnant this concept may seem to many modern readers, it represents an important corollary to the fundamental biblical belief that YHWH was the Lord of history.

The idea of holy war, as presented in Joshua and other Deuteronomistic writings, carries with it both a rationalization for annihilating one's foes and a rigorous code of military etiquette that places under a sacred **herem** (ban) all persons and valued objects associated with the enemy. The initial failure to capture **'Ai** makes abundantly clear just how severe divine judgment against Israel can be when the rule of *herem* is ignored. A Judahite named Achan takes a shawl and some silver and gold as booty; when his crime is uncovered, he and his family, and even his flocks, are themselves placed under a *herem* and stoned to death, clearly with the intent of removing this stain of covenant disobedience from the rest of the Israelite nation. That this rule could be relaxed, however, is clear both from the tale of the Gibeonites, who convince Israelite leaders that they have come from a distant land and so do not fall into the lethal category of "neighbors" (Josh. 9:3–27), and from the later account of the destruction of Hazor, where booty is taken rather than destroyed (11:14).

Nevertheless, the idea that YHWH is prepared to annihilate Israel's enemies, and ultimately all of the world's great empires, is deeply embedded in texts that portray YHWH as a warrior-god (Exod. 15:3) and lives on in the pages of later prophetic and apocalyptic literature. In Joshua, this idea assumes particularly graphic form in the battle for Gibeon (Ch. 10), where YHWH appears to fight alongside the Israelite armies, hurling down huge hailstones that crush the opposing forces (10:11). Even the "Anakim," described in the Book of Numbers as "giants" who so intimidated the Israelite spies that they felt like "grasshoppers" (13:33), are either driven out of the land or annihilated, as YHWH finally makes good on his promise to the patriarchs to set aside the land of Canaan as Israel's patrimony (Josh. 11:22–23).

JOSHUA AS A SECOND MOSES

At the helm of Israel's advancing forces, is Joshua, Moses' one-time assistant and divinely appointed successor. In many ways, Joshua is more successful than his predecessor, winning battle after battle and enjoying the full support of the Israelite tribes. For all that, however, the author chooses to represent Joshua as a small-scale replica of Moses, one whose life experiences parallel those of his mentor. Like Moses, Joshua is commissioned directly by God, both as a military commander and a covenant bearer, and he is repeatedly warned (in familiar Deuteronomic language) to keep the words of the Law on his lips and in his mind. He, too, is allowed to pass miraculously through a body of water—this time the Jordan River—while the Ark of the Covenant is being carried at the head of the procession (Josh. 3–4). He is also privileged to speak with an angelic warrior who cautions him to take off his sandals because he is standing on holy ground (5:13–15); once again, we are looking at a scene that is reminiscent of the commissioning of Moses in Exodus 3.

Joshua's action after the victory at 'Ai, where he continues to hold out his dagger until the battle is over, looks suspiciously like a duplication of Moses' victory posture during the battle with the Amalekites (where Moses held his hands aloft), and at the conclusion of this episode, Joshua engraves in stone a copy of the "law of Moses" (8:32). When old age overtakes him, Joshua summons the tribal leaders to appear before him at Shechem (Ch. 24), whereupon he delivers a farewell address in miniature, in obvious imitation of Moses' farewell discourses in Deuteronomy. After briefly reviewing the history of Israel's covenant with YHWH, Joshua then calls the people to witness against themselves that they have freely chosen to worship the God of the Exodus, and even goes so far as to draw up a body of statutes to be included in the "book of the law of God" (24:26); shortly thereafter, he dies. This replay of the final episodes of Deuteronomy is designed, of course, to make a critical point: Just as Moses began the process of revealing and implementing God's *torah* to Israel, so Joshua will complete that process, realizing all of the unfulfilled promises — for example, the conquest and distribution of the land of Canaan — that Moses was unable to fulfill during his lifetime. The continuity of the covenant drama is therefore preserved by having a previously minor character assume a major role.

THE CONQUEST AND ARCHAEOLOGY

The historicity of the conquest narratives has long been in question, and contemporary archaeology generally views the Israelite invasion as presented in Joshua with skepticism. If one assumes (as most historians do today) that the Exodus was a thirteenth-century-B.C.E. event, then the physical evidence for Israel's sudden appearance in Canaan at the end of that century or the beginning of the twelfth century is both sparse and ambiguous. Excavated sites like Hazor and Debir apparently witnessed significant destruction during this era, though there is no conclusive evidence that this devastation was the result of an "Israelite" incursion. Elsewhere, evidence of armies overrunning fortified cities is either undiscovered or nonexistent. This is particularly true of Jericho, where extensive excavations have turned up no sign of fortifications or of any significant concentration of city-dwellers. As for 'Ai — whose name means "ruin" — it appears to have been uninhabited throughout most of the second millennium B.C.E., and the story of its capture and destruction looks suspiciously like an etiological narrative designed to explain the meaning and origin of the city's name.

What archaeologists can affirm about this era, however, is that, during the late Bronze Age, biblical Canaan and Transjordan saw a relatively sudden increase in the number of small, unfortified villages throughout this territory. No one can state for sure how many of these farming communities were actually populated by Israelites. The Book of Judges provides a very different picture of Israelite political fortunes after the death of Joshua, and the Book of Joshua seems to offer a rather idealized portrait of

Figure 12.3   Some archaeologists believe that this monolith may be the stone that Joshua erected at Shechem to hear and bear witness to YHWH's covenant with Israel (Josh. 24:26–28). Located forty-one miles north of Jerusalem between Mount Ebal and Mount Gerizim, Shechem was an ancient Canaanite sanctuary that became the first religious center of Israel's tribal confederacy.

the early years of the conquest, perhaps as a didactic prologue to the far more pessimistic interpretation of Israel's plight that dominates Judges and 1 Samuel.

One of the more speculative (and intriguing) interpretations of the conquest, one that finds in Joshua 24 a clue to the complex identity of the Israelite tribes, focuses on the covenant renewal ceremony at **Shechem** (Figure 12.3). Instead of viewing Israel as a single, homogeneous social and cultural unit, this theory finds two historically and religiously distinctive communities: one loyal to the Canaanite god El and the other committed to a desert deity named YHWH. These two segments of what will ultimately become the composite group known as Israel—the Elohist and the Yahwist—finally converge in Shechem under Joshua's charismatic leadership and swear loyalty to YHWH and his covenant. Even though the Elohist tribes are not likely to have actually experienced the Exodus, they now embrace that collective memory as their own. This may help to explain the extraordinary emphasis given to both circumcision and the observance of the Passover prior to the battle of Jericho, as well as the surprising tension that erupts between the Transjordanian tribes (Reuben, Gad, and Manasseh) and the rest of tribal Israel over the question of an altar (Josh. 22).

SOURCES FOR JOSHUA

The Book of Joshua contains a reference to a now-lost book titled the **Book of Jashar,** which may have served as one of the literary sources for Joshua, as well as for 2 Samuel. We cannot be certain about the contents of this book, or even the significance of its title—does it, for instance, mean the "Book of the Just," or is it simply a book written by a scribe named Jashar? However, based on the brief passages quoted in Joshua 10:12–13 and 2 Samuel 1:17–27, it would appear to have been a collection of war hymns and heroic narratives that focused on the period from Joshua through the early monarchy. Clearly, its popularity and religious authority were sufficient to allow the author(s) of Joshua to quote from it and then cite the source. This practice of quoting from or alluding to another text is not confined to the books of Joshua and Samuel; the Book of Numbers, for example, quotes from the Book of the Wars of the Lord (Num. 21:14–15), and 1 and 2 Kings repeatedly refer to collections of historical narratives known as the Annals of the Kings of Israel and the Annals of the Kings of Judah. Evidently, Deuteronomistic historians like the author of Joshua had multiple sources from which to derive primary or corroborative information about their subjects.

But of all the sources to which the author of Joshua might have turned, the most important must have been the Book of Deuteronomy—or at least a Deuteronomistic tradition from which a distinctive vocabulary and worldview could then be derived. In fact, the influence of Deuteronomistic thinking can be found everywhere in Joshua—from the prostitute **Rahab,** who has not only heard the story of the Exodus but also knows that "the LORD your GOD is GOD in heaven above and on earth below" (2:11), to the Gibeonites, who seem remarkably well informed about the details of Deuteronomy 20:10–18 and the protocol of peacemaking it lays out. More important, however, is the pervasive recognition in Joshua that the conquest of Canaan and Israel's tenure on the land it is about to occupy are covenant gifts from God that carry with them a reciprocal obligation of service and obedience to God's will. In the most explicit echo of Deuteronomic language imaginable, Joshua calls upon the tribes to choose whom they will serve—the gods of the "Amorites" or YHWH—with no possibility of syncretism or compromise (Josh. 24:14–15). The "either . . . or" logic of this concluding argument resonates throughout the DH and finally forms the basis of the exclusionary monotheism of the Latter Prophets, for whom YHWH alone is the proper object of Israel's worship and the sole guarantor of its continued existence.

QUESTIONS FOR REVIEW

1. What are the principal theories of Israel's origins, and how do they differ from one another? Which of these theories appears to be supported by the largest body of evidence?

2. What use does the Book of Joshua make of the Deuteronomic thesis that loyalty to YHWH ensures victory over one's foes?

QUESTION FOR REFLECTION AND DISCUSSION

How is our understanding of both the patriarchal and Exodus narratives affected by the possibility that ancient "Israel" was a composite social entity, made up of various ethnic groups, some of them Canaanite? How important is it that Moses and the Exodus be "real" (historically verifiable)?

TERMS AND CONCEPTS TO REMEMBER

'Ai
Book of Jashar
Gibeon
herem

Jericho
Palestine
Rahab
Shechem

RECOMMENDED READING

Boling, Robert G. *Joshua.* Garden City, N.Y.: Doubleday, 1982.

———. "Joshua, Book of." In D. N. Freedman, ed., *The Anchor Bible Dictionary,* Vol. 3, pp. 1002–1015. New York: Doubleday, 1992.

Dever, William G. *What Did the Biblical Writers Know and When Did They Know It? What Archeology Can Tell Us about the Reality of Ancient Israel.* Grand Rapids, Mich.: Eerdmans, 2001.

Finkelstein, Israel, and Siberman, Neil Asker. *The Bible Unearthed: Archeology's New Vision of Ancient Israel and the Origin of its Sacred Texts.* New York: Free Press, 2001.

Gottwald, Norman K. *The Tribes of Yahweh: A Sociology of the Religion of Liberated Israel, 1250–1050* B.C.E. Maryknoll, N.Y.: Orbis Books, 1979.

Gunn, David M. "Joshua and Judges." In Robert Alter and Frank Kermode, eds., *The Literary Guide to the Bible,* pp. 102–121. Cambridge, Mass.: Harvard University Press, 1987.

Isserlin, B. S. J. *The Israelites.* London: Thames & Hudson, 1998.

McDermott, John J. *What Are They Saying About the Formation of Israel?* Mahweh, N. J.: Paulist Press, 1998.

Soggin, J. Alberto. *Joshua.* Philadelphia: Westminster Press, 1972.

CHAPTER 13

YHWH's Warriors

The Book of Judges

Key Topics/Themes The Book of Judges marks a transition in the history of the conquest from success to failure, though, as with Joshua, its interpretation of events is entirely consistent with the Deuteronomistic view of Israel's fate and fortunes. With Joshua's death, the people of Israel find themselves without a centralized leadership or even a single personality whom everyone can look to for direction. The generations of the Exodus have indeed passed away, and now leadership devolves to the level of the tribe or clan. It is at this point that the figure of the "judge" (Hebrew, *shofet*) emerges. The biblical judge rarely exercises any of the powers or responsibilities of a modern jurist; Deborah, dispensing justice under her palm tree, is clearly the exception, not the rule. Most of the judges whose exploits are recorded for us are warriors whose charismatic ("spirit-filled") personalities and/or success on the battlefield evoke the respect and even devotion of their contemporaries. Not all of these figures have heroic tales associated with them; some are merely names mentioned in passing. The total number of judges, however, is twelve, which suggests to scholars an intent by the author of Judges to impose a schematic pattern, reflective of the number of tribes, upon the various accounts of localized warfare collected in this book.

The Book of Judges

MAJOR AND MINOR JUDGES

Viewed structurally, the Book of Judges has six developed narratives, each recounting the distinctive exploits of a particular figure. These are the "major" judges, as distinct from the "minor" figures, who are often little more than names on a page:

MAJOR JUDGES	Jephthah
Othniel	Samson
Ehud	MINOR JUDGES
Deborah	Shamgar (3:31)
Gideon	Tola (10:1–2)

Jair (10:3–5)	Elon (12:11–12)
Ibzan (12:8–10)	Abdon (12:13–15)

Almost all of these judges are "unattached" warriors who serve no one but themselves and YHWH. They are not associated with the tribal leadership or with any intertribal organization (similar to the **amphictyonies**, or "leagues" of city-states that existed in Greece) that scholars speculate may have come into being at this time. Gideon, in fact, does not appear to have been anything but a farmer when he was drafted into the service of YHWH, and, to make matters worse, he and his family seem to have been followers of Baal (hence, his "other" name, *Jerubbaal*, meaning "let Baal plead") (Figure 13.1). The autonomy, and even marginality, of these judges is clearly reflective of the progressive disintegration of political authority during the period from roughly 1200 to 1020 B.C.E. and gives added weight to the author's repeated observation that "in those days there was no king in Israel, and every man did what was right in his own eyes" (21:25).

A REVERSAL OF FORTUNES: JUDGES AS A HISTORICAL DOCUMENT

The Book of Judges opens with what appears to be a transitional account of territorial acquisition following the death of Joshua, as the Deuteronomistic historian offers a brief account of battles fought by the tribe of Judah, culminating in the capture and apparent destruction of Jerusalem (1:8), followed by further conquests as far south as the Negev. However, the landscape of near-total victory, laid out for us in Joshua, is quickly redrawn as tribe after tribe meets armed resistance that it cannot overcome. By the time we get to the exploits of the tribe of Benjamin, it becomes clear that Judah's earlier destruction of Jerusalem was either an exaggeration or a misrepresentation: The Jebusites continue to hold the city (1:21; once called **Jebus**), and Jerusalem will not fall into Israelite hands until David conquers it centuries later (2 Sam. 5:6–10). Israel's lightning invasion of Canaan has suffered a reversal, and the Israelites find themselves withdrawing to (or perhaps peaceably settling into) the more defensible highlands.

Although Deborah and Barak are forced to defend their territory against seemingly superior Canaanite forces (Judg. 4–5), the principal threat to Israelite hegemony over Canaan comes from outsiders and not from the indigenous population. For Ehud and his contemporaries, it is the **Moabites** (Ch. 3); for Gideon's generation, it is the **Midianites** and the **Amalekites** (Chs. 6–7). Jephthah and Samson struggle against the Ammonites and the **Philistines,** respectively (Chs. 11–16). This pattern of sporadic invasion, to which Israelite armies respond on an improvised and regional basis, is wholly consistent with the power vacuum that exists in Canaan following the death of Rameses III in 1153 B.C.E. and it certainly is compatible with Judges' ac-

Figure 13.1   This bronze statuette of a bull— seven inches long and five inches high—was found at a Palestinian cultic site dating from the period of Israel's judges (c. 1200 B.C.E.). Representing masculine strength and virility, the bull was commonly associated with both Baal and YHWH.

count of a politically decentralized Israelite society whose leadership exists only at the tribal level and that is ultimately beset by intertribal warfare. The decline of the late–Bronze Age city-state, which contemporary archaeologists have labored to document, provides a suitable backdrop for the gradual "ruralization" of Israel and the inevitable regional tensions that follow as the Israelites become geographically dispersed and politically fragmented. In sharp contrast, then, to the picture of intertribal unity and cooperation in Joshua, Judges provides us with a contrasting (and perhaps more historically reliable) account of Israel's often chaotic emergence as a nation from its tribal origins. At the same time, it gives us a more sobering view of the internal as well as external dynamics of this era, along with a potentially tragic reading of the often fragile relationship Israel enjoys with YHWH.

DEUTERONOMISTIC HISTORY AND THE CONQUEST

The Book of Judges frames its accounts of warfare and political turmoil with one simple and repetitive thesis, a theology of victory and defeat central to the entire Deuteronomistic History:

> Then the Israelites did what was wrong in the eyes of the LORD, and worshipped the Baals; and they abandoned the LORD, the GOD of their ancestors who had brought them out of the land of Egypt; they followed other gods, from among the gods of the peoples who were all around them, and bowed down to them; . . . So the anger of the LORD was kindled against Israel, and he gave them over to plunderers who plundered them; . . . Then the LORD raised up judges, who delivered them out of the power of those who plundered them. Yet they did not listen even to their judges; for they lusted after other gods and bowed down to them. . . . Whenever the LORD raised up judges for them, the LORD was with that judge, and he delivered them from the hand of their enemies all the days of the judge. . . . But whenever the judge died, they would relapse and behave worse than their ancestors, following other gods. . . . (Judg. 2:11–19)

Israel's fortunes, then, are to be understood as part of a cycle of covenant obedience and disobedience. God's need to be both compassionate and judgmental keeps the cycle going just as surely as does Israel's incapacity to remain loyal to YHWH for more than a generation. To be even more precise, what we witness in Judges is something like a spiral movement in history, whereby Israel's periodic sinfulness — its repeated failure to pass the "test" of covenant faithfulness that YHWH has set as the precondition of military victory — sinks it ever deeper into a condition of moral anarchy and alienation. The implication of this argument seems to be

that, given Israel's propensity for covenant breaking, something other than (and presumably more effective than) the charismatic leadership of the judges is needed if the covenant relationship is not to be lost forever. Exactly *what* that "something other" should be is left unanswered at the end of Judges, even as the story of Abimelech's localized "monarchy" (Ch. 9) leaves the reader in some doubt that a king is the answer to Israel's woes.

The Era of the Judges

It follows, then, that in each account we are given of a judge's exploits there are at least two concerns: How does God (at least temporarily) effect the redemption of a specific generation by utilizing the peculiar attributes of a particular warrior, and what is the aftermath of that redemptive act? In some narratives, the heroic "attribute" that enables the judge to rescue his or her people from oppression may be no more than raw courage and a skillful stroke of the sword. In the story of **Ehud,** left-handedness is also an asset in enabling him to approach the Moabite king Eglon and assassinate him. Just before Ehud draws his sword (presumably from his right side, where no one would expect to find it), he confides to Eglon, ironically, that he has "a word from God" (Judg. 3:20) to impart to him. What follows is a political murder framed as an act of divine judgment. In fact, all of the judges can be seen as carrying out God's will in battle, and no matter how flawed they may be as individual moral agents, their role in history is finally understood in Deuteronomistic terms.

DEBORAH AND JAEL

Of all of the judges, **Deborah** is the closest to what might be thought of as a figure of conventional religious authority. For one thing, she is not only a judge; she is also a "prophetess" (Hebrew, *isha n'viah*) and a person of sufficient esteem that a powerful general like **Barak** turns to her for support. With some irony, she warns Barak that their victory will be attributed to her and not to him—a risk that he is apparently willing to take to be assured of divine assistance in his engagement with Canaanite forces. Nor is she the only woman of her era to serve as an instrument of divine redemption. An even more obscure woman, named **Jael,** who is identified simply as the wife of Heber the Kenite (Judg. 4:17), is responsible for the death of the Canaanite general Sisera, and when she drives a tent peg through his head, she accomplishes what her male warrior counterparts could not. This inversion of gender roles is all the more remarkable because women are almost never associated in biblical literature with this kind of violence. The celebratory Song of Deborah that follows this incident in Chapter 5 elaborates on the previous chapter's account of this murder, focusing at last on the anguish and thwarted expectations of Sisera's mother, who awaits her son's triumphant return. What Deborah's song also reveals, however, is the dangerous uncertainty of intertribal cooperation in a time of crisis. Not only are the tribes disloyal to YHWH; they are also often indifferent, if not antagonistic, to one another.

GIDEON, ABIMELECH, AND JEPHTHAH

The Song of Deborah underscores another peculiar tendency of this period: the increasing fragmentation of Israelite society. While Deborah records (in a poem that is thought to be one of the oldest poetic compositions of the Hebrew Bible) the names of the tribes that came to her aid—Ephraim, Benjamin, Machir (a clan of Manasseh), Zebulun, and Issachar—she also chides those tribes that stayed away. Clearly, neither she nor any other judge can rely on assistance from any other tribe or region. In fact, after **Gideon** has completed his divinely assisted victory over the Midianites, it is all he can do to placate the warriors of Ephraim and assure them that he has no intention of excluding them from the glory of defending Israel against its enemies (Judg. 8:1–3). **Jephthah,** of course, is much less successful in defusing the anger of the Ephraimites,

and no sooner does he defeat the Ammonites in battle than he must defend himself against an assault from the Ephraimite army (12:1–6). Intertribal rivalries are threatening to destroy what little solidarity still exists among the Israelites, and once more we see the effects of the decentralization of power and authority following Joshua's death.

In some respects, both Gideon and Jephthah are among the unlikeliest of candidates for the role of judge in Israelite society. Gideon's family, as noted earlier, is a Baal-worshiping family; indeed, one of the first things God commands Gideon to do is to tear down the altar of Baal and the Asherah figure that stands beside it (much to the disgust of his neighbors!). As for Jephthah, he is the son of a prostitute, and his half-brothers deny him any portion of his father's patrimony. The only reason the Gileadites turn to him for help is that, in the interim, he has become a minor warlord. His peculiar vow, which ultimately entails the sacrifice of his virgin daughter, may seem on the surface to resemble Abraham's near-sacrifice of Isaac. In this instance, however, Jephthah is not responding to a divine commandment, nor need he have pronounced the vow at all to be assured of God's support for his campaign. Curiously, the text betrays no embarrassment over the sacrifice and even attempts to integrate the ceremony of mourning for Jephthah's daughter into the ritual cycle of Israelite worship (Judg. 11:40), though nowhere else in the Hebrew Bible is there a reference to such a practice, nor are any of the other judges inspired by the *ruach* (spirit) of YHWH to offer up human victims for sacrifice.

Abimelech may appear at first glance to be a less marginal figure than his father, Gideon, and certainly a much less disreputable figure than Jephthah; when he becomes "king" of Shechem, he is, in a sense, merely accepting an offer already made to his father in the previous chapter. However, Gideon rejects that offer decisively, because God alone is Israel's "ruler" (Judg. 8:24). Like Samuel after him, Gideon rejects the very idea of a monarchy grounded in some notion of "divine right," and Abimelech's conduct on assuming his throne (he slaughters seventy of his brothers) makes very clear his fundamental unfitness to rule. Neither heredity nor charismatic authority can provide assurance or continuity of leadership, and so each generation must rely on the deliverer YHWH sends to it, however problematic he (and sometimes she) may appear.

SAMSON AND DELILAH

There is surely no more problematic (or colorful) figure in Judges than **Samson,** yet of all the warrior figures we survey in this book, he is, paradoxically, the weakest. Samson's weakness is to be found not in his body, of course, but rather in his moral will, and in many ways he is the most tragic of all the figures we encounter in this book. His birth, like so many auspicious births in the Hebrew Bible, is heralded by an angel (or "man of God" as he is alternately identified [13:6]), who twice informs Manoah and his wife that the boy who is about to be born to them must be brought up as a **Nazirite.** In the Book of Numbers (6:1–21), the Nazirite vow—which entails not drinking wine, not eating forbidden food, not cutting one's hair, and not coming in contact with a corpse—is presented as a "term" vow of special ritual purity rather than as a lifelong condition. But in the Samson narrative, the hero's superhuman strength (presumably, a physical manifestation of charisma) is linked directly to the preservation of this vow and to the length of his hair. Samson's interest in Philistine women, however, surpasses his dedication to YHWH, and in a moment of weakness he yields to the repeated demands of his Philistine lover, **Delilah,** thus placing in her treacherous hands the means of his own destruction.

Some scholars see in the story of Samson a remnant of a solar myth—Samson's name in Hebrew, *Shimshon,* means "little sun"—and trace his rise and fall as a warrior to the rising and setting of the sun. Many scholars also find in Samson's biography a fairly explicit warning against exogamy: Marry a non-Israelite woman, the story seems to be saying, and a man can expect her to betray him to her kin sooner or later. What is abundantly clear, however, is that Samson's character flaws (like those of

Saul, still later) are the source of his undoing. Although he exacts a spectacular vengeance on the Philistines at the conclusion of his tale, he is of little use to his fellow Danites or to Israel generally during the span of his career.

The War Against Benjamin

Two later narratives, equally reflective of the turmoil of this era, round out the history of the judges. The first (Judg. 18) concerns an Ephraimite named Micah, who constructs a private shrine, complete with **teraphim** (or "household gods," as the term is commonly translated), and who then hires a wandering Levite to serve as the shrine's "priest." In the very next chapter, this same Levite is lured away by representatives of the tribe of Dan who are searching for some territory they can inhabit safely. That many of the tribes have not found a secure foothold within Canaan is evident throughout the Book of Judges, in obvious contradiction to the prevailing view of Joshua. The second episode, involving a different Levite, carries the theme of disorder and unrest to a new level of horror, as we witness a gang rape and murder committed in the town of **Gibeah,** in Benjamite territory. The entire incident seems to have been written about with a similar episode from Genesis 19 (the near-assault on Lot's house by the men of Sodom) in mind. But at the conclusion of this appalling crime, when the unnamed Levite discovers the body of his murdered concubine on the doorstep, yet another "crime" is committed against the woman as he dismembers her corpse and sends a portion of it to every tribe in Israel. The Benjamites, for reasons unexplained, refuse to turn over the culprits responsible for this murder to an intertribal council, and war ensues. As a result, the Benjamites are virtually decimated, and almost comic means must be employed to rescue the tribe from oblivion.

As a coda to the violence and near-chaos of this period, this incident prepares us, psychologically, for the movement toward monarchy and a hoped-for restoration of political and spiritual order in the books of Samuel to come. It is also instructive to note that Saul, Israel's first king, is a Benjamite: a weak king chosen from the weakest tribe.

QUESTIONS FOR REVIEW

1. Why is the history of the conquest described in cyclic terms in Judges? And what role do the judges play within that historical cycle?

2. Which women play a prominent role in Judges? Does this sudden focus on the women of Israelite society tell us something about the sociopolitical instability of this era?

QUESTION FOR REFLECTION AND DISCUSSION

What conclusions does the Deuteronomistic author of Judges apparently draw from the repeated failures of Israel's tribal leaders to ensure either Israel's self-preservation or its fulfillment of covenant obligations? Is Israel unequal to the task of nation building and divine service, no matter who leads it?

TERMS AND CONCEPTS TO REMEMBER

Abimelech	Jebus
Amalekites	Jephthah
amphictyonies	Midianites
Barak	Moabites
Deborah	Nazirites
Delilah	Philistines
Ehud	*ruach*
Gibeah	Samson
Gideon	teraphim
Jael	

RECOMMENDED READING

Boling, Robert G. *Judges.* Garden City, N.Y.: Doubleday, 1975.

Cross, Frank M. *Canaanite Myth and Hebrew Epic: Essays in the History of the Religion of Israel.* Cambridge, Mass.: Harvard University Press, 1973.

Fretheim, Terence E. *Deuteronomic History.* Nashville, Tenn.: Abingdon Press, 1983.

Hackett, Jo Ann. "'There Was No King in Israel': The Era of the Judges." In Michael D. Coogan, ed., *The Oxford History of the Biblical World,* pp. 132–164. Oxford: Oxford University Press, 1998.

Webb, Barry G. *The Book of Judges: An Integrated Reading.* Sheffield, England: JSOT Press, 1987.

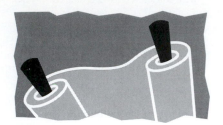

CHAPTER 14

The Birth of the Monarchy

The Books of 1 and 2 Samuel

Key Topics/Themes The canonical books we know today as 1 Samuel and 2 Samuel were originally one long and unbroken narrative tracing the rise of the monarchy in the late eleventh century B.C.E. The separation of this narrative into two distinct books was probably accomplished by the translators of the Septuagint, who presumably found it difficult to incorporate the entire history contained in these two books into one scroll, given that the Greek text (unlike biblical Hebrew) contained vowels as well as consonants. Their decision to effect a break in the Samuel narrative after the death of Saul was a wise one, however. Quite apart from a question of scribal convenience, the story of Israel's first king and his tragic demise marks the dramatic end of a very important phase in the development of the monarchy in Israel.

The Book of 1 Samuel

Though both books bear his name, **Samuel** dominates only the first twelve chapters of 1 Samuel, and he is soon eclipsed in importance by David, the boy-warrior-turned-king whose rise to power is made possible both by Samuel himself and by Israel's worsening political situation. Still, Samuel is a major player in this narrative, and he serves as a perfect transition figure from the era of the judges to the era of the kings. He is perhaps the only figure in biblical narrative to play three roles simultaneously — those of prophet, judge, and priest — and, like the court prophets who come after him (particularly Nathan), he is closely involved with the monarchy as an institution and with the two young kings he helps to place on Israel's throne. Yet, ironically, Samuel's view of the monarchy is distinctly unfavorable, and he does his best to dissuade the tribal leaders who demand that he appoint a king over them:

These will be the ways of the king who will reign over you: he will take your sons and appoint them to his chariots and to be his horsemen, and to run before his chariots; . . . He will take your daughters to be perfumers, cooks, and bakers. He will take the best of your fields, vineyards, and olive orchards, and give them to his courtiers. He will take one-tenth of your grain and your vineyards and give it to his officers and his courtiers. He will take your male and female slaves, and the best of your cattle and donkeys, and put them to his work. He will take one-tenth of your flocks, and you shall be his slaves. (1 Sam. 8:11–17)

Yet, for all his opposition to the monarchy, Samuel is instrumental in providing a sacral basis for kingship by the very act of anointing Israel's first two kings; like priests, kings receive their authority from God and so must be consecrated to him. And for all his disapproval of the institution, it is Samuel who secretly anoints David, thus making possible the rise to power of Israel's most glorious king. This fundamental ambivalence toward monarchy as such is never resolved in the books of Samuel, and one might argue that David's later crimes and moral failures represent an implicit indictment of the office he occupies. In contrast to the treatment of the Davidic dynasty in 1 Chronicles, 1 and 2 Samuel offer portraits of men who are—as Samuel first warned—corrupted rather than ennobled by the power they wield, or simply unequal to the task of governing a "holy nation."

SAMUEL AND SAUL

Scholars have identified three distinct narrative cycles within the larger story of Israel's emergence from the chaos of the era of the judges. The first cycle focuses on Samuel himself, tracing his career from birth to death. Like Samson, Samuel is conceived through an act of divine beneficence when his barren mother, Hannah, vows to consecrate her as-yet-unborn child to the life of a Nazirite. As a child, Samuel serves as attendant to the priest Eli at the northern shrine center of Shiloh, and it is there that Samuel first exhibits signs of his prophetic vocation when he predicts the demise of Eli's house and a judgment against Eli's sons, who have abused their authority as priests (1 Sam. 2:34). Ironically, Samuel's sons turn out to be just as corrupt as Eli's, and for all his credibility as a seer, Samuel displays only modest skills as a military commander. In fact, it is under his presumptive leadership that Israel suffers its greatest humiliation, when the Philistines seize the Ark of the Covenant and briefly hold it as a trophy of war (1 Sam. 4–6), and not until David appears on the scene does Israel see the tide of battle turn decisively in its favor. As a father and political leader, then, Samuel seems largely a failure, and he is certainly out of step with the politics of those tribal leaders who soon clamor for a warrior-king.

SAUL'S REIGN

The second cycle of stories focuses on **Saul**—his rise from obscurity, his initial successes, and his subsequent tragic descent into madness, failure, and death. Samuel plays a key role in the articulation

of every phase of the Saul saga, and even after his death, Samuel's spirit rises from the Underworld to predict Saul's defeat and death in battle. As a transitional figure in the development of the monarchy, Saul emerges as everything that David is not. Plagued by a sense of his own inadequacies, and indecisive (albeit courageous) in battle, Saul more closely resembles the weakest of the judges who preceded him. No sooner does Samuel anoint him Israel's first king than he falls in with a band of prophets whose ecstatic behavior he suddenly begins to imitate (1 Sam. 10:10–13)—a distant echo of the charismatic authority conferred on the judges, and ultimately on Joshua and Moses as well. Yet for all that, Saul cannot sustain these powers and soon finds himself in conflict with Samuel, repeatedly disregarding Samuel's orders of battle and sacrifice. The final break between them occurs in Chapter 15 when Saul neglects (or refuses) to execute the Amalekite king Agag, whom he has taken captive. Samuel denounces Saul, whose decision to hold Agag hostage he portrays as an act of disobedience to YHWH. He then proceeds to warn Saul that "the LORD [YHWH] has torn the kingdom of Israel from you, and has given it to a neighbor of yours, who is better than you" (15:28). That "neighbor," of course, turns out to be David, and in the very next chapter—in what might be seen as a self-fulfilling prophecy—Samuel ensures the destruction of Saul's dynasty by secretly anointing David Israel's next king.

The rapid decline of Saul's political authority and the inexorable deterioration of his mental state proceed hand in hand, and it soon becomes clear that the author-redactor of the Samuel books has chosen to portray Saul as David's foil. The final act of Saul's personal and political tragedy drives that point home as we are witness to the ironic spectacle of Israel's king, driven by fear and despair, turning to a necromancer (the "woman" of En-dor) for divine counsel (1 Sam. 28:7–25). At the time of his death, Saul is alienated from just about everyone he has been close to: David, whose ambition Saul dreads; his son **Jonathan,** whose weakness he deplores; and Samuel, whose departed spirit, summoned from Sheol (Hades in the Septuagint), is almost unwilling to speak to him. Most of all, Saul is alienated from God, who will not communicate with him through "normal" prophetic channels, and the removal of divine favor from a king undermines the legitimacy of that ruler in the eyes of biblical historians and prophets alike. The monarchy is viable, 1 Samuel suggests, only as long as God wishes to preserve it; this highly conditional view of Israel's throne will be challenged and partly transformed, as we will see, in 2 Samuel.

As the arc of Saul's career descends, the arc of David's rises, and the asymmetrical relationship of these two narratives reveals, once again, that David is the true "hero" of the Samuel books. The Davidic cycle of stories is clearly a composite of different, and at times conflicting, narrative traditions, all of which contribute to the rather complex portrait of a morally ambiguous ruler and man. Unlike Saul, who is a grown man when he assumes the throne, David is a mere boy when Samuel secretly anoints him king, and not much older when he defeats **Goliath.** That variant traditions existed concerning David's age and exploits is obvious. In Chapter 16 David is recommended to Saul as both a fighter and a harp player, and he is a member of Saul's household from that moment on (1 Sam. 16:18–23). But in the very next chapter, David is presented to us anew as a boy tending his father's flock in Bethlehem, and when he first meets Saul, it is clear that David has no connection to the court or to the king at all (17:20–37). Even the credit for having defeated Goliath is taken away from David in a later chapter of 2 Samuel, where one Elhanan is honored for having killed Goliath of Gath (2 Sam. 21:19).

Yet all of these variant traditions converge on one central belief: that David, as warrior-king and the progenitor of a dynasty that will champion the cause of YHWH, will not only protect Israel from its enemies but finally elevate the newly created monarchy to an almost sacral status. But before David can assume the throne, he must overcome several formidable obstacles, the most obvious being Saul and his family. David's marriage to Saul's daughter Michal places him within striking distance of the throne, and his friendship with Jonathan ensures that no possible rivalry between them

will occur. However, Saul's growing antagonism toward David, fueled by jealousy and mental instability—and no doubt by a clear perception of David's ambitions—drives him to ever more desperate measures to ensure that David will not be Israel's next king, culminating in his attempts on David's life. And all to no avail; David escapes Saul's clutches for the same reason that he escaped death at the hands of Goliath: From the moment of his anointing, David has enjoyed divine protection and has, in fact, entered into a special covenant with God, which will become quite explicit once Saul has died and he has ascended to the throne. Through all his travails, however, and even when his life is in danger, David is portrayed as never once lifting his hand to subvert or rebel against Saul's authority: "GOD forbid," David tells his men, "that I should harm my master, the LORD's anointed" (1 Sam. 23:6)—an important point for any historian who wishes to exculpate David from the charge that he conspired to destroy Saul and seize the kingdom.

At the conclusion of 1 Samuel, David's situation seems quite perilous, though not nearly as hopeless as Saul's. Not only does David manage to survive a surprise attack by the Amalekites on his encampment at Ziklag (1 Sam. 30), but he is even able to recoup his losses by counterattacking the Amalekite foe, thereby reassuring his men that he will protect what is theirs by the sword. More important, however, David diplomatically shares a portion of the spoils with the elders of Judah, thus positioning himself for his elevation to power as Judah's king.

The Book of 2 Samuel

DAVID'S RISE AND FALL

With Saul's death, the political situation in Israel becomes, at first, increasingly confused. The southern tribe of Judah quickly choose David to be their "king," while Saul's son **Ishbosheth** (elsewhere referred to by the Baalist name of "Ishbaal") is made ruler over a coalition of northern tribes, and intertribal warfare soon follows, reminiscent of the anarchic struggles that characterized the period of the judges. David's forces gain ground, but it is not until Ishbosheth is assassinated by two of his own officers, Rechab and Baanah, that the northern tribal leaders can bring themselves to offer the crown of a united kingdom to David. Though no one suspects David of having been behind the killing of Ishbosheth (whose murderers he quickly dispatches), and though he seems to enjoy widespread support among the people, nevertheless hostility toward David among northerners, and especially among Saul's family, persists, only to flare up in the time of Absalom's rebellion.

David clearly owes many of his early battlefield successes to his commander-in-chief, **Joab,** though he attempts, from time to time, to distance himself from this ruthless and somewhat volatile general, whose savage personal feuds with rival military leaders Abner and Amasa threaten to embarrass David and his court. However, Joab soon becomes indispensable to David; David may curse Joab for his unprovoked acts of violence, and even order his execution near the end of his life, but during the long years of his reign, David increasingly came to rely on Joab's unquestioning loyalty and ruthlessness.

After having established himself in a secure political and military position, David seizes a Jebusite city, **Jerusalem,** to be the site of his new capital. David's motives for selecting a fortified non-Israelite city as the geographical and spiritual center of his new kingdom may have been varied, but at the very least he seems determined to transcend the tribal rivalries that made political unity impossible under the judges by creating a capital that, in effect, belongs to none of the tribes, including his own. That Jerusalem — identified as Salem in both Genesis (14:18) and the Book of Psalms (76:2) — appears to have been associated with the Canaanite god El may also have figured in David's evident determination to merge a political capital with a shrine center, thereby blurring the distinction between monarchy and theocracy. Certainly, David's decision to recover the Ark of the Covenant and house it in Jerusalem appears to reflect a desire to identify himself and his regime directly with YHWH. In Chapter 7, David even offers, through his court prophet **Nathan,** to construct a permanent sanctuary for the ark, only to receive a polite refusal from YHWH, coupled with an extraordinary promise:

> The LORD has told you that he would build up your royal house. When your life ends and you rest with your forefathers, I will set up one of your family, one of your own children, to succeed you and I will establish his kingdom. It is he who shall build a house in honor of my name, and I will establish his royal throne forever. I will be his father, and he shall be my son. . . . Your family shall be established and your kingdom shall stand for all time in my sight, and your throne shall be established forever. (2 Sam. 7:11–16)

This covenant-style commitment to the Davidic dynasty — often referred to as the **Davidic,** or **Royal, Covenant** — bears some resemblance to the patriarchal covenant in that both reflect a belief in an unconditional attachment of the Deity to an individual or to his descendants. The difference here, of course, is that divine protection is being accorded to a ruling family, and YHWH is spoken of as the ruler's "father," an image that is repeated in the psalm literature as well (Pss. 2, 89). As a "charter myth," the Royal Covenant confers a degree of legitimacy and permanence on the Davidic line that no other ruling family can claim, and, not surprisingly, this tradition of dynastic perpetuity was preserved in Judah and in those biblical writings that clearly reflect a southern Israelite bias.

After David establishes a special covenant relationship with YHWH and racks up a string of victories over Israel's foes, his reputation as a warrior-king and a servant of God reaches its apogee, but it is at precisely this point in his career that a sudden reversal in fortune occurs from which David and his family never really recover. In Greek drama, this type of reversal is often referred to as a *peripeteia* — an unexpected and even tragic twist in a character's destiny — and, as in Greek drama, this change in David's fortunes is directly linked to a character flaw. David's affair with **Bathsheba,** and the subsequent conspiracy to kill her husband, **Uriah,** reveals a depth of selfishness and amorality in David not witnessed earlier. To his credit, David sees immediately how appalling his conduct has been when Nathan, in the form of a parable (2 Sam. 12:1–7), accuses him of having "stolen" Bathsheba. Far from defending his conduct, David accepts his guilt and then does penance for his sins, but his contrition comes too late to deter divine punishment. The brunt of YHWH's anger will fall on his children, who, one after another, commit crimes of violence and disloyalty that mimic their father's sins.

The rape of **Tamar** (Absalom's sister) by **Amnon** (Absalom's half-brother) and the subsequent revenge killing of Amnon by **Absalom** are the crimes of a dysfunctional family at war with itself. The subsequent revolt against David's rule led by Absalom is a public tragedy, and one that reveals not only Absalom's corrupt nature (and David's almost incomprehensible indulgence of his rebellious son) but also a lingering disaffection with David among the northern tribes. Seemingly, Absalom has only to raise the flag of rebellion to be followed by those whose battle cry is "What share have we in David? / We have no lot in the son of Jesse / Away to your homes, O Israel" (2 Sam. 20:1). The loyalty of figures like Joab and the counselor Hushai, and Absalom's own foolishness, prevents David from losing both his throne and his life, but unhappiness with David's rule and that of his house persists through the next generation and surfaces at the beginning of Rehoboam's reign (cf. 1 Kings 12–13). What is just as disturbing, however, is David's growing weakness of will and mind, as he sits mourning pathetically for the son who tried to destroy him ("O, my son! Absalom my son, my son Absalom! If only I had died instead of you!" [2 Sam. 18:33]). Joab is finally able to restore David to some sense of duty to his loyal followers, but David clearly can no longer keep his private feelings from undermining his public responsibilities.

The concluding events of David's reign are related at the end of 2 Samuel in a series of miscellaneous chapters (21–24) consisting of heroic tales, genealogies, sacred poetry (the text of Psalm 18), and a twice-told cautionary tale of census taking and divine punishment. The last of these episodes (2 Sam. 24) is perhaps the most revealing of David's decline, when he is "incited" by God to take a census of all able-bodied men of military age in his kingdom. When 1 Chronicles 21 tells this same story, the "inciter" of David's action is "Satan," but in 2 Samuel, it is YHWH alone who provokes David into a decision that he will later bitterly regret, and for which Israel will pay in the form of a plague. The limits of royal power — and, indeed, of human initiative — are nowhere better illustrated than in this enigmatic anecdote; David's only choices are among a variety of punishments that he and his subjects are forced to bear. The final act of David's life and career is reserved for the opening chapters of 1 Kings, where the succession to David's throne is reserved for a son who is scarcely mentioned in 2 Samuel: Yedidiah, better known as Solomon. That David's grasp on power has already begun to weaken, however, is evident even before his chosen heir replaces him on the throne. Unlike Saul, who at least died the death of a warrior in battle, David languishes at the center of a political and familial world that is rapidly spiraling out of his control.

FROM CHIEFDOM TO MONARCHY

The transition from Saul's short reign (c. 1020–1000 B.C.E.) to David's much longer period of rule over a united kingdom (c. 1000–961 B.C.E.) marks a shift in leadership from a type commonly termed "chiefdom" to a form of political rule that begins to resemble what one thinks of as a "monarchy." In a chiefdom, tribal affiliations and kinship relationships mean much less than they do for the tribe-centered leadership we find during the period of the judges. And although a chief may draw on the resources of his native tribe — as Saul does when he returns to his hometown of Gibeah, in Benjamin, for support (1 Sam. 15:34) — he will attempt to create a standing army through which he can control a larger territory and project his influence over neighboring states. Still, like the judges before him, the chief is essentially a charismatic warrior whose authority derives largely from his divinely appointed prowess in battle, and there is no certainty, upon his death, that one of his sons will succeed him.

In a monarchy, in contrast, political leadership is at an even further remove from family and tribal ties, with the rudiments of a court administration and even a bureaucracy in place. Kingdoms are usually larger than chiefdoms and require the services of a greater number of military and diplomatic personnel. And not infrequently kings surround themselves with mercenaries, like David's Kerethite and Pelethite guards (essentially Philistine warriors; cf. 1 Sam. 15:18), whose loyalty is assured. Most important, however, in a true monarchy, leadership is understood to be dynastic. Although disputes within a royal family over precisely who will succeed the king may erupt from time to time, the principle of dynastic succession — the belief that only a king's son may succeed him in power — is never seriously questioned.

Of the two reigns described in 1 and 2 Samuel, David's most nearly resembles a monarchy in scope and character. Not only are David's military exploits more spectacular than those of Saul — and consequently, the territory captured much greater — but his rule over a united, posttribal kingdom is more complete and more centralized. David's transformation of Jerusalem into both the political and religious capital of his kingdom is of the utmost strategic importance precisely because it shifts the focus of national life away from regional centers of earlier tribal loyalty (such as Shechem) to the central city where the royal court and the holiest of sanctuaries are to be found. Moreover, the very concept of a Royal Covenant, according to which David's lineage alone is entitled to divine protection and ultimate political authority, further distances David and his heirs from the tribal and chiefdom forms of rule that precede his ascent to power. That David and his heirs can claim to be YHWH's "sons" (as in 2 Sam. 7:14 or, later, in Pss. 2:7; 89:26-7), a claim that was not only honored by later generations but even embellished by prophetic writers (cf. Isa. 11), suggests just how far Is-

raelite political discourse has come since the days of Samson and Jephthah. Like other Near Eastern monarchs, David rules by divine "right," and although he is far too human a figure to take on divine attributes, he is nevertheless assured that his royal line will enjoy an immortality that he personally has been denied ("your throne shall be established forever" [2 Sam. 7:16]). (Box 14.1 discusses the concept of monarchy in the ancient Near East.)

Sources for Samuel

The composite nature of the two books of Samuel becomes clear when one considers the apparent literary and historical sources from which the Deuteronomistic historian drew his material (but see also Box 14.2):

1. A collection of Saul stories, some involving Samuel, through which Saul's rise from obscurity to kingship to defeat and death can be traced (1 Sam. 8-15, 28-31)
2. Narratives centering on David's rise to power, overlapping with Saul's diminishing powers (1 Sam. 16-2 Sam. 5)
3. A Court History (also referred to as a Succession Narrative) of David's reign through to his death (2 Sam. 9-20; 1 Kings 1-2)

In addition to these major segments of the Samuel/Saul/David story, there are smaller narrative units — apparent reflections of other historical traditions that are interpolated into the central narrative:

1. Narratives relating the birth and prophetic call of Samuel that serve as a bridge between the history of the judges and the early monarchy (1 Sam. 1-3, 7)
2. An account of the Ark of the Covenant, its capture by the Philistines, and its return to Israel (1 Sam. 4:3-7:2; also 2 Sam. 6-7)
3. An appendix of miscellaneous materials — psalms, lists, and stories — that round out the David saga (2 Sam. 21-24)

BOX 14.1
Kingship in Israel and the Ancient Near East

The idea of kingship is one of the foundational concepts of the ancient Near Eastern society, but it is also one of its more problematic ones. It is little wonder, therefore, that the idea of kingship in Israel embodies many of the conflicting attitudes that surround this high office. Among the ancient civilizations that interacted with, and to some extent influenced, biblical Israel, we find two radically different ways of thinking about kings and gods. In Egypt, the pharaoh is perceived as a divine being, descended from the gods. As the reincarnated form of the god Horus, the pharaoh is often depicted as a figure with more than human powers who serves as a bridge between heaven and earth. Ideally, the pharaoh governs his people in accordance with the divinely revealed rules of justice and order (referred to, in Egyptian, as *ma'at*). At his death, the pharaoh's *ka,* or immortal spirit, enters eternity, and his successor becomes the new incarnation of Horus, completing an unbroken cycle of death and rebirth.

The Mesopotamian concept of kingship, in contrast, is both more humanized and more complex, in that it acknowledges the king's mortality while preserving his heroic character. The legendary figure of Gilgamesh, for example, who is portrayed in the epic narrative that bears his name as partly human and partly divine, is destined to die; his search for immortality is finally thwarted by the very gods he had earlier defied, and he is forced to settle for a relatively short life of unparalleled glory and power. Nevertheless, he, like his Egyptian counterparts, is expected to govern justly and to receive heavenly counsel through divination and dreams.

The monarchy in Israel exhibits traits that suggest both an Egyptian and a Mesopotamian influence while preserving characteristics distinctive to itself. Thus, the Royal Covenant, expounded by the court prophet Nathan in 2 Samuel 7:4–16, bears a striking resemblance in language and tone to the Egyptian belief that the reigning pharaoh was a god's "son" and therefore protected from harm by his divine father. In Psalms 2 and 89, YHWH declares David to be both his "begotten" son and his "first-born," the unique object of his steadfast love, thereby reaffirming the notion of an enduring Davidic dynasty that is like no other on earth. The Chronicler echoes these sentiments in his concluding elegiac portrait of David (1 Chron. 29:9–25), offering the reader the image of a sacralized monarchy, committed to the divine sanctuary and to the glory of God. The warrior-king at last becomes the priest-king, who, like the prophets, can serve as a spokesman for YHWH and call on him in the hour of need.

The counterpoint to this tradition of sacralized monarchy can be found throughout the Tanak, and particularly in cautionary texts like Deuteronomy 17:14–20, where the Israelites are instructed to appoint a king who obeys the Torah strictly and who "fears" YHWH enough to keep a copy of the law at his side at all times. Of all the kings of Israel and Judah, only Josiah comes even close to embodying this ideal, and he dies ingloriously in battle. Of the vast majority of Israel's kings, both north and south, the author of the Book of Kings has only one observation to make: "he did what was evil in the sight of the Lord, just as his ancestors had done," thereby summing up the history of a particular reign — and, finally, of the monarchy as such — as a cumulative failure, and as one of the principal causes of Israel's downfall.

By desacralizing the monarchy and by subordinating the will of the king to the *torah* of YHWH, biblical historians subvert the dual tradition of the monarch as divinity and as hero and offer, instead, a countertradition of YHWH as Israel's only "king" (see Pss. 96–99).

BOX 14.2
Were Tales in Genesis Devised to Support the Davidic Monarchy?

In attempting to date the various documents now incorporated into the Torah, scholars consider such questions as the author's purpose and original audience. Why and for whom specifically did he write? If a case can be made for a particular period or set of circumstances in Israel's history that fits the writer's intent and recipients, this evidence can help pinpoint the probable time of composition. Although many elements in the Torah suggest that it assumed its final form after the Babylonian exile in the sixth century B.C.E., parts of the Genesis narrative seem particularly relevant to the political situation of David and Solomon (tenth century B.C.E.). According to some proponents of this theory, many stories in Genesis function to justify or validate the actions and policies of David, Solomon, and their heirs. If this assumption is correct, some of the tales about Israel's ancestors, paralleling events in the reigns of Davidic rulers, may have been shaped to support the Davidic monarchy long before the Babylonians brought the dynasty to an end (587 B.C.E.).

STORY IN GENESIS	REPORT ABOUT THE DAVIDIC DYNASTY
1. God promises Abraham that "kings shall come from you" (Gen. 17:6).	1. David establishes a monarchy despite opposition from tribal leaders who insist that only YHWH is Israel's king (cf. 1 Sam. 8:4–32).
2. YHWH promises Abraham the region extending from "the river of Egypt to . . . the river Euphrates" (Gen. 15:18).	2. David extends Israel's borders to include the territory promised to Abraham (2 Sam. 8:3; cf. 1 Kings 4:21; 8:65).
3. One of the four rivers of Eden is the Gihon (Gen. 2:13).	3. David captures Jerusalem—a Canaanite stronghold—and centers his capital around the Gihon spring, a water source reminiscent of humanity's original paradise home.
4. Abraham pays a tithe to Melchizedek, the Canaanite king-priest of Salem (site of Jerusalem) (Gen. 14:18–24).	4. David retains Zadok, High Priest of Canaanite Jerusalem, as his High Priest; Solomon uses forced labor (a form of taxation) to build the Jerusalem Temple (1 Kings 5:13–17; 9:15)
5. Genesis emphasizes the close kinship of Israel and its future neighboring states; Jacob's twin brother, Esau, "is Edom" (36:1); Ammon and Moab are descended from Abraham's nephew Lot (Gen. 19:36–38).	5. David incorporates the states of Edom, Moab, and Ammon into his kingdom, making them part of the Israelite "family" (2 Sam. 8).
6. YHWH declares that Esau (Edom) will "serve" Jacob (Israel) (Gen. 25:23).	6. "All the Edomites became David's servants" (2 Sam. 8:14; cf. 1 Kings 11:14–17).
7. Abraham prepares to sacrifice his son, Isaac, on Mount Moriah (Gen. 22), considered the future site of Jerusalem.	7. Solomon erects YHWH's Temple on the traditional site of Isaac's "binding," the only place Israel's required sacrifices to YHWH are permitted (cf. Deut. 12; 1 Kings 8).
8. Throughout Genesis, God favors younger sons, preferring Abel to Cain, Jacob to Esau, Joseph to his older brothers, and Ephraim to Manasseh.	8. God favors David over his older brothers and grants the succession to one of David's youngest sons, Solomon (1 Sam. 16:6–13; 1 Kings 1–2).
9. Judah, eponymous founder of David's tribe, has an affair with Tamar; after she tricks him into admitting his guilt, he is forgiven (Gen. 38).	9. Judah's royal descendant, David, has an adulterous affair with Bathsheba; after confessing his guilt, he is forgiven (2 Sam. 11–12).

For a more complete discussion of this topic see Gary A. Rendsburg, "Biblical Literature as Politics: The Case of Genesis," in Adele Berlin, ed., *Religion and Politics in the Ancient Near East,* pp. 47–70 (Bethesda, Md.: University of Maryland Press, 1996).

The artful blending of these diverse traditions is made possible by a sustained sense of divine purpose underlying all of the apparent chaos of Israel's growth pains. Like the judges who precede them, Samuel, Saul, and David are covenant bearers in whom YHWH entrusts some measure of responsibility for the survival of Israel as a political entity and as a confessional community. Understood in that light, the fate of the ark or the impact of prophetic personalities on national life is just as important as the emergence of a monarchy out of the confusion of tribal politics.

QUESTIONS FOR REVIEW

1. Summarize the opposing views of monarchy that we encounter in 1 Samuel, and consider to what extent the later history of the kings of Israel and Judah bears out Samuel's warnings in Chapter 8.

2. How does the Royal (or Davidic) Covenant put the monarchy in a different light? Why is it necessary to anoint kings in Israel, and how is that practice related to the idea of God's "adoption" of the House of David?

3. Consider the pattern of David's life and his reign: At what point do things begin to go very badly for him, and why?

QUESTION FOR REFLECTION AND DISCUSSION

The transition from tribal rule to monarchy seems almost inevitable in 1 and 2 Samuel, and the glamour of David's early reign simply reinforces the impression that Israel will not have fulfilled its destiny until a king reigns in Jerusalem. But can it also be said that these books contain a countertradition of skepticism toward kingship as such, along with a critical history of royal personalities who assumed power, only to fail?

TERMS AND CONCEPTS TO REMEMBER

Absalom	Joab
Amnon	Jonathan
Bathsheba	Nathan
Davidic, or Royal,	Samuel
Covenant	Saul
Goliath	Tamar
Ishbosheth	Uriah
Jerusalem	

RECOMMENDED READING

Cross, Frank M., ed. "The Ideologies of Kingship in the Era of the Empire: Conditional Covenant and Eternal Decree." In *Canaanite Myth and Hebrew Epic: Essays in the History of the Religion of Israel.* Cambridge, Mass.: Harvard University Press, 1973.

Friedman, Richard E. *The Hidden Book in the Bible.* San Francisco: HarperSanFrancisco, 1998.

Halpern, Baruch. *The First Historians: The Hebrew Bible and History.* San Francisco: Harper & Row, 1988.

McCarter, P. Kyle. *1 Samuel.* Garden City, N.Y.: Doubleday, 1980.

———. *2 Samuel.* Garden City, N.Y.: Doubleday, 1984.

Myers, Carol. "Kinship and Kingship: The Early Monarchy." In Michael D. Coogan, ed., *The Oxford History of the Biblical World.* Oxford: Oxford University Press, 1998.

Parallel Stories of Israel and Judah

The Books of 1 and 2 Kings

Key Topics/Themes Although divided into two volumes, the books of Kings form an unbroken narrative, beginning with the death of David and succession of Solomon, continuing with the division of Israel into two rival kingdoms — the larger northern realm of Israel and the smaller southern state of Judah — and culminating with Israel's destruction by Assyria (721 B.C.E.) and Judah's fall to Babylon (587 B.C.E.). Giving unequal coverage to the various kings of Israel and Judah, the two books contain three major parts: (1) the reign of Solomon (1 Kings 1–11), (2) the breakup of the Solomonic kingdom and an interweaving history of rulers in Judah and Israel (1 Kings 12–2 Kings 17), and (3) after Israel's elimination by Assyria, a history of Judah until the Babylonian exile (2 Kings 18–25). Consistently applying Deuteronomic principles to this theologically oriented account, the author-editors ascribe the political and military defeat of both Israel and Judah to their rulers' collective failure to worship YHWH alone, at the single place he had designated, the Jerusalem Temple.

As the final — and longest — segment of the Deuteronomistic History (DH), the two books of Kings span a period of approximately 400 years, from the glory days of King Solomon's reign over a united, prosperous Israel in the mid-tenth century B.C.E. to one of his royal descendants' humiliating captivity in Babylon four centuries later. The last-recorded event in 2 Kings, the release of Judah's deposed ruler, **Jehoiachin,** from a Babylonian prison took place about 562 B.C.E. and thus provides the earliest possible date for the composition or final redaction of the book in its present form. Written from the perspective of the Babylonian exile, the canonical edition of 1 and 2 Kings presents the national cataclysm as tragic and complete, the inevitable result of Israel's cumulative sins.

Two Editions of the Deuteronomistic History

THE FIRST EDITION

Many scholars believe that, before the present edition of Kings was produced, an earlier and much more optimistic version of the work existed, one that culminated in an enthusiastic description of the reforms of King **Josiah** (ruled 640–609 B.C.E.). Composed at the height of Josiah's triumphant religious and military campaigns, when he consolidated national worship at the Jerusalem sanctuary and reconquered part of the northern territories that Assyria had previously occupied, the first edition of Kings portrayed Josiah's reign as the joyous fulfillment of Torah promises for land, blessing, and divinely favored kings. Awarding Josiah unequivocal praise, the DH writers state that he pleased YHWH more than any other king since David (2 Kings 22:2) and describe him as the embodiment of Deuteronomy's foremost command:

> Before him there was no king like him, who turned to the LORD [YHWH] with all his heart, with all his soul, and with all his might, according to the law [*torah*] of Moses; nor did any like him arise after him. (2 Kings 23:25; cf. Deut. 6:4–5)

In its original form, the DH had a remarkable literary symmetry. The first edition began with an account of Joshua's stunning military victories and covenant renewal ceremony and ended in 2 Kings with a description of Josiah's retaking of part of the Promised Land and conducting similar covenant rituals. Backed by YHWH's invisible armies, Joshua successfully led Israel in a holy war, capturing Canaanite strongholds and smashing Canaanite altars. At the conclusion of the DH narrative, Josiah acts as a second Joshua, leading troops to reclaim areas of the northern kingdom and systematically demolishing all places of worship that compete with the approved sanctuary at Jerusalem (cf. Josh. 1–11, 23–24; 2 Kings 23). Both men are portrayed as national heroes, warriors, and enforcers of Yahwism who exemplify Deuteronomic piety in action. Joshua's assembling the tribes to swear exclusive allegiance to YHWH (Josh. 24)—with a stone monument erected to witness the oath—is paralleled by Josiah's holding a comparable rite beside the Temple's pillars (Josh. 24:24–28; 2 Kings 23:3). Besides emulating Joshua in subjugating Canaanite territory and toppling unauthorized shrines, Josiah also takes measures to reclaim the divine presence, purging the Temple of altars to foreign gods that his predecessors had introduced into the sanctuary.

THE SECOND EDITION

After Josiah's early death (609 B.C.E.) and Judah's fall to Babylon, however, Deuteronomistic editors were compelled to revise the first edition's neatly symmetrical presentation of Israel's history. The reforms of Josiah could no longer be seen as a fulfillment of the divine promises, but merely as a brief hiatus in the nation's tragic downward spiral. In revising the DH to explain YHWH's abandonment of the covenant people to their enemies, editors modified the account to reflect the devastating historical reality, adding a new conclusion (2 Kings 23:26–25:29) and inserting several passages that foreshadow the exile. By scattering brief references to the coming national defeat at strategic points in the narrative, the redactors changed the tone and direction of the narrative flow, their intimations of calamity making the ultimate disaster appear inevitable. (For some of the redactors' later interpolations, see Deuteronomy 4:26–27; 28:36, 63–64; Joshua 23:16; 1 Kings 9:7; 11:35–36; 15:3–4; 2 Kings 8:18–19; 20:16–19; etc.)

Reviewing their nation's history in the glaring light of Judah's desolation, DH editors found a way to explain God's decision to rescind the covenant and overthrow the Davidic dynasty—which YHWH had promised would govern his people forever (2 Sam. 7). Although they retained YHWH's unequivocal vow to David, postexilic editors of Kings rephrased later versions of the Davidic Covenant to conform to subsequent events, making them *conditional* on the kings' loyalty to YHWH (cf. 1 Kings 9:4–9). In assessing the cause of national failure, redactor(s) of the DH history concluded that King Manasseh personally bore the chief responsibility. Despite Josiah's perfect loyalty, his predecessor had sinned so grievously that YHWH could not forgive it:

> Still, the LORD did not turn from the fierceness of his great wrath, by which his anger was kindled

against Judah, because of all the provocations with which Manasseh had provoked him. The LORD said, "I will remove Judah also out of my sight, as I have removed Israel; and I will reject the city that I have chosen, Jerusalem . . ." (2 Kings 23:26–27)

The sins of Josiah's grandfather would be visited on his descendants because "the LORD was not willing to pardon" (2 Kings 24:4; cf. Exod. 20:5).

SOURCES FOR KINGS

In compiling the history of Israel's and Judah's kings, the Deuteronomistic author drew on both oral traditions, such as tales about the prophets **Elijah** and **Elisha,** and several written documents. Royal archives that list the notable achievements of Israelite and Judean rulers are frequently cited, including the Book of the Acts of Solomon (1 Kings 11:41), the Book of the Annals of the Kings of Israel (1 Kings 14:19), and the Book of the Annals of the Kings of Judah (1 Kings 14:29). These court records would probably have offered more extensive coverage of individual rulers' economic, political, cultural, and social accomplishments than the DH writer(s) cared to preserve. Unfortunately, none has survived.

A NARROW STANDARD OF JUDGMENT

The Deuteronomistic criteria for evaluating the effectiveness of a given king have almost nothing to do with his military victories or his economic policies. In the DH view, it does not matter whether a king is successful in extending the nation's territory, defeating its enemies, or even rendering ethical judgment to the poor and defenseless (the last a major concern of Israel's prophets). The narrator's judgment focuses almost exclusively on the issue of centralizing YHWH's worship at "the place that the LORD your God will choose . . . as his habitation to put his name there" (Deut. 12:5). Although the place is not specified in Deuteronomy, the author-editors assume it to be Jerusalem, site of Solomon's Temple. Because DH writers regard all other sanctuaries—including ancient shrines at Bethel and Shechem where Abraham, Jacob, and Joshua offered sacrifices—as illegitimate, any ruler who does not vigorously enforce the centralization of YHWH's cult at Jerusalem is vehemently condemned. Although Israel had worshiped YHWH at "high places" (rural hilltop altars) from time immemorial, the Deuteronomistic standard requires their total destruction. The few kings of Judah, such as Hezekiah and Josiah, who campaign to eliminate all shrines outside Jerusalem are the only rulers to win DH approval. Not one of the northern kings receives a passing grade.

When the Davidic kingdom splits into two separate nations after Solomon's death, rulers of the northern state do not wish their subjects to worship only at the southern capital, Jerusalem. According to 1 Kings 12, the first northern king, **Jeroboam I** (ruled 922–901 B.C.E.) established rival sanctuaries at either end of his domain, in the north at Dan and in the south at Bethel. This "sin of Jeroboam"— erecting golden calves on which YHWH was thought to be invisibly enthroned—automatically prevents any northern monarch from pleasing God. Although a contemporary historian might point out that Judah's centralizing royal, political, and religious functions at its own capital—and denouncing as apostate all who choose to worship elsewhere—shows considerable self-interest, in the DH view, Jerusalem is the only place where YHWH accepts the sacrifices mandated by Mosaic Law.

The Reign of Solomon

Given the vast importance that the DH accords the Jerusalem Temple, it is not surprising that the books of Kings devote more space to describing the reign of Solomon, the Temple's builder, than to any other king (1 Kings 1–11). First Kings opens with an account of King David's last days and the court intrigues, led by the prophet Nathan and David's wife Bathsheba, to have her son, **Solomon,** rather than David's oldest son, **Adonijah,** succeed to the throne. (The story of Solomon's succession is probably based on the same Court History that underlies 2 Samuel 9–20.) Even on his deathbed, David behaves like a typical Near Eastern monarch, reminding Solomon that, although he has promised to spare surviving enemies who participated in Absalom's revolt, his successor is bound by no such vow. Taking his father's hint, Solomon begins his administration by murdering not only Adonijah but also David's loyal general Joab and numerous others who might threaten the security of his crown. In a special blessing, YHWH then grants him a "wise and discerning mind" (1 Kings 3:4–15), so that he soon earns international fame for the astuteness of his policies.

ISRAEL'S PROSPERITY

Although the final verdict on Solomon's long reign is decidedly critical (1 Kings 11), most of the narrative expresses strong admiration for his material accomplishments, particularly his wealth and extensive building program. Solomon's largest project is the royal palace, which includes a special mansion for his most important wife, the daughter of an unnamed pharaoh, with whom he forms a political alliance. Covering 11,250 square feet, the palace is much larger than the Temple (2700 square feet), almost as if the sanctuary (on which the narrative focuses) were a religious extension of royal power (cf. 6:2; 7:2). Built to house the Ark of the Covenant, on which YHWH's "glory" is enshrined, the Temple is a windowless rectangular edifice whose floor plan resembles that of other sanctuaries that archaeologists have recently excavated in Syria and Phoenicia (Figure 15.1). According to 1 Kings 8, Phoenician architects, designers, and artisans played a major role in constructing the Temple. **Hiram,** a Phoenician king who was one of Solomon's chief partners in a lucrative international trade, supplied both materials and skilled craftsmen. Despite his large income from commercial enterprises and increasingly heavy taxation of Israel's citizens, however, Solomon is eventually forced to cede twenty Galilean towns to Hiram to pay off his debts (9:10–14).

DEDICATION OF THE TEMPLE

The first Israelite king to be raised in an urban palace rather than in the rural villages and pastures, Solomon assumes more of the trappings of royal privilege than his two predecessors. The extent to which royal power has increased since the days of King Saul is evident in Solomon's assumption of priestly duties in dedicating the Jerusalem Temple. Whereas Samuel publicly withdrew support from Saul when the king offered sacrifices, in the Temple ceremony Solomon, apparently without opposition, takes over priestly functions, not only consecrating the sanctuary but also making both animal and grain sacrifices (1 Kings 8:62–65; cf. 1 Sam. 13:8–15). In the minds of many Israelites, particularly in the north, the Jerusalem Temple may have seemed too much like a dynastically controlled royal chapel (cf. 1 Kings 12).

In recounting the Temple's consecration, the narrator draws a fine distinction between the older Tabernacle theology and the later Deuteronomic concept of YHWH's connection with the Jerusalem sanctuary. In Exodus, YHWH appears to take up residence in his tent-shrine, his "glory" encamped among the Israelites (Exod. 40:34–38). In contrast to Exodus's sense of divine immanence—reinforced in 1 Samuel when the young Samuel experiences YHWH literally standing and speaking to him in the Tabernacle (1 Sam. 3:10)—the DH insists that a transcendent YHWH places only his "name" in the Temple. Although both the Exodus writer and the Deuteronomistic historian employ the same symbol of divine presence—a "cloud" that envelops both Tabernacle and Temple as a sign of YHWH's acceptance—the Deuteronomistic author makes clear that no earthly shrine can hold the Deity. The long dedicatory prayer ascribed to Solomon, a thoroughly Deuteronomistic composition, emphasizes that, although YHWH accepts the Temple, in reality "the highest heavens can not contain [him], much less the house that [Solomon has] built" (1 Kings 8:27). At the very moment that witnesses the fulfillment of Genesis's promise of the divine presence—or at least YHWH's "name"—abiding with Israel, the postexilic redactor inserts

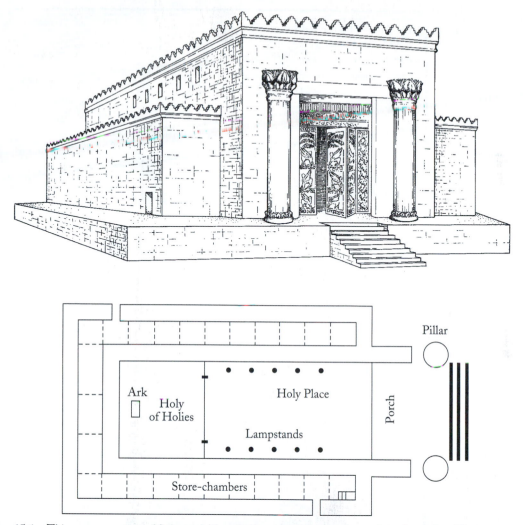

Figure 15.1 This reconstruction of Solomon's Temple shows both the exterior and the floor plan. The Davidic kings and their court theologians insisted that Jerusalem's royal sanctuary was the only place on earth at which YHWH would accept sacrificial offerings, thus compelling Israelites to travel to the national capital to fulfill their Torah obligations.

an ominous reminder that YHWH's future support depends on Israel's Torah observance. YHWH warns Solomon that his oath to preserve the Davidic line depends on wholehearted obedience to covenant laws. Describing an appearance to Solomon immediately after the Temple's dedication, the redactor shows YHWH explicitly warning the king that the "house" he has just sanctified with his presence will become a "heap of ruins," the condition to which Babylonian armies had reduced it at the time the book was edited (1 Kings 9:8–9; cf. 25:8–17).

After the generally positive evaluation of Solomon's accomplishments — his unprecedented opulence, fame, wisdom, and diplomatic prowess (1 Kings 10) — the narrator's final estimate of the

Figure 15.2 Map of the Kingdom of David and Solomon (c. 1000–922 B.C.E.) At its height, the Davidic kingdom incorporated the territories of several neighboring states, including Edom, Moab, and Ammon.

king's significance seems almost incongruous. Chapter 11, which marks a change in attitude toward Solomon and severely criticizes his taking of foreign wives (he is said to have married 700 princesses and appropriated 300 concubines), was probably interpolated by a postexilic redactor, who sought to find in Solomon's reign causes for the nation's subsequent misfortunes. From the redactor's perspective, Solomon compromised his Yahwistic faith by allowing his wives to worship their national gods, even building altars for these deities in the Temple precincts (Ch. 11). Although DH judges Solomon primarily from a religious standpoint, the king's economic policies played a more important part in the breakup of Israel that followed his death. Ignoring the old tribal allocations of Israelite territory, Solomon divided the country into twelve administrative districts, with each obligated to provide supplies for the royal court one month of every year. Even more unpopular was Solomon's practice of compelling Israelite citizens to work on his building projects, possibly using forced Israelite labor to construct the Temple (1 Kings 4:7–19; 5:13–18; cf. 9:15–22). In thus portraying the negative aspects of Solomon's administration, the DH implicitly evokes Samuel's impassioned warning about the grave disadvantages of establishing a monarchy (1 Sam. 8:10–18), as well as Deuteronomy's critical description of kings who behave much as Solomon did (Deut. 17:14–20).

Despite his failure to follow YHWH as his father, David, had done, Solomon is allowed to die peacefully (c. 922 B.C.E.), although his heirs will lose the largest part of the kingdom (Figure 15.2). The region of Judah, however, the nucleus of the Davidic realm, is to remain under his successors' control so that "David may always have a lamp before me in Jerusalem, the city where I have chosen to put my name" (1 Kings 11:12–13, 35–36; cf. assurances given to later Davidic rulers in 1 Kings 15:3–4; 2 Kings 8:18–19).

The Divided Kingdom

JEROBOAM'S REVOLT

Rehoboam (ruled 922–915 B.C.E.), Solomon's successor, foolishly refuses to lighten the crushing burden of taxes and forced labor that Solomon imposed on the people. Rehoboam's arrogant rejection of the northern tribes' plea for a more humane administration sparks a widespread revolt against the House of David. The ten northern tribes withdraw from the united kingdom to form their own independent state —**Israel**— repudiating any tie to the Davidic line:

> What share do we have in David?
> We have no inheritance in the son of Jesse!
> (1 Kings 12:16 [cf. 2 Sam. 20:1])

The uneasy alliance that Saul and David forged between the southern and northern tribes, with their different religious and political cultures, thus proves to be fragile and temporary. Only the southern tribes of Judah and Benjamin remain loyal to the Davidic dynasty and its sanctuary at Jerusalem. Although much smaller and poorer than its northern rival, as a political state **Judah** will survive Israel by 200 years, permitting Tanak writers to record the subsequent history of the divided kingdom from an exclusively Judean viewpoint.

After Israel's secession, Kings records the history of a divided people, alternately describing individual reigns in Israel and then those in Judah (1 Kings 12–2 Kings 17; see the lists of kings in Table 15.1). The Deuteronomistic narrator fits the reports on all rulers into a rigid formula. The introduction to the kings of Israel includes a statement relating the Israelite monarchs' dates to those of contemporary kings in Judah; the name of the capital city; the length of the reign; and a stereotypical condemnation of the king, invariably asserting that "He did what was evil in the sight of the LORD" (because he did not support the Jerusalem cult). In introducing Judean rulers, the narrator follows a similar pattern, connecting the ascension of a Judean monarch with

Table 15.1   Events and Rulers in the Divided Kingdom

APPROXIMATE DATE B.C.E.	MESOPOTAMIA AND EGYPT	ISRAEL	JUDAH	HEBREW PROPHETS
	Twenty-second Dynasty of Egypt (935–725)	Jeroboam I (922–901)	Rehoboam (922–915)	
	Pharaoh Shishak invades Palestine (c. 918)		Abijah (915–913)	
			Asa (913–873)	
900		Nadab (901–900)		
		Baasha (900–877)		
		Elah (877–876)		
		Zimri (876)		
		Omri (876–869)	Jehoshaphat (873–849)	
	Shalmaneser III (859–825) of Assyria	Ahab (869–850)		Elijah (Israel)
850		Ahaziah (850–849)	Jehoram (849–842)	
	Battle of Qarqar (853)	Jehoram (849–842)	Ahaziah (842)	Elisha (Israel)
	Hazael of Syria (842–806)	Jehu's Revolt (842)	Athaliah (842–837)	
800		Jehu (842–815)	Joash (837–800)	
		Jehoahaz (815–801)	Amaziah (800–783)	
		Jehoash (801–786)		Amos (Israel)
		Jeroboam II (786–746)	Uzziah (Azariah) (783–742)	Hosea (Israel)
750	Tiglath-pileser III of Assyria (745–727)	Zechariah (746–745)		
		Shallum (745)	Jotham (742–735)	
		Menahem (745–738)		
		Pekahiah (738–737)	Ahaz (735–715)	Isaiah (Judah)
	Shalmaneser V (726–722)	Pekah (737–732)		
		Hoshea (732–724)		Micah (Judah)
	Twenty-fourth Egyptian Dynasty (725–709)			
725		Fall of Israel (722/721)	Hezekiah (715–687)	
	Sargon II of Assyria (721–705)			
	Twenty-fifth Egyptian Dynasty (716–663)			
700	Sennacherib (704–681)			
	Assyrian invasion of Judah (701)			
			Manasseh (687–642)	
	Esarhaddon of Assyria (681–669)			
	Ashurbanipal (668–627)			
650	Twenty-sixth Egyptian Dynasty (664–525)		Amon (642–640)	

Table 15.1   *(continued)*

Approximate Date B.C.E.	Mesopotamia and Egypt	Israel	Judah	Hebrew Prophets
			Josiah (640–609)	Jeremiah
			Deuteronomic reforms (621 and following)	Zephaniah
				Nahum
	Fall of Nineveh (612)		Jehoahaz (609)	
	Pharaoh Necho (610–594)		Jehoiakim (609–598/597)	
600	Battle of Carchemish (605)		Jehoiachin (598/597)	
	Growth of Neo-Babylonian Empire under Nebuchadnezzar (605–562)		First Babylonian sack of Jerusalem (598/597)	Habakkuk
			Zedekiah (597–587)	Ezekiel
			Fall of Jerusalem (587)	Jeremiah
			Babylonian captivity (587–538)	

Source: In general, this table follows the dates derived from W. F. Albright, *Bulletin of the American School of Oriental Research*, 100 (December 1945), and adopted by John Bright, *A History of Israel* (Philadelphia: Westminster Press, 1972), pp. 480–481.

the currently reigning king of Israel; giving the king's age when he came to the throne and the name of the queen mother; and measuring his performance against that of David. Like the universally condemned kings of Israel, the majority of Judean kings are similarly dismissed for doing "evil" and for being disloyal to YHWH and the Jerusalem cult.

In the description of Jeroboam's revolt against the Davidic dynasty, the rebel is at first portrayed as potentially a champion of the Yahwist faith, rescuing it from Solomon's laxity in tolerating foreign cults. As the prophet **Ahijah** reveals, Jeroboam — a former Solomonic courtier, now a rebel who has the support of Egypt's Pharaoh Shishak — is YHWH's choice to lead the northern tribes back to covenant loyalty (1 Kings 11:26–40). As the first ruler of the northern kingdom, however, Jeroboam proves a great disappointment, primarily for establishing centers of YHWH worship outside of Jerusalem (Chs. 12–13). Jeroboam's unpardonable "sin," giving royal support to rival shrines at Dan and Bethel, is continued by all of Israel's subsequent rulers, a policy that earns all of them a negative rating. Al-

though the DH accords him only a few lines, **Omri** (ruled 876–869 B.C.E.), Israel's sixth king, was so effective that, long after his dynasty had fallen, the emperors of Assyria still referred to Israel as the "land of Omri."

ELIJAH AND KING AHAB

Considerably more space is allotted to the misdeeds of Omri's successor, King **Ahab** (ruled 869–850 B.C.E.), who takes a Phoenician princess, the infamous **Jezebel,** as his queen. A native of Tyre, one of Phoenicia's most important port cities, and a devout worshiper of Baal, Jezebel is depicted as corrupting her husband's entire country. Ahab's endorsement of his wife's Baal worship brings him into confrontation with the most formidable prophet that Israel has yet produced, Elijah the Tishbite, who stages a public contest between YHWH and Baal on Mount **Carmel** near the Mediterranean coast (1 Kings 18). Despite their ritual antics, the Canaanite priests fail to rouse Baal to action, but Elijah's God sends fire from heaven,

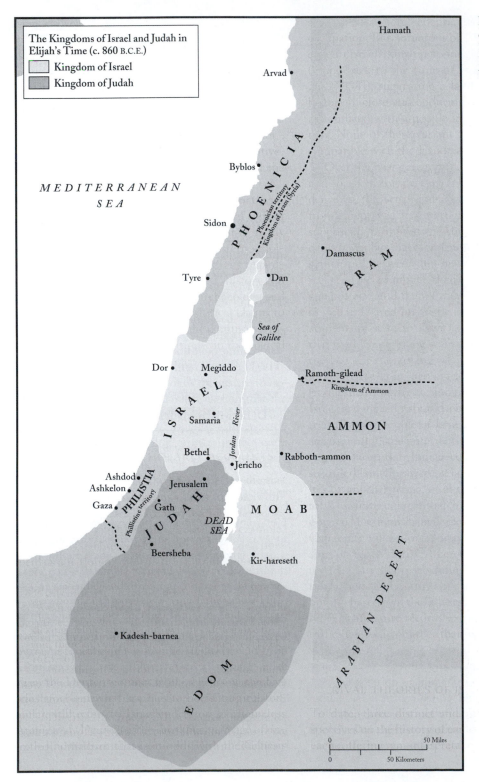

Figure 15.3 Map of the Kingdoms of Israel and Judah in Elijah's Time (c. 860 b.c.e.)

consuming both sacrifice and altar. Triumphant, Elijah slaughters the priests of Baal and announces that YHWH is ending the long drought that has afflicted the country.

Driven from his homeland by Jezebel's death threats, the solitary prophet — who believes that he is the only person still faithful to YHWH — retreats to the desert origin of his faith, Horeb/Sinai. Hidden in the same rocky cleft that once sheltered Moses, Elijah, too, encounters YHWH — not in wind, fire, earthquake, or other spectacular phenomena, but in a "sound of sheer silence" (1 Kings 19:11–12). YHWH then commissions Elijah to return to the political arena, anointing new leaders who will presumably carry out the divine will more effectively than Ahab: Hazael in Syria, Jehu in Israel, and Elisha in the prophetic realm (19:9–16).

Illustrating the need to replace Ahab, the narrative shifts to describe the king's unjust prosecution of **Naboth,** whose vineyard he covets. Following Jezebel's counsel, Ahab abuses provisions of the Mosaic Law by bribing witnesses falsely to accuse Naboth of blasphemy, for which he is stoned and his property forfeited to the crown (1 Kings 21). When Elijah denounces the king's sin, Ahab repents, causing YHWH to delay his punishment, though shortly afterward the king is killed at the Battle of Ramoth-Gilead (Ch. 22). Not only does Elijah survive his royal prosecutors, whose deaths he helps to hasten, but he soon receives the most spectacular validation of any Israelite prophet — a public ascent to heaven (see below). (Figure 15.3 shows the kingdoms of Israel and Judah in Elijah's time.)

2 Kings

THE ELIJAH–ELISHA CYCLE

Because the two parts of Kings are really a single book, the account of Israelite and Judean rulers continues uninterrupted in 2 Kings. Preparing readers for the coming destruction of the northern kingdom, described in 2 Kings 17, this section opens with an episode illustrating YHWH's ongoing conflict with the Omrid dynasty. When King Ahaziah, who lies dying after falling from an upper story of his residence, sends to inquire of "Baal-zebub, the god of Ekron" about his chances of recovery, Elijah intercepts the king's messenger and predicts Ahaziah's certain death. "Is it because there is no God in Israel," Elijah demands, "that you are going to inquire of Baal-zebub," a derisive term meaning "lord of the flies" that biblical writers commonly use for Baal. But when Ahaziah sends a captain and fifty men to bring Elijah to him, the prophet has YHWH consume them with fire from heaven, a fate that also befalls a second contingent of soldiers. Although a third group persuades Elijah to descend from his hilltop retreat and visit the king, the prophet's message does not change, and Ahaziah dies for his disloyalty — the same fate the entire nation will soon experience (2 Kings 1:2–17).

Even when Israelite kings reject Baal in favor of YHWH, however, the Deuteronomistic narrator still judges them adversely. After Jehoram, one of Ahab's sons, inherits the throne, he separates himself from his parents' Baalism, tearing down "the pillar of Baal that his father had made." Nonetheless, the author categorizes him as doing "evil" because he "clung to the sin of Jeroboam," maintaining YHWH's altars at Dan and Bethel (3:1–3).

Chapters 2–8 continue the Elijah–Elisha cycle, interspersing folk legends about the prophets' miracles with archival material about royal alliances, battles, and political intrigues. Elijah's prophetic career reaches a spectacular climax when a "chariot of fire" pulled by fiery horses carries him, as in a "whirlwind," to heaven. The only other figure in the Hebrew Bible besides Enoch (Gen. 5:21) to be "taken" by God and thus to escape ordinary death, Elijah became the object of later prophetic speculation — that he will return to earth before God's final judgment day (2 Kings 2; cf. Mal. 4:5–6).

Inheriting both Elijah's spirit and his prophetic mantle, Elisha continues his mentor's work, performing even more miraculous acts that mark him as a "man of God." Although some of Elisha's miracles, such as his parting waters to cross a river dryshod or resuscitating the only son of a hospitable woman, are virtual duplications of Elijah's activities, others are unique to him. Elisha causes an iron ax head to float on water, turns poisoned soup edible, multiplies twenty barley loaves to feed 100 men, and cleanses a Syrian leper; he also foretells droughts, famines, military victories, and royal deaths.

JEHU'S BLOODY PURGES

A political kingmaker as well as a seer, Elisha secretly sends a messenger to anoint a new Israelite monarch—**Jehu,** a former captain of Ahab's guard. Supported by the army, Jehu (ruled 842–815 B.C.E.) then plunges the nation into a bloodbath (2 Kings 9–10). Citing Elijah's curse on Ahab's dynasty, Jehu massacres all of Ahab's surviving sons, grandsons, friends, priests, and administrators, totally annihilating the royal family and its supporters. His treatment of Jezebel, who is thrown from an upper window to the courtyard below, where she is eaten by dogs, is particularly savage. With **Jehonadab,** who shares his zeal for YHWH, Jehu then assembles all known Baal worshipers in the great temple that Ahab built in **Samaria,** the capital city, and orders eighty executioners to butcher them all. Baal's shrine is demolished and the site turned into a public latrine.

For all his Yahwist fanaticism, however, Jehu does not entirely win the Deuteronomistic writer's approval. In neglecting to remove Jeroboam's golden calves from Bethel and Dan, he is judged not to have served YHWH wholeheartedly. Nor was Jehu an effective king: his purges and massacres may have pleased some Yahwists, but he so depleted the nation's supply of trained leaders that Israel rapidly lost territory on every side. When Jehu died after a reign of twenty-eight years (of which only the violent first year is described in Kings), he left Israel politically weak, without allies, and considerably smaller in size than it had been under Omri and Ahab (2 Kings 10:32–35).

Jehu's low international status is graphically depicted on the Black Obelisk, a stone monument erected by Shalmaneser III (ruled 859–825 B.C.E.), head of the Assyrian Empire (Figure 15.4). The obelisk is inscribed with five scenes depicting representatives from five different nations—including Israel—bringing tribute to the Assyrian monarch. One panel shows Jehu, or his ambassador, forehead to the ground, groveling before his foreign master (Figure 15.5). A roughly contemporary inscription on another monument, the Moabite Stone, records that, after having been conquered by Omri (whose military successes the DH studiously ignores), Moab broke free of Israel's "oppression," a national liberation supposedly achieved by the power of **Chemosh,** the national god of Moab. A tribute to Chemosh's redemption of his people, the Moabite Stone shows that Israel's neighbors in the mid-ninth century B.C.E. had developed a theology of history similar to that which many biblical authors express. As the DH attributes all of Israel's political and economic misfortunes to YHWH's wrath, so the Moabite inscription portrays Moab's former domination by Israel as evidence of Chemosh's anger and the subsequent throwing off of Israel's yoke as the result of the god's blessing (Figure 15.6). Ironically, Moab's ability to break free of Israel was a consequence of the country's internal strife, culminating in Jehu's Yahwist excesses, which so sapped Israel's strength that previously subject nations such as Moab were able to regain—and keep—their independence. Although Elisha prophesies that a confederation of the kings of Israel, Judah, and Edom will conquer "every fortified city" of Moab, the expedition fails. According to 2 Kings 3, when King Mesha, desperate to end the coalition's siege of his city, sacrifices his firstborn son, such "wrath" ensues (from Chemosh?) that the Israelite attackers give up and withdraw (3:4–27; see also Box 7.2, "YHWH and Child Sacrifice").

A QUEEN FOR JUDAH

An indirect result of Jehu's extermination of both Israelite and Judean kings was the elevation of a queen to Judah's throne, her reign the only interruption of the Davidic line in its entire history. A daughter of Omri (or perhaps of Ahab and Jezebel), **Athaliah** (ruled 842–837 B.C.E.) was the wife of Jehoram, king of Judah. (Their son Ahaziah is not

Figure 15.4 A witness to the Assyrian Empire's once irresistible might, the Black Obelisk of Shalmaneser III (859–825 B.C.E.) pictures representatives from five different regions — including King Jehu of Israel — bringing tribute to the Assyrian king. After Assyria destroyed the northern kingdom of Israel (721 B.C.E.), Judah maintained a precarious existence by stripping the Temple of its treasures to keep Assyrian armies at bay (2 Kings 18:13–16).

to be confused with the Israelite king of the same name whose death Elijah had predicted.) When Jehu murdered both Jehoram and Ahaziah (his heir) about 842 B.C.E., Athaliah seized control of Judah. Emulating Jehu's example, Queen Athaliah ordered the execution of all of Ahaziah's male offspring (her grandsons), rival heirs to the crown. Only one prince escaped; the chief priest, Jehoiada, secretly hid Ahaziah's infant son, **Jehoash** (also called Joash), in the Jerusalem Temple.

After Athaliah reigned successfully for six years, the priest Jehoiada masterminded a palace revolt in which Athaliah was murdered and the seven-year-old Jehoash placed on the throne. According to the Deuteronomistic narrator, Jehoash distinguished his long reign (837–800 B.C.E.) by doing "what was right in the sight of the LORD" (2 Kings 12:2). Nevertheless, perhaps because he allowed his subjects to continue sacrificing to YHWH outside Jerusalem, Jehoash's administration endured various humiliations, including turning over the entire national treasury to King Hazael of Syria to keep him from invading Judah. Despite the author's qualified approval, Jehoash, like his grandmother, came to a violent end, murdered by conspirators (12:17–20).

THE ASSYRIAN INVASION AND FALL OF SAMARIA

Although the northern kingdom enjoyed renewed prosperity under such kings as **Jeroboam II** (ruled 786–746 B.C.E.), revolution and violent changes of rulership continued to destabilize Israel. As Israel declined politically, a new threat appeared: After centuries of relative inactivity, **Assyria** began a period of vigorous military expansion, swallowing up lesser kingdoms and peoples as its armies marched

Figure 15.5 This panel of the Black Obelisk shows Jehu, king of Israel, groveling before the Assyrian emperor Shalmaneser III, to whom he pays tribute. The Deuteronomistic writers describe Jehu's revolt against Ahab's dynasty (842 B.C.E.) as a Yahwist-inspired movement (2 Kings 9:1–10:36). However, as a result of Jehu's butchery of Israel's former ruling class, the nation was fatally weakened and eventually destroyed. Ironically, the Black Obelisk identifies Jehu as "son of Omri," founder of the royal line that the Yahwist usurper exterminated.

from Mesopotamia to Egypt. As its power and territorial acquisitions increased, so did Assyria's ability to command tribute from weaker states. When Israel's last king, Hoshea (ruled 732–724 B.C.E.), hoping for Egyptian help, stopped payments to Assyria, Assyrian armies laid siege to Samaria, which **Sargon II** captured and destroyed in 722 B.C.E. Because it was Assyria's policy to deport defeated populations to discourage further rebellions, thousands of Israel's leading citizens were forcibly relocated elsewhere in the Assyrian empire, and foreigners were moved into former Israelite territory.

According to the Deuteronomistic commentary in 2 Kings 17, Israel's fall resulted from its repeated offenses to YHWH, its toleration of Baal cults, and its worship at unauthorized "high places." YHWH remained concerned about this portion of the Promised Land, however, for, displeased with the new settlers, he afflicted the region with marauding lions. Recognizing that the "god of the land" required appeasement, Assyrian administrators dispatched a previously exiled priest of YHWH to teach the inhabitants how to worship Israel's God properly, ending the "plague" of lions. In its distinctively southern bias, the Judean writer's account of the ten "lost" tribes and the origin of the area's non-Israelite population is not, in the opinion of most

scholars, historically reliable. Although an ethnically mixed group—known as **Samaritans** (after Israel's former capital of Samaria)—supplanted the older tribal units, they continued to worship YHWH. Deuteronomistic prejudice against the Samaritans, who maintained sanctuaries competing with that in Jerusalem, colors the biblical account of their origins.

Judah Alone

ASSYRIA AND HEZEKIAH

Although Judah escapes the northern kingdom's fate, Assyrian aggression remains a long-term threat to its continued existence. Second Kings 18–20 describe the reign of **Hezekiah** (715–687 B.C.E.), whose policy toward Assyria, alternating between submission and outright rebellion, brings mixed results. The narrator praises Hezekiah for his vigorous enforcement of Deuteronomic principles, abolishing the "high places" and centralizing national worship at the Jerusalem sanctuary. Asserting Judean autonomy against Assyrian influence, Hezekiah tears down the paraphernalia of Canaanite and other foreign cults that had infiltrated Judean religious practices. Besides demolishing the poles and sacred pillars—symbols of the tree of life associated with the Canaanite goddess Asherah (whom some scholars believe was revered alongside YHWH, perhaps as his divine consort)—Hezekiah also destroys the bronze serpent (called Nehushtan) that Moses had fashioned in the desert to cure people bitten by poisonous snakes (Num. 21:9). As a symbol of healing, the bronze image apparently has become an object of veneration and hence a threat to Yahwist purity. No icon or relic, even one associated with Moses, can be allowed to deflect worship from YHWH alone.

Although the narrative compares Hezekiah to King David in his faithfulness to YHWH (2 Kings 18:3–8), the generally favorable DH attitude toward his reign also includes an element of ambivalence. The text states that YHWH accompanied Hezekiah so that "wherever he went, he prospered" and seems to approve of the king's revolt against Judah's Assyrian oppressors. At the same time, Hezekiah's success is perilously close to failure: His refusal to pay Assyria tribute incites **Sennacherib** (ruled 704–681 B.C.E.) to invade Judah (701 B.C.E.), capture most of its important towns, and levy a ruinously heavy fine on the nation. Hezekiah is forced to strip the Temple of its decorations and treasure, paying Sennacherib enormous sums of silver and gold, and then to submit again to the Assyrian yoke. Although one of Hezekiah's leading advisors, the prophet Isaiah, correctly forecasts that Jerusalem will survive the Assyrian siege unscathed, the king ends his twenty-nine-year reign impoverished and ruling over only a scrap of his former domain.

JERUSALEM'S DELIVERANCE

Assyrian and biblical versions of Sennacherib's invasion of Judah differ strikingly, causing some historians to suppose that they refer to two separate campaigns. According to Assyrian records carved on a hexagonal prism by Sennacherib, Hezekiah was made "a prisoner in Jerusalem, his royal residence, like a bird in a cage"—though the prism says nothing of Assyria's failure to capture the city.

Figure 15.6   The enormously important Moabite Stone, found in 1868, records the victories of Mesha, king of Moab, over the northern state of Israel (ninth century B.C.E.). Grateful to Chemosh, the Moabite national god, for liberating him from the Israelite domination imposed by Omri and Ahab, Mesha articulates a Canaanite mirror image of the Deuteronomistic philosophy of history: "As for Omri, king of Israel, he humbled Moab many years, for Chemosh was angry at his land. And his son followed him and he also said, 'I will humble Moab.' In my time he spoke (thus), but I have triumphed over him and over his house, while Israel hath perished for ever!"

According to 2 Kings and a parallel account in Isaiah 36–37, Jerusalem's escape is attributed to divine intervention. In a single night, YHWH's Angel of Death strikes down 185,000 Assyrian soldiers, forcing Sennacherib to lift his siege and return to Nineveh. The biblical version has some indirect confirmation from nonbiblical sources, including the Greek historian Herodotus, who states that swarms of mice chewed through the soldiers' bowstrings, a reference some commentators interpret as an outbreak of rodent-carried bubonic plague that decimated Assyrian ranks (*Histories*, Bk. 2, 141). After the Assyrian war machine's initial success in laying waste to most of Judah and slaying thousands of its inhabitants, the invaders' final victory had seemed inevitable, making their sudden withdrawal from Jerusalem appear a miracle. Jerusalem's deliverance may have contributed to a popular belief that the holy city would never fall into enemy hands — a view that the prophet Jeremiah would later attack (Jer. 7, 26).

Second Kings 20 relates an incident that evidently took place before Sennacherib's invasion, when Hezekiah still possessed great wealth. Attempting to recruit Babylon as an ally against Assyria, Hezekiah foolishly takes the Babylonian ambassador on a tour of his richly furnished palace and overflowing treasury, displaying all of Judah's economic resources to the foreigner's gaze. Appalled at the king's rashness, Isaiah prophesies that the country's entire wealth will be swept away to Babylon — a direct allusion to Nebuchadnezzar's sacking of Jerusalem more than a century later. Probably added during the postexilic DH revisions, this passage depicts a morally ambivalent Hezekiah. When Isaiah informs him that the disaster still lies in the future, the king finds the news "good," because "there will be peace and security in [his] day" (20:12–19).

MANASSEH'S REIGN

Whereas Hezekiah is judged favorably, the Deuteronomistic writer regards his son **Manasseh** (ruled 687–642 B.C.E.) as the extreme low point in the annals of Judean kings. Hezekiah swept away the "high places" throughout Judah, but Manasseh not only rebuilds them but also erects altars to foreign gods in the Temple itself. Reversing his father's Yahwist reforms, Manasseh commits virtually every covenant violation ever perpetrated by any king of Israel or Judah, including rampant Baalism, black magic, and human sacrifice. Promoting a syncretism abhorrent to Judah's prophets, Manasseh sets up a "carved image of Asherah," perhaps conceived as YHWH's female companion, in the Jerusalem sanctuary. Charged with worse crimes than those perpetrated by the Canaanites whom Israel displaced, Manasseh nonetheless reigns for more than half a century, longer than any other Davidic ruler.

The Book of Chronicles, written at least two centuries after the DH, adds a surprising conclusion to Manasseh's story, one not even hinted at in 2 Kings. According to 2 Chronicles, Manasseh is taken captive to Babylon, where he undergoes a sudden conversion to Yahwism, repenting his former misdeeds. Moved by his prayer, YHWH permits Manasseh's restoration to Judah's throne, after which the humbled and penitent king conducts a thoroughgoing religious reform anticipating that of Josiah. (The Chronicler cites the "records of the seers" as the source of this remarkable tale [2 Chron. 33:11–20]; see Chapter 27.) If the Deuteronomistic editors knew about a tradition in which Manasseh was transformed into an ardent Yahwist reformer, they found no place for a repentant Manasseh in their theology of history. The sorcerer-king is singled out as the primary cause of Judah's demise, and his character is allowed no redeeming qualities (2 Kings 21:10–17; 23:26–27).

Josiah: The Deuteronomistic Hero

With the ascension of Josiah, Manasseh's grandson, Judah enters a new era in the development of Yahwistic faith. Reviving the policies of his ancestor Hezekiah, Josiah (ruled 640–609 B.C.E.) fulfills both the letter and the spirit of Deuteronomy's commands to honor one God and sacrifice to him at one sanctuary only. Although some of its legal traditions may have been compiled in the northern kingdom several generations earlier, Deuteronomy (or at least its nucleus, Chapters 12–26) became Josiah's chief instrument in revitalizing Judah's national faith. Found during Temple repairs — renovations that probably involved removing Manasseh's Baalistic shrines and images — Deuteronomy brought an updated version of the Mosaic legacy to general public notice. The narrator indicates that both king and people were previously unfamiliar with Deuteronomy's statutes and penalties and notes that holding a Passover ceremony, so important in the Pentateuch, is now considered an innovation. According to 2 Kings 23, no comparable Passover celebration was previously observed, during either the period of the judges or that of the monarchy (23:21–23).

Taking advantage of Assyria's rapid decline in the late seventh century B.C.E., Josiah extends his reforms into the former northern kingdom, obliterating altars and desecrating tombs throughout the countryside. His campaign of national renewal is cut short, however, when Egypt's Pharaoh **Necho II** (ruled 610–595 B.C.E.) invades the area on his way to aid the last remnants of Assyrian leadership in northern Syria. Whereas Necho wanted a weakened Assyria to survive as a buffer state between Egypt and the newly revived empire of Babylon, Josiah may have hoped to rid Judah of all foreign occupation or, failing that, to support Babylon against Assyria. Attempting to intercept Necho's army, Josiah is killed at the Battle of Megiddo, thus bringing his Deuteronomic reforms to a premature end and leaving Judah in the hands of weak or incompetent successors.

The Last Days of Judah

In 612 B.C.E., Assyria's capital, Nineveh, falls to the combined forces of the Medes and Babylonians. Although Pharaoh Necho rushes into the power vacuum that Assyria's collapse opens in the Near East, the Egyptians are soon defeated by **Nebuchadnezzar,** king of Babylon, at the Battle of **Carchemish** (605 B.C.E.). The tiny state of Judah now must submit to the Babylonian yoke; its last kings are merely Nebuchadnezzar's tribute-paying vassals.

Josiah's son **Jehoiakim** (ruled 609–598 B.C.E.), whom Nebuchadnezzar placed on Judah's throne, unwisely rebels but dies before the Babylonians can retaliate, leaving his son and successor, Jehoiachin, to suffer the consequences of the revolt. In 598/597 B.C.E., Jehoiachin and his family are taken as prisoners to Babylon, the Temple is stripped of its treasures, and 10,000 members of Judah's upper classes are deported to Mesopotamia (2 Kings 24). Nebuchadnezzar then appoints Jehoiachin's uncle **Zedekiah** (ruled 597–587 B.C.E.) king in his place.

When Zedekiah, too, rebels against Babylon, Nebuchadnezzar besieges and destroys Jerusalem and its Temple. Without comment, the last verses of 2 Kings 25 tersely describe the holy city's devastation: The Babylonians demolish the city walls, shatter the Temple's bronze pillars and set the structure afire, loot and burn surrounding villages, and carry off much of the remaining population, leaving only the poorest citizens behind. Nebuchadnezzar appoints a Judean leader, Gedaliah, governor of the ruined city, but even that token of survival is lost when Judean nationalists murder Gedaliah. Fearing Babylonian retaliation, many of the remaining peasants flee to Egypt.

Has YHWH Abandoned His People Forever?

The flight of Jerusalem's impoverished inhabitants to Egypt brings the story of Israel full cycle, back to the conditions under which their pre-Mosaic ancestors lived, as strangers in a foreign land. Groping to find moral sense in the national catastrophe, the Deuteronomistic History blames the victims: The covenant community deserved to suffer because it broke faith with YHWH. Apostate rulers like Manasseh led the way, but the people, mixing YHWH's worship with that of Baal, Asherah, and other deities, sinned so grievously that a righteous Deity could not refrain from punishing them. Prophetic witnesses to the disaster who were also influenced by the Deuteronomic view of history, such as Jeremiah, similarly attributed Judah's demise to its covenant violations (see Chapter 19). Striving to understand God's intentions in having abandoned them to their enemies, Judean exiles in Babylon reworked Israel's ancient written and oral traditions about Abraham and his descendants to produce the remarkable epic of Israel's creation and fall, Genesis through 2 Kings. In the crisis of God's apparent absence from his people, editors appended to Deuteronomy YHWH's ominous warning, a portent of their plight in exile: "I will hide my face from them; I will see what their end will be" (Deut. 32:20). The same redactors, however, also included assurances that YHWH would someday overthrow Israel's oppressors, restore their prosperity, and reaffirm the covenant partnership (Deut. 33:26–29; cf. Deut. 30:1–5), a future return from exile to the Promised Land (see Chapter 22).

QUESTIONS FOR REVIEW

1. Explain why scholars think that there were two editions of the Deuteronomistic History. What events during the reign of Josiah would seem to be a fulfillment of the ancient promises to Israel and stimulate the production of an optimistic history of the covenant people? What events after Josiah's death necessitated a revision of an earlier edition of the DH? Explain your answer.

2. Describe the accomplishments of Solomon's reign. In what ways was the Temple closely linked to the Davidic monarchy? How were Phoenician architects and artisans involved in constructing YHWH's "house"? What specifically Deuteronomistic ideas appear in the account of Solomon's dedication of the sanctuary (1 Kings 8)?

3. Why did Israel split into two different kingdoms following Solomon's death? What was the "sin of Jeroboam," and how does the installation of rival shrines in the northern kingdom influence the writer-redactor's judgment of the northern rulers?

4. Outline the conflicts between Israel's rulers, such as Ahab and Jezebel, and the prophets Elijah and Elisha. How was the rivalry between worshipers of YHWH and those of Baal involved in Jehu's overthrow of the royal dynasty of Omri and Ahab? Who was Naboth, and how were Torah precepts used against an innocent man?

5. How did Jehu's bloody purges of Baal worshipers lead to the installation of a queen on Judah's throne, the only non-Davidic ruler during the lifetime of the Davidic monarchy? Did Jehu's forcibly imposed Yahwism result in growth and prosperity for his nation?

6. Describe the fall of Israel and the Assyrian threat to Judah and Jerusalem. How did Hezekiah respond to Assyria's invasion of his territory? How did Jerusalem escape the fate of Samaria?

7. Contrast the policies of Manasseh and Josiah. Which king ruled longer? Which king was cut down in his prime? Do the respective fates of Manasseh and Josiah illustrate the theory of history formulated in Deuteronomy? Explain your answer.

8. What happened to Judah and Jerusalem in 587 B.C.E.? What issues about the partnership between YHWH and the covenant people did this event raise?

QUESTIONS FOR REFLECTION AND DISCUSSION

1. In narrating the historical experiences of Israel and Judah, what theological lessons do the Deuteronomistic historian-redactors draw? Why are so few Judean kings (and none in the northern kingdom) judged worthy according to Deuteronomistic standards? How would you judge the specific criteria used to evaluate a particular monarch's moral success? Why do you find it adequate or inadequate in weighing an individual ruler's success or failure?

2. According to the Deuteronomistic History, why did YHWH abandon his people to the Babylonians? Why does the DH single out Manasseh as personally responsible for Judah's destruction? What theological and psychological benefits result from assigning responsibility for this national disaster to the covenant community itself? Is it more psychologically acceptable to blame human failure for loss and suffering than to confront the possibility that Israel's divine patron failed to protect his flock?

TERMS AND CONCEPTS TO REMEMBER

Adonijah	Jezebel
Ahab	Josiah
Ahijah	Judah
Assyria	Manasseh
Athaliah	Manasseh's sins
Carchemish	Mount Carmel
Chemosh	Naboth
division of Israel and	Nebuchadnezzar
Judah	Necho II
Elijah and Elisha	Omri
Elisha's political role	Rehoboam
Hezekiah	Samaria
Hiram	Samaritans
Israel	Sargon II
Jehoash	Sennacherib
Jehoiachin	Solomon
Jehoiakim	two editions of
Jehonadab	Deuteronomistic
Jehu	History
Jeroboam I	Zedekiah
Jeroboam II	

RECOMMENDED READING

Cogan, Mordechai, and Tadmor, Hayim. *2 Kings.* Garden City, N.Y.: Doubleday, 1988. A detailed commentary emphasizing historical and linguistic issues.

Gray, John. *I and II Kings: A Commentary.* Philadelphia: Westminster Press, 1970. Places this theological history of Israel and Judah in its ancient Near Eastern context.

Jones, Gwilym H. *1 and 2 Kings.* 2 vols. Grand Rapids, Mich.: Eerdmans, 1984. A historical-critical examination of the texts.

Long, Burke O. *1 Kings, with an Introduction to Historical Literature.* Grand Rapids, Mich.: Eerdmans, 1984. Focuses on literary analysis of the text.

———. *2 Kings.* Grand Rapids, Mich.: Eerdmans, 1991. Addresses literary issues.

Seow, Choon-Leong. "The First and Second Books of Kings: Introduction, Commentary, and Reflections." In *The New Interpreter's Bible,* Vol. 3, pp. 3–295. Nashville, Tenn: Abingdon Press, 1999. A helpful introductory analysis of the text, with historical and theological discussions.

Walsh, Jerome T. *1 Kings.* Collegeville, Minn.: Liturgical Press, 1996. Offers a literary approach.

CHAPTER 16

The Nature and Function of Israelite Prophecy

Spokespersons for God

Key Topics/Themes The role played by prophets in Israel is not unlike that played by prophets in other ancient Near Eastern cultures. The *navi*—the most commonly used Hebrew word to designate a "messenger" of YHWH—is one who is called by God or who speaks on his behalf, and whose speech is therefore understood to be divinely commissioned or inspired. The Greek word *prophetes*, from which the term *prophet* is derived, means much the same thing: someone appointed by God to speak in his name and to proclaim his will. This singular role could be filled by men or women, though in a patriarchal society like ancient Israel's, it is hardly surprising that the majority of prophetic personalities were men. However, at least two of the women who are designated as prophets—Deborah (Judg. 4–5) and Huldah (2 Kings 22:14–20)—perform the same directive function as their male counterparts, in that they have an opportunity not only to articulate the divine point of view but also to affect history and help to implement the divine plan for Israel. Viewed collectively, then, the prophets should be seen not as mere observers of or commentators on current events but as divinely appointed intermediaries and even as active participants in an unfolding drama of judgment and redemption.

The Spokespersons for God

MOSES THE ARCHETYPE

Within the context of Pentateuchal traditions, Moses is clearly the archetypal representation of the prophet. Though both Abraham and Joseph are referred to as "prophets" and are summoned by God to uphold the covenant relationship, it is Moses who performs nearly all of the functions prophetic personalities were expected to carry out. To begin with, he is the recipient of direct and unambiguous communications from YHWH:

> When there are prophets among you,
> I the LORD make myself known to them
>   in visions;
> I speak to them in dreams.
> Not so with my servant Moses; . . .
> With him I speak face to face—clearly, not
>   in riddles. (Num. 12:6–8)

Moreover, he witnesses a theophany at Sinai/Horeb that the assembled Israelite masses can only dimly perceive: To them, YHWH speaks in thunder; with Moses, he uses intelligible speech. And, as a sign of their particular intimacy, YHWH allows Moses to glimpse either his "back" (Exod. 33:23) or his "face" (Exod. 33:11). There are limits to this intimacy, however, and at the risk of self-contradiction, the author-redactor of Exodus concludes Chapter 33 with the observation that YHWH's face "shall not be seen"—not even by Moses. Nevertheless, Moses is given the unique privilege of revealing YHWH's will to the world in the form of statutory law and ethical-theological proclamations. However, Moses is not only the human voice of divine revelation but also (at least within the Deuteronomic tradition) the exemplary servant of YHWH whose entire adult life is dedicated to God's service, and at his death the Deuteronomist can exclaim: "Never since has there arisen a prophet in Israel like Moses" (Deut. 34:10).

SAMUEL AND HIS SUCCESSORS

Yet, for all this praise, the name and figure of Moses virtually disappear from the Deuteronomistic History after Joshua. The eighth-century-B.C.E. prophet Hosea can exclaim:

By a prophet the LORD [YHWH] brought
Israel up from Egypt,
and by a prophet he was guarded . . .
(Hos. 12:13)

Nevertheless, the "classical," or literary, prophets seem to have forgotten Moses' name, seldom mentioning him in conjunction with the Exodus. In fact, prophecy as a social institution, and certainly as a literary tradition, seems to develop in tandem with the monarchy, and as the monarchy disappears by the fifth century B.C.E., so does prophecy (or at least those prophetic writings considered appropriate for canonization). The reasons for prophecy's "decline" are a matter of conjecture, but the connection between the monarchies and the prophetic class, in both the northern and southern kingdoms, is often very close and politically ambiguous.

Samuel's dual role in the formation of the monarchy—he is both bitterly opposed to it (1 Sam. 8:4–22) and instrumental in the election of Saul and David to the throne—is often replicated in later centuries by prophets who are sometimes supportive and at other times contemptuous of the king and his policies, and who are not reluctant to intervene in the intrigues that surround the royal court. Nathan, for example, confronts David over the assassination of Uriah (2 Sam. 12), denouncing him in God's name, and later prompts Bathsheba to demand that David appoint Solomon as his successor. In the next generation, the prophet Ahijah takes an even more direct role in the disputes between Solomon and northern tribal leaders by inviting Jeroboam to rebel against his royal patron and become king of a secessionist northern kingdom (1 Kings 11:26–40).

ELIJAH AND DEFIANCE OF ESTABLISHED AUTHORITY

Perhaps the boldest attempt by any prophet to oppose a monarchy and directly affect the course of history is that undertaken by Elijah in his struggle with Ahab and Jezebel; in Elijah's career, we can discern a pattern of personal revelation, spiritual proclamation, and political engagement that becomes normative for many prophets after the ninth century B.C.E. Like Moses, Elijah is privileged to experience YHWH directly in the form of a theophany on Sinai/Horeb (1 Kings 19), and like Nathan, he is instructed by God to confront Ahab and denounce him for his crimes against Naboth (1 Kings 21). However, Elijah's greatest challenge to Ahab's authority and to the religious culture of Israel is to be found in his attack on the priests of **Baal** on Mount Carmel (1 Kings 18). By first exposing Baalism as a fraud and then leading a massacre of its priests, Elijah not only places the demands of YHWH before the prerogatives of the king but actually denies the moral legitimacy of Ahab's reign and in so doing places the prophet above the king in the spiritual hierarchy of Israel. Such defiance of established authority in the service of God becomes a familiar pattern by the eighth and seventh centuries

BOX 16.1
The Order of the Prophets' Appearances

Like other contributors to biblical literature, the prophets of Israel and Judah appeared largely in response to urgent political or ethical crises that troubled the covenant community. Editors of the Hebrew Bible placed collections of the prophets' oracles immediately after the Deuteronomistic History, thus emphasizing the prophetic role in the course of events that led to the destruction of both Israel and Judah. As a group, the prophets bear witness to the covenant people's repeated failures to heed YHWH's warnings about the national disasters that would result from disloyalty to him. Most of the prophets belong to one of three critical periods, in each of which the covenant community faced a military or religious crisis that threatened its existence: (1) the Assyrian threat (eighth century B.C.E.), (2) the Babylonian invasion (sixth century B.C.E.), and (3) the restructuring of Judah after the Babylonian exile (late sixth and fifth centuries B.C.E.).

THE ASSYRIAN CRISIS (EIGHTH CENTURY B.C.E.)

Amos A Judean called to prophesy in the northern kingdom of Israel during the mid-eighth century B.C.E., Amos reverses popular assumptions about the "Day of YHWH," which was then apparently believed to be a future time when God would decisively intervene in history to punish Israel's enemies and vindicate his chosen people. Instead, Amos declares that when YHWH appears it will be to punish Israel along with other nations that foster social and economic injustice. Vigorously denouncing the upper classes' exploitation of the poor, Amos predicts national collapse and exile, with only an afterthought of restoration to the land for a "remnant" of the exiled community.

Hosea A native of Israel, Hosea compares his nation's worship of Baal to the breaking of a marriage bond. Although, like Amos, Hosea argues that economic disparity between rich and poor will bring divine punishment, he also emphasizes YHWH's *hesed* (steadfast love), likening God's concern for Israel to that of a devoted father for his disobedient son.

Isaiah of Jerusalem A prophet intimately associated with the Jerusalem sanctuary and Davidic royal family, Isaiah echoes the northern prophets in denouncing the ruling classes' acquisitiveness and callous disregard for the poor. Active during the time of the Assyrian invasion of Judah, he counsels Judean rulers to place their complete trust in YHWH's power to protect the city. He also predicts that a Davidic heir will establish universal peace and justice.

Micah Unlike his contemporary, Isaiah, Micah is a rural villager who unequivocally condemns rich urban landowners who "skin" and "devour" the peasant farmers. Criticizing the Jerusalem kings who permit such practices, Micah declares that the city and the Temple will be destroyed (Mic. 3:9–12).

THE DECLINE OF ASSYRIA AND RISE OF BABYLON (LATE SEVENTH AND EARLY SIXTH CENTURIES B.C.E.)

Zephaniah Compiled during Josiah's reign (640–609 B.C.E.), the oracles of Zephaniah begin with an account of YHWH's resolve to destroy all life on earth and end with the glad announcement that God has repealed his judgment, restoring Judah to his favor (a change of tone probably stemming from Josiah's religious reforms).

Nahum Shortly before Nineveh's fall (612 B.C.E.), Nahum rejoices over Assyria's destruction.

Habakkuk Faced with Babylon's imminent conquest of Judah, Habakkuk ponders YHWH's fairness, concluding that the righteous person must have faith in God's ultimate justice.

THE BABYLONIAN EXILE AND PROMISED RESTORATION OF JUDAH (SIXTH CENTURY B.C.E.)

Jeremiah Active during the reigns of Judah's last kings (Josiah to Zedekiah, c. 626–587 B.C.E.), Jeremiah argues that Babylon is God's instrument of justice used to punish Judah for its sins. Presenting Judah's fate as a result of covenant breaking, Jeremiah then envisions a future covenant between YHWH and his people, a bond that will not be broken (Jer. 31:31). Unlike his predecessor Isaiah, who also advised Judean rulers during foreign invasions, Jeremiah sees little merit in the Temple or the Davidic dynasty.

Obadiah Obadiah condemns the neighboring state of Edom for joining the Babylonians in looting Judah (587 B.C.E.).

(continued)

BOX 16.1 *(continued)*

Ezekiel A priest and mystic exiled in Babylon during Judah's last years (after 597 B.C.E.), Ezekiel envisions YHWH, too holy to remain dwelling in a corrupted sanctuary, as abandoning the Jerusalem Temple. Ezekiel's denunciations of Judean sins are balanced by his visions of Judah's future resurrection to renewed life with YHWH at a gloriously restored holy city.

Second Isaiah Living among the Judean exiles in Babylon during Cyrus the Great's rise to power (c. 550–539 B.C.E.), this anonymous prophet (known as Second Isaiah) explicitly advocates monotheism, declaring that YHWH is the *only* God (Isa. 40–55). He also promises that YHWH will stage a "new exodus," bringing his people back from exile to a splendidly rebuilt Judah. Second Isaiah's four Servant Songs depict the redemptive role of Yahweh's chosen agent, Israel.

AFTER THE EXILE: AN INCOMPLETE RESTORATION (LATE SIXTH AND FIFTH CENTURIES B.C.E.)

Haggai Under Zerubbabel, a Davidic descendant whom the Persians appointed governor of the partly restored postexilic community, Haggai promises that YHWH will cause the wealth of nations to flow into Jerusalem if the Judeans will obediently rebuild the Temple.

Zechariah A contemporary of Haggai (c. 520 B.C.E.), Zechariah produces a series of mystic visions involving the rebuilt Temple, the High Priest Joshua, the Davidic governor Zerubbabel, and YHWH's fu-

ture intentions for the covenant people. A later hand added Chapters 9–12.

Third Isaiah The third section of Isaiah (Chs. 56–66) includes oracles from almost the whole period of Israelite prophecy, including the work of a postexilic prophet, referred to as Third Isaiah, who is sharply critical of the imperfectly restored Judah's religious failures.

Joel Of uncertain date, the collection ascribed to Joel contains a series of apocalyptic visions that depict plagues and other sufferings signaling the Day of YHWH. Calling his hearers to repentance, Joel foresees a climactic outpouring of the divine spirit upon all humanity.

Malachi This anonymous prophet (the book's title merely means "my messenger") also predicts a coming judgment on the frightening day of YHWH's visitation. Promising that an unidentified agent will appear to purify the Temple cult, Malachi ends by announcing the reappearance of the ninth-century Israelite prophet Elijah.

Jonah A humorous tale of a narrow-minded prophet who anticipates (and resents) his God's compassion for Gentiles, this prose work differs in form and content from all other books of prophetic literature. Highlighting YHWH's decision to spare Nineveh, Assyria's hated capital, Jonah seems to offer an implicit criticism of traditional Israelite prophecy, which tended to emphasize YHWH's violent judgments on both Israel and its enemies.

B.C.E., when we see Amos rebuke both a king and his priest (Amos 7:10–17), and Jeremiah pronounce a sentence of death on both a doomed priesthood and an equally doomed king (Jer. 7, 38). Though several prophets appear to have come from priestly families, and though their advice is repeatedly sought out by kings and commoners alike, the prophets as a class seem to keep their distance from both the Temple and the royal court, preserving an independence that reflects their self-perception as YHWH's servants alone. (Box 16.1 discusses the succession of prophets.)

Forms and Characteristics of Prophecy

ECSTATIC PROPHECY

As in other Near Eastern cultures, Israelite prophets exhibit a range of behaviors and personality traits that distinguish them from both priests and wisdom teachers. At one end of the prophetic continuum is the **ecstatic prophet,** whose frenzied gestures were understood to be the result of divine possession. Saul, for example, exhibits precisely this type of behavior twice in his career (1 Sam. 10:9–12; 19:23–24) when, filled with the *ruach elohim* (spirit of God), he strips his clothes off and falls to the ground, lying naked for a day and a night. Anthropologists sometimes describe such behavior as part of an **incubation ritual** in which a prophet enters a state of altered consciousness by lying on an animal skin or on the ground, awaiting some revelation from the gods. In Saul's case, of course, such behavior seems sudden and inexplicable—hence the proverb "is Saul *also* among the prophets?" (1 Sam. 10:12)—but for the priests of Baal whom Elijah challenges, ecstatic and even self-mutilating actions are perfectly conventional ways of summoning Baal to their aid:

> Then they cried aloud and, as was their custom, they cut themselves with swords and lances until the blood gushed out over them. As midday passed, they raved on until the time of the offering of the oblation, but there was no voice, no answer, and no response. (1 Kings 18:28–29)

The Orphic and Dionysian cults in ancient Greece practiced similar rites, all of them seemingly based on some form of **sympathetic magic,** through which the attention of divine beings could be attracted by loud noises and frenzied motions. Some of Ezekiel's prophetic seizures, especially those in which "the hand of the Lord God" falls upon him, may even be explained by comparing them with the common experience of ecstatic visionaries who understand prophecy to be an outside force that takes possession of both body and mind.

DIVINATION

Another common form of prophecy in the ancient world—*divination*—also seems to have had its counterpart in Israel, in spite of Balaam's assertion to the contrary ("surely there is no divination in Israel" [Num. 23:23]). When David, for example, cannot decide whether to pursue the Amalekites who have raided the village of Ziklag, he summons the priest Abiathar and "consults" the **ephod,** fully expecting a prophetic (that is, directive) response (1 Sam. 30:7–8). What Israelite prophets do *not* do is

predict the future by examining the entrails of animals or by studying patterns of bird flights—two common methods of augury or divination in antiquity. However, the ability to predict future events and, more important, to ascertain the likelihood of success or failure for any human venture is widely assumed to be the mark of the prophet in any age. Deuteronomy 18:22 is quite explicit on that point: "If a prophet speaks in the name of the Lord but the thing does not take place or prove true, it is a word that the Lord has not spoken." Jeremiah's contemporaries certainly assumed as much when they imprisoned him for predicting the defeat of Judah at the hands of the Babylonians (Jer. 26) and then turned to him when the very disaster he had foreseen was about to overtake them (Jer. 37). Both Isaiah and Ezekiel are consulted by their contemporaries, hoping for a glimpse of the future from a "seer" (*roeh* in Hebrew literally means "one who sees" or who possesses second sight) who can discern the future because YHWH has already revealed it to him. This very talent allows Samuel to inform Saul that his lost donkeys have already been found (1 Sam. 9:20) and enables Isaiah to predict (at the request of King Ahaz) that Judah's enemies will be crushed by the Assyrian army (Isa. 7:14–17).

Shifts in Prophetic Focus and Influence

For all their skill in "divining" the future, Israel's prophets were primarily neither fortune-tellers nor dream interpreters (the two most common offices performed by court prophets in the ancient world). With the obvious exception of Joseph and Daniel, prophets in Israel did not hire themselves out to foreign kings as persons skilled in **oneiromancy** (the interpretation of dreams) or any other form of divination. The primary task of an Israelite prophet was to be a truth-teller by declaring the word and the will of YHWH to his contemporaries, and the principal "truth" that the prophets were summoned to proclaim was the true nature of the covenant relationship. As the prophets interpreted that relationship, Israel was bound, intimately and reciprocally, to YHWH through a network of conditional and unconditional promises, past associations, and future expectations. Like a husband or a father — and both metaphors are employed repeatedly in prophetic literature to characterize God's feelings for Israel — YHWH expects that some measure of loyalty and obedience will follow from his self-revelation to Israel and the giving of *torah*. And when Israel is neither loyal nor obedient, the response is an intermixture of divine sorrow and anger, followed by rejection:

> You have played the whore with
> many lovers;
> and would you return to me?
>   says the LORD.
> Look up to the bare heights,
>   and see!
> Where have you not been
>   lain with? . . .
> You have polluted the land
>   with your whoring and
>   wickedness.
> Therefore the showers have been
>   withheld,
> and the spring rain has not
>   come;
> yet you have the forehead of
>   a whore,
> you refuse to be ashamed.
> Have you not just now called to
>   me,
>   "My father, you are the friend
>   of my youth —
> will he be angry forever,
>   will he be indignant to the
>   end?" (Jer. 3: 1–5)

This mixed message is what the prophets themselves refer to as the "burden" of prophecy, especially for prophets writing before or during the Babylonian exile. Although the possibility of Israel's reconciliation to YHWH is never ruled out during the 300 years of preexilic prophetic writing, the prevailing view in this literature is that Israel has rejected every opportunity for genuine repentance and must

therefore submit to divine judgment in the form of dispossession from the land. This "reading" of Israel's history is, of course, identical with the interpretation of Israel's fate in the concluding chapters of Deuteronomy and throughout the historical writings known as the Deuteronomistic History. As previously noted, the Former and Latter Prophets are in essential agreement on the meaning and causes of the exile. And although the belief that a "remnant" of Judean exiles will return before long (once YHWH's anger has abated) is repeatedly expressed — in Amos (9:9–15) and Jeremiah (30:1–22), for example, where this theme appears amid repeated predictions of utter disaster — nevertheless, the preexilic prophets are quite consistent in their assertion that Israel has undermined the covenant relationship and must suffer the consequences.

This view undergoes a marked shift in both emphasis and perspective, however, in postexilic prophetic literature. Even though prophets like Second Isaiah and Zechariah are not willing to forget Israel's sins, they are clearly determined to preach God's forgiveness of them:

> Comfort, O comfort my
>   people,
> says your God.
> Speak tenderly to Jerusalem,
>   and cry to her
> that she has served her term,
>   that her penalty is paid,
> that she has received from the
>   LORD's hand
> double for all her sins. (Isa. 40:1–2)

But more important than the lifting of divine censure or the restoration to Judah (for those exiles who heeded the prophetic summons to return from Babylon) is the promise of a more glorious future than Israel has ever known and the appearance of a distinctly eschatological note in the writings of postexilic prophets:

> For I am about to create new
>   heavens
> and a new earth;
> the former things shall not be
>   remembered

or come to mind.
But be glad and rejoice forever
    in what I am creating; . . .
The wolf and the lamb shall feed
    together,
the lion shall eat straw like
    the ox;
but the serpent—its food shall
    be dust!
They shall not hurt or destroy
    on all my holy mountain,
      says the LORD. (Isa. 65:17–18, 25)

This vision of human and cosmic renewal marks a clear departure from earlier prophetic traditions, and the more postexilic writers stress the novelty of this "new world order," the more radical their break with the past comes to seem. For writers who embrace an eschatological view of history, both Israel and the peoples of the world are about to witness a fundamental change in the nature of reality, or perhaps simply a fulfillment of the initial promise of the creation myth that all things (humanity included) will be "very good." That not all postexilic prophets subscribe to this visionary forecast is clear from the writings of figures like Malachi and Haggai, who fret, as their preexilic predecessors did, over Israel's shortcomings (see Hag. 2:10–19; Mal. 1–2). Nevertheless, the prospect of a new beginning and the possibility of a transformed covenant relationship grips most of the prophetic writers of this period, and one can even see an anticipation of this theme in Jeremiah 31 and Ezekiel 37, as visions of spiritual and national rebirth become both more frequent and more urgent. The later appearance of apocalyptic literature—in Zechariah and, especially, Daniel—represents a further development of this tendency of postexilic thought with the symbolic encoding of this argument in texts meant to be understood by only the very few. Prophecy begins, therefore, as an open proclamation of YHWH's judgment of Israel and the world. But as it draws toward its canonical end, prophetic writing becomes increasingly esoteric in its language and perspective, and increasingly remote from the historical urgencies of classical prophetic speech and discourse. The growing pop-

ularity of apocalyptic literature in the postexilic period signals, therefore, not only a growing disenchantment with history but perhaps also a growing disbelief in the prophet as an effective intermediary for YHWH. The closing of the biblical canon and the growing conviction among Diaspora Jews that the era of prophecy had come to an end are surely not unrelated events; with the cessation of direct communication from God, the process of transcribing divine speech must also come to an end, and with it the unfolding epic of Israel's engagement with YHWH.

Paradoxically, then, the decline of prophecy seems to be linked, in part, to the very process of canonization through which the survival of the prophetic tradition and of individual works of prophecy was assured. However, other forces, cultural and political, were clearly at work undermining the authority of prophetic personalities or limiting the impact of their pronouncements. Even within the context of canonical prophetic literature, one can begin to see the growth of a corrosive skepticism directed at prophecy as such, and not simply at the credibility of a particular would-be prophet:

> Mortal, what is this proverb of yours about the land of Israel, which says, "The days are prolonged, and every vision comes to nothing"? (Ezek. 12:22)

Ezekiel's response to this display of collective disbelief in the value of prophetic discourse is to simultaneously decry false prophets while accusing Israel of faithlessness and rebellion. But the anxiety behind this "proverb" clearly indicates a growing culture of doubt that is reflected in the writings of late postexilic prophets—and particularly Haggai and Malachi—who find it necessary to remind their audiences both that YHWH still dwells among them (Hag. 2:4–5) and that indifference to his word and insincerity of worship can only deepen divine alienation from Israel. However compelling the Deuteronomic reading of Israel's fate must have seemed to Israel's prophets and historical redactors, it does not appear to have gained universal acceptance by the late sixth century B.C.E. (for example, Eccles. 8:17).

But the turn away from prophecy may also reflect a shift in the center of both secular and religious authority, as the monarchy is replaced during the Persian period (c. 539–332 B.C.E.) by a priestly theocracy, of which Ezra is the earliest embodiment. Once the priesthood becomes the repository of Israel's collective memory and the principal interpreter of its covenant and epic history, the conscience and the historical consciousness of the nation is now in priestly hands and will remain there until the rise of freelance exegetes of the Torah, later known as rabbis. In such a culture, the prophet begins to seem to many a redundant intermediary for YHWH, and the priest, whom Malachi describes as a "messenger of the LORD of Hosts" (Mal. 2:7), gradually assumes the prophet's teaching and censoring functions.

QUESTIONS FOR REVIEW

1. What role does the prophet play in Israelite culture? From whom does the prophet derive his or her authority?

2. Why did kings like David and Solomon maintain court prophets? What function did they perform?

3. How does ecstatic prophecy differ from divination? What implements might a diviner employ to engage in prophecy?

4. What shift in focus occurs in postexilic prophecy? Which new themes do later prophetic writers emphasize, and how does that reflect Israel's new political situation?

QUESTIONS FOR REFLECTION AND DISCUSSION

1. How can we explain both the preeminence of Moses within the Pentateuchal traditions and his virtual disappearance from later prophetic writings?

2. What is the primary responsibility of an Israelite prophet? What do prophets mean when they speak of the "burden" of prophecy?

3. How do the teachings and pronouncements of the prophets relate to the central themes of the Deuteronomistic History? To what extent is prophecy in Israel an outgrowth of the thinking behind the DH?

TERMS AND CONCEPTS TO REMEMBER

Baal	*navi*
divination	oneiromancy
ecstatic prophet	*roeh*
ephod	*ruach elohim*
incubation ritual	sympathetic magic

RECOMMENDED READING

Barton, John. "Prophecy (Postexilic Hebrew)." In D. N. Freedman, ed., *The Anchor Bible Dictionary*, Vol. 5, pp. 489–495. New York: Doubleday, 1992.

Blenkinsopp, Joseph. *A History of Prophecy in Israel*. Louisville, Ky.: Westminster/John Knox Press, 1996.

Brueggemann, Walter. *Hopeful Imagination: Prophetic Voices in Exile*. Philadelphia: Fortress Press, 1986.

Huffmon, H. B. "Prophecy (Ancient Near Eastern)." In D. N. Freedman, ed., *The Anchor Bible Dictionary*, Vol. 5, pp. 477–482. New York: Doubleday, 1992.

Lindblom, Johannes. *Prophecy in Ancient Israel*. Philadelphia: Fortress Press, 1963.

Schmitt, John J. "Prophecy (Preexilic Hebrew)." In D. N. Freedman, ed., *The Anchor Bible Dictionary*, Vol. 5, pp. 482–489. New York: Doubleday, 1992.

Prophets to the Northern Kingdom

The Books of Amos and Hosea

Key Topics/Themes The earliest examples of literary prophecy we possess date from the second half of the eighth century B.C.E. and naturally reflect the political and theological concerns of that era. The growing power and presence of the Assyrian Empire loom in the background of the books of Amos and Hosea, along with a palpable sense of doom hanging over the northern kingdom of Israel. Both prophets foresee an imminent judgment from God about to descend on Israel, and ultimately on Judah as well, and the cause of divine anger in each case is traced back to two things: Israel's apostasy and its corrupt, socially exploitative society.

Ironically, both Amos and Hosea begin their ministry during the reign of Jeroboam II (786–746 B.C.E.), a reign notable for its length, relative tranquility, and general prosperity. However, what Amos found in the northern kingdom was wealth in the hands of a few and destitution for the many, and a spirit of moral complacency among the very class of people most responsible for social inequities. But beyond these common failures of social conscience, Hosea found an even more appalling lack of commitment to YHWH and to the covenant, and a seemingly incurable attachment to foreign gods. Israel's disloyalty, as they saw it, expressed itself in two not unrelated ways: as indifference to the plight of the poor and the weak, and as an equal indifference to God's demands for obedience and exclusivity of worship. This double failure, as surely as Assyria's imperial ambitions, foretold predictable tragedy for the Israelites in general and for the

northern kingdom in particular, which the Assyrians overran and destroyed in 722 B.C.E.

The Book of Amos

THE HISTORICAL AMOS

The eighth-century-B.C.E. prophet **Amos** is traditionally placed third in the collection of Minor Prophets, but contemporary biblical scholars consider him to be the first prophet whose writings and pronouncements have come down to us in book form. The superscription of his book places his ministry during the reign of **Jeroboam II** (786–746 B.C.E.) in Israel and the reign of Uzziah (783–742 B.C.E.) in Judah, and, even more specifically, "two years before the earthquake." The earthquake to which this passage refers was serious enough to have left traces at Hazor and memorable enough for Flavius Josephus, the first-century-c.e. Jewish historian, to recall and connect with other events of this era. It is customary, then, to place the period of Amos's ministry at midcentury, though the Book of Amos evidently underwent significant redaction after the Babylonian exile.

Amos himself is identified in the text as a shepherd, a herdsman, and a pruner of sycamore trees — obviously, all agricultural tasks. What emerges from these several references is a composite portrait of an *am haaretz* (man of the countryside) who is nevertheless remarkably well informed about the politics of the northern kingdom, even though he comes from Tekoa, a small village not far from Jerusalem (and therefore within the southern kingdom of Judah). More important, when challenged by the High Priest Amaziah at the northern shrine of Shiloh, Amos insists that he is neither a prophet nor the "son of a prophet" (7:14). If, as biblical scholars contend, "son of a prophet" is really an allusion to a community or guild of prophets, then what Amos appears to be saying is that he is not a professional "seer" who makes his living at court or who offers his prognosticative talents to the highest bidder, in the manner of Balaam. Instead, he insists, he responded to YHWH's summons:

> . . . and the Lord [YHWH] took me from following the flock, and the Lord said to me, "Go, prophesy to my people Israel." (Amos 7:15)

Amos's independence from — and opposition to — the religious and political establishment of his time becomes, in later generations, the pattern of Israelite prophecy. Even when the prophet in question appears to come from a priestly family, his attitude toward the priesthood, the Temple, and everything associated with the cultic life of Israel is often very negative, if not altogether dismissive. As a class, the Latter Prophets emerge, in the words of one contemporary scholar, as a group of "dissident intellectuals" whose only loyalty is to God and the covenant, and whose principal task is to bring YHWH's judgment before their fellow Israelites.

THE KINGDOM OF ISRAEL UNDER JEROBOAM II

Ironically, the period of Amos's prophetic mission was a time of comparative peace and prosperity, during which the northern kingdom expanded its territories and new wealth began to flow into Israel as a result of its control of major trade routes. As long as Assyria remained in a state of political and military decline, Israel flourished, and archaeologists have found evidence of a higher standard of living in the excavations of Samaria — Israel's capital from the period of Omri on — and other northern cities than can be found in earlier periods. Amos's description of (presumably aristocratic) women lying on beds of ivory (6:4) does not appear to be at all exaggerated, nor is it likely that much of this wealth trickled down to the lower classes. Indeed, much of what Amos has to say about the moral character of the northern kingdom reflects his view of Israelite society as callous and indifferent to the poor, and at times brutally exploitative:

> Ah, you that turn justice to
>   wormwood,
> and bring righteousness to
>   the ground! . . .
> Therefore because you trample
>   on the poor
> and take from them levies
>   of grain,
> you have built houses of
>   hewn stone,
> but you shall not live in them;
> you have planted pleasant
>   vineyards,
> but you shall not drink
>   their wine. (Amos 5:7, 11)

What appalls Amos, however, is not simply the presence of social injustice but, even more, the complacency of the ruling classes, the smugness of those who live "at ease in Zion" (6:1), convinced that their behavior is irreproachable. In fact, the tragic paradox of such behavior is that the very people who are ignoring the social imperatives of covenant law — that is, the need to care for the poor, the fatherless, and the widowed — imagine that they are completely devoted to YHWH. Amos observes, mockingly, how zealously the privileged classes of Israel bring sacrifices to the northern shrines of Bethel and Gilgal (4:4), but to no avail because they have ignored the poor whom God entrusted to their care. Sounding a theme that many prophets after him will echo, Amos (speaking for YHWH) disdains Israel's worship and finds its insincerity intolerable:

> I hate, I despise your festivals,
>   and I take no delight in your
>   solemn assemblies.
> Even though you offer me your
>   burnt offerings and grain
>   offerings,
> I will not accept them; . . . (Amos 5:21–22)

Instead, Amos goes on to argue, it is righteousness and justice alone that God desires, and no outward show of piety can substitute for true compliance with covenant morality. The loss of Israel's wealth and power, which Amos foresees amid the splendor of the northern cities, will soon follow YHWH's judgment, and in his indictment of the north Amos leaves only the barest hope that "the God of hosts will be gracious to the remnant of Joseph" (5:15).

ISRAEL AND THE NATIONS

Amos's pronouncements of doom are not confined to the northern kingdom, however, and the opening chapter of his book begins with a series of denunciations of Israel's enemies and neighbors. The theological assumption that underlies this collective indictment is, of course, a familiar one in prophetic literature — namely, that YHWH is Lord of history and so every nation is subject to his will and judgment. The novelty in Amos's argument, however, appears in Chapter 2, where, after denouncing the Edomites and the Moabites for their various crimes, he turns (in YHWH's name) on Judah and Israel, condemning both kingdoms for their apostasy and moral indifference. This sudden shift in perspective may well have startled Amos's audience — in all likelihood, they expected this oracle to contain nothing more than "patriotic" assurances of YHWH's hatred of their foes — but it is entirely consistent with his critical view of both the covenant and Israel's place among the nations. For Amos, Israel's relationship with God is both unique and universal. YHWH has chosen to reveal himself to Israel alone ("You only have I known of all the families of the earth" [3:2]), but he has also "brought up" other peoples to their land ("Did I not bring Israel up from the land of Egypt, and the Philistines from Caphtor and the Arameans from Kir?" [9:7]). And, as the God of various "exoduses," he possesses the power and the right to turn around the very history he has created. Thus, having brought the Israelites out of slavery, he can very well send them back into exile and enslavement if they prove themselves repeatedly unfaithful to his *torah* — and that is precisely what Amos warns he will do. Though the Israelites may have thought and spoken of YHWH as if he were their war god ("The Lord is a warrior" [Exod. 15:3]), it is now against treacherous Israel that he will turn his power, reversing the course of history and seemingly ending the special relationship that has endured since Sinai/Horeb.

Amos embodies this message in a series of dirge-like oracles and visions of judgment through which he attempts to communicate the inevitability of Israel's destruction. Comparing Israel both to Sodom and Gomorrah and to Egypt (4:10–11), Amos recalls all of the punishments to which YHWH has subjected Israel in the past, hoping for a collective change of heart. The time has passed, however, for healing the breaches in the covenant, and what lies ahead is only the spectacle of devastation and the death of the nation:

> On that day, says the Lord God,
>   I will make the sun go down
>   at noon,
>   and darken the earth in
>   broad daylight.
> I will turn your feasts into
>   mourning,
>   and all your songs into
>   lamentation;

I will bring sackcloth on all loins,
　　and baldness on every head;
I will make it like the mourning
　　for an only son,
　　and the end of it like a
　　　　bitter day. (Amos 8:9–10)

The "day" of which Amos speaks, and to which he refers elsewhere as the "day of the Lord" (5:18), apparently reflected a popular notion that, at some future era, Israel would triumph over its enemies with the assistance (or possibly intervention) of YHWH. Amos is not the only eighth-century-b.c.e. prophet to allude to this idea of the **Day of the Lord**; Isaiah refers to a "day" of divine judgment and providential action several times (Isa. 2:12–22; 4:1–6; 11:10–16; 13:9–16), and most of these references are to a time of terrible suffering and loss, and not a time of national celebration. By setting himself against the prevailing mood of self-satisfaction and chauvinistic expectations, Amos places the covenant relationship outside of the framework of what his northern contemporaries would have thought of as "normative" religion. Amos's YHWH will not be bought off by ceremonies and sacrifices; nor will he underwrite Israel's political ambitions. YHWH is not Israel's patron god—he is the God who "made the Pleiades and Orion" and who turns darkness into light (Amos 5:8); he is a cosmic, not a national, deity. It is *this* God whom Israel is summoned to "meet," and in Amos's mind the confrontation of sinful Israel and the Creator of the universe can only end in tragedy for the nation that has betrayed him. Each of Amos's visions reinforces this message, as he envisions Israel first overtaken by locusts (7:1–3), then devoured by fire (7:4–6), and finally measured against a plumb (vertical) line (7:7–9) that demonstrates the extent to which YHWH's people fail to "measure up."

Yet, for all that YHWH's judgment against Israel appears sweeping and definitive, the Book of Amos ends with a consoling epilogue that reverses at least some of the predictions of doom that lie at the heart of this work:

For lo, I will command
　　and shake the house of Israel
　　　　among the nations
as one shakes with a sieve,
　　but no pebble shall fall to
　　　　the ground.
All the sinners of my people shall
　　die by the sword,
who say, "Evil shall not
　　overtake or meet us."
On that day I will raise up
　　the booth of David that is
　　　　fallen,
and repair its breaches,
　　and raise up its ruins,
　　and rebuild it as in the days of
　　　　old . . . (Amos 9:9–11)

This promise of restoration, focusing as it does on the Davidic monarchy, suggests not only a southern, Judean, origin for these verses but also a post-exilic date of composition, when Judah, too, lay in ruins and had not yet been rebuilt or reinhabited. That an apparently interpolated passage like this could find its way into the text of Amos is hardly surprising; many prophetic books show evidence of a later redaction that seems to alter the tone and perspective of an original utterance. Indeed, most of the prophetic books that follow offer similar messages of reconciliation with YHWH once the period of divine punishment has run its course.

The Book of Hosea

Traditionally placed first among the Minor Prophets, **Hosea** was a contemporary of Amos, and his ministry was centered in the northern kingdom. In fact, Hosea is perhaps the only native prophet of the kingdom of Israel whose writings have been preserved, though somewhat poorly; the Book of Hosea presents more linguistic and editorial problems than any other prophetic text. That Hosea's speeches and writings were edited long after the fall of Israel in 721 b.c.e. seems fairly obvious to biblical scholars. But even the casual reader can see in the postscript to this book ("Those who are wise understand these things those who are discerning know them" [14:9]) the hand of a later, presumably Judean, redactor who urges his readers — in the language of contemporary wisdom teachers — to reflect on all that this eighth-century-B.C.E. prophet has revealed.

Unlike Amos, however, Hosea is far less concerned with Israel's crimes of social injustice. For Hosea, the root sin of both Israel and Judah is **apostasy,** which the prophet conceives of as a type of "infidelity," and it is from this offense that all other crimes seem to flow. Central to Hosea's indictment of his nation is his belief that Israel possesses neither *knowledge* of YHWH nor *loyalty* to him, that "she" (note the feminine gender of Israel) has "betrayed" YHWH with other gods and so deserves nothing less than to be cast out of his presence and divorced by him. This bold metaphor of covenant loyalty and disloyalty is sustained through the first three chapters of Hosea and remains one of its defining concepts. For centuries, Hosea has been thought of as the "prophet of love," though in fact he is just as unsparing in his judgment of Israel's spiritual failures as any of his successors.

THE HISTORICAL CONTEXT

Though the superscription of this book places Hosea's ministry during the reign of Jeroboam II (786–746 B.C.E.) and his contemporaries in Judah, it is fairly clear from the content of several oracles that he lived through the tumultuous period following Jeroboam's death. During that period, no less than six kings assumed power in Israel, and almost every one of them died violently. Little wonder, then, that Hosea could exclaim, mockingly:

> I will destroy you, O Israel;
>   who can help you?
> Where now is your king, that he
>   may save you?
> Where in all your cities are
>   your rulers,
> of whom you said,

> "Give me a king and rulers"?
> I gave you a king in my anger,
>   and I took him away in
>   my wrath. (Amos 13:9–11)

Of course, Israel's internal instability may well have reflected the growing anxiety in all of the smaller states of the region caused by the resurgence of Assyrian power under **Tiglath-pileser III** (ruled 745–727 B.C.E.) and the threat of imminent invasion posed by his armies as they marched westward. Israel's ill-fated alliance with the Philistines and the Arameans could not stop the Assyrian advance, nor did the willingness of Hoshea (Israel's last king, not to be confused with the prophet) first to pay tribute to Tiglath-pileser III and then to withhold it from his successor, Shalmaneser V, ultimately stave off disaster. Shalmaneser's campaign against the northern kingdom began in 725 B.C.E. and ended in 721 with the fall of the capital city of Samaria and the deportation of a significant portion of the Israelite population (see 2 Kings 17:1–6). A modern historian, viewing the geopolitical situation in the latter part of the eighth century B.C.E., might easily conclude that Israel's armies were no match for Assyria's and that her defeat was inevitable. For Hosea, however, the cause of Israel's destruction could be found only in her alienation from YHWH and the withdrawal of his protecting love.

YHWH'S DISLOYAL MATE

Hosea's marriage to a woman known only as **Gomer,** daughter of Diblaim, has long puzzled biblical scholars, who cannot decide whether the references to this personage are to be taken literally or figuratively. Those who see Gomer as a real, historical individual proceed to view the biographical elements of the first three chapters as the experiential counterpart of God's message; just as YHWH has discovered the depth of Israel's unfaithfulness, so Hosea discovers Gomer's adultery. In this sense, his life becomes a microcosm of his nation's tragedy. Those who insist on a figurative reading of these chapters, in contrast, argue that the true focus of these passages is not on Hosea's domestic travails but rather on *Israel's* faithlessness, for which Gomer—who may be nothing more than a fictitious personality—serves as a dramatically convenient personification.

Whichever interpretation of Gomer's historicity one adopts, however, she is clearly a representation of Israel's failure to live up to its covenant responsibilities—principally, its commitment to monotheism. The syncretism that lies behind Hosea's indictment of Israelite apostasy is evident in both the historical and the prophetic literature; from a later, Deuteronomistic, perspective, the kingdom of Israel is seen, from its very beginnings, as an apostate community, steeped in the worship of golden calves and Canaanite deities (2 Kings 17:7–17). It is to a culture that treats YHWH as if he were merely one of a "host" of deities that Hosea turns, pleading on YHWH's behalf—and speaking in his voice— that they address him as "my husband" (Hebrew, *ishi*) rather than "my Baal" (*ba'ali*) (2:16). This play on words turns on both a linguistic and a theological ambiguity. *Ba'al* can mean nothing more than "lord and master," and in a patriarchal society like ancient Israel's, it is not uncommon for wives to address their husbands as "my *ba'al*." The very same word capitalized, however, can also be understood to refer to the Canaanite fertility god **Baal,** and it is precisely this ambiguity of reference that goes to the heart of Israel's spiritual dilemma. Like his ninth-century-B.C.E. predecessor Elijah, Hosea calls upon his fellow Israelites to renounce Baal and the calf-god of Samaria (possibly a representation of the Canaanite El), as well as any other deity to whom they have attributed their good harvests and collective safety. It is to YHWH alone that they can turn because, whatever Israel may think, he is the sole source of fertility and life itself:

> She did not know
>> that it was I who gave her
>> the grain, the wine, and the oil,
> and who lavished upon her silver
>> and gold that they used for Baal. (Hos. 3:8)

It is Israel's failure to know on whom its fortunes really depend that leads to its "divorce" and all the misfortunes that follow. In what is perhaps the most

often-quoted passage in this book, Hosea warns his contemporaries that because they have "sowed the wind" they will inevitably "reap the whirlwind" (8:7) and that exile and suffering will be their fate. That Hosea holds the king and the priesthood largely responsible for Israel's apostasy is clear from his repeated denunciations of both (4:6–9; 5:1–2; 6:9–10; 7:7). But even the prophets are ultimately to blame for Israel's failure to "know" who YHWH really is and what he demands: "my people are destroyed for lack of knowledge," God declares (4:6), and whatever insight a true prophet might provide into the now-dysfunctional covenant relationship, it comes too late to avert judgment.

Nevertheless—and here Hosea departs most dramatically from Amos—YHWH can neither forget nor deny the love he once felt for Israel, *and still feels.* YHWH's longing to be reconciled to Israel, therefore, is just as strong as his determination to punish this "whoring" generation, and at key intervals his feelings shift from anger to sorrow and finally to hope, as the possibility of *t'shuvah* (understood as meaning both "repentance" and "return") suddenly looms before him:

> How can I give you up, Ephraim?
>> How can I hand you over,
>>> O Israel? . . .
> My heart recoils within me;
>> my compassion grows warm
>> and tender.
> I will not execute my fierce anger;
>> I will not again destroy
>>> Ephraim . . . (Hos. 11:8–9)

These are not divine mood swings, however, but rather an expression of divine *hesed,* of an inextinguishable love. And more than any other prophet of his time, Hosea preserves a tradition that defines the covenant as everlasting and, to that extent, unconditional. In a moving counterpoint to the failed-marriage theme that runs throughout his book, Hosea portrays YHWH as offering to marry Israel again and forever, only this time "in righteousness and in justice, in steadfast love, and in mercy" (2:19). In fact, it is on this note that the entire book concludes. Recalling the Exodus as a time of divine nurturing and trust—as well as rebellion (11:1–11)—Hosea depicts YHWH as a father unable to cast aside the beloved son he once cared for and determined to renew a relationship that at first seemed beyond repair. Hosea's sense of YHWH's faithfulness and of his capacity for forgiveness as well as judgment will become, in time, one of the conceptual anchors of Deuteronomic theology.

QUESTIONS FOR REVIEW

1. What, according to Amos and Hosea, are Israel's principal crimes? Does Israel's covenant with YHWH entitle it to special consideration, or will it be judged just as severely as its neighbors?

2. What is the Day of the LORD? How does Amos's understanding of this concept differ from the popular understanding of his day?

3. How can Hosea speak of Israel's "marriage" to YHWH? How does the idea of *hesed* relate to this metaphor?

QUESTION FOR REFLECTION AND DISCUSSION

How can both Amos and Hosea speak of God's rejection and destruction of Israel in one breath and then hold out the prospect of reconciliation in the next? Does this apparent inconsistency in the prophetic argument suggest a fundamental uncertainty surrounding God's nature or something like a dialectical relationship between divine mercy and judgment?

TERMS AND CONCEPTS TO REMEMBER

Amos	*hesed*
apostasy	Hosea
Baal	Jeroboam II
Day of the LORD	Tiglath-pileser III
Gomer	*t'shuvah*

RECOMMENDED READING

Amos

Auld, A. Graeme. *Amos.* Sheffield, England: JSOT Press, 1986.

Coote, Robert B. *Amos Among the Prophets: Composition and Theology.* Philadelphia: Fortress Press, 1981.

Paul, Shalom M. *Amos: A Commentary on the Book of Amos.* Minneapolis: Fortress Press, 1991.

Willoughby, Bruce E. "Amos, Book of." In D. N. Freedman, ed., *The Anchor Bible Dictionary*, Vol. 1, pp. 203–212. New York: Doubleday, 1992.

Hosea

Anderson, Francis I., and Freedman, David N. *Hosea.* Anchor Bible, Vol. 24. Garden City, N.Y.: Doubleday, 1980.

Mays, James L. *Hosea.* Philadelphia: Westminster Press, 1969.

Seow, C. L. "Hosea, Book of." In D. N. Freedman, ed., *The Anchor Bible Dictionary*, Vol. 3, pp. 291–297. New York: Doubleday, 1992.

CHAPTER 18

The Assyrian Crisis

Isaiah of Jerusalem, Micah, Zephaniah, and Nahum

Key Topics/Themes Active when Assyrian power was at its zenith, threatening to destroy the covenant community, two eighth-century-B.C.E. prophets—Isaiah of Jerusalem and his contemporary Micah—interpreted the meaning of political events for YHWH's people. Isaiah's oracles are embedded in Chapters 1–39 of the book bearing his name; the remaining chapters (40–66) contain the work of two later prophets influenced by his thought. Zephaniah, who lived during King Josiah's reign, when Assyria was in decline, first predicted global destruction and then, perhaps responding to Josiah's reforms, proclaimed that YHWH had pardoned Judah. Late in Josiah's reign, Nahum rejoiced over Assyria's final collapse and the fall of Nineveh, its capital.

Israel's prophets appeared largely in response to specific social and political crises that troubled the covenant community. The earliest of the "writing prophets"—those whose words were compiled in their names—were active during the second half of the eighth century B.C.E., when the Near Eastern political scene was undergoing rapid change. In the northern kingdom, Amos and Hosea warn that Israel's economic exploitation of the poor and its failure to worship YHWH exclusively will result in dire consequences to the nation (see Chapter 17). Although Amos and Hosea do not directly invoke the agent of Israel's impending punishment—the military expansion of Assyria and its threat to both Israel and Judah—the brutal fact of Assyrian aggression provides the historical background for the prophets' negative view of Israel's future. In the southern kingdom of Judah, four prophets—Isaiah, Micah, Zephaniah, and Nahum—explicitly address the Assyrian menace, viewing this revived Mesopotamian power as the instrument of divine wrath.

After centuries of relative weakness, during the reign of Tiglath-pileser III (745–727 B.C.E.), a newly energized Assyria began a series of military conquests, rapidly subjugating much of the Near East (Figure 18.1). In addition to seizing the throne of Babylon, Tiglath-pileser subdued Syria and Palestine, forcing small states such as Israel to pay enormous sums of tribute (2 Kings 15:19–20). When Israel later revolted against Assyrian oppression, Shalmaneser V (ruled 726–722 B.C.E.) laid siege to Samaria, the Israelite capital. Shalmaneser's successor, Sargon II (ruled 721–705 B.C.E.), captured Samaria, destroying the city and deporting many of the former kingdom's inhabitants to Mesopotamia (2 Kings 17; see Chapters 3 and 15). Although Judah also paid heavy tribute to Assyria, it, too, eventually revolted, under King Hezekiah, inciting Sennacherib (ruled 704–681 B.C.E.) to launch a frightening assault on Jerusalem. The prophet Isaiah's advice to Hezekiah during the prolonged Assyrian threat to Judah's center of worship forms an important part of his message.

230

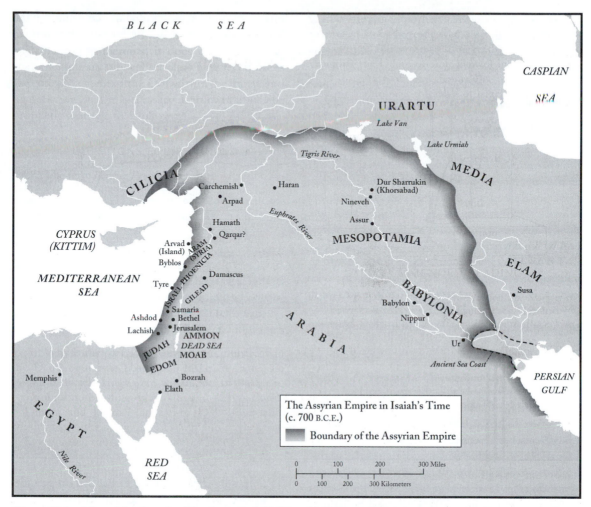

Figure 18.1   Map of the Assyrian Empire in Isaiah's Time (c. 700 B.C.E.)

The Book of Isaiah

Preeminent among the prophetic books, Isaiah contains some of the most memorable passages in the Hebrew Bible, including visions of a future world peace in which all of creation, both human and animal, is subject to YHWH's rule. Although traditionally regarded as the work of a single prophet, contemporary scholars believe that the Book of Isaiah is an anthology of prophetic literature that spans almost the entire era of Israelite

prophecy, from the mid-eighth to the early fifth century B.C.E.. Most scholars divide the book into three different parts, each representing a different historical period and a different author.

The first section of the book (Chs. 1–39) contains the oldest material, oracles by **Isaiah of Jerusalem,** the historical prophet for whom the entire collection is named. Isaiah was active between 742 and 701 B.C.E., a turbulent time that witnessed Assyria's destruction of Israel and threatened engulfment of Judah as well. Most of Isaiah's genuine sayings, embedded amid later prophetic and editorial additions, express advice to Davidic kings during the Assyrian threat and warnings of judgment against Judah for its sins. In contrast, in Chapters 40–55, the time of judgment is past, and the prophet (who is never identified by name after Chapter 39) utters words of comfort and encouragement to a community exiled in Babylon and about to be released by Cyrus of Persia. The book's abrupt change of setting from the Assyrian crisis to the Babylonian captivity and from oracles of doom to oracles of hope, as well as differences in literary style, vocabulary, and theology, indicates a change of author, whom scholars dub Second Isaiah. The book's final ten chapters, encompassing a miscellany of oracles from almost the whole range of biblical prophecy, are thought to include passages from another anonymous prophet, Third Isaiah, who lived in Judah after the exiles' return from Babylon. (In this text, Second Isaiah is considered in Chapter 20, and Third Isaiah in Chapter 21.)

Isaiah of Jerusalem (Isaiah 1–39)

According to the book's opening verse, Isaiah of Jerusalem served as prophet and counselor to three Judean kings: Jotham, Ahaz, and Hezekiah. Beginning about 742 B.C.E., shortly after King Uzziah's death and the ascension of Jotham, Isaiah's career continued until at least 701 B.C.E. and perhaps as late as 687 B.C.E.—a span of forty to fifty-five years. In Chapter 6, which scholars think describes his call to prophesy, Isaiah recounts a mystical experience in the Jerusalem Temple that shaped both his concept of divine holiness and his sense of mission to the Judean people. Suddenly transported to God's throne room in heaven (which the earthly Temple symbolized), Isaiah experienced a vision of YHWH presiding over the divine council and surrounded by myriads of **seraphim,** fiery creatures equipped with three sets of wings. Overwhelmed by the seraphim's praise of God's incomparable holiness and by a corresponding awareness of his own imperfection, Isaiah felt his lips symbolically cleansed by a burning coal, and he volunteered to

carry YHWH's word to Judah. Drawing on the later experience of his fellow Judeans' stubborn refusal to heed his message, however, he presented his inability to persuade his hearers to change their ways as predestined (determined beforehand by divine decree) (6:1–13).

THE STRUCTURE OF CHAPTERS 1–39

Although editors did not arrange Isaiah's pronouncements either chronologically or topically, scholars have related various portions of the book to three principal crises of Isaiah's lifetime: the Syro-Ephraimite War (735–734 B.C.E.), Hezekiah's temptation to ally Judah with Egypt (c. 711 B.C.E.), and the Assyrian invasion of Judah (701 B.C.E.). In their present form, Chapters 1–39 contain both Isaiah's authentic sayings and material later added to expand and update his message. This section is commonly divided into six parts:

1. Prophetic denunciations against wrongdoing in Judah and Jerusalem, interspersed with visions of universal peace under a Davidic ruler (1–12)
2. Prophecies of judgment against foreign nations (13–23)
3. Eschatological visions of cosmic judgment and restoration (24–27), the Little Apocalypse, probably dating to the Persian period
4. Denunciations of Judah and Jerusalem (28–33), probably dating to the Assyrian invasion
5. Additional oracles of judgment and blessing (34–35), probably from the exilic period
6. Prose excerpts from 2 Kings showing Isaiah's interaction with Hezekiah (36–39)

TWO POSSIBLE FATES

A preface to the whole collection of oracles ascribed to Isaiah of Jerusalem, Chapter 1 provides a survey of his major prophetic themes. Like most Israelite prophets, Isaiah ranges between pronouncements of utter doom, on the one hand, and proclamations of glorious future blessings, on the other. For Isaiah, the opposite poles of destruction and salvation are not contradictory; they represent two different possible fates for the covenant community. If Judah's leaders persist in exploiting the poor and governing unjustly, they are doomed, but if they obey YHWH by placing human welfare above profit, they will prosper (Isa. 1:17; cf. 3:13–15; 5:8–20; 10:1–4). The quality of Judah's future depends on the ruling class's willingness to show compassion and provide social justice:

> If you are willing and obedient,
> you shall eat the good of the land;
> but if you refuse and rebel,
> you shall be devoured by the sword.
>   (Isa. 1:19–20)

The nation's destiny is not fixed because, if the people change their behavior, YHWH is willing to forgive, informing wrongdoers that, though their "sins are like scarlet, they shall be like snow" (1:18).

As if to illustrate the universal benefits of transforming Judah into a just society, later redactors follow YHWH's plea for compassion with one of Isaiah's most optimistic oracles — a vision of global peace with an exalted Jerusalem as the center of the new world order (Isa. 2:1–4). As Zion, the Jerusalem hill on which Solomon's Temple stood, becomes the new holy mountain, YHWH extends his "instruction" (and covenant?) to encompass all peoples. Now inscribed on the United Nations Plaza in New York City, Isaiah's promise that all nations will convert their "swords" and other implements of war into "plowshares," instruments of peace, expresses a long-held and as-yet-unrealized ideal in Western culture.

In considering the standard by which Isaiah judges the ruling class's abuse of power, it is important to note that Isaiah never refers explicitly to the Mosaic Covenant. Instead of appealing to the Sinai/Horeb tradition, as Amos and Hosea commonly do, Isaiah emphasizes YHWH's special relationship with the Davidic dynasty in Jerusalem, a concept with which his urban audience was more familiar. This reliance on the Davidic royal line and the sanctity of the Davidic capital may explain why Isaiah regards every threat to Jerusalem and its

anointed kings as an opportunity for the nation to demonstrate its absolute trust in YHWH's sworn oath to preserve and protect David's heirs. The prophet repeatedly urges Judah's rulers to remain "quiet" in the face of military threats, avoiding foreign entanglements and relying exclusively on YHWH's promise to David (cf. 2 Sam. 7).

THE SYRO-EPHRAIMITE CRISIS

Isaiah's policy of trust is well illustrated by his prophetic advice during the Syro-Ephraimite War of the mid-730s B.C.E. As scholars reconstruct events, various Palestinian states, led by "Aram" (Syria) and "Ephraim" (Israel, so named for its most important tribe), apparently formed a coalition to resist Assyrian expansion into the area. When the kings of Syria and Israel besieged Jerusalem to force King **Ahaz** of Judah (ruled c. 735–716 B.C.E.) to join their alliance, Isaiah counseled a passive reliance on YHWH to keep his vow to David and deliver the holy city (Ch. 7).

Ignoring Isaiah's advice, Ahaz negotiated with Assyria, and, thanks to Assyrian influence, the Syro-Ephraimite siege of Jerusalem was lifted. In saving his capital from the political coercion of neighboring Syrian and Israelite kings, however, Ahaz made it subservient to Assyria, so that Judah was reduced to the level of a vassal state in the Assyrian Empire. Regarding Ahaz's compromise as a betrayal of YHWH, Isaiah then announces that Assyria will soon become the "rod" of God's anger to punish Judah for the king's lack of faith (7:18–25; 10:5–6, 28–32). Should Assyria exceed its mandate to chastise his people, however, YHWH will in turn destroy it (10:7–19).

As a pledge that YHWH will rescue his people from the Syro-Ephraimite crisis, Isaiah states that a young woman, perhaps Ahaz's wife, will conceive and bear a son, whose name, **Immanuel**—"GOD (El) is with us"—signifies that YHWH is present to protect his people (7:13–15). By the time the child is old enough to make wise decisions, Isaiah states, both Syria and Israel will have collapsed, ending their threat to Judah. Because both Damascus and Samaria, the respective capitals of these two neighboring states, were destroyed by Assyria within the next several years, Isaiah's confidence was vindicated by the event.

The heir born to Ahaz and his queen was Hezekiah, whose ascension to Judah's throne was perhaps the occasion for Isaiah's famous poem in Chapter 9, which provides the text for a joyful chorus in Handel's *Messiah:*

> For a child has been born for us,
> a son given to us; . . .
> His authority shall grow continually,
> and there shall be endless peace for the throne
>   of David and his kingdom. (Isa. 9:7)

Although Israel and other nearby states were crushed by Assyria, this coronation hymn for the new Davidic ruler predicts a flourishing Judah, secure because of God's pact with David (9:2–21). So forceful is Isaiah's Immanuel prophecy, with its optimism for Judah's divinely appointed monarchy, that—after the Davidic throne had been permanently overthrown—later generations viewed it as a messianic prediction. A term meaning "anointed" and applied to all Davidic kings, **messiah** later became identified with a future heir of David who would restore David's kingdom and vindicate YHWH's people. In the Christian New Testament, Jesus of Nazareth is portrayed as the royal figure whom Isaiah foretold, although the historical Jesus did not reestablish the Davidic monarchy or free the covenant community from its political oppressors.

HEZEKIAH'S ALLIANCE WITH EGYPT

The prophet's attention was drawn from a future peaceable kingdom to more immediate political concerns in 711 B.C.E., when the Assyrians attacked the city of **Ashdod,** which bordered on Judah's southwest frontier. This time, Egypt attempted to form a defensive alliance of Canaanite states to protect its own borders. To dissuade King Hezekiah from involving Judah in this coalition, Isaiah paraded naked through the streets of Jerusalem for three years, graphically illustrating the public humiliations of defeat and slavery that would result

from relying on Egypt instead of YHWH to save them from the Assyrians (Ch. 20). Although Hezekiah did not then commit himself to Egypt—depending on this unreliable nation, Isaiah says, is equivalent to leaning on a broken reed that pierces the hand of the one who grasps it (36:6)—a decade later Hezekiah did join Egypt in an anti-Assyrian coalition. Although this "unholy" alliance elicits some of Isaiah's harshest condemnations of Judah's king, courtiers, and other national leaders (Chs. 28–31), later editors inserted a passage into the collection asserting that even Egypt will learn to "know" and worship YHWH (19:19–22). Perhaps most surprising, this interpolation states that Egypt and Assyria will join forces with Israel to form a trio of Near Eastern powers that, together, will be a "blessing in the midst of the earth" (19:23–24).

ASSYRIA'S ASSAULT ON JERUSALEM

In 701 B.C.E., the Assyrians made their inevitably violent response to Hezekiah's move toward autonomy. Sweeping down from the north, **Sennacherib** (704–681 B.C.E.), one of Assyria's most formidable warrior-kings, cut off Judah's communication with Egypt and laid siege to Jerusalem—exactly as Isaiah feared (29:1–4; see Chapter 15). Although Hezekiah at first followed Isaiah's advice not to surrender, the Assyrian capture and demolition of all forty-six fortified towns in Judah, leaving Jerusalem a solitary oasis in a desert of total devastation, eventually forced the king to capitulate (Figure 18.2). The horrors of the Assyrian invasion are vividly depicted in artwork adorning Sennacherib's palace in Nineveh; one bas-relief shows Assyrian battalions attacking Lachish, one of Judah's largest walled cities, with Assyrian soldiers impaling captives on wooden stakes (see Figure 11.2). Sennacherib spares Jerusalem, but Hezekiah is compelled to pay a staggering price for his resistance—"three hundred talents [about eleven tons] of silver and thirty talents [one ton] of gold" (2 Kings 18:14–16), a huge payoff for Jerusalem's deliverance not mentioned in the edited version of 2 Kings that concludes the collection of First Isaiah's oracles (Isa. 36–39; cf. 2 Kings

Figure 18.2   The cuneiform inscription on this hexagonal prism proclaims Sennacherib's military triumphs over Palestinian states and their Egyptian allies. Sennacherib, emperor of Assyria (704–681 B.C.E.), boasts that his armies overwhelmed Judah, his siege of Jerusalem trapping King Hezekiah (715–687 B.C.E.) "like a bird in a cage." Accounts of Sennacherib's invasion and Jerusalem's deliverance appear in 2 Kings 18:13–19:37 and Isaiah 36:1–37:38.

18:13–20:19). His attempt at independence having failed, Hezekiah has to cede large parts of his kingdom to Assyria and resume his role as Assyrian vassal.

The apparent conflict between Sennacherib's archival report boasting that he sealed Hezekiah in his capital "like a bird in a cage" (see Chapter 15) and the Isaiah–2 Kings claim that the Assyrian army withdrew from Jerusalem because YHWH's angel slew 185,000 troops in a single night remains unresolved. Some scholars postulate that the two accounts refer to two different invasions, one in 701 B.C.E. and a second some time later. Whether there were one or two sieges of Jerusalem, for Isaiah the significant fact was that David's city escaped the destruction inflicted on all other Judean settlements, suggesting that Jerusalem, where YHWH had placed his "name," enjoyed divine protection.

In addition to Isaiah's authentic proclamations, Chapters 1–39 also contain a variety of later interpolations. One section, known as the Little Apocalypse (Chs. 24–27), probably dates from a period after the exile when Judah was a small part of the Persian Empire. Presenting visions of a future world judgment, this literary unit emphasizes YHWH's universal sovereignty. Although some passages apparently express new beliefs about life after death (25:7; 26:19–21), most scholars believe that these verses do not refer to an individual's posthumous fate but rather, like Ezekiel's celebrated "valley of dry bones," symbolically portray the "resurrection" or rebirth of the covenant community from its political demise (cf. Ezek. 37). Allusions to Babylon's fall, such as the poem in Isaiah 14, are also postexilic and were probably composed by members of a prophetic school that preserved and edited the work of Isaiah of Jerusalem.

Because they were delivered as assurances of hope to captive Judeans in Babylon, the oracles of Second Isaiah (Chs. 40–55) are discussed in Chapter 20. Addressed to returned exiles in Judah, the pronouncements of Third Isaiah are reviewed in Chapter 21.

The Book of Micah

Micah, fourth and last of the eighth-century-B.C.E. prophets, was a younger contemporary of Isaiah of Jerusalem. Active between about 740 and 700 B.C.E., he directed his earliest prophecies against Israel's religious sins, predicting the northern kingdom's fall to Assyria (1:2–7). Unlike Isaiah, who may have belonged to Judah's aristocracy, Micah was a native of Moresheth, a village in the foothills southwest of Jerusalem. A man of the people, Micah takes a country-dweller's dim view of urban life and what he sees as its deplorable corruption. Regarding the city as a stronghold of the exploitative ruling classes, a tainted environment that will doom Jerusalem as it did Samaria, Micah denounces the greed and tyranny of merchants and landowners (2:1–5, 6–11; 3:1–4; 6:9–14). From his rural perspective, the prophet condemns not only the acquisitiveness of the rich who gobble up the property of impoverished farmers but the entire urban establishment, including its corrupt princes, judges, and priests and its false prophets whose oracles for hire support the privileged classes (3:9–12; cf. 7:1–4).

Whereas Isaiah criticized the policies of individual kings while supporting the institutions of the Davidic dynasty and Temple cult, Micah shows them little respect. He scornfully denies that the sanctuary's presence in Jerusalem will protect the capital from harm and predicts that both city and Temple will be reduced to rubble (3:1–3, 9–12). Excoriating the Jerusalem nobility and priesthood (6:1–2, 9–16), he also rebukes professional seers

who offer deceptive comfort and who fear to tell the people unwelcome truths (3:5–8). Micah even rejects the belief that Israel's God requires animal or any other formal sacrifice. In the book's most celebrated passage, he—or a later disciple—argues that YHWH asks only for acts of justice and love and for people to walk humbly in the divine presence (6:6–8). For many commentators, Micah presents a classic statement of the insight of the prophet warring against the ritualism of the priest.

Although they were both active during the reign of Hezekiah, neither Isaiah nor Micah mentions the other's work, perhaps because of the differences in their respective backgrounds and attitudes toward Judah's leading institutions. According to many scholars, Micah's original pronouncements about Judah were largely negative, but later editors added several optimistic passages predicting Judah's future glory (4:1–5:15; 7:8–20). One oracle of world peace is expressed in almost exactly the same words as that of Isaiah, giving a very un-Micah kind of approval to the centrality of Jerusalem and its Temple in the divine plan (4:1–4; cf. Isa. 2:2–4). The references to Davidic promises and to a faithful remnant returning to Judah after exile, at which time all citizens will sit under their vines and fig trees in prosperous tranquility (Mic. 2:12; 4:4–8), also seem to have been inserted into Micah's work by later hands. The famous prophecy that Bethlehem one day will become the birthplace of a ruler whose "origin is from of old, from ancient days" (5:2)—generally viewed as a messianic oracle—is similarly judged a later addition.

Although in its present form Micah seems to include oracles composed after the prophet's lifetime, the book nonetheless represents the typical prophetic paradox in which YHWH inspires words of both severe judgment and redeeming hope. In compiling prophetic sayings, later editors commonly attached words of encouragement even to the most severe denunciations, concluding such works as Amos, Hosea, and Micah with visions of future reconciliation and peace (cf. Amos 9:11–15; Hos. 14:2–10; Mic. 7:8–20). Despite Micah's sweeping attacks on Judah's principal authorities, his sayings were preserved on a scroll and housed in the Temple, a structure whose destruction he foretold (cf. Jer. 26:16–18).

The Book of Zephaniah

THE DAY OF THE LORD

In **Zephaniah,** we return to themes first sounded by Amos—but now greatly intensified. Amos startled his listeners by announcing that the Day of the Lord would be cataclysmic for Israel, a time of darkness and suffering, but Zephaniah expands the idea of negative judgment to a cosmic level in which YHWH exterminates *all* life on earth:

> I will utterly sweep away everything
> from the face of the earth, says the Lord.
> I will sweep away humans and animals,
> I will sweep away the birds of the air
> and the fish of the sea. . . .
> I will cut off humanity from the face of the earth
> (Zeph. 1:2–3)

Reversing his life-giving activity in Genesis, YHWH will annihilate all creation, from nonhuman species to great kings, so that "their blood shall be poured out like dust and their flesh like dung" (Zeph. 1:14–17). On the day of his "jealousy," YHWH will consume the earth, reducing it to a sterile wasteland (1:18). (Zephaniah's sweeping declaration of God's resolve to exterminate every living thing contrasts markedly with YHWH's post-Flood statement in Genesis 8:21 that he will "never again curse the ground because of humankind . . . nor will [he] ever again destroy every living creature as [he had] done.")

Although we do not know what specific conditions triggered the prophet's vision of God's extreme violence, he was active during the reign of King Josiah (640–609 B.C.E.), perhaps before the king initiated his Deuteronomic reforms. The Judah that Zephaniah denounces so vehemently was probably a country still under Manasseh's lingering influence, so contaminated by the ruler's idolatries

that YHWH's wrath was considered as inevitable as it was extreme. Apparently, Zephaniah was the first prophet (of whom we have any record) to speak out after the long silence that Manasseh and his immediate successor, Amon, presumably imposed on champions of the "YHWH alone" movement.

After categorically asserting that YHWH will spare nothing that lives, Zephaniah concedes that a few humble people who keep the commandments may "perhaps . . . be hidden on the day of the Lord's wrath" (2:3). In fact, Chapter 2 implies the survival of a faithful remnant, for after neighboring countries—Philistia, Moab, and Ammon—have been obliterated, Judean survivors will confiscate their land (2:6–7, 9–10).

CURSES AND PROMISES

In Chapter 3, Zephaniah attacks the "soiled, defiled" leaders of Jerusalem, calling them "evening wolves" who prey on the poor and who have learned nothing from the examples of other cities that YHWH has destroyed. As a result, YHWH will assemble the nations to pour out his fury on Judah (3:8). After describing a bleak future for humanity, however, Zephaniah concludes by offering an unexpected ray of hope. In a series of terse oracles, he predicts that Gentile nations will come to worship YHWH (3:9–10; cf. Isa. 2:1–4; Mic. 4:1–5), that a repentant Israel will again seek its God (Zeph. 3:11–13), and that scattered exiles will be freed from their oppressors (3:19–20).

An uncharacteristically joyous oracle may represent Zephaniah's response to the beginning of Josiah's reforms, which moved YHWH to avert his anger:

> Sing aloud, O daughter Zion;
> shout, O Israel!
> Rejoice and exult with all your heart,
> O daughter Jerusalem!
> The Lord has taken away the judgments against
> you,
> he has turned away your enemies.
> The king of Israel, the Lord, is in your midst;
> you shall fear disaster no more. (Zeph. 3:14–15)

Zephaniah's sudden optimism about Judah's future may express a belief that Josiah's cleansing of the Temple and his reintroducing the Passover and other Mosaic observances have restored God's presence to the community. Josiah's military successes — God is now seen as a "warrior who gives victory" (3:17) — may have indicated to the prophet that YHWH had changed his mind about eradicating a nation stained by Manasseh's sins. In any case, Zephaniah's image of YHWH happily joining in the musical chorus of national festivals (3:17) represents a striking shift in his vision.

The Book of Nahum

Of **Nahum**'s personal life or theological beliefs we know nothing except that his message is unlike that of any other known biblical prophet. He neither decries his people's sins nor prophesies their punishment; instead, his entire book is composed of three poems rejoicing over the ruin of Nineveh, capital of the Assyrian Empire. His gloating, unmitigated by compassion, contrasts markedly with the merciful attitude toward Nineveh's inhabitants expressed in the Book of Jonah (see Chapter 21).

THE FALL OF NINEVEH

Nahum probably wrote circa 612 B.C.E., either while the combined army of Medes and Babylonians was besieging the Assyrian capital or shortly after the city's capture. A major historical event, the fall of Nineveh to a Medo-Babylonian coalition, permanently ended Assyrian hegemony in the Near East. Nahum was not alone in celebrating Assyria's demise, for the empire that had destroyed Israel and humiliated Judah was notorious for its widespread cruelties, which routinely included the deportation of entire populations, the torture and mutilation of captives, and the chaining of prisoners with metal hooks in their jaws (Figure 18.3).

Nahum sees Nineveh's collapse as evidence of YHWH's vengeance on Assyrian excess (1:2–3);

although YHWH employed the empire as his corrective "rod" to punish Judah and other states, Assyria behaved with such arrogant savagery that it earned divine retribution. Utilizing vivid poetic images, Nahum describes armed legions marching against Nineveh and plundering its treasures (Ch. 2). The enumeration of Assyria's harrowing crimes is equally eloquent (Ch. 3).

In typical prophetic fashion, Nahum interprets Nineveh's fate as part of YHWH's intention to improve the condition of his covenant people. Released from Assyrian bondage, both Judah and a restored Israel will enjoy a new era of freedom and security (2:2), "for never again shall the wicked invade you" (1:15). Despite his assurance of future safety, however, only three years after Nahum's prophecy, Pharaoh Necho II invades Judah, killing King Josiah at Megiddo as Egyptian troops march northward to support remnants of the Assyrian army at Haran (2 Kings 23:29–35). Egypt largely controls Judah's affairs until about 605 B.C.E., when the Babylonians defeat Egyptian forces at the Battle of Carchemish and assume jurisdiction over Canaan, reducing Judah once again to vassal status.

QUESTIONS FOR REVIEW

1. During the eighth century B.C.E., when the threat of Assyrian invasion loomed on the horizon, which prophets were active in the northern kingdom of Israel? What oracles about social and economic justice did they deliver? While Assyria threatened Judah, how did the message of Isaiah of Jerusalem differ from that of his contemporary Micah?

2. Because of differences of style, vocabulary, assumed political background, and content of the prophetic oracles in different parts of the Book of Isaiah, scholars believe that it is an anthology of prophetic sayings rather than the work of a single historical prophet. What are some of the differences in the political situation and the nature of the message between Isaiah 1–39 and Isaiah 40–55? Why does the Assyrian threat dominate in the first part of the book but not the second?

3. What were the concerns of Isaiah of Jerusalem? How does he advise kings, such as Ahaz and Heze-

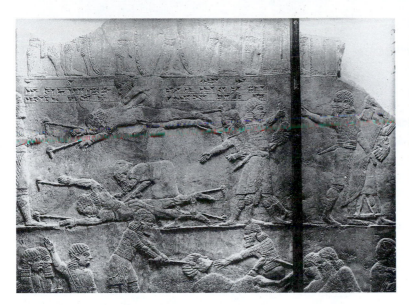

Figure 18.3 Dominating the ancient Near East for two and a half centuries, the Assyrians effectively discouraged revolt by a policy of terror. This Assyrian bas-relief depicts the torturing and flaying alive of captives — defeated soldiers and civilian prisoners alike. When Nineveh, Assyria's capital, was about to fall to a coalition of Medes and Babylonians in 612 B.C.E., the prophet Nahum saw the event as YHWH's punishment of a bloodthirsty nation (Nah. 3).

kiah, to behave during the Assyrian threat? In what terms does Isaiah describe the birth of a royal son and Davidic heir?

4. What momentous event occurred in the northern kingdom in 721 B.C.E.? What happened during Sennacherib's siege of Jerusalem in 701 B.C.E.?

5. What famous oracle do Isaiah of Jerusalem and Micah have in common? How do most of their pronouncements differ? Read Micah 6:6–8 and interpret its meaning for a Judean audience.

6. Summarize Zephaniah's vision of the Day of the LORD. What does YHWH threaten to do to the entire world? What change in Judah's governance may have prompted Zephaniah to add a joyous message to his sayings?

7. What historical event does Nahum celebrate?

QUESTIONS FOR REFLECTION AND DISCUSSION

1. How are the prophetic oracles forecasting Judah's punishment related to the political situation in the late eighth century B.C.E.? Why do the prophets typically view foreign military invasions as resulting from the covenant people's misdeeds? How does As-

syria function as God's "rod of correction"? Analyze the prophets' presuppositions connecting historical events with Judah's loyalty or disloyalty to YHWH. How would a contemporary historian's analysis of Assyrian aggression against a small state like Judah differ from that of the eighth-century prophets?

2. Why are the majority of prophetic oracles devoted to conveying YHWH's negative judgments on both his people and their foreign oppressors? Why are so few concerned with optimistic visions of the future? Why have the prophecies forecasting the destruction of Israel, Judah, Assyria, and Babylon been fulfilled, while those envisioning a time of universal world peace have not?

TERMS AND CONCEPTS TO REMEMBER

Ahaz and the Syro-
  Ephraimite crisis
Ashdod
Assyrian crisis
Immanuel
Isaiah of Jerusalem
Isaiah's visions of
  universal peace
Little Apocalypse
messiah

Micah's oracles on
  exploiting the poor
Nahum's rejoicing over
  Nineveh's fall
prophecy of Immanuel
Sennacherib
seraphim
Zephaniah's version of
  the Day of the LORD

RECOMMENDED READING

Isaiah of Jerusalem (Isaiah 1–39)

Blenkinsopp, Joseph, ed. *Isaiah 1–39: A New Translation and Commentary* (Anchor Bible, Vol. 19). New York: Doubleday, 2000. A scholarly analysis of Isaiah of Jerusalem.

Childs, Brevard S. *Isaiah and the Assyrian Crisis.* Studies in Biblical Theology, no. 3. London: SCM Press, 1967.

Daves, Eryl W. *Prophecy and Ethics: Isaiah and the Ethical Tradition of Israel.* Sheffield, England: JSOT Press, 1981.

Hayes, John H., and Irvine, Stuart A. *Isaiah the Eighth-Century Prophet.* Nashville, Tenn.: Abingdon Press, 1987.

Kaiser, Otto. *Isaiah 1–12.* Philadelphia: Westminster Press, 1972.

———. *Isaiah 13–39.* Philadelphia: Westminster Press, 1974.

Millar, William R. "Isaiah, Book of (Chaps. 24–27)." In D. N. Freedman, ed., *The Anchor Bible Dictionary,* Vol. 3, pp. 488–490. New York: Doubleday, 1992. Discusses the apocalyptic passages incorporated into the Isaiah collection.

Seitz, Christopher R. "Isaiah, Book of (First Isaiah)." In D. N. Freedman, ed., *The Anchor Bible Dictionary,* Vol. 3, pp. 472–488. New York: Doubleday, 1992.

Tucker, Gene M. "The Book of Isaiah 1–39." In *The New Interpreter's Bible,* Vol. 6, pp. 27–305. Nashville, Tenn.: Abingdon Press, 2001. Includes extensive commentary.

Micah

Anderson, Francis I., and Freedman, David N., eds. *Micah: A New Translation and Commentary* (Anchor Bible, Vol. 24E). New York: Doubleday, 2000.

Hillers, Delbert R. *Micah.* Philadelphia: Fortress Press, 1984.

Laberge, Léo. "Micah." In R. E. Brown et al., eds., *The New Jerome Biblical Commentary,* 2nd ed., pp. 249–254. Englewood Cliffs, N.J.: Prentice-Hall, 1990.

Mays, James L. *Micah.* Philadelphia: Westminster Press, 1976.

Simundson, Daniel J. "The Book of Micah." In *The New Interpreter's Bible,* Vol. 7, pp. 533–589. Nashville, Tenn.: Abingdon Press, 1996. Offers textual interpretation.

Wolff, Hans W. *Micah: A Commentary.* Minneapolis: Augsburg Press, 1990.

Zephaniah

Achtemeier, Elizabeth. *Nahum-Malachi: Interpretation.* Atlanta: John Knox Press, 1986. Includes commentary on Zephaniah.

Bennett, Robert A. "The Book of Zephaniah." In *The New Interpreter's Bible,* Vol. 7, pp. 659–704. Nashville, Tenn.: Abingdon Press, 1996.

Szeles, M. E. *Habakkuk and Zephaniah: Wrath and Mercy.* Grand Rapids, Mich.: Eerdmans, 1987. A helpful study.

Nahum

Baker, David W. *Nahum, Habakkuk and Zephaniah.* Donners Grove, Ill.: Inter-Varsity Press, 1988.

Garcia-Treto, Francisco O. "The Book of Nahum." In *The New Interpreter's Bible,* Vol. 7, pp. 592–619. Nashville, Tenn.: Abingdon Press, 1996. Provides useful commentary.

CHAPTER 19

The Babylonian Threat

The Books of Jeremiah, Habakkuk, and Obadiah

Key Topics/Themes As witnesses to the last decades of Judah's collective existence and to the early decades of the Babylonian exile that followed, Jeremiah, Habakkuk, and Obadiah offer us an extraordinary lens through which to view some of the most tragic events in Israel's history. Jeremiah's ministry extends from the reign of Josiah (beginning in 623 B.C.E.) to some time after the murder of Gedaliah in 582 B.C.E., and during that time, he is compelled first to predict and then to endure the destruction of the kingdom of Judah at the hands of the Babylonian king Nebuchadnezzar. Of Habakkuk and Obadiah, we know very little except that they appear to be Jeremiah's near-contemporaries and their pronouncements seem to resonate with the same anxiety over Judah's fate and anguish over its past sins that characterize Jeremiah's response to contemporary events. (Figure 19.1 shows the various empires at Jeremiah's time.)

The Book of Jeremiah

More than any earlier prophet (even Elijah), **Jeremiah** becomes an object of public scorn for what appears to be his "disloyalty" in proclaiming that the Babylonians are nothing less than the instrument of divine judgment, sent to Judah to punish the people for their abandonment of the covenant — a conviction that is expressed with equal fervor by Habakkuk (1:6–11), though not with the same consequences. At the risk of his life, Jeremiah attempts to convince both king and commoner that the only realistic course of action open to Judah is submission to **Nebuchadnezzar** and a renewal of commitment to YHWH's *torah*, but his warnings and pleas fall on deaf ears. The final chapter of the Deuteronomistic History — the defeat and exile of Judah — is therefore played out for all three prophets with a sense of inevitability that rivals the classical Greek concept of *moira* (destiny). Nothing — not even belated acts of collective penance — can turn aside YHWH's justifiable wrath.

THE STRUCTURE OF JEREMIAH

Like the books of Isaiah and Ezekiel, Jeremiah is clearly a composite work that can be broken down into four discrete segments: (1) oracles delivered during the reign of Jehoiakim and Zedekiah (Chs. 1–25), (2) biographical narratives combined with prophecies of redemption and restoration (Chs. 26–45), (3) prophetic diatribes against the "nations" (Chs. 46–51), and (4) a concluding historical postscript taken largely from 2 Kings 24–25 (Ch. 52). Jeremiah 36 provides a clue as to how this material may have initially been gathered, and by

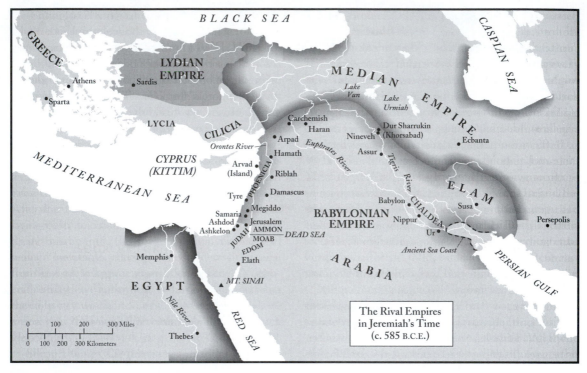

Figure 19.1   Map of the Rival Empires in Jeremiah's Time (c. 585 B.C.E.)

whom, for it is in this chapter that Jeremiah receives these instructions from God:

> . . . take a scroll and write on it every word that I have spoken to you about Jerusalem and Judah and all the nations, from the day I first spoke to you in the reign of Josiah down to the present day. (Jer. 36:2)

The "present day" is the fourth year of the reign of Jehoiakim (605 B.C.E.), but the actual writing of this scroll was done by a scribe, **Baruch ben Neriah,** who may have served Jeremiah as a disciple, private secretary, and, ultimately, redactor. Scholars speculate that this scroll consisted largely of the material now found in Chapters 1–25, which then served as the nucleus of a much larger collection of writings, some attributed to Jeremiah himself and some contributed by Baruch and others. This complex process of composition may account for the fact that the Book of Jeremiah often presents mate-

rial out of chronological sequence or with no apparent transition from one body of writings to another. Little wonder, therefore, that Jeremiah seems to contradict himself on some of the most basic questions of Israel's fate, as when he pronounces a seemingly irrevocable doom over Judah and Jerusalem:

> Thus will I shatter this people and this city as one shatters an earthen vessel so that it cannot be mended, and the dead shall be buried in Topheth because there is no room elsewhere to bury them. (Jer. 19:11)

Later, however, Jeremiah offers the following:

> I am with you and will save you, says the LORD. I will make an end of all the nations amongst whom I have scattered you, but I will not make an end of you; though I punish you as you deserve, I will not sweep you clean away. (Jer. 30:11)

That Jeremiah's understanding of YHWH's intent could change after the destruction of Judah had become reality is not so remarkable, after all. And, like his eighth-century-B.C.E. predecessors, Hosea and Isaiah of Jerusalem, he seems to hold ambivalent views on the possibility of Judah's recovery of its covenant with God and its land. What remains constant, however, throughout the forty years of his ministry, is his perception of YHWH as the guiding force behind history. And if, as one recent scholar has suggested, Baruch ben Neriah was, in fact, the editorial hand behind both the Deuteronomistic History and the Book of Jeremiah, one can easily understand why the combined theme of divine judgment and retribution figures so centrally in each of these narratives.

YHWH'S LAWSUIT AGAINST JUDAH

At the core of Jeremiah's prophetic indictment of Judah is the Deuteronomic conviction that YHWH's covenant with the people of Israel is both a conditional and an unconditional agreement. As a conditional "treaty" with the Deity, the covenant survives only as long as Israel is prepared to honor the terms of their agreement and obey the commandments of God. The Josianic reform described in 2 Kings 22–23 is based on the premise that national catastrophe can be averted only by a collective gesture of repentance and renewal, sentiments that Jeremiah echoes many times before the final curtain is brought down on Judah's hopes for survival:

> Come back to me, apostate Israel, says the LORD, I will no longer frown on you. For my love is unfailing, says the LORD, I will not be angry forever. Only you must acknowledge your wrongdoing, confess your rebellion against the LORD your GOD. Confess your promiscuous traffic with foreign gods under every spreading tree, confess that you have not obeyed me. (Jer. 3:13)

But whether out of conviction that Josiah's reforms have failed—hence the renewed apostasies of Manasseh—or out of the belief that the cumulative sins of Judah are so enormous that no gesture of contrition could possibly avail, Jeremiah returns repeatedly to the assertion that the people of Israel, and most especially its religious and secular leaders, have forfeited all hope of mercy and will have to pay the penalty of defeat and exile before any hope of divine forgiveness can be entertained. Part of that penalty is the loss of Jerusalem and of Solomon's Temple. Although Jeremiah appears to be from a priestly family, he heaps scorn on those who imagine that the "Temple of the LORD" is inviolable and so cannot be overrun or destroyed by an enemy:

> You steal, you murder, you commit adultery and perjury, you burn sacrifices to Baal, you run after other gods whom you have not known; then you come and stand before me in this house, which bears my name, and say "We are safe"; safe, you think, to indulge in all these abominations. Do you think that this house, this house which bears my name, is a robbers' cave? (Jer. 7:9–11)

On this point, Jeremiah parts company with the first Isaiah, who declared—on the occasion of the Assyrian invasion and siege of Jerusalem in 701 B.C.E.—that "the LORD of Hosts, like a bird hovering over its young, will be a shield over Jerusalem" (Isa. 31:5). Clearly, Jeremiah is convinced that divine patience with Judah is at an end and that YHWH's "case" against apostate Judah allows for no other judgment than its destruction. So inexorable does Judah's fate appear, in fact, that Jeremiah can speak of his nation as a shattered vessel that cannot be mended (Jer. 19:11).

EXILE, RESTORATION, AND COVENANT RENEWAL

However, having proclaimed doom upon his generation, Jeremiah then proceeds to offer his contemporaries both practical advice and visionary assurances of national restoration and redemption. To the exilic community in Babylon, Jeremiah sends a letter urging them to build houses, to marry, and to pray for the welfare of the host nation (29:1–8). Over two generations will pass, he predicts, before YHWH once again takes up the cause of the exiles and returns them to their land. And if one dates Jeremiah's prediction of a "full seventy years" (29:10)

Figure 19.2 An artist's reconstruction of Babylon at the time of King Nebuchadnezzar (605–562 B.C.E.), founder of the Neo-Babylonian Empire and conqueror of Judah (587 B.C.E.), illustrates the city's massive fortifications. During their captivity in Babylon, Judah's former ruling classes reedited and/or produced much of the literature that now forms the Hebrew Bible. The towering ziggurat at the left, an artificial mountain crowned with a chapel to the Babylonian gods, is characteristic of Mesopotamian religious architecture; its predecessors at Ur and elsewhere may have inspired the "Tower of Babel" legend (Gen. 11).

of Diaspora existence prior to Judah's restoration from Nebuchadnezzar's initial invasion in 598–597 B.C.E., then Jeremiah is not that far off (Figure 19.2). In 539 B.C.E., Cyrus of Persia conquers Babylon, and the following year, he issues an edict permitting the people of Judah to return to their land. Second Isaiah responds to this happy change of fortune by declaring Cyrus YHWH's "messiah" (Isa. 45:1–4). Although Jeremiah never mentions how (or by whose hand) this miracle of national renewal will be accomplished, the conviction that God has not withdrawn his love or compassion from Judah altogether persists throughout his book.

This idea reaches its theological climax in Chapter 31, where Jeremiah first reassures his contemporaries that, proverbial wisdom and Exodus 34:7 notwithstanding, the sins of the fathers will not descend automatically on the sons: "the man who eats sour grapes shall have his own teeth set on edge" (Jer. 31:30). He then goes on, in a more visionary vein, to predict a time when

> I will make a new covenant with Israel and Judah. It will not be like the covenant I made with their forefathers when I took them by the hand and led them out of Egypt. . . . But this is the covenant which I will make with Israel after those days, says the LORD; I will set my law within them and write it on their hearts; I will become their GOD and they shall become my people. No longer need they teach one another to know the LORD; all of them, high and low alike, shall know me, says the LORD, for I will forgive their wrongdoing and remember their sin no more. (Jer. 31:31–34)

Nowhere does the Book of Jeremiah more powerfully reflect the Deuteronomic tradition than in this passage, where the prophet touches upon two central themes of Deuteronomic teaching: the need to internalize *torah* and the certainty that YHWH will, after a suitable period of collective contrition, restore the people of Israel and Judah to his love and protection (Deut. 30:1–10). In fact, Jeremiah decisively dismisses the very possibility that Israel and its covenant with God could disappear forever (Jer. 31:36) and even foresees in some detail the rebuilding of Jerusalem and its walls. The unconditionality of these promises is reminiscent of the Royal or Davidic Covenant of 2 Samuel 7:11–16, where YHWH's pledge to preserve David's line in perpetuity rises above whatever morally contingent circumstances may attend the history of Israel's monarchy; God will remain loyal, even when his covenanted people do not. And unlike the covenant renewal movement of Josiah's reign, this restoration will last forever. It is this assurance of ultimate reconciliation, more than anything else, that allows a defeated and exiled Judah to rebuild itself and to reformulate its shattered covenant with YHWH.

THE WEEPING PROPHET

The Book of Jeremiah offers us a better, more sustained glimpse into the inner life of a prophet than perhaps any other work of prophetic narrative. Jeremiah is often presented to us—through both first- and third-person perspectives—as an anguished and conflicted personality, torn between the prophet's need to proclaim the word of God and personal anger and grief at the human toll the prophetic calling exacts. Like Job, he curses the day he was born (cf. Job 3:3 with Jer. 20:14–18), and, as in Ecclesiastes, he wishes that he had never been born rather than witness the sorrow he is compelled to behold (cf. Eccles. 4:3 with Jer. 20:17–18). He experiences prophecy as a "writhing of the bowels" and a "throbbing" of the heart (Jer. 4:19) and even accuses God of having deceived him and then alienated him from his countrymen (20:7–10). Like Moses, Jeremiah appears genuinely reluctant to assume the prophetic mantle, and like Elijah, he comes very close to losing his life at the hands of enraged kings and royal courtiers (26:7–15 and 38:4–13). To complete his misery, he is forbidden to marry or to enter a house of either mourning or feasting (16:1–9), thus isolating him from a normal life of social interaction. Even the men of his native village, Anathoth, threaten to kill him if he continues to prophesy (11:21).

For all his manifest unpopularity, however, Jeremiah is practically abducted and taken to Egypt in the wake of Gedaliah's assassination (43:1–7). His stature as YHWH's prophet remains, ironically, undiminished near the end of his life—and this in spite of the fact that he bitterly denounces the Judahite exiles who disregard his warnings against abandoning the land of Judah. In opposition to those who argue that Judah's woes are the consequence of neglecting not YHWH but the **Queen of Heaven** (possibly the Canaanite Asherah, thought of as YHWH's consort [44:17–18]), Jeremiah once again affirms the basic Deuteronomistic principle of cumulative guilt and accountability:

> The LORD did not forget those sacrifices which you and your fathers, your kings and princes and the people of the land burnt in the cities of Judah and in the streets of Jerusalem, and they mounted up in his mind until he could no longer tolerate them. . . . This calamity has come upon you because you burnt these sacrifices and sinned against the LORD and did not obey the LORD or conform to his laws, statutes, and teachings. (Jer. 44:21–23)

Yet, despite his indignation over Judah's spiritual blindness and obstinacy, Jeremiah can still weep over Judah's terrible defeat (9:1) and compose lamentation upon lamentation over the corpses of his countrymen and over the ruins of Zion itself (9:17–22 and 14:17–22). More important, however, while in prison, he decides to purchase a tract of ancestral land as a gesture of enduring attachment to both the land and the covenant promises that YHWH has made to Israel (32:6–44). The same God who could rescue his people from slavery in Egypt, Jeremiah reasons, is capable of restoring them to the land from which he banished them, thus completing the cycle of penance and redemption that began with Israel's invasion of Canaan (Judg. 2:10–22). Though Jeremiah describes his destiny as having been sealed even before the moment of his birth ("Before I formed you in the womb I knew you" [Jer. 1:5]), Israel's fate remains open. Although he will never live to see it, he can at least envision a future Davidic kingdom whose righteousness will reverse the tragic spiral of both past and present history (23:5–6).

In the wake of Judah's destruction, then, and the loss of both Temple and monarchy, one thing remained of its still vital religious culture: the prophetic understanding of YHWH's justice and of the precarious, yet enduring, covenant relationship that still bound Israel to its God.

The Book of Habakkuk

Along with Nahum and Joel, the Book of Habakkuk is one of the shortest books of the Hebrew Bible—and also one of the most puzzling. Contemporary scholars remain divided over its structure and meaning, and given the absence of a super-scription that might identify the prophet with a particular reign or era, no consensus exists over its probable dating. References to the **Chaldeans** (the Babylonians)—both as invaders and as future objects of divine punishment—would seem to place this book within the time span of Jeremiah, or at least within the political context of the late seventh century B.C.E., but beyond that nothing is known about either the prophet himself or the length of his prophetic ministry. Curiously, **Habakkuk** is identified explicitly in the opening verse of the first chapter as a *navi,* or "prophet," a title that no other pre-exilic prophet seems to have claimed for himself, which has led some scholars to speculate that he may have been a "professional" seer or have had some association with the Temple cult. What is clear, however, is that he (or his editor) understood his oracle to be a *massa,* or "burden," a term employed by Ezekiel and other prophets to signify any prophetic speech that seeks to explain and justify YHWH's actions to an uncomprehending audience.

DIVINE JUSTICE AND THE BABYLONIAN THREAT

Habakkuk begins with a complaint that is also a lament, as the prophet struggles with a problem that neither he nor the author of Job is able to resolve: the spectacle of unjust suffering in a world filled with violence and wickedness. The Deuteronomic response to such a crisis of faith inevitably focuses on Israel's sins; whatever calamity overtakes the nation is seen as just punishment for covenant violations. Habakkuk, however, assumes a much more ambiguous (or perhaps ambivalent) position, decrying both the "wicked" who "surround the righteous" (Hab. 1:4) and the Babylonian armies that appear to be the very instruments of divine judgment (cf. Jer. 21:4–7). Unlike Abraham's conversation with YHWH over the fate of Sodom and Gomorrah (Gen. 18), Habakkuk's dialogue with God leads to no final affirmation of the justness of the afflictions visited upon Judah. Instead, we are left, at the conclusion of Chapter 1, with the prophet's

bewilderment at God's "silence" in the face of Babylonian cruelty.

Chapter 2 takes a very different tack, and here we can see the emergence of a limited **theodicy** that attempts to justify YHWH's "delay" in responding to the prophet's pleas for retaliatory justice. The "plunderer" of nations (again, presumably, Babylon), Habakkuk is assured, will itself be plundered by the very peoples it has victimized; punishment for this wrongdoer has only been delayed, not denied. The prophet's responsibility in this interim period is to counsel patience and to live in faithful adherence to the very covenant YHWH only *seems* to have forgotten about but, in fact, is sure to honor. The arrogant may swagger and the foolish may turn to idols, but the "cup" of divine judgment is "in the Lord's right hand" (Hab. 2:16) and the conqueror will at last be forced to drink from it. In the meantime, Habakkuk is advised, the "world" is to remain silent, secure in the conviction that YHWH "is in his holy temple" (2:20).

A PSALM OF YHWH'S TRIUMPH

Chapter 3 appears to be a separate literary unit, and some scholars have speculated that it may be the work of another author. In form, it closely resembles the liturgical poetry of the Book of Psalms and even employs the musical term *selah,* a term used throughout the Psalter and commonly understood to be a signal to the Temple orchestra. And though this composition refers to itself as a "prayer" (Hebrew, *tefilah*), it appears to be a psalm of divine victory over foes human and divine:

> Was your wrath against the
>   rivers, O Lord? . . .
> or your rage against the sea,
> when you drove your horses,
>   your chariots to victory?
> You brandished your naked bow,
>   sated were the arrows at your
>   command.
>   You split the earth with rivers.
> The mountains saw you,
>   and writhed . . . (Hab. 3:8–10)

The anthropomorphic imagery of these verses not only echoes the language of Psalm 77 but even suggests comparisons to Canaanite and Babylonian epic literature. One can easily imagine the same poetic statements made on behalf of Baal and Marduk, both warrior-gods who engaged in battle with the "sea." As an addendum to the first two chapters, this poem seems to move Habakkuk's theodicy in yet another direction, toward a mythological vision of cosmic struggle in which YHWH emerges, at last, as the master of his universe as well as Lord of history. At a critical moment, then, in the life cycle of biblical faith, Habakkuk reaffirms a conviction that earlier generations had expressed within a probably henotheistic context: that no matter how many rivals — human or heavenly — YHWH may face, he will defeat them, and at last humankind will behold the execution of his divine plan.

The Book of Obadiah

Consisting of only one chapter, the Book of Obadiah is the shortest book of the Hebrew Bible, and it reflects conditions in Judah some time after the Babylonian invasion and exile. The focus of this book is twofold: first, on the neighboring kingdom of **Edom** and its role in Judah's defeat, and, second, on YHWH's punishment of both Edom and the "nations" on the Day of the LORD. About **Obadiah**— whose name means "YHWH's servant"— we know virtually nothing, except that, like his predecessor Nahum, he looks forward to the utter destruction and humiliation of Israel's enemies and the restoration of the Judahites to their land.

TREACHEROUS ESAU

Obadiah's indictment of Edom is based on two perceived wrongs, one immediate and one remote in time. Like Jeremiah — whose very language Obadiah deliberately echoes — he accuses the Edomites of heartlessly pillaging a "brother" in his moment of tragedy and defenselessness:

You should not have joined in the
　gloating over Judah's
　disaster
　on the day of his calamity.
You should not have looted
　his goods
on the day of his calamity. (Obad. 1:13)

Other prophetic writers of this period express equal bitterness over Edom's behavior — for example, Lamentations 4:21 and Ezekiel 25:12–14 — and Obadiah seems to be tapping into a deep vein of popular disgust with the Edomites for having occupied a portion of southern Judah in the wake of the Babylonian defeat of Judah's armies. For this "crime," Obadiah promises, YHWH will exact commensurate punishment by allowing Edom, in turn, to be overrun by its enemies.

But not content with Edom's immediate betrayal of its neighbor, Obadiah harks back to the struggle between Jacob and Esau as both a precedent and a paradigm for the present struggle. The intimation is that Edom — whose descent is traced from Esau (Gen. 25:30)— has been treacherous and violent from the start, and that, just as the struggle between the patriarchal twins was resolved in Jacob's favor at the beginning of Israel's history, so it will be resolved in his favor again; only this time, Esau/Edom will be "cut off" forever, and "Mount Zion" will rule over "Mount Esau."

YHWH'S "DAY" OF TRIUMPH

Judah's revenge on Edom, however, will serve only as the prelude to an even greater triumph, which all the nations will witness on the Day of the LORD. In common with his more triumphalist counterparts (cf. Joel 3), Obadiah envisions an approaching time of destruction and national vindication in which "the house of Jacob shall be a fire, and the house of Joseph a flame" (Obad. 1:18), consuming everything in its path. When the dust settles on this era of end time warfare, Israel, Obadiah predicts, will possess even more territory than was taken from it during the Babylonian invasion, and its enemies will be forced to drink the same bitter potion of defeat that Judah was once forced to swallow. "As you have done," Obadiah warns Israel's foes, "it shall be done to you" (1:15). With that prognostication Obadiah joins the ranks of eschatological prophets for whom Israel's return from exile will be accompanied by a global reordering of the balance of justice and power on earth.

QUESTIONS FOR REVIEW

1. What view of the Babylonian conquest of Judah do Jeremiah and Habbakuk share? How can they be so unpatriotic as to view their nation's enemy as YHWH's "instrument"?

2. In how many ways, according to Jeremiah, have the people of Judah violated the covenant and alienated themselves from God? To what extent does Jeremiah's indictment of Judah reflect the influence of Deuteronomistic thinking?

QUESTIONS FOR REFLECTION AND DISCUSSION

1. What hope for the more distant future do Jeremiah, Habbakuk, and Obadiah hold out to their contemporaries? How will the nations that have attacked and destroyed Judah be dealt with by YHWH? And what will the future of the covenant be?

2. Compare the underlying theodicy of collective sin and collective punishment that Jeremiah and his contemporaries clearly endorse with the more problematic views of a postexilic prophetic writer like Zechariah. Why do preexilic prophets place such stress on Israel's responsibility for its own destruction?

TERMS AND CONCEPTS TO REMEMBER

Baruch ben Neriah
Chaldeans
Edom
Habakkuk
Jeremiah

Nebuchadnezzar
Obadiah
Queen of Heaven
theodicy

RECOMMENDED READING

Jeremiah

Blank, Sheldon H. *Jeremiah*. Philadelphia: Westminster Press, 1986.

Bright, John. *Jeremiah*. Anchor Bible, Vol. 21. Garden City, N.Y.: Doubleday, 1965.

Holladay, William L. *Jeremiah: A Fresh Reading*. New York: Pilgrim Press, 1990.

Ludrom, Jack R. "Jeremiah (Prophet)." In D. N. Freedman, ed., *The Anchor Bible Dictionary*, Vol. 3, pp. 684–698. New York: Doubleday, 1992.

———. "Jeremiah, Book of." In D. N. Freedman, ed., *The Anchor Bible Dictionary*, Vol. 3, pp. 706–721. New York: Doubleday, 1992.

Habakkuk

Haak, Robert D. *Habakkuk: Translation and Commentary*. Leiden: Brill, 1992.

Obadiah

Wolff, Hans W. *Obadiah and Jonah*. Minneapolis: Augsburg, 1986.

CHAPTER 20

Prophets in Exile

The Book of Ezekiel and Second Isaiah

Key Topics/Themes Ezekiel and the pseudonymous author scholars have called Second Isaiah (or Deutero-Isaiah) are prophetic voices that speak to us from a critical, albeit somewhat obscure, period in Israel's history: the interval between the Babylonian conquest of 587 B.C.E. and the first generation of Jews to return from Babylon following Cyrus's edict of 538 B.C.E. Each must minister to an expatriate community that is initially crushed by defeat and exile, and then, a generation later, elated by the prospect of national restoration. Between them, Ezekiel and Second Isaiah reflect the full spectrum of collective emotions: from resentment and despair over YHWH's abandonment of Israel to rising hope that both the covenant and the nation itself can be renewed without a repetition of the spiritual errors of the past.

Of the two prophets, Ezekiel — writing in the wake of a forced deportation of priests and members of the Judean ruling class — seems more consumed by anger and grief. Like the classical prophets who preceded him, Ezekiel stresses Israel's culpability and foresees ultimate disaster for a nation that cannot or will not repent. Once tragedy has struck, however, the burden of Ezekiel's witness shifts from divine rejection and punishment to reconciliation and eventual restoration. For Second Isaiah, however, the worst has already occurred: Jerusalem and the Temple have been destroyed, and Judah has become a province of first the Babylonian and then the Persian Empire. Rather than denounce his contemporaries or rehearse the Deuteronomic view of Israel's tragedy, Second Isaiah adopts the role of consoler and spiritual guide, reassuring his fellow Jews in exile that Israel's "debt" to God has been paid in full. Ezekiel's vision of national restoration has now become an imminent possibility. In language evocative of a second exodus, Second Isaiah foresees an era of renewed intimacy and trust, as Israel becomes what God had always intended it to be: his faithful "servant" and a "light" to the nations.

The Book of Ezekiel

Like Jeremiah, his older contemporary, **Ezekiel** is a prophet of the Babylonian exile, and he appears to have been removed to Babylon during the first deportation of 597 B.C.E. His earliest prophecies date from 593 B.C.E., and while the kingdom of Judah still stood, Ezekiel, like so many prophets before him, warned his contemporaries of imminent divine judgment and of the national catastrophe to follow. Unlike an Amos or a Hosea, however, Ezekiel lived to see the fulfillment of these warnings and, later, to envision a future of collective restoration and spiritual rebirth. Yet, in spite of all the world-changing events he lived through, and more than any other literary prophet, Ezekiel focuses intently and unremittingly on his own inner life, speaking in the first person and relating visionary experiences of a mystical, and possibly hallucinatory, character. His style of writing is like no one else's, full of metaphors and symbols that often defy literal translation, and no prophet has given a more vivid (or puzzling) account of the impact that prophecy had on his mind and body:

> The hand of the LORD came upon me there, and he said to me, Rise up; go out into the plain, and there I will speak to you. So I rose and went out into the plain; the glory of the LORD was there, like the glory which I had seen by the river Kebar, and I threw myself down on my face. Then a spirit came into me and stood me on my feet, and spoke to me: Go, he said, and shut yourself up in your house. You shall be tied and bound with ropes, man, so that you cannot go out among the people. I will fasten your tongue to the roof of your mouth and you will be unable to speak; . . . But when I have something to say to you, I will give you back the power of speech. (Ezek. 3:22–27)

Whether any of these directives is to be understood literally or figuratively — whether Ezekiel really remained mute for a lengthy period or was actually bound by ropes and confined to his house — is a point of disputation among scholars that may never be resolved. What is clear from this passage, and from many others, is that Ezekiel's response to the divine summons, wildly eccentric as it may initially seem, is a calculated sequence of dramatic gestures, each symbolizing the captive nature of the people of Judah and the imperative nature of God's rebuke of Judah's sins. For Ezekiel, the power of divine speech supersedes human discourse, and, like his doomed nation, Ezekiel is bound over to God's will. This mysterious, and occasionally overwhelming, sense of God's presence in both history and the prophet's own consciousness is one of the hallmarks of Ezekiel's sensibility.

EZEKIEL'S PROPHETIC WARNINGS

Roughly two-thirds of the Book of Ezekiel is devoted to oracles of divine judgment, whether against Judah or against the nations that surround

it, but it is in the opening chapter (where neither God's anger nor Judah's impending doom is mentioned) that Ezekiel establishes the visionary framework within which prophecies of both catastrophe and hope will take on a cosmic as well as historical significance. For centuries after the Hebrew Bible's final redaction, Jewish mystics studied this chapter carefully, hoping to find in it some hidden clue to the mystery of the divine nature; first-time readers of this text are likely to find it baffling, and even surreal.

Ezekiel's vision begins with a storm wind and clouds of fire, out of which emerge four winged creatures, suggestive of guardian figures of Mesopotamian myth, that possess both human and animal features (Figure 20.1). Above the heads of these creatures, however, is a movable throne that has all the mobility of a chariot, and the mysterious figure seated on that throne becomes the focus of Ezekiel's otherworldly gaze:

> Above the vault over their heads there appeared, as it were, a sapphire in the shape of a throne, and high above all, upon the throne, a form in human likeness. I saw what might have been brass glowing like fire in a furnace from the waist upwards; and from the waist downwards I saw what looked like fire with encircling radiance. Like a rainbow in the clouds on a rainy day was the sight of that encircling radiance; it was like the appearance of the glory of the LORD. (Ezek. 1:26–28)

This is not the first time the imagery of fire and of storm clouds has been associated with the divine presence (see Exod. 3:1–6 and Deut. 4:10–15), of course, nor is it the sole reference to an awe-inspiring radiance emanating from that presence (consider Exodus 34:18, where Moses asks to see God's **kavod**, commonly translated as "glory" or "splendor," only to appear later in that chapter with a glowing face). Even the winged creatures who are mysteriously attached to this chariot-throne are familiar figures from Israel's cultic tradition, having earlier stood in the Holy of Holies in Solomon's Temple (1 Kings 6:23–28). What is new, however, is the systematic evasiveness that characterizes Ezekiel's depiction of YHWH, suggesting that any

Figure 20.1   This stone cherub, over ten feet tall, once guarded the entrance to an Assyrian palace at Calah (Nimrud). A hybrid creature associated with Mesopotamian religion, the cherub commonly has a human face (symbolizing intelligence), the body of a bull or lion (representing strength), and the wings of an eagle (indicating its supernatural swiftness as the gods' emissary). YHWH's cherub guards the tree of life (Gen. 3:24), and a pair of cherubim extend their wings over the Ark of the Covenant, figuratively sheltering God's throne (Exod. 37:6–9; Ps. 99:1). In Ezekiel's vision, cherubim with four faces, grotesque beasts far removed from the chubby infants of popular tradition, draw YHWH's heavenly chariot (Ezek. 1, 10).

The moment this same deity enters the arena of history, however, he becomes the more familiar figure of providential justice, the "judge of all the earth" in Abraham's phrase (Gen. 18:25), that we encounter elsewhere in Pentateuchal and prophetic literature. Ezekiel is appointed God's "watchman" (Ezek. 3:17) to carry messages of reproach to the people of Judah, reminding them of their own unfaithfulness and of the treachery and rebellion of all previous generations of the people of Israel. God addresses Ezekiel as *ben adam*—literally, "son of Adam," but commonly translated as "son of man"—and repeatedly asks him to act out the very punishments his countrymen are about to suffer. Thus, in Chapter 4, Ezekiel is commanded to draw a picture of Jerusalem and to construct a model of a siege engine, keeping his face turned toward the city while doing so. Then he is instructed to lie on his left side for 190 days and on his right side for 40 days, followed by an indefinite period of being tied up in ropes. All of this presumably is a symbolic reenactment of Israel's and Judah's transgressions and of the enslavement to an invading power (in this case, Nebuchadnezzar's Babylon), which acts as God's instrument of judgment (4:4–8). The theatrical nature of these demonstrations aside, the essential content of Ezekiel's message is entirely consistent with Deuteronomistic theology: Israel has repeatedly sinned, violating its covenant with God in every conceivable way, and now its fate is sealed. In fact, the often grotesque ceremonies of self-inflicted torture that Ezekiel undergoes all convey the same, almost nightmare-like, impression of a terrible and irresistible doom.

ISRAEL'S REDEMPTION AND INDIVIDUAL RESPONSIBILITY

If Ezekiel had been commissioned to say only that Judah had at last exhausted God's patience, with its women weeping for **Tammuz** (8:14)—a Babylonian fertility deity whose descent into the Underworld was a central rite in agricultural renewal ceremonies—then he would have had no more to say to his contemporaries than his eighth- and seventh-century-B.C.E. prophetic counterparts, for whom

image of the deity—anthropomorphic or non-anthropomorphic—represents at best a linguistic approximation of an unapproachable divine reality. Like the God who speaks to Job out of the whirlwind, Ezekiel's blazing ruler of the heavens can be glimpsed only as long as he remains in his transcendent domain.

Israel's chief sin was its apostasy. In fact, Ezekiel has much more to say, and the line of argument he develops seems to speak directly to the concerns of the exiled Judeans in Babylon. Like Jeremiah, Ezekiel is well aware of a growing disenchantment with prophets and prophecy among his contemporaries, and of feelings of cynicism and disbelief:

> What is this proverb current in the land of Israel: "Time runs on, visions die away"? Say to them, These are the words of the LORD GOD: I have put an end to this proverb; it shall never be heard in Israel again. Say rather to them, The time, with all the vision means, is near. There will be no more false visions, no specious divination among the Israelites, for I, the LORD, will say what I will, and it shall be done. (Ezek. 12:21–25)

This sense of imminency, of dire events about to occur, no doubt reflects the heightening political fears of the period between 597 and 587 B.C.E., as both the Judean community in exile and Judeans still living in the land of Israel under Zedekiah's rule awaited the final act in the struggle between Judah and Babylon. But it also reflects an internal conflict within Israelite culture itself over the value and efficacy of prophecy. This conflict is just as visible in Chapters 13 and 18 of Deuteronomy as it is in Ezekiel, suggesting that repeated invasions of the land of Israel, from the eighth through the sixth century B.C.E., had taken their toll on the faith of the average Israelite in YHWH's saving power. Clearly, some Israelites (in exile or not yet in exile) had already concluded that God's "glory" had indeed departed from Jerusalem, that YHWH had cast them off or dismissed them from his mind, and that prophecy had become either unreliable or irrelevant.

To these spiritually alienated Judeans, Ezekiel makes two distinct responses. He reminds them, first, that, under covenant, both individuals and the entire community are judged by God and, second, that YHWH has always longed for their repentance, not their annihilation. Thus, and without dismissing the idea of corporate (group) responsibility that looms so large elsewhere in biblical literature, Ezekiel emphasizes the responsibilities of individuals and the possibilities for the forgiveness of sins open to each individual:

> What do you mean by repeating this proverb in the land of Israel: "The fathers have eaten sour grapes, and the children's teeth are set on edge"? As I live, says the LORD GOD, this proverb shall never again be used in Israel. Every living soul belongs to me; father and son alike are mine. The soul that sins shall die. (Ezek. 18:2–4)

Of course, Jeremiah also objected to this same proverb (Jer. 31:29–30), and probably for the same reasons: This popular saying reeks of fatalism and moral passivity, placing the responsibility for obedience or disobedience to God's commandments on some earlier generation. However, Ezekiel goes one step further when he insists that the sins of one generation will never again carry over to the next. This is a striking departure from the logic of Exodus 34:7 and similar texts, where the sins of the fathers quite clearly define and determine the fate of succeeding generations. By implicitly taking issue with the Mosaic principle of inherited guilt, Ezekiel offers his fellow exiles an alternative view of both divine justice and the individual's role in the larger scheme of salvation. In contrast to the books of Kings, where enormous stress is placed on the persistence of wrongdoing at the highest levels of society and on the cumulative, intergenerational nature of Israel's unfaithfulness, Ezekiel carefully separates the moral life of the father from that of the son. He even tries to distinguish discrete phases of an individual's life, to demonstrate that YHWH will ultimately review the ultimate direction and goal of the life before passing judgment on it. Such a view of divine subtlety, as well as divine justness and mercifulness, on the microcosmic level allows Ezekiel to turn, in later chapters, from oracles of collective doom to prophecies of national restoration without seeming to contradict himself.

EZEKIEL'S VISIONS OF THE FUTURE

Chapter 33 marks a turning point in Ezekiel's ongoing arraignment of Judah and its neighbors. In this chapter, Ezekiel learns for the first time that

Jerusalem has fallen to the Babylonians; he regains his powers of speech, and he returns to a theme first introduced in Ezekiel 18:

> You complain, "We are burdened by our sins and offenses; we are pining away because of them; we despair of life." So tell them: As I live, says the LORD GOD, I have no desire for the death of the wicked. I would rather that a wicked man should mend his ways and live. Give up your evil ways, give them up; O Israelites, why should you die? (Ezek. 33:10–11)

That divine judgments are neither gratuitous nor irrevocable was clear to earlier prophets, and presumably to their audiences as well, but in the present circumstances Ezekiel finds it necessary to restate the obvious. His fellow exiles have lost faith either in themselves or in YHWH, or both. Ezekiel must now reassure them of at least two things: that God is still with them in exile and that the door is not closed to forgiveness and to the possibility of a return to their land.

This possibility becomes a visionary certainty in what may be the most influential chapter in Ezekiel, Chapter 37:

> The hand of the LORD came upon me, and he carried me out by his spirit and put me down in a plain full of bones. . . . they covered the plain, countless numbers of them, and they were very dry. He said to me, "Man, can these bones live again?" I answered, "Only thou knowest that, LORD GOD." He said to me, "Prophesy over these bones and say to them, O dry bones, hear the word of the LORD. This is the word of the LORD GOD to these bones: I will put breath into you, and you shall live." (Ezek. 37:1–5)

This oracle is not, it should be noted, a promise of general resurrection for all humankind (though in later centuries both Jewish and Christian commentators read it in precisely that way) but rather an affirmation of Israel's national rebirth and restoration to its native land. The prophet himself underscores this reading by insisting on the symbolic nature of this vision and by declaring (on YHWH's behalf) "I will settle you on your own soil" (37:14). But the most remarkable part of this promise is that

this act of deliverance is not made contingent on the fulfillment of Israel's collective penance (as in Hosea 14:1–7 and many other prophetic texts). Ezekiel offers us a vision of renewal that combines elements of Genesis 1—where God extends his life-giving *ruach* (commonly translated as "spirit," but here rendered as "breath") to a lifeless cosmos—and Genesis 2—where God infuses his *nishmat chayim* (spirit of life) into the claylike shell of Adam, making him a *nefesh chayah* (living soul)—to convey the idea that YHWH's deliverance of Israel from exile will be an act of re-creation, an act of unsolicited compassion and generosity, as was the first act of creation. Nor will this new covenant community, Ezekiel assures his readers, ever again be estranged from God; once more, they will be one nation, governed by a Davidic king and obedient to YHWH's *torah*.

However, before this new and everlasting kingdom can be securely established, Israel must defend itself against a mortal enemy Ezekiel identifies simply and mysteriously as **Gog** from the land of **Magog.** Scholars have entertained a number of conjectures as to who or what Gog may represent, but Gog is likely nothing more than an archetypal figure of menace, a composite of Israel's enemies, and one whose threatened violence will be neutralized by God. Force of arms, Ezekiel here insists, will never prevail against the will of YHWH, and when this final victory over evil and arrogance is achieved, all nations will see the earth-shattering power of Israel's Deity:

> On that day, when at length Gog comes against the land of Israel, says the LORD GOD, my wrath will boil over. In my jealousy and in the heat of my anger I swear that on that day there shall be a great earthquake throughout the land of Israel. The fish in the sea and the birds in the air, the wild animals and all reptiles that move on the ground, all mankind on the face of the earth, all shall be shaken before me. Mountains shall be torn up, the terraced hills collapse, and every wall crash to the ground. I will summon universal terror against Gog. (Ezek. 38:18–21)

At this moment, history-based prophecy gives way to eschatology, and Ezekiel offers us an end time scenario, complete with cosmic upheaval, out of which an unprecedented future will arise. Thus, a vision of Israel's restoration becomes a vision of the world's renewal.

For Ezekiel, who was born into a priestly family, an essential part of Israel's restoration is a rebuilding of the now-destroyed Solomonic Temple, and the final section of this book (Chs. 40–48) provides a series of blueprints for both the new building itself and the theocracy that will govern the restored Temple. This theocracy centers on one priestly line — the **Zadokite** line — that traces its origins back to David's administration (2 Sam. 8:17) and that serves as a substitute for the Levite clans, whose role now becomes subordinate to that of the Zadokites (Ezek. 40:46). In these chapters, Ezekiel is clearly intent on revisiting and rewriting the ecclesiastical traditions of the Pentateuch, hoping perhaps to redeem an institution and a religious caste (to which he himself belonged). Earlier prophets (Amos, Isaiah, and Jeremiah, particularly) had seemingly rejected the sacrificial system and the priesthood on the grounds that both had become hopelessly corrupt. But Ezekiel takes a different course, envisioning a future Israel in which the sacral offices of the Mosaic tradition are once again pure and upright. Coming full circle at last, Ezekiel foresees God's return to the sanctuary from which his "glory" had earlier departed:

> He led me to the gate, the gate facing eastwards, and I beheld the glory of the GOD of Israel coming from the east. His voice was like the sound of a mighty torrent, and the earth shone with his glory. The form that I saw was the same as that which I had seen when he came to destroy the city, as that which I had seen by the river Kebar, and I fell on my face. (Ezek. 43:1–3)

A life-giving stream, Ezekiel discovers, now flows out from under the rebuilt Temple's walls, fertilizing the once-barren land (or valley of dry bones) and producing a lush vegetation suggestive of the Garden of Eden (47:1–12). Once restored to God's favor, Israel will enter upon an idyllic existence that will realize, at last, YHWH's vision for humanity.

Second Isaiah (Isaiah 40–55)

One of the Hebrew Bible's greatest poets, the anonymous prophet known as Second Isaiah brought a message of hope and consolation to his fellow exiles during the last years of the Babylonian captivity (c. 540 B.C.E.). Announcing that Judah's time of punishment is fulfilled, Second Isaiah proclaims that YHWH not only has fully pardoned his people but also is granting them freedom, guiding them on a "new exodus" out of Babylon and back to the Promised Land.

To mark the transition from the oracles associated with Isaiah of Jerusalem (Chs. 1–39) to those of the unnamed poet who carried on Isaiah's prophetic tradition almost two centuries later (Chs. 40–55), postexilic editors inserted a long prose excerpt from 2 Kings. The interpolated passage ends with Isaiah warning King Hezekiah that all his wealth will one day be "carried to Babylon" and that his descendants will serve as eunuchs "in the palace of the king of Babylon" (Isa. 39:5–7). From this point on, neither the name of Isaiah nor the Assyrian threat that preoccupied him is mentioned. Henceforth, all references to the Near Eastern political scene concern Assyria's successor, Babylon, which is already about to fall, and the rise of a new dominant power, that of the Medes and Persians.

CYRUS OF PERSIA

Urging the dispirited exiles to see these international developments as evidence of God's hand at work, Second Isaiah (Deutero-Isaiah) emphasizes that Israel's God remains in full control of human history, directing political events to redeem his captive people. YHWH's agent in delivering the exiles is **Cyrus the Great,** king of Persia, whose armies were then sweeping through the Near East. Although Cyrus does not "know" YHWH, the Persian leader is nonetheless God's instrument of change, winning a series of astonishing victories, beginning with his conquests of Media (549 B.C.E.) and Lydia (546 B.C.E.). Viewing Cyrus's triumphs

Figure 20.2   The Cyrus Cylinder, describing Cyrus the Great's capture of Babylon (539 B.C.E.), illustrates the radically different ways in which non-Israelites and biblical writers interpreted the same historical events. Second Isaiah views Cyrus, liberator of Jewish captives, as YHWH's national deliverer, his "messiah" (Isa. 45:1–3). Whereas the author of 2 Chronicles shows Cyrus attributing his victories to YHWH (2 Chron. 36:23), the cylinder presents Cyrus ascribing them to the chief Babylonian god, Marduk, who inspires the Persian conqueror to restore the Near Eastern gods' neglected altars. The editors who arranged the Hebrew Bible's contents regarded Cyrus's actions as so important that they made his order to rebuild the Jerusalem Temple the climactic final act in the Hebrew Bible canon, completing the creation sequence begun in Genesis 1:1.

as evidence of divine action, Second Isaiah declares that he is the "shepherd" who fulfills God's purpose of restoring the Judean community and rebuilding Jerusalem and the Temple, which the Babylonians had destroyed (44:28–45:6; cf. 41:1–9, 25–29; 48:12–16, 20–22). Unlike Isaiah of Jerusalem, the exilic prophet does not look to a Davidic heir to rehabilitate the covenant community; instead, he declares that Cyrus is YHWH's "anointed," his "messiah" (45:1).

Because Second Isaiah refers to Babylon's fall to Cyrus as imminent but not yet accomplished (Ch. 47), his oracles were probably delivered shortly before 539 B.C.E., when Cyrus captured the city. A year after Cyrus took Babylon, the prophet's optimistic view of him as a liberator was vindicated by

the Persian king's policy that encouraged all groups who had been deported to Babylon to return to their respective homelands. Although Second Isaiah regards Cyrus's liberation of exiles as if it were directed exclusively to the Judean community, the Persian emperor apparently pursued a general policy of repatriation and restoration of local shrines in the lands he conquered. Nor, in spite of the Judean prophet's pronouncements, did he ascribe his conquests to YHWH. According to the Cyrus Cylinder, an artifact inscribed with an account of Babylon's capture, Cyrus officially attributed his success to Marduk, chief god of the Babylonian pantheon, who delivered his city to the Persians because Babylonian rulers had neglected Marduk's cult (Figures 20.2 and 20.3).

Figure 20.3 The splendor of Nebuchadnezzar's Neo-Babylonian Empire is reflected in this museum reconstruction of the ceremonial Gate of Ishtar, Babylonian goddess of love, fertility, and war. While upper-class Jews were held captive in Babylon (587–538 B.C.E.), they probably witnessed the annual New Year's festival in honor of Marduk, creator of heaven and earth, which featured an elaborate parade that passed through these portals. Note that the figures decorating the enameled brick include a serpent with legs (a dragon), reminiscent of the Genesis serpent.

THE OMNIPOTENCE OF JUDAH'S GOD

Although he views a single group—Judean exiles—as occupying the center stage of world history, Second Isaiah, more than any prophet before him, makes categorical declarations about the uniqueness, universality, and eternity of the biblical God. Without beginning or ending, YHWH alone is the creator and ruler of the cosmos; other gods do not exist: "they are all a delusion, their works are nothing; their images are empty wind" (41:29).

Even Marduk (also called Bel) and his divine son, Nebo, supposedly responsible for Babylonian political supremacy, are nonentities, powerless before Judah's incomparable God:

> . . . for I am GOD and there is no other;
> I am GOD, and there is no one like me,
> declaring the end from the beginning,
> and from ancient times things not yet done . . .
>   (Isa. 46:9–10)

For Second Isaiah, God's will is irresistible, shaping human history in unforeseen ways to achieve his people's salvation. Because he is all-powerful and all-wise, YHWH alone can predict the covenant community's restoration and guarantee its future reality:

> Who has announced from of old the things to
>   come?
> Let them tell us what is yet to be.
> Do not fear, or be afraid;
> have I not told you from of old and declared it?
> You are my witnesses!
> Is there any god besides me?
> There is no other rock; I know not one.
>   (Isa. 44:7–8)

To the poet, YHWH is both transcendent and immanent: From his heavenly perspective, mighty nations and empires are insignificant, no more than "a drop from a bucket" (Isa. 41:15). Although he effortlessly commands the innumerable stars of heaven (representing the members of his celestial council), he also reaches out to earth, inspiring his frightened and exhausted people to trust in the restoration of Judah's fortunes and giving them "wings like eagles" for the journey home (40:25–31).

In creating the covenant community anew, YHWH extends to his people as a whole his promise to David, encompassing all the faithful in his "everlasting covenant" (55:3–5). Summoning the Judean exiles to a new role on the world stage, YHWH will make them "a light to the nations" (42:6) and witnesses to his glory (43:10), a culmination of the ancient promise to Abraham that his descendants ultimately would be a source of universal blessing. For exiles unable to grasp the magnitude of God's pardon and redemption, YHWH reminds them that his plan for Israel exceeds the limits of human imagination:

> For my thoughts are not your thoughts.
> nor are your ways my ways, says the Lord.
> For as the heavens are higher than the earth,
> so are my ways higher than your ways
> and my thoughts than your thoughts.
>
> (Isa. 55:8–9)

THE SERVANT SONGS

One of the most distinctive components of Isaiah 40–55 is the series of poems known as the **Servant Songs** (42:1–4; 43:8–13; 49:1–6; 50:4–9; 52:13–53:12). In most of the songs, Israel is explicitly designated as God's "servant" (cf. 43:10), a people commissioned to represent YHWH in the world. In one of the songs, however, the poet seems to describe an individual rather than the people as a whole (52:13–53:12), portraying him as one "despised and rejected of men: a man of sorrows and acquainted with grief" (53:3, King James Version). Known as the Suffering Servant, the unidentified figure in this poem is misunderstood, grouped with sinners, and condemned to an agonizing, humiliating defeat. Many scholars think that this poem voices a new development in biblical attitudes toward the meaning of suffering. Traditional views, such as those of most Israelite prophets and the Deuteronomistic writers, held that the covenant community's misfortunes resulted from its sinful disobedience. In Second Isaiah's poem, however, the afflicted person, though guiltless, willingly accepts the punishment for others' wrongdoing, courageously enduring pain on their behalf:

> Surely he has borne our infirmities and carries our
>   diseases;
> yet we accounted him stricken, struck down by
>   God, and afflicted.
> But he was wounded for our transgressions,
>   crushed for our iniquities;
> upon him was the punishment that made us
>   whole, and by his bruises we are healed.
>
> (Isa. 53:4–5)

Speculations about the identity of the Suffering Servant abound, ranging from the covenant people collectively to a single person who represents Israel, perhaps the prophet himself. The belief that sin and its penalty can be transferred from the community as a whole to a sacrificial object also appears in Leviticus 16, which prescribes a ritual in which the priest transmits the people's sins to a sacrificial goat, which is then sent away to die in the desert. Some scholars believe that this **scapegoat** ceremony may have given rise to a reevaluation of the meaning of suffering in which individual sufferers bear the consequences of communal guilt.

Although the early Christian community identified the Suffering Servant with Jesus of Nazareth (cf. Acts 8:29–35), most scholars now look for an interpretation that respects the integrity of the Hebrew Bible. As noted previously, some commentators think that the one who suffered undeservedly was the prophet himself. Certainly, by preaching that Cyrus of Persia was God's tool in overthrowing Babylon, the prophet invited retaliation from the Babylonian authorities, as well as from members of his own community who had accepted the status quo and feared that Second Isaiah's subversive message would worsen their situation. Other biblical literature dealing with the exile suggests that accommodation to Babylon was encouraged: Jeremiah had urged submission to Babylon's rule, and Daniel, though written later, similarly portrays Judean leaders serving honorably in the Babylonian government (Dan. 1–5). To some exiles, Second Isaiah's political oracles were probably seen as a threat to their community's welfare. The persecution, imprisonment, and possible death of the anonymous servant—followed, after Cyrus's defeat of Babylon, by public vindication—may reflect the prophet's personal experiences as understood by the disciples who collected, edited, and interpreted his life and teaching.

One of the most influential of all biblical prophets, Second Isaiah not only proclaimed an absolute **monotheism** but also promoted a radical understanding of contemporary political events—the decline of Babylon and the rise of Persia under Cyrus—as concrete evidence of YHWH's control of history. Seeing the imminent return to Judah as a new exodus, the prophet defines the covenant community's new task as witnessing to YHWH's incomparable power, wisdom, and saving purpose, bringing "light" to a previously dark world.

QUESTIONS FOR REVIEW

1. After the fall and destruction of Jerusalem, how does Ezekiel (like his near-contemporary Jeremiah) prepare his people for the future? What hope does he hold out to them for returning to their homeland?

2. How does Ezekiel's view of the Temple differ from that of Jeremiah or Isaiah of Jerusalem? In what way is the rebuilding of the Temple part of an End time scenario for Ezekiel?

3. List some differences between the historical circumstances of Isaiah of Jerusalem and those of the prophet known as Second Isaiah. Why do Chapters 40–55 deal with promises of consolation and return to the homeland rather than imminent threats of national punishment, as found in Chapters 1–39? Why is Second Isaiah's message often called a "book of consolation"?

4. To what historical figure does Second Isaiah look for the release of his people? How would the conquests of this foreign leader be meaningful to an audience of Judean exiles in the mid-sixth century B.C.E., but not to Judeans two centuries earlier, the time of Isaiah of Jerusalem?

5. What passages in Isaiah 40–55 can you cite to illustrate the prophet's monotheism? What contributions does this writer make to the developing biblical concepts of God? What "new thing" does Second Isaiah see YHWH accomplishing for his people? How does the prophet encourage his audience's faith in their future?

6. What are the Servant Songs? Describe some speculations about the identity of the "Suffering Servant" in Isaiah 53. Explain the concept of vicarious suffering for others' benefit.

QUESTIONS FOR REFLECTION
AND DISCUSSION

1. Why do Ezekiel's contemporaries express disbelief in prophets and prophecy? Hadn't they just been given sufficient proof that what the preexilic prophets had warned would happen had, in fact, occurred? How do you explain this apparent discrepancy?

2. Why does God repeatedly address Ezekiel as *ben adam* (son of man)? Does this title cast Ezekiel into a special relationship with God, or is he merely being addressed as a representative of humanity?

3. How do you interpret Second Isaiah's identification of Cyrus the Great as YHWH's "messiah," or divinely anointed king? Why does this prophet designate a foreign ruler for this role rather than a descendant of David? After reviewing the discussion of the exile and partial restoration of the covenant community under Persian rule in Chapter 3, explain Cyrus's importance in the biblical tradition (see also Chapters 22 and 27).

4. How does Second Isaiah's portrayal of God resemble that depicted in Exodus and Numbers? How does it differ from many other biblical descriptions of the Deity?

TERMS AND CONCEPTS TO REMEMBER

Cyrus the Great
Ezekiel
Gog and Magog
kavod
monotheism
scapegoat

Second Isaiah/Deutero-
    Isaiah
Servant Songs
Tammuz
Zadokites

RECOMMENDED READING

Ezekiel

Boadt, Lawrence. "Ezekiel, Book of." In D. N. Freedman, ed., *The Anchor Bible Dictionary*, Vol. 2, pp. 711–722. New York: Doubleday, 1992.

Eichrodt, Walter. *Ezekiel*. Philadelphia: Westminster Press, 1970.

Greenberg, Moshe. *Ezekiel, 1–20*. Garden City, N.Y.: Doubleday, 1983.

Klein, Ralph W. *Ezekiel: The Prophet and His Message*. Columbia: University of South Carolina Press, 1988.

Zimmerli, Walther. *Ezekiel*, 2 vols. Hermenica. Philadelphia: Fortress Press, 1979, 1983.

Second Isaiah (Deutero-Isaiah)

Baltzer, Klaus. *Deutero-Isaiah: A Commentary on Isaiah 40–55*. Minneapolis: Fortress Press, 2001. Reinterprets the author as a prophet at the time of Jeremiah.

Blenkinsopp, Joseph, ed. *Isaiah 40–55: A New Translation and Commentary* (Anchor Bible, Vol. 19A). New York: Doubleday, 2002. A major new scholarly analysis.

Childs, Brevard S. *Isaiah.* Old Testament Library. Louisville, Ky.: Westminster/John Knox Press, 2000. Places the message of Second Isaiah in historical continuity with the oracles of Isaiah of Jerusalem.

Clifford, Richard J. "Isaiah, Book of (Second Isaiah)." In D. N. Freedman, ed., *The Anchor Bible Dictionary,* Vol. 3, pp. 490–501. New York: Doubleday, 1992. A good introduction.

Gottwald, Norman K. *The Hebrew Bible: A Socio-Literary Introduction.* Philadelphia: Fortress Press, 1985. Includes an insightful analysis of Second Isaiah's sociopolitical circumstances among the Judean exiles in Babylon.

Muilenburg, James. "Introduction and Exegesis to Isaiah 40–66." In G. A. Buttrick, ed., *The Interpreter's Bible,* Vol. 5, pp. 151–773. New York and Nashville, Tenn.: Abingdon Press, 1956. An older but still substantial analysis of the messages of Second and Third Isaiah.

North, Christopher R. *Isaiah 40–55.* New York: Macmillan, 1964.

———. *The Suffering Servant in Deutero-Isaiah,* 2nd ed. New York: Oxford University Press, 1956. A helpful review of different interpretations of the "servant" passages.

Westermann, Claus. *Isaiah 40–66.* Philadelphia: Westminster Press, 1969. A standard work.

CHAPTER 21

After the Exile

Israel's Last Prophets — Haggai, Zechariah, Third Isaiah, Joel, Malachi, and Jonah

Key Topics/Themes Writing during the era of Persian ascendancy, the last of Israel's prophets — a diverse group that included Haggai, Zechariah, Third Isaiah, Joel, Malachi, and Jonah — touched on a range of prophetic themes. Inspired both by optimism about Israel's future and suspicion of the people of Palestine, the late prophets at once urged the rebuilding of the Temple, reported mystic visions of the restored Temple, criticized the restored community for its religious failures, predicted apocalyptic events, and offered moral fables about YHWH's universality and compassion.

With Cyrus's conquest of Babylon in 539 B.C.E., the political situation in Judah changed for the better, as Judean exiles in Babylonia were encouraged to return home and to rebuild both Jerusalem and its Temple. No longer a kingdom, Judah (referred to in Persian as *Yehud)* became a province in the Persian Empire and was granted at least some measure of self-government, with a dyarchic (two-person) leadership consisting of a governor and a High Priest. Interestingly, the Persians selected Zerubbabel, Jehoiachin's grandson, to be Judah's governor, replacing his uncle, Sheshbazzar, in about the year 520 B.C.E. Like Nehemiah, Zerubbabel returned to Judah with the full blessing of the Persian court, and probably with the understanding that he would represent Persian as well as Judean interests in Jerusalem.

Once in Jerusalem, however, Zerubbabel and the High Priest, Joshua, became the focal point of prophetic expectations, as the prophets began to campaign vigorously for a rapid rebuilding of the Temple and a full restoration of Israel's religious life. As a representative of the royal Davidic line, however, Zerubbabel also became the focus of proto-messianic expectations, and it is hardly surprising to discover — in both Haggai and Zechariah, books by two of his contemporaries — broad hints of eschatological signs that portend the overthrow of the Persian Empire and the recovery of Judah's independence. Whatever their expectations may have been, the Persians remained firmly in control of Judah until the late-fourth-century-B.C.E. conquest of Persia and all of its territories by Alexander the Great (c. 330 B.C.E.). Nevertheless, the belief that YHWH had chosen Zerubbabel as his "signet ring" (Hag. 2:23), through which to accomplish wonders, certainly motivated the prophets of this generation to prod their contemporaries to renew and deepen their commitment to God and to his worship.

Table 21.1   Neo-Babylonian and Persian Empires

Approximate Date B.C.E.	Events in Babylon or Persia	Events in Judah
625	Nabopolassar of Babylon (626–605)	
600	Nebuchadnezzar creates Neo-Babylonian Empire (605–562)	First captivity of Jerusalem (598/597)
		Ezekiel prophesies in Babylon
	Nebuchadnezzar conquers Judah (587)	Fall of Jerusalem and deportation of Jews (587)
	Amel-Marduk (562–560)	
	Neriglissar (560–556)	Exile
550	Nabonidus (556–539)	
	Cyrus (550–530) captures Babylon (539), founds Persian Empire	Second Isaiah in Babylon
		Cyrus issues edict freeing Jews (538)
		Jewish remnant returns to Judah
		Zerubbabel, governor of Judah
	Cambyses (530–522) extends Persian Empire to include Egypt	Haggai and Zechariah
	Darius I (522–486)	Temple is rebuilt (520–515)
500		
	Persia invades Greece, is defeated at Marathon (490)	Joel
	Xerxes I (486–465) launches second Persian invasion of Greece (480–479)	Malachi
	Artaxerxes I (465–424)	
450		
425	Xerxes II (423)	Nehemiah comes to Jerusalem (445)
	Darius II (423–404)	
400	Artaxerxes II (404–358)	Ezra issues reforms; final (?) edition of Torah is promulgated
350	Artaxerxes III (358–338)	
	Arses (338–336)	
	Darius III (336–331)	
	Alexander the Great of Macedonia (336–323) conquers Persia, Egypt, Mesopotamia, western India, etc.; begins Hellenistic period	

Accompanying this spirit of renewal, however, were feelings of suspicion and resentment toward the ethnically mixed population of Palestine (and particularly Samaria), coupled with the conviction that the restored Judean community should be led exclusively by returnees from Babylon. Such sentiments, expressed openly in the books of Ezra and Nehemiah, form the backdrop of the Book of Jonah and help to explain its plea for tolerance and religious understanding for people outside the covenant. (Table 21.1 summarizes key events and figures in this era.)

The Book of Haggai

As the tenth book in the Book of the Twelve (the collection of "minor" prophets), **Haggai** bears a very close relationship to the Book of Zechariah. Both works appear to have been written shortly before the completion and rededication of the Second Temple in 516 or 515 B.C.E. In fact, many scholars today view the books of Haggai and Zechariah as a composite work, with overlapping dates and personalities. It is chiefly to **Zerubbabel** and **Joshua** that Haggai's message is delivered, and they are both instructed by God to hasten the building of his "house" (the Second Temple). Indeed, Haggai repeatedly chides both the leaders and the people of Judah to pay less attention to their own needs and much more attention to the worship of the one God from whom all of the blessings of renewed prosperity will flow:

> Go up to the hills and bring wood and build the house, so that I may take pleasure in it and be honored, says the LORD. You have looked for much, and, lo, it came to little; and when you brought it home, I blew it away. Why? says the LORD of hosts. Because my house lies in ruins, while all of you run off to your own houses. Therefore the heavens above you have withheld the dew, and the earth has withheld its produce. (Hag. 1:8–10)

The logic of this argument, of course, is the logic underlying the Deuteronomistic History, whereby all rewards and punishments are presented as contingent on Israel's service to and obedience of YHWH. Whatever lack of success the returnees have experienced farming the land can therefore be attributed to YHWH's disfavor and to their own manifest selfishness in denying him the thanks he is due. Any hope of a change in present conditions, Haggai goes on to say, will depend on the willingness of the restored Judean community to respond to his warnings and to overcome whatever apathy or reluctance has prevented them from completing a building project that began almost twenty years before the beginning of his ministry.

NEW HEAVENS, A NEW EARTH, AND A NEW JUDAH

Haggai's tone changes markedly in the second and final chapter of this short book, as his focus shifts from the incomplete Temple to the not-yet-restored Judah, and his language and sentiments suddenly become openly eschatological:

> Once again, in a little while, I will shake the heavens and the earth and the sea and the dry land; and I will shake all the nations, so that the treasure of all nations shall come, and I will fill this house with splendor, says the LORD of hosts. (Hag. 2:6–7)

Reassuring his audience that the divine **kavod** ("glory" or "splendor") will return to Judah and to the new Temple, Haggai insists that the people first purify themselves, lest the sacrifices they offer become impure as well. Some scholars interpret this reference to impurity as a rejection of any participation in the rebuilding process by the mixed population of Samaria — subsequently known as **Samaritans** — whose sincerity and trustworthiness were doubted by the newly established Judean leadership (Ezra 4:1–5 and Neh. 4:7–8). Other scholars have suggested, however, that Haggai's message is not a politically encoded attack on Judah's northern neighbors, but rather a rebuke of the Judeans themselves and their spiritually naive assumptions that they can enjoy the fruits of the earth without first paying proper homage to God and obeying his word.

But having made this point, Haggai concludes his work by invoking, once again, the vision of new heavens and a new earth — of an eschatological future, in short — in which all of the kingdoms of the earth will fall by the sword and, as a result, Judah will once again live to see its freedom and sovereignty restored. The very same God, Haggai assures his contemporaries, who could accomplish the Exodus from Egypt can also, surely, bring about this latter-day redemption from slavery. As we will see, the prophet Zechariah developed this apocalyptic scenario with even greater fervor and detail than his contemporary Haggai.

The Book of Zechariah

The Book of Zechariah, the longest book in the collection of Minor Prophets, dates, at least in part, from the same period as the Book of Haggai (c. 520–518 B.C.E.). Some scholars have argued that **Zechariah** and Haggai should be viewed as a composite work in which the pronouncements of one flow into the visions of the other, and both Haggai and Zechariah reflect the profound changes in Israel's fortunes that follow the conquest of the Babylonian Empire by Cyrus the Great in 539 B.C.E. Cyrus's decree permitting the Jews to return to Judah and rebuild the Temple created a new set of political and religious challenges for the exiled Judean community. In the Book of Zechariah, we can see how, a generation later, during the reign of Darius I (522–486 B.C.E.), at least one postexilic prophet rose to those challenges. The ups and downs of the restoration period that culminated in the rebuilding of the Temple in 515 B.C.E.— described at length in Ezra 3–6 — and the uncertain political situation of the Persian-appointed governor, Zerubbabel, serve as a backdrop to this book and help to explain Zechariah's anxiety over the sincerity of Israel's commitment to the worship of YHWH. Yet, in spite of his doubts, as well as Deuteronomistic reflections on the consequences of Israel's apostasy, he tries to impart to his contemporaries his conviction that the renewal of Israel's spirit and of its relationship with YHWH will at last be accomplished in their time, though "not by might, nor by power, but by my spirit, says the LORD of Hosts" (Zech. 3:6).

Contemporary scholars tend to view the Book of Zechariah as two books in one, subdivided into Chapters 1–8 — presumably the work of the "historical" Zechariah — and Chapters 9–14 — attributed to an author or authors commonly designated as "Deutero-Zechariah" (or "Second Zechariah"). Both the style and content of these two parts differ markedly, and by the final chapter of this book, the prophetic message of Zechariah clearly has evolved from one of visionary proclamation and moral advocacy to one of eschatological fervor and expectation.

THE HISTORICAL ZECHARIAH

The first eight chapters of the Book of Zechariah center on seven interlocking visions, each reflective of the condition of Judah in the generation following Cyrus's decree. Zechariah is given a night vision of a horseman riding a red horse amid a stand of myrtle trees (1:8), surrounded by other, variously colored, horses. An angelic interpreter appears and explains that they represent angelic "patrols" whose presence is a sign of world peace. Invoking divine compassion upon Judah and Jerusalem, the angel then assures Zechariah that Judah's period of penance is over and that YHWH has at last "returned" to Jerusalem; the rebuilding of the Temple, stalled for almost two decades, can and should resume. Subsequent visions follow — of four horns, four blacksmiths, and a man taking the measure of Jerusalem (1:18–2:5) — but the message is basically the same: The restoration of the people to the land and of the Temple in Jerusalem will proceed unchecked; the exile is at last over. Indeed, the very nations that earlier had plundered Judah will now turn to its people and plead to be accepted into the community of YHWH (8:23).

A RESTORATION OF DAVIDIC KINGS?

Like Haggai, Zechariah seems to have pinned his hopes for the rebuilding of the Temple and the spiritual renewal of Judah on two men: Zerubbabel, appointed by Darius to be Judah's governor, and Joshua, the High Priest. Unlike Haggai, however, Zechariah seems inclined to defend rather than criticize the political and ecclesiastical leadership of the restored Judean community. In one of the more memorable visions in this book, he sees Joshua arraigned before YHWH, with an "angel of the LORD" and "the Satan" standing on either side. Acting in his role as heavenly prosecutor, the Satan is prepared to accuse Joshua of some unspecified sin when he is rebuked by YHWH, who then declares that Joshua is "a brand plucked from the fire" (Zech. 3:2). As if to confirm YHWH's vindication of Joshua, the angel then proceeds to have the High

Priest's filthy garments removed and replaced by "festal apparel." This symbolic removal of guilt, and the promise of covenant renewal that accompanies it, culminates in a more explicit eschatological promise of a future Davidic ruler, whom Zechariah refers to as "my servant the Branch" (3:8). Zechariah is not the only prophet to employ this apparently messianic term to designate Judah's rightful ruler; Isaiah (4:2; 11:1) and Jeremiah (23:5; 33:15) also speak of a "branch" of the house of David who will rule over a restored and unified kingdom in the days to come.

However, the identity of this "branch" remains something of a mystery, and it is not at all clear whether Zechariah intended to designate Zerubbabel or Joshua as his principal agent of divine redemption. In Chapter 4, Zerubbabel is presented to us as one who will not only lay the foundations of the Temple but also, "plummet [plumb line]" in hand, complete its rebuilding (4:8–10). Haggai also holds Zerubbabel in the highest esteem — even referring to him as YHWH's "signet ring" (Hag. 2:23) — but in contrast to Zechariah, Haggai assigns Zerubbabel a clearly messianic role as the instrument of divine judgment against the nations. In Zechariah, however, that role apparently is reserved for Joshua, who is envisioned as wearing a crown and who is explicitly identified as the "Branch" who will restore both the Temple and the monarchy (6:11–13). Unfortunately for both prophets, Zerubbabel seems to disappear from biblical history at this point; conceivably, he was removed from his position by Persian authorities. Zechariah certainly has nothing more to say about him or about Joshua, and the focus of his prophecy shifts from the human agents of Judah's redemption to the material and spiritual fulfillments of the coming age.

"SECOND ZECHARIAH"

The second part of the Book of Zechariah — which may well be the work of a school of writers rather than a single author — contains a group of diverse oracles whose themes are often explicitly eschatological and whose tone is often stridently chauvin-istic. Three ideas dominate this section of the book: first, that YHWH will bring judgment against Judah's neighbors at the same time that he gathers the remnant of his people back to Zion; second, that the nations will make war, with all its accompanying horrors, against Judah and Jerusalem; and third, that YHWH himself will intervene on Judah's behalf, destroying its enemies and establishing himself as the "king over all the earth" (14:9).

The "universalism" with which this section of the Book of Zechariah concludes — that is, the promise that all of the "families of the earth" will worship YHWH alone — may seem to be contradicted by the expectation of savage global conflict. But, as in the books of Daniel (7–12) and Ezekiel (38–39), we see unfold a dialectical scenario in which apocalyptic writers call for a climactic struggle to precede the end time and the establishment of the kingdom of God and/or the perpetual rule of a Davidic king. However, for Zechariah, the end time will mean not only the definitive end of all threats to Judah's existence but also an end to both idolatry and "prophesy" (13:2), though whether the latter term refers to "false" prophecy, or to any form of prophecy at all, remains unclear. A certain distrust of mantic prophecy (prophecy that entails the use of quasi-magical means to obtain oracular powers) has long characterized the prophetic movement, as reflected in Amos's declaration that he is neither a prophet nor the son of a prophet (Amos 7:14). Zechariah's declaration that, in days to come, "prophets" will be ashamed to boast of visionary powers (Zech. 13:4) seems to reflect the views of an eschatological "group" within the postexilic community for whom an end to the prophetic tradition was a necessary concomitant to the end of history. That the authors of the Book of Zechariah belonged to such a group is, of course, a matter of speculation, but it is clear that by the late Hellenistic period (second and first centuries B.C.E.) momentum was gathering within Judaism to close the biblical canon and declare an end to prophetic revelation.

Third Isaiah (Isaiah 56 – 66)

The unknown prophet whom scholars call Second Isaiah had inspired his fellow exiles in Babylon with oracles of hope, proclaiming a splendid future for a restored Judah and Jerusalem (Isa. 40–55; see Chapter 20). After Cyrus the Great's decree of 538 B.C.E. paved the way for all peoples displaced by Babylonian conquerors to return to their respective homelands, a contingent of Judean exiles trudged back to Judah, now subject to the Persian Empire. Instead of reentering the restored paradise that Second Isaiah had envisioned, however, the refugees encountered only ruin and devastation, with both the holy city and its sanctuary still heaps of rubble. With Judean cities "a wilderness" and Jerusalem "a desolation" (64:10–11), the returned exiles suffered from extreme disappointment, poverty, and deprivation. Assuming Second Isaiah's role as prophetic comforter, the anonymous postexilic seer known as Third Isaiah defines his mission as offering similar reassurance:

> The spirit of the LORD GOD is upon me,
> because the LORD has anointed me,
> he has sent me to bring good news to the op-
>   pressed. (Isa. 61:1)

Third Isaiah describes his audience as consisting of "prisoners," "the brokenhearted," and "those who mourn in **Zion** [Jerusalem's sacred hill on which Solomon's Temple had stood]" (61:1–3). Proclaiming both "the year of the LORD's favor" and divine "vengeance" on Judah's oppressors, the prophet declares that the covenant community will rise from its ashes:

> They [the returned exiles] shall build up the an-
>   cient ruins,
> they shall raise up the former devastations;
> they shall repair the ruined cities." (Isa. 61:4)

As Isaiah of Jerusalem two centuries earlier had chastised the upper classes, which had defrauded the poor, Third Isaiah emphasizes that Judah's future prosperity depends not on reviving cultic sacrifices but on caring for "the hungry," "the naked," and "the homeless poor" (58:7). Only then will the restored community become the world's "light," a beacon of social and economic justice that his exilic predecessor foretold (58:10; 60:1–3; cf. 42:6). Instead of an arid desert, Judah will then become "like a watered garden," a veritable Eden in which God could dwell (58:11, 14).

Expanding on Second Isaiah's message about God's omnipotence and universality, Third Isaiah declares that the covenant arrangement now embraces whole classes of people who previously were excluded, including foreigners (perhaps non-Israelite refugees who joined the Judean exiles in returning from Babylon) and "eunuchs" (male officials in Near Eastern bureaucracies were routinely castrated). Foreigners and eunuchs who keep the Sabbath and "hold fast [the] covenant" are now authorized to serve at the sanctuary, for the new Temple will be "a house of prayer for all peoples" (56:1–8; cf. 66:18–23). Whoever rejects idols to worship YHWH "shall possess the land and inherit [God's] holy mountain," their voluntary commitment to Israel's God making them heirs to all the divine promises (57:13).

Unlike his contemporaries Haggai and Zechariah, Third Isaiah neither raises expectations for a revival of the Davidic monarchy nor argues that renewed prosperity depends on rebuilding the Temple. Indeed, the prophet asserts that the Temple is virtually irrelevant to the Deity, for whom all "heaven" is a "throne" and the earth merely a "footstool":

> What is the house that you would build for me,
> and what is my resting place? (Isa. 66:1)

For Third Isaiah, who addresses the concerns of an impoverished society struggling to survive, YHWH will vindicate the restored community by inundating it with "the wealth of the nations" (61:6). As in the days of Solomon, a flourishing international trade will attract riches to Jerusalem, "so that nations shall bring you their wealth, with their kings led in procession. . . . The glory of Lebanon shall come to you" (60:6–13).

The eschatological visions of universal peace and plenty that close this segment of Isaiah are perhaps the most enduring part of the prophet's legacy. Looking beyond the bleak present to "new heavens and a new earth," a global paradise in which humans and animals dwell peacefully together, the prophet encompasses all humanity in his vision of cosmic harmony (65:17–25; 66:22–23; cf. 2:1–4; 11:6–9). Such prophetic expectations of a divinely renewed creation persist into the Greco-Roman period, when both Jewish and Christian writers composed apocalypses imagining the imminent fulfillment of the Book of Isaiah's hopes for a God-ruled future (see Chapter 29; cf. the New Testament books of Revelation [21:1–4] and 2 Peter [3:13]).

The Book of Joel

The Book of Joel, traditionally placed after Hosea as the second book in the collection of the Minor Prophets, presents a double challenge to readers. Nothing can be inferred from the superscription of this book about when **Joel** lived and taught, nor can we even be certain that the entire book, short as it is, is the work of a single author. Structurally, Joel seems to divide itself into two parts: Chapters 1– 2:17 speak of a terrifying plague of locusts that are devouring the land, and Chapters 2:18–3:21 envision a time of judgment and redemption, when not only the locusts but Judah's regional enemies as well will be gone. Historically, the setting of Joel's oracles seems to many scholars to be postexilic. The economic hardships he refers to, the absence of any mention of a king, and the prominence of the priesthood in his thinking — all suggest the economic and political conditions of Judah in the late sixth century B.C.E. However, references to an approaching army in Chapter 2 might be construed as a prophetic warning of an imminent Babylonian invasion, and Joel traditionally has been viewed as a preexilic figure, if only because of the centrality of the Day of YHWH in his discourse.

DEVASTATION AND REDEMPTION

Those who stress the unity of this book see the locust plague of the first chapter as a prologue to the message of deliverance from tragedy that emerges in Chapters 2 and 3. Echoing the classical prophets of the eighth and seventh centuries B.C.E., Joel urges his readers to repent their sins and to return to God, who, he assures them, is "slow to anger, and abounding in steadfast love" (2:13). The consequence of such repentance, he goes on, will be the removal of the "northern army" that threatens Judah and the restoration of the land to a condition of fertility. No longer will Israel have to fear either nature or human malice, once YHWH is to be found in the "midst" of his people.

The scenario of destruction and re-creation that follows YHWH's intervention in history — the ultimate focus of Joel's message — presents readers with both a comprehensive and a programmatic view of the Day of YHWH. Alternating between visions of cosmic terror and idyllic renewal, Joel foresees two completely different fates assigned to Israel and its enemies. In Judah restored, Joel proclaims, the "mountains shall drip sweet wine, the hills shall flow with milk" (3:18), and Jerusalem will be inhabited forever. As for Egypt, Edom, Tyre, Sidon, and Philistia, however, the Day of YHWH will prove to be a moment of horrific and irreversible doom:

> I will show portents in the heavens and on earth, blood and fire and columns of smoke. The sun shall be turned to darkness, and the moon to blood, before the great and terrible day of the LORD comes. (Joel 2:30)

YHWH himself, in the guise of a warrior-god, will avenge in blood all of the cruelties and injustices visited on Israel by its neighbors, and all of the nations of the world will be summoned to the "valley of Jehoshaphat" to be arraigned before the court of divine justice. This "valley" appears to be an imaginary spot — or, more precisely, a metaphor for "standing in judgment" — whose name ("YHWH has judged" in Hebrew) conveys the essence of Joel's understanding of what the Day of YHWH represents. It is a time of divine punishments and re-wards, an apocalypse of retribution and salvation, and a definitive turning point in the history of the covenant relationship. At last, the promise that Israel will become a holy nation is about to be realized, but instead of becoming a "kingdom of priests," it is now destined to become a nation of prophets:

> I will pour out my spirit on
> all flesh;
> your sons and your daughters shall
> prophesy,
> your old men shall dream
> dreams,
> and your young men shall
> see visions.
> Even on the male and female
> slaves,
> in those days, I will pour out
> my spirit. (Joel 2:28)

Unlike Isaiah, however, Joel does not envision a universal sharing of divine gifts or a gathering of all peoples on the Temple mount; mockingly (and in a deliberate inversion of the Isaian image), Joel urges the nations to "Beat your plowshares into swords" (3:10), because Israel's vindication demands their destruction. In sharp contrast to Amos, and indeed to most preexilic prophets, Joel does not dwell on Israel's sinful past or present. Nor does he predict that either the locusts or the invading army he envisions in the first two chapters will last beyond a brief but indefinite period of national travail. What he does emphasize, however, is YHWH's determination to honor his covenant pledge to preserve and defend Israel against its foes, and he repeatedly refers to the vindication of Israel as one of YHWH's principal objectives during this period of judgment and global catastrophe. The barely concealed nationalism underlying these visions is as marked in Joel as it is in Nahum, enhanced by the addition of apocalyptic sentiments and predictions. For Joel, as for many later apocalyptists, Israel's restoration and the world's end are coterminous events, each testifying to YHWH's supreme power over both history and the cosmos.

The Book of Malachi

Placed last on the scroll containing the Twelve (Minor) Prophets, the short Book of **Malachi**—titled an "oracle" in the superscription—reflects conditions in Judah a few generations after the return from the exile. Active at some time between the rededication of the Jerusalem Temple in 515 B.C.E. and about 450 B.C.E., the prophet presents many of his oracles in the form of a fictional dialogue between God and speakers representing the partly restored covenant community. In these disputations, which mainly focus on the sacrificial cult at the rebuilt sanctuary, God complains that people and priests insult him by offering defective animals, whereas covenant instruction requires perfect, unblemished sacrifices (Chs. 1–2; cf. Lev. 22:17–25; Deut. 15:21). In contrast to Gentiles (non-Judeans), whom he claims provide a "pure offering" as they worship Israel's God, YHWH's laments that his own people, who have the most reason to be grateful to him, sacrifice only "blind," "lame," or "sick" creatures (Mal. 1:6–14).

The book's title, *Malachi*, means "my messenger" and is probably not the name of the prophet, an anonymous figure about whom no information is given. The title may have been taken from 3:1, a passage in which YHWH announces that he is sending "my messenger" to "prepare the way" for God's imminent appearance at the Temple, a divine inspection of Judah's inferior sacrificial system that will resemble a "refiner's fire," separating dross from gold (3:1–4; cf. 1:1). Although emphasizing that YHWH arrives to cleanse the offensive rituals at the Jerusalem sanctuary, the author (whom we call Malachi to avoid confusion) broadens his charge to include the people's ethical obligations to other members of the covenant community. Those who take economic advantage of alien residents, "widows," and "orphans" or who "oppress the hired workers in their wages" risk divine judgment (3:5).

Returning to cultic matters, Malachi accuses the people of "robbing God" for not paying their tithes (one-tenth of their incomes) to maintain the Temple and its priesthood. If they are faithful in this, he promises, they again will receive divine favor, transforming Judah into "a land of delight" (3:8–12). In the book's most frequently cited passage, Malachi appears to condemn divorce, perhaps in response to the policies of Ezra and Nehemiah, postexilic leaders who forced Judean men to cast off their foreign wives (3:13–16; cf. Ezra 10:3, 44; Neh. 13:23–29). Some commentators argue, however, that Malachi is here borrowing Hosea's image of a marriage pact between God and people, in which the human partner has been unfaithful (cf. Hos. 3:10–12).

Responding to those who question God's justice (3:17), Malachi declares that God will intervene to champion the righteous and punish the wicked in a fiery day of judgment. Compiling a "book of remembrance" containing the names of those who revere him, YHWH will spare them "on the day" that he acts (3:16–18). Although divine fire will consume evildoers, the faithful will behold "the sun of righteousness" rising "with healing in its wings," causing them to leap joyfully "like calves" over the ashes to which the wicked have been reduced. As a harbinger of this "great and terrible day of the LORD" (an eschatological image derived from Amos), YHWH will send his messenger, whom an appendix reveals to be none other than the prophet Elijah (4:5).

In editing this compilation of anonymous oracles, redactors appended two passages—a command to observe all the Mosaic "statutes and ordinances" (Mal. 4:4) and the identification of Elijah, whom a whirlwind had transported to heaven, as the eschatological messenger. In both Protestant and Roman Catholic editions of the Bible, Malachi appears as the last book of the Old Testament, making the appended references to Israel's *torah* and prophets a thematically appropriate transition to the New Testament. The allusion to Elijah's return to reconcile "parents to their children" resurfaces in the Christian Gospels, in which John the Baptist is named as the promised mediator (cf. Mark 9:11–12; Matt. 17:9–13).

The Book of Jonah

In both literary form and content, the Book of Jonah differs strikingly from other prophetic works in the Hebrew Bible. Rather than a collection of oracles that addresses an ethical issue or political emergency, Jonah is a brief narrative relating the misadventures of a prophet who fails utterly to understand the God who summons him to warn the inhabitants of Nineveh, capital of the hated Assyrian Empire, of impending judgment. In some respects, Jonah is a comedy in which the humor derives from rhetorical exaggeration and the spiritual limitations of the central figure, who interprets YHWH's graciousness as a cruel joke made at his personal expense. Although **Jonah** was almost certainly written during the postexilic period, the fictional title character apparently takes his name from a prophet who lived during the reign of Jeroboam II, who ruled Israel during the eighth century B.C.E. (2 Kings 14:25).

In most biblical accounts, prophets are described as overcoming their initial reluctance to accept God's call and then prophesying as commanded. In Jonah, however, the prophet is not only reluctant but deliberately disobedient and consistently resentful of God's use of him. When called to preach in Nineveh, Jonah—perhaps suspecting that YHWH's kindness may lead him to spare that hated city—heads in the opposite direction. Aboard a foreign ship sailing to Tarshish (probably Spain) in the remote western Mediterranean, Jonah falls asleep during a raging storm that YHWH has conjured up to halt his prophet's cowardly flight.

Although they are Gentiles who worship foreign gods, the sailors on Jonah's ship are portrayed as just and reasonable men, open to hearing the word of Israel's God. Casting lots, they learn that Jonah is the cause of the storm that threatens to capsize them, but they are too humane to throw the Israelite jinx overboard. Only after begging YHWH's forgiveness do they hurl Jonah into the sea, where God has arranged for a large fish to swallow him.

Chapter 2 consists largely of Jonah's desperate prayer from the belly of the sea creature. In this poetic passage, Jonah likens his predicament to being immersed in the original watery chaos that preceded creation and to the helpless state of the dead in Sheol, begging God to rescue him. YHWH then orders the fish to spew Jonah out, depositing him onshore.

The humor of the totally improbable dominates Chapter 3. After his "resurrection" from the fishy grave, Jonah again hears YHWH's voice ordering him to go to Nineveh, described as so gigantic a metropolis that it takes three days to traverse it. Announcing his message as brutally as possible in a single sentence—"Forty days more, and Nineveh shall be overthrown!"—Jonah is unpleasantly surprised at the people's reaction. The entire Assyrian population, from the king on down, immediately repents; even the animals wear sackcloth, a garment of mourning and self-abasement, as if they, too, hope that YHWH will repent and spare their city. Approving of the Assyrians' response, YHWH rewards their improved behavior by deciding not to obliterate them.

Furious at such divine softheartedness, Jonah disapprovingly paraphrases the Exodus passage that describes YHWH as "a gracious God and merciful, slow to anger, and abounding in steadfast love" (4:2–3; cf. Exod. 34:6–7; Num. 14:17–19). As Jonah implies, it is one thing for Israel's God to manifest *hesed* (steadfast love) to his own people, but quite another for him to bestow it on a Gentile nation that does not explicitly worship him. Feeling betrayed because YHWH did not vindicate his preaching by producing a spectacular catastrophe, Jonah asks to die. YHWH has but one question for him: "Is it right for you to be angry?" (4:5).

While the prophet sulks in solitude outside Nineveh's gates, YHWH attempts to teach Jonah a much-needed lesson that might bring him closer to the divine perspective. First causing a leafy bush to grow, providing shade "to save him from his discomfort," YHWH then sends a worm to kill the plant. Smoldering with resentment, the prophet again asks for death, his death wish contrasting sharply with God's concern for human life (4:6–8).

The book concludes with a conversation in which Jonah and his God discuss the implications of the plant's short life. How, YHWH asks, can the prophet regret the death of a mere bush and not understand YHWH's concern for the 120,000 humans living in Nineveh, people who "do not know their right hand from their left, and also many animals?" (4:9–11). The prophet who has learned that nowhere on land or sea can he escape YHWH's reach is now also asked to contemplate the implications of YHWH's universality. As Amos and Second Isaiah recognized, Israel enjoys a special relationship with God but does not have exclusive claim to divine care—the same Deity who created Israel also directs the destinies of other nations (Amos 9:7; Isa. 42:4–6; 45:1–6, etc.). The author does not state whether Jonah was able to embrace this larger perspective, leaving the question for readers to ponder.

QUESTIONS FOR REVIEW

1. Haggai and Zechariah were active during the late sixth century B.C.E. when a Judean "remnant" had returned to Jerusalem from Babylon. Although their prophetic oracles have been revised by postexilic editors, it is still possible to discern that both prophets apparently hoped for a restoration of Davidic rule. Who was Zerubbabel, and what was his expected role in a restoration of the monarchy? What role did Joshua the High Priest play?

2. How did Haggai and Zechariah try to persuade the returned Judeans to rebuild the Jerusalem Temple? What benefits to the people did they say would occur if YHWH's sanctuary was restored?

3. How does the work of "Second Zechariah" differ in form and content from that of the historical prophet? Describe his apocalyptic interests.

4. The reality of life under Persian domination in a partly restored Judea contrasted with earlier prophetic promises. How did postexilic disappointments in the present serve to stimulate Third Isaiah's ecstatic visions of a future "new heavens and a new earth"?

5. How does Joel balance threats of absolute destruction of all earthly life with promises of future salvation? What will the "Day of YHWH" bring to the world?

6. How does Malachi reinterpret the "Day of YHWH" to include traditions about the return of the prophet Elijah, who was carried alive to heaven in a fiery chariot?

7. How does Jonah react when YHWH commands him to preach divine judgment on Nineveh? Why does he try to run away? Are his anxieties about YHWH's mercy, even to Gentiles, justified?

QUESTIONS FOR REFLECTION AND DISCUSSION

1. In comparing the concerns and themes voiced by the postexilic prophets, do you see any major changes in their messages from the prophecies delivered earlier by Amos, Hosea, Micah, and Isaiah of Jerusalem? Does the book of Jonah contain a critique of traditional Israelite prophecy? Explain.

2. The Israelite institution of prophecy began shortly after the creation of the Davidic monarchy and ended a generation or two after its dissolution. What reasons can you give for the cessation of prophecy in the covenant community?

TERMS AND CONCEPTS TO REMEMBER

Elijah, return of
Haggai
Joel's visions of cosmic destruction
Joel's visions of divine inspiration
Jonah's message to Nineveh and its effects
Joshua
kavod
Malachi's "messenger of the covenant"
"new heavens and a new earth"

postexilic Jerusalem
province of Judea
question of intermarriage and divorce
Samaritans
Second Temple
Second Zechariah, eschatology of
universalism
YHWH's wrath and mercy
Zechariah
Zerubbabel
Zion

RECOMMENDED READING

Haggai and Zechariah

Ackroyd, Peter R. *Exile and Restoration: A Study of Hebrew Thought in the Sixth Century B.C.E.* Philadelphia: Westminster Press, 1968.

Meyers, Carol, and Meyers, Eric. "Zechariah 1–8." In *The Anchor Bible Dictionary,* Vol. 6, pp. 1061–1065. New York: Doubleday, 1992.

Petersen, David L. *Haggai and Zechariah 1–8.* Philadelphia: Westminster Press, 1984.

———. "Zechariah 9–14." In *The Anchor Bible Dictionary,* Vol. 6, pp. 1065–1068. New York: Doubleday, 1992.

Wolff, Hans. *Haggai.* Minneapolis: Augsburg, 1988.

Joel

Hiebert, Theodore. "Joel." In *The Anchor Bible Dictionary,* Vol. 3, pp. 873–880. New York: Doubleday, 1992.

Kapelrud, Arvid. *Joel Studies.* Uppsala, Sweden: Almquist & Wiksells, 1948.

Wolff, Hans. *Joel and Amos.* Philadelphia: Fortress Press, 1977.

Third Isaiah

Emmerson, Grace I. *Isaiah 56–66.* Old Testament Guides. Sheffield, England: Sheffield Academic Press, 1992.

Hanson, P. D. *Isaiah 40–66.* Louisville, Ky.: Westminster/John Knox Press, 1995.

Stuhlmueller, Carroll. "Deutero-Isaiah and Trito-Isaiah." In R. E. Brown et al., eds., *The New Jerome Biblical Commentary,* 2nd ed., pp. 329–348. Englewood Cliffs, N.J.: Prentice-Hall, 1990. Discusses the work of Second and Third Isaiah in the prophets' historical context.

Malachi

Hanson, Paul D. "Malachai." In J. L. Mays, ed., *Harper's Bible Commentary,* pp. 753–756. San Francisco: Harper & Row, 1988.

Ogden, Graham S., and Deutsch, Richard R. *Joel and Malachi: A Promise of Hope, a Call to Obedience.* Grand Rapids, Mich.: Eerdmans, 1987.

Schuller, Eileen M. "The Book of Malachi." In *The New Interpreter's Bible,* Vol. 7, pp. 843–877. Nashville, Tenn.: Abingdon Press, 1996.

Jonah

Ceresko, Anthony R. "Jonah." In R. E. Brown et al., eds., *The New Jerome Biblical Commentary,* 2nd ed., pp. 580–584. Englewood Cliffs, N.J.: Prentice-Hall, 1990.

Fretheim, Terence E. *The Message of Jonah.* Minneapolis: Augsburg, 1977.

Magonet, Jonathan. "Jonah, Book of." In D. N. Freedman, ed., *The Anchor Bible Dictionary,* Vol. 3, pp. 936–942. New York: Doubleday, 1992. A short introduction to issues raised in the book.

Trible, Phyllis. "The Book of Jonah." In *The New Interpreter's Bible,* Vol. 7, pp. 463–529. Nashville, Tenn.: Abingdon Press, 1996. A sensitive reading of this paradoxical view of Israelite prophecy.

———. *Rhetorical Criticism: Context, Method, and the Book of Jonah.* Minneapolis: Fortress Press, 1994. Demonstrates the relationship between literary artistry and Jonah's theological message.

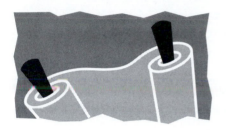

CHAPTER 22

Introduction to the Writings

Reevaluating Israel's Life with God

Key Topics/Themes The third major division of the Hebrew Bible, and the last to be adopted into the canon, the Writings (Kethuvim) are as diverse in content as they are in literary form, ranging from devotional poetry (Psalms), to books of practical and speculative wisdom (Proverbs, Job, and Ecclesiastes), to theological histories reinter-preting Israel's past (1 and 2 Chronicles). Although some books in the Writings, such as the Psalms, contain preexilic material, most of the documents reflect the difficulties of the covenant community's postexilic readjustment, when Judah was subject to Persian domination.

After the Exile: A Reinterpretation of Judah's Religious Mission

After the Babylonian exile, nothing in the covenant community was ever again the same. Although successive waves of Judean exiles returned to Jerusalem following Cyrus's decree encouraging repatriation in 538 B.C.E., postexilic restoration was only partial. Despite the prophecies of Haggai and Zechariah (see Chapter 21), neither the Davidic dynasty nor the former state of Judah was restored. Known then as the province of Judah (Ezra 5:8; later called **Judea**) and restricted to the territory surrounding Jerusalem, the Judean homeland was reduced to a small subunit of the Persian Empire. Except for a brief interval when the Maccabees (Hasmoneans) ruled (142–63 B.C.E.), the Judean people never again enjoyed political independence (see Chapters 28 and 29). Persian administrators, following an

imperial policy of promoting local religions in the Persian Empire, supported the reestablishment of YHWH's cult at a rebuilt Jerusalem Temple, but the harsh reality of postexilic life seemed a mockery of Second Isaiah's visions of a glorious future. Only a tiny scrap of the land promised to Abraham's descendants was still theirs, and an increasingly large number of YHWH's people were living far from their homeland in the **Diaspora,** the scattering of Jews abroad in **Gentile** (non-Jewish) nations.

The Postexilic Community

Although Persia did not grant the province of Judah political autonomy or allow Davidic heirs to reestablish the throne, it actively encouraged Judah's religious function, mandating an official edition of the Mosaic Torah (Ezra 7) and at least partially subsidizing reconstruction of the Temple. Instead of being ruled by Davidic kings who strove to make

273

BOX 22.1
The Writings: Responses to Judah's Postexilic Experience

"Can these bones live?" When YHWH asked this question of Ezekiel, who was then a captive in Babylon, the covenant people resembled desiccated skeletons scattered in a boneyard. The nation of Judah had perished in the flames rising from Jerusalem and Solomon's Temple. Further, as had happened to many other small states crushed by the Babylonian juggernaut, it looked as if Judah would vanish forever, buried in history's graveyard. YHWH, however, regarded Judah's political death and interment—punishment for its faithlessness—as only a temporary state: "these bones [that were] the whole House of Israel" would live again. In Ezekiel's vision of his nation's future resurrection, the prophet witnesses YHWH's miraculous reenactment of Adam's creation. Infusing Judah's apparently lifeless corpse with his spirit, YHWH re-creates a people for his name (Ezek. 37:1–14).

The third principal division of the Hebrew Bible, the Writings (Kethuvim), provides the wide-ranging responses of postexilic authors to the radically changed circumstances of the covenant community. As Ezekiel had envisioned old bones infused with new life, so writers living after the exile labor both to revive Judah's old institutions, such as the Temple cult and priesthood, and to interpret anew YHWH's con-

tinuing purpose for Judah. Simultaneously preserving ancient traditions and infusing them with new meaning, the author of 1 and 2 Chronicles retells Israel's history from a priestly perspective in which the postexilic priesthood can, as community leaders, be viewed as the logical successors to the Davidic kings, the best of whom devotedly supported the sanctuary cult. Opening his revised history with an extensive genealogy that links Adam, God's first human creation, with both Levite priests and Davidic kings, and concluding with Cyrus's resuscitation of the Judean state, the Chronicler emphasizes the continuity of his community's past and present.

The unknown author of Ruth fashions another re-creation of Israel's past by placing his gentle heroine back at the time of the Judges, even before the monarchy was established. At the same time that he celebrates an idealized past, picturing a far more peaceful environment than that depicted in the Book of Judges, Ruth's author tackles issues of exclusivity that had long troubled the covenant people. Perhaps deliberately protesting Nehemiah's law compelling all Israelite men to divorce their non-Israelite wives, the writer portrays Ruth, a Moabite woman—and presumably a former worshiper of Chemosh—as entirely sympathetic. Although the Torah portrayed

their nation a political force in the Near East, the former monarchical state became a theocracy, a "God-ruled" society led by priests. The covenant community's historical transition from an independent kingdom aspiring to play a role in international politics to a people deprived of political influence and subservient to Persian authority also marks a change in the Judeans' understanding of their relationship with YHWH. No longer governed by divinely appointed kings or involved in the political arena, Judah refocused its energies on its religious mission and priestly heritage.

Many of the books included in the Writings illustrate the postexilic community's focus on priestly concerns, particularly YHWH's formal worship at

the Second Temple. In editing this final section of the Tanak, postexilic editors placed the Psalms, a compendium of hymns and other songs performed at the Second Temple, at the head of the collection. The books of Chronicles, which reinterpret the role of Davidic kings to portray them as advocates of priestly Temple rituals, are given the climactic end position (Box 22.1). In this arrangement, the Writings—and the Hebrew Bible as a whole—conclude with the proclamation of Cyrus, king of Persia, who invites Jews from throughout his empire to return to Jerusalem and support YHWH's sanctuary (2 Chron. 36:22–23).

Between Psalms and Chronicles, which bracket the Writings, redactors assembled a richly diverse foreign women, whether Moabite or Midianite, as wanton temptresses who caused Israelite men to sin, and hence to deserve death (cf. Num. 31:1–20; Deut. 7:1–16; 20:17–18), the story of Ruth celebrates marriage between a foreign widow and her Yahwist husband, clearly implying that it fulfills the divine will.

In the Writings, poets and sages also explore the possible meanings of Israel's prolonged suffering and incomplete restoration, creating such masterpieces as Job and Ecclesiastes. Rejecting the simplistic Deuteronomic thesis that equated prosperity with religious obedience, and misery with sin, the authors of these wisdom books boldly question conventional biblical teachings, including traditional concepts of God. Representing a broad spectrum of literary categories, from lyric poetry and short fiction to lengthy historical narratives, the Writings bear eloquent testimony to the diverse ways in which Judah's postexilic thinkers creatively refocused and reinterpreted their religious legacy.

BOOKS OF THE WRITINGS

- Psalms (an anthology of deeply felt religious poetry)
- Proverbs (a compilation of wise sayings and largely practical and conventional wisdom)
- Job (a philosophical exploration of YHWH's ethical character and relationship to humanity)
- Ecclesiastes (a sage's quest for meaning and delight in paradox)
- Ruth (a short story about a Moabite woman's new life in Israel during the time of the judges)
- Song of Songs (a collection of erotic love poems)
- Lamentations (an anguished complaint about YHWH's destruction of his people)
- Esther (a short story about Jewish survival in a foreign empire)
- Ezra (a composite account of Ezra, the priest-scribe who brought the Torah from Babylon to re-create the covenant community in postexilic Jerusalem)
- Nehemiah (a narrative about rebuilding Jerusalem's fortifications under Persia's sponsorship)
- Daniel (an apocalypse, or revelation, that includes mystical visions of events leading to the end time; the last-written book in the Hebrew Bible canon, discussed in its historical context in Chapter 28)
- 1 and 2 Chronicles (a priestly revision of the Deuteronomistic History, emphasizing the Temple cult)

anthology of sacred literature that differs significantly from the other two parts of the Hebrew Bible. Although derived from many different sources, the material in the Torah is thematically bound together by YHWH's series of promises to the patriarchs and the Sinai/Horeb agreement he made with their descendants. The theologically oriented narratives of Joshua through Kings (the Former Prophets) are unified by the author-editors' controlling intent to show YHWH as Lord of history, expressing his will through Israel's rise and fall. Even the fifteen books of the Latter Prophets, for all their disparate responses to changing political and religious circumstances over a period of four centuries, form a comparatively coherent tradition.

In contrast, the Writings present a wide range of viewpoints, reflecting the multifaceted religious, social, and psychological struggles of a covenant community living under foreign political control.

Whereas the long line of prophets began during the early monarchy and largely ended a few generations after Judah's return from the exile, the Writings in their present form belong primarily to the postexilic era (approximately the fifth to the second centuries B.C.E.). Extremely varied in both literary form and theological content, the Writings include some unexpected selections from Hebrew literature, ranging from erotic lyrics in the Song of Songs to a militaristic celebration of national survival in Esther, a volume that makes no direct reference to

God. (As if to rectify this omission, however, the Greek translation of Esther in the Septuagint interpolates a series of prayers and other passages to demonstrate that the heroine was Torah-observant and obedient to the divine will; see Chapter 29.)

A Brief Survey of the Writings

Placed first in the Writings, Psalms is a collection of devotional poetry that sets the tone for this part of the Tanak, which as a whole explores the complex nature of Israel's difficult postexilic partnership with YHWH. The 150 individual lyrics in this book run the gamut of religious feeling, from exulting praise of God to bitter complaints about his treatment of Israel. Although many were probably composed during the period of the Davidic monarchy and sung at the coronation of Davidic kings, others reflect the postexilic situation, expressing bewilderment and disappointment at YHWH's apparent failure to honor his promises to David or to provide the national blessings enumerated in Genesis and Deuteronomy. Raising issues of divine justice that are addressed throughout the Writings, several psalmists confront the painful disparity between the ancient promises and the bleak historical realities. Psalm 89 directly charges YHWH with breaking his word to David, to whom he had sworn:

> I will not violate my covenant, or alter the word
>   that went forth from my lips.
> Once and for all I have sworn by my holiness: I
>   will not lie to David.
> His line shall continue forever,
> and his throne endure before me like the sun . . .
>   (Ps. 89:34–36)

Babylon's overthrow of the Davidic line—never to be restored—appears to invalidate YHWH's sworn oath:

> But now you have spurned and rejected him
>   [David and his heirs];
> you are full of wrath against your anointed.

> You have renounced the covenant with your
>   servant;
> you have defiled his crown in the dust.
>   (Ps. 89:38–39)

YHWH's repudiation of the Davidic Covenant, which brought into question the trustworthiness of the Deity's promises, was not the only theological issue that troubled the postexilic Judean community. In striving to understand their God's intentions, devout Judeans confronted another paradox: the more faithful they were to YHWH, worshiping him exclusively, the more they suffered from injustice and oppression. As the poet of Psalm 44 observes, God's promise to protect those loyal to him—the major premise of Deuteronomy—was not fulfilled in Judah's actual historical experience. In contrast to ancient traditions about YHWH's saving acts in the remote past, the postexilic God seems indifferent to the massacres and other violence inflicted on his people:

> You have made us like sheep for slaughter,
> and have scattered us among the nations.
> You have sold your people for a trifle,
> demanding no high price for them.
>   (Ps. 44:11–12)

Rejecting the Deuteronomic assumption that suffering results from sin, the psalmist insists that his community has kept its Torah obligations:

> All this has come upon us,
> yet we have not forgotten you,
> or been false to your covenant.
> Our heart has not turned back,
> nor have our steps departed from your way,
> yet you have broken us. . . . (Ps. 44:17–19)

Ironically, it is precisely *because* of their commitment to YHWH that his worshipers suffer:

> *Because of you* we are being killed all day long,
> and counted as sheep for the slaughter.
> Rouse yourself! Why do you sleep, O Lord?
> Awake, do not cast us off forever!
> Why do you hide your face?
>   (Ps. 44:22–24; emphasis added)

Although the covenant people survived their many afflictions, YHWH's refusal to come to their aid as he had in Moses' day — as if he were now asleep or absent — perplexed many of the authors whose works appear in the Writings, particularly the wisdom writers (see Chapter 25).

Not vouchsafed an answer to the problem of YHWH's increasing "hiddenness," the psalmists as a group focused on the covenant people's obligations as a worshiping community, emphasizing the importance of **liturgy,** a body of ceremonial rites performed in public worship (see Chapter 24). Liturgical concerns are similarly evident in the books of Chronicles, which are largely preoccupied with Temple rituals, enumerating the duties of singers, priests, Levites, and others in carrying out the sacrifices and other formal practices of YHWH's cult. In editing the Hebrew Bible, priestly scribes gathered five short books — Ruth, Song of Songs, Ecclesiastes, Lamentations, and Esther — together to form a small anthology within the Writings known as the **Megillot.** Also called the *Festival Scrolls,* the Megillot were designed to serve a liturgical purpose: At each of the five principal festivals in the Jewish religious calendar, one of the five documents was read aloud (see Chapter 26). Although the content of these five works is extremely diverse — Ruth is a bucolic love story, Esther a secular tale justifying Jewish military self-defense, Ecclesiastes a skeptical meditation on self-contradictory wisdom and divine hiddenness, Lamentations a passionate complaint over YHWH's abandonment of Jerusalem, and the Song of Songs a celebration of sexual enjoyment — all were employed to serve the postexilic community's resolve to worship YHWH alone.

The historical narratives of Ezra and Nehemiah, which describe sociopolitical conditions in Judea under Persian domination, emphasize both a reorganization of postexilic society and the importance of teaching *torah* requirements to a dejected population. Both books are concerned about preserving the covenant community as a worshiping body while subject to foreign control (see Chapter 23). Unlike any other book in either the Prophets (where it typically appears in Christian Old Testaments) or the Writings (where Jewish editors placed it), Daniel is an **apocalypse,** a "revelation" or "unveiling" of unseen realities in the spirit world and of future events. Composed during a time of intense persecution in the mid-second century B.C.E., this apocalyptic work surveys the covenant people's history — cast in the form of prophecy — from the Babylonian exile to the Hellenistic era (see Chapter 28). The last-written book of the Hebrew Bible, Daniel also deals with issues of keeping Jewish identity and *torah* obligations in the Diaspora, where pressures on Jews to conform to foreign cultures were pervasive.

Whereas many books in the Writings are closely associated with observing Judean Temple rituals and/or maintaining Jewish worship in the Diaspora, other texts in this part of the Tanak — the wisdom literature — embody a wide spectrum of responses to the covenant people's historical experience of both prosperity and extreme suffering. The compilation of largely conventional observations in Proverbs offers commonsense advice on the value of behaving prudently, serving God, and attaining a good life. In contrast, Job, a book of speculative wisdom, radically departs from most biblical portraits of God, challenging conventional piety to reconcile the Deity's presumed goodness with the universal prevalence of injustice and undeserved pain. As a paradigm of the covenant community's tragic losses during and after the Babylonian exile, Job raises ethical and theological issues that no theologian has yet satisfactorily resolved (see Chapter 25). (Two later wisdom books, Ecclesiasticus and the Wisdom of Solomon, are discussed with the Apocrypha in Chapter 29.)

With a few exceptions, this text discusses the Writings in the canonical order of the Hebrew Bible, beginning with Psalms and ending with 1 and 2 Chronicles. For coherence, however, the wisdom books, including Ecclesiastes, are covered together, with the simpler practical counsel of Proverbs discussed before Job's profound exploration of cosmic justice and the problem of evil. A special case, Daniel is examined in the context of the

Maccabean Revolt and the apocalyptic movement (see Chapter 28).

QUESTIONS FOR REVIEW

1. What diverse categories of literature appear in the third major division of the Hebrew Bible, the Writings? In what ways — subject matter, themes, and theological concerns — do these books typically differ from the Torah and the Prophets?

2. To what new foreign power was the covenant community subject after some leading exiles returned to Jerusalem from Babylon? How do some passages in the Writings criticize YHWH for failing to keep his promise to maintain an heir of David on Judah's throne? What crisis of faith resulted from the incompleteness of the postexilic restoration?

3. How do some of the Writings, such as the collection of Psalms, express the partly restored community's new sense of its function as a worshiping community?

QUESTION FOR REFLECTION AND DISCUSSION

Whereas the first two parts of the Hebrew Bible, the Torah and the Prophets, focus on presenting YHWH's requirements — legal, ethical, and ritual — for the covenant people, the Tanak's third division, the Writings, includes some of the postexilic community's varied responses to God's sometimes puzzling behavior. Late in the Babylonian exile, Second Isaiah proclaimed that YHWH was about to rescue his people by staging a "new exodus." Why, then, does YHWH not visibly intervene on his covenant people's behalf, as he did during the Exodus from Egypt? Why, when the postexilic community is thoroughly united in YHWH's worship at a rebuilt Temple in Jerusalem, does God seem to grow progressively more "hidden" or "absent" from human history?

TERMS AND CONCEPTS TO REMEMBER

apocalypse
complaints about
    YHWH's inaction
Diaspora
diverse genres in the
    Writings
Gentile
liturgy (in Second
    Temple)
Megillot
partial postexilic
    restoration
postexilic priestly
    theocracy
province of Judea
skeptical wisdom
    literature

RECOMMENDED READING

Albertz, Rainier. *A History of Israelite Religion in the Old Testament Period.* Vol. 2, *From the Exile to the Maccabees.* Louisville, Ky.: Westminster/John Knox Press, 1994. Traces social and theological developments manifest in documents of the postexilic period.

Birch, Bruce C.; Brueggeman, Walter; Fretheim, Terence E.; and Petersen, David L., eds. *A Theological Introduction to the Old Testament.* Nashville, Tenn.: Abingdon Press, 1999. Includes a chapter on postexilic books reflecting multiple crises in Judea's partly restored community.

Henshaw, T. *The Writings: The Third Division of the Old Testament Canon.* London: Allen & Unwin, 1963. Includes historical background and analysis of individual books.

Morgan, D. F. *Between Text and Community: The "Writings" in Canonical Interpretation.* Minneapolis: Augsburg Fortress, 1990. Examines the various documents addressing the diverse needs of the postexilic community.

Stern, Ephraim. *Material Culture and the Land of the Bible in the Persian Period, 538–332 B.C.* Jerusalem: Israel Exploration Society, 1982. Surveys archaeological evidence about Judean life under Persian rule.

Weinberg, Joel P. *The Citizen Temple Community.* JSOT Sup. 151. Sheffield, England: JSOT, 1992. A collection of essays exploring social and economic conditions of the Second Temple period.

CHAPTER 23

The Postexilic Readjustment

The Books of Ezra and Nehemiah

Key Topics/Themes Set against the backdrop of the return to Judah — or *Yehud*, as it was known in Persia — by thousands of Judean exiles, the books of Ezra and Nehemiah record the difficulties facing the repatriated Judean community and the far-reaching changes in social policy and self-perception that characterize this community from the late sixth through the fifth century B.C.E. The perspective from which the events of this era are seen, however, is explicitly theological and designed to serve as a model for future generations of Jews, both in the land of Judah and in Diaspora communities. The stated purpose for which Ezra is sent to Judah is to ensure that the *torah* of YHWH is being faithfully observed and that offerings of silver and gold made to Israel's God on behalf of the Persian court are faithfully delivered to their destination (Ezra 7:12–26). However, Ezra (and later Nehemiah) is primarily concerned with two things: the need to bring an end to assimilationist tendencies within the Judean community and the equally urgent need to promulgate the Torah, in both the inclusive and exclusive sense of that word (that is, the expressed will of God versus the text of the Pentateuch). His mission will not be complete, therefore, until the religious and ethnic boundaries of Jewish identity are reestablished, in conformity with the values and ideals of the Babylonian Jewish community.

The Book of Ezra

Contemporary scholars generally agree that the books of Ezra and Nehemiah were originally a single book bearing the name *Ezra* and were only later subdivided into two separate works. No agreement exists, however, on precisely when these books were written or whether they once formed part of a larger historical work that included the writings of the Chronicler. However, because the time span of events in Ezra and Nehemiah extends from approximately 538 B.C.E. to 400 B.C.E., it is probably safe to assume that they were either written or redacted some time after this period — perhaps during the early fourth century B.C.E. Several books in antiquity circulated under the name of *Ezra*, but only this text was made a part of the Jewish canon. A later work of apocalyptic character, commonly designated as 2 Esdras, was included in the expanded Christian canon, along with other intertestamental writings designated as apocrypha in most English Bibles (see Chapter 29).

Both **Ezra** and **Nehemiah** offer us a theological interpretation of political decisions made both in Persia and in Judah. The policies of the Persian court throughout this period were designed to ensure the stability of Persia's far-flung empire, and there can be little doubt that both Nehemiah and Ezra were seen as politically trustworthy representatives of the exiled Judean community who could be relied on to carry out imperial orders. Uncertainty over the territorial ambitions of Greece and Egypt, as well as the geographical importance of

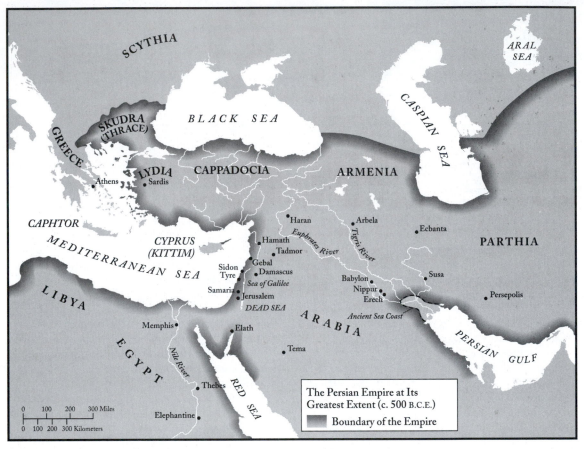

Figure 23.1   Map of the Persian Empire at Its Greatest Extent (c. 500 B.C.E.)

Palestine to the Persian Empire, would have made the journeys of Ezra and Nehemiah necessary for purely diplomatic reasons.

REBUILDING THE TEMPLE

The Book of Ezra begins with a supposed quotation from a royal edict issued by the Persian king **Cyrus the Great,** who, in 538 B.C.E., permitted Judean exiles living in Babylon to return to their homeland for the express purpose of rebuilding their Temple in Jerusalem (Figure 23.1). Though no copy of this edict has ever been found, it is certainly consistent with Cyrus's (and, later, Persian) policy of according subject peoples sufficient autonomy to regulate

their internal affairs and worship their gods. Toward that end, the returning Judeans are given back the sacred vessels that were taken from the Temple by **Nebuchadnezzar,** and, under the leadership of one **Sheshbazzar,** a prince of the exiled royal family, over 42,000 Judeans make the journey.

By the third chapter, however, no further mention is made of Sheshbazzar, and the leadership of this community passes to **Zerubbabel,** a governor of Davidic descent, and a priest named Joshua. Both of these figures are named and invoked by the prophets Haggai and Zechariah, and it is under their combined leadership that the rebuilding of the Temple begins in earnest, though not without conflict. Opposition to the rebuilding of the Temple comes from two sources: the indigenous population of mixed descent, later known as Samaritans, whose offer to help rebuild the Temple is bluntly rejected by Joshua and Zerubbabel; and the governor of the province "Beyond the River," Tattenai, who may have viewed a restored Judean Temple (and, still later, rebuilt city walls) as the first stage of a potential political rebellion. Tattenai challenges the legality of the entire project, inspiring the new Persian king, **Darius,** to search his archives, only to discover that authorization for the rebuilding came directly from his predecessor, Cyrus. In a plot twist that Diaspora writers were particularly fond of, Darius not only allows the rebuilding to continue but also insists that the cost be borne by Tattenai and his subjects; he even threatens with royal punishment anyone who impedes the reconstruction effort. As in the Book of Esther, the Jews' "adversaries" are defeated, and political intrigue becomes the instrument through which God's purposes are accomplished.

EZRA'S MISSION

Ezra's entrance into this narrative is the final chapter of the story of homecoming and renewal, and he arrives in Jerusalem in 458 B.C.E. with at least two objectives. King **Artaxerxes** has sent him with a tribute of silver and gold for "the GOD of Israel, whose dwelling is in Jerusalem" (Ezra 7:15), and with the understanding that he is to reestablish not only the sacrificial system of the newly restored Temple but also a judicial system that will ensure obedience to the laws of YHWH and of Persia (Figure 23.2). Ezra, however, has something else in mind. On learning that intermarriage with the surrounding peoples became commonplace during the period of the exile, he openly mourns and denounces the "faithlessness" of the indigenous Israelite population and then orders the Israelite men who have turned to him for guidance to make a collective confession of sin and to divorce their foreign wives.

However disturbing Ezra's course of action may be to modern religious and political sensibilities, it is hardly inconsistent with earlier biblical traditions, particularly those enshrined in the Pentateuch. The

Figure 23.2   This silver figurine from the court of Artaxerxes I (465–424 B.C.E.) shows the kind of tunic, trousers, and hood that biblical figures such as Ezra, Nehemiah, and Haman may have worn, as officials associated with the Persian emperor's court. After Cyrus the Great defeated Babylon in 539 B.C.E. and encouraged former captives to restore the cults of their respective national gods, the Judeans returned to Palestine, rebuilt YHWH's Temple, and enjoyed two centuries of Persia's comparatively tolerant rule.

Deuteronomic code is particularly stern and explicit on this point, defending the ban on **exogamy** on specifically religious grounds:

> Do not intermarry with them, giving your daughters to their sons or taking their daughters for your sons, for that would turn away your children

from following me, to serve other gods. Then the anger of the LORD would be kindled against you, and he would destroy you quickly. (Deut 7:3)

Although other biblical texts and traditions take a much more benign or even indifferent view of intermarriage (the Book of Ruth, for example), the link between exogamy and apostasy is drawn repeatedly in biblical literature—throughout the Book of Hosea and in 1 Kings' commentary on Solomon's love of "foreign women" (11:1–8)—and it is clearly understood by Ezra and his contemporaries that widespread exogamy is proof that Israel has, once again, "broken faith" with YHWH. Ezra's grief, then, and the collective penance he enjoins on the people of Judah have little to do with social or ethnic "exclusivism." Rather, as a scribe and teacher of *torah,* he is calling on his people to rebuild not only the sanctuary of YHWH but also their covenant relationship with him, which, as the prophets before him often observed, has to be an exclusive one.

The Book of Nehemiah

THE RETURN TO JERUSALEM

The narrative of Nehemiah begins more than a decade later than that of Ezra, and it assumes the form of a first-person account (or memoir) of Nehemiah's attempts to rebuild both the walls of Jerusalem and the religious spirit of Judah. As cupbearer to King Artaxerxes I (ruled 464–423 B.C.E.), Nehemiah is able to obtain from the king both letters of safe passage back to Judah and instructions to the governors of the region to provide him with materials for the rebuilding of the Temple fortress gates and the city walls. But, as in the time of Zerubbabel, Nehemiah's plans for restoration are opposed by the very authorities who are supposed to assist him, and once again a Judean leader is accused of secretly planning a revolt against Persian authority. Yet, in spite of such opposition, the gates and walls are rebuilt, and Nehemiah is finally appointed governor

of Judah with a mandate not only to defend Jerusalem from its hostile neighbors but also to lighten the burdens of the common people, whom earlier governors had cruelly exploited.

PROCLAIMING THE TORAH

It is at this point in the narrative (Ch. 8) that Ezra makes his appearance, bringing with him the "book of the law of Moses, which the LORD had given to Israel" (Neh. 8:1). Precisely what this "book" contains cannot be determined from the passages that follow, but biblical scholars have long assumed that this scroll (Hebrew, *sefer torat Moshe*) consisted of some portion, if not the whole, of our present Pentateuch. Reading this text aloud before the assembled masses in Jerusalem, Ezra urges the people to observe the festival of **Sukkoth** (or Tabernacles), and he instructs them in the making of a *sukkah* (hut), as prescribed in the Book of Leviticus (Lev. 23:39–43). He then proceeds, in Chapter 9, to offer a lengthy summary of covenant promises and of Israel's apostasies, culminating in a curiously ambivalent profession of faith that ironically juxtaposes images of slavery in Egypt with assertions of divine justice and faithfulness:

Here we are, slaves to this day—slaves in the land you gave to our ancestors to enjoy its fruit and its good gifts. Its rich yield goes to the kings whom you have set over us because of our sins; they have power also over our bodies and over our livestock at their pleasure, and we are in great distress. (Neh. 9:36–37)

Just what Ezra's role may be at this juncture, or what connection he may have to Nehemiah, is unclear from the two chapters that allude to his presence and teaching, and his sudden appearance in and then disappearance from the Book of Nehemiah further complicates whatever narrative or historical sequence the Ezra and Nehemiah narratives presuppose. When, in Chapter 13, the reading of the "book of Moses" resumes, the people are once again admonished not to marry the women of **Ashdod, Ammon,** and **Moab.** But it is Nehemiah, not Ezra, who denounces and even beats those who have violated this commandment, though the names of other priests and Levites are included in this history. It is almost as if Ezra's campaign against exogamy, years earlier, had never occurred, or, more likely, an overlap of traditions made it possible to attribute essentially the same action or policy to these two different figures.

Though he is obliged to journey to the court of Artaxerxes for a time, Nehemiah finally returns, only to discover that the people of Judah have, yet again, reverted to type and forgotten their covenant responsibilities. Nehemiah acts swiftly to end widespread neglect of the Sabbath and the equally widespread practice of intermarriage. Reminding his fellow Judahites — in true Deuteronomic fashion — of the terrible consequences of collective indifference and disobedience to the *torah* that have already befallen them, Nehemiah proceeds to "cleanse" Judah of "everything foreign" (13:30) and to reestablish the covenant-centered society Judah was always intended to be. Nehemiah's establishment of a virtual **theocracy** thus reverses the downward spiral of Israel's history. Although the restoration of the exiles to their homeland did not prove to be anything like the glorious visions of national and world redemption that readers of Second Isaiah had come to expect, still Jeremiah's promise of return ("I will bring them back to this place, and I will settle them in safety" [Jer. 32:37]) has at last been fulfilled.

Historical Sources and Narrative Sequence

The source materials that the author of Ezra/Nehemiah drew on most likely include the following: the prophetic writings of Haggai and Zechariah, documents of various kinds from the period of Cyrus to Artaxerxes, census lists and genealogies, and the "memoirs" of both Ezra and Nehemiah. In the process of arranging this material in narrative form, however, the author duplicates and interpolates references to personalities and events in a particularly problematic way, and scholars have puzzled over the gaps and seeming discrepancies of this narrative, though to little avail. Especially problematic is the relationship between Ezra and Nehemiah, and the question of which of them really came first. Even casual readers notice the obvious duplication of story line in Nehemiah, where the very reforms that Ezra has presumably already carried out are reintroduced as if nothing had been done over a decade before. Nor is it even clear that Ezra, whose cameo role in the Book of Nehemiah allows him suddenly to enter the narrative in Chapter 8 and to exit it just as unceremoniously at the end of Chapter 9, actually precedes Nehemiah, though the chronologies of their respective books would seem to necessitate that interpretation. The realization that the public assembly scenes in Ezra (Ch. 10) and Nehemiah (Chs. 8 and 9) closely resemble each other suggests that we are, once again, looking at two overlapping accounts of the same event, with each version reflecting the different perspectives of their probable sources.

What is clear, however, from both the Ezra and the Nehemiah narratives, is that Judah is about to embark on a new chapter in its long and often contested relationship with YHWH. But this time, it will do so without a king and without even the pretense of national sovereignty; as the prophetic era draws to a close, it must learn to manage with only an "interpreter" of *torah* for religious guidance. All of the elements of a theocracy are in place, and for approximately the next 300 years, that is the only form of local government Judah will know.

QUESTIONS FOR REVIEW

1. Which figure in Persian history made it possible for the exiled Jews of Babylon to return to their homeland? What was Persian policy toward Judah thereafter?

2. Why do Ezra and Nehemiah pressure Israelite men to divorce their non-Israelite wives? How would the author of the Book of Ruth have responded to this demand?

QUESTION FOR REFLECTION AND DISCUSSION

What possible connection exists between Ezra's attempt to make the postrestoration Judean community a *torah*-centered society and the apparent cessation of prophecy? Are we witnessing, during the era of Ezra and Nehemiah, a shift in religious authority from prophet to priest?

TERMS AND CONCEPTS TO REMEMBER

Ammon
Artaxerxes
Ashdod
Cyrus the Great
Darius
exogamy
Ezra (Esdras)
Moab

Nebuchadnezzar
Nehemiah
Sheshbazzar
sukkah
Sukkoth
theocracy
Zerubbabel

RECOMMENDED READING

Blenkinsopp, Joseph. *Ezra-Nehemiah: A Commentary.* Philadelphia: Westminster Press, 1988.

Fensham, F. Charles. *The Books of Ezra and Nehemiah.* Grand Rapids, Mich.: Eerdmans, 1982.

Klein, Ralph W. "The Books of Ezra and Nehemiah." In *The New Interpreter's Bible*, vol. 3, pp. 661–851. Nashville, Tenn.: Abingdon Press, 1999.

Meyers, Jacob M. *Ezra, Nehemiah.* Garden City, N.Y.: Doubleday, 1965.

Williamson, H. G. M. *Ezra and Nehemiah.* Sheffield, England: JSOT Press, 1987.

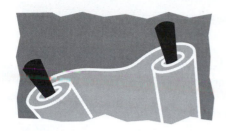

CHAPTER 24

Worshiping at the Second Temple

Hebrew Poetry and the Book of Psalms

Key Topics/Themes A major component of the Tanak, particularly the Writings, Hebrew poetry typically employs the techniques of metaphor and parallelism to convey its message. An anthology of devotional lyrics, the Book of Psalms encompasses a broad spectrum of responses to Israel's historical experience, particularly the prolonged theological crisis that followed Babylon's destruction of Judah in 587 B.C.E., with the attendant loss of Davidic kingship, land, and Temple. The collection of 150 poems, traditionally divided into five separate books, represents a variety of poetic genres that are generally categorized by their literary form and/or content. The most common classifications include the hymn, or song of praise (Pss. 8, 19, 78, 100, 103, 104, 114, 117, and 150); psalms of thanksgiving (Pss. 18, 30, 40, 66, 116, and 118); laments, both individual and collective (Pss. 10, 22, 38, 42, 43, 44, 51, 58, 59, 69, and 74); royal psalms associated with Davidic kings (Pss. 2, 45, 51, 72, 89, and 110); enthronement psalms proclaiming YHWH as king (Pss. 93 and 95–99); psalms of blessing or cursing (Pss. 109 and 137); and psalms of wisdom, instruction, or meditation (Pss. 1, 33–37, 49, 52, 73, 90, 112, 119, and 128).

Hebrew Poetry

Approximately one-third of the Hebrew Bible is written in poetry. The Pentateuch and the Deuteronomistic History contain numerous short poems, ranging from Adam's rapturous verse about Eve's creation (Gen. 2:23), to Miriam's song at the great sea (Exod. 15:21), to Deborah's victory hymn (Judg. 5:1–31), to David's lament over Jonathan's death (2 Sam. 1:19–27). Poems are scattered intermittently throughout the prose narratives in Genesis through 2 Kings, and many books in the Latter Prophets and the Writings are composed almost entirely in poetry, including not only the books of Isaiah, Jeremiah, Ezekiel, and the Twelve but also Psalms, Proverbs, Lamentations, and Job.

SIMILE, METAPHOR, AND ALLEGORY

Like those of other cultures, Hebrew poets use a variety of rhetorical devices to achieve their effect. In the Song of Songs, two lovers are shown ecstatically comparing each other's bodies to luscious fruits, domestic and wild animals, and even topographical features, celebrating in almost grotesque imagery their own joy in sexual love. Employing a series of **similes**— comparisons using "as" or "like"— the speaker admires his beloved's luxuriant hair and complete set of dazzlingly white teeth:

> Your hair is like a flock of goats,
> moving down the slopes of Gilead.
> Your teeth are like a flock of shorn ewes
> that have come up from the washing,
> all of which bear twins,
> and not one of them is bereaved.
> (Song of Sol. 4:1–2)

The poetic complaints in Lamentations also evoke strong emotions, but these are feelings of pain and sorrow at the desolation of Jerusalem. Here, the poet uses a **metaphor,** an implied comparison that portrays the city as a captive woman, dirty and dressed in rags:

> Her uncleanness was in her skirts;
> she took no thought of her future;
> her downfall was appalling,
> with none to comfort her. (Lam. 1:9)

Mixing prose passages with short poems, Ecclesiastes offers an emotionally detached contrast to Lamentations' passionate grief, citing traditional—and sometimes contradictory—examples of prudential wisdom in poetic couplets. Yet, the author concludes his skeptical comments with a singularly haunting poem that compares the body of a dying man to an old house. Creating a poetic **allegory,** a narrative in which one object or action functions as a symbol of something else, the author depicts the decrepitude and failing senses of extreme age as a crumbling edifice, worn out and ready to collapse:

> in the day when . . . the women who grind cease working because they are few, and those who look through the windows see dimly; when the doors on the street are shut, and the sound of the grinding is low . . . (Eccles. 12:3–4)

Unable to chew, see, or hear, the aged person prepares for his "eternal home," the grave.

PARALLELISM

In contrast to English poetry and that of other Western nations, Hebrew poetry does not use rhyme or regular meter, although many poetic lines have a strongly rhythmic quality. Instead, the biblical poetic line is notable for its terseness, repetition of key words or phrases, vivid imagery, and, above all, various kinds of parallelism. The most characteristic feature of Hebrew poetry, **parallelism** involves expressing similar ideas in similar verbal structures. In *synonymous* parallelism, an idea articulated in the first line is repeated in slightly different words in the second, a device the psalmists frequently employ:

> The heavens are telling the glory of GOD;
> and the firmament proclaims his handiwork.
> (Ps. 19:1)

> Praise the LORD, all you nations!
> Extol him, all you peoples! (Ps. 117:1)

> For who is GOD except the LORD [YHWH]?
> And who is a rock besides our GOD? (Ps. 18:31)

In one of the many variations of synonymous parallelism, the second line offers a specific example to illustrate the general statement made in the first. In Psalm 106, the poet cites a famous instance in which the Israelites proved ungrateful to the God who had rescued them from Egypt:

> Our ancestors, when they were in Egypt,
> did not consider your wonderful works;
> they did not remember the abundance of your
>   steadfast love,
> but rebelled against the Most High at the Red
>   Sea. (Ps. 106:7)

A set of two couplets from the same poem emphasizes related aspects of Israel's deliverance by repeating the first statement in parallel but slightly different form:

> He rebuked the Red Sea, and it became dry;
> he led them through the deep as through a desert.
> So he saved them from the hand of the foe,
> and delivered them from the hand of the enemy.
> (Ps. 106:9–10)

In *antithetical* parallelism, one line makes a statement, and the next line expresses its opposite. Proverbs offers many examples of this form:

> A wise child makes a glad father,
> but a foolish child is a mother's grief. (Prov. 10:1)

A slack hand causes poverty,
but the hand of the diligent makes rich.
(Prov. 10:4)

The clever see danger and hide;
but the simple go on, and suffer for it.
(Prov. 22:3)

Synthetic or *formal* parallelism is not, strictly speaking, parallelism at all. In this poetic form, the first line expresses a thought, the second adds a new idea, and the third completes the statement. David's lament over the fallen Saul and Jonathan illustrates this pattern:

I am distressed for you, my brother Jonathan;
greatly beloved were you to me,
your love to me was wonderful,
passing the love of women. (2 Sam. 1:26)

PERSONIFICATION

In some poetic books, such as Proverbs, the author employs **personification,** the imparting of human attributes to an idea or abstract concept, such as wisdom. Proverbs depicts divine Wisdom, the Deity's primary attribute, as a woman who roams city streets, imploring foolish young men to listen to her and avoid her opposite, the "loose woman," whose ways lead to death (Prov. 8:1–11; cf. 1:20–33; 2:16–22; 5:3–23). In Proverbs 8, the writer personifies Lady Wisdom as God's firstborn, not only giving her cosmic stature but also making her the mediator between the human and divine realms:

Before the mountains had been shaped,
before the hills, I was brought forth —. . .
When he established the heavens,
I was there . . .
then I was beside him, like a master worker,
and I was daily his delight. . . . (Prov. 8:25, 27, 30)

Existing before the created world, Lady Wisdom serves as a witness to the stages by which the cosmos developed, her balanced phrases offering first-hand testimony to God's creative activity. With its rhythmic repetitiveness, concrete images, and varieties of parallelism, biblical poetry awakens the imagination and stirs the feelings, inspiring readers to wonder and reflect.

The Book of Psalms

For many readers, the Book of Psalms represents the quintessence of Hebrew poetry. Containing 150 individual lyrics composed at different times over a span of perhaps six centuries, this poetic collection expresses virtually the full range of Israelite religious experience. From the heights of ecstatic praise to the depths of utter despair, Israel's poets respond in amazingly diverse ways to the ever-changing historical circumstances that affected their relationship to Israel's God. In the Torah and through the prophets, YHWH spoke to his covenant people; in the Psalms, individual members of the community reply to God, exulting in his glorious presence in or grieving over his mysterious absences from Israel's communal life.

A distinguishing feature of this collection is its emphasis on the Davidic monarchy. Both the poets who created the individual psalms and the editors who later compiled and edited them were profoundly attached to the House of David. Whereas some of the older psalms were written to commemorate events during the Davidic dynasty, such as the coronation and enthronement of kings, others were composed long after the Babylonian exile had brought a permanent end to the monarchy. Like Isaiah of Jerusalem, the prophet who emphasized YHWH's special relationship to David's royal line, many of the preexilic psalmists celebrated the close link between Israel's God and his anointed rulers. After the exile, some poets continued to evoke hopes connected with the Davidic Covenant, although they most typically emphasized the sovereignty of Israel's true ruler, YHWH.

Despite their thematic association with the Davidic monarchy, the psalms are as diverse in religious feeling as they are in historical origin. Ranging from declarations of complete trust and confidence in divine protection (Pss. 23, 91) to sorrowful complaints about God's apparent failure to shield his people from disaster (Pss. 44 and 89, quoted in Chapter 22), the psalms explore both the heights and the depths of Israel's troubled partnership with YHWH.

The book's title comes from the Greek *psalmoi,* which refers to instrumental music and, by extension, the words accompanying the music. In translating the psalms, the editors of the Septuagint used *psalmoi* to render the Hebrew title *Tehillim,* which means "praises." Although each psalm has its own compositional history, as a collection the Psalms represent the lyrics performed — to the accompaniment of pipes, trumpets, flutes, harps, cymbals, tambourines, and other musical instruments — at the Second Temple as part of YHWH's worship.

"DAVIDIC" AUTHORSHIP

The tradition that David composed the psalms probably owes much to his popular reputation as a musician and poet (1 Sam. 16:23; Amos 6:5). Phrases such as "of David" that are attached to particular psalms are annotations by later editors and may mean only that the psalm thus denoted is "in the manner of David" or that it concerns one of David's royal successors. (Grammatically, this phrase, in Hebrew, may also indicate that a particular poem was written *for* a Davidic prince.) Besides associating many psalms with Israel's idealized king, editors noted that other poets also contributed to the anthology: Psalm 72 is attributed to Solomon, Psalm 90 to Moses, and various others to Asaph and the sons of Korah. Numerous psalms are clearly post-Davidic, such as Psalm 72, which laments the destruction of the Jerusalem Temple, and Psalm 137, which describes conditions during the Babylonian exile. Of the 150 psalms, 116 have titles or superscriptions indicating authorship, setting, or directions to the Temple musicians. All are thought to be late scribal additions to the texts.

Scholars believe that the present anthology of Psalms was put together by uniting several smaller subcollections, including these:

- Davidic psalms in which the name YHWH predominates (Pss. 3–41)
- Davidic psalms in which *Elohim* is the preferred term for God (Pss. 51–72) (Psalm 14 and Psalm 53 are virtually identical, except that the former uses the divine name.)

- Two subcollections ascribed to the sons of Korah (Pss. 42–49, 84–88), perhaps a guild of Temple singers — the "Korahites" — named in 1 Chronicles 9:19, 31; 12:6
- A group credited to Asaph (Pss. 50, 73–83) (cf. 1 Chron. 16:5 or 2 Chron. 29:13)
- A set of psalms emphasizing YHWH's kingship (Pss. 93–99)
- A unit known as "songs of ascents" (Pss. 120–134), presumably sung as worshipers "ascended" Zion, the hill upon which the Temple stood
- Two subsets of thanksgiving psalms using the imperative "hallelujah" (praise YHWH) (Pss. 111–118, 135–136, 146–150)

Combining these subcollections, as well as other lyrics, into the canonical Book of Psalms, postexilic editors then divided this poetry anthology into five separate books, perhaps to resemble the Torah's division into five volumes. Each of the first four books closes with a distinctive benediction (41:13; 72:19; 89:52; 106:48), calling on worshipers to "bless" God. Book 1 contains Psalms 1–41, some of which may be among the oldest in the collection; Book 2, Psalms 42–72; Book 3, Psalms 73–89; Book 4, Psalms 90–106; and Book 5, Psalms 107–150. Psalms 1 and 2 act as a general introduction to the entire collection. Psalm 150 is a **doxology,** an expression of praise to God that typically concludes a confession of faith, that rounds off the collection as a whole.

CATEGORIES OF PSALMS

Early in the twentieth century, Hermann Gunkel pioneered modern techniques of analyzing the psalms critically, classifying them according to their literary form, presumed liturgical function, or topical content. As noted shortly, different psalms take different forms, in part depending on the occasion for which they were composed, such as royal coronations or weddings, laments for personal or national suffering, petitions for divine help, and songs of thanksgiving for help received. Although scholars now recognize that many psalms combine several different literary genres, mixing lament with praise and expressions of trust—and that some are too distinctively individual to be labeled at all—Gunkel's basic categorizations remain useful. In surveying the most common classifications of psalms, it should be remembered that these religious lyrics embody both private prayer and public worship, and that all were performed at the Second Temple as communal expressions of Israel's complex and ever-evolving partnership with God.

Hymns or Songs of Praise   In composing songs of praise, the poet typically cited specific reasons for which God deserved Israel's worship: his creation of the world and his saving intervention in Israel's history. Psalm 8 honors God for establishing an orderly universe, fashioning humanity in his divine image, and placing human beings, who are only a "little lower than GOD," at the apex of his earthly hierarchy:

> You have given them [humanity] dominion
> over the work of your hands;
> you have put all things under their feet. (Ps. 8:6)

Psalm 104, which seems to be a Hebrew poet's revision of a much older Egyptian hymn to the solar deity worshiped by Pharaoh Akhenaton, pays tribute to YHWH's creative wisdom and might while incorporating typical Near Eastern motifs of earth originating amid a watery chaos:

> You stretch the heavens out like a tent,
> you build your palace on the water above; . . .
> You fixed the earth on its foundations,
> unshakable for ever and ever,
> you wrapped it with the deep [primal watery
>   abyss] as with a robe,
> the waters overtopping the mountains.
> At your reproof the waters took to flight,
> they fled at the sound of your thunder,
> cascading over the mountains, into the valleys,
> down to the reservoir you made for them;
> you imposed the limits they must never cross
>   again,
> or they would once more flood the land. . . .
> Glory for ever to Yahweh!
> May Yahweh find joy in what he creates. . . .
>   (Ps. 104:3, 5–9, 36, Jerusalem Bible)

Although they were composed at different times, both Genesis 1 and Psalm 104 picture God as effortlessly subduing the primal, chaotic waters. Other psalms, however, evoke ancient myths in which YHWH had to fight primordial monsters of chaos, such as Rahab or Leviathan, at the time of creation:

> Yet, God, my king from the first,
> author of saving acts throughout the earth,
> by your power you split the sea in two,
> and smashed heads of monsters on the waters.
> You crushed Leviathan's heads,
> leaving him for wild animals to eat,
> you opened the spring, the torrent,
> you dried up inexhaustible rivers.
>   (Ps. 74:13–15, Jerusalem Bible; cf. Isa. 27:1;
>   Job 3:8; 41:1–34)

Echoing Baal's mythical battle against Yamm (the all-encompassing sea) and Marduk's brutal splitting in two of Tiamat, the primal ocean, Psalm 89 depicts YHWH conquering Rahab, a personification of watery chaos:

> You control the pride of ocean,
> when its waves ride high, you calm them;
> you split Rahab in two like a carcass
> and scattered your enemies with your mighty arm.
>   (Ps. 89:9–10, Jerusalem Bible; cf. Job 9:13;
>   26:12–13; see also Chapter 25 and Figure 25.3)

In addition to his acts of creative majesty, God is to be praised for his faithfulness in guiding and directing Israel's history. Psalm 78 surveys YHWH's mighty deeds in rescuing Israel from Egypt, nurturing his people in the Sinai wilderness, and choosing David to shepherd the covenant community. In those ancient days, the poet recalls, YHWH aroused himself from sleep to fight for Israel: "like a hero fighting-mad with wine, the Lord woke up to strike his enemies on the rump and put them to everlasting shame" (Ps. 78:65–66, Jerusalem Bible). Psalm 105 similarly reviews Israel's distant past, when YHWH made his promises to Abraham and Jacob, brought plagues upon his people's Egyptian oppressors, and turned the Canaanites' territory over to Israelite tribes.

A subset of the psalms of praise, known as the "Songs of Zion," centers on Jerusalem, the city made holy by God's invisibly dwelling in the Temple that stood on **Zion,** a prominent hill that psalmists endow with characteristics of Eden, the original site of God's earthly visitations (Pss. 46, 48, 84, 87, 122). Two of these psalms (46 and 48) seem to reflect a belief in Zion's invincibility, a confidence supposedly guaranteed by YHWH's having placed his "name" there. (Prophetic views of Jerusalem's impregnability differ strikingly; while Isaiah expresses confidence in YHWH's protection [see Chapter 18], Jeremiah declares that the sanctuary's presence could not save the city from Babylon [Jer. 7, 26] [see Chapter 19].)

Psalms of Thanksgiving   Psalms of thanksgiving are typically prayers offered in gratitude for God's having saved or delivered the psalmist from danger (Pss. 18, 30, 40, 66, 116, 118). They commonly begin with expressions of praise, describe the situation that formerly threatened or troubled the poet—such as life-threatening illness, endangerment from war, or the machinations of enemies—gratefully acknowledge God as the source of deliverance, and, in some cases, exhort bystanders to share in the thanksgiving. In Psalm 30, the poet compares his former suffering to a descent into Sheol, the Underworld housing the dead:

> O LORD [YHWH], you brought my soul from
>   Sheol,
> restored me to life from among those gone down
>   to the pit. (Ps. 30:3)

In his distress, the poet reminds God that he will gain nothing by allowing his servant to die, for Sheol's eternally silent inhabitants can offer him no worship:

> To you, O LORD, I cried, . . .
> "What profit is there in my death,
> if I go down to the pit?
> Will the dust praise you?
> Will it tell of your faithfulness?" (Ps. 30:8–9)

Now that YHWH has rescued the poet from death, turning his "mourning into dancing," his worshiper can rejoin the living to praise God at his Temple. (For a description of Sheol, see Box 25.1.)

Laments   Poems that emphasize sorrow, grief, mourning, or regret are classified as laments or complaints and feature both individual and communal supplications. Some individual laments, such as Psalm 55, are personal petitions that first praise God and then ask for rescue from the petitioner's enemies and for vengeance on them. Although many laments are concerned with forgiveness of personal sins (Pss. 38, 51), some are genuine complaints, implying that God has been unaccountably slow to redress injustice (Pss. 10, 58, 59).

Psalm 22, which opens with the plaintive cry "My GOD, my GOD, why have you forsaken me?" is a mixed genre combining lament with praise. Following graphic descriptions of the poet's suffering, the psalm introduces a petition begging for the Deity's help (22:1–21). Although the poem begins in bleak despair, following the petition (22:19–21), it changes abruptly to an exulting hymn of praise that culminates in a confident declaration of YHWH's sovereignty (22:22–29). In the last two lines, the poet declares that both he and "a people yet unborn" will "proclaim [God's] deliverance," ensuring a continuity of worship into the far-distant future (22:30–31). With its striking contrast between the poet's initial grief and his later resolve to praise YHWH, this lament, moving from sorrow to joy, illustrates an important theme in the Psalms: Although YHWH's people may endure almost unbearable pain, their God remains present with them, an everlasting source of spiritual renewal. Redemption, in fact, is found in the midst of suffering.

Several communal laments focus on the Babylonian conquest that stripped Israel of its essential identity and institutions, including land, kingship, and sanctuary. Gunkel observed that many of these collective laments follow a structural pattern, typically beginning with an invocation that addresses God. Psalm 74, a communal dirge lamenting the Temple's destruction, asks the Deity if this national calamity means that he has permanently severed his covenant ties:

> O GOD, why do you cast us off forever?
> Why does your anger smoke against the sheep of
>   your pasture? (Ps. 74:1)

In the second part, the complaint, the psalm speci- fies the reasons for the lament. In Psalm 74, God is invited to inspect the pitiful ruin of his holy place:

Pick your steps over these endless ruins:
the enemy have sacked everything in the
    sanctuary.
They roared where your assemblies used to take
    place, . . .
Axes deep in the wood, hacking at the panels,
they battered them down with mallet and hatchet;
then, GOD, setting fire to your sanctuary,
they profanely razed the house of your name to
    the ground. (Ps. 74:3–4, 6–7)

The poem next opposes the lament with a confes- sion of trust, asserting the poet's reliance on God. After citing YHWH's mythic battle against Levia- than, recalling his primordial triumphs, Psalm 74 affirms God's continuing mastery of creation, man- ifest in earth's seasonal cycles:

Yours is the day, yours also the night;
you established the luminaries and the sun.
You have fixed all the bounds of the earth;
you made summer and winter. (Ps. 74:16–17)

This expression of confidence in the Deity's ability to act is followed by a petition in which God is asked to take action to remedy the problem. Urging YHWH not to "forget" his worshipers, the poet asks God to "remember" both the blasphemer who publicly despoiled his holy place and the covenant people who depend on his vindication:

Remember this, O LORD, how the enemy scoffs,
and an impious people reviles your name.
Do not deliver the soul of your dove to the wild
    animals; . . .
Have regard for your covenant, . . .
Rise up, O GOD, plead your cause. . . .
                              (Ps. 74:18, 20, 22)

Although absent in two of the greatest communal laments, Psalms 44 and 74, some complaints close with a statement of thanksgiving in which the poet vows to tell the community of faith what God has accomplished.

Psalm 44, which also adheres to Gunkel's pat- tern, contrasts the mighty deeds YHWH performed

in the remote past—actions the current genera- tion has only heard about—with the misery the people experience in the present. This lament is particularly noteworthy for its rejection of the tra- ditional Deuteronomic view that only disobedience will bring disaster to the covenant community. The psalmist flatly states that the people have re- mained faithful to their covenant vow and that they suffer simply because they keep YHWH as their God. After describing the massacres and humilia- tions their enemies regularly inflict on the commu- nity, the poet asserts:

All this has come upon us, yet we have not for-
    gotten you,
or been false to your covenant;
Our heart has not turned back,
nor have our steps departed from your way;
yet you have broken us . . .
Because of you we are being killed all day long,
and accounted as sheep for the slaughter.
                              (Ps. 44:17–19, 22)

These communal laments, including the second half of Psalm 89, which implies that God has bro- ken his sworn oath, collectively form a persistent theme illustrating God's odd inaction or apparent refusal to honor his ancient covenant promises (see Chapter 22). In preparing their final edition of Psalms, the redactors intermixed these laments with royal psalms—songs focusing on the Davidic kings—and enthronement psalms, lyrics praising YHWH as Israel's true and abiding ruler. This jux- taposition of negative and positive theological con- fessions effectively mirrors the ever-fluctuating sor- rows and joys of a worshiping community that finds its God in both darkness and light.

Psalms of Blessing and Cursing Another sub- category—psalms of blessing and cursing—may appear ethically disturbing to modern sensibilities attuned to the concept that religion teaches the re- turn of good for evil. Psalm 1, for example, arbi- trarily divides all people into two mutually exclu- sive classes—the righteous and the wicked—and promises doom for the latter, with no shades of gray allowed. In Psalm 109, the poet enthusiastically lists disasters with which the writer asks God to afflict those who offend him. These include the wish that his enemies be condemned by a corrupt judge, punished for the sins of their ancestors, and tormented by the certainty that their orphaned children will be driven in poverty from their homes. Psalm 137, which begins in lyric beauty ("By the rivers of Babylon —"), concludes in vindictive fury, invoking a blessing on avengers who will seize Babylonian infants and dash out their brains against a rock (137:8–9).

Royal Psalms   Classified by their content rather than their literary form, royal psalms commemorate events and issues involving Davidic kings. Scattered throughout the entire collection, royal psalms vary widely in subject and mood, ranging from the celebration of a royal wedding (Ps. 45) or the coronation of a new ruler (Pss. 2, 72, and perhaps 110), to a review of God's original promises to David that culminates in a bitter complaint about the Deity's historical failure to honor his commitment to the Davidic dynasty (Ps. 89). Along with Psalm 1, Psalm 2 serves as a general introduction to the whole book, raising the issue of divinely ordained kingship. The psalm opens by describing a revolt against "the LORD [YHWH] and his anointed," directly associating the rule of God with political submission to his earthly representative, the king whose head is **anointed** (rubbed with holy oil by a priest) at the time of his installation in office. Historically, the rebellious kings were probably princes of neighboring states, such as Edom or Moab, who attempted to break free from Israel's domination after the death of a Davidic ruler and before his successor could consolidate his position. Viewed as part of the collection as a whole, however, this psalm introduces a theme that runs throughout the book: Whereas Davidic monarchs may have been God's agents for governing his people, YHWH himself is Israel's real king. An assertion that YHWH rules the world, with or without Davidic kings and despite apparently unending human opposition, is perhaps Psalms' most pervasive message.

In Psalm 110, YHWH addresses the king as "my LORD," vowing to subdue his enemies, shattering all opposition.

> The LORD has sworn and will not change his
>   mind,
> "You [the king] are a priest forever
> according to the order of Melchizedek."
>
>   (Ps 110:4)

This passage is unique in connecting the ruler with the mysterious figure of Melchizedek, the king-priest of Salem to whom Abraham paid tithes (Gen. 14:17–20). As many scholars have noted, the poet's attempt to present the king as both monarch and priest suggests that this particular psalm was composed, not for a Davidic king, but for one of the Hasmoneans, non-Davidic Maccabean rulers who reigned in Judah from about 142 to 63 B.C.E. Although they were not descendants of Aaron, progenitor of Israel's priestly class, the Hasmoneans appropriated the office of High Priest, as well as that of king (see Chapters 28 and 29). They may have tried to legitimate their holding both offices by claiming descent from the king-priest Melchizedek. If these speculations are valid, psalms that eventually became part of the canon were still being composed in the late second or early first century B.C.E.

Enthronement Psalms   Although the Davidic dynasty was overthrown in 587 B.C.E. and never restored, in at least some circles, hope remained that YHWH would someday remember his promise and appoint a descendant of David to lead his people. The explicit, unequivocal language of the Davidic Covenant assured that in some future generation God would at last "remember" his word. In the meantime, the covenant community was to recognize that YHWH still reigned, over the "nations" as well as Judah. The enthronement psalms (93, 95–99) extol YHWH as supreme monarch —"a great King above all gods" (95:3). "Exalted far above all gods," he is "most high over all the earth" (97:9). His ceaseless reign is evident not only in the mystery and beauty of nature (93:3–4; 96:6) but also in his "righteousness" and "truth" (96:13) and his strengthening presence among believers (97:10–12). Despite human rebellion and resistance to his reign, he continues as universal sovereign:

> The LORD [YHWH] is king: let the peoples tremble!
> He sits enthroned upon the cherubim; let the earth quake!
> The LORD is great in Zion;
> he is exalted over all the peoples. (Ps. 99:1–2)

Psalms of Wisdom and Instruction   Although the world at large may not perceive YHWH's kingdom, several poets indicate the proper human response to divine rule. To some scholars, psalms that employ words typical of Israel's sages or teachers of wisdom, such as "instruction," "teaching," and the "law of the LORD," seem to comprise an identifiable category (Pss. 33–37, 49, 52, 73, 90, 112, 119, 128). Some biblical wisdom, such as that contained in Proverbs, is characterized by the advice to pursue a virtuous life and follow the divine will by embracing good and rejecting evil. The first psalm, with its plea to avoid the wicked and "delight . . . in the law of the LORD," echoes wisdom principles, as does Psalm 37, which urges readers not to envy the material success of the wicked, who will ultimately fail, but to emulate YHWH's love and compassion, qualities that ensure divine approval. The poet states that, despite having lived to old age, he has never seen "the righteous forsaken or their children begging bread" (37:25). Somewhat less optimistically, Psalm 34 states that the "afflictions of the righteous" are many but that they are sustained by the divine presence (34:19–20).

The Religious Power of the Psalms   In the Torah and the prophetic books, God speaks to humanity through Moses or the prophets. In the Psalms, the covenant people speak to God, sometimes praising his past actions in delivering Israel and other times questioning the way in which he governs the cosmos. Even when fearing that YHWH is absent or "asleep," the psalmists persist in an ongoing dialogue with their God, alternately voicing supreme confidence in his power to save, bewilderment at his present inaction, and confidence in his rule as universal king. Accepting both adversity and joy as inevitable components of their community's collective life, the psalmists affirm the redemptive value of the divine–human bond.

QUESTIONS FOR REVIEW

1. Describe some key characteristics of Hebrew poetry, and give some examples of parallelism, simile, metaphor, allegory, and personification. Which books of the Hebrew Bible are composed chiefly in poetry? What effects can poetry achieve that prose usually cannot?

2. Define the term *liturgy,* and explain the liturgical functions of the Book of Psalms. Why did the editors of this poetic collection indicate that the psalms were "by [or 'in the manner of'] David"? What other poets are alluded to in the anthology? For what kinds of occasions were many of the psalms written?

3. What qualities or concerns typify the principal categories of psalms, such as the hymn of praise, the lament or complaint, the royal or enthronement psalm, and the psalm of wisdom or instruction? How do the psalmists maintain a dialogue with God? What do they commonly ask of YHWH?

QUESTIONS FOR REFLECTION AND DISCUSSION

1. From your reading of various psalms, including Psalms 44 and 89, discuss the people's complaints about God's absence or apparent inattentiveness during critical periods in Israel's history. Why is YHWH sometimes said to be "asleep"?

2. The traditional attribution of Psalms to King David reenforces the strong historical connection between the Davidic monarchy and the Temple, where the psalms were performed as part of worship services. Why were Israel's officially recognized poets so supportive of the Davidic dynasty, even after it had ceased to exist? How were divine promises to David for an eternal throne reinterpreted in the postexilic covenant community?

TERMS AND CONCEPTS TO REMEMBER

allegory	parallelism
anointed rulers	personification
categories of psalms	Psalms' connection with
dialogues with God	monarchy and Temple
doxology	simile
Hebrew poetry	Zion
metaphor	

RECOMMENDED READING

Alter, Robert. *The Art of Biblical Poetry.* New York: Basic Books, 1985.

Anderson, Bernard W. *Out of the Depths: The Psalms Speak for Us Today.* Philadelphia: Westminster Press, 1974. A sensitive interpretation of the psalms' continuing relevance.

Berlin, Adele. *Biblical Poetry Through Medieval Jewish Eyes.* Bloomington: Indiana University Press, 1991. An important work of critical interpretation.

———. *The Dynamics of Biblical Parallelism.* Bloomington: Indiana University Press, 1985. A helpful explanation of how parallelism functions in the biblical texts.

———. "Introduction to Hebrew Poetry." In *The New Interpreter's Bible,* Vol. 4, pp. 301–315. A concise discussion of the characteristics of biblical poetry.

———. "Parallelism." In D. N. Freedman, ed., *Anchor Bible Dictionary,* Vol. 5, pp. 155–162. New York: Doubleday, 1992. A concise and useful introduction.

Gunkel, Hermann. *The Psalms: A Form-Critical Introduction.* Translated by T. M. Horner. Introduction by James Muilenberg. Philadelphia: Fortress Press, 1967. A standard work by the pioneer of the form-critical method.

Kugel, James A. *The Idea of Hebrew Poetry: Parallelism and Its History.* New Haven, Conn.: Yale University Press, 1981. A valuable historical-critical study.

McCann, J. Clinton, Jr. "The Book of Psalms." In *The New Interpreter's Bible,* Vol. 4, pp. 641–677. Asserts that the five books of psalms are structured theologically, juxtaposing royal celebrations, complaints, and laments with songs exulting in God's cosmic reign.

Mowinckel, Sigmund. *The Psalms in Israel's Worship,* Vols. 1 and 2. Translated by D. R. Ap-Thomas. Nashville, Tenn.: Abingdon Press, 1962. Like Gunkel's, a fundamental study.

Sarna, Nahum M. *Songs of the Heart: An Introduction to the Book of Psalms.* New York: Schocken Books, 1993. Places the psalms in the context of the ancient Near East and relates them to later rabbinic interpretation.

Wilson, Gerald H. *The Editing of the Hebrew Psalter.* SBLDS 76. Chico, Calif.: Scholars Press, 1985. A seminal analysis of Psalms' literary and theological organization.

CHAPTER 25

Israel's Wisdom Writers

The Books of Proverbs, Job, and Ecclesiastes

Key Topics/Themes When the sixth-century-B.C.E. prophet Ezekiel warns his contemporaries that disasters are about to befall them, he identifies three types of religious authorities to whom they are likely to turn (in vain): "they shall keep seeking a vision from the prophet; instruction shall perish from the priest, and counsel from the elders" (Ezek. 7:26). These "elders" from whom "counsel" (Hebrew, *etsah*) can be obtained are also referred to, in other texts, as "wise men" and "wise women," and the wisdom (Hebrew, *hochmah*) they dispense is a kind of moral understanding that is fundamentally different from the revealed knowledge of prophets and priests. Even though the Book of Proverbs assures us that wisdom comes from YHWH's "mouth" (Prov. 2:6), no wisdom writer of the Hebrew Bible claims to base his knowledge on a vision from God, nor does he speak in God's voice or assume the role of divine advocate to Israel or to the nations of the earth. Instead, the wise man of Israel — like his counterparts in Egypt and Mesopotamia — bases his counsel on experience, that is, on his own close observation of life and on the reflections of generations who preceded him.

Introduction to Wisdom Literature

Whether wisdom teachers in Israel ever regarded themselves as an identifiable intellectual class — what modern societies generally refer to as an "intelligentsia" — is a matter of scholarly controversy today. It is certainly possible that "schools" of wisdom were established at the courts of Israel and Judah, perhaps connected to the training of royal scribes. But it is just as likely that much of the moral instruction found in works like the Book of Proverbs ultimately derives from what might be called "folk wisdom," or a common heritage of moral insight and traditional values that may long have existed in oral form. Whatever its source, wisdom found its emblematic hero in the figure of King Solomon, who, in 1 Kings, asks God for "an understanding mind" and the ability to "discern between good and evil" (3:9). Such was the esteem in which Solomon was held in later ages that no less than three canonical wisdom texts were attributed to him — the Song of Songs, Proverbs, and Ecclesiastes — as well as a flock of noncanonical works, from the Wisdom of Solomon to the Odes of Solomon and the Psalms of Solomon. Modern biblical scholars generally view this tradition as unsupported by any evidence that might reasonably link Solomon to these books, but his reputation as Israel's wisest king would have been sufficient, in antiquity, to have authenticated such claims and to have led to the incorporation of these works within the biblical canon. Certainly, the notion that wisdom was a divine gift might have sprung from traditions surrounding Solomon's early career and from the belief that the wise ruler is one whose heart knows the "fear" (or, better, "awe") of YHWH and who understands the inevitable consequences of sin (Prov. 1:7).

Perhaps the most striking difference between **wisdom literature** and other forms of moral instruction and psychological analysis in the Tanak—and certainly the characteristic that differentiates it most sharply from prophecy—is the absence in wisdom writing of any reference to the Mosaic Covenant, or the Exodus, or the exile. The world of wisdom literature is curiously ahistorical, existing apart from any reference to specific historical eras or events and focused mainly on the behavior of individuals, in either a family or a community setting. Wisdom writers seem to be unconcerned with or unaware of Israel's struggle to survive and to know nothing of divine threats or promises. They are just as indifferent to the cultic life of Israel, inasmuch as they neither comment on the Jerusalem Temple or the multitude of hill shrines condemned by prophet after prophet nor reflect on the goodness or corruption of kings.

What does concern wisdom writers, however, is the presence or absence of *order*—whether moral, social, or metaphysical—and particularly the consequences of disorder in a universe that should reflect divine rationality and justice. Those wisdom writers whose view of the balance of order and disorder is generally positive tend to embrace a philosophy akin to the Deuteronomic thesis and find that, by and large, goodness is rewarded in this life, and evil punished. The Book of Proverbs clearly endorses this view when it declares,

> . . . the path of the righteous is
>   like the light of dawn,
> which shines brighter and
>   brighter until full day.
> The way of the wicked is like
>   deep darkness;
> they do not know what they
>   stumble over. (Prov. 4:18–19)

Similar sentiments are to be found in the stories of Joseph and Daniel, as well as in deuterocanonical works like the Wisdom of Solomon and Ecclesiasticus (the Wisdom of ben Sirach; see Chapter 29). The advice that follows echoes the generally optimistic worldview of the "conventional" wisdom tradition: People who work hard, obey God's commandments, and avoid the pitfalls of immorality and conceit will know both prosperity and contentment. Humanity's primary duty, then, is first to discern and then to obey the divine will as it is expressed in the order of the cosmos that YHWH has created.

However, the more negative or "critical" view of the balance of good and evil—or of the place of wisdom in a world where goodness and obedience to YHWH seem somehow irrelevant to human destiny—also finds its voice in the books of Ecclesiastes and Job, and even the Deity himself cannot avoid being called to account for the universe he has created. The boldness and skepticism that surface in these books may well reflect a postexilic disenchantment with the hopeful and perhaps naive belief that the moral economy of the world could be explained simply by superimposing a Deuteronomic schema on the individual life in the hopes of demonstrating the rewards of *torah* observance. In the absence of a clearly defined and universally accepted myth of the afterlife, Diaspora wisdom teachers had, of necessity, to explain the cruelties and inequities of life without reference to a system of posthumous rewards and punishments. They therefore limited the focus of their observations to this world rather than the next (Box 25.1). This is why the author(s) of Job can speak not only of **Sheol** and the afterlife but also of the present life in the most despairing tones:

> Are not the days of my life few?
>   Let me alone, that I may find a
>   little comfort
> before I go, never to return,
>   to the land of gloom and deep
>   darkness,
> the land of gloom and chaos,
>   where light is like darkness. (Job 10:20–22)

This is also why the wisdom author can urge his readers to accomplish whatever little they can in this world, because there is neither "knowledge [nor] wisdom in Sheol, to which you are going" (Eccles. 9:10). Of all the postexilic writings that are in any way affected by or related to the wisdom movement

BOX 25.1
Sheol — The Biblical Underworld

When Job asks, "If mortals die, will they live again?" (14:14), his rhetorical question about the possibility of an afterlife is answered in the negative; unlike trees that may revive after being cut down, the dead remain permanently dead (14:18–22). In contrast to the Egyptians, who went to great lengths to preserve their dead in the hope of future life, the ancient Israelites did not embrace a doctrine of posthumous immortality. The covenant people's relationship with YHWH did not extend beyond the grave, an assumption that intensifies Job's need for divine justice in the present life. Instead of a future reward in heaven, YHWH's worshipers anticipated only endless confinement in Sheol, a dark, subterranean abyss that indiscriminately housed all the dead, good and evil alike.

Reminding God that only the living can serve or praise him, a psalmist begs for his life to be spared:

> For in death there is no remembrance of you,
> in Sheol, who can give you praise?
> (Ps. 6:5; cf. Isa. 38:18–19)

Another biblical poet suggests that keeping worshipers alive works to the advantage of a God who requires praise: "What profit is there in my death, if I go down to the Pit [another term for Sheol]? Will the dust praise you? Will it tell of your faithfulness?" (Ps. 30:9). A third psalmist reminds YHWH that the dead, no matter how devout, can no longer bear testimony to his miraculous deeds:

> Do you work wonders for the dead?
> Do the shades rise up to praise you?
> Is your steadfast love declared in the grave, . . .
> Are your wonders known in the darkness,
> or your saving acts in the land of forgetfulness?
> (Ps. 88:10–12)

Death breaks the bond between God and humanity: "those who go down to the Pit cannot hope for your faithfulness" (Isa. 38:18). The most Job can hope for in Sheol is oblivion and respite from pain (Job 3:17–19).

The author of Ecclesiastes offers a similarly bleak view, urging the wise to savor the joys of this life because even the righteous can expect no posthumous blessings:

> The living know that they will die, but the dead know nothing; they have no more reward, and even

the memory of them is lost . . . never again will they have any share in all that happens under the sun. . . . Whatever your hand finds to do, do with your might; for there is no work or thought or knowledge or wisdom in Sheol, to which you are going. (Eccles. 9:5, 10)

Postexilic leaders in Judea may have emphasized a negative view of the afterlife to discourage older folk beliefs about the dead, beliefs the Israelites once probably shared with their Canaanite neighbors. Many ancient societies assumed that the dead not only continued to exist in another dimension but also could communicate with the living, helping relatives and harming enemies. The biblical name *Sheol* is thought to derive from the verb *sha'al*, "to ask," perhaps a reference to the ancient and widespread practice of inquiring of the dead. A passage in Deuteronomy explicitly condemns anyone who "consults ghosts or spirits, or who seeks oracles from the dead" (Deut. 18:10–11), showing that the custom was not unknown in the covenant community. An offense to YHWH punishable by death (Lev. 19:31; 20:6, 27), consultation with diviners or fortune-tellers is seen as tantamount to relying on rival sources of supernatural power. The Hebrew Bible's only example of necromancy (eliciting prophetic speech from the dead) is Saul's notorious visit to the medium of En-dor, where a female necromancer conjures up the spirit of the prophet Samuel, illustrating an old belief that the ghosts of the departed could be summoned from Sheol to foretell the future (2 Sam. 28:3–25).

Although one psalmist declares that YHWH can be present in both heaven *and* Sheol (Ps. 139:7–8), it was not until the Book of Daniel was written in the second century B.C.E. that a biblical author unambiguously promises the faithful a future life. Other passages, such as the vision of "dry bones" coming back to life in Ezekiel 37, refer not to individuals but to Judah's restoration after its political "death" in Babylonian captivity. For Daniel, postmortem existence takes the form of a resurrected body, in which the just will awake to "everlasting life," while the covenant breakers will experience "shame and everlasting contempt" (Dan. 12:1–3).

Perhaps the most optimistic vision of the afterlife appearing in the Old Testament is expressed in the

(continued)

BOX 25.1 *(continued)*

apocryphal Wisdom of Solomon (first century B.C.E.). The Hellenistic writer, deeply influenced by Greek ideas about the soul's intrinsic immortality taught by such philosophers as Pythagoras, Socrates, and Plato, rejects traditional biblical concepts about the soul's gloomy fate in Sheol, declaring that "God created us [humans] for incorruption, and made us in the image of his own eternity" (Wisd. of Sol. 2:23). Offering a solution to the problem of undeserved suffering, the author states that God's faithful servants, no matter how unjustly afflicted, will be compensated in the next world:

> But the souls of the righteous are in the hand of
>   GOD, and no torment will ever touch them.
> In the eyes of the foolish they seemed to have died,
>   and their departure was thought to be a disaster,
>   and their going from us to be their destruction, but
>   they are at peace.
> For though in the sight of others they were punished,
>   their hope is full of immortality. (Wisd. of Sol. 3:1–4)

in Israel, only the Book of Daniel holds out the prospect of a general resurrection in which "many of those who sleep in the dust of the earth shall awake, some to everlasting life, and some to shame and everlasting contempt" (Dan. 12:2). In the absence of such a belief, however, "critical" wisdom is left to reflect on the obvious and disheartening truth that "the race is not to the swift" and that "time and chance" seem to be the determinants of human destiny (Eccles. 9:11).

Nevertheless, whether a defining, morally significant order of things is to be found in this world or in some other, future, existence, the search for wisdom in Israel goes on. For writers of critical wisdom books, the quest for moral understanding is precisely that — a "quest" or uncertain pursuit of insights hidden from public view:

> But where shall wisdom be
>   found?
> And where is the place of
>   understanding?
> Mortals do not know the way to
>   it,
> and it is not found in the land
>   of the living . . .
> It is hidden from the eyes of all
>   living,
>   and concealed from the birds of
>   the air. (Job 28:12–13, 21)

God alone, the author of Job continues, knows wisdom's hiding place, and the sum of what we have been able to ascertain of divine wisdom is the ne-

cessity of obeying his commandments and holding him in awe. The *torah*-obedient life emerges, then, as a middle ground between despair over an inability ever to find the moral essence of life and overconfidence in one's own goodness or in the goodness of life itself.

The Book of Proverbs

As the principal source of "practical" wisdom teaching in the Tanak, the Book of Proverbs plays an important role in formulating what many Israelites would have seen as a normative view of the content and function of wisdom in their society. Though ascribed to Solomon — who, according to tradition, is supposed to have written over 3000 proverbs (1 Kings 4:29–33) — the Book of Proverbs is widely viewed today as a compilation of maxims and poems from many hands. In fact, the book itself reveals something of the diversity of its sources by citing the wisdom teachers Agur (Prov. 30:1–14) and Lemuel (Prov. 31:1–9), about whom we know nothing apart from their sayings in this collection. That wisdom writing was an international enterprise is well known to biblical scholars today, and it is now possible to trace the potential origin of biblical proverbs back to an Egyptian or Mesopotamian source. One obvious, non-Israelite source of biblical wisdom is the Egyptian sage Amenemope,

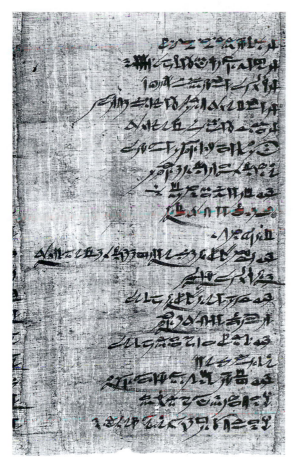

Figure 25.1 An ancient Egyptian papyrus recording the Wisdom of Amenemope (c. 1200 B.C.E.) contains sage advice that was later incorporated in the Book of Proverbs (22:17–24:22). The wisdom movement permeated virtually the entire ancient Near East, creating an international legacy shared by Egypt, Mesopotamia, and Israel.

nature, and the etymology of the word *mashal* suggests that the underlying intent of any proverb is to inspire readers to better "govern" their lives or adopt rules of life designed to promote contentment and well-being. Wisdom writers generally, and the authors of Proverbs specifically, do not claim to impart divine revelation to their audience. Although they trace the ultimate origin of wisdom itself back to YHWH—"the fear of the LORD [YHWH] is the beginning of knowledge" (Prov. 1:7)—proverbial wisdom is clearly experientially based knowledge, derived from reflections on the good life over many generations. Thus, many of the maxims in the Book of Proverbs are presented as parental advice:

> Hear, my child, your father's
> instruction,
> and do not reject your mother's
> teaching . . . (Prov. 1:8)

The underlying assumption here and throughout this book is that the younger generation has much to learn from the collective experience of earlier generations. This view of the superior wisdom of the elders is common to most traditional cultures, and it would certainly have appealed to wisdom teachers who were connected in any way to Israel's most venerable cultural institutions, the royal court and the Temple. It is not unlikely, therefore, that the earliest wisdom teachers served as royal counselors or as scribes whose task it was to train a younger generation of scholars and diplomats to take their place in Israel's court bureaucracy.

THE VALUE OF WISDOM

Perhaps the most important lesson wisdom writers-as-parents attempt to communicate to the young is the folly of acting on impulse (particularly sexual impulses) and the need for diligence and conscientiousness. Admonitions to work hard and not be idle ("Go to the ant, you lazybones, consider its ways, and be wise" [Prov. 6:6]) are often coupled with warnings against bad companions and immoral women. Most of this advice is clearly intended for young men, eager to make their way in the world, but some is directed at young women as

whose recovered sayings parallel those found in Proverbs 22 and 23 (Figure 25.1).

THE *MASHAL*

The basic literary unit of this book is the **mashal,** or proverb (the English word comes from the Latin *proverbia*), a brief, didactic saying, often based on a close observation of life. Proverbs are directive in well. The concluding chapter of Proverbs contains an extended acrostic poem (in which every line begins with a different letter of the alphabet in alphabetical sequence) that describes the character and duties of the ideal wife-mother, whose life obviously revolves around the home and whose virtues are reflected in the well-being of her family:

> A capable wife who can find?
>   She is far more precious than
>   jewels. . . .
> She seeks wool and flax,
>   and works with willing hands. . . .
> She considers a field and buys it;
>   with the fruit of her hands she
>   plants a vineyard. . . .
> She looks well to the ways of her
>   household,
> and does not eat the bread of
>   idleness. (Prov. 31:10–27)

The stable family unit, like the law-abiding society, is clearly the conservative ideal that Proverbs is promoting, along with a generally pragmatic view of the consequences of morally indifferent behavior. In this regard, wisdom teaching has much in common with the Deuteronomic tradition in that it stresses the rewards accruing from hard work and good behavior, as well as the punishments life itself will inflict on those who lie or cheat or ignore parental warnings.

However, nowhere is wisdom more highly praised in this book than in Chapter 8, where it is personified in the figure of a young woman who stands at the crossroads and at the gates of the city, promising great treasure to those who heed her instruction. As a figurative extension of divine moral intelligence, Wisdom is described as the first-created of YHWH's beings and as the central metaphor of what appears to be a hymn to God's creative powers:

> The LORD created me at the
>   beginning of his work,
> the first of his acts of long ago . . .
> Before the moutains had been
>   shaped,
> before the hills, I was brought
>   forth —

> when he had not yet made earth
>   and fields,
> or the world's first bits of soil.
> When he established the heavens, I
>   was there,
>   when he drew a circle on the
>   face of the deep,
> when he made firm the skies
>   above, . . .
> then I was beside him, like a
>   master worker . . . (Prov. 8:22–30)

In later Jewish and Christian philosophy, this extended figure of speech takes on a life of its own, merging curiously with the Stoic concept of the Logos. But within the context of the Hebrew Bible, "Lady Wisdom" (as this figure is sometimes called) remains nothing more than an exalted way of referring both to YHWH the Creator and to the rationality of his creation. In the light of this metaphor, the pursuit of wisdom becomes an attempt to understand the moral underpinnings of the universe and the mind of the Creator who brought it into being. Unlike the Book of Job, however, Proverbs conjures up a scenario of world creation that affirms rather than questions the fundamental moral intelligibility of the nonhuman cosmos. "The LORD has made everything for its purpose" (Prov. 16:4), the author of Proverbs declares, and in such a divinely ordered world, no moral or immoral act goes unnoticed or unrewarded.

Knowing all this, the wise will accept divine *musar* (Prov. 1:2)—meaning "discipline," though this term is often mistranslated as "instruction"—as both an expression and a logical consequence of the awe with which they regard the Creator. Only the fool, Proverbs asserts repeatedly, will turn aside from YHWH and his counsel, and in place of the prosperity that awaits the lovers of wisdom, only disaster and Sheol await those who prey on the innocent (Prov. 1:12). References to the Underworld in Proverbs, however, are not connected to any developed afterlife myth, and, consequently, the judgments that overtake the wicked are limited to this life, with the ultimate punishment being an untimely and grief-filled death. As the foolish disregarded YHWH throughout their lives, so he will disregard them when they call on him in their final hours (Prov. 1:24–31).

Yet, for all its assurances that a good life will be YHWH's reward to the wise, Proverbs is realistic enough to recognize that prosperity is never universal and that happiness is only a relative good. In counseling virtue and its rewards, it therefore cautions readers against unreasonable or purely materialistic expectations:

> Better is a dry morsel with
>   quiet
> than a house full of feasting
>   with strife. (Prov. 17:1)

At times, in fact, the author of Proverbs can sound not unlike the author of Ecclesiastes, acknowledging, for example, the practical value of a bribe (Prov. 17:8) or the inevitable arrogance of the rich (Prov. 18:23). For all the seeming cynicism of such observations, however, Proverbs remains consistent in its praise of the virtues of loyalty, humility, and thrift, and confident that a loose tongue and unchecked desires ultimately will destroy both the individual and the community.

The Book of Job

A bold challenge to traditional views of God, the Book of Job dramatizes the plight of an innocent man whose intellectual honesty prevents him from portraying himself as sinful in order to validate conventional ideas about divine justice. Asserting his right to be heard, Job demands that God, who is both Accuser and Judge, appear in court to offer evidence that would justify treating a righteous person as if he were a criminal (Figure 25.2). Cosmic in scope, Job ranges throughout the traditional three-story universe, from sessions of the divine council in heaven, to images of an earthly courtroom where conventional ideas about God are placed on trial, to speculations about Sheol, the underground abode of the dead (see Figure 7.1). The book climaxes with YHWH's longest self-disclosure in the Hebrew Bible (38:1–41:34).

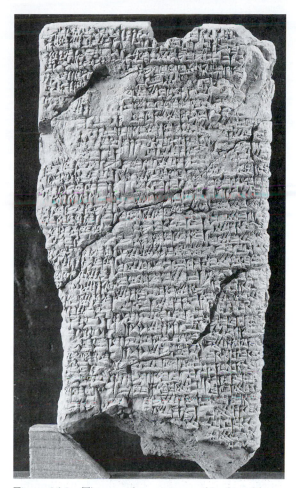

Figure 25.2 The cuneiform script on this clay tablet narrates a Sumerian variation of the Job story. Like the Book of Job, this text records the humiliating ordeals of a righteous man who nonetheless clings to his faith and is at last delivered from his undeserved sufferings. The problem of evil, with its conflict between the concept of a benign God and the fact of unmerited human pain, was a perplexing theme explored in Egyptian, Babylonian, and Israelite literature.

ISSUES OF THE POSTEXILIC AGE

Although scholars do not agree on when Job was written, the general time of its composition can be inferred from the theological issues it confronts. The oldest extant reference to the title character was recorded during the Babylonian exile, when the prophet Ezekiel mentioned three ancient figures who were considered models of righteousness — Noah, Danel (not the biblical Daniel), and Job (Ezek. 14:14, 20). Although Ezekiel says nothing specific about Job, he may have had in mind a tradition about Job's patience while suffering, a motif emphasized in the folktale that opens the biblical book (cf. Job 1:22; 2:9–10). In its questioning of God's right to prosecute a person of exemplary goodness "for no reason" (2:3), however, the book is far more than an edifying study of the hero's fortitude and loyalty under severe testing. The Tanak's most fully developed **theodicy**— a literary attempt to reconcile beliefs about divine goodness with the prevalence of evil—Job seems to express the deepest concerns of the postexilic era, when old assumptions about rewards for faithfulness and penalties for wrongdoing had lost much of their former authority.

For Job's author, previous attempts to explain his community's suffering and the equity of God's judgments were insufficient. In dealing with the crisis of their nation's destruction, the Deuteronomistic redactors attributed both Israel's fall and Judah's collapse to their failure to obey YHWH's commands. According to the Deuteronomic theory of history, the covenant people were a collective entity, a corporate body that prospered or suffered together, not only for their own actions but also for those of their ancestors. Thus, Judah was annihilated because YHWH found the sins of one of its last kings to be unforgivable (2 Kings 23:26–27; see Chapter 15). While in exile, Ezekiel proposes a variation on the old principle of collective community responsibility: Henceforth, YHWH will deal with his people in a new way, judging each generation according to its individual merits, rather than making it pay for the past sins of its ancestors or the future errors of its descendants (Ezek. 18). Declaring that YHWH takes no "pleasure in the death of anyone" but wishes all to live, Ezekiel states that God will look favorably on new generations who turn from their parents' misdeeds to follow Torah commands.

While stating that God will, after the exile, judge each generation individually, Ezekiel nonetheless insists on preserving the old Deuteronomic formula that equated good conduct with divine blessings. Despite his innovations, Ezekiel clearly presupposes that YHWH will favor the good and condemn only the wicked. Because it is unthinkable that YHWH behaves unjustly, all individuals must deserve whatever evils befall them.

Some wisdom writers advocated similar views. According to the Book of Proverbs, God's world manifests an intrinsic moral order in which all thoughts and actions have predictable consequences. Proper "fear of the Lord" and diligent, prudent behavior will result in prosperity and honor, whereas disloyalty to YHWH and evil deeds will ultimately bring failure and shame. Like the Deuteronomists, the authors of practical wisdom postulated a cosmic system of ethical cause and effect that equitably determined the degree of good or evil present in human lives. In times of peace and relative social stability, this philosophy seemed to work, and Israel's sages, who presumably were examples of the policies they preached, taught their students that *torah*-keeping, honesty, and hard work almost invariably translate into economic success and public reputation.

After Babylon's destruction of Judah, however, when thousands of *torah*-abiding people permanently lost family, health, land, and possessions, confidence that righteous behavior could ensure a good life was less easy to entertain. Observing widespread injustice that turned the Deuteronomic thesis on its head — with foreign overlords cruelly exploiting even the most obedient of YHWH's people — the anonymous author of Job could accept neither Deuteronomy's simplistic theories nor Ezekiel's implication that human misery always derives from sin. Combining traditional reverence for YHWH with an acutely critical intelligence and demand for moral logic, Job's author protests comfortable but outmoded notions about the connection between good behavior and good fortune. Creatively expanding on folklore about Job (Ezek. 14:14, 20), the writer, in some of the Hebrew Bible's greatest poetry, forcefully illustrates his conviction that old theological claims about the certainty of divine justice were woefully inadequate to explain the apparently random and arbitrary nature of human pain.

DIFFERENT NAMES OF GOD

Although most of the book is in poetry (Job 3:1–42:6), Job opens and closes with brief prose narratives. In the prose sections framing the central poetic drama, the Deity is YHWH; in the poetic dialogues that make up most of the book, however, the personal name of Israel's covenant patron is almost entirely absent (except in 12:9). Instead, Job frequently addresses God as El (or its variation, *Elohe*) or, less often, as *Shaddai*, an archaic title that occurs in Genesis but is otherwise rarely used in the Bible. (Exodus 6 states that, prior to the time of Moses, YHWH was known only as *El Shaddai*.) Not until the drama's final act, when YHWH speaks to Job from a violent storm, does the poet consistently invoke the Deity's personal name (Chs. 38–41).

THE PROSE PROLOGUE: YHWH AND THE DIVINE COUNCIL

An Innocent Victim The prologue (Job. 1–2) presents Job as a thoroughly admirable and godly person who in no way deserves the torments inflicted on him. Described as "blameless and upright, one who feared God and turned away from evil" (1:1; 1:8; cf. 2:3), he is a model of humanity created in God's image, one who enjoys a harmonious relationship with his Creator. So scrupulous is Job about not offending God that he offers sacrifices for his children in case they, even in thought, have sinned. No wonder YHWH declares that "there is no one like [Job] on the earth" (Job 1:8). Although Job's "friends" will vigorously dispute it, seeking to exonerate God by making Job guilty, Job's innocence is absolutely essential to the book's theological meaning. Commending Job's moral excellence, YHWH himself regards the man as faultless (1:8; 2:3; cf. 42:7). The friends' attempt to uncover some secret flaw in Job's character or behavior—an effort in which many commentators have joined—is misguided, distracting attention from the real issue, the inadequacy of conventional ideas about God and the divine-human relationship.

Although Job's exemplary character differentiates him from most people, he is also a universal type, the person of goodwill found throughout history. For this reason, the writer makes him not an Israelite but a native of Uz (a region south of Edom) who lived long before Israel's birth. Belonging to the patriarchal age, Job is not a member of the covenant community. As an archetypal figure who endeavors to please God in every aspect of his life, however, Job has an unwritten covenant with God, who, as proverbial wisdom later assumed, administers a just universe. When Job, still honoring his commitment to YHWH, is suddenly plunged into extreme misery, readers are forced to confront the mystery of God's refusal to banish evil from his world.

YHWH's Heavenly Court Job's troubles begin in heaven, where YHWH has called an assembly of divine beings—the *bene ha elohim* (sons of the gods)—which includes "the Satan," a member of YHWH's council who serves as the Deity's prosecuting attorney. At this point in Satan's historical evolution, *Satan* is not a proper name (the Hebrew text uses the definite article, for "the Satan"), and the Satan is not YHWH's adversary but his servant, a celestial functionary whose task is to seek out and expose any disloyalty in God's human subjects (Box 25.2). Ironically, it is YHWH who initiates Job's ordeal by drawing the Satan's attention to Job's perfect devotion, as if to cite a conspicuous example of one whose virtue affirms God's wisdom in creating humanity (Job 1:6–8). Accepting his ruler's implied challenge, the Satan suggests that Job will not remain loyal if deprived of children, property, and reputation. For reasons known only to himself, YHWH accepts this challenge, withdrawing the protective "fence" with which he had previously shielded Job from misfortune.

Stripped of divine protection, Job immediately experiences the power of chaos—the sudden injection of violent change into his formerly stable environment. Predatory nomads sweep away his flocks and herds; the "fire of God" consumes his sheep and

BOX 25.2
Evolution of the Satan Concept

Readers who think of **Satan** as a supernatural embodiment of evil, a powerful rebel against God who presides over an underworld of fire and brimstone, may be puzzled at the Hebrew Bible's portrayal of him as a regular member of YHWH's heavenly council. In Job, he is included among the "sons of God," a celestial being whose role is limited to carrying out YHWH's orders (Job 1–2; cf. Zech. 3). Despite the later popular mythology that transforms "the Satan" into a God-defying "Prince of Darkness," responsible for all the world's ills, the Tanak grants him no independence from God.

Although commonly regarded as synonymous with the Hebrew *Satan*, the term **devil** is absent from the Tanak (and occurs relatively infrequently in the New Testament). Derived from the Greek word *diablos, devil* means "accuser" or "slanderer." Even in the Christian Bible, the Greek devil and the Hebrew Satan are not explicitly linked together until the author of Revelation so identifies them, equating Satan, the devil, and the Genesis serpent who tempted Eve (Rev. 12:12; cf. Gen. 3). This correlation took place late in biblical history, however, appearing first in noncanonical works such as the books of Adam and Eve (see Chapter 30).

THE SATAN AND THE HEBREW BIBLE

Although Revelation identifies the two figures, the Satan of the Hebrew Bible is not precisely the same entity as the devil of the New Testament. The concepts expressed by these two different terms developed independently of each other. The word *satan* derives from a Hebrew root meaning "obstacle"; personified (given human qualities), it means "opposer" or "adversary." In the Tanak, the Satan has an adversarial relationship with humanity, but not with God, whose servant he remains.

According to historians of religion — scholars who analyze the evolution of religious ideas and beliefs — the concept of Satan developed from the negative qualities once attributed to God. In this view, the Satan figure is essentially the "dark side," or psychological "shadow," of YHWH's ethically ambivalent

character (see Chapter 4). Tracing in chronological order the biblical references to Satan provides evidence that the violent and destructive traits formerly considered part of the divine nature were eventually ascribed to the Satan. The tension between contrasting aspects of the biblical God — who is both Creator of light and life and a sometimes vindictive destroyer — is thus partly resolved. God can be seen as all-good and all-loving, while the Satan becomes responsible for the undesirable realities of existence.

In an early stage of this theological development, some biblical writers saw all things, good and evil alike, emanating from a single source — YHWH. A form of **monism** — a belief that the universe contains only one divine principle — this view held that YHWH alone caused both joy and sorrow, both prosperity and suffering (cf. Deut. 28). In the oldest literary strand of the Pentateuch, the Yahwist shows YHWH first creating life and then regretting it, annihilating most life forms on earth (Gen. 2, 6–8). At this stage in Israel's religious thought, YHWH is not only giver of life and pitiless executioner but also tormentor and deceiver. After first selecting Saul to be Israel's first king, YHWH then rejects him, driving Saul to madness by dispatching an "evil spirit" to torment him (1 Sam. 16:14–23). God also sends a "lying spirit" to lead King Ahab to his doom (1 Kings 22:18–28). Both of these texts show "evil" (defined from a human viewpoint and applied exclusively to disobedient persons) as one of the means YHWH employs to effect his will. As late as the sixth century B.C.E., Second Isaiah depicts YHWH as the originator of both light *and* dark, good *and* evil (Isa. 45:7).

Taking another step in the development of the Satan figure, some of Israel's thinkers placed the source of human trouble not in YHWH alone but also among the *bene ha elohim* (literally, "sons of the gods") who form YHWH's heavenly court. These unnamed divine beings, which may include some of the ethically undeveloped deities that YHWH denounces in Psalm 82, include the Satan, who has the job of "accusing" YHWH's people and testing their loyalty (Zech. 3:1–9; Job 1–2). Although the Satan is by this time viewed as separate from YHWH himself, he remains completely under the Deity's control, doing nothing without God's express permission. He functions as God's obedient agent, a facet of the divine personality. As YHWH's prosecuting attorney who tempts the divine judge to punish the innocent, the Satan also directly takes over God's previous role as destroyer, using the natural elements to kill Job's children and plunge the man of faith into despair. In contrast, in Zechariah's vision of the celestial throne room, YHWH resists the adversary's attempt to persuade him to afflict his people; in this case, the Deity's compassion and mercy prevail. (It is important to remember that in each of the few Tanak passages in which the Satan appears he is always *humanity's* adversary, not God's.)

A clear example of the Satan's assumption of the more sinister aspects of YHWH's character occurs in the two accounts of King David's census. In the first version, which was probably written before the Babylonian exile, YHWH puts it into David's head to sin by taking a census of Israel — always hated by the people because it was done for purposes of taxation and military conscription. David's census taking angers God, who then punishes not the king who ordered it but the people at large, sending a plague that kills thousands of Israelites (2 Sam. 24:1–25). In a second telling of this episode, written hundreds of years later, it is not YHWH who inspires David's census but the Satan; YHWH only punishes it (1 Chron. 21:1–30). The centuries that elapsed between the compositions of these two parallel accounts apparently witnessed a significant change in the covenant community's theological viewpoint. It was no longer possible to see YHWH as both the *cause* of sin and the one who punished it. The contradictory actions that the author of Samuel had ascribed to God the Chronicler now separates, assigning the cause of David's guilt to the Satan.

ZOROASTRIANISM AND LATER JUDEO-CHRISTIAN THOUGHT

After the Babylonian exile, when Judea was dominated by the Persian Empire, new religious ideas gradually infiltrated Jewish thinking. **Zoroastrianism,** the official Persian religion, viewed the universe as dualistic, ruled by two opposing supernatural forces of good and evil. The powers of light were led by Ahura Mazda, while those of darkness were directed by his opposite, Ahriman, the Zoroastrian devil. According to the religion's founder, the prophet Zoroaster, at the end of time a cosmic battle between good and evil would result in Ahriman's defeat and the triumph of good. Until then, the two competing forces would struggle incessantly, generating the mixture of creative peace and destructive violence that characterizes human life.

With its hierarchy of angels and demons, system of posthumous rewards and punishments, and concept of an all-good deity waging war against a wicked opponent, Zoroastrianism profoundly influenced later Judeo-Christian ideas about the nature of Satan, who eventually became the enemy not only of humankind but of God as well. Significantly, no biblical literature written before the Persian period names individual angels or depicts the Satan as an autonomous entity. Only in postexilic books like Tobit and Daniel are particular angels such as Michael, Gabriel, and Raphael, and demons such as Asmodeus, given personal names. With the influx of Greek and other foreign ideas following Alexander's conquest of the Persian Empire, including Judea, in the fourth century B.C.E., views of an afterlife populated with angels and demons proliferated (see the discussions of 2 Esdras in Chapter 29 and Enoch in Chapter 30). By New Testament times, Persian, Greek, Syrian, and other originally non-Jewish ideas had been thoroughly assimilated by the covenant community and rigorously subordinated to the religion of YHWH. After the first century C.E., however, Judaism rejected many of these Persian and Greek influences, denying many books that incorporated these concepts a place in the Tanak. The canonical Hebrew Bible grants the Satan little space and scant respect.

For additional information about the historical development of the Satan, see Jeffrey B. Russell, "Hebrew Personification of Evil" and "The Devil in the New Testament," in *The Devil: Perceptions of Evil from Antiquity to Primitive Christianity,* pp. 174–220 and 221–249 (Ithaca, N.Y.: Cornell University Press, 1978). See also Elaine Pagels, *The Origin of Satan* (New York: Random House, 1995). Presenting a "social history of Satan," Pagels shows how religious sects, particularly the Essenes and some New Testament authors, associated their opponents with demonic influences.

shepherds; and a fierce wind demolishes the house where his children are feasting, killing them all. Robbed of everything he holds dear by chaotic forces of earth, air, and sky, Job still blesses YHWH's name (1:1–2:21). As if tempting God to doubt further the integrity of his human creation, the Satan next persuades YHWH to infect his faithful worshiper with a painful and disfiguring disease, although YHWH protests that such persecution is unjustified, stating that his cynical agent has "incited" God against Job "for no reason" (2:3). In contrast to YHWH, who yields to pressure from Satan, Job rejects his wife's despairing plea to "curse God, and die." Courageously, Job resolves to live, persisting in his quest to understand the nature of his drastically changed relationship with the Deity.

THE CENTRAL POETIC DRAMA

Job's Lament   In Chapter 3, the action shifts from the heavenly court to Job's dungheap; in a long monologue, he prays to have the process of creation reversed, asking for a return to the primal darkness that shrouded all before God illuminated the cosmos (cf. Gen. 1:1–2). If light and life are mere vehicles for pain, it is better not to exist or, once born, to sink quickly into the oblivion of Sheol, the dark subterranean realm where the human dead remain in eternal nothingness (cf. Eccles. 9:5, 10; see also Box 25.1). Job's agony is intensified by God's silence, the total absence of any communication that would give his pain ethical meaning. His evocation of **Leviathan,** the mythical dragon of chaos, the "fleeing serpent"—embodiment of darkness and disorder that YHWH is portrayed as having subdued but not having eliminated during creation— expresses Job's direct experience of chaotic evil and anticipates the imagery in YHWH's final speech at the end of the drama, when God depicts himself as the proud owner of this monster (cf. Job 3:8; 26:10–14; 41:1–34).

The Central Debate   After delivering his anti-creation hymn, Job is joined by three friends— **Eliphaz, Bildad,** and **Zophar**—exponents of the religious orthodoxy contained in Proverbs and the Deuteronomistic writings. Throughout the book, the three do not move from their initial position— that Job's present misery must result from some vile but unknown sin. Championing long-accepted views of God, they argue, with increasing vehemence, that Job is guilty because God is just. An infallible sign of divine displeasure, Job's suffering confirms his error.

The book's central section is arranged in a series of debates between Job and his accusing friends: In three cycles of dialogue, each friend gives a speech, and Job, in turn, replies. In the last cycle, Job offers a final statement in which he reviews his life for any deed that might have offended God (Chs. 29–31). As the debates become more heated, Job's early patience gives way to a realization of two unorthodox truths: His humanity entitles him to innate moral rights, which God has violated; and if he is innocent and God is truly all-powerful, then the Deity must be responsible for the evil that he and all other people endure.

In Chapters 9 and 10, Job asks God to appear before him in human form so that their conflict can be settled in terms of legal justice. Even while demanding that God present evidence to prove Job's alleged wrongdoing, Job realizes that he has no chance to argue his cause before the Almighty. Anticipating YHWH's climactic discourse, Job describes God's control of nature, the irresistible force that reduces all mortals to insignificance. Furthermore, Job recognizes that the power that afflicts him is the same power that will judge him:

> Though I am innocent, I cannot answer him;
> I must appeal for mercy to my accuser.
> If I summoned him [to a courtroom] and he answered me,
> I do not believe that he would listen to my voice.
> For he crushes me with a tempest,
> and multiplies my wounds without cause; . . .
> If it is a contest of strength, he is the strong one!
> If it is a matter of justice, who can summon him?
> (Job 9:15–19)

Acknowledging God's power, Job can only conclude that, in practice, he makes no effort to distinguish between the innocent and the guilty:

It is all one; therefore I say
he destroys both the blameless and the wicked.
When disaster brings sudden death,
he mocks at the calamity of the innocent.
The earth is given into the hands of the wicked;
he covers the eyes of the judges —
if it is not he, who then is it? (Job 9:22–24)

With courage born of his realization that good people can be more compassionate and ethically responsible than the biblical God appears to be, Job suggests that God, who seems to revel in exercising his omnipotence, also must learn what it means to be human, to experience the universe from the human perspective:

I will say to GOD, Do not condemn me;
let me know why you contend against me.
Does it seem good to you to oppress,
to despise the work of your hands
and favor the schemes of the wicked?
Do you have eyes of flesh?
Do you see as humans see?
Are your days like the days of mortals,
or your years like human years,
that you seek out my iniquity and search for
    my sin,
although *you know that I am not guilty,*
and there is no one to deliver out of your hand?
                    (Job 10:2–7; emphasis added)

Reversing the traditional wisdom that asks us to look at things from the Deity's viewpoint, Job asks that God develop greater empathy for the human condition, experiencing his imperfect world as mortals must, without the divine prerogatives of omniscience, immortality, and immunity to pain.

In the final speech by one of Job's "false comforters," Bildad attacks the notion that any human can deserve God's favor, denigrating all mortals as mere "maggots" and "worms" (25:6; cf. similar views expressed by Eliphaz in 4:17–21 and 15:14–16 and by Zophar in 11:5–12). This attempt to justify human suffering by uniformly reducing humanity to moral baseness — an assumption to which Job also refers (9:2; 12:9; 14:4) — is sometimes used to support conventional beliefs about divine justice. The friends' emphasis on humankind's inborn depravity culminates historically in the later

Christian doctrine of **original sin,** which asserts that all humans inherit from Adam an inescapable tendency to sin, resulting in their blanket condemnation by a righteous Deity. Job's author, however, makes no reference to the Genesis story about the first couple's disobedience or its alleged consequences for humanity. When YHWH later appears to Job, he categorically rejects the friends' arguments and makes no allusion to humankind's supposedly innate sinfulness (42:7).

Elihu's Interruption   Between Job's final challenge to God (Chs. 29–31) and God's appearance in the whirlwind that logically follows it (Chs. 38–41), redactors inserted a lengthy speech by **Elihu,** a character whom the text has not previously introduced. Perhaps scandalized by Job's unorthodox theology, the writer of Elihu's discourse attacks Job for refusing to make things easy by simply confessing his sins (perhaps including self-righteousness) and thereby restoring the comforting view of God's perfect justice. Rehashing the three friends' arguments, Elihu adds little to the discussion, although he claims to resolve the problem that Job's case presents. Absurdly self-confident, Elihu presumes to speak "on God's behalf":

I will bring my knowledge from far away,
and ascribe righteousness to my Maker.
For truly my words are not false;
one who is perfect in knowledge is with you.
                    (Job 36:3–4)

After six chapters of Elihu's empty rhetoric, readers may well feel that the opening question in YHWH's first speech applies to him rather than to Job: "Who is this that darkens counsel by words without knowledge?"

YHWH'S REVELATION OF HIS UNIVERSE

As Job foresaw in Chapter 9, when God at last appears, it is not in human form to explain why he subverts his assumed principles of justice by allowing the wicked to thrive and the good to suffer. Indeed, YHWH appears in a superhuman display of power, celebrating his own strength and creative ingenuity and refusing to address any of Job's anguished questions. Speaking from the whirlwind as if to express the intractable, amoral energy of the natural world he has created, YHWH emphasizes the enormous gap between divinity and humanity. In his first speech (38:1–39:30), he parades images of cosmic grandeur before Job's dazzled eyes. Sardonically, he demands that Job inform God about the miracle of creation, astronomical phenomena, and the curious habits of wildlife. He invites Job to share his creative pride in the world of animal violence, such as the fearless warhorse that delights in battle (39:19–25). In his final horrific example, YHWH describes the eagle or vulture whose "young ones suck up blood," feasting on the bodies of the dying, oblivious to their pain (39:27–30).

Looking for the bread of understanding, Job is handed a scorpion, a catalogue of impersonal natural wonders, and a pitiless survey of predatory nature, "red in tooth and claw." When YHWH asks if Job, now deluged with examples of the savage and inexplicable, is ready to give up, Job merely replies that he will speak no more. Is Job's retreat into silence before God's self-revelation an act of reverent submission, or does it represent the numbness of moral shock?

Apparently unsatisfied with Job's wordless acquiescence, YHWH then launches into a second long discourse, in which he strikes at Job's deepest fear: that in the absence of a comprehensible divine ethic, humans will have to create—out of emptiness—their own meaning of life. When YHWH asks, "Will you even put me in the wrong? Will you condemn me that you may be justified?" (40:8), Job's response must be no, for he has no wish to justify himself at the Deity's expense. He merely asks YHWH to administer the cosmos according to ethical principles that will encourage good conduct in human life. As he earlier observed, YHWH's tolerance of the present system appears to support "the wicked," who commonly triumph over their moral betters.

YHWH next invites Job to examine the divine regulation of human society, asking him if he can duplicate the divine thunder that (when it chooses) can obliterate the wicked (40:9–14). But YHWH does not linger over his strangely inconsistent enforcement of justice in human affairs. Instead, he demands that Job consider the significance of two frightening monsters—Behemoth and Leviathan—that seem totally alien to human concerns. "The first of the great acts of GOD," **Behemoth** is a creature so powerful, so grotesque, and so removed from any possible relation to normal human experience that God's admiration for the monster compels Job to realize that the world is not a place designed primarily for humankind's benefit. When YHWH equates Behemoth and humanity, telling Job, "I made [it] just as I made you" (40:15), he reveals a universe that is God centered, a creation in which humans and dangerous beasts coexist, both the offspring of God. (This view contrasts markedly with that in Genesis 1:26–31, in which humanity, the pinnacle of creation, is divinely authorized to hold all other life forms in submission.)

Scholars formerly thought that Behemoth and Leviathan were, respectively, the hippopotamus and the crocodile. However, with the discovery of Ugaritic texts referring to Baal's defeat of Lothan, the primeval sea dragon, we now know that Leviathan is a mythological beast symbolizing the chaos that existed before creation and that periodically reasserts itself, threatening to unravel the world order. The Canaanite Lothan and Hebrew Leviathan are variant forms of **Rahab,** another version of the chaotic dragon that YHWH subdued when imposing order on the cosmos (Ps. 89:9–10). In Job, YHWH describes Leviathan in mythic terms, as a dragon belching fire and smoke (Job 41:18–21), at whose approach even "the gods are afraid" and thrown into a frenzy (41:25). Yet, terrifying as it is, YHWH delights in the brute:

> On earth it has no equal, a creature without fear.
> It surveys everything that is lofty; it is king over
>   all that are proud. (Job 41:33–34)

YHWH's allusion to Leviathan's supremacy among the "proud" recalls his earlier declaration that he *can* subdue the "proud" and the "wicked" who oppress others (40:9–14), although he chooses to do so only intermittently. As he tolerates the monster of chaos, amoral energy that has not been assimilated

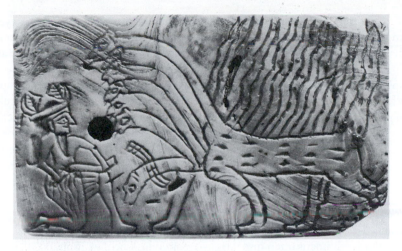

Figure 25.3   Mesopotamian God Battles a Seven-Headed Dragon Dating from the Sumerian Early Dynastic period (c. 2800–2600 B.C.E.), this plaque is believed to show the Sumerian god Ninurta, a divine warrior and son of Enlil, who functions as a cosmic savior by defeating the primal monster of chaos. Biblical writers preserved aspects of this conflict myth in references to YHWH's struggles with Leviathan, another name for the primeval serpent (cf. Ps. 74:12–17; Job 3:8; 26:13; 41:1–34; Isa. 27:1). The mythical dragon rears his seven heads again in the New Testament Book of Revelation, where, identified with Satan and the devil, he is cast from heaven by the archangel Michael (Rev. 12:3, 9; 13:1; 17:3).

into cosmic order, he apparently also incorporates arbitrary violence and unmerited suffering into his cosmic system.

Hearing YHWH's acknowledgment of Leviathan's role in the world, Job withdraws his questions about divine justice (42:2–3). The universe is as it is, an unfolding process in which light and dark, gentle and savage, and good and evil are intrinsic components. Leviathan, the dragon that periodically rears its head to shatter the peace of both nature and humanity, is perhaps a manifestation of the same mysterious, disruptive force that YHWH has made part of the cosmic whole (Figure 25.3). Absolute sovereign, YHWH is unlimited by merely human concepts of right and wrong, a monistic view that Second Isaiah also expresses:

I am the LORD, and there is no other.
I form light and create darkness,
I make weal and create woe;
I the LORD do all these things. (Isa. 45:6–7)

In portraying his universe, YHWH assigns no role to the Satan, either as an agent who tests the loyalty of humankind or as a theoretical source of cosmic evil and rebellion. For the author of Job, as well as Second Isaiah, YHWH's unity and omnipotence leave no room for any competing supernatural entity.

After disclosing the divine paradox that encompasses polar opposites of light and dark, YHWH asks Job to intercede for his three friends, because Eliphaz, Bildad, and Zophar "have not spoken of me what is right, as my servant Job has" (Job 42:7). Whereas the three friends defended a traditional concept of God, Job dared to point out the perplexing disparity between standard notions of divine justice and the facts of real life, whereby people do not always receive what they ethically deserve. After experiencing God directly in the whirlwind, Job abandons his attempt to find moral logic in the divine governance of the world, for YHWH has revealed himself to be far more concerned with the complex phenomena of the universe he has created than with resolving issues of good and evil that trouble humans.

After accepting Job's intercession for his friends, however, YHWH restores all of Job's possessions twice over, again placing his worshiper in the secure and prosperous environment he inhabited before God removed the "fence" that shielded Job from harm. Although Job is given ten more children, they are not the same children he lost as a result of the controversy between YHWH and his celestial prosecutor. Dispenser of both "weal" and "woe," YHWH administers a world in which — contrary to conventional wisdom — humans often find it agonizingly difficult to distinguish random chance from divine providence.

The Book of Ecclesiastes

Though one of the five **Megillot** and an integral part of the traditional liturgy (it is customarily read on Sukkoth / Tabernacles), Ecclesiastes is surely the most problematic work within the canonical wisdom tradition, and the most difficult to relate to normative wisdom traditions. Its tone, viewpoint, and underlying message are so persistently skeptical, occasionally to the point of nihilism, that it is difficult to understand how this book came to be incorporated into the biblical canon in the first place. Though contemporary scholars are virtually unanimous in regarding Ecclesiastes' allusive references to Solomon — "the son of David, king in Jerusalem" (1:1) — as a literary fiction, ancient readers clearly took this suggestion of authorship seriously and, assuming that Solomon was indeed the author of this book, concluded that he chose, for whatever enigmatic reasons, to refer to himself as **Koheleth.** Even today, no one is quite sure what the name *Koheleth* actually means and whether it should be understood as a personal name, a pen name, or a title. In any case, in antiquity, the mere association of this work with the Solomonic tradition of divinely bestowed wisdom was probably enough to legitimate

this book of reflections in the eyes of its priestly editors and to counteract whatever doubts they may have had about its acceptability as a book of inspired teachings.

About the identity and background of its author, we can only speculate. The Septuagint translators rendered the name *Koheleth* as "Ecclesiastes," deriving that word from the Greek word for "assembly" (*ecclesia*), reasoning that the name *Koheleth* must itself derive from the Hebrew verb *kahal*, meaning "to assemble." Just *what* Koheleth is supposed to have assembled is unclear. But the prevailing view today is that he was a *hakham*, or wisdom teacher, who gathered students around him or who imparted his unconventional teachings to an attentive audience. The English words *teacher, speaker,* and *preacher* are obviously approximations of what the name *Koheleth* may have meant — that is, if we are to understand it as a functional term rather than as a personal noun. As for the historical setting of this book, most scholars are convinced that Ecclesiastes is not only a postexilic composition but a rather late one at that, most likely reflecting attitudes and literary influences prevailing during the Hellenistic period. The era following the conquest of Palestine by Alexander the Great (333 B.C.E.) brought Judean society into direct contact with Greek culture, and it is not unlikely that a professional sage living in Jerusalem in the late fourth century B.C.E. would have been affected by new, philosophically challenging ideas. The language of Ecclesiastes reinforces the impression that it is a relatively late work, in that it incorporates both Persian loan words (that is, words borrowed from the Persian language) and Aramaic verb forms. But even without such evidence, scholars would be inclined to distance this book from more conventional wisdom writings like Proverbs simply as a way of explaining its remarkably disillusioned perspective.

THE LIMITS OF HUMAN UNDERSTANDING AND THE USES OF IRONY

Central to Koheleth's view of the human predicament is his conviction that, no matter how great the effort, human wisdom cannot account for the anomalies and bitter contradictions of life:

When I applied my mind to know wisdom, and to see the business that is done on earth, how one's eyes see sleep neither day nor night, then I saw all the work of God, that no one can find out what is happening under the sun. (Eccles. 8:16–17)

This note of incomprehension is sounded whenever Koheleth attempts to reach even the most provisional comprehension of a life that is often as frustrating to the intellect as it is subversive of the moral sense. In fact, the only conclusion Koheleth allows himself is that the very effort to understand life is pointless or, as he often expresses it, "vanity" and a "chasing after wind." Yet, for all his repeated declarations that it is impossible to reach any conclusions about life, Koheleth does make a number of incisive observations about the nature of human existence and the prospects for happiness in a world that seems designed solely for the purpose of defeating and destroying all human enterprises. Here again, the motif of "vanity" surfaces, as Koheleth explores the various ways in which human beings seek either fulfillment or insight:

> I searched with my mind how to cheer my body with wine — my mind still guiding me with wisdom — and how to lay hold on folly, until I might see what was good for mortals to do under heaven during the few days of their life. I made great works; I built houses and planted vineyards for myself; I made myself gardens and parks, and planted in them all kinds of fruit trees. . . . Whatever my eyes desired I did not keep from them; I kept my heart from no pleasure, for my heart found pleasure in all my toil, and this was my reward for all my toil. Then I considered all that my hands had done and the toil I had spent in doing it, and again, all was vanity and a chasing after wind, and there was nothing to be gained under the sun. (Eccles. 2:3–11)

It is the ultimately transitory character of all types of human happiness and all forms of human endeavor that haunts Koheleth's mind, along with the realization that, however successful one may be in pursuing one's life goals, death cancels everything out. From that terminal perspective, success is merely another form of failure.

Underlying these observations are two radical, and ultimately related, assumptions: Death means annihilation, and not only of the body but also of all the dreams and desires the mind and body can possibly experience in this life; and God's existence — though never to be doubted — has no direct bearing on the course of human life or on the destiny of individuals. No biblical writer, in fact, is as direct or as unambiguous as Koheleth in his view of Sheol as the sole form of an afterlife in which there is "no work or thought or knowledge or wisdom" (Eccles. 9:10). And although God, Ecclesiastes assures us, "will bring every deed into judgment" (12:14), the manner of that "judgment" is never made explicit, nor is it ever connected to events in the Underworld. Death, therefore, becomes a vast nothingness that swallows up both joy and misery, reducing all of the distinctions on which moral discourse is based — distinctions of justice/injustice, truth/falsehood, and righteousness/wickedness — to mere differences of language and perspective, not differences in destiny. This realization of the irrelevance of the moral life to one's personal fate becomes the source of Koheleth's "cynicism," as he ponders the implications of living in a world in which the same fate (death) overtakes the wise man and the fool, the just and the unjust.

At his most despairing, Koheleth rejects life itself as something not worth desiring or preserving:

> Again I saw all the oppressions that are practiced under the sun. Look, the tears of the oppressed — with no one to comfort them! On the side of their oppressors there was power — with no one to comfort them. And I thought the dead, who have already died, more fortunate than the living, who are still alive; but better than both is the one who has not yet been, and who has not seen the evil deeds that are done under the sun. (Eccles. 4:1–3)

If nonexistence is preferable to existence, then it might be argued that creation itself was the Creator's mistake and that bringing new life into this unredeemable world simply replicates that original error. Koheleth does not appear willing to carry this thesis to its logical conclusion, though later, Gnostic writers were more than willing to do so.

More often than not, however, Koheleth is content simply to question the "profit" in pursuing a life of wisdom and goodness. At most, he concedes that it is more pleasurable to satisfy one's needs in this life than to suffer deprivation, and for that reason, he urges his readers to eat and drink and derive whatever enjoyment they can from life because all of these pleasures will, before long, be cut short by death. To some scholars, such sentiments are oddly reminiscent of Epicurean philosophy, which held that all life forms are transient gatherings of atomic particles, governed by chance and destined to disintegrate at the moment of death. To others, Koheleth's counsel of self-gratification seems strikingly similar to the advice of Siduri in the *Epic of Gilgamesh,* who urges the hero of that poem to give up his quest for immortality and find satisfaction in the ordinary pleasures of life. Of course, Ecclesiastes embraces neither the materialist metaphysic that underlies Epicurean thought nor the hedonism that is embodied in Siduri's speech. But, then, neither does he reflect on the covenant, on *torah,* or on any of the basic faith claims that undergird biblical theology. And even when Ecclesiastes occasionally echoes more conventional wisdom sentiments — asserting, for example, that God both observes and tests us (3:18) or that we are to guard our tongues lest we provoke his judgment (5:2–7) — such observations have no final bearing on the sustaining insight of this book: namely, that no effort of mind or heart can endow life with a value or meaning it does not possess. God is surely in heaven (5:2), Koheleth insists, but here on earth, no sign of the moral order of his universe can be found.

THE CYCLES OF LIFE

When Koheleth does reflect on the order (as opposed to the disorder) of things, his image of life often assumes a cyclical pattern. In the opening chapter, for example, he compares the passage of human generations first to the diurnal cycle of sunrises and sunsets, then to the circuitous movements of wind currents, and finally to the suggestively circular flow of streams into the sea. More evocatively, in Chapter 3, he depicts the whole of life as an alternating sequence of "seasonal" events in which all things

are assigned a "time to be born, and a time to die" (Eccles. 3:2). Powerful as this composite image is, however, there is no hint in this poem or in anything that follows it of any release from this cycle of perpetually recurring events. Ecclesiastes confines us to a world of temporal/biological repetition in which there can never be anything "new under the sun," nor any transcendent moment of divine revelation (like Sinai) that moves history and humankind beyond the endlessly repetitive rhythms of nature. What is most conspicuously missing from Koheleth's worldview, then, is the mostly linear perspective that dominates the Deuteronomistic History or the equally linear thrust of apocalyptic thought. There is nothing in Ecclesiastes' universe to look back on or forward to, and therefore no possibility of divine or human novelty. Neither the Exodus nor the Day of the LORD has any place in this scenario. It is tempting to describe Koheleth's perspective as not merely ahistorical but *antihistorical;* nothing that has happened or that may happen, to Israel or to the world, can alter the "vanity" of things.

The concluding chapter of Ecclesiastes seemingly reverses the thrust of Koheleth's argument by counseling its readers to "fear God and keep his commandments" (12:13), and modern scholars suggest that these verses may well be an interpolation designed to bring Ecclesiastes "into line" with the prevailing sentiments of the conventional wisdom tradition. But whatever the original intent of the author-redactor of Ecclesiastes may have been, Chapter 12 serves as a didactic frame for the rest of this book, reminding us that "the sayings of the wise are like goads" (12:11) and that the one thing most readers of wisdom books must be goaded into acknowledging is the transitory character of all desires — perhaps even the desire for life itself. By admonishing his readers to trust God rather than books (of which, he assures us, "there is no end"), Koheleth is not so much contradicting himself as moving his reflections into another domain, where failure and despair have no place, and the only truth is obedience to an omniscient (albeit remote) deity. This "turn" toward the transcendent may conceivably be an afterthought or even represent another authorial voice, but it is entirely consistent with the general direction of speculative wisdom writing in Israel. As in the Book of Job, a magisterial deity, seemingly disconnected from the world of human striving and the quest for ultimate knowledge, serves to anchor an otherwise subversive narrative in a reality removed from human inquiry. It is enough, Koheleth seems to be saying, that God exists beyond the range of our inquisitive minds and that he sees into our hearts even if we cannot see into his. In the presence of such a deity, obedience and awe are the only appropriate responses.

QUESTIONS FOR REVIEW

1. What are the principal differences between the more "conventional" or "practical" wisdom books like Proverbs and the "critical" wisdom books like Ecclesiastes and Job? Do these different types of wisdom writing actually embody different (and incompatible) worldviews?

2. Do the writers of Job and Ecclesiastes offer readers anything resembling an explanation for the presence of evil in the world? Or do they simply accept the reality of injustice and misfortune as an inevitable part of the scheme of things?

3. How do the counsels and moral equations of Proverbs relate to the Deuteronomistic History and its underlying thesis of collective rewards and punishments?

QUESTIONS FOR REFLECTION AND DISCUSSION

1. Why were the books contained in the Writings (Kethuvim) section of the Hebrew Bible apparently the last to be canonized? Was it simply a matter of date of composition, or were some of these books troubling to religious authorities? And why would works as seemingly secular as the Song of Songs or Ecclesiastes, or as provocative as Job, be included in a collection of sacred writings at all?

2. Critical wisdom books offer us a skeptical and possibly subversive view of God and of the balance of good and evil in his world. Is there a way of reading Job and Ecclesiastes that allows readers to preserve

some of the more conventional values and perspectives of the Torah and the Prophets without suppressing the interrogative, and even pessimistic, ideas found in each of these books?

TERMS AND CONCEPTS TO REMEMBER

Behemoth	monism
bene ha elohim	*musar*
Bildad	nature of YHWH's
devil	universe
Elihu	original sin
Eliphaz	Rahab
Epic of Gilgamesh	Satan
hakham	Sheol
Koheleth	theodicy
Leviathan	wisdom literature
mashal	Zophar
Megillot	Zoroastrianism

RECOMMENDED READING

Proverbs and Ecclesiastes

Bergant, Dianne. *Israel's Wisdom Literature: A Liberation-Critical Reading.* Minneapolis: Fortress Press, 1997.

Crenshaw, James L. *Ecclesiastes.* Philadelphia: Westminster Press, 1987.

———. *Old Testament Wisdom: An Introduction,* rev. ed. Louisville, Ky.: Westminster/John Knox Press, 1998.

Gordis, Robert. *Koheleth: The Man and His World.* New York: Jewish Theological Seminary of America Press, 1951.

McKane, William. *Proverbs.* Philadelphia: Westminster Press, 1970.

Scott, R. B. Y. *Proverbs, Ecclesiastes.* Anchor Bible, Vol. 18. Garden City, N.Y.: Doubleday, 1965.

Job

Crenshaw, James L., ed. *Theodicy in the Old Testament.* Philadelphia: Fortress Press, 1983.

Dhorme, Edouard P. *A Commentary on the Book of Job.* Translated by H. Knight. London: Thomas Nelson, 1967. A reprint of a major study of Job, first published in 1926.

Gordis, Robert. *The Book of God and Man: A Study of Job.* Chicago: University of Chicago Press, 1965.

Habel, Norman C. *The Book of Job.* The Cambridge Bible Commentary. New York: Cambridge University Press, 1975. Offers NEB text and perceptive analysis.

Hone, Ralph E., ed. *The Voice out of the Whirlwind: The Book of Job*. San Francisco: Chandler, 1960. Includes the King James Version of the text of Job and a collection of interpretive essays.

Kallen, H. M. *The Book of Job as a Greek Tragedy*. New York: Moffat, Yard, 1918. A stimulating comparison of Job to the tragedies of Aeschylus and Euripides.

Levenson, Jon D. *Creation and the Persistence of Evil*. San Francisco: Harper & Row, 1988. A lucid study of divine omnipotence and the problem of evil.

MacKenzie, R. A. F., and Murphy, R. E. "Job." In R. E. Brown et al., eds., *The New Jerome Biblical Commentary*, 2nd ed., pp. 466–488. Englewood Cliffs, N.J.: Prentice-Hall, 1990. Offers a more conventional reading of the poem.

Mitchell, Stephen. *The Book of Job*. San Francisco: North Point Press, 1987. A fresh translation and insightful commentary.

Newsom, Carol A. "Job, Book of." In *The New Interpreter's Bible*, Vol. 4, pp. 317–637, Nashville, Tenn.: Abingdon Press, 1996. Includes theological interpretation.

Penchansky, David. *The Betrayal of God: Ideological Conflict in Job*. Literary Currents in Biblical Interpretation. Louisville, Ky.: Westminster/John Knox Press, 1992.

Pope, Marvin H. *Job*. Anchor Bible, 5th ed. Garden City, N.Y.: Doubleday, 1978. A translation with many useful notes.

Sanders, Paul S., ed. *Twentieth-Century Interpretations of the Book of Job: A Collection of Critical Essays*. Englewood Cliffs, N.J.: Prentice-Hall, 1968. Offers a variety of viewpoints.

von Rad, Gerhard. *Wisdom in Israel*. Translated by J. D. Martin. Nashville, Tenn.: Abingdon Press, 1973. An excellent theological study.

CHAPTER 26

Four Books of the Megillot (Festival Scrolls)

Ruth, Lamentations, Song of Songs, and Esther

Key Topics/Themes The five books that make up the Megillot collection — Ruth, Song of Songs, Ecclesiastes, Lamentations, and Esther — have at least one thing in common: They are "Festival Scrolls," traditionally associated with some of the principal religious events of the Jewish calendar (Table 26.1). The practice of reading these books as part of a religious ceremony may date back to the late Second Temple era (first century B.C.E.), which could explain why these books are found grouped together in the Masoretic text of the Hebrew Bible. However, apart from their liturgical function, these five works have little else in common; in fact, they are as diverse as any five books can be. Ruth, for example, a love story set in the time of the judges, allows us to trace the genealogy of King David back to a Moabite woman who embraces Israel and its God. Lamentations is a collection of dirges that lament the destruction of Jerusalem by the Babylonians, and its author explicitly assigns blame for this tragic event to sinful Israel itself. As for Esther, it is a tale of intrigue, courage, and revenge, set in the time of Xerxes I (ruled 486–465 B.C.E.), whose heroine never once appeals to YHWH for help or even mentions his name — not unlike the Song of Songs, a collection of love poems that celebrate the drama of human sexual desire apart from any connection to the Deity or his attachment to Israel. Yet, despite (or possibly because of) this diversity of theme and tone, these books did appeal to Diaspora audiences, which evidently craved something other than prophetic and historical narratives or codes of law. These books speak to some of the deepest human emotions — anxiety, skepticism, grief, and love — and do so within literary genres that set them apart from the rest of the Hebrew canon, giving each work its own distinctive flavor and purpose. (Because it forms an integral part of Israel's wisdom tradition, Ecclesiastes is discussed along with Proverbs and Job in Chapter 25.)

The Book of Ruth

The Book of Ruth is one of the more memorable novellas of the Hebrew Bible, and other than the Book of Esther, it is the only canonical book of the Hebrew Bible whose principal figure is a woman. In fact, two women occupy a central position in this narrative — **Naomi** and her daughter-in-law **Ruth** — and together the relationships they create, with each other and with God, are unprecedented in biblical literature. The importance of the Book of Ruth was recognized even in antiquity; Ruth was read at the Feast of Shavuoth (Pentecost) and was placed first in the Megillot. In the Septuagint, however, Ruth was placed between the Book

Table 26.1   The Megillot and Associated Festivals

Book	Festival
Ruth	**Pentecost**—a late-spring harvest festival
Song of Songs	**Passover**—the annual holiday that commemorates the end of slavery for the Israelites in Egypt
Ecclesiastes	**Feast of Tabernacles,** or *Feast of Booths*—the autumn agricultural feast of thanksgiving
Lamentations	**Fast of the Ninth of Av** (July–August)—a day of mourning for the destruction of the Jerusalem Temple by the Babylonians in 587 B.C.E. and the Romans in 70 C.E.
Esther	**Purim,** or *Festival of Lots* (February–March)—the celebration of Jewish deliverance from Persian attack

of Judges and 1 Samuel, presumably because its story is set in the time of the judges, and that is where most English Bibles place it today.

THE HISTORICAL SETTING: A QUESTION OF INTERMARRIAGE

Placing the story of Ruth and Naomi within the historical setting of the era of the judges is especially problematic for modern readers, because nothing in this book reflects the violence or political turmoil of this period. Relations between Moab and Judah seem peaceful enough for a Judahite family to pass back and forth between Bethlehem and the Moabite midlands without hindrance and without so much as a hint of ethnic or religious hostility. Though Ruth is referred to repeatedly as the "Moabitess," no one in Bethlehem seems to care that she is a foreigner or to object when she marries **Boaz.** Such generosity of spirit is in sharp contrast to the Deuteronomic tradition, which portrays the Moabite and the Ammonite peoples as both inhospitable and totally unacceptable as marriage partners:

> No Ammonite or Moabite shall be admitted to the assembly of the LORD. Even to the tenth generation, none of their descendants shall be admitted to the assembly of the LORD, because they did not meet you with food and water on your journey out of Egypt, and because they hired against you Balaam son of Beor . . . to curse you. You shall never promote their welfare or their prosperity as long as you live. (Deut. 23:3–6)

This contrast in attitudes becomes even more striking when one consults the books of Ezra and Nehemiah, where returning Judahite males are bitterly chided for having married foreign wives or simply ordered to divorce them (Ezra 9–10; Neh. 13:23–27). Such intermarriage clearly was regarded by postexilic writers as an act of treachery against YHWH or as a temptation to apostasy and was repeatedly condemned. Moreover, regional conflict between Israelites and Moabites, like that alluded to in Judges 3, would have made such a union unlikely at best. That King David is described as a descendant of such a union suggests that, for the unknown author of Ruth, the issue of intermarriage was far from a closed issue, in spite of the traditions arrayed against it. Obviously, the author's intent is to elevate the stature of at least one Moabite woman until she ranks as an equal to "Rachel and Leah who together built up the House of Israel" (Ruth 4:11).

RUTH, NAOMI, AND BOAZ

What is even more remarkable about this narrative is its focus on the lives of two obscure women who, beset by misfortune, cling together for mutual support and hope. Indeed, Ruth's profession of loyalty to Naomi is one of the classic biblical expressions of love and devotion between two people:

> Do not press me to leave you
> or to turn back from following you!
> Where you go, I will go;

where you lodge, I will lodge;
your people shall be my people
and your GOD my GOD.
Where you die, I will die —
there I will be buried.
May the LORD do thus and so to me,
and more as well,
if even death parts me from you! (Ruth 1:16–17)

As for Ruth's future husband, the wealthy land-owner Boaz, his goodness and magnanimity are no less extraordinary than Ruth's, and from their first encounter, he displays the exemplary virtues of a pious Israelite male. Following the commandment of God to leave a portion of a field or a vineyard for the poor to glean (harvest or gather from) (Deut. 24:19–21), Boaz generously offers to let Ruth glean in his fields and in no one else's and then exercises a special caution by ordering his young men to leave her alone. When Boaz later discovers Ruth lying by his feet while he sleeps on the threshing floor, he responds with something more than generosity after she informs him that he is a near-kinsman and therefore eligible to marry her. His willingness to wed her no doubt reflects not only his romantic interest in her but also his appreciation of her loyalty and discretion, as well as his perception that she has sought refuge under the "wings" of the Lord God of Israel (Ruth 2:12).

Boaz's behavior at this moment, therefore, embodies two central thematic concerns: the rewards that will come, sooner or later, to those who commit themselves to YHWH's providence, and the importance of *hesed*, or kindness, in all relationships, whether human or divine. In Boaz's view, YHWH has placed Ruth in his care, and he would be remiss in his devotion to the God of Israel if he turned her away or denied the obvious affection he feels for her. This is particularly true in light of the obligation laid on the near-kinsman (the *goel*, or "redeemer," in Hebrew) by the Levirate law, which the Book of Deuteronomy describes in the following way:

When brothers reside together, and one of them dies and has no son, the wife of the deceased shall not be married outside the family to a stranger. Her husband's brother shall go into her, taking her in marriage, and performing the duty of a husband's brother to her, and the firstborn whom she bears shall succeed to the name of the deceased brother, so that his name may not be blotted out in Israel. But if the man has no desire to marry his brother's widow, then his brother's widow shall go up to the elders at the gate. . . . Then the elders of his town shall summon him and speak to him. If he persists, saying, "I have no desire to marry her," then his brother's wife shall go up to him in the presence of the elders, pull his sandal off his foot, spit in his face, and declare, "This is what is done to the man who does not build up his brother's house." Throughout Israel his family shall be known as "the house of him whose sandal was pulled off." (Deut. 25:5–10)

As a potential *goel*, Boaz can act responsibly *and* follow the dictates of his heart, or he can behave as selfishly as the even nearer kinsman who refuses to marry Ruth when the prospect of inheriting Elimelech's property is offered to him. Curiously, nothing is said in Ruth about spitting in anyone's face or removing anyone's sandal as a sign of disgrace. But this nameless relative serves, nevertheless, as an effective foil to Boaz, who gladly performs his duty to God and to the widow with whom he has fallen in love. Nor is the overlapping of motivations here a problem for the author of Ruth; Boaz is allowed to act out of both self-interest and devotion to *torah* without having personal desire undermine or compromise obedience to the law.

That the fruit of this union is pleasing to YHWH is manifestly clear by the end of the story. Boaz has fulfilled his Levirate obligations and found the perfect wife, while Naomi's bitterness has been removed by the birth of a grandson whom neighboring women refer to as *her* son. The culminating proof of divine acceptance of this marriage comes at the very conclusion of the narrative, which reveals, for the first time, just who Ruth really is: the great-grandmother of King David, and therefore the source, along with Boaz, of Israel's greatest dynasty. That a Moabite woman could be the ancestress of Israel's most glorious king is commonly perceived to be an implicit rebuttal to postexilic views of intermarriage and a reminder of the belief that, within the prophetic tradition at least, non-Israelites would one day be called on to declare their allegiance to YHWH. For many scholars, then, the theological subtext of Ruth — its implied universalism and its view of a benevolent deity who quietly and indirectly leads human beings closer to him and toward their own happiness — is even more important than the story of family life that occupies the foreground of the narrative.

STRUCTURE AND DATING

Viewed as a literary composition, the Book of Ruth exhibits numerous signs of artful arrangement and linguistic subtlety. The narrative is divided into two roughly symmetrical parts: The first focuses on the travails of the family of Elimelech, and more specifically on the journey of Naomi and Ruth back to Judah and their adjustment to life there; the second focuses on the unfolding relationship of Ruth and Boaz and on its happy consummation. The unstated premise of both parts of this story is that, though YHWH has taken away, he can restore. Thus, what Naomi and Ruth lost in Moab, they will regain in Judah through the *hesed* of Israel's God and through their mutual devotion. This argument is embodied in narrative form through a series of binary oppositions that define the pattern of three interwoven lives, moving from famine to feasting, from death to life, from widowhood to marriage, and, finally, from bitterness to joy. Within this framework, major characters are realized with extraordinary economy. From just a few deft strokes, for example, we come to understand both Naomi's despair over the loss of her menfolk and her determination to see her daughter-in-law Ruth succeed where she has failed.

Questions surrounding the authorship and date of composition of Ruth, however, have proved far more controversial than views on its literary excellence, and a number of competing hypotheses have arisen to explain why, how, and when Ruth may have been written. Scholars who stress the theme of intermarriage and who focus on Ruth's status as an ethnic outsider tend to favor a postexilic date of composition, seeing the book as a whole as a kind of polemic against a religious establishment (typified by Ezra and Nehemiah) that insists on the nar-rowest view of covenant fellowship and that warns against the threat posed by an apostate (non-Israelite) wife. To bolster their view that Ruth is a comparatively late composition, they cite the presence of words of Aramaic origin, departures from the Deuteronomic tradition, and the general absence of social/historical realism as proof that the author of Ruth lived centuries after the period of the judges and so was able to paint an idealized portrait of that era.

Those who favor an earlier, preexilic, dating of Ruth have found a "classical" Hebrew style present in this work. They even speculate that Ruth may have existed as an oral folktale centuries before any attempt at literary redaction was made, thus giving some credibility to the ancient Jewish tradition that the prophet Samuel was the author of Ruth. In fact, if we compare the account of Hannah's conception of Samuel in the opening chapter of 1 Samuel to that of the conception and birth of Obed in Ruth, we can see why the editors of the Septuagint chose to place the story of Ruth's baby just before the story of Hannah's. Both women are compensated by YHWH for the barrenness and turmoil of theirs lives, and each in her way serves as a model of faith and trust in God.

The Book of Lamentations

Lamentations is the work that is chanted in sorrow when Jews gather each year to mourn the destruction of Jerusalem. According to tradition, the city fell to the Babylonians on August 9, 587 B.C.E., and again on the same day and month to the Romans in 70 C.E. The five poems in this little book vividly express the people's collective grief at the loss of their holy city. Whereas the prophetic books record public pronouncements of doom against the Judean capital, Lamentations (particularly Chs. 2 and 4) embodies the private anguish of individuals who witnessed the fulfillment of YHWH's harsh judgment.

The name "Lamentations" derives from the Greek *Threnoi* and the Latin *Threni*, both of which are translations of the Hebrew title *Qinoth*, meaning "dirges." The more common Hebrew name, however, is *Eikhah,* referring to the opening phrase "How [lonely sits the city]" (1:1). Although Lamentations appears immediately after the Book of Jeremiah in most English editions of the Old Testament, in the Hebrew Tanak, it is placed among the Writings as one of the Megillot (Festival Scrolls).

Probably because Jeremiah is the great prophet of Jerusalem's doom (see Chapter 19), a relatively late tradition attributes Lamentations to him. The book itself does not mention the writer, and many scholars believe that it is the product of two or three anonymous poets, who may have been eyewitnesses to the horrors of the famine, starvation, and slaughter they describe. The oldest poems appear in Chapters 2 and 4, which were written shortly after Nebuchadnezzar's armies besieged and destroyed Jerusalem. Chapters 1 and 3 were composed somewhat later, in the sixth century B.C.E., and Chapter 5 during the postexilic period. Carefully structured, the first four poems are **acrostics:** Each has twenty-two verses, one for each of the twenty-two letters of the Hebrew alphabet, in which the first word of each verse begins with a different letter of the alphabet in sequential order. Chapter 5 also has twenty-two verses, but these are not arranged alphabetically.

From such artful wordplay, it is apparent that Lamentations is not a spontaneous outpouring of emotion, although the poets' feelings run deep and many passages are extremely moving. In Chapter 2, the poet emphasizes both the totality of Jerusalem's ruin and the dehumanization of its population, which hunger has driven to cannibalism:

> Look, O Lord, and consider!
> To whom have you done this?
> Should women eat their offspring,
> the children they have borne?
> Should priest and prophet be killed
> in the sanctuary of the Lord? (Lam. 2:20)

"Slaughtering [Judah's inhabitants] without mercy," YHWH has given his enemies reason to rejoice, while his people are subjected to intolerable conditions (2:21–22).

Adhering to the Deuteronomic assumption, the poets of Chapters 1, 2, and 4 agree that Jerusalem's fall resulted from the people's sins, particularly those of the priests and prophets who had falsely promised deliverance (4:13). Considering the thoroughness and duration of the covenant community's devastation, however, the poets question YHWH's intentions toward his worshipers. Will the extremity of the people's suffering at last move God to show pity?

Writing long after the exile had ended, the author of Chapter 5 reflects on the fact that the people's hardships and suffering continue unabated during a disappointingly inadequate restoration. Still under a foreign yoke, the people are enslaved in their own homeland, relentlessly exploited by taskmasters as harsh as those in Egypt. Facing the paradoxical conflict between prophetic promises and historical reality, the poet wonders aloud if God has permanently abandoned his worshipers and begs for a *genuine* restoration:

> Why have you forgotten us completely?
> Why have you forsaken us these many days?
> Restore us to yourself, O Lord . . .
> renew our days as of old—
> unless you have utterly rejected us . . .
> (Lam. 5:20–21)

The Song of Songs

Referred to variously as the Song of Songs, the Song of Solomon, and Canticles, this collection of love poems is the only example of erotic poetry in the Hebrew Bible. Similar anthologies of love poetry are to be found in Babylon and Egypt, and numerous parallels (of romantic sentiment and imagery) have been drawn between individual poems or metaphors in the biblical Song and corresponding Egyptian and Babylonian poetic traditions. Like other Near Eastern love poets, the author of the Song of Songs celebrates both the exaltation and the anguish of sexual longing and fulfillment, invokes the beauty of nature, and tactfully avoids the subject of marriage. And like its Near Eastern counterparts, the Song of Songs seems to have been written as a secular entertainment.

No scholarly consensus exists today over why the Song of Songs was written or how it made its way into the biblical canon. Though traditionally ascribed to King Solomon (as are Proverbs and Ecclesiastes), the opening verse—"The Song of Songs, which is Solomon's"—could just as well have been translated "which is *for* Solomon." Modern scholars have been inclined to regard this superscription as nothing more than a literary fiction or convention, linking Solomon with the poem. Similarly, references to a "king" or to Solomon himself (Song 8:11) are presumed to be part of a network of associations with Solomon and his court that may well have been responsible for the admission of this volume into the canon as one of the Solomonic wisdom books. But apart from this ancient tradition, no evidence of authorship or even date of composition can be found within the text itself. As a consequence, theories abound as to what the Song of Songs is really about and why these poems were written in the first place.

A CELEBRATION OF EROTIC LOVE

Read simply as an anthology of love lyrics, the Song of Songs can be seen as an unabashed celebration of what Proverbs 30:19 calls "the way of a man with a girl." Not only does the Song of Songs exalt sexual desire, but it draws a varied portrait of young lovers caught up in the sometimes painful longing for the beloved:

> You have ravished my heart, my
>   sister, my bride,
> you have ravished my heart
>   with a glance of your eyes,
> with one jewel of your necklace. (Song 4:9)

Some commentators claim to have found traces of a courtship narrative, binding together the seemingly disconnected verses of this book in the form of an exchange of praises and vows; others prefer to view this volume as an anthology of shifting moods and venues, with the lover and his beloved professing mutual admiration and desire, often in the form of dialogues. That many of these poems seem to presuppose secrecy or separation as the precondition of this love affair may help to explain why love is so often sought but rarely consummated. But no reason is ever given why the lovers cannot profess their love for each other openly or simply resolve their longing for one another in marriage.

One of the more distinctive (and to modern readers, distracting) poetic conventions employed throughout the Song of Songs is the catalogue of sensual delights each of the lovers finds in the other:

> How beautiful you are, my love,
>   how very beautiful!
> Your eyes are doves
>   behind your veil.
> Your hair is like a flock of goats,
>   moving down the slopes of
>   Gilead.
> Your teeth are like a flock of
>   shorn ewes
>   that have come up from the
>   washing,
> all of which bear twins,
>   and not one among them is
>   bereaved.
> Your lips are like a crimson
>   thread
> and your mouth is lovely. (Song 4:1–3)

In later Arabic love poetry, this same rhetorical device is referred to as the *wasf,* and we are obviously dealing here with a poetic tradition that is both ancient and rooted in a consciously stylized form of language. The object of such praise is clearly to magnify the image of the beloved and to suggest that her beauty is all the more precious to her lover because she combines in herself all of the splendors of the natural world. Moreover, any reading of such passages as "your neck is like the tower of David" (Song 4:4) that overlooks the inherent artificiality of this metaphoric tradition is likely to miss the imaginative boldness (and even theatricality) of such comparisons.

FIGURATIVE READINGS OF THE SONGS

Historically, both Christians and Jews have found it theologically expedient to read the Song of Songs as something other than a collection of love poems, and these nonliteral interpretations are often referred to as "allegorical" readings of this text. In the context of early Judaism, the rabbis clearly saw the Song of Songs as God's love song to Israel, in which the desire of the lovers is translated into divine longing for the renewal of Israel's spiritual "intimacy" with YHWH. Adopting a parallel approach to these poems, the early church interpreted them as Christ's love song to the church or, later, his "wooing" of the individual soul.

Both of these interpretive strategies can be seen as extensions of one of the more powerful and recurrent images of the covenant relationship in prophetic literature, the marriage metaphor, in which YHWH is the "husband" to Israel's "bride." In Hosea 2:16, for example, Israel is instructed to address God as "my husband" and to abandon her lovers, and similar statements and images can be found in Jeremiah (2:2; 3:1–2), Isaiah (1:21), and Ezekiel (16:8–43; 23:1–45). At the very least, what such interpretations of these songs presuppose is the existence of multiple levels of meaning in any biblical text — in this case, a partly hidden metaphor of the divine courtship of Israel to which other biblical texts pay explicit homage. There seems little doubt, furthermore, that the allegorical method was employed to silence critics of the Song of Songs who view this poetry simply as sensual and therefore profane.

A similarly nonliteral method of reading is employed by some modern exegetes of the Song of Songs who see in it multiple references to a half-buried cultic ceremony. According to this theory, the Song of Songs originally was a pagan liturgy celebrating the union of a god and goddess as part of a fertility ritual. Only later did it undergo a kind of "demythologization" until it became, at last, a dialogue between human lovers in which a "king" or a shepherd takes the place of a divine suitor. Israelite worship of the "Queen of Heaven" (Jer. 44:17) would seem to give some substance to this rather speculative reconstruction of the prehistory of the Song of Songs, though the poems themselves exhibit no such references. The idea that love songs like these may also have found their way into rural wedding ceremonies — another possible point of origin for this collection — in which the bride and groom recited portions of the Song of Songs as a kind of liturgy, has captured the fancy of a number of biblical translators and editors, though, again, no evidence of such a practice in ancient Israel has yet been unearthed.

GENDER AND COURTSHIP

What may be the most intriguing aspect of the Song of Songs, seen from a contemporary, post-feminist perspective, is the prevalence of the female voice. The Song of Songs is the only book of the Hebrew Bible that foregrounds the feelings of a woman in love and allows her more than equal time to express those feelings with startling candor:

> My beloved thrust his hand into
> the opening,
> and my inmost being yearned
> for him.
> I arose to open to my beloved,
> and my hands dripped with
> myrrh . . . (Song 5:4–5)

That most such expressions are presented from a woman's rather than a man's point of view and that no mention is made anywhere in the poem of the beloved's father — though several references are made to a mother and brothers — suggest to some modern scholars that the probable author of the poems was a woman who shrewdly sought to pass off her work as the youthful utterances of King Solomon, whose many wives no doubt made him seem a romantic figure to later generations. What is certain, however, is that within the dialogue setting of these poems a woman's voice — strong, passionate even, and self-conscious — can be heard for the first and last time in biblical literature.

The Book of Esther

The Book of Esther is commonly viewed today as a historical romance set in the era of Xerxes I, who ruled the Persian Empire from 486 to 465 B.C.E. (Figure 26.1). The Hebrew name assigned to this monarch is **Ahasuerus**, and the unnamed author of Esther spins a tale about a young and beautiful Israelite-in-exile, variously named **Esther** or

Figure 26.1 This bas-relief at Persepolis, the Greek-designed capital of the Persian Empire, shows an enthroned Darius I (522–486 B.C.E.), with his son and successor, Xerxes I (486–465 B.C.E.), standing directly behind him. Both emperors launched ill-fated invasions of Greece, only to be routed by the Athenians and their allies at Marathon (490 B.C.E.) and Salamis (480 B.C.E.).

Hadassah, who enters Ahasuerus's harem upon the disgrace (and presumed divorce) of the reigning queen, **Vashti.** Esther's uncle **Mordecai,** a devout Jew and shrewd counselor to his niece, also plays a major role in this story, as does a royal advisor to the king named **Haman,** whose hatred of Mordecai nearly spells disaster for all of the Jews living within the Persian Empire. With the exception of Ahasuerus, these characters apparently all were fictional creations, and the story of their intertwined lives seems to have been conceived as a patriotic fiction, designed to strengthen the resolve of the Diaspora Jewish community to withstand the hostility of their non-Jewish neighbors and hope for a brighter and more secure future in the land of their exile.

As a Festival Scroll, the Book of Esther provides the "script" for the minor festival of Purim. The very name of this festival — possibly derived from the Babylonian word *puru,* meaning "lots" — points to the episode in the Book of Esther in which Haman draws lots to determine the date on which the Jews of Persia are to be massacred (3:7). It has been theorized that the entire book was conceived as a means of providing a pseudohistorical setting for an often bacchanalian celebration of nationalist sentiments within the Persian Jewish community. The decision to include the Book of Esther within the biblical canon did not go unchallenged in antiquity, and given the largely secular nature of this narrative — the Hebrew version of Esther does not refer to God even once — one can easily understand why later religious authorities were troubled by its status as a "holy" book. Undoubtedly, the popularity of the festival itself ensured that the book pre-

serving the festival narrative would survive and ultimately attain canonical status.

HISTORY INTO FICTION

As a work of the historical imagination, Esther interweaves some reliable information about the Persian Empire during the fifth century B.C.E. with a melodramatic tale of imminent catastrophe and redemption. Much of the historical background of this tale appears to have been taken from secondary sources like Herodotus's *History* (which was written in the fifth century B.C.E.) and other books that would have provided a fairly accurate account of Persian names and court customs, but some of the "data" provided by the author of Esther clearly are inaccurate and seem to be the product of his imagination. Thus, we have no historical record of a Persian queen named Vashti, nor of any queen of Jewish descent named Esther. The Persian Empire consisted of 20, and not 127, provinces (Figure 26.2); and it does not appear that any Persian monarch ever gave an order to massacre his Jewish subjects or to allow them, in turn, to massacre their would-be murderers. Indeed, the numbers of Persians killed during the final attack on the Jewish community is so large (75,000 according to Esther 9:16) that it seems quite unlikely that any contemporary or later Persian historian would have neglected to mention it. As for Esther herself, even if she had been eligible to marry the king in the first place — and the only reliable information we possess on that subject suggests that Ahasuerus's bride would have been chosen from the Persian nobil-

Figure 26.2   This bas-relief depicts a Persian satrap, or governor. The Persians divided their enormous empire into twenty administrative units called satrapies, each locally autonomous but ruled by the emperor's appointed governor. As the books of Ezra, Nehemiah, and Esther reveal, some upper-class Jews, including those from priestly families, rose to influential positions within the Persian administration. Because the Persians did not permit the restoration of the Davidic royal line, many priests assumed leadership roles in postexilic Judah.

ity—she would have had to have been almost a hundred years old to have been taken into exile during the period of Nebuchadnezzar, and therefore not likely to have dazzled the king with her beauty.

Some scholars suggest that the real origin of the story of Esther is to be found in myth rather than in fictionalized history, and they have pointed to a resemblance between the names Esther and **Ishtar,** the Babylonian goddess of love and war, and between Mordecai and **Marduk,** the most powerful of the Babylonian warrior-deities, as proof of a mythic subtext in Mordecai's confrontation with Haman. According to this hypothesis, the story of Esther's exposure and triumph over Haman is really (symbolically) the triumph of Marduk over his supernatural enemies, represented in the Esther narrative by Haman and his ten sons, all of whom are hanged. And the fact that YHWH is never referred to, or cited as the source of the Jews' deliverance, merely

reinforces the impression that the remote origins of the Esther story are to be found outside Israelite religion and folklore altogether. At the conclusion of the book, reference is made to the "annals of the kings of Media and Persia" (10:2), a nonextant work whose existence is attested to only in this passage and whose content can only be guessed at. Still, the fact that the author of Esther even alludes to this "lost" book suggests the presence of other, outside, sources for this narrative that we can no longer access today.

SURVIVAL IN THE DIASPORA

Whatever its ultimate sources may have been, the Book of Esther, like the Book of Daniel, tells a story of survival against the odds within a Diaspora culture that, at first, seems strangely inhospitable to its Jewish subjects. Though we have no evidence of any concerted action or discriminatory policy against the Jews during the Persian period (extending roughly from 539 B.C.E. to the era of Alexander's conquests of the Middle East in 334 B.C.E.), both Daniel and Esther express deep anxiety over the fate of Jews for whom total assimilation and subsequent loss of religious identity is not an option. The Hellenistic era witnessed a heightening of these fears, largely as a result of the encroachments of Hellenism on second-century-B.C.E. Judaism and the overt hostility of Antiochus IV (see Chapter 28 for a discussion of the Maccabean Revolt). But the Book of Esther suggests that fear of persecution may well have preceded the reality by 200 to 300 years.

Interestingly, in both Daniel and Esther, it is the individual of piety or courage (or both) who champions the cause of his or her people and faith. Mordecai's remark to Esther that her ascent to royalty may have been calculated for "just such a time as this" (Esther 4:14) underscores this theme and hints discreetly at a belief in the providential intervention of heroic personalities at a time of crisis — a belief that goes back to the Book of Judges. The Book of Esther makes no explicit reference to the issue of religious loyalty (though Esther does request that the Jews of Susa fast on her behalf [4:16], and fasting is generally construed in the Hebrew Bible to be a form of petitionary prayer to YHWH), but this does not exclude the possibility that a potential loss of both faith and national identity weighed heavily on the minds of Jewish writers from the fourth century B.C.E. right up to the Maccabean Revolt of 164 B.C.E. And if we establish a probable date of composition (and later redaction) for both Esther and Daniel that is no earlier than this window of time, then a strong argument can be made that both books (or at least the first six chapters of Daniel) are examples of a peculiar postexilic genre, the **Diaspora novella,** as some scholars have termed it, whose principal themes are loyalty to YHWH and collective preservation through heroic action. The Greek version of the Book of Esther, in contrast to the earlier Hebrew text, does mention God's name repeatedly, and in that version of the narrative Esther emerges as a heroine of faith and valor.

Unlike Judith, the heroine of the deuterocanonical book that bears her name, Esther does not assume the role of female warrior, nor is she required (like Jael in Judges 4:17–22) to drive a stake through Haman's head or heart. Esther's weapons are those of the courtier, and it is by virtue of her beauty and the clever manipulation of her enemy that she is able to save her people from certain disaster. Her heroism, like that of Daniel (to whom she is so often compared), is the heroism of an uprooted minority that must live by its wits in a world where power is permanently in the hands of others and where dreams of national restoration and empowerment have no place.

QUESTIONS FOR REVIEW

1. What do the books of the Megillot have in common, and why were they grouped together as a literary unit in the Masoretic Text?

2. How do Ruth and Esther display initiative in a world dominated by men? Are their actions truly heroic or merely resourceful?

3. Why was a book of erotic poetry — namely, the Song of Songs — incorporated into the biblical canon? Is its subject matter far too secular for a collection of sacred writings?

QUESTIONS FOR REFLECTION AND DISCUSSION

1. Why did the writers of the Megillot, like their counterparts in the wisdom tradition, focus so intently on human subjects, intimate feelings, and individual personalities? Are these books more humanistic in their outlook than books of prophecy and sacred poetry?

2. What kind of audience would have found a Diaspora novella like Esther inspiring, or a collection of love poems like the Song of Songs entertaining? Would the same audience have read Lamentations with equal pleasure?

TERMS AND CONCEPTS TO REMEMBER

acrostics	Marduk
Ahasuerus (Xerxes I)	Mordecai
Boaz	Naomi
Diaspora novella	Passover
Esther	Purim
Fast of the Ninth of Ab	Ruth
Feast of Tabernacles	Shavuoth (Pentecost)
Haman	Vashti
Ishtar	

RECOMMENDED READING

Ruth

Brenner, Athalya, ed. *A Feminist Companion to Ruth.* Sheffield, England: Sheffield Academic Press, 1993.

Campbell, Edward F. *Ruth.* Anchor Bible. Garden City, N.Y.: Doubleday, 1975.

Lamentations

Dobbs-Allsopp, F. W. *Weep, O Daughter of Zion: A Study of the City Lament Genre in the Hebrew Bible.* Rome: Pontifical Institute Press, 1993.

Glatt-Gilad, David A. "Lamentations." In Paul J. Achtemeier, ed., *The HarperCollins Bible Dictionary,* pp. 587–588. San Francisco: HarperSanFrancisco, 1996. A helpful introduction that emphasizes parallels to other ancient Near Eastern dirges and laments.

Provan, Iain W. *Lamentations.* New Century Bible Commentary. Grand Rapids, Mich.: Eerdmans, 1991. An informative commentary.

Westermann, Claus. *Lamentations: Issues and Interpretation.* Translated by C. Muenchow. Minneapolis, Minn.: Fortress, 1994. An insightful study.

Song of Songs

Bloch, Ariel, and Blach, Chana. *The Song of Songs with an Introduction and Commentary.* New York: Random House, 1995.

Brenner, Athalya, ed. *A Feminist Companion to Song of Songs.* Sheffield, England: Sheffield Academic Press, 1993.

Gordis, Robert. *The Song of Songs and Lamentations,* rev. ed. New York: KTAV, 1974.

Murphy, Roland E. "Song of Songs, Book of." In D. N. Freedman, ed., *The Anchor Bible Dictionary,* Vol. 6, pp. 150–155. New York: Doubleday, 1992.

Pope, Marvin. *The Song of Songs.* Anchor Bible. Garden City, N.Y.: Doubleday.

Esther

Berg, Sandra B. *The Book of Esther.* Chico, Calif.: Scholars Press, 1979.

Craig, Kenneth. *Reading Esther: A Case for the Literary Carnivalesque.* Louisville, Ky.: Westminster/John Knox Press, 1995.

Moore, Carey. *Esther.* Anchor Bible. Garden City, N.Y.: Doubleday, 1975.

CHAPTER 27

Reinterpreting Israel's History

The Books of 1 and 2 Chronicles

Key Topics/Themes Because the restoration of Judah following the return from exile was only partial and still incomplete — the Davidic monarchy was not reestablished and Judah remained under foreign control — it became desirable to reevaluate Israel's past in terms of what the covenant community had actually become in the postexilic era. Based largely on 1 and 2 Kings, the books of Chronicles retell Israelite history from a priestly vantage point, portraying the Davidic monarchs as primarily forerunners of the priestly aristocracy that administered the Second Temple.

The Chronicler: A Priestly Revisionist

Recognizing that YHWH, Lord of history, had drastically changed the direction of Israel's historical development, postexilic writers undertook the necessary task of reinterpreting the covenant community's past to depict it as a prologue to their unexpectedly diminished present. A century or two after the exiles' return to Judea, an anonymous scribe known as the **Chronicler** again surveyed Israelite history, this time concentrating on the center of national worship, the Jerusalem Temple. For the Chronicler, Israel's destiny was not necessarily to exercise political power on the world stage but to promote YHWH's cult with ethical and ritual purity — a revisionist view that historical events seemed to validate. Most of the promises made to Israel's ancestors in Genesis, particularly those for a secure homeland and a line of kings, no longer seemed attainable. YHWH had permanently re-

moved both the Davidic monarchy and Judah's political freedom. Almost all that remained was a belief in the divine presence, symbolized by the Holy of Holies in the rebuilt Temple.

AUTHORSHIP

Because of their generally consistent priestly orientation, the four books of 1 and 2 Chronicles, Ezra, and Nehemiah are commonly assigned to the same writer. Recently, however, many scholars have disputed the claim that the same person — the Chronicler — was responsible for all four narratives, pointing to differences in attitude and theology that distinguish Ezra and Nehemiah from the two books of Chronicles. Although some scholars argue that the same priestly redactor provided the final editing of all four volumes, preserving older material that differed from his viewpoint and adding commentary to impart thematic unity, more recently, a majority of scholars have concluded that the author of Chronicles was different from that of

326

Ezra-Nehemiah. The prominence he gives to the Levites in their role as Temple singers and functionaries certainly suggests that he belonged to that group.

SOURCES AND THEMES

The books of 1 and 2 Chronicles are largely rewrites of Samuel and Kings, but with a significant change in emphasis. Instead of portraying David and Solomon as creators of a powerful — though short-lived — Israelite kingdom, the Chronicler depicts them as priest-kings whose main concern was always the building, furnishing, and maintenance of the Jerusalem Temple. The stream of Israel's history thus flows, not toward the goal of political success and status in the international arena, but toward the properly regulated liturgy at the Jerusalem sanctuary — a religious mission that could be carried out regardless of Judea's postexilic lack of political autonomy (2 Chron. 35:16–19; 36:22–23).

The Chronicler draws mainly from 2 Samuel and 1 and 2 Kings, although he also borrows genealogical lists from the Pentateuch and passages from various psalms to fill out his account. In addition to his canonical sources, the writer also refers to otherwise unknown documents, such as the "records of the seer Samuel, . . . the records of the prophet Nathan, and . . . the records of the seer Gad" (1 Chron. 29:29–30; see also references to Solomon's archives [2 Chron. 9:29] and those of Hezekiah [2 Chron. 32:32]). Although the Chronicler may have utilized some historically reliable material not included in the Deuteronomistic History, it is now impossible to verify the historicity of his extensive interpolations, such as descriptions of Hezekiah's religious reforms (2 Chron. 29–31) or Manasseh's alleged repentance (2 Chron. 33). As many commentators have observed, the embellished account of Manasseh's sins, his deportation to Babylon, and the purification of the Jerusalem cult after his return to Jerusalem exactly parallel what happened to Judah. In the Chronicler's revisions, Manasseh comes to embody the covenant people's collective experience, that of a sinner redeemed by suffering and repentance.

The two parts of Chronicles were originally one volume, until the Septuagint editors divided the work into two scrolls titled *Paralipomenon,* meaning "what was omitted" — that is, information not previously included in the books of Samuel and Kings. When translating the Vulgate, Jerome called the work *Chronicon,* the Latin name from which the English title is derived. This closely approximates the Hebrew title, *Dibre Hayamim,* which means "annals" (literally, "the book of acts of days").

Unlike the books of Kings, 1 and 2 Chronicles do not offer a parallel account of the monarchies of the divided kingdoms of Israel and Judah. By the Chronicler's era, expectations for a reunion of the two nations had probably died out, and the history of the northern kingdom seemed no longer relevant. Focusing almost exclusively on Judah's story, the author refers to Israel only when it concerns Judean affairs.

The Book of 1 Chronicles

First Chronicles devotes the first nine chapters to a survey of world history — all in the form of an extensive genealogy that begins with Adam and ends with a list of prominent Judeans (particularly Levites) who returned from the Babylonian captivity to Jerusalem (1:1–9:34). The narrative proper opens with a negative evaluation of Saul's reign, encapsulated in a brief account of the king's visit to the medium of En-dor and his ensuing death, which serves as a foil for the divine blessings heaped on Saul's successor, David. The book's remaining twenty chapters are largely an uncritical celebration of David's accomplishments, illustrating the principle that faithfulness to YHWH brings divine favor and national success.

In Chapters 11–29, David is portrayed not as a military and administrative leader (as he is in 1 and 2 Samuel) but essentially as a religionist whose reign is devoted to supervising elaborate preparations for the Temple that his heir, Solomon, will later build in Jerusalem. David is thus shown as eagerly contributing to the sanctuary's financial support and recruiting the artisans and musicians necessary for its construction and liturgy. In his revisionist view of David's career, the Chronicler introduces a number of significant changes in his Deuteronomistic sources; his innovations include the following:

- Making Saul's failure as king a divine judgment caused by his visit to the necromancer of Endor, an obvious betrayal of the Yahwist cult (10:13–14)
- Having David proclaimed king over all Israel at Hebron (12:23–40), whereas historically only the tribe of Judah acknowledged him there (cf. 2 Sam. 2)
- Interpolating a long prayer given by David when he brings the Ark of the Covenant to Jerusalem, thus clothing the monarch in priestly garb (1 Chron. 16:7–36)
- Insisting that David contributed enormous sums of gold toward building the Temple, thereby providing a good example to later Judeans (22:14–16; 28:14–19).
- Stating that David was responsible for assigning the Levites — cantors, gatekeepers, and bakers — their Temple duties, thus making a direct connection between the Davidic monarchy and the later Temple liturgy
- Asserting that David determined the plans, furnishings, and functions of the Temple and that Solomon merely carried them out (28:1–31)
- Removing all references to David's misdeeds, including his adultery with Bathsheba and responsibility for Uriah's murder
- Attributing to David a final speech in which he urges generous financial support for the construction and upkeep of the Temple (29:1–10)
- Implying that David transferred the reigns of power to Solomon while he was still alive and that Solomon ascended the throne without opposition (29:22–28)
- Substituting Satan for YHWH as the source of David's decision to make a census of the people, thereby removing from God the moral responsibility for this act (21:1; cf. 2 Sam. 24:1)

RETOUCHING ROYAL PORTRAITS

In portraying David as primarily a proto-priestly organizer of future Temple liturgy, the Chronicler not only omits any reference to the king's adulteries and murderous plotting but also deletes from the record such violent actions as David's ruthless elimination of Saul's heirs. Ignoring Absalom's revolt against his father, as well as other rebellions and palace intrigues that shadowed the later years of David's administration, the Chronicler allows Solomon to mount Israel's throne without having to shed a brother's blood (1 Chron. 29:22–28).

As his revisions of the Deuteronomistic History indicate, the Chronicler's purpose is not to compose a historically accurate narrative or to provide fresh insights into David and Solomon (whose questionable conduct he consistently ignores) but to insist that, from the inception of the Davidic monarchy, Judah's principal mission was to worship YHWH wholeheartedly and according to precise *torah* rituals. In the second half of his narrative, he demonstrates that the failure of Judean kings to enforce correct worship at the Jerusalem Temple led to the monarchy's demise. In addition to showing how royal faithlessness and lack of zeal for YHWH's sanctuary contributed to the nation's downfall, the Chronicler blames the people as a whole for their religious errors (cf. 2 Chron. 36:14), an element missing from the Deuteronomistic History, which places responsibility for Judah's collapse squarely on Manasseh's shoulders (2 Kings 24:3–4). By extending responsibility to the entire community for causing the national disaster, the writer hopes to rouse his postexilic audience from its collective apathy and rekindle zealous communal participation in the national worship at Jerusalem.

The Book of 2 Chronicles

The Chronicler's second volume begins by enthusiastically describing the glories of Solomon's reign and ends by summarizing the text of Cyrus's decree mandating the return of all Judean expatriates to

Jerusalem. Although he includes a description of the conflict between Solomon's heir Rehoboam and the rebel Jeroboam that led to the division between Judah and Israel, he does not — unlike 2 Kings — provide a parallel account of the two kingdoms' monarchies. By the Chronicler's era, expectations for a reunion of the two nations had probably died out and the history of the northern kingdom no longer seemed relevant. Focusing on Judah's story, the author refers to Israel only when it concerns Judean affairs.

FROM SOLOMON TO HEZEKIAH

The first nine chapters recount the splendors of Solomon's legendary wealth and ambitious building projects, highlighting the construction, ceremonial dedication, and divine consecration of the Temple (Figure 27.1). As he had idealized David, so the author portrays Solomon in a consistently positive light, retaining nothing of 2 Kings' criticism of the monarch's later reign (2 Chron. 1–9; cf. 2 Kings 11). The Chronicler does, however, preserve the earlier account of the confrontation between Rehoboam and the rebellious northern tribes that withdraw from the Davidic realm when the new king refuses to modify his harsh policies. To emphasize the link between the monarch's fidelity to YHWH and his political fortunes, the writer creates an expanded version of Pharaoh Shishak's invasion of Judah and looting of the Temple treasury, humiliating results of Rehoboam's having "abandoned the law of the LORD" (2 Chron. 12:1–12).

After the split between Judah and Israel, the Chronicler rapidly scans the line of Judean rulers, pausing to elaborate on the reigns of four kings whose religious policies he endorses — Asa, Jehoshaphat, Hezekiah, and Josiah. Expansively rewriting Kings' story of Hezekiah, the author devotes four chapters (Chs. 29–32) to the king's religious reforms, presenting them in a way that anticipates Josiah's later and more thorough centralization of the Jerusalem cult. Portrayed as a zealous enforcer of the "one God, one sanctuary" ideal, Hezekiah makes a clean sweep of all rival shrines outside the capital, smashing their sacred objects.

Figure 27.1 The Hebrew inscription on this pottery fragment, which dates from the eighth or seventh century B.C.E., refers to the "gold of Ophir." According to the books of Kings and Chronicles, King Solomon imported vast quantities of this precious metal from Ophir, famous for the high quality of its gold. Although Egyptian documents also refer to Ophir, its location, perhaps somewhere in eastern Africa, is now unknown.

He is also depicted as conducting extensive Temple renovations and instituting a nationwide Passover celebration, even dispatching envoys to the northern tribal territories (by then under Assyrian occupation), inviting all to participate in the Jerusalem rites (Ch. 30). Using phrases almost identical to those the Deuteronomistic History applied to Josiah, the Chronicler states that "since the time of Solomon . . . there had been nothing like this in Jerusalem" (30:26; cf. 35:18 and 2 Kings 23: 22–23).

MANASSEH'S SINS AND REPENTANCE

Between the approved reigns of Hezekiah and Josiah came that of **Manasseh,** whose forty-five-year reign exceeded that of any other ruler of Judah or Israel. The Chronicler agrees with the Deuteronomistic History on Manasseh's "abominable" crimes, which include burning his son as a religious sacrifice, but then adds that this practitioner of "evil" underwent a remarkable conversion, an event about which 2 Kings is entirely silent. According to 2 Chronicles 33, after the Assyrians imprison Manasseh in Babylon, the former sorcerer suddenly turns to YHWH, who pardons the repentant king and restores him to his Judean throne (although the writer does not explain how this astonishing reversal occurs). Safely back in Jerusalem, Manasseh initiates religious reform, cleansing the Temple of the foreign shrines he previously installed there and rebuilding YHWH's altar. The Chronicler states that a copy of the prayer by which Manasseh persuades YHWH to rescue him is preserved in the "annals of the seers" (or, in some manuscripts, the "annals of Hozai" [2 Chron. 33:19]). The document called the Prayer of Manasseh and included in the Apocrypha is not the same work to which the Chronicler refers (see Chapter 29).

Perhaps the most striking addition that the Chronicler makes to this narrative of Judah's last Davidic kings is his innovative retelling of the circumstances surrounding King Josiah's death. After following 2 Kings' account of Josiah's thoroughgoing reforms — and a greatly expanded description of Josiah's Passover observances in Jerusalem — the writer inserts an episode featuring a dramatic confrontation between Josiah and Pharaoh Necho. Leading Egyptian armies through Judah's territory en route to rescuing the last remnants of Assyria's empire at Carchemish, Necho is — astoundingly — depicted as a prophet of YHWH who sends messengers to warn Josiah that the pharaoh is actually carrying out God's orders. Understandably refusing to see Necho as speaking "from the mouth of God," Josiah intercepts the pharaoh's troops, is shot by archers, and, fatally wounded, is brought back to Jerusalem to die (2 Chron. 35:20–24). Apparently unable to accept the fact that the Davidic monarch most conspicuously effective in reestablishing YHWH's worship was struck down while bravely defending his homeland, the Chronicler felt compelled to provide a reason for Josiah's untimely death — he failed to recognize the foreign invader as YHWH's oracle!

Whereas the Deuteronomistic historian portrays Josiah as faultless and blames Manasseh's sins for Judah's fall to Babylon (2 Kings 23:24–28), the Chronicler, strangely, exonerates Manasseh by granting him repentance and then ascribes the abrupt termination of Josiah's praiseworthy reforms to the king's inability to hear YHWH's voice in an unlikely — and biblically unprecedented — source. Adhering to Deuteronomy's theory of history even while freely revising the Deuteronomistic narratives, the Chronicler insists on an inflexible law of error and punishment.

THE PLACEMENT OF CHRONICLES IN THE CANON

Although the events that 2 Chronicles narrates took place before those recorded in Ezra and Nehemiah, editors chose to accord the books of Chronicles the climactic end position in the Hebrew Bible. In thus arranging the postexilic historical narratives out of chronological sequence, the editors had Cyrus — whom Second Isaiah identified as YHWH's "Messiah," or Anointed One (Isa. 45:1) — utter the last words heard in the biblical canon. Whereas the Hebrew Bible's first speaker is God — commanding the world into existence — its final speaker is a mortal, a non-Israelite leader whose decree brings the covenant community back into existence, restoring YHWH's people to their Promised Land. A Gentile conqueror who espouses the Judean cause and authorizes rebuilding its fallen Temple, the Persian emperor acts within the human realm to accomplish the divine will. Cyrus, to whom "the LORD [YHWH], the God of heaven, has given . . . all the kingdoms of the earth," calls on Jews scattered throughout the world to reassemble in Jerusalem: "Whoever is among you of all his people, . . . Let him go up!" (2 Chron. 36:22–23).

QUESTIONS FOR REVIEW

1. Why did a postexilic writer compose a new history of the covenant community, 1 and 2 Chronicles, that largely duplicates the material in 1 and 2 Kings? What theological goal motivated the Chronicler to produce a revised edition of Judean history?

2. List some of the significant changes the Chronicler made in reediting his primary source, the Deuteronomistic History. How did this author reinterpret the reigns of David and Solomon? What changes did he make in describing the reigns of Manasseh and Josiah?

3. From a postexilic viewpoint, what religious institution in Judea was the most important facet of the partly restored covenant community? How did the Chronicler regard the transition from monarchy to priestly administration of the covenant people?

4. What historical figure made Judah's restoration possible? What imperial power controlled Judea between about 539 and 330 B.C.E.?

QUESTIONS FOR REFLECTION AND DISCUSSION

1. Why did YHWH not restore the covenant people as an independent political state as in the days of King David? Why was the Davidic monarchy not restored in fulfillment of YHWH's unconditional promise in 2 Samuel 7 and Psalm 89?

2. In what ways did Judea's postexilic leadership reevaluate and revise the covenant community's primary function? Do you think that YHWH's purpose was better served by an administration of priests than it was by Davidic rulers?

TERMS AND CONCEPTS TO REMEMBER

Chronicler
Cyrus's decree
Josiah's encounter with
    Pharaoh Necho
Manasseh

postexilic theocracy
repatriation of Judean
    exiles
revisions in Manasseh's
    biography

RECOMMENDED READING

Ackroyd, Peter R. *The Chronicler in His Age.* JSOT Supplement Series, 101. Sheffield, England: JSOT Press, 1991.

Allen, Leslie C. "The First and Second Books of Chronicles." In *The New Interpreter's Bible,* Vol. 3, pp. 299–659. Nashville, Tenn.: Abingdon Press, 1999.

Klein, Ralph W. "Chronicles, Book of 1–2." In D. N. Freedman, ed., *The Anchor Bible Dictionary,* Vol. 1, pp. 992–1002. New York: Doubleday, 1992.

Meyers, Jacob M. *1 Chronicles.* Garden City, N.Y.: Doubleday, 1965.

———. *2 Chronicles.* Garden City, N.Y.: Doubleday, 1965.

Noth, Martin. *The Chronicler's History.* JSOT Supplement Series, 50. Sheffield, England: JSOT Press, 1987.

CHAPTER 28

Keeping Torah in a Hostile World

The Diaspora, the Maccabean Revolt, Apocalypticism, and the Visions of Daniel

Key Topics/Themes In the aftermath of the destruction of Jerusalem in 587 B.C.E. and the deportation of thousands of Judeans to Babylonia, a new social and institutional reality began to emerge among Judeans in exile: the creation of established communities of Judeans (later to be called "Jews") living permanently outside the land of Israel. During the centuries that followed, and in spite of the return to Judah by some portion of the exiled Judean community, these **Diaspora** populations of Babylonia, Egypt, Syria, North Africa, and Asia Minor continued to grow. By the first century of the common era, significant numbers of Jews could be found scattered throughout the Mediterranean and the Middle East.

This novel situation demanded both resourcefulness and a measure of group solidarity, as Diaspora Jews were faced with the seemingly contradictory task of assimilating successfully to their new environment while remaining true to their ancestral faith. As long as the Temple in Jerusalem stood, Diaspora communities were obliged to contribute funds to its upkeep and periodically to make pilgrimages on one or more of the major festival days. By demanding a degree of cultural (and, more specifically, religious) autonomy within the societies in which they lived, Diaspora Jews sought to limit the influence of first Babylonian and then Persian and Hellenistic civilizations on their way of life by preserving and then redacting their sacred literature. During this postexilic era, however, Jews

living in the Diaspora faced, for the first time, a type of hostility directed at them by their "host culture," a hatred based on the perception that they constituted an alien and unassimilable social entity, thereby representing a threat to that society. Or, as Haman describes the Jews to Ahasuerus, emperor of Persia, in the Book of Esther: "There is a certain people scattered and separated among the peoples in all the provinces of your kingdom; their laws are different from those of every other people, and they do not keep the king's laws, so that it is not appropriate for the king to tolerate them" (3:8).

It is against this backdrop of perceived cultural distance and the threat of collective violence against Jews by their more powerful enemies that we must consider both the impact of the Maccabean Revolt and the growth of apocalypticism in the second century B.C.E. For those who longed for the reestablishment of an independent Jewish kingdom, the victories of the Maccabees must have seemed the fulfillment of a long-deferred dream, but the instability of the Hasmonean dynasty that followed and the growing presence of Roman power in the eastern Mediterranean clearly convinced others that nothing less than direct divine intervention would assure the preservation of a *torah*-centered Israel or bring to an end the precarious and endangered existence of the very Diaspora communities for whom the Book of Daniel was written.

332

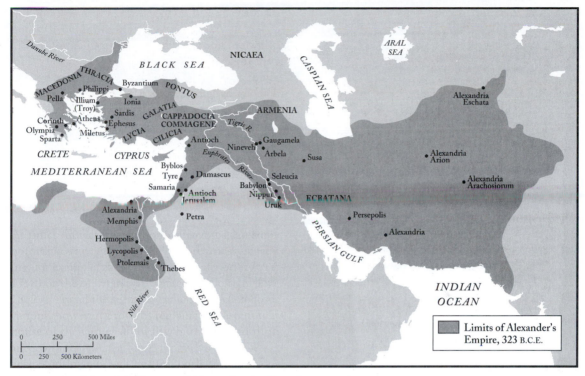

Figure 28.1   Map of the Empire of Alexander the Great (323 B.C.E.)

Judaism Versus Hellenism

While the Persian Empire lasted (539–330 B.C.E.), the Jews of *Yehud*—the Persian name for Judah—enjoyed a comparatively uneventful existence, living under the political authority of provincial governors and under the religious authority of their own High Priests. This situation changed dramatically in the late fourth century with the appearance of Alexander the Great (356–323 B.C.E.), whose lightning conquests of Greece, Persia, Egypt, Afghanistan, and western India enabled him to amass the largest empire the world had ever seen (Figure 28.1). Alexander's untimely death at the age of thirty-two led to the dismemberment of his empire, with huge segments controlled by his successors (Table 28.1). At first, **Palestine**—the name by which Greek geographers knew Judah and its surrounding territo-

ries—was ruled by the **Ptolemies,** a successor dynasty that ruled Egypt for three centuries. But in 199 B.C.E., the **Seleucids,** who ruled Syria and whose empire extended from Asia Minor to Mesopotamia, seized control of what was formerly the land of Israel (Figure 28.2).

But whether the Jews found themselves living under Ptolemaic or Seleucid authority, the dominant culture to which they were exposed was a globalized form of Greek culture known as **Hellenism**—a general term designating the arts, philosophy, and religious practices of Greek-speaking peoples throughout the lands conquered by Alexander. Many Jews, particularly the wealthy and socially prominent, found Hellenistic civilization quite attractive and willingly embraced Greek values and lifestyles, often by blending Hellenistic and Judaic cultural traits. One obvious example of this synthesis of cultures is to be found in the translation of

Table 28.1   Hellenistic Successors of Alexander the Great (336–323 B.C.E.)

| Approximate Date B.C.E. | Rulers over Palestine | | Events in Judah |
	Egypt (Ptolemies)	Syria (Seleucids)	
323	Ptolemy I Lagi (323–285)		
		Seleucus I (312–280)	
300			
	Ptolemy II Philadelphus (285–246); Alexandrine Jews begin translation of the Torah and Prophets (Septuagint Bible)		
		Antiochus I (280–261)	
		Antiochus II (261–246)	Judah under Ptolemaic control
250			
	Ptolemy III Euergetes (246–221)	Seleucus II (246–226)	
		Seleucus III (226–223)	
		Antiochus III (223–187)	
	Ptolemy IV Philopator (221–203)		
200	Ptolemy V Epiphanes (203–181)	Seleucids capture Palestine (200–198/197)	Judah under Seleucid control
	Ptolemy VI Philometer (181–146)	Seleucus IV (187–175)	Persecution of Jews; desecration of the Temple (168 or 167)
		Antiochus IV Epiphanes (175–163)	
		Antiochus V (163–162)	Maccabean revolt under Mattathias (d. 166) and Judas Maccabeus (d. 160); rededication of the Temple (165 or 164)
150		Demetrius I (162–150	
			Judah independent under Hasmoneans (142–63)

some portion of the Hebrew Bible (presumably, at first, the Pentateuch) into Greek—a translation known as the **Septuagint**—which was undoubtedly done as a concession to Greek-speaking Egyptian Jews whose Hebrew skills were too poor to allow them to read their Scriptures in their original language (see Chapter 2). The practice of assigning Greek names to Jewish children, in Palestine as well as in the Diaspora, is another clear sign of cultural adaptation to and assimilation into Hellenistic society (Figure 28.3).

The Maccabean Revolt and Its Aftermath

However, the Jewish response to Hellenistic culture was never universally positive, and with the ascent of **Antiochus IV Epiphanes** (ruled 175–163 B.C.E.) to the Seleucid throne, the relationship between Jews and their Greek-Syrian overlords degenerated into open conflict. Historians have long speculated on the motives behind Antiochus's sud-

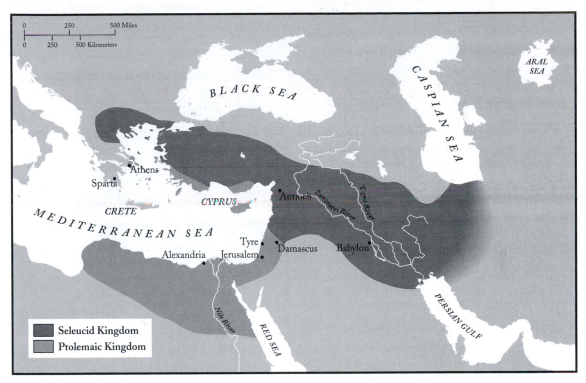

Figure 28.2   Map of the Seleucid and Ptolemaic Kingdoms After Alexander's death in 323 B.C.E., his vast empire was divided among his military successors. General Ptolemy assumed control of Egypt, while another general, Seleucus, ruled Syria and Mesopotamia. The Ptolemaic and Seleucid dynasties repeatedly fought each other for control of Palestine.

den and violent persecution of the Jews of **Judea** (as that portion of southern Palestine having Jerusalem at its geographical center was later known). Military reversals in his war against the Ptolemies and a growing need for funds seem to have prompted him, in 167 B.C.E., to undertake a policy of "forced Hellenization," which included destroying copies of the Torah, barring circumcisions, preventing Jews from observing the Sabbath and other festivals, and, most important, seizing the Temple and its treasury. The Judean response was not long in coming.

The Maccabean Revolt, as the armed Judean rebellion against Antiochus and his policies is commonly known today, began later that year in the village of Modein, not far from Jerusalem, when a

local priest named Mattathias and his sons killed both a royal commissioner and a Jew who had agreed to sacrifice to the Greek gods. Gathering an army of loyal Jews around him, Mattathias's eldest son, Judah (known as the "Maccabee" or [God's] "Hammer"), undertook a guerilla-style military campaign against numerically superior Seleucid forces. After several decisive victories, he was able to retake most of Jerusalem and the Temple, three years to the day (according to Jewish tradition) after Antiochus had polluted it by transforming it into a house of worship dedicated to **Zeus** (Figure 28.4). However, part of Jerusalem was still under Seleucid control, as was much of Judea; several more years of fighting remained before the sons of Mattathias and their followers could claim real control

Figure 28.3   This mosaic, in which Alexander of Macedonia (left) defeats the Persian emperor Darius III (right center) at the Battle of Issus (333 B.C.E.), pictures a decisive moment in later biblical history. Alexander's conquest of the older Near Eastern centers of power, including Egypt, Palestine, Mesopotamia, and Iran, introduced a new era in which Greek language, art, literature, science, and philosophy transformed the biblical world.

of Judean territory. (A more detailed discussion of the Maccabean Revolt can be found in Chapter 29, in connection with 1 and 2 Maccabees.)

Following Antiochus's death in 163 B.C.E., and after Judah's death in battle, Jonathan, the oldest surviving son of Mattathias, assumed leadership of the Judean rebels. In 152 B.C.E., a claimant to the Seleucid throne signed a peace treaty with him, appointing him to the position of High Priest. Thus began the **Hasmonean** dynasty, whose name derives from *Hashmonay* (presumably the name of one of Mattathias's ancestors), and it was this dynasty that governed Judea from 160 to 63 B.C.E. through a succession of priest-kings. This newly reclaimed autonomy, which Judea had not known since the Babylonian conquest, apparently inspired two very different responses from second- and first-century-B.C.E. religious writers, whose reaction to the Maccabean Revolt and its aftermath was largely negative. One such group, referred to collectively as

hasidim (pious ones) gradually withdrew their support for the Hasmonean dynasty, viewing the appointment of Mattathias's sons to the high priesthood as an act of usurpation. The Essenes, and specifically the Qumran community (to be discussed in Chapter 31), certainly shared this view, and their growing disapproval of the Jerusalem priesthood seems to date from this period.

Other pietists, however, were not content simply to withdraw themselves or their support from the Hasmonean religious establishment. Instead, they looked forward with increasing fervor to the day when the corrupt Hasmonean regime would be replaced with a true theocracy and all wicked governments would fall before the overwhelming power of angelic armies, sent by God to cleanse the earth of its evil and bring about an era of holiness and redemption. Writers of apocalyptic works certainly reflect the more radicalized sentiments of this second community, and it is to this distinctive form of

Figure 28.4   Statue of Zeus (or Poseidon) Holding a (Vanished) Thunderbolt This larger-than-life bronze (c. 460 B.C.E.) probably represents the king of the Olympian gods. Zeus was both a personification of storm and lightning and the heavenly enforcer of justice, lawful order, and cosmic harmony. Unlike the Judeo-Christian God, who is eternal, Zeus is the descendant of older generations of gods who ruled the universe before him.

largely postexilic literature that we now turn our attention.

Apocalyptic Literature

One of the more distinctive genres of the late prophetic period is the apocalyptic narrative, which, at first glance, may seem only marginally intelligible, thanks to its bewildering language and imagery. The term *apocalyptic* derives from the Greek *apoka-lypsis,* meaning a "revelation," or disclosure, of something hidden from common view. In a biblical context, that "something" turns out to be the pattern and meaning of history, for Israel and the world.

A RADICAL THEODICY

The Book of Daniel is the only canonical book that contains a significant amount of apocalyptic material, but it is certainly not the only work influenced by apocalyptic thinking. The Book of Isaiah (Chs. 24–27, 62–66), for example, speaks of "new heavens and a new earth" (65:17) that will mark the culmination of Israel's covenant relationship with YHWH, and the Book of Ezekiel (Chs. 30, 37–39) envisions a time of world conflict, cosmic upheaval, and national renewal:

> On that day there shall be a great shaking in the land of Israel; the fish of the sea and the birds of the air, and the animals of the field, and all creeping things that creep on the ground, and all human beings that are on the face of the earth, shall quake at my presence, and the mountains shall be thrown down, and the cliffs shall fall, and every wall shall tumble to the ground. . . . So I will display my greatness and my holiness and make myself known in the eyes of many nations. Then they shall know that I am the LORD. (Ezek. 38:19–23)

The first six chapters of the Book of Zechariah strike a similar note, complete with visions of angels who serve not only as instruments of divine judgment but also as heavenly interpreters of divine revelation.

But it is only in the Book of Daniel (Chs. 7–12) that a full-scale scenario of the end time is laid out in elaborate detail, complete with scenes of a heavenly court (including the Deity seated on a throne), reports of cosmic as well as earthly struggles, and highly symbolic accounts of the rise and fall of successive empires, ending with the establishment of a "kingdom of heaven" and the resurrection and final judgment of the dead. And because the ultimate focus of Daniel and many other apocalyptic narratives is on the "end" of history, it is common to describe apocalyptic writings as exhibiting an **eschatological** outlook—its name derived from the Greek *eschaton,* meaning "last things" (or, in this context, last days)—though not all apocalyptic works offer a definitive vision of humanity's final hours. Permeating this end time drama is a combined sense of the imminence and the inevitability of divine judgment, as well as the underlying conviction that the evil kingdoms of this world cannot last forever. At the heart of Daniel and other apocalyptic writings, therefore, is a radical **theodicy**—that is, a defense of divine justice—that demonstrates through visions and esoteric interpre-

tations of Scripture just how the balance of good and evil will be restored and true piety rewarded once the world as we know it has ceased to be.

UNIQUE CHARACTERISTICS OF APOCALYPTIC WRITING

Though many scholars view apocalyptic literature as an outgrowth of later prophetic thought, apocalyptic writing clearly reflects a heightened sense of urgency brought on by some crisis of faith or by persecution, or both. The Book of Daniel certainly seems to confirm this observation in that it appears to have been redacted during Antiochus's persecution of devout Jews who refused to submit to his policy of forced assimilation. But even when the conflicts, and corresponding challenges to faith, are largely internal—as seems to be the case in Zechariah—apocalyptic scenarios reflect a growing impatience and anxiety within the community of the faithful over the timing and finality of divine judgment. Indefinite postponements of the "Day of YHWH" must surely have led to a skeptical attitude toward prophecy as such, as in the Book of Ezekiel, when the exiles from Judah complain that "the days are prolonged, and every vision comes to nothing" (Ezek. 12:22). To reply to and combat such doubts, apocalyptic writers moved beyond their prophetic counterparts in their assurances that YHWH would act decisively, and soon, to change both Israel's and the world's condition forever.

Perhaps the most striking departure from an earlier prophetic perspective, however, is the relative absence of Deuteronomic thought and rhetoric from apocalyptic literature. No longer do we read again and again about Israel's apostasies, of its "promiscuities" and social crimes requiring divine punishment. Although apocalyptists concede the painful facts of Israel's sinful past, the focus of their concern shifts dramatically to visions of divine intervention and world transformation:

> On this mountain the LORD of
> Hosts will make for all
> Peoples

A feast of rich food, a feast of
    Well-aged wines, . . .
And he will destroy on this
    Mountain
The shroud that is cast over all
    Peoples,
The sheet that is spread over all nations;
He will swallow up death
    Forever.
Then the Lord God will wipe
    Away the tears from all
      Faces,
And the disgrace of his people he
    Will take away from all
    The earth. . . . (Isa. 25:6–8)

The universality of such promises is as remarkable as the novelty of the events foreseen—in this case, a world without death. And the suddenness with which this fundamental change in human existence will occur signals that we are about to turn a corner in human history and leave all of the old woes and sins behind.

The historical trajectory of apocalyptic literature inevitably leads one beyond the limits of the biblical canon to an intertestamental literature in which the expectation of imminent and miraculous deliverance from evil becomes even more pronounced. Books like 1 Enoch and 2 Esdras, for example, plunge us into a world of cosmic and ethical dualism, where the entire universe appears to be caught up in a struggle between opposing supernatural forces. Human suffering is related directly to this world-shattering struggle, and our sense of the progression of historical time gives way to a more mythic scheme of long "ages" or periods as human history is telescoped into a series of conflict-ridden epochs. The finality of this struggle—the sense that time is running out and that divine patience with human frailty is at an end—lends a combined note of desperation and feverish expectation to apocalyptic projections of cosmic and terrestrial warfare, as apocalyptists attempt to measure the distance between the present and the end time (cf. Daniel's "a time, two times, and a half-time" [Dan 7:25]).

Just as striking, however, is the extraordinary passivity that seems to characterize human agents within apocalyptic narratives. These mortal beings can only await the predestined catastrophes and redemptions already planned in heaven and about to be executed on earth. Understandably, when violence of cosmic proportions is about to be unleashed on the human race, mere human actions cannot possibly be seen as altering the course of things. Or, as the author of Daniel 8 observes, when the evil "king of bold countenance" (presumably Antiochus IV) is at last broken, it will not be accomplished "by human hands" (Dan 8:25). The initiative for historical change and conflict resolution lies entirely within God's hands, where, apocalyptists suggest, it has always been. Just as the Deity could bring a universe into being without help or opposition, so he can uncreate that universe when it suits him. (Box 28.1 discusses the characteristics of apocalyptic writing.)

The Book of Daniel

The book of Daniel is really two books in one. Chapters 1–6 consist largely of didactic tales in which the title hero, Daniel, remains true to his faith under adverse circumstances; in Chapters 7–12, the same Daniel who earlier interpreted other people's dreams now recounts his own apocalyptic visions of the end time. Most biblical scholars today are convinced that Daniel was one of the last books of the Hebrew Bible to be written or edited before the canon was regarded as "closed," and the terminal date most often given for its composition and/or redaction is 164 B.C.E. If, as many scholars suspect, Daniel was written amid the persecution of Palestinian Jews during the reign of Antiochus IV—and with the express intention of strengthening their resistance to his policy of forced assimilation—then we can easily understand why an obscure and legendary figure like Daniel would have appealed to Jews of the Maccabean era.

BOX 28.1
The Characteristics of Apocalyptic Writing

As works of prophecy declined and claims of prophetic inspiration became more difficult to substantiate, a new form of revelatory narrative began to emerge in Israel, one that exhibited traits that distinguished it from both prophetic and wisdom literature.

UNIVERSALITY

Unlike prophetic writers, apocalyptists create visionary scenarios of global proportions, often depicting the rise and fall of great empires or portraying the fate of the entire human race. And though biblical apocalyptists are clearly concerned with Israel's survival, as well as with its crucial role in the shaping of human destiny, they are just as concerned with the broad sweep of history and the struggle waged in both heaven and earth between the "godly" and the "ungodly." What follows, then, is a perceptible enlargement of dramatic perspective beyond what one normally encounters in prophetic literature, in which Israel's passage from exile to redemption is set against the backdrop of an entire universe moving inexorably toward divine judgment.

VESTIGES OF ANCIENT MYTHS

Apocalyptic writings often reveal traces of ancient mythological systems whose ideas and imagery were partially preserved in biblical poetry. In Psalm 74 and Isaiah 25:7, for example, we can hear distant echoes of a familiar "combat myth," so common in Babylonian and Canaanite epic literature, in which gods engage in life-and-death struggles that determine the future of the cosmos. Within the context of the biblical worldview there can be no doubt, of course, that Israel's God will crush "Leviathan" and swallow Death (the Canaanite *Mot*) forever. But in the more schematic "two-story universe" of the apocalyptic imagination, hosts of angels and demons confront each other in an ongoing cosmic war that will end only when God or his Messiah intervenes to create an everlasting kingdom of peace and justice (Dan. 10:13–21; 12:1–7). That human agents, acting on their own initiative, cannot bring an end to injustice and war is one of the key critical assumptions underlying all apocalyptic thinking.

ESOTERIC REVELATIONS AND ENCODED LANGUAGE

Apocalyptic narratives purport to be supernatural revelations, often of a private nature, imparted to a wisdom figure of great fame (like Daniel, Enoch, or Ezra). The agent through whom this revelation is given is almost always an angel, and the revelatory experience may be part of an upper-world journey or a dream vision. Because such revelations are shared with only a chosen few, the language and syntax of these visions are often obscure and secretive in nature.

SOURCES OF DANIEL

Aside from this book, which bears his name, Daniel appears nowhere else in the Hebrew Bible, nor do other postexilic writers refer to him—with one possible exception. The prophet Ezekiel twice refers to a **Danel,** who may or may not be the same figure we encounter in the Book of Daniel. Ezekiel's first reference occurs in Chapter 14, where he observes:

> Even if those three men were living there [in Israel], Noah, Danel and Job, they would save none but themselves by their righteousness. (Ezek. 14:14)

By placing Danel (or Daniel?) alongside Noah and Job, Ezekiel appears to be holding up three ancient, virtuous, non-Israelite role models of personal integrity as a reproach to his contemporaries, but nowhere does he suggest that Daniel might be one of his fellow exiles. Later, in Chapter 28, Ezekiel again alludes to a Danel, whose wisdom he contrasts with the folly of the present (28:3), but the whole point of this allusion would have been lost had a sixth-century-B.C.E. Daniel still been living.

A more likely source for the Daniel of this book, and quite possibly for Ezekiel's two references, can be found in Canaanite folklore. Archaeological dis-

Employing code words and vague images, apocalyptists either hint at imminent catastrophes or present the passage of time symbolically in a way that, paradoxically, encourages their readers to keep the faith while discouraging them from engaging in realistic chronological calculations. The fact that many apocalyptic narratives apparently were written in times of political and religious oppression may explain why apocalyptists use encoded animal symbolism (for example, the four beasts in Daniel 7–8) and other techniques of concealment to portray ongoing conflicts that threaten their community and their faith.

COSMIC AND ETHICAL DUALISM

The war of good against evil, or light against dark, often assumes a dualistic character in apocalyptic literature. History is a battlefield, apocalyptists believe, where human and divine forces converge to wage the final struggle for control of the cosmos, and nations are either for God or against him. There is no middle ground in this conflict, and the faithful must endure until the end. The apocalyptic view is therefore as exclusivist as it is uncompromising, and its depiction of God's nature necessarily emphasizes his punitive and relentless qualities. God's principal role in apocalyptic writings is that of omnipotent judge and executioner; he is the Creator who wills a violent end to his creation. Although his justice cannot be questioned, he emerges as a supreme figure of fearsome and destructive power. No consideration is given in apocalyptic thought either to a progressive amelioration of the human condition or to a collective moral transformation — via acts of repentance — of the human race. The mass of humankind is clearly doomed, and apocalyptic literature holds out hope for only the chosen few.

ESCHATOLOGICAL PREOCCUPATIONS

The belief that history is moving inexorably toward some finite and irreversible end is crucial to apocalyptic thinking. Speculations about the end time (Greek, *eskaton*) abound in apocalyptic narratives, and (not coincidentally) apocalyptists are the earliest biblical writers to portray the afterlife as well as the "day" of judgment. And while earlier biblical writers were content to place the souls of the deceased within the shadowy Underworld of **Sheol,** apocalyptists embrace both the idea of resurrection and that of postmortem punishments. By extending the arc of providential judgment beyond this earthly life, apocalyptic writers are able to resolve those nagging doubts about God's justice that surface in both Ecclesiastes and Job by constructing a consistent, otherworldly theodicy. Thus, if the faithful cannot be rewarded in this life, then in the world to come divine providence will at last be vindicated and wickedness decisively punished. Unlike the prophets, whose perceptions of time are generally limited to the present or to the not-too-distant future, apocalyptists extend the horizon of biblical narrative until a historical symmetry emerges: Just as there was a beginning to historical time, they argue, so there will be an end — and at that end, God will act directly to undo and correct all that human perversity and disobedience have done to undermine his creation.

coveries at the site of the ancient Syrian city of Ugarit (now called Ras Shamra), dating back to the fourteenth century B.C.E., reveal the existence of a Canaanite folk hero and king named Danel who — like the biblical Solomon — was esteemed for his fairness and his wisdom. It may well be that the biblical Daniel is a "borrowed" literary type-figure who was inserted into the history of the Babylonian and Persian captivity and who for dramatic purposes was made a member of the Judean aristocracy and a prominent personality at court. In each of the stories in which he appears, Daniel exhibits a wisdom similar to that of his legendary Canaanite namesake, with one important difference: Daniel's wisdom is of the "mantic" variety, meaning that he is gifted with quasi-prophetic powers of understanding and a unique ability to interpret dreams. In this respect, he more nearly resembles the patriarch Joseph, with whom he shares a number of traits. Like Joseph, Daniel is a captive in a strange land, and, also like him, he raises himself from obscurity to fame on the strength of his mind-reading and dream-interpreting abilities. Where Daniel differs sharply from Joseph, and even from a Diaspora heroine like Esther, is in his determination to remain loyal to YHWH, risking his life in defense of his faith.

INTERPRETING DREAMS AND RESISTING ASSIMILATION

The Daniel who appears in five of the first six chapters of this book is clearly conceived as an exemplary Jew who meets every challenge to his faith with courage and shrewdness. In Chapter 1, for example, Daniel, along with his friends **Shadrach, Meshach,** and **Abednego,** are being groomed for life at the court of the Babylonian king **Nebuchadnezzar.** Rather than eat forbidden foods, however, Daniel and his friends opt for a vegetarian diet, on which they prosper, proving that it is possible to observe the biblical dietary code in a foreign land, albeit with some restrictions and adaptations. In Chapter 6, however, Daniel faces a much more formidable challenge when he is ordered by the Persian king Darius to cease offering petitions (presumably, petitionary prayers) to any god and to offer them to the king instead. Daniel ignores this decree, is thrown into a lions' pit, and is promptly saved by divine intercession. Much the same fate awaits Shadrach, Meshach, and Abednego in Chapter 3 when they are cast into a fiery furnace for refusing to bow before the golden image of a Babylonian divinity. An angel is sent into the furnace to protect them, and they emerge unharmed, to the astonishment of Nebuchadnezzar, who then offers both protection and social advancement to the would-be martyrs. In each case, the moral of the story is the same: If people remain steadfast in their commitment to the God of the covenant, he will keep faith with them.

Yet, for all the dangers that surround him, Daniel is able to ingratiate himself with the Babylonian court by virtue of his extraordinary talent for dream interpretation. **Oneiromancy**—the practice of divination through dream interpretation—was a valued skill in the courts of ancient Near Eastern rulers, and Daniel's quasi-supernatural abilities lead to his rapid advancement at court, where he easily outshines the court magi. In Chapter 2, Daniel performs the seemingly impossible task of telling Nebuchadnezzar not only what his dream meant but also what it was that he had dreamt in the first place. In Chapter 4, Daniel once again explains the meaning of a dream that had baffled all other dream interpreters, and in Chapter 5, he decodes a heavenly inscription for "King" **Belshazzar.** In each case, the message that Daniel must impart to his royal patrons is a grim and ironic one. In Chapter 2, he informs Nebuchadnezzar that a succession of kingdoms will follow his own, each weaker than the one before it (gold, silver, bronze, and iron); in Chapter 4, he predicts that Nebuchadnezzar will be banished from human society for a time; and in Chapter 5, he translates the handwriting on the wall for Belshazzar, to whom he reveals that his days are numbered. Clearly, it is the reliability of the interpretation, and not the outcome of the dream, that endears Daniel to his royal patrons. What none of them can grasp, however, is that their power and their kingdoms are doomed to extinction and that only one "kingdom" will ever endure:

> In the period of those kings the GOD of heaven will establish a kingdom which shall never be destroyed; that kingdom shall never pass to another people; it shall shatter and make an end of all these kingdoms, while it shall itself endure for ever. (Dan. 2:44)

The later chapters of Daniel have a great deal more to say about this everlasting kingdom, but much of the irony that surrounds Daniel's dream interpretations derives from our recognition that the royal patrons whom Daniel serves, when seen from a divine perspective, are ultimately powerless to shape their own fate or the destiny of other nations. It is God's will alone, the author of Daniel insists, that determines the outcome of every human action, and of history itself.

DANIEL'S VISIONS OF THE END TIME

Chapters 7–12 contain a series of apocalyptic visions, each of which embodies a common eschatological projection of a not-too-distant future. In this future time, the kingdom of God will at last prevail over all its adversaries, but only after a protracted war in heaven and on earth has been waged for control of this world:

At that moment Michael shall appear, Michael the great captain, who stands guard over your fellow countrymen; and there will be a time of distress such as has never been since they became a nation till that moment. But at that moment your people will be delivered, every one who is written in the book: many of those who sleep in the dust of the earth will wake, some to everlasting life, and some to the reproach of eternal abhorrence. The wise leaders shall shine like the bright vault of heaven, and those who have guided the people in the true path shall be like the stars for ever and ever. (Dan. 12:1–3)

Chapter 7 offers one version of this composite scenario, complete with esoteric symbolism and a glimpse of the heavenly throne. In the first part of the chapter (7:1–8), Daniel has a vision of four "beasts," following one another in swift succession and each representing, allegorically, a different Near Eastern empire: a lion with eagle's wings (Babylon); a bear with ribs in its mouth (Media); a winged leopard with four heads (Persia); and a monstrous creature with iron teeth, bronze claws, and ten horns (Macedonian Greece and the successor kingdoms of the Ptolemies [Egypt] and the Seleucids [Syria]). Suddenly a smaller horn appears, and the focus of the narrative shifts to this figure, whom most scholars identify as Antiochus IV. If, as contemporary biblical scholarship assumes, the whole point of this allegory is the successive defeat of kingdom after kingdom, culminating in the final defeat of the most fearsome of Israel's conquerors — Antiochus's policy of forced Hellenization provoked the Maccabeans into open revolt against his rule — then the underlying and specifically political purpose of these narratives suddenly becomes clear. Israel will not be destroyed at last, no matter how "ferocious" and seemingly invincible its enemies may appear:

In the last days of those kingdoms, when their sin is at its height, a king shall appear, harsh and grim, a master of stratagem. His power shall be great, he shall work havoc untold; . . . He shall challenge even the Prince of princes [presumably, God] and be broken, but not by human hands. (Dan. 8:23–25)

However, Daniel's visionary reenactment of Israel's fate at the hands of diverse conquerors also contains a scene in heaven, where, like Ezekiel, Daniel is privileged to behold God's likeness, seated on a fiery throne:

. . . thrones were set in place and one ancient in years took his seat, his robe was white as snow and the hair of his head like cleanest wool. Flames of fire were his throne and its wheels blazing fire; a flowing river of fire streamed out before him. Thousands upon thousands served him and myriads upon myriads attended his presence. The court sat, and the books were opened. (Dan. 7:9–10)

This scene of thrones and flames and "myriads" of spirits would have been familiar to readers of earlier scriptural texts, and even non-Jews in the ancient Near East would have found the general contours of this upper-world vision quite acceptable. With its multiple layers of anthropomorphic imagery, this passage offers one version of an archetypal myth that the books of Job (Chs. 1–2), Isaiah (Ch. 6), Exodus (Ch. 24), and Psalms (2, 82, 104), as well as Ezekiel (Ch. 1), all allude to: a vast projection of human monarchy onto the heavens. Here, all the trappings of royal power and mystery can be seen, and an ambiguously human deity, majestically robed and seated on his splendid throne, presides over a court of attendant angels.

What is apparently new in Daniel's vision, however, is the sudden entrance of another heavenly figure, identified simply and enigmatically as *k'var enosh* (literally, "one like a son of man"), on whom God will bestow earthly dominion, thereby bringing an end to the reign of mortal rulers. Later generations of Bible commentators, both Christian and Jewish, understood this figure to be a messianic redeemer, though the author of Daniel never actually uses this title. What is clear, however, is that human effort alone will not avail against the evil power wielded by the "little horn" (Figure 28.5). Only intervention from the upper world will suffice to rescue Israel from destruction and to establish the "everlasting sovereignty" of the "saints," who presumably will share dominion with the "one like a

Figure 28.5 The notorious "little horn" of Daniel's vision (Dan. 7:8, 20–22, 24–26; 11:21–45), Antiochus IV Epiphanes (175–163 B.C.E.) was the Seleucid ruler of Hellenistic Syria who profaned the Jerusalem Temple by erecting a statue of Olympian Zeus there, an "abomination" that resounds through the books of Daniel and 1 Maccabees. Shown in profile on this Greek coin, Antiochus IV tended to identify his rule with that of Zeus, king of the gods.

son of man." Just who these "saints" (or "holy ones" [Aramaic, *kaddishin*]) of YHWH might be has prompted endless conjecture among readers of this text. However, if they can be identified with Jewish pietists of the Maccabean period who were just as opposed to Antiochus as Judah Maccabee and his supporters but who were unwilling to join his armed revolt, then this invocation of divine intervention may well represent their response to those who urged them to take up arms against their Greek-Syrian oppressors. Indeed, the entire Book of Daniel may conceivably have been intended to console as well as vindicate this very segment of second-century-B.C.E. Judean society.

REDEMPTION AND RESURRECTION

It soon becomes clear, however, that the establishment of a kingdom of God is only one stage in an unfolding drama of cosmic struggle and universal redemption. In Chapter 8, Daniel receives instruction from the angel **Gabriel** on Israel's fate in the end time, and in Chapters 9–12, that instruction is expanded (by an unnamed angelic mentor) to incorporate the fate of all peoples in the "days to come." Once more, reference is made to a "contemptible creature" (again, presumably, Antiochus) who has made desperate war against the "Holy Covenant" (11:30). Yet, for all his power, the "Book of Truth" (11:2) reveals that his campaign of conquest and terror will end in failure and death. At that moment, everyone whose name appears in "the book" will be rescued, and even those who have died will undergo a resurrection to "everlasting life"; still others (Antiochus and those who opposed YHWH?) will be subject to the "reproach of eternal abhorrence" (12:2). While all of this is happening, **Michael,** the great warrior-"prince" of Israel, will wage war in heaven with the warrior-prince of Persia (10:13–14), thus evoking an image of parallel worlds in turmoil, with the fate of earthly armies hinging on the success of heavenly "hosts." This spectacle of a modified **theomachy**—in which lesser deities make war on each other to achieve predominance — may be viewed as a residual memory fragment of the collective culture of the ancient Near East, as in the *Enuma Elish,* where Marduk and his opponents fight to the death for control of the cosmos. Such a subtext seems wildly incompatible, of course, with the generally monotheistic thrust of biblical literature and of the Book of Daniel itself. Still, it is impossible not to notice that even heaven itself is not immune to internecine warfare and angelic opposition to the will of YHWH.

CANONICITY AND HISTORICITY

The Book of Daniel may well have been one of the last books admitted to the biblical canon, and a close reading of this text reveals just how problematic it is for contemporary scholars. Even in the ancient world, doubts were cast on its authenticity, and today, the vast majority of biblical scholars incline toward a very "late" date for Daniel's era of composition and redaction. Daniel is the only truly bilingual book in the Hebrew Bible—roughly half of it is written in Aramaic (2:4–7:28)—and therefore is likely to have been written for a postexilic audience thoroughly at home in Aramaic as well as Hebrew. Daniel also is replete with historical errors and with variant historical traditions at odds with those in other books of the Bible. One such "error" appears in the opening verses of the book, where we read that Nebuchadnezzar conquered Judah and Jerusalem during the reign of Jehoiakim (not Jehoiachin, his son) and then carried him off to Babylon. This assertion contradicts the account of this era given in 2 Kings 24, which itself is at variance with 2 Chronicles 36. More distractingly, Chapter 5 informs us that Belshazzar "the King," son of Nebuchadnezzar (Babylonian texts identify him as a prince and son of King Nabonidus), was conquered by Darius the Mede, who was neither a Mede nor the conqueror of Babylon (Cyrus of Persia conquered Babylon in 539 B.C.E.). This same Darius is later identified as the son of Ahasuerus (Xerxes I) (Dan. 9:1), though, in fact, Ahasuerus was Darius's son, and the Medes did not overrun Babylon. Such mistakes are, perhaps, easier to comprehend if we assume that the author-redactor of Daniel wrote at a time far removed from the beginnings of the Babylonian exile, and with only a sketchy idea of the succession of Babylonian and Persian kings.

One fairly widespread view of the Book of Daniel today is that it is best seen as a Diaspora novella, in which accuracy of historical reference is far less important than didactic focus. The aim of the Daniel author, clearly, is not to recount events from 606 B.C.E. to 536 B.C.E. (the stated time span of these narratives) in the manner of the Chronicler. Rather, it is to tell a series of inspiring stories about an exemplary Diaspora figure—not unlike Esther—whose apocalyptic visions surpass even the eschatological longings of the major prophets. In Daniel's end time world, the dead as well as the living will experience judgment and redemption, and Israel's centuries-long penance will come to a glorious end. As a work of visionary propaganda, then, Daniel rises above history (as do virtually all apocalyptic writers) in order to envision human events from a more-than-human perspective.

QUESTIONS FOR REVIEW

1. What are the characteristics of apocalyptic literature? How does an apocalyptist's view of history differ from a prophet's?

2. What does the term *eschatology* mean? Where do we find eschatological themes in the Book of Daniel?

3. What were the causes of the Maccabean Revolt? Who were the Hasmoneans, and what connection did they have to the Maccabean leadership?

4. What portrait of Diaspora life does the Book of Daniel paint for its readers? What sort of role model does Daniel provide for contemporary readers?

5. What does the word *Hellenism* refer to? In what ways were the Jews of the late fourth through the first centuries B.C.E. influenced by Hellenism?

QUESTIONS FOR REFLECTION AND DISCUSSION

1. Why did some Jews living during the Hasmonean era turn toward apocalyptic writings and eschatological ideas? What is so attractive about the idea of the "end of history," and how can that idea be related back to the political situation of Judea and the Jewish Diaspora during the Hasmonean period?

2. Why did a segment of the hasidim movement withdraw its support for the Maccabean leadership and later distance itself from the Hasmonean dynasty? What evidence do we have that the author of Daniel sympathized with this group?

TERMS AND CONCEPTS TO REMEMBER

Abednego	Belshazzar
Antiochus IV Epiphanes	Danel
apocalyptic literature	Diaspora

eschatology
Gabriel
hasidim
Hasmonean
Hellenism
Judea
Meshach
Michael
Nebuchadnezzar
oneiromancy

Palestine
Ptolemies
resurrection
Seleucids
Septuagint
Shadrach
Sheol
theodicy
theomachy
Zeus

RECOMMENDED READING

Collins, John C. *The Apocalyptic Imagination: An Intro-duction to Jewish Apocalyptic Literature.* Grand Rapids, Mich.: Eerdmans, 1998.

——. "Daniel, Book of." In D. N. Freedman, ed., *The Anchor Bible Dictionary,* Vol. 2, pp. 29–37. New York: Doubleday, 1992.

——, ed. The Encyclopedia of Apocalypticism, Vol. 1. New York: Continuum, 2002.

Hanson, Paul D. *Old Testament Apocalyptic.* Nashville, Tenn.: Abingdon Press, 1987.

Hartman, Louis F., and De Lella, Alexander A. *The Book of Daniel.* Garden City, N.Y.: Doubleday, 1978.

Russell, D. S. *Daniel, An Active Volcano: Reflections on the Book of Daniel.* Louisville, Ky.: Westminster/John Knox Press, 1989.

——. *The Method and Message of Jewish Apocalyptic: 200 B.C.–A.D. 100.* Philadelphia: Westminster Press, 1964.

Stone, Michael. *Scriptures, Sects and Visions: A Profile of Judaism from Ezra to the Jewish Revolts.* Philadelphia: Fortress Press, 1980.

CHAPTER 29

The "Second Canon"

Books of the Apocrypha

Key Topics/Themes In finalizing the canon of the Hebrew Bible (Tanak), Jewish editors rejected approximately fourteen documents that had been included in the Greek Septuagint edition of the Jewish Scriptures. Accepted by the early church as deuterocanonical, these books, known as the Apocrypha, are part of Catholic and Orthodox editions of the Old Testament. Containing works of poetry, wisdom, prose fiction, and historical narrative, the Apocrypha explore important ideas in the development of Hellenistic Jewish thought.

As noted in Chapter 1, Catholic and Orthodox editions of the Old Testament include about fourteen books or parts of books that Jewish editors did not accept in the Hebrew Bible (Tanak). Except for 2 Esdras, most of these documents—the **Apocrypha**—first appeared in the Septuagint, the Greek edition of the Jewish Scriptures used by the early Greek-speaking Christian community. The Christian church eventually classified these books as *deuterocanonical*—as belonging to a later "second canon." Composed primarily during the last centuries B.C.E., such works as 1 and 2 Maccabees and the Wisdom of Solomon provide an important link between the Old and New Testament periods, when Jewish thought was profoundly influenced by Greek ideas. In Catholic and Orthodox Old Testaments, the apocryphal books are interspersed among the Prophets (Nevi'im) and the Writings (Kethuvim); when included in Protestant editions of the Bible, such as the Revised English Bible and the New Revised Standard Version, the apocryphal books are grouped together as a separate unit between the Old and New Testaments.

Most of the apocryphal books were composed in the same literary forms as those in the Writings of the Hebrew Bible—short stories (Judith and Tobit), wisdom literature (Ecclesiasticus and the Wisdom of Solomon), historical narratives (1 and 2 Maccabees), and an apocalypse (2 Esdras) (Table 29.1). In addition, in the Septuagint, Esther and Daniel incorporated extensive passages that do not appear in the Hebrew/Aramaic texts, such as long

Table 29.1 *Deuterocanonical (Apocryphal) Books*

The Hebrew Bible (Tanak) omits fourteen books or parts of books that some Christian churches regard as part of the Old Testament. This table presents the canonical status — the acceptance or rejection — of the deuterocanonical (apocryphal) writings by various representative groups. A dash (—) indicates that the writing is not accepted. An empty circle (○) indicates that the book is not part of the canon but is given some religious value. A dark circle (●) indicates that the writing is included in the Bible but is not equal in authority to the Old and New Testaments. A dark square (■) means that the book is accepted as part of the Old Testament.

| | | | | EASTERN ORTHODOX | |
BOOK	JEWISH	PROTESTANT	ROMAN CATHOLIC	GREEK	RUSSIAN
1 Maccabees	—	○	■	■	●
2 Maccabees	—	○	■	■	●
Additions to Daniel	—	○	■	■	●
Tobit	—	○	■	■	●
Judith	—	○	■	■	●
Additions to Esther	—	○	■	■	●
Baruch	—	○	■	■	●
Letter of Jeremiah	—	○	■	■	●
Ecclesiasticus (ben Sirach)	—	○	■	■	●
Wisdom of Solomon	—	○	■	■	●
2 Esdras (4 Ezra)	—	○	○	■	●

For additional information on deuterocanonical and extracanonical works, see James H. Charlesworth, "Biblical Literature: Apocrypha and Pseudepigrapha," in Mircea Eliade, ed., *The Encyclopedia of Religion*, Vol. 2, pp. 173–183 (New York: Macmillan, 1987).

prayers highlighting Esther's allegiance to Torah rules and narratives emphasizing Daniel's extraordinary skills as a sage. Varied in both content and literary quality, deuterocanonical writings include some notable milestones in the evolution of religious thought, ranging from folklore about angels and demons (Tobit), to practical applications of wisdom (Ecclesiasticus), to innovative ideas about the afterlife (Wisdom of Solomon), to the conflict between secular culture and Torah loyalty (1 Maccabees), to the concept of heavenly rewards for martyrdom (2 Maccabees). In surveying the Apocrypha, we will first examine those books appearing in Catholic editions of the Old Testament, including 1 and 2 Esdras and the Prayer of Manasseh (part of the Latin canon until 1546). Other documents, such as 3 and 4 Maccabees and Psalm 151, which are revered in the Greek Orthodox tradition, are discussed as part of the **Pseudepigrapha,** a large and extremely diverse body of Jewish literature produced during the Greco-Roman era (see Chapter 30).

The Book of Tobit

Although the Septuagint editors placed Tobit among the historical books, along with Chronicles and Ezra-Nehemiah, it is really a work of imaginative fiction. The action is ostensibly set in the seventh century B.C.E. when many Israelites from the northern kingdom were removed from their homeland and resettled throughout the Assyrian Empire (cf. 2 Kings 17), but the book really addresses issues of a much later period — the problems of Hellenistic Jews living in the Diaspora (scattering abroad).

Probably composed during the third or second century B.C.E., Tobit dramatizes the conflicts that sometimes arose between devout Jews and their Gentile rulers. In this context, Nineveh, the Assyrian capital in which much of the story takes place, represents the kind of foreign environment in which Diaspora Jews struggled to maintain their ancestral faith.

A JEWISH DIASPORA FAMILY

The unknown author's purpose is to encourage Jewish exiles to cultivate Torah obedience and adherence to received tradition, including family solidarity and charitable giving. Although the narrative focuses largely on a single family's everyday affairs, it is designed to illustrate a larger theme: Israel's God hears — and answers — the prayers of persons loyal to him, rewarding their fidelity with material success (cf. Deut. 28). This theme is dramatized in a skillfully constructed plot consisting of three closely interwoven stories. The book's central figure is Tobit, an exemplary Jew who scrupulously observes all Torah requirements but who suffers the illnesses and privations of a latter-day Job. A subplot involves his kinswoman Sarah, a beautiful virgin whose seven husbands have all been killed on their wedding night by the jealous demon Asmodeus. A second subplot concerning Tobit's son Tobias, who travels to Media, exorcizes the demon, and marries Sarah, effectively ties all the narratives together.

Tobit's story is joined to Sarah's by the Deity's hearing their simultaneous prayers for death:

> At that very moment, the prayers of both of them were heard in the glorious presence of GOD. So Raphael [an angel] was sent to heal both of them: Tobit, by removing the white film from his eyes so that he might see GOD's light with his eyes; and Sarah, daughter of Raguel, by giving her in marriage to Tobias and by freeing her from the wicked demon Asmodeus. (Tob. 3:16–17)

Tobit is praying to die because, for piously burying the bodies of slaughtered Israelites, he has not only incurred the wrath of the Assyrian king and been stripped of all his possessions but also been blinded by bird droppings (2:9–3:6). Sarah, unhappy that a maid has accused her of murdering her seven bridegrooms, similarly longs to end her life (3:7–15). Although God has already resolved to help them, the characters themselves must take action before the divine intervention can be accomplished. To relieve his poverty, Tobit sends his son Tobias to Ecbatana, a site in the Near Eastern country of Media (modern Iran), to claim money that Tobit entrusted to a relative, Raguel, who is also Sarah's father.

Disguised as a traveler named Azariah, the archangel Raphael guides young Tobias to Ecbatana, provides detailed instructions on the use of fish parts to expel Asmodeus (who flees to Egypt, where an angel binds him), and permits the union of Tobias and Sarah. Raguel, who had spent the wedding night digging a grave for his new son-in-law, is astounded the next morning that Tobias is still alive. On Tobias's triumphant return to Nineveh with the money and a new wife, Raphael also cures Tobit's blindness with fish gall (11:10–15).

A treasure trove of Hellenistic Jewish social customs and beliefs, Tobit incorporates several traditional folk motifs, two of which folklorists have identified as the tale of the Grateful Dead (telling of an impoverished hero who is rewarded for giving proper interment to an unburied body) and the tale of the Monster in the Bridal Chamber (describing a demon who jealously slays a new husband on the night of his marriage). In addition, Tobit includes a classic journey theme, in which a young man travels to a strange land to acquire treasure and a bride, commonly with supernatural assistance.

Combining elements of Jewish popular piety and folklore, Tobit also deals with such matters as guardian angels (5:21; 12:12–13), sacrificial obligations (1:6–7), dietary restrictions (1:10–12), personal prayers (3:2–15; 8:5–8), the importance of traditional burial (1:17–19; 2:3–8; 14:12), the power of demons and the use of fish entrails in exorcizing them (3:8; 6:6–8; 8:1–3), seven angels at the heavenly court (12:15), and the value of wise parental advice (4:3–19). Tobit's views on angels — guardian spirits who act as benign intercessors

(12:12)—and demons who afflict human victims seem to reflect the influence of Persian Zoroastrianism, with its doctrine of warring sprits of good and evil (see Chapter 25).

The last chapters—Tobit's thanksgiving psalm (Ch. 13) and an epilogue recounting his advice that Tobias and Sarah leave Nineveh to escape the city's impending destruction (Ch. 14)—may be later additions. The final section, in which Tobit prophesies Nineveh's fall and Jerusalem's glorious restoration, contains a prediction notable for its universality: "the nations in the whole world will all be converted and worship God in truth" (14:6).

The Book of Judith

Like Tobit, Judith is a historical romance composed by an anonymous writer during the Hellenistic period and set in the distant past. The book begins with a glaring historical error—that Nebuchadnezzar (ruled 605–562 B.C.E.) reigned in Babylon over the Assyrians, when in reality his father, the previous king of Babylon, had already destroyed Nineveh years before (612 B.C.E.)—an anachronism that may have been intentional, to show at the outset that the book should not be mistaken for factual history. The author probably used the Babylonian setting to address difficulties of his own time—specifically, the Seleucid persecution of the Jews under Antiochus IV (ruled 175–165/164 B.C.E.). The book's fictionalized Nebuchadnezzar, then, represents Antiochus, the tyrant who tried to eradicate Judah's religion (1 Macc. 1:14–50; Dan. 3:3–15), against whom the author encourages Jews to rise in armed revolt, asserting that Israel's God will defend his people if they remain faithful (Jth. 13:11; 16:17).

A NATIONAL HEROINE

Judith was probably written about 100 B.C.E., significantly after the Maccabees had driven the Syrians from Palestine and established a Hasmonean dynasty. The heroine's name, the feminine form of "Judah," literally means "female Judean" and may be intended to symbolize the covenant community or to remind readers of Judas, its Maccabean leader. Judith embodies the traditional biblical heroism of the solitary Israelite successfully defeating a foreign superpower, as Jael killed Sisera (Judg. 4:12–24; 5:25–30), Samson slew the Philistines (Judg. 16), and David vanquished Goliath (1 Sam. 17). Judith's triumph over Holofernes, the Assyrian commander, signifies her people's victory over their collective enemies.

The Book of Judith is divided into two parts. The first (Chs. 1–7) states that, after conquering Media, Nebuchadnezzar sent Holofernes to punish countries that had not supported his campaign. Victorious in subjugating various other nations, the seemingly invincible Assyrian armies lay siege to the Samaritan town of Bethulia (which in Hebrew may mean "House of YHWH"), a fortified site that may symbolize Jerusalem, which the historical Antiochus had sacked. When Bethulia is ready to submit, the ruler Uzziah decrees that Israel's God be given another five days to rescue his people.

In the second part (Chs. 8–15), Judith, a beautiful and pious widow, berates Jewish leaders who would put their God to the test and volunteers to save the city herself. After offering a prayer, she perfumes herself, dresses in her most luxurious clothes and jewelry, and covertly enters the Assyrian camp, pretending to defect because of her admiration for Holofernes. Flattered, the Assyrian commander invites the seductive woman into his tent, where, after plying him with wine, she seizes his sword and cuts off his head.

Stowing the head in her travel bag, Judith and the maid who accompanied her convey it to Jerusalem, where it is displayed on the city wall. Unnerved by their leader's decapitation, the Assyrian soldiers withdraw, allowing the Jews to loot their camp. Judith dedicates her share of the booty to the Jerusalem Temple. In an epilogue, Judith hails her God for protecting his people (16:17). After living to a ripe old age, Judith is honored by her compatriots as a national heroine.

Although Judith was written at a time when using deceit to overthrow an enemy could be regarded as an act of religious piety, the book is more than a nationalistic war story. Judith's emphasis on the power of Israel's God to deliver an obedient people echoes a theme recurrent in biblical history: It is not "by sword or spear" that Israel carries the day, but only through the will of its God, who can save by the frail hand of a lone woman (cf. Judg. 9:52–54; 1 Sam. 17:46–47).

Additions to Esther

The Septuagint edition of Esther contains six parts (totaling 107 verses) not found in the Hebrew Bible. Although these interpolations originally may have been composed in Hebrew, they survive only in Greek texts. When Jerome prepared the Latin Vulgate, he removed the Additions from the main body of the book and placed them at the end (Additions to Esther 10:3a–16:24, according to Jerome's ordering of the text). Recent English editions that include the Apocrypha handle the textual problems in various ways. The Jerusalem Bible inserts the Additions in Esther's main text but prints them in italics to distinguish them from the Hebrew narrative. The New Revised Standard Version prints the added passages apart from the Hebrew text, as a separate document among the Apocrypha.

Because the Hebrew Bible's version of Esther's story contains neither prayers nor even a single reference to God, Greek redactors apparently felt compelled to give this secular tale a more explicitly religious orientation, alluding to "God" or the "Lord" fifty times. The six different insertions, perhaps representing several different redactors writing at different times, emphasize such topics as the efficacy of prayer and the Deity's saving power (13:8–18; 14:3–19; 15:8). One addition forms a new introduction to the book, giving Mordecai an apocalyptic dream that places the Jews' defense against Persian attack in the context of God's ultimate victory over all worldly opposition (11:2–12).

A rigorously devout practitioner of Torah Judaism and Kosher dietary laws (not mentioned in the original), the Esther of the Greek version refuses to eat the emperor's food (14:17) and finds her marriage to a Gentile husband, Emperor Artaxerxes, repellent (14:15). These added touches highlight the importance of holding fast to Jewish customs, a lesson for readers in the Diaspora who might be tempted to neglect Torah rules in order to assimilate into Gentile society. Transformed into a model of legal rectitude, Esther despises the regal "splendor" accorded her as queen, regarding her public honors as a "filthy rag" and "loathing" the fact that she shares her bed with an "uncircumcised" and "alien" king (14:14–18).

Some of the Additions also heighten the narrative's dramatic tension, increasing the suspense of Esther's unsolicited interview with Artaxerxes by articulating her dread of what may happen if she displeases her master (the emperor has absolute power of life and death over his subjects) (15:16–19). Redactors also attempted to lend plausibility to the story by reproducing the alleged text of Artaxerxes' letter condemning Haman, who turns out to be a Macedonian spy, fully discrediting him as not only a hypocrite but also a traitor to the throne. Praising the emperor's Jewish subjects, the decree commands them to defend themselves when attacked (16:1–24). Expanding on elements in the Hebrew original, the Additions present Jewish courtiers as loyal to their foreign rulers but operating in an atmosphere poisoned by intrigue and treachery instigated by jealous rivals. But the Additions also advance a more comprehensive outlook, injecting into a violent story of Jewish patriotism a reverent proclamation of divine omnipotence. Ultimately, even Artaxerxes testifies that Israel's God reigns supreme (16:4, 21).

Additions to Daniel

THE PRAYER OF AZARIAH AND THE SONG OF THE THREE YOUNG MEN

The Greek version of Daniel includes, among many briefer interpolations, three relatively long poetic and narrative passages not found in the Hebrew canon. The first of these additions, known as the

Prayer of Azariah and the Song of the Three Young Men, consists of psalms or hymns reputedly sung by Daniel's companions, Shadrach, Meshach, and Abednego, while confined in a Babylonian furnace. These songs are inserted into the Hebrew/Aramaic text between verses 23 and 24 of Daniel 3 (forming vv. 3:24–90 in Catholic editions). Following the order established in Latin editions, the added short stories of Susanna and Bel and the Dragon usually are appended at the end of Daniel, appearing, respectively, as Chapters 13 and 14.

The opening poem, the Prayer of Azariah (the Hebrew name of Abednego), is a lament confessing Israel's collective sins and beseeching its God for mercy, though, oddly, the psalm never alludes to Azariah's fiery ordeal. The references to Israel's suffering under "an unjust king, the most wicked in all the world" (3:32, Catholic editions) and to the suppression of the Temple services (3:38–40) suggest that the poem may have been composed during the persecutions of Antiochus IV, perhaps about the same time that the eschatological visions of Daniel 7–12 were composed.

The choral song that the three Jewish youths sing in unison (3:52–90) is a fervent hymn of praise extolling Israel's God and invoking the natural elements—earth, air, sea, and all living creatures—to honor the Deity. Some critics have suggested that this poem, which resembles the canonical Psalm 148 in thought and Psalm 136 in literary form, may be a popular hymn of thanksgiving for Maccabean military victories. Experts are not agreed, however, on either the exact time of composition or the original phrasing of these poems. Like other Additions to Daniel, they may have been written in Hebrew, Aramaic, or Greek during the late second or early first century B.C.E.

SUSANNA

Because Daniel is still a "young lad" when the action takes place, this cleverly plotted narrative is sometimes placed at the beginning of the Book of Daniel, although, following the order of Latin editions, it usually appears as Chapter 13 in Catholic editions. Enhancing Daniel's reputation as a sage,

this section is commonly viewed as the world's first detective story.

While living in Babylon during the exile (587–538 B.C.E.), Susanna, a beautiful and virtuous young wife, rejects the lustful advances of two Jewish elders who are also judges. When they spitefully accuse her of adultery and their testimony results in her condemnation to death, God, acting through Daniel, inspires the youth to demand a more thorough investigation. Separating the elders, who then give contradictory evidence, he exposes them as guilty of bearing false witness, consigning them to the fate they had planned for Susanna (Figure 29.1). Although it teaches a moral lesson about the obligations of Jewish magistrates in the Diaspora to behave justly, this short fiction is as suspenseful and entertaining as it is didactic. Its skillful juxtaposition of a young woman embodying youthful innocence and vulnerability and two aging community leaders whose overwhelming "passion" for her incites them to betray the trust placed in their office makes the story of Susanna a timeless glimpse into the psychological complexities of human sexuality.

BEL AND THE DRAGON

The third Addition, usually appearing as Chapter 14, recounts three incidents demonstrating both Daniel's superior powers of deduction and the deceitful machinations of Gentile priests who try to discredit him. In the first episode, Daniel proves to "King Astyages" (Cyrus of Persia, who now rules at Babylon) that the great statue of **Bel** (the Babylonian god Marduk) does not consume the food left before it but that the offerings are eaten by lying priests and their families (14:1–22). Disabused of his superstition, Cyrus orders the priests and their relatives slain and commissions Daniel to destroy Bel's altar and temple.

In the next section, Daniel poisons a dragon, or large serpent, to show his credulous ruler that it is not a divinity but a mortal reptile (14:23–27). When Babylonian subjects who had revered the serpent learn that Daniel has killed it, they accuse the king of acting like a "Jew" and persuade him to throw the foreign troublemaker into a lions' pit,

Figure 29.1 The difficulties that some early Christians experienced in Greco-Roman society are perhaps echoed in this third-century-C.E. painting of an episode from the Additions to Daniel. Two elders, representing accepted religious authority, point accusingly at Susanna, whom they falsely charge with immorality. Daniel (left) observes the scene, about to pronounce on Susanna's innocence.

where he remains for six days. During this period, an angel carries the prophet Habakkuk (holding him by the hair) from Judea to Babylon so that he can feed Daniel and then returns the prophet to Palestine. When the king discovers on the seventh day that Daniel remains uneaten, he releases him, praises his God, and hurls Daniel's accusers into the pit, where the lions promptly devour them (14:28–42).

As in the other Additions, the author dramatizes the saving power of prayer, insisting that Israel's God never "forsakes those who love [him]" (14:38). Consistent with the Hebrew/Aramaic text of Daniel, the Greek redactors insist that the Deity watches over persons who remain faithful to his commandments and reject the snares of idol-worshiping Gentiles.

The Book of Baruch

A composite work to which at least three different writers contributed, Baruch purports to be a prophetic book written by Jeremiah's secretary early in the Babylonian captivity (cf. Jer. 32:12; 36:4–10).

As the only volume in the Apocrypha to imitate the prophetic mode of speech, much of Baruch consists of paraphrases from the canonical Hebrew Bible, including passages from Daniel 9, Job 28, and Isaiah 40–66. Although set during the Babylonian exile, the book actually deals with the problems of Diaspora Jews living in the Greco-Roman world. Estimates of the dates of composition for its various parts range from 200 to 60 B.C.E.

Baruch is commonly divided into two main sections, each of which contains two subdivisions. The opening statements (1:1–38) present several confusing contradictions. The author claims that the book was written in Babylon five years after the Babylonians burned Solomon's Temple (thereby dating it to 582 B.C.E.) (1:2), but he also represents the exiles asking the High Priest and his assistants in Jerusalem to offer prayers at "the house of the LORD" (1:14), as if it were still standing. Equally problematic is the assertion that Baruch read "the words of this book" to deported Judeans living in Babylon (1:1–4), when events related in the book did not occur until long after the supposed time of the public reading.

The first division includes an introduction (1:1–14) and a longer section, largely based on Daniel

9:4–19, that portrays the Judean exiles confessing the sins that had caused their nation's downfall and beseeching divine mercy (1:15–3:8). In the manner of Israel's classic prophets, a subsection contains an oracle promising that the scattered exiles will be returned to their homeland (2:27–35).

The second part, apparently by a different author, opens with a didactic hymn praising Israel's God for revealing his wisdom in the Mosaic Torah (3:9–4:4). Echoing motifs from Second Isaiah and Lamentations, the next unit contains poems of hope and comfort, as well as expressions of sorrow for Jerusalem's sufferings. The poet realizes that Judah's misfortunes are punishment for its violation of the covenant but foresees a joyous return to the Promised Land (5:1–9).

The Letter of Jeremiah

Although some ancient Greek manuscripts place this document after Lamentations, both Latin editions and most English Bibles that include the Apocrypha attach it to Baruch, where it appears as Chapter 6. Ostensibly a letter from Jeremiah to Judeans about to be exiled to Babylon, this pseudonymous document is, in fact, a much later work, apparently modeled on the historical Jeremiah's letter of advice to his exiled compatriots (Jer. 29). Estimates on the date of composition range from 317 to about 100 B.C.E.

The writer's principal theme is the evil of idolatry, on which his attack is the most virulent and extensive in biblical literature except for that in the Wisdom of Solomon (cf. Wisd. of Sol. 13:1–15:17). Although the only foreign god specifically mentioned is Bel (Marduk) (Bar. 6:4), scholars believe that the author is really denouncing Hellenistic deities whom Jews of the Diaspora might, for social and political reasons, have been seduced to worship. "Babylon" thus functions as a symbol of Greco-Roman cultures in which Jews struggled to keep their monotheistic commitment.

Like the author of Daniel, who similarly faced the historical fact that Jeremiah's prediction of Judah's full restoration did not occur after "seventy years" of Gentile oppression, the writer here interprets Jeremiah's time period as really meaning "seven generations" (Bar. 6:3; cf. Jer. 29:10; Dan. 9:24). Assuming that a biblical generation is forty years (Num. 32:13), he concludes that the covenant community will endure exile until the end of the fourth century B.C.E. The letter thus updates older biblical promises, making them relevant to his Diaspora audience.

The Book of Ecclesiasticus (the Wisdom of Jesus Son of Sirach)

The longest wisdom book in either the Tanak or the Apocrypha, Ecclesiasticus is also the only deuterocanonical writing whose author, original translator, and date are known. The writer identifies himself as Jesus Son of Sirach (50:27), a professional teacher of wisdom who conducted a school or house of learning in Jerusalem (51:24) (Figure 29.2). In a preface to the main work, the author's grandson reveals that he brought the book to Egypt, where he translated it from Hebrew into Greek at a date equivalent to 132 B.C.E.; his grandfather had composed it in Jerusalem about 180 B.C.E. The title, which means "church book," may reflect either its extensive use in Christian worship or the fact that the church, unlike the Jewish editors of the Tanak, received it into the canon.

Written in the tradition of Proverbs, Ecclesiasticus (also commonly referred to as Sirach) is a collection of wise sayings, moral essays, hymns to divine Wisdom, practical advice to the young and inexperienced, private meditations, thoughtful reflections on the human condition, and detailed instructions on proper social behavior. Like the sages who compiled Proverbs, Sirach perceives an ordered design in the universe and counsels others to conform their lives to it. A learned, respected, influential representative of upper-class Palestinian Judaism, he reveals a personality that is genial, pragmatic, and urbane. Writing in the relatively

Figure 29.2 Discovered at Masada, the hilltop fortress where the last important band of Jewish rebels held out against Roman armies (73 C.E.), this fragment of the Book of Ecclesiasticus (Wisdom of Jesus Son of Sirach) is approximately 2000 years old.

peaceful decades before Antiochus IV began his attacks on the Jewish faith, Sirach believes that life can be a positive experience for Torah observers who conduct themselves with prudence, insight, and shrewdness.

WISDOM AND THE GOOD LIFE

Firmly grounded in the biblical tradition oriented toward worthy goals of the present life, Sirach resembles the author of Ecclesiastes in rejecting notions of human immortality or posthumous rewards (see Chapter 25). "Human beings," he writes, "are not immortal" (Ecclus. 17:30), and all the dead, regardless of individual merit, are relegated to the permanent oblivion of Sheol (14:12–19; 38:16–23). The only form of posthumous identity available to humans involves the production of children and the maintenance of a good reputation (44:13–15). Eschewing apocalyptic enthusiasms, Sirach focuses on the benefits of wisdom applied to the art of life. The first forty-two chapters of his book, containing many brief aphorisms interspersed with

longer poetic discourses, offer advice and admonitions on diverse topics: the fear of God as the basis of wisdom (1:20; 32:14–33:3), appropriate humility (3:17–26), generosity to the poor (4:1–11; 7:32–40), advantageous friendships (6:5–17; 12:8–19; 22:19–32), trust in God (2:1–23; 11:12–30), humanity's ethical responsibilities (16:24–17:13), female spite (25:13–36), qualities of a good wife (26:1–23), proper manners and control of drinking at banquets (31:12–32:17), honor for physicians and respect for scholars (38:1–15; 31:1–15), and the human predicament and fate of the wicked (40:1–11; 41:5–16). Living in a comparatively stable era in which the wise could earn a fair share of affluence and social prestige, Sirach regards the world as fundamentally just, with God rewarding the righteous and punishing evildoers. Silent on the great issue of cosmic injustice dramatized in Job, he did not live to face the dilemma created by Antiochus's attempts to eradicate the Torah faith, when devout Jews suffered precisely *because* of their loyalty to covenant principles (see the discussion on 1 and 2 Maccabees).

A HYMN TO WISDOM

Like the author of Proverbs 8, Sirach personifies Wisdom as a gracious female figure who dwells with God in heaven but also communicates with humankind. In Chapter 24, he praises Lady Wisdom as not only God's first creation, a direct expression of eternal divinity, but also an inhabitant of earthly Zion and the source of Israel's divine teaching. Speaking before the celestial assembly, Wisdom proclaims her intimacy with God:

> I came forth from the mouth of the Most High,
> and covered the earth like a mist. . . .
> Before the ages, in the beginning, he created me,
> and for all the ages I shall not cease to be.
> In the holy tent [Tabernacle] I ministered before him,
> and so I was established in Zion.
> Thus in the beloved city he gave me a resting place,
> and in Jerusalem was my domain.
>
> (Ecclus. 24:3, 9–11)

Sirach adds a new dimension to Wisdom's praise, explicitly identifying her with the Torah, God's revelation to Israel:

> All this [Wisdom's speech] is the book of the covenant of the Most High GOD, the law [torah] that Moses commanded us as an inheritance for the congregation of Jacob. (Ecclus. 24:23; cf. 19:20)

Whereas most wisdom writers almost never refer to either the Mosaic Covenant or Israel's checkered historical experience in trying to keep it, Sirach at a stroke combines the Wisdom and Torah traditions, equating heavenly Wisdom with God's instructions to Moses. (The view that the Torah is eternal and preceded the world's creation is also voiced in the noncanonical Book of Jubilees; see Chapter 3.)

In Chapter 42, Sirach offers a more conventional wisdom hymn, describing the physical universe as reflecting divine glory. Like Psalm 19, the poem invites readers to discover God in the wonders of creation (42:15–43:33). Immediately after, Sirach introduces the book's most famous section: "Let us now sing the praises of famous men," celebrating the exemplary faith of Israel's ancestors. A eulogy of twenty-nine biblical heroes, from Enoch and Abraham to Josiah and Nehemiah, this poetic passage reflects Sirach's personal viewpoint on Israel's past. He not only devotes more space to praising Aaron (Israel's first High Priest) than to Moses (Israel's preeminent leader and lawgiver); he also declines even to mention Ezra, the scribe credited with formulating the postexilic Torah. Many scholars believe that the omission of Ezra is deliberate—a result of Sirach's dislike of an emerging religious movement that claimed Ezra as a forerunner, the Pharisee party. Sirach's particular beliefs, including his interest in priestly ritual and his rejection of belief in angels, demons, or a future resurrection—all associated with the **Pharisees**—may indicate his identification with an incipient rival party, the **Sadducees.** (These two groups figure prominently in the New Testament; see Chapter 31.)

Sirach's tribute to Israelite ancestors climaxes in the praise of Simon the High Priest (c. 225–200 B.C.E.), whom Sirach lauds as embodying the best of his nation's traditions (50:1–24). As intercessor between God and the covenant community, Simon was privileged to enter the Temple's Holy of Holies annually on the Day of Atonement (cf. Lev. 16) and there pronounce the divine name YHWH, which by Hellenistic times was considered too sacred to utter publicly. The book concludes with an epilogue containing Sirach's hymn of personal thanksgiving (Ecclus. 51:1–12) and an autobiographical summary of the rewards of pursuing Wisdom (51:13–30).

In Sirach's view, God's law remains fixed and unchanging, complete for all time; his corollary assumption, that the cosmos is justly administered according to discernible moral laws favoring the righteous and punishing the wicked, resembles that given in Proverbs and imparts a somewhat static quality to his teaching. Offering assurance that divine justice inevitably prevails and that, through hard work, the exercise of Torah ethics, and prudent behavior, one can attain the benefits of a good and godly life, Sirach provides guidelines for living in a well-ordered world. (His reluctance to address such Jobian issues as the problem of evil and undeserved suffering, however, may make his insights appear less relevant in times of moral crisis and violent disruptions of the social order.) Although his book did not gain entry into the Jewish canon, its popularity among many Hellenistic Jews is attested to by twentieth-century discoveries of large fragments of the Hebrew text at sites ranging from Cairo, Egypt, to Qumran and Masada in Palestine.

The Wisdom of Solomon

A JEWISH-GREEK SYNTHESIS

Although it presents itself as King Solomon's counsel to the world's rulers, this brilliant collection of poems, proverbs, and sage meditations was probably composed by an anonymous Greek-educated Jew living in Alexandria, Egypt, during the last century B.C.E. Like most of the apocryphal works, the book is directed to Jews living in the Diaspora, many of whom were moved to give up their ancestral traditions by the virtually irresistible lure of Greek culture and philosophy or under the pressure of Gentile discrimination. The author's familiarity with Greek philosophical terms and concepts (Wisd. of Sol. 8:7, 19–20; 12:1), as well as his commitment to the Jewish Scriptures, suggests that his work is an attempt to reconcile these two contrasting traditions by showing that the biblical revelation not only anticipates the best in Greek thought but is superior to it.

To demonstrate Judaism's ethical and religious superiority, the author argues that his tradition offers a view of world history and divine justice that will appeal to the moral and rational Gentile. A creative synthesis of Jewish and Greek ideas, the Wisdom of Solomon makes a significant contribution to biblical theology, particularly in its visions of future immortality for the righteous and of Wisdom acting as a savior figure in human life. The book can be divided into three parts: the value of Wisdom (a divine spirit) and the promise of a joyous afterlife (Chs. 1–5); the origin, character, and function of Wisdom (Chs. 6–9); and God's Wisdom operating throughout world history (Chs. 10–19).

Defining Wisdom as a "kindly spirit" emanating from an all-knowing God, the opening section vividly contrasts two views of human life. Whereas the wicked misuse reason, thinking that human existence is not only ephemeral but also meaningless, the righteous, symbolically held "in the hand of God" (3:1), benefit from divine reason and receive the gift of immortality (Chs. 2–3). Confronting the problem of unmerited suffering raised in Job, the author foresees a future life that compensates for all earthly ordeals. Although evildoers may prosper on earth and oppress the good, the soul's survival in a posthumous existence guarantees that divine justice ultimately prevails. Asserting that "God created us for incorruption, and made us in the image of his own eternity" (2:23), the author assures his readers that physical death of the righteous is only an illusory defeat, for death is transcended by the soul's eternal communion with God (3:1–9).

Although skeptics may think that the good people whom they wronged will perish utterly, their victims' sufferings were merely a test to reveal their true worth, qualifying virtuous souls eventually to judge and rule over the world (3:2–8). Evil deeds are thus used for a higher good, serving to exalt the righteous and ultimately punish their perpetrators (3:10).

THE CHARACTER AND VALUE OF WISDOM

Numerous Greek concepts appear in the second part of the book, which features "Solomon's" praise of Lady Wisdom, the conveyer of immortality (cf. 6:1; 8:13). The speaker, who takes personified Wisdom as his "bride" (8:2), implies that the soul exists in heaven prior to its earthly existence (8:19–20; 9:15). This belief in an immaterial, preexistent soul that leaves the spirit realm to become incarnate (take on flesh) in an earthly body and, at death, escapes its human form to return to heaven expresses a widespread Hellenistic belief derived from the teachings of Greek philosophers such as Pythagoras, **Socrates,** and **Plato.** (The author's creative association of Wisdom, the soul's temporary incarnation, and a postmortem ascent to immortal life in heaven received further development in the New Testament Gospel of John, which applies these concepts to Jesus [cf. John 1:1–14].)

The influence of Greek ethical philosophy also appears in the author's celebration of the four classical virtues, which were later adopted as the four cardinal virtues of Christian morality:

> And if anyone loves righteousness, her labors are virtues;
> for she teaches self-control and prudence,
> justice and courage;
> nothing in life is more profitable for mortals than these. (Wisd. of Sol. 8:7)

WISDOM'S ROLE IN HUMAN HISTORY

In the third section of his book, the author presents an idealized survey of early humanity (Ch. 10) and of Israel's history (Chs. 10–19), contrasting the Deity's judgments on unbelieving Gentiles with his tender care for the covenant people, to whom Wisdom lent strength and understanding. Emphasizing God's benevolence and mercy, these passages depict Wisdom as a savior who rescues, guides, and inspires those who seek her. Using the illustration of God's delivering the Israelites from Egypt, the writer shows that Israel benefited from the same natural elements used to inflict the ten plagues on Egypt: Whereas God, through Moses, brought water from a rock to slake the people's thirst, he made the Nile's waters undrinkable for the Egyptians by changing them to blood. Thus, "one is punished by the very things by which one sins" (Wisd. of Sol. 11:16). This extended reinterpretation of the Exodus is repeatedly interrupted by various digressions, including reflections on divine power and mercy (11:17–12:22) and a long denunciation of idolatry (13:1–15:17), reminiscent of Second Isaiah's scornful estimate of Babylonian gods (cf. Isa. 40, 46). The concluding reinterpretation of biblical history may have been intended to inspire hope among Diaspora Jews that Israel's God would again intervene to aid them as he had their distant ancestors.

In the next-to-last chapter, the author introduces a concept that was to exert a powerful influence on Christian thought. He describes Wisdom as God's "all-powerful word" leaping down "from heaven, from the royal throne," to take up residence in a "land that was doomed." Carrying, "the sharp sword of [God's] authentic command," this cosmic figure "touched the heaven while standing on the earth," linking the realms of matter and spirit (Wisd. of Sol. 18:15). Perhaps only a generation or two after the Wisdom of Solomon was written, another learned Jew living in Alexandria expanded on this concept of a celestial "word" (Greek, *Logos*) as a divine intermediary. **Philo Judaeus,** interpreting the opening verses of Genesis in which God spoke light into existence, designated this divine utterance—the Word (Logos)—as the agent of creation. Stoicism, a Greek philosophy popular with many upper-class Romans, had similarly used "Word" (Logos) to denote the principle of cosmic reason that created and shaped the universe. Philo's usage, integrating Jewish Scripture with Greek philosophy, eventually resurfaces in the Gospel of John, which adapted it to portray the prehuman Jesus, whom John identified as the "Word" active at creation (John 1:1). The Wisdom of Solomon's usefulness in formulating later Christian doctrine may explain not only why the book was widely read in Christian circles (Paul paraphrases it in his letters to the Romans and Corinthians) but also why it appears in the Muratorian Canon, a list of New Testament books its author considered authoritative.

The Prayer of Manasseh

The shortest independent book in the Apocrypha, this devotional poem of only fifteen verses is supposedly the work of King Manasseh, whom 2 Kings 21 condemns as the most wicked monarch in Judah's history. Although the incident is not mentioned in the Kings account of his long reign, 2 Chronicles alleges that the Assyrians took Manasseh captive to Babylon, where, by repenting of his sins—including idolatry, sorcery, and human sacrifice—he won YHWH's forgiveness and was restored to his throne. Back in Jerusalem, Manasseh reportedly purged the city of "foreign gods," removed an idol from the Temple, and rebuilt YHWH's altar (2 Chron. 33:5–10).

Although the Chronicler notes that Manasseh's prayer was preserved in the "records of the seers" (2 Chron. 33:19), scholars do not believe that the apocryphal work, composed during the second or first century B.C.E., is based on the earlier source. Echoing the psalms of individual lament, such as Psalms 69–71, the poem is theologically important because it emphasizes both the genuineness of a sinner's repentance and God's willingness to pardon and redeem even the guiltiest (Pr. of Man. v. 7).

The Book of 1 Maccabees

A vividly detailed account of Jewish struggles to defend their ancestral religion against enforced **Hellenization**—the adoption of Greek culture and practices—1 Maccabees describes events in Palestine during the turbulent second century B.C.E. In remarkably terse, matter-of-fact prose, the book recounts a war for Jewish religious and political independence in which a particular family—the Maccabees—leads the covenant people from a state of foreign oppression to one of national autonomy. Emphasizing the Maccabees' crucial role in achieving Jewish freedom, the narrative opens with a description of **Antiochus IV** (ruled 175–163 B.C.E.) and his attempts to unify the diverse peoples of his empire (which then controlled Palestine) by Hellenizing the entire population (Ch. 1). Antiochus's edicts forbidding Torah study, circumcision, Sabbath keeping, and observance of Kosher dietary restrictions trigger an uprising led by Mattathias and his sons (Ch. 2), culminating in a prolonged guerilla war conducted by **Judas Maccabeus** (Chs. 3–9); after Judas's death, the revolt is carried on by his brothers Jonathan (Chs. 9–12) and Simon (Chs. 13–16), who succeed in driving Syrian armies from their homeland. Simon's son, John Hyrcanus I, becomes the first king-priest of a new Maccabean (Hasmonean) dynasty ruling over a politically independent Judea (Figure 29.3).

Like the Hebrew text of Esther, 1 Maccabees narrates Jewish battles against Gentile oppression without referring to miracles, divine intervention, or any other supernatural agency. Writing about 100 B.C.E., the anonymous narrator portrays his leading characters, the Maccabean family, as Torah loyalists, but he never attributes their military or political victories to God's direct help, though he does imply that faithful Jews who are willing to die to defend their faith will achieve success.

Although widely viewed as an inspiring history of Jewish self-determination, the author probably had a specific political agenda. Recent commentators point to a passage describing the defeat of Joseph and Azariah, two Jewish patriots who fought the Syrians apart from the Maccabean family: "Thus the people suffered a great rout because, thinking to do a brave deed, they did not listen to Judas and his brothers. But they did not belong to the family of those men through whom deliverance was given to Israel" (1 Macc. 5:61–62). Without direct Maccabean leadership, the author implies, even the most heroic acts are doomed to failure, a perspective suggesting that the book was composed primarily to validate the Maccabean (Hasmonean) dynasty.

ANTIOCHUS IV'S PERSECUTION AND THE MACCABEAN REVOLT

In a brief preface, 1 Maccabees provides background for the events that follow, summarizing Alexander the Great's conquest of Persia, the spread of Greek culture, and his successors' division of Alexander's empire (see Table 28.1). Palestine was first awarded to Ptolemy of Egypt but was seized by the rival Seleucids of Syria shortly after 200 B.C.E. Although many Jews voluntarily embraced Greek ways, many others—known as the **hasidim** (pious ones) adamantly resisted what they regarded as an unacceptable compromise of their faith. Government-sponsored Hellenization greatly intensified under Antiochus IV, who met Jewish resistance by outlawing the practice of Judaism altogether, burning copies of the Mosaic Torah and forbidding sacrifice to any gods but those of Greece. Mothers

Figure 29.3   Map of Palestine in the Maccabean Period (c. 168–63 B.C.E.)

Palestine in the Maccabean Period
(c. 168-63 B.C.E.)

Kingdom of Alexander Janneus

who had their infant boys circumcised were punished by having their babies slain, with the bodies then tied around the mothers' necks. To enforce his prohibitions, Antiochus stationed a garrison of Syrian soldiers in Jerusalem, building a massive fortress near the Temple. In a final outrage, the king erected a statue of the Olympian Zeus in the Temple courtyard and sacrificed pigs on YHWH's altar, rendering the shrine ceremonially unclean.

Mattathias Whereas some Jews, enticed by Greek culture and philosophy, voluntarily supported Antiochus's policies, others reluctantly acceded, out of fear. Among those who defied the king was the village priest **Mattathias.** When a fellow villager obeys Antiochus's representative by eating a mouthful of pork, Mattathias kills both the offending Jew and the official. With his five sons—John, Simon, Judas, Eleazar, and Jonathan—he then flees to the neighboring hill country (1 Macc. 2).

After Syrian troops massacre 1000 Jews who refuse to defend themselves on the Sabbath, Mattathias and his followers prudently decide that self-defense does not violate Sabbath rules. Fighting a guerilla war against the occupying army, Mattathias's group destroys numerous pagan altars and forcibly circumcises many Jewish boys. When near death, Mattathias appoints the most capable of his sons, Judas Maccabeus (Greek, the "Hammer" [God's instrument of warfare]) as his successor to continue the fight.

Judas Maccabeus Chapters 3–9 form a tribute to the heroic service of Judas Maccabeus to the Jewish nation. Against tremendous odds, he defeats the Syrians in several decisive battles. Marching into Jerusalem, he accomplishes his main religious objective: reclaiming the Temple and purifying the altar that Antiochus has polluted. Judas then institutes the joyous festival of dedication—known today as **Hanukkah**—according to tradition, exactly three years to the day after Antiochus had defiled the sanctuary. When Antiochus unexpectedly dies in 163 B.C.E., Judas concludes an armistice with the Syrians, assuring his people the right to practice their hereditary religion. After hostilities are re-

newed three years later, Judas defeats the Syrian general Nicanor, who had threatened to burn the Temple.

Among Judas's most historically significant actions is his decision to sign a treaty of friendship with Rome, the powerful new empire then arising in the West. Writing before Roman armies took over Judea in 63 B.C.E., the author ironically portrays Rome as the champion of peace and international stability, the protector of smaller states that willingly place themselves within its sphere of influence (Figure 29.4).

Jonathan After Judas falls in battle, his brother Jonathan becomes leader of the Jews (160–142 B.C.E.). Sharing his predecessor's charismatic gifts, Jonathan rallies the people against further Syrian aggression. Alexander, the new claimant to the Syrian throne, shrewdly concludes a peace settlement with Jonathan in 152 B.C.E. and appoints him High Priest, by this time a political as well as religious office. This act establishes a line of Hasmonean kings (named for a Maccabean ancestor) that lasts until 40 B.C.E., when the Romans appoint Herod I king of the Jews. During later political turmoil, however, Jonathan is lured into the Syrian camp and treacherously slain (1 Macc. 9:23–12:53).

Simon The last of Mattathias's five sons, Simon now assumes military leadership and eventually the high priesthood as well. Although he marshals an army, he fights fewer battles than did his brothers; relying more on diplomacy and guile than military force, Simon bribes Syrian troops to withdraw and secures peace for seven years. Taking advantage of the lull and of Syria's internal strife, Simon builds a series of fortresses around Judea and forms an alliance with the Syrian ruler, who confirms his appointment as High Priest and also releases the Judeans from taxation. This pact (142 B.C.E.) effectively affirms Jewish autonomy and marks Judea's emergence as an independent state.

John Hyrcanus In 134 B.C.E., however, the Syrians again attack, and many Jews are killed or imprisoned. The aged Simon commissions two of his

Figure 29.4 The coin on the right was struck during the reign of John Hyrcanus II (67–40 B.C.E.), the Hasmonean ruler who invited the Roman occupation of Judea in 63 B.C.E. The bronze coin on the left features a menorah, the seven-branched lampstand kept in the Temple, and was issued during the brief reign of Antigonus (40–37 B.C.E.), last of the Hasmonean dynasty. Herod I, the Roman-appointed king of Judea, had Antigonus beheaded and ruthlessly eliminated all other Hasmonean claimants to the throne.

sons, Judas and John, who lead the Jewish army victoriously against the invaders. After Simon and two of his sons, Mattathias and Judas, are murdered by Simon's traitorous son-in-law, John (surnamed "Hyrcanus"), Simon's other son, becomes Judah's priest-king (1 Macc. 16), the last event recorded in Old Testament history. (For a survey of Judean history in Roman times, see Chapter 31.)

Although 1 Maccabees may have originated as a superior example of dynastic propaganda, the book offers a generally accurate portrayal of a chaotic era in which the competing forces of Greek culture and Jewish tradition clashed head-on. Without evoking supernatural elements in his narrative, the author nonetheless demonstrates that loyalty to the Mosaic Torah, coupled with courage and skill in battle, resulted in both religious freedom and the creation of a new Jewish state. (For a very different response to the crisis of Antiochus's persecutions, a mystical invocation of divine intervention, see the discussion of Daniel in Chapter 28.)

The Book of 2 Maccabees

A Greek work, probably written in Alexandria, Egypt, after 124 B.C.E., 2 Maccabees is not a continuation of the history of 1 Maccabees but a revised version of events related in the first seven chapters of the earlier book. According to the compiler's preface (2:19–32), the book is an edited abridgment of a five-volume historical work (since lost) by "Jason of Cyrene," who is otherwise unknown. The period covered is approximately 176–161 B.C.E.

Whereas 1 Maccabees is a comparatively straightforward and plausible account of the Jewish revolt against Syria, the second book's credibility is undermined by its emphasis on exaggerated numbers, unlikely miracles, and supernatural apparitions. The writer of 2 Maccabees, who interprets the events he describes theologically, not only presents the rebellion's success as an act of God (11:13; 15:27)

BOX 29.1
Torah Loyalism, Martyrdom, and the Reward of Future Life

The persecutions of Antiochus mark the first time in biblical history that Jews died not for defending their country militarily against foreign invaders but merely for practicing their faith. The Book of 2 Maccabees paints horrific pictures of faithful Jews paying for their integrity with torture, mutilation, and death. When Eleazar, a ninety-year-old Torah instructor, spits out the pig's flesh that Antiochus's soldiers have forced on him, he is bludgeoned to death. Even worse were the agonies endured by seven young brothers who similarly refused to pass the king's test of religious conformity by eating what the Torah forbade. One by one, before their mother's eyes, they are scalped, their heads flayed, their tongues cut out, and their hands and feet lopped off; then, still conscious, they are thrust into huge pans and slowly fried alive (2 Macc. 7).

As martyrs who willingly died in a religious cause, the anonymous seven brothers not only served as models for other Jews forced to choose between life and Torah loyalty but also voiced a belief that their unspeakable sufferings would be compensated for in a future life. Expressing a conviction that God will resurrect the faithful dead—a view that enters the biblical record only with the Hellenistic Book of Daniel (12:1–3)—the second brother places his martyrdom in the light of eternity: "The King of the world will raise us up, since it is for his laws that we die, to live again for ever" (2 Macc. 7:9). Appearing initially in the crisis ignited by enforced Hellenization, the concept that enduring a painful but holy death would lead to immortality ultimately exerted a pervasive influence on both the Hellenistic Jewish and the early Christian communities.

---

but repeatedly injects commentary about such matters as divine guidance and future retribution for Israel's enemies into his narrative (5:17–20; 6:12–17; 8:36; 12:40), along with such typical Pharisaic doctrines as belief in a bodily resurrection (7:9; 14:46).

CORRUPTION, PERSECUTION, AND MARTYRDOM

The book opens with two letters from Palestinian Jews to their fellow Jews in Egypt, urging them to observe Hanukkah, the December festival commemorating the Temple's rededication (2 Macc. 1:1–2:18). These letters are probably an editor's later addition appended to the compiler's original introduction (2:19–32), a review of literary sources that were probably included to establish authorial credibility. The main narrative describes the increasing corruption of two pre-Maccabean High Priests, Jason and Menelaus (Chs. 3–4); the cruelty of Antiochus IV's persecutions of faithful Jews (Chs. 5–7); the military successes of Judas Maccabeus, which

culminate in his purification of the Temple (Chs. 8–10); and Judas's subsequent battles against such Syrian foes as Nicanor, chief general of Demetrius I, one of Antiochus's successors (Chs. 10–15).

Despite the doubtful historicity of some episodes, 2 Maccabees is an effectively written account, providing colorful illustrations of the greed and treachery of Jason and Menelaus, renegades who betray their own people for personal gain. Particularly memorable are the author's depictions of the tortures endured by Jews who refused to obey Antiochus's decrees ordering them to violate Torah commands, epitomized by the eating of pork. Eleazar, ninety years old and a distinguished teacher, is bludgeoned to death; even worse is the fate of seven brothers, who, in the sight of their mother, are systematically mutilated and slowly burned alive under Antiochus's fiendish supervision (Chs. 6–7; Box 29.1).

Emphasizing the courage and nobility of Jewish martyrs ready to die for their faith, the author offers an ingenious philosophy of suffering to account for Israel's woes. Antiochus and similar tyrants are merely the Deity's human instruments for disciplining the covenant people. Paradoxically, the martyrs' extreme pain is a sign of divine benevolence: Whereas God allows Gentile nations to multiply their crimes and guilt — implying that future retribution will be all the more severe — Israel is punished *before* its collective sins have "reached their height" (6:12–17), sparing the people greater misery in the end. Thus, the countless disasters that befall faithful Judeans constitute visible proof that their God has *not* deserted them.

The author's other distinctive views include a promised resurrection of the dead (7:9; 14:46), a belief the efficacy of prayer to relieve the dead from sin (12:43–45), a doctrine that the righteous dead can intervene on behalf of the living (15:12–16), and a concept that God created the world out of nothing *(ex nihilo)* (7:28). Although such beliefs may have been held by only a limited number of Hellenistic Jews, they became widely accepted in Roman Catholicism, which draws on 2 Maccabees for several doctrines, including prayers for souls in purgatory and the intercessory prayers of saints.

(The books of 3 and 4 Maccabees are discussed among the Pseudepigrapha in Chapter 30.)

The Book of 1 Esdras (3 Ezra)

Although they were deleted from the canon of Roman Catholic Old Testaments at the Council of Trent in the sixteenth century C.E., the two apocryphal books ascribed to Ezra remain canonical in Eastern Orthodox editions of the Old Testament. First Esdras, the earlier work, appears in the Septuagint, but 2 Esdras, the last-written document in the Apocrypha, was composed too late (c. 100 C.E.) for inclusion. Adhering largely to the Jewish canon (the Tanak), Jerome (c. 348–420 C.E.) did not accept most of the Apocrypha for his Latin translation, the Vulgate. Many Old Latin editions, however, included both 1 and 2 Esdras, for many centuries according them deuterocanonical status in the Western church.

Probably composed during the second century B.C.E., 1 Esdras is largely a Greek revision of some postexilic narratives from the Tanak, a retelling of biblical history from the reforms of Josiah to those of Ezra. Freely drawing on 2 Chronicles (Chs. 35–36), most of Ezra, and part of Nehemiah (7:73–8:12), this volume contains only one section that has no parallel in the canonical books, a legendary tale about the superiority of Jewish wisdom at the court of Darius, emperor of Persia (1 Esd. 3:1–5:6).

The book opens with an account of Josiah's elaborate celebration of the Passover at the Temple in Jerusalem in the late seventh century B.C.E., a narrative based on 2 Chronicles 35. Like the Chronicler, the author of 1 Esdras promotes a priestly view of Judah's history, emphasizing Temple rituals, prescribed festivals, and Levitical rites, duties, and prerogatives. Highlighting the covenant people's legal and liturgical obligations, the book concludes with Ezra's proclamation of the Mosaic Torah to the Judean exiles who have returned from Babylon. The one original episode concerns Zerubbabel, a descendant of King David who is depicted as an intimate of the Persian ruler. Like similar anecdotes in Esther and Daniel that illustrate the rewards of keeping Torah commands in the Diaspora, this passage contrasts the lofty ethical insights of Jewish sages with the more limited vision of their foreign counterparts. Based on a traditional Near Eastern form of court entertainment in which courtiers engaged in a battle of wits, the story features three young guardsmen of Emperor Darius, each of whom is asked to nominate what he regards as the strongest force in the world. After Darius and his noblemen judge the merits of their respective nominations, they will award "rich gifts and prizes" to the winner. Three of the contestants' nominations — wine, the king, and women — suggest the typical values of courtiers familiar with both the amusements and political realities of an imperial administration. In the original version of the contest, "women" probably won the prize, for the narrator insists that even kings are subject to their beauty. Zerubbabel, whose suggestion ingeniously combined "women ... and truth," then explains that even stronger than the sway of feminine charm is the power of truth, "which lives and rules forever" (1 Esd. 4:28). Champion of a loftier ethic than his Persian companions, Zerubbabel is judged the winner and is rewarded by a royal appointment to govern Judah and restore its fortunes (3:1–4:43).

The Book of 2 Esdras (4 Ezra)

Written at almost the same time as the New Testament Book of Revelation (c. 100 C.E.), 2 Esdras is the only apocalypse included in the Apocrypha. Although dropped from Catholic editions in the sixteenth century C.E., the book now appears in some modern editions of the Old Testament, such as the Revised English Bible and the New Revised Standard Version. In its present form, 2 Esdras is a composite document; the central section (Chs. 3–14) was composed by a Jewish visionary in either Hebrew or Aramaic about thirty years after the Romans had destroyed Jerusalem in 70 C.E. After the book was translated into Greek, an anonymous Christian editor added the first two chapters (c. 150 C.E.) to restore the proper worship of Israel's God. Approximately a century later, another Christian redactor appended Chapters 15 and 16, providing a Christian framework to this first-century Jewish apocalypse.

EZRA'S THEODICY

Attributed to Ezra, the priestly scribe credited with assembling the Mosaic Torah while exiled in Babylon (cf. Ezra 7), the core chapters were actually composed by an unknown Jewish author who lived more than five centuries after Ezra's time. Like his ancestors during the Babylonian exile, the author of 2 Esdras 3–14 had witnessed the humiliating overthrow of his people's holy city and Temple, a catastrophic triumph of Gentile power over the covenant community that called God's justice into question. The pseudonymous writer, who finds himself in a position analogous to that of the his-

torical Ezra, draws on the resources of apocalyptic discourse to find some meaning or purpose in the national disaster. Chapters 3–14 present a series of seven eschatological visions, of which the first three are cast in the form of philosophical dialogues between Ezra and various angels who defend God's handling of historical events. These celestial messengers counter Ezra's repeated questioning of divine ethics with attempts to justify the Deity's ways to humankind. Most readers find Ezra's questions more penetrating than the conventional answers he receives.

If Babylon (Rome) is God's chosen instrument to punish his people, Ezra asks, why are Babylonians (Romans) so much worse behaved than the Jews whom they oppress? Why has God allowed an enemy nation that mocks him to annihilate those who at least try to worship him (2 Esd. 3:25–32)? Is it not better to remain unborn than to live and suffer without knowing why (4:12)? The angels' replies express the apocalyptic stereotype: God will dispense justice in good time. The flourishing of wickedness is only temporary; it will be terminated according to a foreordained time table (4:27–32), and the divine schedule is not humanity's concern. As Ezra observes, however, he does not presume to inquire into heavenly mysteries; rather, he seeks only to learn that which human intelligence is able to comprehend:

> To what end has the capacity for understanding been given me? For I did not mean to ask about ways above [exclusively God's domain], but about things which pass by us every day, why Israel . . . whom you love [is] given to godless tribes. (2 Esd. 4:22–23)

The wrenching disparity between the divine promises to Israel and the miserable historical reality constitutes a paradox that the Deity does not explain.

THE AFTERLIFE

Ezra is concerned about not only the earthly plight of his people but also the condition of their souls after death. Reluctantly agreeing that many act wrongly while only a few are righteous, he none-theless disputes the justice of condemning sinners to unending torment without any further chance of repentance. Chapter 7 juxtaposes graphic de-scriptions of salvation and damnation, offering the most detailed portrayal of the afterlife in the Old Testament:

> Then the place of torment shall appear, and over against it the place of rest; the furnace of hell shall be displayed, and on the opposite side the paradise of delight . . . here are rest and delight, there fire and torment. (2 Esd. 7:36–38)

As in Revelation and the parable of Lazarus and the Rich Man in Luke's Gospel (all composed during the last decades of the first century c.e.), the plea-sures of the blessed are enhanced by a clear view of sinners in eternal pain.

THE ESCHATOLOGICAL FUTURE

In Chapter 9, 2 Esdras changes from a Job-like theodicy to a typically apocalyptic preview of the world's end. Ezra's fourth vision depicts a woman who, mourning her first son, is suddenly trans-formed into a thriving city. Uriel, one of the book's angelic mediators, explains that the woman is Jeru-salem, her lost son the destroyed Temple, and the splendid city a future glorified Zion (Chs. 9–10; cf. Rev. 12, 21–22). In Chapters 11 and 12, the author portrays Rome as a mighty eagle that now domi-nates the earth but that is destined to disappear when a lion (the Messiah) appears to judge it for its perse-cution of the righteous (11:38–12:34). The sixth vision underscores the certainty of the Messiah's ex-pected appearance and his righteous overthrow of unbelievers who oppress Jerusalem (Ch. 13).

The two final chapters, a Christian appendix from the third century c.e., dramatize the Deity's coming vengeance on the wicked. Predicting a swarm of terrors and calamities, the book assures readers that the ungodly nation (Rome), as well as all other empires that persecute the faithful, will fall and that the guilty will be consumed by fire (Chs. 15–16).

QUESTIONS FOR REVIEW

1. Define *deuterocanonical* and explain its applica-tion to the category of books also known as the Apoc-rypha. Why do Catholic and Eastern Orthodox edi-tions of the Old Testament contain documents not included in the Hebrew Bible (Tanak) or Protestant Old Testament? What role did the contents of the Greek Septuagint play in the early church's acceptance of a larger canon than that of the Jewish Scriptures?

2. During what historical period were most of the deuterocanonical books (the Apocrypha) written? What issues of the Diaspora do they typically address? How does Tobit illustrate the problems of Jews living abroad in Gentile territories? What examples of Hel-lenistic Jewish folklore does it include?

3. Describe the actions by which Judith became a national heroine. Who is Holofernes, and how does his fate illustrate the power of Judith's God? What other characters in the biblical tradition resemble Ju-dith in their solitary performance of heroic deeds (all viewed as representing divine empowerment)?

4. Esther is the only book in the Hebrew Bible that does not mention God. How do the Additions to Esther give the story a more religious orientation?

5. Summarize the Additions to Daniel. How does Daniel rescue Susanna from her false accusers? How does he demonstrate to foreign rulers the superiority of his God?

6. In canonical Jeremiah, who was Baruch? How does advice contained in the Letter of Jeremiah apply to Diaspora Jews?

7. To what general category do Ecclesiasticus and the Wisdom of Solomon belong? Who was Jesus Son of Sirach? When, where, and in what language did he write, and how did his book come to be translated into Greek? With what document does Sirach identify Lady Wisdom? How does the author of the Wisdom of Solomon portray Lady Wisdom, and how is this important in the development of Judeo-Christian ideas? What Greek ideas does this book introduce into the biblical tradition?

8. Identifying and defining all the terms and his-torical figures involved, describe Antiochus IV's policy of enforced Hellenization and the resistance of Torah loyalists (the hasidim). Who were Mattathias and Ju-das Maccabeus, and how did they respond to Syrian

oppression? How did the Maccabean family succeed in reestablishing an autonomous Jewish state? What dynasty did they found? What event does the festival of Hanukkah commemorate?

9. Explain how the martyrdom of faithful Jews, such as the seven sons and their mother described in 2 Maccabees, is associated with the rise of a new belief—resurrection to a future afterlife.

10. Identify the canonical status of 1 and 2 Esdras. Summarize the single original episode included in 1 Esdras. To what literary genre does 2 Esdras belong, and what historical disaster for the Jewish people does it address? How does 2 Esdras deal with questions of divine justice and an afterlife of rewards and punishments?

QUESTIONS FOR REFLECTION AND DISCUSSION

1. Discuss some of the political, cultural, and religious consequences of Alexander the Great's conquest of the eastern Mediterranean world (see Chapter 3). How do the voluntary Hellenization of many Jews and the Maccabean Revolt fit into the larger picture of the Hellenistic age created by Alexander and his successors?

2. In what specific ways do such works as Tobit, Judith, Baruch, and 1 and 2 Maccabees offer encouragement and counsel to members of the covenant community scattered abroad in the Diaspora? What message do these writings have for communities of faith today?

3. Discuss the nature and function of personified Wisdom in Ecclesiastes and the Wisdom of Solomon, explaining the role she plays in human history. How does the Wisdom of Solomon link divine Wisdom to Torah faithfulness and immortality? How do these new ideas add an important dimension to the problem of divine justice and undeserved suffering dramatized in older wisdom books like Job?

TERMS AND CONCEPTS TO REMEMBER

Antiochus IV (Epiphanes)
Apocrypha
Bel
deuterocanonical books
Esdras's (Ezra's) theodicy
Hanukkah
hasidim
Hasmonean dynasty
Hellenization
Judas Maccabeus
martyrdom and resurrection
Mattathias
Pharisees
Philo Judaeus
Plato
Pseudepigrapha
Sadducees
Socrates
Torah loyalty in a Diaspora setting
Wisdom as creative Word (Logos)
Wisdom as Torah

RECOMMENDED READING

General Works

Albertz, Rainer. *A History of Israelite Religion in the Old Testament Period: Vol. 2: From the Exile to the Maccabees.* Translated by John Bowden. Louisville, Ky.: Westminster/John Knox Press, 1994. Offers authoritative sociohistorical background on the period in which the Apocrypha and much of the Pseudepigrapha were composed.

Charles, R. H., ed. *Apocrypha and Pseudepigrapha of the Old Testament.* 2 vols. Oxford: Clarendon Press, 1913. A monumental work of scholarship.

Charlesworth, James H., ed. *The Old Testament Pseudepigrapha. Vol. 1: Apocalyptic Literature and Testaments. Vol 2: Expansions of the "Old Testament" and Legends, Wisdom and Philosophical Literature, Prayers, Psalms and Odes, Fragments of Lost Judeo-Hellenistic Works.* Garden City, N.Y.: Doubleday, 1983, 1985. Contains contemporary translations and extensive scholarly annotation.

Cohen, Shaye J. D. *From the Maccabees to the Mishnah.* Philadelphia: Westminster Press, 1987. An informative survey of Jewish thought from c. 200 B.C.E. to 200 C.E.

Coogan, Michael D.; Brettler, Marc Z.; and Newsom, Carol, eds. *The New Oxford Annotated Bible with the Apocrypha/Deuterocanonical Books,* 3rd ed. New York: Oxford University Press, 2001. Provides extensive scholarly commentary on the NRSV texts.

Harrington, Daniel J. *Invitation to the Apocrypha.* Grand Rapids, Mich.: Eerdmans, 1999. A good introductory guide to the deuterocanonical literature.

Hengel, Martin. *Jews, Greeks, and Barbarians: Aspects of the Hellenization of Judaism in the Pre-Christian Period.* Philadelphia: Fortress Press, 1980. A shorter study of Jewish and Greek cultures in the last centuries B.C.E.

———. *Judaism and Hellenism.* 2 vols. London: SCM Press, 1974. A comprehensive, detailed study of the interactions of Greek and Jewish thought in the Hellenistic period.

Nickelsburg, George. *Jewish Literature Between the Bible and the Mishnah.* Philadelphia: Fortress Press, 1981. A major study of Jewish writings in the Greco-Roman period.

Stone, Michael. *Scriptures, Sects, and Visions: A Profile of Judaism from Ezra to the Jewish Revolts.* Philadelphia: Fortress Press, 1980. A concise, clearly written exposition of major developments in Jewish thought from the postexilic restoration to the revolts against Rome.

Tobit and Judith

Nowell, Irene. "The Book of Tobit." In *The New Interpreter's Bible,* Vol. 3, pp. 973–1971. Nashville, Tenn.: Abingdon Press, 1999. Offers an introduction and commentary.

Wills, Lawrence M. "The Book of Judith." In *The New Interpreter's Bible,* Vol. 3, pp. 1073–1183. Nashville, Tenn.: Abingdon Press, 1999. Discusses the book as a Hellenistic literary romance.

Additions to Daniel, Additions to Esther, and Baruch

Crawford, Sidnie W. "The Additions to Esther." In *The New Interpreter's Bible,* Vol. 3, pp. 943–972. Nashville, Tenn.: Abingdon Press, 1999. A helpful commentary.

Moore, Carey A. *Daniel, Esther, and Jeremiah: The Additions.* Anchor Bible, Vol. 42. Garden City, N.Y.: Doubleday, 1977. Gives new translations and commentary.

Ecclesiasticus (Sirach) and the Wisdom of Solomon

Crenshaw, James L. "The Book of Sirach." In *The New Interpreter's Bible,* Vol. 5, pp. 601–867. Nashville, Tenn.: Abingdon Press, 1997. Provides background, commentary, and analysis.

Kolarcik, Michael. "The Book of Wisdom." In *The New Interpreter's Bible,* Vol. 5, pp. 435–600. Nashville, Tenn.: Abingdon Press, 1997. Offers extensive commentary and analysis of this important Hellenistic text.

Reese, James M. *Hellenistic Influence on the Book of Wisdom and Its Consequences.* Rome: Biblical Institute Press, 1970. A significant study.

Skehan, Patrick W., and Di Lella, Alexander A. *The Wisdom of ben Sira.* Garden City, N.Y.: Doubleday, 1987.

Smith, John G. *Ecclesiasticus: Or the Wisdom of Jesus Son of Sirach.* Cambridge Bible Commentary on the New English Bible. London: Cambridge University Press, 1974.

Winston, David. *The Wisdom of Solomon.* Anchor Bible, Vol. 43. Garden City, N.Y.: Doubleday, 1979. A recent translation with scholarly annotations.

Wright, Addison G. "Wisdom." In R. E. Brown et al., eds., *The New Jerome Biblical Commentary,* 2nd ed., pp. 510–522. Englewood Cliffs, N.J.: Prentice-Hall, 1990. A good introduction to the book's Hellenistic-Jewish background.

1 and 2 Maccabees

Doran, Robert. "1 Maccabees." In *The New Interpreter's Bible,* Vol. 4, pp. 1–178. Nashville, Tenn.: Abingdon Press, 1996. Provides historical background to the Maccabean Revolt and detailed annotation of the text.

———. "2 Maccabees." In *The New Interpreter's Bible,* Vol. 4, pp. 179–299. Nashville, Tenn.: Abingdon Press, 1996. Discusses sources and major themes.

Goldstein, Jonathan A. *1 Maccabees: A New Translation with Introduction and Commentary.* Anchor Bible, Vol. 41. Garden City, N.Y.: Doubleday, 1976. Provides valuable background information and interpretive notes.

———. *2 Maccabees: A New Translation with Introduction and Commentary.* Anchor Bible, Vol. 41A. Garden City, N.Y.: Doubleday, 1976. Also includes historical-critical discussions.

1 and 2 Esdras (3 and 4 Ezra)

Metzger, Bruce. "The Fourth Book of Ezra." In James Charlesworth, ed., *The Old Testament Pseudepigrapha,* Vol. 1, pp. 516–559. Garden City, N.Y.: Doubleday/Anchor Books, 1983. Offers textual history and commentary.

Meyers, Jacob M. *1 and 2 Esdras.* Anchor Bible. Garden City, N.Y.: Doubleday, 1974. Recent translations with notes and commentary.

CHAPTER 30

The Pseudepigrapha
Noncanonical Writings of the Late Biblical Period

Key Topics/Themes A large number of Hellenistic Jewish compositions, not included in any official canon of the Hebrew Bible/Old Testament, are known as the Pseudepigrapha (documents falsely attributed to eminent writers of the distant past, such as Abraham, Enoch, or Moses). Like the books in the canonical Writings and the Apocrypha, the pseudepigraphal works encompass a wide range of literary genres, including poetry, apocalyptic works, and prose narratives.

In addition to the Apocryphal books that are or were at one time regarded as deuterocanonical in Catholic and/or Orthodox churches, Jewish authors of the Greco-Roman period also composed a large number of other documents that apparently were never part of any recognized canon. Written between about 250 B.C.E. and 200 C.E., a body of literature known as the **Pseudepigrapha** addressed many of the same Diaspora concerns found in the Apocrypha. Derived from two Greek words, *pseudos* (meaning "deceit" or "untruth") and *epigraphe* (meaning "writing"), the Pseudepigrapha are typically works incorrectly ascribed to famous biblical figures such as Adam, Enoch, Noah, Abraham, Moses, or Isaiah. Some, however, such as the Letter of Aristeas, do not claim illustrious authorship. In literary form, they range from apocalypses and sacred legends to devotional poetry and creative reinterpretations of canonical narratives. Like the Apocrypha, the Pseudepigrapha were written in Hebrew, Aramaic, or Greek. Because of space limitations, we will discuss only a representative selection of these books, particularly those that express ideas important to Hellenistic Judaism and/or early Christianity. (For the complete texts, see James Charlesworth's *The Old Testament Pseudepigrapha* in "Recommended Reading.")

The Book of 1 Enoch (the Ethiopic Book of Enoch)

A composite document, 1 Enoch incorporates diverse material composed as early as the third century B.C.E. and as late as the first century C.E. Although the book, originally written in Hebrew and/or Aramaic, had fallen out of use centuries before the only complete copy was found in an Ethiopic translation in the eighteenth century, 1 Enoch was once widely read. Aramaic fragments of the book have been found among the Dead Sea Scrolls and at Masada, the Herodian fortress where

Figure 30.1 Built as a fortress retreat by King Herod, during the Jewish Revolt, Masada served as the rebels' last holdout against Roman troops. According to Josephus, in 73 C.E. Masada's occupying force of 1000, including some women and children, committed mass suicide rather than become Roman slaves.

the last survivors of the Jewish Revolt against Rome perished about 73 C.E. (Figure 30.1). Apparently accepted in some Christian circles, 1 Enoch is quoted as Scripture in the New Testament epistle of Jude.

First Enoch is the oldest of three extant books ascribed to the biblical Enoch, listed in Genesis as one of the patriarchs who lived before the Flood. A person of exemplary righteousness, Enoch did not experience ordinary human death because "God took him," presumably transporting him alive to heaven (Gen. 5:24). The tradition of Enoch's mysterious ascension into the divine presence inspired a host of legends about his unparalleled knowledge of celestial secrets, which are supposedly revealed in the books bearing his name.

Containing some of the oldest examples of Jewish apocalyptic literature, the earliest parts of 1 Enoch anticipate visions of the spirit world and predictions of the end time that later appear in Daniel and the New Testament Book of Revelation. Like the author of Daniel, the writer of 1 Enoch refers to angels as the "Watchers" and describes sessions of God's heavenly court. Written about 170 B.C.E., the section known as the Ten Weeks Apocalypse (91:12–17; 93:1–10) divides human history into epochs symbolically represented by successive "weeks" of years, culminating in a final judgment when the righteous are separated from the wicked. The book's latest segment, which many scholars think was added during the first century C.E. or slightly earlier, is the Book of

Similitudes (Parables). This book describes a mysterious figure called the "Son of Man," who is later identified as Enoch himself, the one whom God transported to heaven and to whom he revealed sacred secrets (1 Enoch 71:14).

An ancient compiler or editor arranged 1 Enoch into five parts, perhaps to emulate the fivefold division of the Pentateuch and Book of Psalms. The first section, the Watchers (Chs. 1–36), expands on the Genesis account of the "sons of God" who mated with mortal women, producing a hybrid race of giants and heroes (cf. Gen. 6:1–4). Describing the fall of these rebellious divine "sons," Enoch is represented as making a tour of heaven and Sheol (the biblical Underworld), where he views a flaming abyss in which the fallen angels are punished (Chs. 17–18, 21; cf. 108:3–7, 15). Enoch's portrayal of the angels' incandescent dungeon resembles ancient Greek myths about the imprisonment of the Titans, divine giants whom Zeus overthrew and confined in Tartarus, the pit below Hades' realm (see Figure 7.1).

Enoch's second section (Chs. 37–71) contains a series of "similitudes," parables on a variety of topics, including the Messiah, the rewards of the virtuous, and the coming judgment by the Son of Man. The third part, the Astronomical Writings (Chs. 72–82), is a miscellaneous compilation of Hellenistic scientific ideas, including accounts of planetary and lunar movements that presuppose earth as the center of the solar system. In the fourth section, the Dream Visions (Chs. 83–90), the author employs a typically apocalyptic device, surveying past events as if they were prophecies of the future, predicting the (then-imminent) global deluge. Having confirmed his prophetic authority, Enoch then offers an allegorical narrative of world history that portrays the covenant people as tame (and gentle) animals and the people of the Gentile nations as wild beasts, symbolism also found in Daniel and Revelation. His account begins with Adam, signified by a white bull, and ends with the appearance of the Messiah as a "lamb" who becomes a "great animal" with black horns.

The final section, the Epistle of Enoch (Chs. 91–108), incorporates some of the book's oldest material, including fragments from a Book of Noah or Book of Lamech that describe the birth of Lamech's miraculously beautiful son, Noah, an angelic being whom God selects to survive the coming Deluge. It also includes an eschatological vision of a New Age that looks back to the prophecies in Third Isaiah (Isa. 65:17; 66:22) and forward to Christian writers' later adaptation of this promise in the New Testament books of Revelation and 2 Peter:

> And the first heavens shall depart and pass away,
> And a new heaven shall appear . . .
> And all shall be in goodness and righteousness,
> And sin shall no more be mentioned forever.
> (1 Enoch 91:16, 17; cf. Rev. 21:1–3;
> 2 Pet. 3:13)

The book concludes with Enoch's last words of encouragement for the pious, who await their God's day of reckoning (Chs. 106–108).

The Book of 2 Enoch (the Slavonic Book of Enoch)

Also called the Slavonic Book of Enoch because it has survived only in a Slavonic translation, 2 Enoch was originally written in Greek. Although the book's present form may represent a Christian edition from as late as the seventh century C.E., it probably originated during the first century C.E. Injunctions to visit the Jerusalem Temple three times a year (51:4) and references to ongoing sacrificial procedures (59:1–2; 61:4; 62:1) indicate that at least these portions of the text were written before 70 C.E.

A first-person narrative, which scholars have divided into sixty-eight brief chapters, the book describes Enoch's ascension to the tenth heaven, where he beholds the face of God and is taught all knowledge; his thirty-day journey back to earth to transmit this wisdom to his sons; and his permanent return to the spirit realm. The first section (Chs. 1–21) offers a fascinating survey of the ten different levels of heaven through which Enoch ascends. Although the concept may seem strange to contemporary readers, the author makes several of of the celestial spheres places of darkness and torment. The "second heaven," for example, is a gloomy prison for rebellious angels (Ch. 7); the "third heaven" is divided into a sensuous paradise for the righteous and a flaming hell for sinners (Chs. 8–10); and the fifth level contains the giant angel who had provoked a rebellion against God and whom Enoch persuades to beseech the Deity for mercy (Ch. 18). Enthroned in the ultimate level, "the tenth heaven," God is portrayed with a face burning "like iron made to glow in fire" (22:1), an awe-inspiring figure of cosmic magnificence.

In the second part of the book (Chs. 22–38), the Deity instructs Enoch in the mysteries of creation and interprets human history from the time of Adam to that of Noah and the Flood. The third division (Chs. 39–66) shows Enoch teaching his sons about the heavenly mysteries he has witnessed and counseling them to study the 366 books he has written to preserve divine wisdom. Expressing a typically apocalyptic viewpoint, Enoch insists that God has predetermined all history, including the course of individual human lives (53:2–3). The final two chapters recount Enoch's final ascension and summarize his extraordinary accomplishments (Chs. 67–68). Resembling some contemporary accounts of the soul's otherworldly journeys, Enoch's visions of the spirit realm exemplify important aspects of late Hellenistic Jewish mysticism.

Although 2 Enoch was composed for a Hellenistic Jewish audience, its graphic descriptions of the afterlife, including both rewards and punishments, had a significant influence on Christian thought. The book's structuring of the spirit world in ten ascending levels reappears in Dante's presentation of heaven in the *Divine Comedy*.

The Letter of Aristeas

In contrast to much of the Pseudepigrapha, the Letter of Aristeas—a highly embellished account of how the Greek Septuagint edition of the Hebrew Bible was made—does not claim to have been written by a famous biblical character from the distant past. The document is supposedly a letter from "Aristeas," a Greek-speaking Jewish member of the court of Ptolemy II (ruled 285–246 B.C.E.), to his brother Philocrates, recounting the origins of the Septuagint. In form, however, it is not a letter preserving eyewitness reports of a literary enterprise but a fictionalized treatise implying that this Greek edition of the Jewish Scriptures represents a phenomenal consensus of Jewish scholarship, an accomplishment worthy of the highest confidence and respect. According to the author (whom we call Aristeas to avoid confusion), when Ptolemy II was informed that his famous library in Alexandria, Egypt, lacked a copy of the Hebrew Bible, the king immediately dispatched Aristeas and Andreas to Jerusalem to obtain the original text, the basis for a new Greek translation.

The book then describes the negotiations with the High Priest Eleazar, the selection of six leading scholars from each of the twelve tribes of Israel, the reception of the seventy-two Jewish experts at the Ptolemaic court, their labors in translating the Hebrew text into Greek, and their production in seventy-two days of absolutely identical translations, the reliability of which is affirmed by the Jewish leaders of Alexandria. In popular usage, this widely distributed Greek edition became known as the "work of the seventy," giving the Septuagint (LXX) its name.

Despite its wealth of concrete detail, scholars regard Aristeas's account as more legendary than historical. It is likely that in the mid-third century B.C.E. a librarian added a Greek transcription or translation of the Pentateuch to the great library in Alexandria. It is also plausible that one of the Ptolemies, who were avid collectors of literature, sponsored the acquisition. The author's depiction of extravagant royal honors showered on the Jewish translators, however, is considered too exaggerated to be historical.

Modern scholars believe that the Letter of Aristeas was composed not by a contemporary of Ptolemy II but by an unknown writer 150 years later. The author was probably an Alexandrian Jew familiar with the Egyptian court, who wrote to demonstrate the authority of the Septuagint Bible used by his community. He also sought to illustrate the superiority of biblical wisdom (manifested in the Torah) to Greek learning by including an extended dialogue between Jewish teachers of the law and Greek philosophers — with the former winning every argument.

Its legendary elements notwithstanding, the Letter of Aristeas testifies to the widespread popularity of the Septuagint in Diaspora Judaism of the Hellenistic era. However, this Greek edition was probably produced not by Hebrew scholars imported from Jerusalem but by scholars in the Alexandrian Jewish community, who first translated the Pentateuch and then, over many decades, gradually added the Prophets (Nevi'im) and the Writings (Kethuvim), eventually including books of the Apocrypha as well. After being adopted by the Greek-speaking churches of early Christianity (it is the version quoted in most New Testament books), the Septuagint was ultimately rejected by the Jewish scholars and editors responsible for the canonical Hebrew Bible.

The Book of Jubilees

The Book of Jubilees takes its name from the author's method of partitioning world history into "Jubilees," or epochs of forty-nine symbolic years, based on the **Jubilee** concept described in Leviticus 25. The writer then subdivides each forty-nine-year period into seven "weeks," each of which contains seven solar years of 364 days. This parsing out of global chronology into precisely defined — and divinely predetermined — units of time is typical of the author's priestly concern with precise distinctions and legalistic compartmentalization.

Jubilees is also known as the "Little Genesis" because it is an extensive revision of the Hebrew Bible's first book, containing interpretive commentary and other interpolations from the vast storehouse of Jewish oral tradition. In this expansion and elaboration of the canonical text, the author provides a virtual **midrash** characteristic of Jewish practice in the Hellenistic era, when the book was written. Derived from a Hebrew word meaning to "inquire" or "search out," midrash refers to the practice of interpreting and explaining biblical texts, a procedure associated with scribes and rabbis (teachers of the Law).

Just as the Chronicler revised and expanded on the books of Kings to give Israel's history a priestly slant (see Chapter 27), so the author of Jubilees reworks the Genesis narrative (and also the first twelve chapters of Exodus) to emphasize the absolute supremacy of the Torah, both in its written text and in the approved oral traditions that interpret it. He therefore presents the patriarchs — Abraham, Isaac, and Jacob — as devoted observers of Mosaic Law and of later oral applications of it. His purpose is to show that the Torah existed prior to the world's beginning, that it embodies the highest values in the universe, and that its deliverance to Moses at Sinai/Horeb was the final manifestation of divine wisdom.

Jubilees portrays an angel relating the whole story, from creation in Genesis 1 to Israel's departure from Egypt in Exodus 12, so that Moses can preserve it in the Pentateuch. The writer's anachronistic approach results in some startling changes to the patriarchal narratives. Abraham, at age fourteen, is said to have rejected his father's idols and embraced a perfect monotheism (Jub. 11:16–18). To the story of Abraham's death, the author appends a long apocalyptic prophecy in which the angel tells Moses of the disasters to come following humanity's disobedience and Israel's failure to honor the covenant. But after the chastened Israelites return to studying the Torah and heeding its commands, their God will restore them to prosperity and long life (23:13–32).

These eschatological prophecies (cf. 1:14–29) help to enliven the writer's otherwise pedantic style, which chiefly focuses on legalistic matters, such as the distinctions between "clean" and "unclean" foods and actions, strict Sabbath observance, and the avoidance of Gentiles and their "idolatrous" religions. The author also devotes considerable space to such ritual practices as circumcision (Ch. 15); ceremonial festivals; obligatory offerings of fruit, grain, and animals; and the statutes regulating women's sexual functions (3:8; 15:31–32; 22:16–20; 30:7–17; 50:6–13).

Some scholars detect a resemblance between Jubilees' legalistic theology and that expressed in several sectarian documents found among the Dead Sea Scrolls (see Chapter 31). The presence of fragments from nine different manuscripts containing the Hebrew text of Jubilees strengthens this view. Although originally composed in Hebrew, a complete text survives only in an Ethiopic version. Both it and Latin translations are taken from a Greek edition of the Hebrew original, which may be dated to about 100 B.C.E.

The Book of 3 Maccabees

The title of this book is misleading, for it has nothing to do with the Maccabees but is a legendary account of how the Jews living in Egypt came to celebrate a joyous festival of deliverance. Its theme — the narrow escape of Diaspora Jews from mass slaughter by their Gentile enemies — strongly resembles that of Esther. Composed in Greek, 3 Maccabees probably originated in Alexandria in the late first century B.C.E.

The book's seven chapters recount two major incidents. In the first, Ptolemy IV Philopater, after defeating the Syrian king Antiochus II at Raphia in 237 B.C.E., attempts to enter the Jerusalem Temple but is stopped by a miraculous judgment (1:1–2:24). In the second, Ptolemy tries to force the Egyptian Jews to worship his gods. When they refuse, he orders them trampled to death by elephants as a public spectacle showing the consequences of disobedience. After the Jews are miraculously saved three times, Ptolemy, now respectful of their God, not only subsidizes an annual celebration of Jewish deliverance but also issues a decree permitting them to execute Jews who compromise their faith (6:22–7:23). The parallel to Ahasuerus's edict allowing the endangered Jews to defend themselves is obvious, as is the resemblance of the Egyptian festival to Purim (see Chapter 26).

The Book of 4 Maccabees

Although 4 Maccabees appears in some manuscripts of the Greek Old Testament, it never attained canonical status. Its creative interpretation of Jewish traditions in terms of Greek philosophy, however, has had a significant influence within some Eastern Orthodox churches. Unlike the first three books named after the Maccabees, this book is not a historical narrative but a philosophical discourse on the proposition that reason reigns supreme over the passions. Thoroughly Greek in language, form, style, and philosophical vocabulary, it is also fully Jewish in its insistence that true wisdom and virtue derive from knowledge of the Torah and absolute fidelity to its principles (1:15–17).

The outstanding example upon which the author draws to illustrate his thesis that reason controls the emotions is the martyrdom of Jews rationally faithful to their law during the persecutions of Antiochus IV. His retelling of the tale of the suffering and deaths of the priest Eleazar and the seven brothers and their mother (cf. 2 Macc. 6–7) is probably why the book received its title.

The author selectively combines Greek and Jewish thought, a theological synthesis in which foreign ideas are used to reinforce and illustrate Jewish traditions. Although he asserts that wisdom is manifested in the four cardinal virtues of classical philosophy — self-control, justice, courage, and temperance (4 Macc. 1:18–35) — he demonstrates the values of the Stoic qualities (duty, endurance, self-control, and service to family and state) through their application to the lives of such biblical models of faith as Joseph (2:2–3), Moses (2:17), Jacob (2:19), David (3:6–18), and the martyrs of the Maccabean period (Chs. 5–17).

As the martyrs' case histories demonstrate, the real source of wisdom is Israel's God; Greek virtues are merely labels for higher attributes known to faithful Jews alone (17:19–18:24). Like Second Isaiah, the writer declares that the righteous suffer vicariously for the sins of the covenant community (1:11; 6:29; 17:21–22; cf. Isa. 53). Borrowing another Greek concept, he asserts that Jews who died for their allegiance to the Torah have attained everlasting life. He stipulates, however, that the immortality of martyrs' souls is not necessarily inherent, as in Platonic philosophy, but is bestowed by God (4 Macc. 14:6; 18:23).

Scholars do not agree on the book's place of composition, with suggestions ranging from Alexandria, to Jerusalem, to Antioch in Syria. It was probably written sometime between the Roman occupation of Palestine (63 B.C.E.) and the destruction of Jerusalem (70 C.E.).

Psalm 151

Appearing in several Greek manuscripts either as an appendix to the canonical Psalms or, as in the Codex Sinaiticus, as an integral part of the Psalms, this lyric poem was ostensibly composed by a youthful David shortly after God had chosen him as Israel's future king. Written in the first person, Psalm 151 voices David's sense of gratitude and wonder at being preferred to his older, taller, and handsomer brothers. A somewhat different Hebrew version of the poem, celebrating David's victory over the Philistine giant Goliath, was found among the Dead Sea Scrolls. Although not regarded as canonical by Catholics, this lyric is accepted in the Eastern Orthodox tradition.

The Testaments of the Twelve Patriarchs

This long, didactic work purports to be the last words or testaments of the twelve sons of Jacob to their descendants. Although modeled on the Blessing of Jacob to his twelve sons (Gen. 49), the Testaments of the Twelve Patriarchs does not for the most part contain prophecies about the individual tribes' future destinies. Rather, it consists mainly of

exhortations by each patriarch, using his own particular character and life history as an example either to avoid or emulate. With their strong emphasis on moral lessons to be drawn from individual lives and on strict adherence to divine principles, the Testaments have much in common with Israel's wisdom literature. But the Testaments also contain much visionary material, including warnings of eschatological judgment typical of apocalyptic works. Combining revelations of divine secrets, such as the nature of angels and the heavenly world, with ethical advice about avoiding such common vices as sexual passion, envy, and deceit, the Testaments constitute a peculiarly mixed genre unusual in the biblical tradition. Although scholars disagree about the work's original language and place of origin, many place its composition in Palestine during the Maccabean period, perhaps between 150 and 100 B.C.E.

Just before their deaths and burials, descriptions of which conclude their deathbed speeches, each of Jacob's twelve sons voices a warning and/or prophecy for Israel. The eldest, Reuben, uses his own case to caution against "the ignorant ways of youth and sexual promiscuity" (T. Reub. 1:6–7; cf. Gen. 35:22; 49:4). (Each of the twelve testaments has its own chapter numbering.) Citing his murderous jealousy of Joseph, Simeon, Jacob's second son, counsels against envy, ending his homily with the admonition to be "obedient to Levi and to Judah" (T. Sim. 7:1)—the two tribes from which a priestly and a royal Messiah will come.

Levi, the son from whom Israel's priests are descended, declares that he was uniquely favored by God, permitted to visit the seventh level of heaven and receive direct divine appointment to the priesthood. Urging his descendants to respect the Torah and seek wisdom, Levi states that he learned from studying the Books of Enoch that his progeny will corrupt the priestly office until a messianic High Priest appears to establish the New Age. Judah, from whom the Davidic line of kings will descend, instructs his offspring to avoid wine, women, and greed and to subordinate themselves to Levi's descendants, the hereditary priests who led the postexilic Judean community. Confirming that his tribe will produce a messianic king, Judah nonetheless emphasizes that this royal figure will be secondary to the priestly Anointed One.

Perhaps because most of their tribal descendants, at the time of writing, lacked the religious or political influence of Levi and Judah, the remaining sons of Jacob focus primarily on ethical advice. Issachar extols the values of a pious country dweller; Zebulun exhorts his progeny to behave charitably; and Dan exhorts against wrath and the bearing of false witness. Naphtali, who has also read Enoch's works, combines ethical counsel with cosmological concerns, commanding his heirs to conduct themselves with piety, purity, and kindliness, thus reflecting the harmony of the cosmos. Warning Israel against the destructiveness of hatred, Gad commends the value of showing brotherly love. Asher, describing the pitfalls of wickedness and deceit, praises the virtues of candor and honesty. Imploring his people to avoid sexual temptation, Joseph delivers a long oration extolling the benefits of self-restraint and chastity. And in the final testament, the youngest son, Benjamin, who refuses any longer to be called "rapacious wolf" (T. Ben. 11:1; cf. Gen. 49:27), summarizes the book's principal theme, exhorting Judeans to "keep the Law of the LORD and his commandments" (10:3–4), underscoring the primary obligation of the covenant community.

The Sibylline Oracles

The **Sibyl,** after whom this collection of prophecies was named, was the title given a series of highly esteemed prophetesses in the Greco-Roman world. Allegedly inspired by the god Apollo, the Sibyl delivered oracles foretelling the fate of individuals and nations; one particularly honored compilation of her prophecies was kept in Rome and consulted by the city's political leaders during times of crisis, such as those precipitated by war, famine, or plague. In Italy, the most famous Sibyl dwelt at Cumae near the Bay of Naples, where her oracles enjoyed such prestige that the Latin poet Virgil made her the guide of Aeneas during the hero's perilous descent into Hades's subterranean realm (*Aeneid,* Bk. 6). The pseudepigraphal Sibylline Oracles represent a highly diverse assemblage of eschatological prophecies composed by different authors over a long span of time, from about 250 B.C.E. to 550 C.E. The oldest oracles were composed by Hellenistic Jews, to which Christian redactors later added considerable material (the introduction to the whole collection is thought to have been written by the Christian editor who assembled the books in the sixth century C.E.). Like the pagan oracular literature on which they are modeled, the Sibylline Oracles were repeatedly edited and revised, both in the form of writers' interpolating "prophecies" about historical events that had already occurred and in the updating of earlier oracles to make them relevant to later generations.

When adopted into the Jewish tradition, the Sibyl was reborn as the daughter-in-law of Noah and thus associated with the very beginning of the post-Flood world (Sib. Or. 3:8–26). In this new guise, she was moved to prophesy both Israelite and Greek history and to denounce both Gentile religions and the Jews' political enemies. In all, approximately fourteen books of oracles were collected, in which pagan, Jewish, and Christian oracles are melded. Of the twelve books that survive intact (others exist only in small fragments), the largest block of primarily Jewish material appears in Books 3–5, the section discussed here. (Books 6–8 are largely of Christian origin.)

A Jewish elaboration of an older pagan document, Book 3 contains a prophecy predicting the Messiah's arrival at a time "when Rome will also rule over Egypt" (Sib. Or. 3:46–61) and warnings of eschatological disaster for foreign nations resisting God's sovereignty (3:573–812). Throughout Book 3, the author rather incongruously blends references to Greco-Roman history and mythology, such as Zeus's overthrow of the Titans, ancient gods who once ruled the universe, with moral exhortations to observe Jewish ethical standards (3:110–570). As an example of divine punishment for Gentile pride, the author includes a paraphrase of the Genesis story of the Tower of Babel (3:97–109), perhaps one of the oldest passages in the book. Amid the forecasts of innumerable cosmic disasters are a few allusions to historical figures that help date some of the oracles. References to the Egyptian monarch Ptolemy VII incline some scholars to believe that most of the document was composed during his reign (145–116 B.C.E.). Passages mentioning later events, such as the second triumvirate (43 B.C.E.) and Cleopatra (c. 30 B.C.E.), were probably inserted at a later date.

Book 4, a series of cryptic utterances in which some historical events are cited as signs of imminent calamity, was written after the catastrophic eruption of Mount Vesuvius in 79 C.E. (Sib. Or. 4:130–136). The veiled predictions of Nero's return from the dead at the head of an invading army (4:137–139; cf. 8:140–155) reflect a belief popular in the later first century C.E. (see also the use of this legend in Revelation 17:8–9).

Although Book 3's contents indicate that it was written in Egypt, Book 4's place of origin is unknown. Book 5, notable for its lament over the fall of Jerusalem (Sib. Or. 5:397–413), probably appeared in Egypt during the late second century C.E. The Christian books were added much later.

The Psalms of Solomon

Written during the political turbulence of the last century B.C.E. when Roman occupying forces moved into Palestine, the eighteen psalms in this book reflect an important development in Judeo-Christian history: the emergence of messianic expectations that directly anticipate later New Testament concepts of Israel's Messiah. Psalm of Solomon 17 envisions a righteous king who will drive the hated foreigners (Romans) from Jerusalem and establish a universal kingdom ruling over both Jews and Gentiles. Composed only decades before the rise of Christianity, this poem is the first known work of Jewish literature to use the terms "son of David" and "Lord Messiah [Christ]," distinctive titles that Gospel writers apply to Jesus of Nazareth. Although Psalm of Solomon 17 portrays the Mes-

siah as sinless and powerful, he is clearly a human rather than supernatural figure, God's agent but not a divine being. His promised activities include gathering together a "holy people" who will be "children of their God," cleansing Jerusalem (presumably including the Temple), and ruling compassionately over the Gentiles. Although a Davidic heir, this "Lord Messiah" apparently achieves his dominion without military conquest because he is "powerful in the holy spirit" and strengthened by "wisdom and understanding." This vision of a peaceful Messiah subduing opponents through the "word of his mouth [his teaching]" foreshadows similar views expressed in the Gospels.

Although these lyrics do not directly claim Solomonic authorship, the resemblance of Psalm of Solomon 17 to canonical Psalm 72, which is ascribed to Solomon, as well as the tradition that the king had composed more than 1000 "songs" (1 Kings 4:32), may have led later editors to add inscriptions attributing the collection to him. Internal allusions to historical events help to date the time of composition: References to Pompey's termination of the Hasmonean dynasty, to his conquest of Judea (PssSol. 8:15–21), and to his death in Egypt (2:26–27) indicate that these passages were written between about 63 and 48 B.C.E. The denunciation of "a man alien to our race" may refer either to Pompey or to Herod the Great, the Roman-appointed local ruler who seized Jerusalem in 37 B.C.E. Scholars estimate that these psalms were written between about 63 and 30 B.C.E.

The specific religious community in which these poems originated is difficult to identify with certainty. References to belief in a future resurrection of the dead (3:12; 13:11; 14:9–10) and individual free will (9:4) suggest some connection with the Pharisees, who espoused these doctrines. Some scholars believe that the poet of Psalms of Solomon 17 and 18, which express strong messianic hopes, may have had some link with the Essenes, the monastic group that lived at Qumran, the site near which the Dead Sea Scrolls were found (Figure 30.2).

Like the canonical Psalms, this compilation embraces a variety of literary genres, including hymns

Figure 30.2 An apocalyptic sect that awaited YHWH's call to battle the Romans, the Essenes maintained a monastic colony at Qumran near the northwest shores of the Dead Sea. After the Essenes had hidden their library—the Dead Sea Scrolls—in nearby caves, the Roman army destroyed Qumran (68 C.E.), the ruins of which have since been excavated.

(PssSol. 2:30–37; 3:1–2; 14:1–10), songs of lamentation (2:19–25; 7; 8:22–34; 16:6–15), and songs of thanksgiving (13:1–4; 15:1–6; 16:1–5). The various genres, however, are typically mixed together in a single poem. Thus, the second psalm opens as a national lament over the Gentile invasion of Jerusalem (2:1–14), changes into a meditation on God's mysterious ways (2:15–18), shifts to a review of history (2:19–21), becomes an urgent petition for divine justice (2:22–25), and, in the succeeding verses, alternates between forms, including a meditation, a hymn, a confession of faith, and an invocation of all people to fear God and praise him (2:28–37). As in the canonical lyrics, the poet draws rigid distinctions between the righteous and the wicked.

The Books of Adam and Eve

Both Hellenistic Jewish and early Christian writers delighted in producing fictional accounts of the first human pair. The Books of Adam and Eve have a complex literary evolution whereby Hebrew writings from the first century C.E. were later extensively redacted by Christian editors. They consist of two supplementary and sometimes contradictory documents: The Life of Adam and Eve *(Vita Adae et Evae)*, which survives in a Latin edition translated from a Greek text, and a parallel Greek narrative that is misnamed the Apocalypse of Moses. Some elements of the composite Adam and Eve story are found only in the Life, others only in the Apocalypse, and still others in both. This discussion summarizes material from both works.

The Life opens with Adam and Eve already expelled from paradise. Unable to survive on their own, they attempt to placate the Deity through prayer and acts of penitence. But Eve, who punishes herself by immersing her body in the icy Tigris River, is again deceived by Satan, this time into abandoning this form of painful expiation, a lapse for which Adam bitterly reproaches her (Chs. 1–11).

When Adam complains that Satan persecutes them without reason, the latter replies that he has good cause to hate humankind: It is because of Adam that this once-glorious being was thrown from heaven. According to Satan, after the first man was created, God commanded all the heavenly host to worship this human image of the divine. Refusing to adore a younger and inferior creature, the devil and those who sided with him were cast out of the celestial abode. By thus observing the Torah's prohibition against idolatry and by applying the biblical law of retaliation, Satan thus instigates the human couple's fall from grace, just as he himself was humiliated for humanity's sake (Chs. 12–17). Unmoved, Adam endures forty days' penance in the Jordan River.

The Life then recounts the births of Cain and Abel, their lethal rivalry, and the arrival of a third son, Seth, followed by the births of sixty additional offspring (Chs. 18–24). Adam informs the adult Seth of an earlier vision in which the Deity described Adam's inevitable death (Chs. 25–29). When Adam actually lies dying, Seth and Eve try to obtain a miraculous healing oil from the "tree of mercy," but the archangel Michael orders them back from the gates of paradise and affirms the finality of Adam's demise. God will make no provision to ease the pain of human mortality until the final judgment (Chs. 30–44; cf. Apoc. Mos. 5–14). Eve then narrates her version of humanity's first disobedience and its dire consequences, illustrated by Adam's actual death at age 930 (Life. 45–48).

After God mercifully transports Adam's soul to a paradise in the third heaven, he revisits earth, accompanied by angels, to entomb Adam's body, as well as that of the hitherto unburied Abel. Adam and all his progeny are then promised a physical resurrection, when soul and body will be reunited (Apoc. Mos. 35–42). Six days later, Eve also dies, praying to be buried in her husband's tomb, the location of which remains unknown. Michael then instructs the orphaned Seth never to mourn on the Sabbath, which is a holy day symbolizing an eschatological future life in the New Age (Life. 49–51; Apoc. Mos. 52–53).

A compendium of highly imaginative speculations about what the life of the first human couple was like following their loss of Eden, the Books of Adam and Eve incorporate some important aspects of Hellenistic Jewish lore. In this midrash on the Genesis tale of humanity's primal break with the Creator, Satan becomes the voice behind the speaking serpent and the source of human sin, a late tradition that profoundly influenced Christian thought. The narrative also introduces a myth of Satan's rebellion against God and subsequent fall from heaven, a theme that reached its fullest expression in Western Christianity with Milton's portrayal of a heroic rebel in *Paradise Lost* (cf. Rev. 12:7–12).

Taken as a whole, the writings of the Apocrypha and Pseudepigrapha provide an illuminating glimpse into the extremely diverse ways in which many different Jewish thinkers struggled to define and promote the covenant community's foundational beliefs and practices during the Greco-Roman era. In many parts of the Diaspora, the attractions of Greek civilization—its art, literature, social institutions, and philosophies—seemed almost irresistible, leading to voluntary assimilation and the adoption of the ways of non-Jewish culture. Although the conflict between Torah loyalty and Greek culture was sometimes violent—as in the Maccabean military response to Antiochus IV's coercive policies—some Hellenistic Jewish literature, such as the Wisdom of Solomon and 4 Maccabees, reflects a creative synthesis of Greek and Jewish traditions. In such fusions of Greek and Jewish ideas, however, both apocryphal and pseudepigraphal authors consistently subordinate Greek philosophical concepts to Torah principles, emphasizing the superiority of the Mosaic revelation. Greeks such as Socrates and Plato may have had wonderful ideas, but the best of Greek philosophy was always anticipated by Moses and the prophets!

In dramatizing the historical conflict between some Gentile rulers and Torah-observant Jews, such Hellenistic works as Daniel and 2 Maccabees introduce new concepts postulating a future life through bodily resurrection that had not previously been a part of the biblical tradition. New ideas about an afterlife of rewards or punishments, derived from both Persian Zoroastrianism and Greek eschatological speculations, not only influenced much Hellenistic Jewish thought but also early

Christian writers, who inherited both the Septuagint edition of the Hebrew Bible (including the Apocrypha) and the pseudepigraphal documents. Early church fathers quoted frequently and approvingly from many of the extracanonical books discussed in this chapter.

After the two Roman destructions of Jerusalem in 70 and 135 c.e., Palestinian Judaism rejected the Septuagint Bible, as well as all the other Hellenistic literature it regarded as noncanonical, abandoning both apocalyptic speculations and accommodations with Greek culture. Whereas the Christian churches appropriated many of the rejected books, containing such diverse ideas as the soul's incarnation and intercessory prayers on behalf of the dead, postwar Judaism rigorously emphasized Torah obedience, reinterpreting Mosaic Law in the absence of Temple and priesthood and applying oral traditions to fulfilling the law in daily life. (See Chapter 31 for a review of Judaism at the close of the biblical period.)

QUESTIONS FOR REVIEW

1. Define the term *Pseudepigrapha* and describe the kinds of books this collection includes. Who was the biblical Enoch, and what pseudonymous books are ascribed to him? Describe the visions of the spirit world depicted in 1 and 2 Enoch.

2. Summarize the origins of the Septuagint as portrayed in the Letter of Aristeas. How does this book's version of events differ from the views of contemporary scholarship?

3. Define *midrash* and apply it to the composition of the Book of Jubilees. What parts of the Torah does this narrative reinterpret? In what ways are the Testaments of the Twelve Patriarchs and the Books of Adam and Eve also midrashim on the Genesis text?

4. Summarize some of the conflicts (and syntheses) between Greek and Jewish culture described in 3 and 4 Maccabees and the Sibylline Oracles. How does Psalm of Solomon 17 present a view of Israel's Messiah that anticipates that of a later messianic movement, early Christianity?

QUESTIONS FOR REFLECTION AND DISCUSSION

1. Drawing on the canonical Daniel, the deuterocanonical 2 Esdras, and the noncanonical 1 and 2 Enoch and the Sibylline Oracles, trace the evolution of apocalyptic ideas about the predestined flow of historical events, the conflicts between covenant loyalty and Gentile political dominance, and the possibility of martyrdom. In what ways have traditional prophetic beliefs about the coming "Day of YHWH" been transformed to include visions about a future divine judgment involving all nations and an afterlife characterized by rewards for fidelity to the Torah and penalties for disobedience?

2. Why do you think that, for many people, beliefs outlined in canonical biblical literature have greater authority than those described in the Apocrypha or Pseudepigrapha? Identify some ideas absent from the Tanak that are now part of many Jewish or Christian belief systems, and explain why you do or do not support them.

TERMS AND CONCEPTS TO REMEMBER

Jubilee
Letter of Aristeas and
   origin of the
   Septuagint
midrash
Psalm of Solomon 17
   (the Messiah)

Pseudepigrapha
Sibyl
tour of ten heavens
trends and themes in
   Hellenistic Jewish
   literature

RECOMMENDED READING

1 and 2 Enoch

Anderson, F. I. "2 (Slavonic Apocalypse of) Enoch." In James Charlesworth, ed., *The Old Testament Pseudepigrapha*, Vol. 1, pp. 101–221. Garden City, N.Y.: Anchor Books/Doubleday, 1983. A new translation with scholarly commentary.

Himmelfarb, Martha. *The Ascent to Heaven in Jewish and Christian Apocalypses.* New York: Oxford University Press, 2001. Includes a discussion of the Enoch literature.

Isaac, E. "1 (Ethiopic Apocalypse of) Enoch." In James Charlesworth, ed., *The Old Testament Pseudepigrapha*, Vol. 1, pp. 5–100. Garden City, N.Y.: Anchor Books/

Doubleday, 1983. A new translation, with detailed annotation.

Nickelsburg, George. *1 Enoch: A Commentary on the Book of 1 Enoch Chapters 1–36, 81–108.* Minneapolis: Fortress Press, 2001. A comprehensive study.

Letter of Aristeas and Book of Jubilees

Davenport, Gene L. *The Eschatology of the Book of Jubilees.* Leiden, Netherlands: Brill, 1971. Examines apocalyptic elements in this midrash of Genesis.

Shutt, R. J. H. "Letter of Aristeas." In James Charlesworth, ed., *The Old Testament Pseudepigrapha,* Vol. 2, pp. 7–34. Garden City, N.Y.: Anchor Books/Doubleday, 1985. A new translation and interpretive introduction.

Wintermute, O. S. "Jubilees." In James Charlesworth, ed., *The Old Testament Pseudepigrapha,* Vol. 2, pp. 35–155. Garden City, N.Y.: Anchor Books/Doubleday, 1985. A new translation and notes placing the book in historical context.

3 and 4 Maccabees

Anderson, H. "3 Maccabees" and "4 Maccabees." In James Charlesworth, ed., *The Old Testament Pseudepigrapha,* Vol. 2, pp. 509–564. Garden City, N.Y.: Anchor Books/Doubleday, 1985. A new translation and commentary.

Testaments of the Twelve Patriarchs and Prayer of Manasseh

Charlesworth, James. "Prayer of Manasseh." In James Charlesworth, ed., *The Old Testament Pseudepigrapha,* Vol. 2, pp. 625–637. Garden City, N.Y.: Anchor Books/Doubleday, 1985. A new translation and extensive notes.

Kee, Howard C. "Testaments of the Twelve Patriarchs." In James Charlesworth, ed., *The Old Testament Pseudepigrapha,* Vol. 1, pp. 775–828. Garden City, N.Y.: Anchor Books/Doubleday, 1983. A new translation and introduction.

Sibylline Oracles and Psalms of Solomon

Collins, J. J. "Sibylline Oracles." In James Charlesworth, ed., *The Old Testament Pseudepigrapha,* Vol. 1, pp. 317–472. Garden City, N.Y.: Anchor Books/Doubleday, 1983.

Wright, R. B. "Psalms of Solomon." In James Charlesworth, ed., *The Old Testament Pseudepigrapha,* Vol. 2, pp. 639–670. Garden City, N.Y.: Anchor Books/Doubleday, 1985. Emphasizes the importance of messianic psalms.

Books of Adam and Eve

Charles, R. H. "The Books of Adam and Eve, with an Introduction." *Apocrypha and Pseudepigrapha of the Old Testament,* Vol. 2, pp. 123–154. Oxford: Clarendon Press, 1913. An old but valuable edition of the texts.

Johnson, M. D. "Life of Adam and Eve." In James Charlesworth, ed., *The Old Testament Pseudepigrapha,* Vol. 2, pp. 249–296. Garden City, N.Y.: Anchor Books/Doubleday, 1985. Offers parallel columns of text from both the Life and the Apocalypse of Moses.

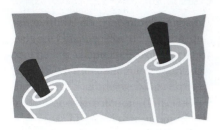

CHAPTER 31

From the Maccabees
to bar Kochba

*Victory, Defeat, and the Emergence
of Postbiblical Judaism*

Key Topics/Themes The period of postbiblical Jewish history that stretches from the Maccabean victory of 164 B.C.E. to Titus's destruction of the Second Temple in 70 C.E. is often designated as the era of the "Second" Commonwealth in Jewish history. This conflict-ridden but highly creative period serves as both a postscript to our study of biblical literature and a preface to the history of the two world religions that claim the Hebrew Bible as a foundational text — namely, Judaism and Christianity. The reestablishment of a Judean kingdom under the leadership of the sons of Mattathias, and the internal divisions within Judean society that this event brings to the surface, is depicted in the first two books of the Maccabees. Here, Jewish pietists and their Hellenized opponents struggle for both political and spiritual dominance within Judea while continuing to wage external war against the Seleucid monarch Antiochus IV and his successors. (Figure 31.1 shows a time line of key events from the end of the Babylonian exile to the second Jewish Revolt.)

The Three "Philosophies"

Much of the primary-level information on which any study of Jewish culture during the Second Temple period is based derives from the writings of the late-first-century-C.E. historian **Flavius Josephus.** Though born into a priestly family, Josephus chose to embrace (for a time) the Judean rebellion against Rome, and when war broke out in 66 C.E., he assumed command of a fortress in the Galilee. Rather than fight to the death, however, Josephus surrendered ingloriously to the Romans and convinced the commanding Roman general, Vespasian (Figure 31.2), that he could be of use as a translator. Thus, he began his career as a writer in the employ of the Flavian household. In light of such a check-

ered political career, it is understandable that modern historians view with reservations at least some of the data and commentary Josephus provides. He was, after all, the Benedict Arnold of his generation and was not above portraying himself and his Roman sponsors in the best possible light. However, two of his major works — *The Jewish War* and *Antiquities of the Jews* — offer the fullest contemporary account of Judean society and thought of any writer of his time, and for lack of any more reliable source, historians of this era turn to Josephus for a portrait of an emergent and evolving Judaism under Hasmonean (and later Roman) rule.

According to Josephus, Jewish religious culture during this era was dominated by three diverse and identifiable "philosophical" communities — the Pharisees, the Sadducees, and the Essenes — each

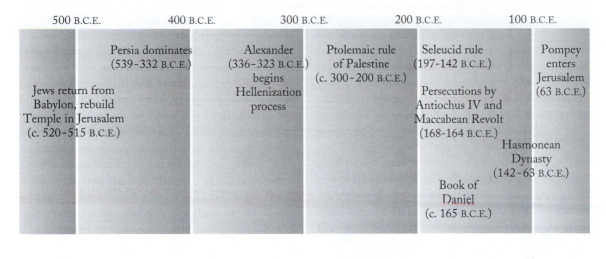

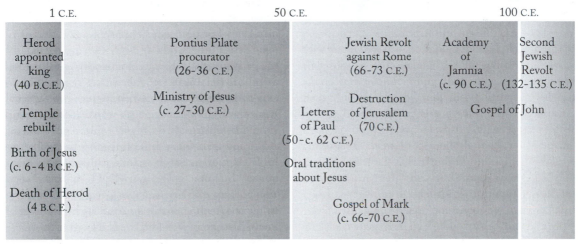

Figure 31.1   Time Line of Key Events from the End of the Babylonian Exile to the Second Jewish Revolt

with its own distinct worldview and equally distinct political agenda. Josephus employs the Greek term *hairesis* (literally, a "choice") to describe these communities, or "voluntary associations," as a modern historian might call them, but these divergent philosophical schools also represented divergent political parties during the reigns of the late Hasmonean kings John Hyrcanus (134–104 B.C.E.) and Alexander Janneus (103–76 B.C.E.). As the Hasmonean era drew to a close, many of the political and religious conflicts that had earlier erupted dur-

ing the Maccabean Revolt continued to divide Judean society.

THE PHARISEES

Josephus leaves no doubt about which of these "philosophies" finally achieved dominance during this era and in the generations of Roman rule that followed. The **Pharisees** enjoyed greater support among the Jewish masses and ultimately exerted greater influence over the course of Jewish history

Figure 31.2   Portrait Bust of the Emperor Vespasian (Ruled 69–79 C.E.) Appointed by Nero to crush the Jewish Revolt (66–73 C.E.), Vespasian conquered Galilee but withdrew from the war after Nero's suicide. A year later, he became emperor. He then appointed his son Titus to carry on the siege of Jerusalem.

than either of their rivals. The name *Pharisee* derives from the Hebrew word *parush*, meaning either "separated from" or "explained," but scholars dispute both the origin and meaning of this term. To be a Pharisee may originally have meant to belong to a community that rigorously separated itself from ritually impure substances and persons in an effort to observe, as fully as possible, biblical laws of purification, diet, and tithing. Alternatively, it may also have referred to a class of Torah scholars who "explained" (that is, resolved) conflicting passages and statutes within the Pentateuch. Some scholars suggest that the Pharisees may have represented a splinter group of hasidim, or "pietists," who

initially joined the Maccabean Revolt but later dissociated themselves from Hasmonean political ambitions. Whatever their origins, the Pharisees emerged as formidable political opponents of Alexander Janneus, who persecuted them for a time but who also advised his wife (Salome Alexandra), on his deathbed, to reach some accommodation with the Pharisees if she wished to reign in peace. And Alexandra apparently did precisely that. By elevating Pharisaic leaders to the position of royal counselors while securing the support of the Sadducean party, she was able to maintain a remarkable degree of tranquility during her short reign (76–67 B.C.E.) and to ensure the survival of the Pharisaic party.

However, what really defined the Pharisees ideologically, in sharp contrast to their Sadducean counterparts, was their belief in what came to be called the **Oral Torah**—a body of interpretive rulings (another meaning of the word *parush*), transmitted orally, that both defined and expanded the range of biblical commandments beyond anything found in the Pentateuch. By attributing such rulings to Moses—in the form of an oral tradition dating back to Sinai/Horeb that the writers of the New Testament would later refer to, dismissively, as the "tradition of the elders" (Mark 7:13)—the Pharisees were able to invoke the authority of a secondary revelation. This enabled them to validate their teachings and invalidate the arguments of their opponents. But no less influential than their conviction that they possessed an authoritative oral tradition was the Pharisees' belief in the immortality of the soul, the resurrection of the dead, and divine judgment of all souls in the afterlife based on their conduct in this life. Ideas that previously had appeared only in late biblical or deuterocanonical texts like Daniel and the Wisdom of Solomon were now part of "normative" Pharisaic teaching, and when these were combined with the conviction that all Jews were bound to fulfill the commandments of God in their daily lives with the same degree of scrupulousness as were the priests in the Temple, the basic elements of a new belief system began to emerge. This form of Judaism would survive the destruction of the Second Temple and could be transported anywhere in the Jewish Diaspora.

That the Pharisees are portrayed in largely negative terms in the New Testament, and particularly in the Synoptic Gospels, is as much a reflection of internal struggles within the early Christian community as it is of any possible differences in judgment between the historical Jesus and his Pharisaic contemporaries. The Gospel writers' depiction of Jesus as opposed to — and opposed by — the dominant religious personalities of his day exists side by side with conflicting accounts of Jesus' Pharisaic-like insistence that the Torah be observed scrupulously (Matt. 5:17–19) and that the commandments of God are as incumbent on the ordinary householder as on any priest or Levite attached to the Temple. That Jesus shared a Pharisaic view of both the Judgment Day and the resurrection of the dead is evident from his teachings and apocalyptic pronouncements (Matt. 24:15–31; Mark 12:11–27). However, the Pharisees' refusal to accept messianic claims made on Jesus' behalf extended to other messianic claimants as well. And it was their reluctance to embrace wholeheartedly an eschatological agenda that ensured the survival of their form of Judaism in the post–70 C.E. era.

THE SADDUCEES

No matter which source we turn to — Josephus, the New Testament, or later rabbinic writings — we find relatively little information on which to base a historically accurate portrait of the **Sadducees.** The term *Sadducee* (Hebrew, *Zaddukim*) appears to derive from the name of a High Priest, **Zadok,** who served both David and Solomon and who is memorialized in the Book of Ezekiel as the ancestor of the only legitimate line of High Priests (Ezek. 40:46). We may never know how many members of priestly families actually belonged to this "party," but Josephus leaves us with the impression that their numbers were never very large and their influence over the common people never very substantial. It would appear, however, that the High Priest was chosen from only Sadducean families.

Because they were representatives of the priestly establishment, the Sadducees' influence could be seen to exist out of all proportion to the number of their actual adherents, an influence that grew under the reigns of John Hyrcanus and Alexander Janneus, only to be eclipsed by that of the Pharisees during the transitional reign of Salome Alexander. Just how much power they exercised during the reign of Herod (37–4 B.C.E.) and the period of direct Roman rule that followed remains problematic. Modern historians see the Sadducees as little more than "wealthy accommodationists" who did whatever they had to do to maintain themselves in a position of authority. That persons of wealth and status might take a more conservative stance in politics and religion is hardly surprising, though we have no certain knowledge of the role the Sadducees played before and during the first Jewish War with Rome (66–73 C.E.). However, the fact that the Zealots targeted members of the priesthood for attack during the war suggests that, in the eyes of Judean rebels, Sadducees of the priestly class were simply Roman collaborators.

Their religious conservatism is easier to define, however, and the views that are attributed to them by our various sources indicate that they were, in most respects, fundamentally opposed to Pharisaic teachings. Thus, in contrast to the Pharisees, the Sadducees rejected the very notion of an oral Torah, insisting that only the received (written) text and its laws possessed any authority. What followed from this strict constructionism was the rejection not only of Pharisaic interpretive authority but also of a belief system that incorporated elements of postbiblical thinking. This explains their repudiation of such characteristic Pharisaic beliefs as the immortality of the soul and the resurrection of the dead. There is little doubt, therefore, that the Sadducees looked on the dynamic, expansionist view of the Torah promoted by the Pharisees as an unacceptable innovation that they, as the appointed priestly guardians of the Torah, were entitled to ignore. That the future of post-Temple Judaism belonged to the Pharisaic party was something the Sadducees could not foresee.

THE ESSENES

The last of Josephus's "philosophies" is perhaps the most elusive and the source of the greatest controversy today. Like the Pharisees, the **Essenes** apparently were an offshoot of the Maccabean-era hasidim, and their name may have been based on an Aramaic cognate for the word *hasid;* certainly, piety and ritual purity were the watchwords of the Essene communities. Our understanding of who and what the Essenes were derives largely from Josephus; from **Philo Judaeus,** a first-century-c.e. Alexandrian Jewish philosopher; and from the Roman historian Pliny. From these three sources, a composite portrait emerges of a community of ascetic separatists who, rejecting the spiritual authority of the Temple priesthood, withdrew from Judean society into quasi-monastic communities. There, they engaged in agriculture, studied and copied holy books (canonical and noncanonical alike), kept themselves in a state of near-absolute ritual purity, and awaited the coming of a messianic era and the Day of Judgment.

Unlike the Pharisaic fellowships, Essenic brotherhoods were open only to a spiritual elite, and full membership in the communities could be achieved only after a period of probation. Furthermore, most Essenes did not marry, presumably reflecting their view of the imminence of divine judgment and cosmic destruction and the arrival of the messiah(s). Josephus estimated their numbers to be around 4000 (compared with an estimated 6000 Pharisees), but he also noted that the Judean population at large viewed the Essenes with great respect, according them a status close to that of prophets.

Qumran and the Dead Sea Scrolls Our sense of how the Essenic movement related to the rest of Judean society has been greatly enhanced, and further complicated, by the discovery of ancient scrolls in caves situated near the Dead Sea — writings commonly known today as the **Dead Sea Scrolls.** In 1947, a Bedouin shepherd boy, investigating a cave near the ancient settlement of **Qumran,** happened upon pottery jars filled with ancient manuscripts (Figure 31.3). Archaeological teams subsequently explored eleven caves in the vicinity of the Dead Sea and discovered the remains of an ancient library belonging, apparently, to members of an Essene-like community that had established itself, sometime during the Hasmonean era, near the northwest corner of the Dead Sea. The manuscripts presumably were placed in the caves for safekeeping, but the virtual destruction of Qumran during the Jewish Revolt of 66–73 c.e. undoubtedly prevented members of this community from retrieving any of the scrolls (Box 31.1).

Today, most scholars view the Qumran community as essentially Essenic in character. They speculate that the community's founder — referred to in Qumran literature as the "Teacher of Righteousness" — may have led his followers into seclusion near the Dead Sea due to the belief that the Hasmonean leadership had hopelessly polluted the Temple by assuming the role of High Priest, thereby usurping the rightful claim of the Zadokite priestly families. Significantly, the Qumran community referred to its members as the ***benai Zadok*** ("the sons or descendants of Zadok," who, for Ezekiel [40:46], represented the only legitimate priestly line) and looked forward to regaining control of the Temple and returning all of Israel to a proper standard of ethical and ritual purity. The entire outlook of this community was shaped by eschatological beliefs and apocalyptic longings. In one of their most revealing writings, commonly referred to as the War Scroll, they envision a conflict of cosmic dimensions in which angelic as well as human armies will storm to victory over the Romans and their allies. According to this view, the whole of humankind is divided into two irreconcilable camps — the children of righteousness and light, and the children of falsehood and darkness. At the moment of divine intervention, Melchizedek (angelic leader of the forces of light) will destroy Satan and all his minions and judge all those, humans and angels, who served evil and defied the good. At this culminating point in history, two messiahs will arrive, one priestly and the other Davidic, and together they will create an ideal Jerusalem and initiate the kingdom of God.

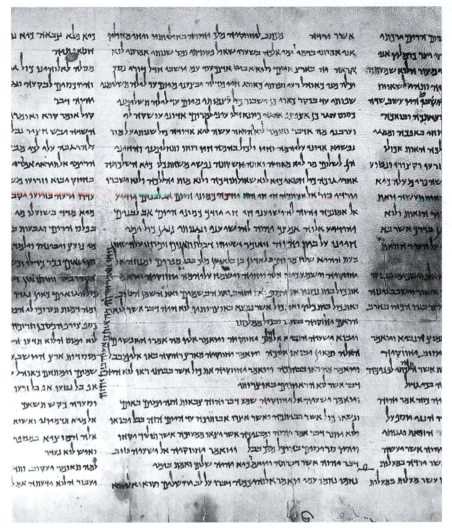

Figure 31.3 This passage is from one of the Dead Sea Scrolls (1Q Isa. 49:12), which were placed in clay jars and hidden in caves near the Dead Sea. The Essene library from the Qumran monastery includes the oldest surviving copies of the Hebrew Bible (Old Testament).

In addition to works that embody elements of this apocalyptic scenario, the Qumran library contained literally hundreds of fragments of canonical biblical texts, deuterocanonical texts such as Tobit, and pseudepigraphal works like 1 Enoch and the Book of Jubilees. Curiously, the one canonical text missing from this collection is the Book of Esther,

a work that may, for all we know, have been excluded from the Qumran canon. In addition, two other types of manuscripts were found among this collection: books peculiar to the Qumran community, describing its constitution and policies, and *pesharim,* or commentaries on biblical books, reflecting the community's singular interpretation of

BOX 31.1
The Dead Sea Scrolls

Among the more than 800 manuscripts found near Qumran, the following are thought to be the most relevant to the study of biblical literature:

1. Copies of biblical texts (in Hebrew, Aramaic, and Greek). With the exception of the Book of Esther, fragments of every canonical book have been found at Qumran, some of which exhibit substantial variations from the "standard" text of the Hebrew Bible (the Masoretic Text, or MT). Perhaps the most significant find, however, is a copy of Isaiah that is remarkably close to the MT version and one of the best preserved. This text is at least 900 years older than any previously known version of Isaiah.

2. Apocryphal and pseudepigraphal texts (such as Tobit, 1 Enoch, the Book of Jubilees, and the Prayer of Nabonidus). It is unclear whether the Qumran community regarded deuterocanonical works like Tobit or pseudepigraphal works like Enoch as "canonical" works of Scripture. What is clear from the inclusion of these books, as well as other writings of similar character, is the community's interest in didactic and apocalyptic literature, and particularly narratives of rescue and redemption from evil.

3. Writings peculiar to the Qumran community (such as the Manual of Discipline, the Zadokite Document, the Temple Scroll, and the Thanksgiving Hymns). Writings like the Manual of Discipline provide a glimpse into the tightly regulated life led by fully initiated members of the Qumran community. These texts reveal a disciplined, hierarchical community of devout sectarians who spoke of themselves as the "children of light," banded together to protect themselves from the "sons of darkness." The Temple Scroll — the longest of the recovered scrolls, measuring over twenty-eight feet — is a compendium of laws and priestly practices related to the Temple, which the Qumran community regarded as polluted and in desperate need of cleansing. The Qumran library also included at least twenty-five hymns of thanksgiving in which the poet — like the biblical psalmist — gives thanks to God for higher spiritual knowledge and deliverance from the evil and foolishness that surround him on all sides.

4. Biblical commentaries (*pesharim* on Habakkuk, Nahum, Isaiah, Psalm 37, and Genesis). A *pesher* is an interpretive reading of a biblical text designed to point out its application to some con-

biblical verses and their contemporary meaning and application. The formal or extended commentaries — on the Psalms and on prophetic books like Isaiah and Habakkuk — follow a standardized pattern of citing a brief passage and then offering an interpretation of that passage without regard to the larger literary context, a method of exegesis replicated in early rabbinic literature. What distinguishes Essenic interpretive literature from Pharisaic (and later rabbinic) biblical interpretations is the obvious eschatological frame of reference adopted quite consistently by the Qumran pietists. For them, the end time was imminent and all previous Scriptures were a foreshadowing of events affecting their community, the true "remnant" of Israel.

The Zealots

No discussion of first-century-C.E. Judean politics and religion would be complete without some description of the most radicalized of contemporary Jews, whom Josephus and the New Testament called the "Zealots." Best described as religiously motivated revolutionaries, the **Zealots** never constituted a single party or political movement. But as a term temporary problem or situation. At Qumran, the explication of such texts presupposed some form of esoteric knowledge, the kind of insight often attributed to the Teacher of Righteousness. In the commentary on Habakkuk, for example, practically every verse is scanned for its hidden eschatological import, and references to the "Chaldeans" are systematically transposed into a first-century-C.E. context and applied to the *Kittim* (presumably, the Romans).

5. Astronomical, apocalyptic, and mystical texts (such as the War Scroll, the Melchizedek Text, and the Angelic Liturgy). The War Scroll provides an apocalyptic scenario of impending warfare between the armies of light and darkness in which the hosts of Satan will be vanquished by the sword of the Almighty. No text in the Qumran library expresses more directly the eschatological expectations of this community or its sense of impending doom for the world. Of similar character is the Melchizedek Text, in which an obscure priest-king of Genesis 14:18–19 is elevated to the position of heavenly intercessor and leader of angelic armies. He is assigned the role of humanity's judge during the final days, and on the Day of Atonement, he will preside over the destruction of Satan and all his minions. On a somewhat lighter note, the Qumran library also includes fragments of messianic horoscopes, predicting what the Messiah will look and sound like.

6. Noncanonical hymns and psalms. A variety of noncanonical poems were found interspersed among canonical psalms. Themes familiar to any reader of the Book of Psalms — such as praise of God and the fruits of wisdom, along with pleas for help and forgiveness of sins — abound, in addition to fragments of what appears to be a Temple liturgy.

What these and many other texts not listed reveal is a library of "sacred" writings much more expansive than the biblical canon we know from either Josephus or later rabbinic literature, and clearly reflective of the sectarian character of this community. Moreover, fragments of canonical biblical texts discovered at Qumran suggest that many of the books of the Hebrew Bible had not yet been "standardized"— that is, no universally agreed-on version of these texts had been accepted by Jewish communities in Palestine or in the Diaspora. As a result, differences in grammar, spelling, and the actual length of certain texts distinguish the Qumran version of the Bible from other versions. It is theorized that the text of the Hebrew Bible remained in a fluid state throughout the period from 100 B.C.E. until the end of the first century C.E., at which time the rabbinic version (commonly referred to as the Rabbinic Recension) appears to have finally become the standard form of the Bible for most Jews.

---

of convenience for groups and/or individuals committed to a policy of rebellion against Rome, coupled with apocalyptic expectations of messianic deliverance, *Zealots* has served historians well. The earliest example of this type of anti-Roman rebellion occurred in 6 C.E., when one **Judas the Galilean** urged his Judean contemporaries not to pay taxes to the Roman Empire — which, not coincidentally, had just instituted direct imperial rule of Judea — and declared that "God alone" was Judea's master. A generation later, in 46 C.E., two of Judas's sons were crucified by the Romans for instigating yet another rebellion against the Roman occupation. Then, at the beginning of the first Jewish War

(in 66 C.E.), Eleazar ben Jair, the leader of a related group of urban revolutionaries known as the *Sicarii* (literally, "dagger men") seized the Dead Sea fortress of **Masada,** which his followers held until 73 C.E., and where (according to Josephus) they committed mass suicide rather than surrender to Roman troops. (Figure 31.4 shows a scale model of first-century-B.C.E. Jerusalem.)

The motivation behind these and other acts of revolutionary violence was clearly a mixture of nationalism and messianism. Leaders emerged who claimed (or whose supporters claimed) a mandate from God for their rebellion and who undoubtedly believed (as did their Essenic contemporaries) that

Figure 31.4   This scale model shows Jerusalem in the first century C.E. The simple flat-roofed tenements housing the general population contrast with the monumental public buildings that Herod I (40–4 B.C.E.) erected. The heavily fortified Temple area appears in the top center.

divine intervention would turn the tide of battle in Judea's favor. Hatred toward Rome had been building steadily throughout much of Jewish Palestine from the moment the Romans imposed direct rule over Judea through a series of appointed governors or "prefects" in 6 C.E. By midcentury, it was clear that only a spark would be needed to set off a major military uprising, which was provided in April of 66 C.E. when the reigning prefect, Florus, helped himself to some of the gold kept in the Temple treasury. For the Zealots, and for many of the common people not affiliated with the Zealot movement, this was the last straw. What ensued was a disastrous four-year war with Rome that ended in the burning of the Second Temple and the decisive defeat of rebel Jewish forces (Figures 31.5 and 31.6).

The final, and most destructive, manifestation of the Zealot "philosophy" (as Josephus terms it) came not in the first century but, rather, in the second, in

the form of the bar Kochba rebellion of 132–135 C.E. The leader of this revolt was one Simon bar Kosiba who gave himself the quasi-political title of *Nasi* (or "prince," in Hebrew) and who was believed to be a messiah figure by some of the most prominent religious leaders of his day, thereby earning the name **bar Kochba** (son of a Star). He established a command center in the southern Judean desert and fought off Roman troops for three years until his defeat in the summer of 135 C.E. The results of what is sometimes called the second Jewish War with Rome were absolutely devastating for the Judean population, with thousands of people enslaved and hundreds of towns and villages destroyed. This debacle put an end to nationalist aspirations among Jews for centuries to come and discredited the very figures who were most closely associated with Zealot politics and the messianic hopes associated with the Zealot movement.

Figure 31.5   This detail is from the Arch of Titus, which the Roman Senate erected in the Forum of Rome about 100 C.E. Created in honor of Titus's victories in the Jewish War, this frieze depicts Roman soldiers carrying off loot from the Jerusalem Temple, including the menorah — the seven-branched candelabrum formerly housed in the sanctuary.

Judaism After the Destruction of the Second Temple

Any discussion of the religious culture that produced the Hebrew Bible must conclude with a series of crucial historical observations. The religious system we call Judaism today, though the result of many centuries of development, did not exist in antiquity in anything like its present form. Perhaps the greatest difference between biblical Judaism and the Judaism practiced after 70 C.E. was the disappearance of the Temple from its central position in Jewish ritual life (Figure 31.7). Once the Second Temple was destroyed, it was no longer possible to bring animal sacrifices to the sanctuary. Thus, of necessity, prayer routines took the place of sacrifice, just as the **synagogue** eventually took the place of the Temple as the spiritual focal point of the Jewish community. The leadership role once exercised by priests was now filled by a new class of religious scholars, commonly referred to as **rabbis,** who provided the community with expert guidance in the following of both biblically based laws and oral traditions of a nonbiblical origin. In time, rabbinical "table fellowships" — small groups of like-minded Pharisaic scholars who ate and studied together — evolved into "academies" that provided not only a curriculum for prospective scholars of the Torah but also a courtlike setting where questions of a ritual

Figure 31.6   Portrait Bust of the Emperor Titus (Ruled 79–81 C.E.) When his father, Vespasian, left him in charge of putting down the Jewish Revolt, Titus laid siege to Jerusalem, capturing the city and burning its Temple in August 70 C.E. He succeeded his father as emperor in 79 C.E. but died after a brief reign.

or ethical nature could be answered authoritatively. Unlike priests, rabbis were chosen not on the basis of heredity but rather on account of their knowledge of the Torah and of biblical law. It was to this class of scholars that the Romans eventually turned for nonpolitical leadership of the Jewish community.

According to one ancient tradition, recorded in rabbinic literature, it was during the final struggle for control of Jerusalem in 70 C.E. that one of the leading Pharisaic scholars of that generation, **Jochanan ben Zakkai,** had himself smuggled out of the city and approached the Roman general (and

soon-to-be emperor) Vespasian, begging him for permission to establish a Torah academy in the seacoast town of Jamnia (or Yavneh). It was there, and at other locations in the Galilee during the second century C.E., that ben Zakkai's successors settled questions regarding the religious calendar and other matters of religious observance. It was also within such a setting that earlier decisions over the scope and content of the biblical canon continued to be debated.

The second major difference between biblical and postbiblical Judaism is the sociohistorical setting within which Jews were compelled to live. The process of territorial displacement known as diasporization had already begun during the biblical period, as evidenced in the books of Esther, Daniel, Ezra, and Nehemiah; in the postexilic portions of Isaiah and Psalms; and, finally, in the apocryphal books of Tobit and Judith. In Daniel's struggle to remain true to his faith, and in Esther's decision to cast her lot with her people-in-exile, we have two archetypal images of the Diaspora Jew, beset by conflicting demands of assimilation and commitment to Torah ideals and group loyalties. Both of these figures resolved this dilemma by remaining true to their ancestral ties and beliefs while continuing to live in a foreign land and serve foreign kings (though not their gods!). In Ezra and Nehemiah, in contrast, we have the example of pious Jews drawn irresistibly back to their ancestral land and moved to restore the Temple destroyed by the Babylonians. For these returnees, the practice of Judaism outside the land of Israel was ultimately unthinkable. Their attitude contrasted sharply with that of Daniel, who presumably was content to turn toward Jerusalem in prayer three times a day (Dan. 6:10) and who continued to lead a Torah-true life in spite of the threats to his faith posed by an alien and sometimes hostile environment. As the Jewish population of Judea decreased after the second century C.E.— chiefly as a consequence of the two wars with Rome — the geographical focal point of Jewish life gradually shifted to Babylon, where rabbinical academies of great stature flourished. By then, the diasporization of Jews and Judaism appeared to be an irreversible tendency.

Figure 31.7   This scale model of Herod's Jerusalem Temple shows his extensive renovations. Begun about 20 B.C.E., the renovations had been completed only a few years before the Romans destroyed it in 70 C.E. According to Josephus, the bejeweled curtain veiling the sanctuary's innermost room, the Holy of Holies, depicted a panorama of heaven.

The third principal difference between biblical and postbiblical Judaism is to be found in the development of a second, oral, Torah — a body of traditional teachings and ritual practices derived or extrapolated from the "written," or canonical, Torah. The canonization of the Hebrew Bible, which most scholars place near the end of the Hasmonean period, brought with it the belief that not only the process of writing sacred books but also the phenomena of prophecy and direct revelation from God had come to an end. Though we have little reliable information on who was responsible for the closing of the biblical canon — ancient Jewish tradition ascribes that authority to Ezra and to the religious scholars who succeeded him — the results of canonical closure are much easier to document. As noted in earlier chapters, the writing of deuterocanonical works continued throughout the Hasmonean and early Roman periods (second century

B.C.E. to the second century C.E.), in clear defiance of any belief in the cessation of prophetic authority. (Figure 31.8 shows the Roman Empire around the turn of the millennium.) But more important, Jewish religious leaders found a way to expand the range and transform the character of biblical law through a process of interpretation that altered profoundly the relationship between the rules that governed priestly sanctity and the everyday religious practices of the Jewish laity. This shift to a more democratic form of Torah observance, in which every home became an extension of (and a partial substitute for) the priestly altar, and in which a divine sanctuary (synagogue) could be found in every community where Jews prayed together, represented a further development of the Pharisaic table fellowships and the decentralized model of the Torah-centered life Pharisaic communities embodied.

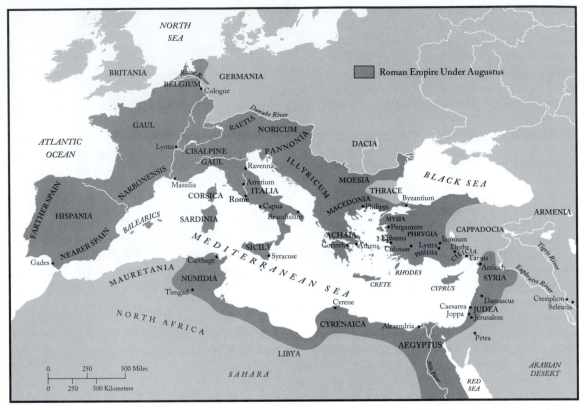

Figure 31.8   Map of the Roman Empire at the Death of Augustus in 14 C.E. With the city of Rome as its administrative capital, the empire governed most of the known world. Its subjects included people of virtually every race, language group, and ethnic background.

The Writing of the Two Talmuds

The final stage in the restructuring of Judaism was marked by the promulgation of a second "Torah"— that is, the Oral Torah presented in written form, commonly known as the **Talmud.** There were two major redactions of the Talmud, the first completed in Palestine during the fifth century C.E. and the second (and more comprehensive version) completed in Babylon near the beginning of the sixth century C.E. When scholars refer to a passage or ruling from *the* Talmud, it is generally the much longer, Babylonian, version, consisting of sixty-three volumes (referred to as "tractates") that they are citing. The subjects covered in these writings

range from criminal and civil law, to ritual protocol, to folklore, with each tractate organized in a loosely topical way. The basis for each general discussion is either a specific passage from the Torah or a current religious practice, often buttressed by specific references to the biblical text. The focus of almost all rabbinic debates and rulings in the Talmud is the need to resolve questions that arise out of attempts to apply biblical commandments equitably and realistically to an ever-changing environment.

The compilation and codification of these discussions and rulings took place in two stages. The first stage, called the **Mishnah** (which translates as "that which is learned by repetition"), was completed at the beginning of the third century C.E. under the supervision of Rabbi Judah the "Nasi" (in this case, the head, or "prince," of a rabbinic court). The probable motive behind this reduction of an originally oral tradition to written form can be found in the growing anxiety among both Palestinian and Diaspora Jews that a renewal of the religious persecutions of the bar Kochba period would lead, once again, to a wholesale slaughter of Torah scholars and to the total loss of their knowledge and wisdom. Only a written account of their debates would enable later generations to reconstruct the pattern of their thoughts and judgments, thereby assuring some continuity of religious practice and thought from generation to generation.

The second stage in this process, referred to as the **Gemara** (meaning "the completion"), took up where the Mishnah left off, representing the further reflections of later generations of rabbinic scholars, commenting on or extrapolating from the decisions of their predecessors. This process was brought to an end in the fifth and sixth centuries C.E. by the virtual canonization of the combined Mishnah/Gemara text and the subsequent omission of alternative traditions from this combined volume. The practice of writing commentaries on the Talmud did, in fact, continue well into the Middle Ages, but by the sixth century C.E., the text of the Babylonian Talmud had stabilized sufficiently that it provided early Judaism with a second "scripture" and a guidebook to Judaism's future development and survival.

The Suppression of Eschatology and the Formation of the Rabbinic Messiah

As leadership of the Jewish community gradually passed, in the first and second centuries C.E., from the priesthood to the lay scholar class (whom we can now refer to as the rabbinate), the focus of normative religious experience in Judaism moved further and further away from the world of apocalyptic eschatology and from the messianic politics to which it gave birth. The very concept of the "mes-

siah" (Hebrew, *mashiach*), which we can trace through multiple mutations from the period of Second Isaiah — for whom even the Persian conqueror Cyrus served as a messianic world redeemer (Isa. 45:1–4) — to the generation of Jesus of Nazareth (c. 4 B.C.E.–30 C.E.), became increasingly problematic in the course of the first century C.E. as messiah after messiah suffered defeat at the hands of the Romans. This was particularly evident after the defeat and death of bar Kochba — on whom many Jews, including the celebrated martyr **Rabbi Akiba,** had pinned their hopes for a divinely assisted victory over the Romans. The widespread destruction and disillusionment that resulted from this rebellion led several leading figures within the rabbinate to repudiate not only bar Kochba and his supporters but also the ideology of the warrior-messiah who would, in the near future, liberate Judea from Roman rule by military means alone. In place of a single, historically recognized "savior," endowed with supernatural powers, the rabbis offered (in tractate Sanhedrin 96–98 of the Babylonian Talmud) a composite figure whose chief characteristics were piety and Davidic descent. This figure would someday liberate his people from foreign oppression, but only when Israel had collectively demonstrated its devotion to God and his Torah.

In contrast to the pre–bar Kochba generation, the post–bar Kochba rabbinate forcefully discouraged speculation on the timing of this now-postponed event. As much as possible, they sought to demystify the figure of the Messiah himself by deliberately ignoring the supernatural qualities that earlier writers (2 Esd. 7:26–44; 13:1–38) had invested him with, focusing instead on the "birth pangs," or spiritual and societal changes, that had to come to pass before this more earthly messiah could appear. This strategy of demystification reflected not only rabbinic Judaism's ongoing struggle with the nascent Jewish/Christian community — and with the messianic claims that it advanced on behalf of Jesus of Nazareth — but also its own increasingly urgent need to construct a viable system of beliefs and religious practices that could withstand the loss of both a homeland and a national savior.

QUESTIONS FOR REVIEW

1. Who was Josephus, and why are his writings crucial to an understanding of the Second Temple period?

2. Into how many distinctive "philosophies" or communities can Judaism of the Second Temple period be subdivided?

3. What are the Dead Sea Scrolls, and why was their discovery of importance to the study of the biblical canon?

4. Who were the Zealots, and what role did they play in the Jewish wars against Rome?

5. Who was Simon bar Kosiba, by what nickname was he known, and what was the outcome of the rebellion he inspired?

6. How many versions of the Talmud were created after the Second Temple period, and what are their contents?

QUESTIONS FOR REFLECTION AND DISCUSSION

1. What were the principal philosophical differences that divided Pharisees, Sadducees, and Essenes from one another? How can we explain the predominance of the Pharisees after the first Jewish War with Rome?

2. Why are the writings of the Qumran community of importance to us today? How do they contribute to our understanding of the diversity of first-century-C.E. Judaism?

3. What motivated the Zealots to rebel against Rome in the face of overwhelming Roman military superiority? Why has Masada become a symbol of that resistance?

4. What are the principal differences between biblical and post–Second Temple Judaism?

TERMS AND CONCEPTS TO REMEMBER

academy of Jamnia
bar Kochba
benai Zadok
Dead Sea Scrolls
Essenes
Flavius Josephus
Gemara
Jochanan ben Zakkai
Judas the Galilean
Masada
Mishnah
Oral Torah
Pharisees
Philo Judaeus
Qumran
rabbi
Rabbi Akiba
Sadducees
Sicarii
synagogue
Talmud
Zadok
Zealots

RECOMMENDED READING

Cohen, Shaye J. D. *From the Maccabees to the Mishnah.* Philadelphia: Westminster Press, 1987.

Horsley, Richard A. "Messianic Movements in Judaism." In D. N. Freedman, ed., *Anchor Bible Dictionary,* Vol. 4, pp. 791–797. New York: Doubleday, 1992.

Neusner, Jacob. *From Politics to Piety: The Emergence of Pharisaic Judaism.* Englewood Cliffs, N.J.: Prentice-Hall, 1973.

Sanders, E. P. *Judaism: Practice and Belief 63 B.C.E. to 66 C.E.* Harrisburg, Pa.: Trinity Press International, 1992.

Shanks, Hershel, ed. *Understanding the Dead Sea Scrolls.* New York: Vintage Books, 1993.

Stone, M. E. *Scriptures, Sects, and Visions: A Profile of Judaism from Ezra to the Jewish Revolts.* Philadelphia: Fortress Press, 1980.

Vermes, Geza. *The Dead Sea Scrolls in English.* New York: Penguin Books, 1997.

Glossary of Major Old Testament Characters, Terms, and Concepts

This Glossary identifies or defines a representative selection of major characters, concepts, places, and terms found in the canonical Hebrew Bible. For a more comprehensive treatment of individual terms, the reader is directed to David Noel Freedman, ed., *The Anchor Bible Dictionary*, Vols. 1–6 (New York: Doubleday, 1992), an indispensable resource. For useful one-volume references, consult Paul Achtemeier, ed., *Harper's Bible Dictionary* (San Francisco: HarperSanFrancisco, 1991); Raymond Brown, Joseph Fitzmyer, and Roland Murphy, *The New Jerome Biblical Commentary*, 2nd ed. (Englewood Cliffs, N.J.: Prentice-Hall, 1990); David Noel Freedman, Alan C. Myers, and Astrid B. Beck, eds., *Eerdmans Dictionary of the Bible* (Grand Rapids, Mich.: Eerdmans, 2000); and B. M. Metzger and M. D. Coogan, eds., *The Oxford Companion to the Bible* (New York: Oxford University Press, 1993).

Aaron The older brother of Moses and first head of the Israelite priesthood, Aaron was the son of Amram the Levite and his aunt Jochebed (Exod. 6:20). Because Moses reputedly had a speech defect, Aaron served as his spokesman before the pharaoh (Exod. 4:14). According to the priestly source in the Pentateuch, which stresses Aaron's special role, Moses anointed him and his four sons as founders of Israel's priesthood (Num. 3:1–3), consecrating them to administer the Tabernacle (see Lev. 8 and Exod. 29). Although he led in the worship of the golden calf (Exod. 32:1–6), Aaron remained in divine favor. His son Eleazar succeeded him as High Priest of Israel.

Aaronites Priestly descendants of Aaron's line (1 Chron. 12:27; Ps. 115:10).

Abednego In the Book of Daniel, the Babylonian name given to Azariah, one of the three Hebrew youths whom Nebuchadnezzar cast into a fiery furnace (Dan. 1–3).

Abel The second son of Adam and Eve (Gen. 4:2) and brother of Cain, who murdered Abel when his animal sacrifice was accepted by YHWH whereas Cain's grain offering was rejected. This story of the first murder (Gen. 4:3–10) occurs in the J portion of the Pentateuch. In Hebrew, the name *Abel* means "breath" or "vanity."

Abigail Wife of Nabal the fool, a wealthy shepherd who denied young David a share of his property. By wisely making a peace offering to David's guerrilla band, Abigail saved her husband's life. After Nabal's death, she married David (1 Sam. 25) and bore him a son, Chileab (2 Sam. 3:3).

Abihu One of Aaron's oldest sons. He and his brother Nadab accompanied their father and Moses part of the way up Mt. Sinai where they encountered YHWH and dined in his presence (Exod. 24:9). In a very different tradition, in which Abihu and Nadab offered "unholy fire" within the sanctuary and were themselves immediately consumed by fire (Lev. 10:1–2). No further explanation is given for their deaths. *See also* Nadab.

Abimelech **(1)** In Genesis, a king of Gerar at whose court Abraham presented his wife, Sarah, as his sister (Gen. 20:1–18). The ruler and patriarch later made a covenant with each other (Gen. 21:22–34). **(2)** A Philistine king at Gerar to whom Isaac passed off his wife, Rebekah, as his sister and with whom he, too, later established a covenant (Gen. 26:1–33). **(3)** In Judges, the son of Gideon who slew his seventy brothers and made himself king at Shechem until he was killed during a siege (Judg. 9).

Abraham In Genesis 12–24, Abraham (at first called *Abram*, meaning "exalted father") is the supreme example of obedience to YHWH and the founder of the Hebrew nation. By divine order, he leaves his adopted home in Haran, in northern Mesopotamia, and travels to Canaan (Palestine), which land is promised to his descendants who are to become a mighty nation (Israel). YHWH later demands that he sacrifice his only son by his wife Sarah. Because of Abraham's willingness to surrender Isaac, YHWH reaffirms the Abrahamic Covenant, by which the patriarch's descendants are to become as numerous as the "sands of the sea" and a source of blessing to all nations. According to Genesis, the twelve tribes of Israel are descended from Abraham's grandson Jacob. The Age of Abraham, a period of mass nomadic movement in the ancient Near East, occurred during the nineteenth or eighteenth century B.C.E.

Abrahamic Covenant The series of promises that YHWH makes to the patriarch Abraham, including vows to give his descendants nationhood, the territory of Canaan, and a line of kings, and to make them a source of universal blessing. In Genesis, YHWH initiates four different versions of this pact (Gen. 12: 2–3; 15:1–21; 17:1–22; and 22:15–18), the visible "sign" of which is circumcision (Gen. 17:11). Like the divine oath to David (2 Sam. 7), the Abrahamic Covenant is unconditional.

Absalom In 2 Samuel, the son of David and Maacah (2 Sam. 3:3). Noted for his physical beauty and fiery temperament, Absalom killed his half-brother Amnon to avenge the rape of his sister Tamar, fled to Geshur in Aram, but was reconciled with his father three years later. He later rebelled against David and drove him from Jerusalem but was defeated and killed by the loyalist Joab (2 Sam. 13–14).

acrostic In Hebrew poetry, a series of lines or verses of which the first words begin with consecutive letters of the alphabet. Examples of this alphabetic sequence are found in Lamentations 1–4 and Psalm 119.

Adam In Genesis, the name *Adam* literally means "ruddy," from the Hebrew for "red"; it possibly derives from an Akkadian word meaning "creature." In the older creation account (Gen. 2:4–4:26), Adam is simply the "man [earthling]," which is not rendered as a proper name until the Septuagint version (c. 250 B.C.E.). New Testament writers typically use Adam as a symbol of all humanity (as in 1 Cor. 15:21–49 and Rom. 5:12–21).

Adonai The Hebrew word for "Lord," a title of honor and majesty applied to the Israelite Deity, particularly during the late postexilic period, as a substitute for the personal name *Yahweh*, which was considered too sacred to pronounce.

Adonijah The son of David who tried unsuccessfully to succeed his father on Israel's throne and whom Solomon put to death (1 Kings 1:9–2:25).

Ahab Son of Omri and king of Israel circa 869–850 B.C.E. Although Ahab practiced the Yahwist religion, he allowed his wife, Jezebel, daughter of a Phoenician ruler, to encourage the Baal cult, which brought the condemnation of the prophet Elijah (1 Kings 17–22). A contemporary of Judah's King Jehoshaphat, Ahab was killed while defending Israel against Assyria's Shalmaneser III.

Ahasuerus (Xerxes) The son of Darius Hystaspes and Atossa, daughter of Cyrus the Great, the Ahasuerus of the Book of Esther is usually identified with Xerxes I (486–465 B.C.E.), who led the second Persian invasion of Greece and was defeated at the Battle of Salamis (480 B.C.E.). There is no record that he ever had a Jewish queen named Esther.

Ahaz King of Judah (c. 735–716 B.C.E.) and father of Hezekiah, who succeeded him. Although Ahaz reigned during the ministries of Isaiah and Micah, he compromised the Yahwist religion to curry favor with Assyria, whose vassal Judah became (2 Kings 16).

Ahijah A northern prophet who first appears during the reign of Rehoboam and who incites Jeroboam to lead the ten northern tribes in a rebellion against Rehoboam's tyrannical rule (1 Kings 11:29–39). Ahijah later denounces Jeroboam for his apostasy and predicts disaster for his royal house (1 Kings 14:1–17).

'Ai The "ruin" in Hebrew, 'Ai was a city reputedly destroyed by Joshua's conquest of Canaan (Josh. 7:2–5; 8:1–29). But archaeology has demonstrated that it had already been abandoned in the thirteenth century B.C.E. when the Israelites entered Palestine.

Akhenaton The Egyptian pharaoh (1364–1347 B.C.E.) who radically altered the state religion, introducing a henotheistic cult of the solar deity Aton and outraging the conservative priests of the Theban state god Amun. Abandoning his original name, Amenhotep IV, Akhenaton founded a new capital, Akheta-ton (now known as Tel el Amarna); archaeologists call his reign the Amarna period.

Akkad (Accad)   The narrow plain of Babylonia lying north of Sumer, locale of the Akkad dynasty, founders of the first real empire in world history (c. 2360–2180 B.C.E.). In Akkad, named for its capital city, were many of the great cities of antiquity, some of which are mentioned in Genesis 10.

Akkadian (Accadian)   (1) the period during which the early Semitic dynasty established by Sargon I dominated Mesopotamia (twenty-fourth to twenty-second centuries B.C.E.). **(2)** The Akkadian language, written in cuneiform script but sharing many features with Hebrew, Arabic, and Aramaic; a Semitic tongue used in Mesopotamia from about the twenty-eighth to the first centuries B.C.E.

Alexander the Great   One of the most brilliant leaders and military conquerors of the classical world. Son of King Philip of Macedonia, Alexander was born at Pella in Macedonia in 356 B.C.E. and died in Babylon in 323 B.C.E. During his relatively brief career, he conquered most of the known world, created an empire that extended from Greece to India, propagated Greek culture throughout the Near East, and instituted a period of cosmopolitanism termed Hellenistic. His influence on Palestine is recounted in 1 Maccabees 1.

Alexandria   A major port city and cultural center founded by Alexander the Great on the Egyptian coast. The home of a large Jewish colony during the Hellenistic period, Alexandria nourished a fusion of Hebraic and Hellenic (Greek) ideas, one result of which was the Greek Septuagint translation of the Hebrew Bible.

allegory   A literary narrative in which persons, places, and events are given a symbolic meaning. Some Hellenistic Jewish scholars of Alexandria tended to interpret the Hebrew Bible allegorically.

Amalekites   According to Genesis 36:12, these nomadic tribes were descendants of Esau who occupied the desert south and southeast of Canaan. Persistent enemies of ancient Israel, the Amalekites attacked Moses' group (Deut. 25:17–19), were defeated by Joshua at Rephidim (Exod. 17) and conquered by Gideon (Judg. 6:33; 7:12), but were still troublesome in Saul and David's time (1 Sam. 15; 30:18).

Amarna Age   A title assigned to the reign of Pharaoh Amenhotep IV (Akhenaton), whose new capital had been built at Amarna, Egypt.

Amarna Letters   During the late nineteenth century, excavations at Tel el Amarna (approximately 190 miles south of Cairo) uncovered a cuneiform library consisting largely of diplomatic exchanges between the Egyptian court and its vassal kingdoms in Syria and Palestine from 1388 to 1362 B.C.E. This correspondence provides us with a vivid picture of the social and political turbulence that affected the reigns of Amenophis III and his son, Amenhotep IV (better known as Akhenaton).

amen   A term derived from a Hebrew work whose root suggests "so be it." Typically used as a confirmation (1 Kings 1:36), implying agreement.

Ammon   (1) A tribal state located northeast of the Dead Sea, one of Israel's traditional enemies. **(2)** David's eldest son, who, having fallen in love with his half-sister Tamar, lures her to his bedroom and then rapes her. To avenge this crime against his sister's honor, Absalom murders his older brother Amnon and then flees from court to avoid punishment (2 Sam. 13).

Ammonites   A Semitic group supposedly descended from Abraham's nephew Lot (Gen. 19:38). Chronic enemies of Israel (1 Sam. 11; 1 Kings 11), they occupied the eastern margin of the Transjordan plateau to harass the Israelites.

Amorites   A Semitic people (called "Westerners" or "highlanders"), who moved into the ancient Near East about 2000 B.C.E. and founded the states of Mari and Babylon, of which Hammurabi is the best-known Amorite ruler. The term was also applied to a tribe living in Canaan before the Israelite conquest (Num. 13:29; 21:26; Judg. 1).

Amos   A shepherd and "dresser of sycamore [fig] trees" from the Judean village of Tekoa who denounced the religious and social practices of the northern kingdom (Israel) during the reign of Jeroboam II (c. 786–746 B.C.E.), Amos was the first biblical prophet whose words were collected and preserved in a book.

amphictyony   A confederation of tribes or cities (typically of six or twelve members) organized around a particular deity's shrine. The term is commonly applied to the league of Israelite tribes during the period of judges (c. 1200–1000 B.C.E.).

Anath A Canaanite agricultural goddess, sister-consort of the fertility god Baal.

angel From a Greek word meaning "messenger," angels were commonly conceived in biblical times as emissaries from the Deity who employed them to communicate his will to humanity. The oldest known rendition of angels in art occurs on the stele of Urnammu, a Sumerian king, but many scholars suggest that Israel's belief in angelology derives from Persian sources. Angels named in canonical Scripture include Michael and Gabriel, although apocryphal and pseudepigraphal literature lists others.

anointed The literal meaning of the Hebrew word *mashiah*, a term applied to Davidic kings who were consecrated in office by the ritual smearing (anointing) of their heads with holy oil. *See* Messiah.

anthropomorphism Attributing human characteristics to something not human; particularly, ascribing human shape and form to a deity.

Antiochus The name of several Syrian monarchs who inherited power from Seleucus I, a general and successor of Alexander the Great. The most famous were Antiochus III, who gained control of Palestine from Egypt in 198/197 B.C.E., and Antiochus IV (*Epiphanes,* or "God Manifest") (175–163 B.C.E.), whose persecution of the Jews led to the Maccabean Revolt.

Anu Head of the older generation of Mesopotamian gods, he is the Babylonian version of the Sumerian sky god An, whose name means "heaven." Regarded as the "father of the gods," he had a temple at Uruk, where he was worshiped into Hellenistic times.

'Apiru Egyptian version of the term *Habiru. See* Habiru.

apocalypse From the Greek *apokalypsis,* meaning to "uncover" or "reveal," the term refers to a special kind of prophetic literature that purports to foretell the future in terms of symbols and mystical visions and deals primarily with eschatological events.

apocalyptic literature A branch of prophetic writing that flourished in Judaism from about 200 B.C.E. to 140 C.E. and greatly influenced Christianity. Works such as Daniel, Enoch, 2 and 3 Baruch, 2 Esdras, and the Christian Book of Revelation are distinguished by cryptic language, symbolic imagery, and the expectation of an imminent cosmic catastrophe in which the forces of Good ultimately defeat the powers of Evil, resulting in the establishment of a messianic rule and consequent transformation of the universe.

Apocrypha From the Greek, meaning "hidden" books. Apocrypha refers to noncanonical or deuterocanonical literature, especially the fourteen books included in the Greek Septuagint and Latin Vulgate Bibles but not in the Masoretic Text of the Hebrew Bible.

apodictic law Law cast in the form of unconditional demands, such as the "thou shalt nots" in the Decalogue (Exod. 20).

apokalypsis English transliteration of a Greek term meaning a "revelation, an unveiling of what is hidden."

apostasy From a Greek term meaning "to revolt," apostasy is the act of abandoning or rejecting a previously held religious faith. An apostate is one who has defected from or ceased to practice his or her religion.

apotheosis In the Greco-Roman context, the elevation of a hero to divine stature, such as the posthumous deification of Alexander or Julius Caesar.

'Aqaba, Gulf of A northern arm of the Red Sea, part of the Jordan rift, which separates the Sinai peninsula from Midian and Arabia.

Aram According to Genesis 10:22, Aram was the son of Shem (a son of Noah) and progenitor of the Arameans, whom the Hebrew Bible identifies with the Syrians (Gen. 24).

Aramaic The langage of the Arameans (Syrians), Aramaic was a west-Semitic tongue used in parts of Mesopotamia from about 1000 B.C.E. The official language of the Persian Empire after about 500 B.C.E., it was spoken by the Jews after the Babylonian exile. Parts of the Hebrew Bible were composed in Aramaic, and a Galilean dialect of Aramaic was probably the language spoken by Jesus.

archetype The primal form or original pattern from which all other things of a like nature are descended. The term refers to characters, ideas, or actions that represent the supreme and/or essential examples of a universal type, as Moses is the archetypal model of prophet and lawgiver.

Ark The rectangular houseboat that Noah built to contain his family and pairs of all animals during the Flood (Gen. 6:14–16).

Ark of the Covenant The portable wooden chest, supposedly dating from Mosaic times (Exod. 25:10–22), that contained sacred artifacts of Israel's religion, such as Aaron's staff and the two stone tablets representing the Decalogue. Sometimes carried into battle (Josh. 6:4–11; 1 Sam. 4), the Ark of the Covenant was eventually brought to Jerusalem and kept in the innermost sanctuary of Solomon's Temple. Its fate after the Temple's destruction is unknown.

Artaxerxes King of Persia (465–423 B.C.E.), son of Xerxes I. According to Nehemiah 2, Artaxerxes commissioned Nehemiah, his Jewish cupbearer, to go to Jerusalem and rebuild the city's walls. Scholars are not agreed on whether Ezra returned to Jerusalem during the reign of Artaxerxes I or Artaxerxes II.

Asa The third king of Judah (c. 913–873 B.C.E.), whose long reign was marked by various religious reforms. The authors of Kings and Chronicles judge him a "good" ruler (1 Kings 15:8–24; 2 Chron. 14:1–16:14).

Ashdod One of the five major cities of the Philistines (Josh. 13:3), where the captured Ark of the Covenant was placed in Dagon's temple (1 Sam. 5:1–8).

Asher The reputed founder of an Israelite tribe that occupied a strip of Palestinian coast between Carmel and Phoenicia (Josh. 17:10–11; 19:24–31; Judg. 1:31–32; 5:17).

Asherah The Hebrew name for the Canaanite goddess Asherat, "Lady of the Sea," a consort of El, Canaan's chief deity, whom the apostate Israelites worshiped at various times (see 1 Kings 11:5; 16:33; 18:19; etc.).

Ashkelon One of the five leading Philistine cities (Josh. 13:3; 2 Sam. 1:20).

Ashurbanipal IV Assyrian emperor (c. 668–627 B.C.E.), grandson of Sennacherib, son and successor of Esarhaddon; called Asnapper in Ezra 4:10.

Assur (Asshur) **(1)** The chief deity of the Assyrians, king of their gods, and personification of war. **(2)** Assyria's first capital, located on the west bank of the Tigris River, site of an earlier Sumerian city. **(3)** The name of the country from which the Assyrians took their name.

Assyria **(1)** A large territory centered along the upper Tigris River in Mesopotamia, including the major cities of Assur, Calah, and Nineveh. **(2)** The empire that dominated the Near East from the eleventh to the seventh centuries B.C.E. and whose leaders destroyed Israel in 721 B.C.E. and besieged Jerusalem in 701 B.C.E. It was destroyed by a coalition of Babylonians and Medes in 612 B.C.E.

Assyrians The "people of Assur," the chief god of Assyria, the Assyrians controlled the Fertile Crescent from about 1100 to 612 B.C.E. Israelite prophets such as Isaiah of Jerusalem regarded them as YHWH's instruments of punishment for Israel's disobedience.

Athaliah The queen of Judah (842–837 B.C.E.), she was the daughter of Omri (or of Ahab and Jezebel). After Jehu murdered her husband, Jehoram, king of Judah, she assumed the throne, the only woman to do so in the entire history of Israel and Judah.

Aton (Aten) The Egyptian sun god whom Akhenaton proclaimed the sole deity to be worshiped, he was represented by a solar disk from which beams of life-giving light emanated.

Atonement, Day of (Yom Kippur) An annual Israelite observance in which the High Priest sacrifices animals ("sin offerings") to effect a reconciliation between YHWH and his people (Lev. 16). In this solemn ritual, the priest symbolically transfers the Israelites' collective sins onto a "scapegoat," which is then banished to the wilderness, to be taken by Azazel (probably a desert demon). The day marked the High Priest's once-yearly entrance into the Temple's Holy of Holies, where, invoking the divine name, he mediates YHWH's forgiveness of Israel's transgressions, making the people again "at one" with their God.

Atrahasis A name meaning "extra-wise," an epithet commonly applied to Utnapishtim, the Mesopotamian hero who was the only man who, with his household, survived the global deluge.

Azazel The unidentified place or demon to which the scapegoat was sent on the Day of Atonement (Lev. 16:8, 10, 26).

Baal A Canaanite-Phoenician term meaning "lord" or "master," the name applied to Canaan's most popular fertility god. Worshiped as the power that caused germination and growth of farm crops, Baal was a serious rival to YHWH after the Israelites settled in Palestine and became dependent on agriculture (Judg. 2:11–14). He is pictured as a god of storm and rainfall in a contest with the Yahwist Elijah on Mount Carmel (1 Kings 18:20–46).

Babel A term meaning the "gate of God," Babel became synonymous with the confusion of languages that typified cosmopolitan Babylon (Gen. 11:4–9). The Tower of Babel, or "House of the Terrace-platform of Heaven and Earth," was a ziggurat. *See* ziggurat.

Babylon An ancient city on the middle Euphrates that was capital of both the Old and Neo-Babylonian empires. Under Nebuchadnezzar II (605–562 B.C.E.), who joined forces with the Medes to defeat Egypt at the Battle of Carchemish (605 B.C.E.) and create the second Babylonian Empire, Babylon destroyed Jerusalem and its Temple (587 B.C.E.). Babylon fell to the Persians in 539 B.C.E. Alexander the Great's plans to rebuild the old sanctuaries ended with his death in 323 B.C.E., and the city never regained its former glory. As the archetypal enemy of God's people, Babylon became the symbol of Satan's worldly power.

Babylonian exile The period between 587 and 538 B.C.E. during which Judah's upper classes were held captive in Babylon. An earlier deportation of Jewish leaders in 597 B.C.E. included the prophet Ezekiel. After Cyrus of Persia conquered Babylon in 539 B.C.E., Jews who wished to do so were encouraged to return to their Palestinian homeland.

Balaam A Bedouin prophet or fortune-teller from Pethor on the Euphrates River whom Balak, king of Moab, hired to curse the Israelites when they attempted to cross Moab on their way to Canaan. YHWH caused the hired soothsayer to turn his curse into a blessing on Israel (Num. 22–24), although another tradition blames Balaam for corrupting the Israelites (Num. 31:8, 15–17).

ban The practice of dedicating all conquered enemies and their property to the victor's god, a policy of holy war that required the mass slaughter of all defeated peoples. According to Deuteronomy, the Israelites were commanded to place all Canaanites under the ban.

Barak An early Israelite judge (military commander), apparently subordinate to Deborah, who fought against the Canaanites oppressing Israel. He failed to capture his chief opponent, Sisera, who was killed by Jael, a woman (Judg. 4–5).

bar Kochba Simeon bar Kosiba (nicknamed *bar Kochba*, meaning "son of a Star") was the messianic leader of a revolt against Roman occupation of Judea that lasted from 132 to 135 C.E. This rebellion is often referred to as the second Jewish War with Rome, and bar Kochba's defeat led several rabbinic scholars of the time to view him as a "false" messiah.

Baruch ben Neriah The secretary and friend of Jeremiah, Baruch (blessed) recorded the prophet's message, which probably became the nucleus of the Jeremiah scroll (Jer. 32:9–14; 36; 43:6). The apocryphal Book of Baruch was attributed to him, as were the apocalypses of 2 and 3 Baruch in the Pseudepigrapha.

Bathsheba The wife of Uriah, a Hittite soldier working in King David's service, Bathsheba's adultery with David and his murder of her husband evoked the denunciation of the prophet Nathan (2 Sam. 11:1–4; 12:1–23). The mother of Solomon, she conspired to place her son on Israel's throne (1 Kings 1:15–17).

Beersheba An ancient well in southern Palestine identified with the Genesis patriarchs (Gen. 21:22–34; 26:23–25, 32–33; 46:1); later a traditional location of the extreme southern border of the Israelite kingdom (Judg. 20:1; 2 Sam. 24:2; 1 Kings 4:25; etc.).

Behemoth A mysterious beast probably derived from Mesopotamian mythology but sometimes identified with the hippopotamus (Job 40:15–24). *See also* Leviathan.

Bel The Babylonian-Assyrian version of Baal, a common name for Marduk, chief god of Babylon (Isa. 46:1–4), sometimes called Merodach by the Jews (Jer. 50:2).

Belial An adjective meaning "not profitable" or "wicked" but used in the Hebrew Bible as a proper name to denote an evil character, as "son of" or "daughter of" (Deut. 13:13; Judg. 19:22; 1 Sam. 10:27).

Belshazzar In Daniel, the last king of Babylon, son of Nebuchadnezzar (Dan. 5:1–31), though archaeological discoveries indicate that he was neither, but merely prince regent for his father, Nabonidus.

Beltshazzar A name meaning "protect the king's life," given to Daniel by his Babylonian masters (Dan. 1:7; 2:26; 4:8, 9).

Benai Zadok Persons claiming descent from Solomon's High Priest, Zadok ben Ahitub, whose genealogy extends back to Aaron's son Eleazar (1 Chron. 6:4–15). The last Zadokite priest to occupy the office of High Priest was Onias, who was deposed by Antiochus IV in 175 B.C.E. *See* Zadok.

Benjamin The twelfth and last son of Jacob, second son of the patriarch's favorite wife, Rachel, and thus full brother of Joseph and half-brother of Jacob's other ten sons. Benjamin figures prominently in Joseph's saga (Gen. 42–44) and is regarded as the founder of the tribe of Benjamin, which, under the Israelite monarchy, occupied territory adjacent to that of Judah (Josh. 18:11–28; Judg. 1:8, 21). When the ten northern tribes seceded from the Davidic monarchy, Benjamin remained with the southern kingdom of Judah (1 Kings 12:21; Ezra 4:1).

Bethel An ancient site, meaning "house of God," associated with the patriarchs Abraham (Gen. 12:8) and Jacob (Gen. 28:11–13, 22). Under the divided kingdom, Jeroboam I built a shrine at Bethel, near Judah's northern boundary (1 Kings 12:32). Amos denounced a prophet at the royal sanctuary there (Amos 7:10–17).

Bethlehem A village about five miles south of Jerusalem, birthplace of David (1 Sam. 17:12) and the place where Samuel secretly anointed him king of Israel (1 Sam. 16:1–2; 20:6). According to Micah 5:2, it was to be the Messiah's birthplace.

Beth-peor An unidentified site east of the Jordan River in Moab, near which the Israelites camped before crossing Jordan and where Moses was buried (Deut. 3:29; 4:46; 34:6).

Bildad One of Job's three friends who dispute with him the meaning of his afflictions (Job 2:11; 8; 18; etc.).

blasphemy Speech defaming the Deity, a capital offense in Hebrew Bible times (1 Kings 21:9–13).

Boaz A wealthy landowner of Bethlehem (Ruth 2:1) who married the Moabite Ruth and became an ancestor of David (Ruth 4:22).

Book of the Covenant The collection of statutes and commandments appearing in Exodus between the giving of the Decalogue and the ratification of the covenant at Sinai/Horeb (Exod. 20:18–23:33), it contains some of the oldest legal material in the Hebrew Bible. This compilation takes its name from Exodus 24:7, where Moses reads from the "book of the covenant."

Booths, Feast of In ancient Israel, an autumn agricultural festival of thanksgiving during which the celebrants erected booths or shelters reminiscent of the wilderness encampments used during Israel's journey from Egypt to Canaan (Exod. 34:22); also known as the Feast of Tabernacles or Sukkoth (Lev. 23:39–44; Neh 8:13–18).

Caesar A hereditary name by which the Roman emperors commemorated Gaius Julius Caesar, great-uncle of Augustus (Octavian), the first emperor.

Cain According to the J (Yahwist) source of Genesis, the first son of Adam and Eve, who slew his brother Abel, thus becoming the archetypal murderer and fugitive (Gen. 4). The "mark of Cain" is not a curse, but a sign that YHWH protected him from his enemies.

Calah An ancient city on the Tigris, one of the early capitals of Assyria (Gen. 10:11–12).

Caleb Along with Joshua, one of the two spies sent to reconnoiter Canaan who brought back a favorable report of Israel's chances (Num. 13:14). For his trust in YHWH, Caleb was allowed to enter Canaan, while all others of his generation died in the wilderness (Num. 13:30; 14:38).

Canaan The Tanak name for the land of Palestine west of the Jordan River, from Egypt in the south to Syria in the north (Gen. 10:19). According to Hebrew tradition, Canaan was the territory promised to Abraham's descendants (Gen. 15:7–21; 17:1–8) and infiltrated by the Israelite tribes during the thirteenth and twelfth centuries B.C.E. (Num. 21; Josh. 1–24; Judg. 1–2).

canon A term derived from the Greek *kanon*, which may be related to the Semitic *qaneh*, a "reed," perhaps used as a measuring rod. In modern usage, a canon is a standard of measure by which a religious community judges certain writings to be authoritative, usually of divine origin. The Hebrew Bible alone is the canon of Judaism, whereas Christianity accepts both it (sometimes including the Apocrypha) and the Greek New Testament. The canon is thus an official list of books considered genuine, worthy to be used in teaching and liturgy, and hence binding in doctrine and morals. The adjective *extracanonical* refers to books not included in the offical canon or list.

Carchemish An important Hittite site in northern Syria that overlooked the main crossing of the Euphrates on the trade route from Assyria to the Mediterranean. In 605 B.C.E., Nebuchadnezzar II defeated the Egyptian forces of Pharaoh Necho II here (2 Chron. 35:20; Jer. 46:2), thus ending Egypt's last significant attempt to reassert its hegemony in the Near East and establishing Babylon as the dominant power.

Carmel The name (meaning "garden" or "orchard") of a hilly range along the western border of Asher (Josh. 19:26), extending from the hill country of Samaria to the Mediterranean where Mount Carmel projects into the sea. Sacred to Baal because of its lush vegetation, Carmel was the site of Elijah's contest with the Canaanite priests (1 Kings 18).

case law Law expressed in conditional terms: If such an act is committed, then such must be the punishment; characteristic of ancient Near Eastern legal forms, including those found in Mosaic Law.

Chaldea A Mesopotamian territory occupied by Semitic Arameans who founded the Neo-Babylonian Empire under Nabopolassar and his son Nebuchadnezzar, first in a brief line of Chaldean rulers (2 Kings 24:2; 25:4–13; Jer. 37:5–12). The Chaldeans were famous for their mastery of astronomy and astrology.

chaos The Greek term designating the original void or abyss that predated the world's creation; in the ancient Near East, it was typically portrayed as a vast, dark waste of boundless sea, out of which the cosmos emerged. *See also* cosmos.

Chedorlaomer King of Elam, a country east of Babylonia on the Persian Gulf (Gen. 14).

Chemosh The national god of Moab to whom children were sacrificed as burnt offerings (Num. 21:29; Jer. 48:7, 13, 46). King Solomon erected an altar to Chemosh (1 Kings 11:7) that was not dismantled until Josiah's reforms more than three centuries later (2 Kings 23:13). Like the Israelites, the Moabites, or "people of Chemosh," attributed their country's defeats and failures to their deity's anger.

cherub, cherubim (pl.) Mythological creatures—part bird, part human, part other animal—that were placed in pairs at each side of the mercy seat of the Tabernacle and, later, in the innermost sanctuary of Solomon's Temple, to protect the sacred relics in the Ark of the Covenant (Exod. 25:18–22). Their images were also embroidered on the veil of the Temple (2 Chron. 3:14) and sculpted on a frieze around the Temple walls and on the bases of the "Molten sea" (1 Kings 6:23; 7:29; 1 Chron. 28:18; Heb. 9:5). Such winged creatures, with a lion's or ox's body, eagle's wings, and human face, were common in ancient Near Eastern art and have been found in Byblos, Nineveh, and elsewhere. Originally the guardians of divine beings, they were later identified with the angels of YHWH's heavenly court.

Chronicler The anonymous author of 1 and 2 Chronicles, who produced a revisionist account of Israel's history from a postexilic, priestly perspective.

circumcision An ancient Semitic operation in which the foreskin of eight-day-old males is removed as a ceremony of initiation into the religion and community of Israel. Circumcision is represented as beginning with Abraham (Gen. 17:10–14) or Moses (Exod. 4:24–46; see also Lev. 1:59; 2:21; 12:3).

Code of Hammurabi The compilation of Sumero-Babylonian laws inscribed on the basaltic stele of Hammurabi (1728–1686 B.C.E.), founder of the first Babylonian Empire. A number of Hammurabi's statutes anticipate those of the biblical Torah.

codex A manuscript book of an ancient biblical text, used to replace the unwieldy scrolls on which the Scriptures were first recorded.

Codex Sinaiticus An ancient Greek edition of the New Testament, which contains several books that supplement the central canon.

conquest of Canaan The gradual occupation of Palestine during the thirteenth and twelfth centuries B.C.E. by previously nomadic Israelites, an idealized account of which is given in Joshua 1–24.

cosmogony A theory or tradition about the origin or birth of the universe (cosmos).

cosmology A theory describing the natural order or structure of the universe.

cosmos The Greek term designating the universe, understood as an ordered system characterized by structure, stability, and harmony. *See also* chaos, cosmogony, and cosmology.

Court History Also called the *Succession Narrative*, it is the account of David's reign and Solomon's succession to Israel's throne, the narrative underlying 2 Samuel 9–24 and 1 Kings 1–2.

covenant **(1)** An agreement or compact between individuals, such as Abraham and Abimelech (Gen. 21:27) or David and Jonathan (1 Sam. 18:3). **(2)** A promise YHWH makes to certain people, such as Noah (Gen. 9:13) and Abraham (Gen. 15:18–21; 17:4–14). **(3)** A legal bond YHWH forms with a chosen group, such as Israel, and the demands he makes in return. The Mosaic or Sinatic Covenant is that from which the Old "Testament" (a synonym for "covenant" or "contract") takes its name (Exod. 20–24, 34; Deut. 29; Josh. 24).

Covenant Code A name given to the collection of ancient Hebrew laws found in Exodus 20:23–23:33, often called the Book of the Covenant (Exod. 24:7).

cult The formalized religious practices of a people, particularly systems of veneration, public rites, and liturgies.

cult legend The oral tradition explaining or validating the sacredness of a particular place or shrine, such as the Genesis stories about Jacob's mystical experiences at Bethel or Peniel.

cuneiform A wedge-shaped system of writing that originated in ancient Sumer circa 3000 B.C.E. and spread throughout Mesopotamia.

Cyrus the Great The founder of the Persian Empire and conqueror of Babylon (539 B.C.E.) who liberated the Jews from captivity and decreed their return to Jerusalem to rebuild the Temple (2 Chron. 36:22–23; Ezra 1:1–8). Second Isaiah calls him YHWH's "shepherd" (Isa. 44:28) and his "Anointed" or "Messiah" (Isa. 45:1).

D *See* Deuteronomist.

Dagon An ancient Canaanite agricultural deity worshiped by the Philistines at Ashdod and Gaza (1 Sam. 5:1–7) and whose Gaza temple reputedly was destroyed by Samson (Judg. 16:23–30).

Damascus The capital of Syria and terminus of ancient caravan routes in the Fertile Crescent. Damascus was supposedly founded by Uz, grandson of Noah's son Shem (Gen. 5:32; 6:10; 10:23), and was visited by Abraham (Gen. 11:31; 12:4; 14:14).

Dan **(1)** The son of Jacob and Rachel's servant, Bilhah (Gen. 30:1–6). **(2)** One of the twelve tribes of Israel, which first occupied a small territory between Judah and Ephraim (Josh. 19:40–48) but later migrated north to an area close to the Jordan source (Josh. 19:47; Judg. 1:34; 18). **(3)** A Danite city formerly known as Laish, where Jeroboam I later established a cult center (1 Kings 12:26–30). As the phrase "from Dan to Beersheba" (Judg. 20:1; 2 Sam. 24:2; 1 Kings 4:25; etc.) indicates, the city of Dan was regarded as the extreme northern boundary of Israel.

Danel An ancient king whose name (Danel) appears in the *Ras Shamrah* epics and who was incorporated into the same tradition as Noah and Job (Ezek. 14:14; 28:3). He is not the same as the character in the Book of Daniel, who is referred to in no other canonical Hebrew Bible work.

Darius The name of several Persian rulers mentioned in the Hebrew Bible. **(1)** Darius I (522–486 B.C.E.), son of Hystaspes, was the emperor whose forces invaded Greece and were defeated at Marathon (490 B.C.E.). He continued Cyrus the Great's favorable treatment of the Jews (Ezra 5–6). **(2)** Darius "the Mede" (Dan. 5:31; 9:1), alleged to have condemned Daniel to the lion's den (Dan. 6:7–26), is unknown to history.

Dathan A Reubenite who rebelled with Korah against Moses and Aaron in the Sinai desert (Num. 16:1–35; 26:7–11).

David The son of Jesse (Ruth 4:18–22), successor to Saul, and second king of the united twelve-tribe monarchy (1000–961 B.C.E.), David expanded Israel's boundaries to their greatest extent, founded a new administrative and religious capital at Jerusalem, and created a prosperous though short-lived Palestinian Empire. His story is told in 1 Samuel 16 through 1 Kings 2; the Chronicler gives an often unreliable, idealized version of his cultic activities (1 Chron. 2, 3, 10–29). So great was David's effectiveness and popularity, especially in retrospect, that he became the prototype of the Messiah figure, who was prophesied to be his descendant (Isa. 9:5–7; 11:1–16; Jer. 23:5; 30:9; Ezek. 34:23–31; etc.).

Davidic Covenant (Royal Covenant) YHWH's vow to keep King David's descendants on Israel's throne "forever." Although later modified to make the divine promise dependent on the Davidic rulers' obedience (1 Kings 8:25–26), God's original promise is unconditional (2 Sam. 7:8–17; Ps. 89:19–37), raising questions about YHWH's fidelity to his word after the Babylonians permanently overthrew the Davidic dynasty in 587 B.C.E. (Ps. 89:38–51).

Day of Atonement (Yom Kippur) *See* Atonement, Day of.

Day of the Lord This phrase is a recurrent eschatological motif in classical prophecy from the eighth through the sixth centuries B.C.E. It signifies a time of global catastrophe and divine judgment upon all of the nations of the earth (including Israel). Amos appears to be the earliest prophet to employ this phrase (Amos 5:18–20), but it is Zephaniah (Zeph. 1:14–18) who gives us the fullest depiction of this "day" as a time of universal suffering and devastation, when the sins of all peoples will finally be exposed and punished.

Dead Sea Known in biblical times as the "salt sea" (Gen. 14:3; Num. 34:3; Josh. 3:16; 12:3), the "sea of the plain [Arabah]" (Josh. 3:16; 12:3), and the "east sea" (Ezek. 47:18; Joel 2:20), this lake, forty-six miles long, was given its present name by Greeks in the second century B.C.E. Occupying a basin into which the Jordan River empties, and located in a geological fault zone that extends from Syria to the Gulf of 'Aqaba and thence into East Africa, it lies 1290 feet below sea level and has a depth of approximately 1200 feet, making it the lowest body of water in the world. With a saline content five times that of the ocean, it supports no fish or other forms of life.

Dead Sea Scrolls   Biblical and other religious manuscripts dating from the second century B.C.E. to the first century C.E., found in caves near Qumran on the northwest shore of the Dead Sea.

Deborah   A judge and prophetess who, with Barak, helped bring about Israel's victories over the Canaanite forces of Sisera (Judg. 4–5).

Decalogue   *See* Ten Commandments.

Delilah   A woman from Sorek whom the Philistines bribed to discover and betray the secret of Samson's strength (Judg. 16). Her name means "coquette" or "flirtatious."

demythologizing   The process of transforming ancient traditions about the gods and their activities into ostensibly historical narratives, such as the biblical writers' adaptations of Mesotamian myths of creation and the Flood to create the Genesis creation and deluge accounts. In the process of demythologization, beliefs about the gods' heavenly council were changed to conform to later Israelite monotheism, with the older deities reduced to subordinate members of YHWH's divine court (Job 1–2).

deuterocanon   The fourteen books or parts of books found in the Greek Septuagint and later editions of the Latin Vulgate—such as Tobit, 1 and 2 Maccabees, and the Wisdom of Solomon—but not included in the Hebrew Bible or most Protestant Old Testaments that Roman Catholics and some others regard as forming a second or later canon. After the Council of Trent, the books of 1 and 2 Esdras and the Prayer of Manasseh were deleted from the deuterocanonical list. When Protestant editions of the Bible include these works, they are typically classed as Apocrypha.

Deutero-Isaiah   *See* Second Isaiah.

Deuteronomic Reformation   The label that biblical scholars apply to King Josiah's reforms of Judah's central cult following 621 B.C.E. The name derives from the assumption that the law book found during Josiah's repairs of the Temple was a form of the Book of Deuteronomy (probably Deut. 12–26) and that the work's insistence on the centralization of Israel's cult at a single (undesignated) sanctuary inspired Josiah's sweeping destruction of all rival shrines (2 Kings 22–23).

Deuteronomist (D)   The unknown writer who compiled and edited the present form of the Book of Deuteronomy. Some scholars believe that he added the introductory material (Deut. 1–11) and appendixes (Deut. 27–34) to the older Deuteronomic code (Deut. 12–26).

Deuteronomistic History (DH)   The books of the Former Prophets (Joshua, Judges, Samuel, Kings) as compiled and revised from older sources by an anonymous author or editorial school deeply influenced by the historical philosophy of the Book of Deuteronomy. The first edition was produced late in Josiah's reign (c. 610 B.C.E.), and a second edition followed Jerusalem's destruction in 587 B.C.E. It was further edited after the Babylonian exile.

devil   The English word commonly used to translate two Greek words with different meanings: (1) *diabolos,* "the accuser" (John 8:44), and (2) *daimonion,* one of many evil spirits inhabiting the world, which were thought to cause disease, madness, and other afflictions (see Matt. 10:25; Mark 3:22; Luke 8; 11:14–16; etc.). In Revelation 12:9, the devil is identified with the Hebrew Satan and the serpent of Genesis.

DH   *See* Deuteronomistic History.

Diaspora   Literally, a "scattering," the term refers to the distribution of Jews outside their Palestinian homeland, such as the many Jewish communities established throughout the Greco-Roman world.

Diaspora novella   A short novel or mid-size narrative written sometime after the Babylonian exile of 587 B.C.E. and with the obvious intent of encouraging the exiled Jewish community to remain steadfast in its faith. A canonical example of this type of literature can be found in the Book of Esther, which is set sometime during the reign of Xerxes I (486–465 B.C.E.), but which may have been written during the late fourth or early third century B.C.E. A deuterocanonical example of this same genre can be found in the Book of Judith, which was probably written sometime during the Hasmonean period (165–37 B.C.E.), even though the story is set during the sixth-century-B.C.E. reign of the Babylonian king Nebuchadnezzar. Both of these narratives focus on the heroic activities of a single (in this case, female) protagonist who is successful in rescuing her community from seemingly certain destruction.

Dinah   The only daughter of the patriarch Jacob, by his wife, Leah, she is raped by Shechem, who wishes to marry her. Insulted by the Canaanite priest's method of courting their sister, Dinah's brothers first deceive Shechem into having himself and his male kin circumcised, and, then, while the Canaanites are in a vulnerable state, slaughter his entire family, an act of treachery that Jacob protests (Gen. 34).

divination   The practice of foretelling the future through supernatural means.

divine council   The heavenly assembly of gods, a concept common throughout the ancient Near East. In Israelite tradition, YHWH presides as king of the council, surrounded by lesser divine beings who serve as his emissaries (Pss. 82, 89; Job 1–2; Zech. 3).

documentary hypothesis   A scholarly theory associated with Julius Wellhausen that argues that the Pentateuch is not the work of one author, but the result of many generations of anonymous writers, revisers, and editors (redactors) who produced the four main literary strands or components found in these five books: J (the Yahwist, c. 950–850 B.C.E.); E (the Elohist, c. 850 B.C.E.); D (the Deuteronomist, c. 650–621 B.C.E.); and P (the priestly component, c. 550–450 B.C.E.).

doublet   A literary term denoting two or more versions, from different sources, of the same material (cf. Gen. 12:10–20; 20:1–18; 26:6–11; Exod. 3:1–20; 6:2–13; 20; Deut. 5; etc.).

doxology   In a religious writing or service, the formal concluding expression of praise or formula ritually ascribing glory to God.

dragon   A symbolic reptile derived from ancient Near Eastern mythology, related to the serpent in Eden (Gen. 3) and identified with the devil and Satan (Rev. 12). *See* Leviathan.

dualism   A philosophic or religious system that posits the existence of two parallel worlds, one of physical matter and the other of invisible spirit. Moral dualism views the universe as divided between powers of Good and Evil, Light and Dark, which contend for human allegiance.

E   *See* Elohist.

Ea   Babylonian god of wisdom, fresh water, and incantation (counterpart of the Sumarian Enki), he was a benefactor to humanity, warning Utnapishtim, ancestor of Gilgamesh, of Enlil's plan to drown the world in a flood and giving the man directions to build an ark and stock it with birds and animals. Ea is the father of Marduk, who later became king of the Babylonian gods.

Ebedmelech   The Ethiopian (Cushite) eunuch who rescued Jeremiah from the cistern where the prophet's enemies had left him to die (Jer. 38:1–13; 39:15–18).

Eber   The legendary ancestor of various Hebrew, Arab, and Aramean tribes (Gen. 10:24–30; 11:15; 1 Chron. 1:18); listed in the New Testament as an ancestor of Jesus (Luke 3:35).

Ebla   A large, ancient Canaanite city (located in modern Syria), Ebla contained an extensive library of clay tablets inscribed in Mesopotamian cuneiform. Compiled during the late third millennium B.C.E., Ebla's archives predate the oldest biblical documents by 1000 years.

ecstatic prophet   Any prophet who reports being "seized" by the spirit of God and who then falls into a state of rapture can be considered an "ecstatic" prophet. Even someone not normally associated with prophetic behavior can experience this type of religious frenzy, as when Saul is suddenly possessed by the spirit of God in the presence of a band of prophets from Gibeah (1 Sam. 10:10–13). Several prophets claim to have been moved by the divine spirit, particularly Ezekiel (3:12; 8:3; 11:1).

Eden   The gardenlike first home of humanity (Gen. 2:8); an earthly paradise from which the first couple was expelled (Gen. 3:24). See also Ezekiel 28:13, where the "king of Tyre" enjoyed an "Eden," possibly a lush forested region (Ezek. 31:18; 36:25; Isa. 51:3; Joel 2:3).

Edom   In Hebrew Bible times, a region or country extending southward from the Dead Sea to the Gulf of 'Aqaba, bordered on the north by Moab, on the northwest by Judah, and on the east and southeast by the Sinai Peninsula (Num. 20:14–21; 2 Kings 3:20; etc.). It was also called "Seir" (Gen. 32:3; Num. 24:18; Judg. 5:4), identified with Esau (Gen. 36:1), and thought to be YHWH's original homeland (Deut. 33:2; Judg. 5:4–5; Hab. 3:3). Famous for its wisdom tradition (Obad. 8; Jer. 49:7), Edom is the setting for the Job story and may have contributed the central ideas of that philosophical work.

Edomites   According to Genesis, descendants of Jacob's twin brother, Esau, "who is Edom" (Gen. 36:1); a Semitic people who occupied the territory southeast of Judah and were among Israel's bitterest enemies (Judg. 11; 2 Kings 8:20–22; Ps. 137:7; Amos 1–2, 9; Ezek. 25:12–14; 35:1–15). The Edomites later infiltrated southern Judea, which in Hellenistic times was called Idumea (Mark 3:8).

Egypt   An ancient nation centered along the Nile River southwest of Palestine, visited by Abraham (Gen. 12:10–20) and settled in by his Israelite descendants (Gen. 41–50) for a reputed 430 years (Exod. 12:40). Moses, raised at the Egyptian court, led the enslaved Israelites from Egypt circa 1280–1250 B.C.E. (Exod. 1–15). Many of Israel's classical prophets advised against turning to Egypt for political or military help (Isa. 30:1–7; 31:1; 36; Jer. 46; Hos. 7:11), although King Solomon had once made an alliance with the pharaohs (1 Kings 9:16–18, 24). Egyptian attempts to restore its hegemony in Palestine were finally ended at the Battle of Carchemish (605 B.C.E.), when Nebuchadnezzar of Babylon defeated Pharaoh Necho's troops.

Ehud   The left-handed judge (military leader) from the tribe of Benjamin who murdered the obese Moabite king, Eglon, at Jericho and then led an Israelite army to rout the Moabite invaders (Judg. 3).

El, Elohim (pl.)   A Semitic term for a divine being. In Canaanite religion, El was the high god, father of lesser deities. In the Hebrew Bible, El, when used as a name for the Israelite Deity, typically occurs as part of a phrase, such as El Shaddai (God of the Mountain), El Bethel (God of the House of God), or El Elyon (God Most High). In its plural form, the Hebrew generic term for deity applied to both the national God (Gen. 1:1; 2:5; etc.) and foreign deities (Exod. 15:2; 11).

Elam   An ancient civilized center across the Persian Gulf from Sumer (now in Iran), supposedly founded by Elam, son of Shem (Gen. 10:22). Chedorlaomer, king of Elam, headed several Babylonian states (Gen. 14:1–11). Elamites later helped Assyria invade Judah (Isa. 11:11; 22:6).

Eleazar   **(1)** The third son of Aaron, a chief of the Levites, who succeeded his father as High Priest (Exod. 6:23; Num. 3:2, 32, 20:25–29; Josh. 14:1). **(2)** In 2 Maccabees, the aged "teacher of the Law" who was bludgeoned to death for refusing to eat pig's flesh (2 Macc. 6:18–31).

Eli   In 1 Samuel 2:22–4:18, an ineffectual judge and priest at Shiloh under whose jurisdiction young Samuel served (1 Sam. 3:1).

Elihu   A young man who condemned Job's alleged self-righteousness (Job 32–37).

Elijah   Literally, "YHWH is my God"; a fiercely Yahwist prophet from the northern kingdom whose anti-Baalism and attacks on Ahab's dynasty had a tremendous impact on Israel's political course during the ninth century B.C.E. and who shaped his nation's prophetic traditions for centuries thereafter (1 Kings 17–19, 21; 2 Kings 1–2). Reportedly carried to heaven in a fiery chariot (2 Kings 2:1–13), he was expected to reappear shortly before the Day of YHWH arrived (Mal. 4:5–6).

Eliphaz   The most moderate and restrained of Job's critics (Job 4, 8, 15, 22–24, etc.).

Elisha   A ninth-century C.E. prophet in the northern kingdom, successor to Elijah (1 Kings 19:15–21; 2 Kings 2:1–15). Like his predecessor, Elisha was a clairvoyant who worked numerous miracles, including the resuscitation of a dead child (2 Kings 4:18–37; 6:32–7:2; 8:7–13; 13:14–19). So great was his prestige that he not only brought an end to the Omri-Ahab–Jezebel dynasty in Israel by having the upstart Jehu anointed king (2 Kings 9:1–13) but also made Hazael king of Syria (2 Kings 8:7–15).

Elohim   *See* El.

Elohist (E)   The scholarly term designating the anonymous author or compiler responsible for the E document, or tradition, in the Pentateuch. The name arose from his characteristic use of *Elohim* to denote the Hebrew Deity.

El Shaddai   Although commonly translated "God Almighty," this term probably means "God of the Mountain," referring to the Mesopotamian cosmic "mountain" inhabited by divine beings. One of the patriarchal names for the Mesopotamian tribal god, it is identified with YHWH in the Mosaic revelation (Exod. 6:3). Except for a few occurrences in Job (5:17; 8:5; etc.), Isaiah (13:6), and Ezekiel (10:5), it appears chiefly in the Pentateuch (Gen. 17:1; 28:3; 35:11, 43:14; 48:3; Exod. 6:3, etc.). *Shaddai* alone appears in Ruth (1:20–21) and Job (13:3; 20:15–20; 31:2; 40:2; etc.).

En-dor   Literally, "fountain of habitation"; a small town southeast of Nazareth, remembered for its medium whom King Saul solicited (1 Sam. 28:7–25).

Enoch   A son of Cain (Gen. 4:17, J's account) or of Jared (Gen. 5:18, P's version) and father of Methuselah (Gen. 5:21). P's statement that "God took him" (Gen. 5:24)—apparently to heaven and without death—strongly influenced later Hebrew notions of immortality and gave rise to a whole body of pseudepigraphal literature in which Enoch is a model of divine wisdom.

Enuma Elish   The Babylonian creation epic that takes its name from the opening phrase (in Akkadian) "when above."

ephod   An apronlike garment worn by the high priest Aaron and his successors (Exod. 28).

Ephraim   (1) The son of Joseph and Asenath (daughter of the priest Potipherah) and adopted by Jacob (Gen. 48:1–20). **(2)** The Israelite territory occupied by the tribe of Ephraim, bordered on the south by Dan and Benjamin, on the west by the Mediterranean, on the north by Manasseh, and on the east by the Jordan River Valley. Shechem (Josh. 21:20) was its most important city and served as an early capital of the northern kingdom (1 Kings 12:1). **(3)** The half-tribe of Ephraim, along with Manasseh, was one of the twelve tribes. After the ten northern tribes seceded (922 B.C.E.) from the Davidic union, Ephraim became dominant in Israel and was commonly used as a synonym for the whole ten-tribe nation.

Epicureanism   Greco-Roman philosophy founded by Epicurus that advocated avoiding pain and pursuing intellectual rather than sensual pleasure. Epicurus taught that the universe is entirely physical, including the human soul, which perishes at death.

epiphany   An appearance or manifestation, particularly of a divine being; typically sudden and accompanied by dramatic natural effects (Exod. 3, 6, 19, 24; Isa. 6; Job 38–42; etc.).

eponym   The person from whom a people or group is reputed to have taken its name (Gen. 36:1).

Erech (Uruk)   An ancient Sumerian city, home of the legendary King Gilgamesh.

Esarhaddon   The son of the Assyrian emperor Sennacherib, Esarhaddon ruled from about 680 to 669 B.C.E., despoiled Tyre and Sidon, colonized Samaria, and reputedly took Manasseh, king of Judah, captive to Babylon (2 Kings 19:37; Isa. 37:38; 2 Chron. 33:11; Ezra 4:2).

Esau   The firstborn son of Isaac and Rebekah, twin brother of Jacob (Gen. 25:25–34), Esau gave up his birthright to his cleverer sibling (Gen. 27–28), thus becoming the prototype of the person who is insensitive to his heritage (Heb. 12:16). He was thought of as the progenitor of the Edomites, traditional enemies of Jacob's descendants (Israel) (Gen. 36).

eschatology   From the Greek, meaning a "study of last things," eschatology is a doctrine or theological concept about the ultimate destiny of humanity and the universe. Having both a personal and a general application, it can refer to (1) beliefs about the individual soul following death, including divine judgment, heaven, hell, and resurrection; or (2) larger concerns about the fate of the cosmos, such as events leading to the Day of YHWH, the final battle between supernatural Good and Evil, judgment of the nations, and the establishment of the Deity's universal sovereignty. Apocalyptic works like Daniel, Revelation, 2 Esdras, and the books of Enoch typically stress eschatological matters.

Essenes   According to Josephus, one of the three major sects of first-century-C.E. Judaism. Semi-ascetic in nature, the Essenes were spiritual descendants of the hasidim (meaning "pious") who had resisted Antiochus IV's attempts to destroy the Jewish religion. Their apocalyptic convictions and certain of their rituals akin to baptism have suggested to some scholars that they were an influence on such representative pre-Christian figures as John the Baptist. They are commonly identified with the Qumran community, which produced the Dead Sea Scrolls.

Esther   The heroine of the canonical book bearing her name, cousin and adopted daughter of Mordecai (Esther 2:15), queen of Persia under Xerxes (Esther 1:1–2:18), Esther became a national heroine by delivering her people from a mass slaughter planned by Haman (Esther 2:19–4:17). The Book of Esther commemorates the Feast of Purim (Esther 9:17–10:3).

Ethiopia   An area of northeast Africa (Abyssinia), which the Hebrews called Cush or Kush, supposedly settled by a son of Ham (Gen. 10:6–8). Classical writers mention a line of Ethiopian queens named Candace, one of whom is cited in Acts 8:27.

etiology   Literally, a statement of causes or origins; in literary terms, a narrative created to explain the origin or meaning of a social practice, topographical feature, ritual, or other factor that arouses the storyteller's interest.

Euphrates River   The longest river of southwest Asia; one of the four streams of Eden (Gen. 2:14), the Euphrates was the extreme northeastern border of Israel's kingdom at its height (2 Sam. 8:3; 10:16; 1 Kings 4:24).

Eve   The first woman, wife of Adam, who derived her name from the Hebrew verb "to live" because she was the "mother of all those who live" (Gen. 3:30).

Evil-merodach   The son and successor to Nebuchadnezzar who reputedly treated well Judah's captive monarch Jehoiachin (2 Kings 25:27–30; Jer. 52:31–34). The name means "man of Marduk."

exegesis   A literary term denoting close analysis and interpretation of a text to discover the original author's exact intent and meaning. Once this has been established, later interpretations may also be considered.

exile   The period during which the Jews were captive in Babylon (587–538 B.C.E.).

Exodus, the   A Greek term meaning a "going out" or "departure." In the Hebrew Bible, it refers to the escape of Israelite slaves from Egypt under Moses' leadership (c. 1280–1250 B.C.E.), an event the Hebrews regarded as YHWH's crucial saving act in their history (Exod. 15; 20:1–2; Deut. 5:6; Josh. 24:1–13; Ps. 105:26–39; Amos 2:10; etc.).

exogamy   The practice of marrying outside of one's tribe or ethnic group; its opposite is endogamy.

exorcism   The act or practice of expelling a demon or evil spirit from a person or place (Tob. 8:1–3).

expiation   In religious terms, the act of making atonement for sin, usually by offering a sacrifice to appease divine wrath (Lev. 16).

Ezekiel   A major prophet of the sixth century B.C.E., exiled to Babylon, who was distinguished by his strange visions and priestly concerns. The name means "God strengthens."

Ezra (Esdras)   A postexilic Jewish priest who returned to Jerusalem from Babylon during the reign of the Persian emperor Artaxerxes (Ezra 7:1) to promulgate the Mosaic Torah and supervise a reformation of the Jewish religion (Neh. 8–10; Ezra 7–10). His influence on later Judaism was so great that he was conceived as the re-creator of the Hebrew Bible and author of several pseudohistorical and apocalyptic works (1 Esd. 8–9; 2 Esd. 14).

faith   In biblical terms, the quality of trust, reliance on, and fidelity to God. The Greek translation of the Hebrew Bible (the Septuagint) uses two terms (*pistis*, *pisteuein*) to express the concept, which the patriarch Abraham exemplified by his trust in YHWH's promises (Gen. 15: 5–6).

Fast of the Ninth of Av   A solemn observance mourning the two destructions of the Jerusalem Temple, the first by the Babylonians (587 B.C.E.) and the second by the Romans (70 C.E.), both in the month of Av (August). The dirges in the Book of Lamentations are read to commemorate the sanctuary's dual fall.

Feast of Dedication   An eight-day Jewish celebration (now known as Hanukkah) instituted in 165 B.C.E. by Judas Maccabeus and held annually on the twenty-fifth day of Kislev (November–December) to commemorate the cleansing and rededication of the Jerusalem Temple, which Antiochus IV had polluted.

Feast of Tabernacles   Also called the Feast of Booths, or Sukkoth, it was a joyous annual celebration of the autumn harvest (late September–early October). Commemorating the Mosaic period when Israel dwelt in tents or huts (booths) in the wilderness, it expressed the people's gratitude to YHWH for supplying them with grain and wine (Exod. 23:16; 34:22; Lev. 23:39–43; Deut. 16:13–15).

Fertile Crescent   The name by which James H. Breasted designated the arch or semicircle of fertile territory stretching from the Persian Gulf on the northeast to Egypt on the southwest and including Mesopotamia, Syria, and Palestine.

firmament   The Hebrew Bible term for the vault or arch of the sky that separated the earthly oceans from the heavenly ocean of rain-giving clouds and in which Elohim placed the sun, moon, and stars (Gen. 1:6–8, 16–20; 7:11; 2 Sam. 22:8; 2 Kings 7:2; Pss. 24:2; 78:23; 104:2, 5; Job 26:11; 27:18).

Flood, the   The global deluge of Noah's day (Gen. 6:5–8:22), based on ancient Mesopotamian flood stories akin to that found in the *Epic of Gilgamesh* and later used as a prototype of world judgment and destruction (Matt. 24:36–41; Luke 17:26–30; 2 Pet. 2:5; 3:5–7).

form criticism   An English rendition of the German *Formsgeschichte,* a method of biblical criticism that attempts to isolate, classify, and analyze individual units or characteristic forms contained in a literary text and to identify the probable preliterary form of these units before their incorporation into the written text. Form criticism also attempts to discover the setting in life (*Sitz-im-Leben*) of each unit—that is, the historical, social, religious, and cultural environment from which it developed—and to trace or reconstruct the process by which various traditions evolved from their original oral state to their final literary form.

fundamentalism   A largely North American Protestant movement, beginning about the turn of the twentieth century, that affirmed the literal factuality of all biblical statements and rejected post-Enlightenment questioning of biblical infallibility.

Gabriel   In the Hebrew angelic hierarchy, one of the seven archangels whose duty it was to convey the Deity's messages. Gabriel explained Daniel's visions to him (Dan. 8:15–26; 9:20–27). The name may mean "person of God" or "God has shown himself mighty."

Gad   **(1)** The firstborn son of Jacob and Zilpah (Gen. 30:1–11; 35:26), Gad was the eponymous ancestor of the Israelite tribe of Gad (Num. 2:14) whose territory was located northeast of the Dead Sea, east of the Jordan River (Num. 32; Deut. 3:16–20). Gad joined the revolt against Rehoboam and was part of the ten-tribe northern kingdom. **(2)** A prophet at David's court (1 Sam. 22:5; 2 Sam. 24; 1 Chron. 21; 2 Chron. 29:25, 29).

Galilee   From the Hebrew term *Galil ha-goyim,* meaning "circle of Gentiles," the name given northern Palestine lying west of the Jordan, an area originally assigned to the tribes of Ashur, Zebulun, and Naphtali, who failed to evict the Canaanites living there (Josh. 19; Judg. 1, 4, 5).

Galilee, Sea of   The major body of fresh water in northern Palestine and source of livelihood to many Galilean fishermen.

Gath   Of the Philistines' five major cities, the one nearest to Hebrew territory (Josh. 13:3; 1 Sam. 17, 27; etc.).

Gaza   The southernmost of the Philistines' five principal cities (Josh. 13:3) where Samson destroyed the temple of Dagon (Judg. 16). During the Israelite monarchy, Gaza marked the southernmost boundary of Judah (1 Kings 4:24).

Gemara   The second part of the Talmud; an extensive commentary, in Aramaic, on the Hebrew Mishnah.

genealogy   A mini-history of descent, either for an individual or a group, listing a succession of fathers and sons. Numerous such lists occur in the Hebrew bible, beginning with the genealogy in Genesis 5 (the generations of Adam) and concluding with the genealogies of Chronicles (e.g. 1 Chron. 8). Given the importance to ancient Israel both of the inheritance customs and of the royal and priestly succession, it is easy to see why these lists were preserved and often used as linking devices between chapters.

Gentile   Someone who is not a Jew, an uncircumcised person, one belonging to the "nations" (Ps. 9:17; Isa. 2:2; Zeph. 2:1; Hag. 2:7).

Gibeah   A small hill town in the territory of Benjamin, prominent in the eleventh century B.C.E. because it was the home of Saul (1 Sam. 10:26) and the first capital of the united monarchy (1 Sam. 13–14; 2 Sam. 21:6).

Gibeon   A city of the Hivites (Horites) (Josh. 9:17; 11:19), whose people deceived Joshua into making a treaty of protection with them (Josh. 9–10), Gibeon became an Israelite cult center (2 Sam. 21:1–9; 1 Kings 3:4–5; 1 Chron. 16:39–40; 2 Chron. 1:3, 13; etc.).

Gideon   Also called *Jerubbaal* (contender against Baal), a military judge who delivered Israel from the Midianites (Judg. 6–8). Although Gideon refused to accept a crown (Judg. 8:22–32), his son Abimelech reigned for three years at Shechem (Judg. 9).

Gilboa   A prominent hill on the west side of the Jordan Valley, site of the battle in which the Philistine armies defeated King Saul and killed three of his sons, including Jonathan, thus clearing the way for David to mount Israel's throne (1 Sam. 31; 2 Sam.1).

Gilead   A rugged highland in central Transjordan located between the Yarmuk and Arnon rivers (Josh. 13; Jer. 8:22; 46:11).

Gilgal   The name of several Israelite towns, including one located southeast of Jericho where Joshua erected twelve stones symbolic of Israel's twelve tribes (Josh. 4:1–9, 20); the site of the confirmation of Saul's kingship (1 Sam. 11:15; 13:4–15); and a cultic center in southwest Samaria associated with a school of prophets, particularly Elijah and Elisha (2 Kings 2:1–4; 4:38).

Gilgamesh   The legendary king of Uruk, hero of the Sumero-Babylonian *Epic of Gilgamesh,* fragments of which date from shortly after 3000 B.C.E., describing his adventures battling Evil and searching for immortality. The Babylonian version incorporates a story of the Flood narrated by Gilgamesh's ancestor Utnapishtim.

Gnosticism   A mystical philosophy that emphasizes secret knowledge (Greek, *gnosis*), cosmic dualism, and God's alienation from the material world.

Gog   The term Ezekiel uses to depict a future leader of Israel's enemies (Ezek. 38) whose attack on the Jerusalem sanctuary will precipitate YHWH's intervention and the ultimate destruction of the wicked (Rev. 20:8).

golden calf   **(1)** An image that the apostate Israelites fashioned out of gold jewelry and other treasures taken from Egypt and that, under Aaron's direction, they worshiped as their deliverer from slavery (Exod. 32:1–6; Deut. 9:16). **(2)** Two calf images that Jeroboam I set up at Bethel and Dan as rivals to the Jerusalem sanctuary were probably not revered as idols in themselves but as visible pedestals of the invisibly enthroned YHWH (1 Kings 12:29).

Goliath   The Philistine giant from Gath whom the young David defeated with a slingshot (1 Sam. 17; 2 Sam. 21:19).

Gomer   The adulterous wife of the prophet Hosea. Gomer serves as a symbolic representation of Israel's apostasy, and Hosea's ambivalence toward his faithless wife perfectly captures YHWH's ambivalence toward sinful Israel.

Goshen   An area in northeastern Egypt where Jacob and his clan settled to escape a Near Eastern famine (Gen. 46:28–34; 47:5–12).

Habakkuk   A prophet of the late seventh or early sixth century B.C.E., perhaps a Levitical temple musician (Hab. 1:1; 3:1, 19), and presumed author of the book bearing his name.

Habiru   An ancient Near Eastern term designating people or clans who were outside the urban social and legal structure. The Habiru appear to have been nomads who raided the settled populations during the Amarna period (fourteenth century B.C.E.) in Palestine. The biblical Hebrews may have been related to this group.

Hades   The Greek term for the Underworld, abode of the dead, named for Zeus's brother Hades, god of the nether regions. In the Septuagint Bible, it is used to translate *Sheol*, the Hebrew word for the gloomy subterranean place where all the dead, good and evil alike, were eternally housed (Gen. 42:38; 1 Sam. 2:6; Job 7:9; Ps. 6:5; Prov. 27:20; Eccles. 9:10; Isa. 38:18; etc.).

Hagar   In Genesis 16, Sarah's Egyptian handmaiden, who bears Abraham's first son, Ishmael. In Genesis 21, the jealous Sarah persuades Abraham to drive Hagar and Ishmael into the wilderness, whence an angel rescues them.

haggadah   Jewish narrative writings dating from the early centuries C.E. that illustrate and interpret the nonlegal portions of the Torah (law).

Haggai   A postexilic prophet who, with his contemporary Zechariah, urged the restored community of Jerusalem to rebuild the Temple (520 B.C.E.).

Hagiographa   A Greek term, meaning "sacred writings," that applies to the third major division of the Hebrew Bible (the Kethuvim), encompassing books of poetry, wisdom, late historical texts (Chronicles-Ezra), and the apocalypse of Daniel.

halakah   A collection of Jewish interpretations and applications of the Mosaic Law dating from the early centuries C.E.; the core of the legal sections of the Talmud.

Ham   According to Genesis, a son of Noah (Gen. 5:32; 6:10; 7:13; 9:18, 22) and the father of Canaan (Gen. 9:22), Ham was considered the progenitor of various nations in Phoenicia, Africa, and west Arabia (1 Chron. 8). The "land of Ham" is usually taken to be Egypt (Pss. 78:51; 105:23; etc.).

Haman   An official at Ahasuerus's (Xerxes') court who attempted to engineer the mass extermination of the Jews (Esther 3, 7).

Hammurabi   The sixth king of Babylon's First Dynasty (1728–1686 B.C.E.) and founder of the first Amorite Empire in Mesopotamia. Hammurabi is best remembered for his law code, inscribed on an eight-foot stone monument in Akkadian cuneiform, whose legal forms resemble those of Hebraic covenant law. *See* Code of Hammurabi.

Hannah   The wife of Elkanah and mother of Samuel (1 Sam. 1). Hannah's lyric prayer (1 Sam. 2:1–10) anticipates the Magnificat of Mary (Luke 1:42–45).

Hanukkah   *See* Feast of Dedication.

Haran   An ancient trade center in northwestern Mesopotamia, about sixty miles above the confluence of the Belikh and Euphrates rivers, Haran was the site of an important moon cult and of Abraham's call to follow YHWH (Gen. 11:28–12:5, 24). The last refuge of the Assyrians, it was destroyed by the Medes about 606 B.C.E. (Zeph. 2:13–15; Nah. 3:1–3).

hasidim   Devout Jews who refused to forsake their religion during the persecutions of the Seleucid monarch Antiochus IV (Epiphanes) (second century B.C.E.).

Hasmoneans   The Jewish royal dynasty founded by the Maccabees and named for Hasmon, an ancestor of Mattathias. The Roman conquest of Palestine in 63 B.C.E. brought Hasmonean rulership and Jewish independence to an end.

Hazel   An Aramean official of Damascus who murdered his king, Ben-hadad II, at the prophet Elisha's instigation (2 Kings 8:7–15; see also 1 Kings 19:15–18), usurped the Syrian kingship, and despoiled parts of Israel and Judah (Amos 1:3; 2 Kings 12; 2 Chron. 22). The name means "God sees."

Hebrew **(1)** A member or descendant of one of a group of northwestern Semitic peoples, including the Israelites, Edomites, Moabites, and Ammonites. According to Genesis 10:21–31 and 11:15, the Hebrews were descended from Eber, great-grandson of Shem (1 Chron. 1:18) and apparently belonged to an Aramean (ancient Syrian) branch of Semites who had originally migrated from Arabia. The Israelites' Aramean ancestry is referred to in the famous creed of Deuteronomy 26:5 (see also Gen. 25:20; 28:5). **(2)** The Semitic language spoken by the Israelites.

Hebrew Bible Also known as the Tanak for its three-fold division into Torah (Divine Instruction), Nevi'im (Prophets), and Kethuvim (Writings), this collection of documents in Hebrew and/or Aramaic is known to Christians as the Old Testament. Catholic and Greek Orthodox editions of the Old Testament include the Apocrypha, books excluded from the Hebrew Bible canon.

Hebron An ancient city nineteen miles southwest of Jerusalem (Num. 13:22), located near the sacred oaks of Mamre associated with Abraham (Gen. 13:18; 18; 35:27), and one of the oldest continuously inhabited sites in Palestine.

Heilsgeschichte A term from German biblical scholarship, usually translated as "sacred history" or "salvation history," which refers to the fact that Hebrew Bible writers told Israel's story not as an objective series of events, but as a confession of faith that their God was operating through the history of his chosen people, directing events in order to save them, or at least those faithful to their covenant relationship.

Hellenism The influence and adoption of Greek thought, language, values, and culture that began with Alexander the Great's conquest of the eastern Mediterranean world and intensified under his Hellenistic successors and various Roman emperors.

Hellenistic Pertaining to Greek (Hellenic) culture disseminated throughout the Near East by the conquests of Alexander the Great (ruled 336–323 B.C.E.) and the administrations of his successors, such as the Ptolemaic dynasty of Egypt and the Seleucid kingdom of Syria.

henotheism The worship of a single god with a belief that other gods exist. Psalm 82 appears to represent a henotheistic stage of Israelite religion, as do such passages as the victory song in Exodus 15.

herem A sentence of total destruction executed against any people whom God has designated as deserving total annihilation. This sentence of death extends to all of their possessions, and even their livestock, and it represents the most extreme form of divine punishment directed against Israel's enemies (see Deut. 13:12–17; Josh. 6:15–21; 1 Sam. 15:1–22).

hermeneutics The study of the methodology of applying the principles and rules of interpreting a biblical text; especially, applying the results of such analysis to a contemporary situation, as one might apply the message of Hosea to modern problems of monogamy and religious faith.

Herod I Herod the Great, the Idumean Roman-appointed king of Judea (40–4 B.C.E.) who completely reconstructed the Jerusalem Temple; he was notorious for reputed cruelty and was almost universally hated by his Jewish subjects.

Hexateuch A term meaning "six scrolls" that scholars use to denote the first six books of the Hebrew Bible—the Torah plus the conquest narrative in Joshua—which some experts believe once formed a continuous account (J).

Hezekiah The son of Ahaz and fourteenth king of Judah (c. 715–686 B.C.E.), Hezekiah ruled during the Assyrian crisis when Sargon II and then Sennacherib overran Palestine. His reign was notable for the prophetic careers of Isaiah and Micah and for sweeping religious reforms, which included purging the Jerusalem Temple of non-Yahwistic elements (2 Kings 18–20; Isa. 22:15–25, 36–39; 2 Chron. 29–32).

hierocracy A form of government controlled and administered by religious authorities; the term characterizes Jerusalem and Judah following the return from exile and the rebuilding of the Temple in the late sixth century B.C.E. and after.

hieroglyphics The ancient Egyptian system of writing in pictorial script.

higher criticism The branch of biblical scholarship that attempts to analyze biblical writings for the purpose of determining their origins, their literary history, and their author's purpose and meaning. Unlike lower criticism, which confines itself to studying the written texts to discover (if possible) the authentic words of the original writers or their redactors, higher criticism endeavors to isolate and interpret the religious, political, and historical forces that produced a given book and caused it in many cases to be revised and reedited by later hands. *See* textual criticism.

Hinnom, Valley of A topographical depression lying south and west of Jerusalem; also called the "Valley of the [Children] of Hinnom" (Jer. 7:32; 2 Chron. 28:3; 2 Kings 23:10; etc.).

Hiram **(1)** The name of a series of rulers of Tyre, an ancient Phoenician seaport, with whom David and Solomon engaged in trade and commerce (2 Sam. 5:11; 1 Kings 5:1; 9:11; 1 Chron. 14:1; 2 Chron. 3; Ezek. 26–28), **(2)** A half-Tyrian, half-Israelite architect and craftsman whom King Hiram sent from Tyre to cast the bronze or copper fixtures and decorations of Solomon's Temple (1 Kings 7:13–51; 2 Chron. 2:13–14; 4:16).

historical criticism Analyzing a written work by taking into consideration its time and place of composition in order to comprehend the events, dates, personages, and other factual elements mentioned in or influencing the text.

Hittites Mentioned forty-seven times in the Hebrew Bible either by this name or as descendants of Heth (a grandson of Ham, son of Noah), the Hittites were among the most powerful people in the ancient Near East. A non-Semitic Indo-European group, they formed an older kingdom (c. 1700–1400 B.C.E.) contemporaneous with the Hebrew patriarchal period (Gen. 23), as well as a later "new kingdom" (c. 1400–1200 B.C.E.). Archaeologists have found remains of their cities in Asia Minor (central Anatolia), northern Mesopotamia, Syria, and Palestine, where the Pentateuch and Joshua list them among the nations occupying Canaan (Gen. 15:20; Exod. 3:8; Deut. 7:1; 20:17; Josh. 3:10; 11:3; 24:11).

The Hebrews from Abraham to Solomon had various commercial and political relations with the Hittites (Gen. 23:1–18; 26:34; Josh. 1:4; Judg. 3:5–6; 2 Sam. 11:2–27; 1 Kings 9:20–22; 11:1; 2 Kings 7:6; 2 Chron. 1:17; 8:7–9; Ezek. 16:3, 45). About 1200 B.C.E., however, the Hittite kingdom in Asia Minor fell to an invading Aegean people, probably Thracians and Phrygians. The Hittites centered near Carchemish in northern Syria were defeated by Sargon II in 717 B.C.E. and absorbed into the Assyrian Empire.

Holiness Code The name given to the body of laws and regulations set forth in Leviticus 17–26 derives from the code's emphasis on holiness (separateness, religious purity) of behavior, which was to distinguish Israel and set its people apart from the rest of the world.

Holy of Holies In Hebrew, a superlative referring to the Most Holy Place, the innermost room of the Tabernacle and Temple, where YHWH was believed to be invisibly present.

Horeb The name that the E and D traditions use for the mountain in the Sinai desert at which Moses received Yahweh's law (Exod. 17:6; 33:6; Deut. 1:2, 6, 19; 4:10, 15; also Ps. 106:19). Called Sinai in the J and P sources, its exact location is unknown. According to 1 Kings 19:1–21, Elijah fled there to renew his prophetic inspiration.

Hosea An eighth-century prophet active in the northern kingdom from before the death of Jeroboam II (c. 746 B.C.E.) until shortly before its fall to Assyria in 721 B.C.E.; the source of the Book of Hosea, first in the printed list of Minor Prophets.

Hoshea (Hosea) The last king of Israel (732–724 B.C.E.).

Huldah A female prophet associated with King Josiah's royal court in Jerusalem who pronounced on the authenticity of a "book of law" thought to be an early form of Deuteronomy. In the biblical record, she is the first person to decide on the authority of a scriptural document and thus stands at the head of the canonizing process (2 Kings 22; 2 Chron. 34).

Hyksos The Egyptian name (perhaps meaning "rulers of foreign lands") for a racially mixed but largely Semitic group that infiltrated and overran Egypt circa 1720–1570 B.C.E., establishing the Fifteenth and Sixteenth dynasties; themselves expelled by the Theban kings Kamose and Ahmose I, who founded the native Egyptian Eighteenth Dynasty. Some scholars believe that the Hebrews entered Egypt during the friendly rule of the Semitic Hyksos and were enslaved when the native Egyptians returned to power.

Hyrcanus The name of John I, son of Simon Maccabeus, Hasmonean king and High Priest of Judah (134–104 B.C.E.). John II (63–40 B.C.E.), a High Priest and puppet ruler installed by Rome, was succeeded by Herod the Great.

Idumea The name, meaning "pertaining to Edom," that the Greeks and Romans applied to the country of Edom, Judah's southern neighbor; the home of Herod the Great.

immanence The divine quality denoting God's presence in the material world, including human society and history.

Immanuel The name (meaning "God is with us") that Isaiah gave to a child whose birth he predicted as a sign to King Ahaz during the Syro-Ephraimite War (late eighth century B.C.E.). Although not presented as a messianic prophecy, it was nevertheless interpreted as such (Mic. 5:3; Matt. 1:22–23).

incubation ritual Any ritual act designed to facilitate communication with the Underworld, often accomplished by lying on the ground or in contact with an animal skin. The closest any biblical text comes to describing such a ritual is found in 1 Samuel 28:8–20 where the woman of En-dor summons up the spirit of Samuel from Sheol.

Isaac The son of Abraham and Sarah (Gen. 21:1–7), child of the covenant promise by which Abraham's descendants would bring a blessing to all the earth's families (Gen. 17:15–22; 18:1–15) but whom YHWH commanded to be sacrificed to him (Gen. 18:1–18). Reprieved by an angel, Isaac marries Rebekah (Gen. 24:1–67), who bears him twin sons, Esau and Jacob (Gen. 27:19–26), the latter of whom tricks his dying father into bestowing the firstborn's birthright on him (Gen. 27:1–45).

Isaiah An eighth-century B.C.E. prophet and counselor of Judean kings, Isaiah of Jerusalem was active during the reigns of Uzziah, Jothan, Ahaz, and Hezekiah (collectively, 783–687 B.C.E.) (Isa. 1:1; 6:1; 7:1–12; 38:1–6). Oracles attributed to this historical figure are found in Isaiah 1–39, particularly in Chapters 1–11, 20, 22, and 28–31. (Ch. 24–27, 33–35, and 36–39 are thought to be by other hands.) Second Isaiah, who lived during the Babylonian exile (587–538 B.C.E.), contributed Chapters 40–55. Third Isaiah, whose work is found in Chapters 56–66, lived during the postexilic period. A complete text of Isaiah, possibly dating from the second century B.C.E., was found among the Dead Sea Scrolls.

Ishbosheth One of Saul's sons who becomes king shortly after his father's death in battle. He is recognized as king by every tribe except Judah, and his two-year reign is brought to an abrupt end when he is assassinated by Rechab and Baanah, who hope for a reward when they present David with Ishbosheth's head — and, by implication, his crown. David is appalled by this crime, and orders the immediate execution of Ishbosheth's murderers (2 Sam. 4:5–12); It

would appear that Ishbosheth's name (meaning "man of shame") was changed by the author-editor of 2 Samuel; the original form of his name apparently was Ishbaal (meaning "man of Baal"), and he is so identified in 1 Chronicles 8:33.

Ishmael The son of Abraham and Sarah's Egyptian handmaiden, Hagar (Gen. 16), Ishmael and his mother were exiled to the desert, where an angel rescued them (Gen. 21). Cited as the eponymous ancestor of twelve princes (Gen. 25:12–16), he is also regarded as the progenitor of the Arabs and a forefather of Mohammed, founder of Islam.

Ishmaelites The name the J document applies to caravan merchants trading with Egypt (Gen. 37:25–28; 39:1) but whom the E document calls Midianites (Gen. 37:28, 36). Although the twelve tribes of Ishmael were a populous nation (Gen. 17:20), the biblical record seldom refers to them.

Ishtar The goddess of love and war in the Assyrian and Babylonian pantheons; the prototype of later fertility and erotic deities such as Ashtoreth, Aphrodite, and Venus (Jer. 44).

Isis An ancient Egyptian goddess, wife of Osiris and mother of Horus, who was worshiped from prehistoric to Roman times. As a beneficent mother who protected her devotees, Isis was pictured in Egyptian art as a madonna with child.

Israel **(1)** The name given Jacob by an unnamed being in Transjordan (Gen. 32:28, J source) and by YHWH at Bethel (Gen. 35:10, P source). Although interpreted as "he has been strong against God" (Gen. 32:28), it probably means "may God show his strength" or "may God rule." **(2)** The Israelite nation descended from the twelve sons of Jacob (Israel); the covenant people chosen at Sinai/Horeb. **(3)** The northern kingdom as opposed to the southern kingdom of Judah during the period of the divided monarchies (922–721 B.C.E.).

Issachar The son of Jacob and Leah (Gen. 30:14–18), the eponymous progenitor of the inland tribe bearing his name (Gen. 49:14–15; Josh. 19:17–23; Deut. 33:18–19; Num. 1:29; 26:25; 1 Chron. 7:2).

itinerary An ancient literary genre dealing with geographical locations and features that mark the stages of a journey narrative. Accounts of the patriarchs' wanderings in Genesis and the Israelites' prolonged trek through the Sinai wilderness in Exodus-Numbers include itineraries.

J   *See* Yahwist.

Jabal   According to Genesis 4:20, a son of Lamech and Adah whom the J source regards as the progenitor of itinerant tent dwellers and keepers of livestock.

Jabesh-gilead   A city built in the rugged country east of the Jordan River, destroyed by Israelites who resented the town's failure to send representatives to a tribal assembly at Mizpah (Judg. 21:8–14). Men from this city rescued the decapitated body of Saul from the Philistines (1 Sam. 11; 31:12; 1 Chron. 10:11–12), for which courageous feat David rewarded them (2 Sam. 2:5–7).

Jachin and Boaz   The names that Hiram, a half-Phoenician craftsman, gave to the twin pillars of copper decorating the entrance to Solomon's Temple (1 Kings 7:13–22; 2 Chron. 3:17). Their exact appearance, religious function and significance, and the meaning of their names are conjectural.

Jacob   The younger of twin sons born to Isaac and Rebekah (Gen. 25:21–26), Jacob is famous for his shrewdness, opportunism, and craftiness. He stole his brother Esau's birthright and Isaac's blessing (Gen. 25:29–34; 27:1–29), acquired great wealth in stock breeding (Gen. 29–30), and absconded with his father-in-law's household gods (Gen. 31:1–21) but later concluded a covenant with him (Gen. 31:22–25). Jacob was also the recipient of several divine visitations: the dream vision of a ladder to heaven at Bethel (Gen. 28) and wrestling with a divine being at Jabbok, Transjordan, after which his name was changed to Israel (Gen. 32:24–32; 33:4), a revelation renewed at Bethel (Gen. 35:1–15).

Father of twelve sons, eponymous ancestors of Israel's twelve tribes (Gen. 46:1–27), Jacob suffered in old age largely because of the temporary loss of his favorite children, Joseph (Gen. 37:2–36) and Benjamin (Gen. 43:1–14), and other filial problems reflected in his deathbed blessings (Gen. 49:1–28). In accordance with his wishes, he was buried in a cave near Mamre, which his grandfather Abraham had purchased from a Hittite (Gen. 49:29–33; 50:7–13).

Jael   The wife of Heber the Kenite (a member of a nomadic tribe of metalworkers), who offered hospitality to Sisera, the Canaanite general, and then murdered him, thus becoming a national heroine in Israel (Judg. 4:11–22; 5:24–31).

Jamnia (Yavneh)   A coastal village in Palestine. *See* Jamnia, Academy of.

Jamnia, Academy of   An assembly of eminent Palestinian rabbis and Pharisees held about 90 c.e. in the coastal village of Jamnia (Yavneh) to define and guide Judaism following the Roman destruction of Jerusalem and its Temple. According to tradition, a leading Pharisee named Yohanan ben Zakkai had escaped from the besieged city by simulating death and being carried out in a coffin by his disciples. Yohanan, who had argued that saving human lives was more important than success in the national rebellion against Rome, was given Roman support to set up an academy to study Jewish law.

Japheth   According to Genesis 5:32, 6:10, 9:18, and 10:1, one of Noah's three sons, the eponymous ancestor of various Indo-European nations, especially Aegean Sea peoples, including the Greeks (Ionians) and Philistines (Gen. 10:1–5).

Jashar, Book of   Apparently a collection of Hebrew poetry (since lost), quoted in Joshua 10:12–13, 2 Samuel 1:18, and 1 Kings 8:53 (Septuagint version only).

Javan   According to Genesis 10:4–5, the fourth son of Japheth and progenitor of the Ionian Greeks and other coastal and island peoples of the northeastern Mediterranean (1 Chron. 1:5, 7).

JE   The designation scholars give the hypothetical document uniting J's (the Yahwist's) account of Israel's beginnings with E's (the Elohist's) parallel narrative. After the northern kingdom of Israel fell to Assyria in 721 b.c.e., refugees may have brought the E document south to Jerusalem, where it was combined with the older J to produce JE, thus preserving E's northern tribal stories about the national ancestors and Exodus.

Jebus   The city held by the Jebusites, an ancient Canaanite tribe (Gen. 10:16; Josh. 11:3; 1 Chron. 1:14; Ezek. 16:3), which later became Jerusalem, it may have been the same town called Urusalim (city of peace) in the Amarna letters and called Salem (city of Melchizedek) in Genesis 14:18–20 (see also Josh. 18:16, 28; Judg. 19:10; 1 Chron. 11:14). David captured the city and made it his capital (2 Sam. 5:7–9; 6–10; 1 Chron. 11:4–9), placed the Ark of the Covenant there (2 Sam. 6:4–5), and purchased from a Jebusite an ancient stone threshing floor (2 Sam. 24:16–24; 1 Chron. 21:15–28) that became the site of Solomon's Temple (1 Kings 6:1–8:66).

Jeduthun   The representative leader or eponymous founder of a guild of Temple singers and musicians (1 Chron. 25:1, 3, 6; 16:40–42) that provided music for services at the Jerusalem sanctuary. This group officiated during the reigns of Solomon (1 Chron. 5:12–13), Hezekiah (2 Chron. 29:14), and Josiah, whose magnificent revival of the Passover liturgies they helped celebrate (2 Chron. 35:15–16). Jeduthun's name appears in the superscriptions of Psalms 39, 62, and 77 and among the list of exiles returned to Jerusalem from Babylon (Neh. 11:17).

Jehoash (Joash)   The name of several Hebrew Bible figures. **(1)** Judge Gideon's father (Judg. 6:11, 31–32). **(2)** A son of King Ahab (1 Kings 22:26–27; 2 Chron. 18:25–26). **(3)** The eighth king of Judah (c. 837–800 B.C.E.), a son of Ahaziah, who reduced Baal worship and repaired the Temple but later had to forfeit some of its treasures to pay Hazael, king of Aram, who besieged Jerusalem. Joash's reign, including the machinations of his grandmother, the queen-regent Athaliah, is recorded in 2 Kings 11–12, 13:10–13 and 2 Chronicles 22:11–24:27. **(4)** The twelfth king of Israel, third of the Jehu dynasty, who recovered some of the Israelite territory that his predecessors had lost to Syria, defeated king Amaziah of Judah, and transported some of the Temple's treasures from Jerusalem to Samaria (2 Kings 13:1–25; 14:8–16; 2 Chron. 25:18–19).

Jehoiachin   The king of Judah (598–597 B.C.E.), son and successor of Jehoiakim. After inheriting the throne at age eight and reigning for only three months and ten days, he was taken captive to Babylon (2 Kings 24:10–12; 2 Chron. 36:9–10), where he remained for the rest of his life. Babylonian records indicate that he was at first accorded favored status but later imprisoned until Nebuchadnezzar's successor, Evil-merodach (Amel-Marduk), released him (562 B.C.E.) and honored him above other captive kings (2 Kings 25:27–30; Jer. 52:31–34).

Jehoiakim   The second son of Josiah, Jehoiakim was made king of Judah about 609 B.C.E., when Pharaoh Necho of Egypt placed him on the throne, deposing his brother Jehoahaz, who had reigned for only three months (2 Kings 23:34; 2 Chron. 36:4). Another brother, Zedekiah, replaced Jehoiakim's heir, Jehoiachin, to become Judah's last Davidic monarch. The Deuteronomistic historians, the Chronicler, and the prophet Jeremiah all denounced his religious policies and misguided attempts to combat Babylonian domination with Egyptian alliances (2 Kings 23:36–24:6; 2 Chron. 36:5–8; Jer. 25–26, 36). Ignoring Jeremiah's advice (Jer. 36:1–26), Jehoiakim died or was assassinated before paying the consequences of his re-

bellion against Babylon (2 Kings 24:6). The Chronicler states that he was chained and carried off to Babylon (2 Chron. 36:6–7), but this was the fate of his son and heir, Jehoiachin (2 Kings 24:12–16; 2 Chron. 36:10).

Jehonadab   The son of Rechab the Kenite (1 Chron. 2:55), he assisted Jehu in massacring King Ahab's family and slaughtering Baal worshipers in Israel (2 Kings 10:14–27). According to Jeremiah 35:1–19, he was a nomadic ascetic who condemned drinking wine, planting vineyards, cultivating fields, and building cities. His support of Jehu's fanatical Yahwism may have been in part a revolt against Ahab's urban culture.

Jehoram   **(1)** A son of Ahab and king of Israel (849–842 B.C.E.) who enlisted King Jehoshaphat's help in quelling Moab's rebellion against paying Israel tribute (2 Kings 3:1–27). Jehu later murdered him (2 Kings 8:25–29; 9:22–26). **(2)** The son of Jehoshaphat and king of Judah (839–842 B.C.E.), he married Ahab's daughter Athaliah and fostered the religion of Baal in Judah (2 Kings 8:16–24; 2 Chron. 21:1–20). His reign was marked by wars with the Arabs and Philistines and by the loss of Judah's control of Edom. The name means "YHWH is exalted."

Jehoshaphat   The son of Asa and king of Judah (873–849 B.C.E.), his name means "YHWH judges." Although the Deuteronomistic historians give him short shrift (1 Kings 15:24; 22:41–51), the Chronicler emphasizes the general success of his twenty-four-year reign (2 Chron. 17:1–21:1), which was marked by important religious reforms; effective wars against Edom, Moab, and Ammon (2 Chron. 20:1–30); and the achievement of relative political security and prosperity for his people.

Jehovah   An English rendering of the divine name created by adding the vowels of *Elohim* and *Adonai* to the four consonants (YHWH) of the Tetragrammaton, the term entered the language via a Roman Catholic Latin translation about 1518 C.E., though the name *Yahweh* is considered a more accurate rendition of the Hebrew original.

Jehu   A son of Jehoshaphat (not the king of Judah) whom the prophet Elisha had anointed king of Israel in 842 B.C.E. (2 Kings 9:1–3), fulfilling an earlier command of Elijah (1 Kings 19:16–17). Thus commissioned by Israel's prophetic guild, Jehu proceeded to slaughter Ahab's family and all connected with it (2 Kings 9:14–10:27), including King Jehoram, King Ahaziah of Judah and his forty-two sons, Queen

Jezebel, Ahab's seventy sons, and numerous other Israelites who worshiped Baal. Jehu's long reign (842–815 B.C.E.) saw Israel's territory shrink to a fraction of what it had been under Omri and Ahab (2 Kings 10:32–33). Although he murdered in YHWH's name, his actions were condemned by the prophet Hosea (Hos. 1:3–5). Nor was he a wholehearted Yahwist (2 Kings 10:31), though his name means "YHWH is He."

Jephthah   The son of Gilead and a harlot, Jephthah was driven as a youth from the area of Gilead by his legitimate brothers (Judg. 11:1–3) but was recalled by Gilead's elders when the Ammonites attacked Israel. An effective military leader, he defeated the Ammonites and was judge (general) in Israel for six years (Judg. 12:7). Best known for vowing to make a burnt offering of the first person he met after the battle if YHWH would grant him victory, he presumably immolated his own daughter, who had come to congratulate him on his success (Judg. 11:29–40; see 2 Kings 3:27).

Jeremiah   One of Israel's greatest prophets, Jeremiah warned Jerusalem and its kings of their misdeeds and of impending doom from the Babylonians for approximately forty years (c. 627–587 B.C.E.) (Jer. 1:1–3). Beginning in the thirteenth year of Josiah's reign (640–609 B.C.E.), he also prophesied during the reigns of Jehoiakim (609–598 B.C.E.), Jehoiachin (598–597 B.C.E.), and Zedekiah (597–587 B.C.E.), continuing after Jerusalem's fall (587 B.C.E.) and during a forced exile in Egypt (Jer. 40–44).

Although persecuted by both government officials and his compatriots for his unpopular (and seemingly treasonous) message that YHWH had forsaken Judah and determined its annihilation, Jeremiah persisted in attacking official policy and denouncing those who trusted in the Temple (Jer. 1:11; 15; 21–22; 25–28; 36–38). After Jerusalem's fall, he was treated well by the Babylonians (Jer. 39–40), but his fellow survivors forcibly transported him to Egypt (Jer. 42–44). His message is known for its promise of a new covenant and a restoration of Judah (Jer. 30–33).

Jericho   One of the world's oldest cities, Jericho's ruins lie near an oasis on the west side of the south Jordan River Valley. Partly excavated by archaeologists, its earliest occupation dates to about 7800 B.C.E. Although according to Joshua 2 and 5:13–6:26 its fortified walls crumbled when the Israelites marched around the city, radiocarbon dating indicates that the site was already abandoned at the time of the conquest (thirteenth century B.C.E.). Jericho was partly rebuilt by Hiel of Bethel during Ahab's reign (869–850 B.C.E.) (1 Kings 16:34), but no evidence of this occupation remains. It was extensively rebuilt during Herod's day (40–4 B.C.E.)

Jeroboam I   An Ephraimite who led the ten northern tribes' secession from the Davidic monarchy and became the first ruler of the northern kingdom (1 Kings 11:26–12:33). Jeroboam I reigned from approximately 922–901 B.C.E. His first capital was Shechem, site of the old tribal confederacy (Josh. 24), but he later moved his administration to Tirzah, his former home and an ancient Canaanite royal sanctuary (1 Kings 12:24–25). The Deuteronomistic historians condemned Jereboam I for establishing rival Yahwist shrines at Bethel and Dan to compete with the Yahwist Temple at Jerusalem, and they condemned him for tolerating the worship of such foreign deities as Chemosh, Ashtoreth, and the Ammonite Milcom (1 Kings 11:33; 12:26–13:34).

Jeroboam II   A descendant of Jehu, son of King Jehonash, and ruler of Israel (786–746 B.C.E.) whose long reign brought relative peace and material prosperity to the northern kingdom, Jeroboam II won major victories over Ben-hadad, king of Syria, and extended Israel's territory so that it included almost all the territory over which David and Solomon had ruled except Judah. The Deuteronomistic account of his reign (2 Kings 14:23–29) gives no indication of its importance. The prophets Amos and Hosea, who were active during the time of Jeroboam II, denounced the country's economic oppression of the poor as well as its widespread materialism.

Jerome   An eminent Christian scholar and teacher (347–419/420 C.E.) known for his translation of the Bible into Latin. *See* Vulgate.

Jerusalem   An ancient Palestinian holy city, sometimes identified with the Salem of Genesis 14:17–20 but more often with Jebus, a city of the Jebusite tribe (Josh. 18:28; Judg. 19:10), Jerusalem became King David's capital after he captured it from the Jebusites (2 Sam. 5:6–10; 2 Chron. 4:5). Solomon centralized the worship of YHWH on a hill called Zion there (1 Kings 5–7; 2 Chron. 2–4), and Jerusalem remained the capital of Judah after the secession of the northern tribes (922 B.C.E.). The city suffered three major destructions: in 587 B.C.E. when the Babylonians razed Solomon's Temple; in 70 C.E. when the Romans destroyed the city and its Herodian Temple; and in 135 C.E. when the Romans decimated the city for the last time.

Jesse The son of Obed and grandson of Ruth and Boaz (Ruth 4:17, 22), Jesse was a Judean shepherd and father of seven or eight sons; including David (1 Sam 16:10–11; 17:12; 1 Chron. 2:12–17), who became king of Israel. He is mentioned in the dynastic prophecies of Isaiah 11:1, 10.

Jethro A shepherd and priest of the Kenites, a Midianite tribe of coppersmiths, with whom Moses took refuge during his flight from Egypt and whose daughter Zipporah he married (Exod. 2:15–22; 18:1–12). Moses apparently identified Jethro's god, YHWH, with El Shaddai, god of the Israelite ancestors (Exod. 3, 6, 18).

Jew Originally a member of the tribe or kingdom of Judah (2 Kings 16:6; 25:25), the term later included any Hebrew who returned from Babylonian captivity and finally encompassed all members of the covenant community scattered throughout the world (Esther 2:5).

Jezebel The daughter of King Ethbaal of Tyre and wife of King Ahab, Jezebel promulgated Baal worship in Israel and persecuted YHWH's prophets (1 Kings 16:29–33; 18:4, 19; 19:1–3). After she perverted the Mosaic Law to confiscate Naboth's vineyard (1 Kings 21:1–16), Elijah predicted her shameful death (1 Kings 21:24–26), a prophecy fulfilled when Jehu threw her body to the dogs to eat during his bloody purge of Ahab's dynasty (2 Kings 9:30–37).

Jezreel **(1)** A fertile valley, known as the Plain of Esdraelon, extending southeast across Palestine from north of Mount Carmel to the Jordan River. **(2)** A fortified city and the site of Naboth's vineyard (1 Kings 21:1–24) and of Jehu's murders of King Joram, of the queen-mother Jezebel (2 Kings 9:24, 30–37), and of all Ahab's heirs (2 Kings 10:1–11).

Joab A son of Zeruiah, half-sister of David (2 Sam. 2:18), Joab was the cruelly efficient commander-in-chief of David's armies who managed the capture of Jerusalem (2 Sam. 5:8; 1 Chron. 11:6–8) and successful wars against the Syrians, Ammonites, and Edomites (2 Sam. 12:26–31; 1 Kings 11:15–17). He murdered Abner, general of the northern tribes under Saul's heir, Ishbaal (2 Sam. 2:18–23; 3:22–30); arranged Uriah's death so that David could marry Bathsheba (2 Sam. 11:6–21); reconciled David and Absalom (2 Sam. 14:28–33) but later murdered

David's rebellious son (2 Sam. 18:9–17); and supported the wrong contender for David's throne (1 Kings 1:5–33), for which he was executed early in Solomon's reign (1 Kings 2:28–34), supposedly on David's deathbed advice (1 Kings 2:5–6).

Job The name apparently dates from the second millennium B.C.E. and may mean "one who comes back to God," a penitent. It may derive from the Hebrew *ayab*, "to be hostile," denoting one whom God makes his enemy. The central character of the wisdom book bearing his name, Job is linked with Noah and Danel as a person of exemplary righteousness (Ezek. 14:14, 20). All three of Ezekiel's heroes were non-Israelites; Job was probably an Edomite.

Jochanan ben Zakkai A Rabbinic scholar of the first century C.E. who, according to Talmudic legend, has himself smuggled out of Jerusalem (in a coffin) during the final siege in 70 C.E. According to this account, his disciples carry him into the camp of the Roman general Vespasian, whereupon ben Zakkai prophecies that Vespasian will be the next emperor of Rome. In gratitude for this favorable prediction, Vespasian grants ben Zakkai the privilege of opening a Rabbinic academy in the seacoast town of Jamnia (Yavneh) thereby ensuring the survival of Judaism after the war.

Joel Although numerous biblical figures bore this name (meaning "YHWH is God"), the best known is the son of Pethuel (Joel 1:1), a prophet of postexilic Judah (perhaps c. 350 B.C.E.).

Jonah A son of Amittai, a Zebulunite from Gath-hepher whom YHWH sent as prophet to warn Nineveh of its impending doom (Jon. 1:1–16). The book's fictional hero is probably not to be identified with the prophet Jonah, cited in 2 Kings 14:25.

Jonathan The son and heir of King Saul (1 Sam. 13:16; 14:49; 1 Chron. 8:33) and famous for his unselfish devotion to young David (1 Sam. 18:1–5; 19:1–7; 20:1–21:1; 23:15–18). Along with his father, Jonathan was killed by the Philistines at the Battle of Gilboa (1 Sam. 31:1; 2 Sam. 1:16), a loss David lamented in one of his most moving psalms (2 Sam. 1:17–27).

Joppa An important harbor of ancient Palestine, located on the Mediterranean coast about thirty-five miles northwest of Jerusalem and now a suburb of Tel Aviv (1 Macc. 10:76; 12:33–34; 13:11; 14:5, 34; 2 Macc. 12:3–4).

Jordan River The main river of Palestine, which occupies a deep north-south rift valley connecting the Sea of Galilee with the Dead Sea (a distance of about sixty-five miles) and forms the boundary between east and west Palestine. The Jordan is mentioned in the narratives concerning Lot, Abraham, and Jacob (Gen. 13:10; 14:12–16; 32:10) but is best known as the last barrier Israel crossed before entering Canaan—an event marked by a miraculous stopping of the river's flow (Josh. 3:1–5:1).

Joseph The son of Jacob and Rachel, who aroused his ten older brothers' jealousy, was sold into slavery and taken to Egypt where, aided by his ability to interpret dreams, he rose to power second only to that of Pharaoh himself. His story is told in Genesis 30:22–24 and Genesis 37–50. The name *Joseph* is used to represent the combined tribes of Ephraim and Manasseh (Josh. 16:1–4) and the northern kingdom (Ps. 80).

Josephus, Flavius An important Jewish historian (c. 37–100 C.E.) whose two major works—*Antiquities of the Jews* and *The Jewish War* (covering the revolt against Rome, 66–73 C.E.)—provide valuable background material for first-century C.E. Judaism and the early Christian period.

Joshua **(1)** The son of Nun, an Ephraimite, Joshua (meaning "YHWH is salvation") was Moses' military assistant (Exod. 17:8–13), in charge of the Tabernacle (Exod. 33:11), one of the two spies optimistic about Israel's prospects of conquering Canaan (Num. 13:1–16; 14:6–9), and chosen to succeed Moses (Num. 27:18–23; Deut. 3:28; 31:23; 34:9). He led the Israelites across the Jordan (Josh. 3), captured Jericho (Josh. 6) and 'Ai (Josh. 7–8), warred against the Canaanite kings (Josh. 10–12), allotted the land to various tribes (Josh. 13:1–22:8), and made a covenant with YHWH and the people (Josh. 24). **(2)** High priest of Jerusalem during the governorship of Zerubbabel (c. 520 B.C.E.). In the third chapter of Zechariah, Joshua appears in a dream-vision as the symbolic representative of a purified priesthood (Ezra 2: 2; 3: 2; Hag. 1: 1, 12, 14).

Josiah The son of Amon (642–640 B.C.E.), Josiah (meaning "YHWH heals") became king of Judah after his father's murder. The outstanding event of his reign (640–609 B.C.E.) was the discovery of a book of the Law (probably an early edition of Deuteronomy) and the subsequent religious reform it inspired (following 621 B.C.E.). Josiah purged Judah and part of Israel's old territory of their rural shrines and "high places," centering all worship at the Jerusalem Temple (2 Kings 23:27). He was killed at Megiddo attempting to intercept Pharaoh Necho's army on its way to support the collapsing Assyrian Empire (609 B.C.E.) (2 Kings 22:1–23:30; 2 Chron. 34:1–35:27).

Jotham **(1)** The youngest son of Jerubbaal (Gideon) (Judg. 9:5), who denounced his brother Abimelech to the people of Shechem for the latter's murder of Jerubbaal's seventy sons (Judg. 9:7–21). **(2)** The son of Uzziah, who was king of Judah as regent for his father (c. 750–742 B.C.E.) and later in his own right (742–735 B.C.E.) (2 Kings 15:32–38; 2 Chron. 27:1–9). The name means "YHWH is perfect."

Jubilee Derived from the Hebrew word for "ram's horn" or "trumpet," the term refers to the sabbatical year described in Leviticus 25:8–24 to be kept every half-century and proclaimed by a trumpet blast on the Day of Atonement. During a Jubilee year, all debts were to be canceled and private property returned to its rightful owners.

Judah **(1)** The fourth son of Jacob and Leah (Gen. 29:35) who, according to the J account, received his father's most powerful blessing (Gen. 49:8) and became the progenitor of the tribe of Judah, which along with that of Ephraim was the most important in Israel's history. David was of this populous tribe, which loyally supported his dynasty (2 Sam. 2:4; 1 Kings 12:20). **(2)** The kingdom of Judah, the southern kingdom of the divided monarchy, was composed chiefly of the tribes of Judah and Benjamin, which supported the Davidic dynasty when the northern ten tribes seceded from the union (922 B.C.E.). It was destroyed by the Babylonians in 587 B.C.E.

Judaism The name applied to the religion of the people of Judah (the Jews) after the northern kingdom of Israel fell (721 B.C.E.) and particularly after the Babylonian exile (587–538 B.C.E.).

Judas Maccabeus The third of five sons of the Judean priest Mattathias, leader of a successful uprising (c. 167–160 B.C.E.) against the Syrian king Antiochus IV. The epithet *Maccabeus* is believed to mean "the hammer," referring to Judas's effectiveness in striking blows for Jewish freedom. His story is told in 1 Maccabees. *See* Maccabees.

Judas the Galilean A Jewish revolutionary who led a revolt against Rome when Quirinius was governing Syria (6 or 7 C.E.) (Acts 5:27).

Judea The Greco-Roman designation for territory comprising the old kingdom of Judah, the name first appears in Ezra 5:8, a reference to the "province of Judaea." During Roman occupation, Judea was the southernmost of the three divisions of the Roman province of western Palestine, the other two of which were Samaria and Galilee (Neh. 2:7).

Judeans The inhabitants of Judea, the Greco-Roman designation of the territory formerly occupied by the kingdom of Judah. The term also designated members of the covenant people living abroad in the Diaspora.

judges (1) In the Book of Judges, charismatic (spirit-filled) men and women who led Israelite tribes or clans mainly by the force of their character; in the period before the monarchy, these leaders rallied some Isralites to fight against oppressors from neighboring Canaanite regions, such as the Moabites or Philistines. There were twelve officially designated as such: Othniel of Judah, Ehud, Shamgar, Deborah, Gideon, Tola, Jair, Jephthah, Ibzan, Elon, Abdon, and Samson, though Eli and Samuel were also spoken of as judges (1 Sam. 4:18; 7:15). (2) In the Hebrew Bible, a civil magistrate (Exod. 21:22; Deut. 16:18), administrator of a judiciary system traditionally organized by Moses (Exod. 18:13–26; Deut. 1:15–17; 16:18–20; 17:2–13; 19:15–20). Under the monarchy, the king became the supreme civil judge (2 Sam. 15:2; 1 Kings 3:9, 28; 7:7).

Judgment, Day of A theological concept deriving from the ancient Hebrew belief that the Day of YHWH would see Israel's triumph and the destruction of its enemies, a confidence the prophet Amos shattered by proclaiming that it would mean calamity for Israel as for all who broke YHWH's laws (Amos 5:18–20). This view prevails in Zephaniah 1:1–2; 3 and Malachi 3:1–6; 4:1–6. Isaiah also refers to "that day" of coming retribution (Isa. 11:10–16; 13:9, 13), while it is given an apocalyptic setting in Daniel 7:9–14, an idea developed in several apocryphal and pseudepigraphal books.

Kadesh The central campsite of the Israelites during their wanderings through the Sinai wilderness (Num. 13:26–33; 20:1–11; 32:8; Deut. 1:19–25).

kavod The Hebrew term for YHWH's "glory" that was believed to be invisibly present in the Jerusalem Temple.

Kenite hypothesis A hypothesis that YHWH was originally the tribal god of the Kenite clan from which Moses and his Hebrew followers borrowed and adapted their religion (Exod. 18:1–12).

Kenites A Midianite clan of nomadic coppersmiths and metalworkers to which Jethro, Moses' father-in-law, belonged (Exod. 18:1–12; Num. 10:29–32; Judg. 1:16; 4:11; 1 Sam. 15:6).

Kethuvim (Ketubim, or Kethubim) The Hebrew term designating the Writings, the third division of the Hebrew Bible: Psalms, Job, Proverbs, Song of Songs, Ecclesiastes, Esther, Ruth, Lamentations, Daniel, Ezra, Nehemiah, and 1 and 2 Chronicles.

Kittim Originally a Hebrew Bible name for the Island of Cyprus and its inhabitants (Gen. 10:4), thought to be descendants of Noah's grandson Javan, it was later applied to Macedonian Greeks (1 Macc. 1:1) and others (Dan. 11:30).

KJV Abbreviation for the King James Version of the Bible, published in 1611.

Koheleth (Qoheleth) The title — meaning the "president" or "preacher" of an assembly or school (*qahal*) — that the otherwise anonymous author of Ecclesiastes (the Greek equivalent of the term) gives himself (Eccles. 1:1; 12:9–10).

koinē The "common" or popular form of Greek spoken by Alexander's soldiers and transmitted as an international language throughout the Greco-Roman world. The Septuagint and New Testament are written in *koinē*.

Korah The son of Izhar, who rebelled against Moses' leadership during the Sinai wanderings (Num. 16–17).

Laban A descendant of Nahor, brother of Rebekah (Gen. 24:29; 25:20), father of Leah and Rachel, and thus father-in-law of Jacob. An Aramean living in Haran, Laban was noted for his duplicity and greed (Gen. 24:29–31:55).

Lachish A major fortified city in Judah about thirty miles southwest of Jerusalem and twenty miles from the Mediterranean coast (2 Kings 14:19; 2 Chron. 11:5–12; 14:6; 32:9; Jer. 34:7).

Lamech According to J, the son of Methuselah and father of Tubal and Jubal (Gen. 4:1–24); according to P, the son of Methuselah and father of Noah (Gen. 5:25–31). His boastful song of vengeance is given in Genesis 4:23–24.

Latter Prophets Also known as the "writing prophets," the term refers to the books of Isaiah, Jeremiah, Ezekiel, and the twelve Minor Prophets.

Law The Torah (meaning "teaching" or "instruction") or Pentateuch, the first five books of the Bible containing the legal material traditionally ascribed to Moses.

Leah Laban's older daughter, whom he married to Jacob by trickery after the latter had worked seven years for her younger sister, Rachel (Gen. 29:16–30:21; 31:14). Although Jacob disliked Leah, she bore him six sons and a daughter: Reuben, Simeon, Levi, Judah, Issachar, Zebulun, and Dinah (Ruth 4:11).

legal procedures Also known as *case law,* or *casuistic law,* this refers to legal decrees phrased in a qualifying manner, commonly in the form "If this happens, then that must be done." Typical of both ancient Mesopotamian law and many statutes in the Mosaic Torah, this form contrasts with the absolute demands of apodictic, or policy, law. *See also* apodictic law, case law, policy law.

legend A term denoting unverifiable stories or narrative cycles about celebrated people or places of the past. Legends grow as the popular oral literature of a people. Their purpose is not to provide historical accuracy but to entertain and to illustrate cherished beliefs, expectations, and moral principles. Scholars consider much of the material associated with the stories of the patriarchs, Moses, and prophets to be legendary.

Levi The third son of Jacob and Leah (Gen. 29:34; 35:23), Levi earned his father's disapproval for his violence in slaughtering tribal neighbors (Gen. 34:30; 49:5–7). He was the eponymous ancestor of the tribe of Levi to which Moses, Aaron, and Miriam belonged (Exod. 6:16; Num. 3:1–39).

Leviathan A mythical sea monster, the ancient Near Eastern dragon of chaos and symbol of Evil that YHWH defeated in creating the universe (Ps. 74:14; Dan. 7:2; Isa. 27:1; Job 41:1–34; see also Rev. 11:7; 12:3; 13:1–8).

Levites The Israelite tribe descended from Levi, son of Jacob (Num. 3; 1 Chron. 5:27–6:81), that was given priestly duties in lieu of land holdings when Israel conquered Canaan (Deut. 18:1–8). According to P, only descendants of Aaron were to be priests (Exod. 28:1; Num. 18:7); the Levites were regarded as their assistants and servants (Num. 18:2–7; 20–32). They served as priests of secondary rank and as Temple functionaries during the postexilic period, which was dominated by a priestly hierarchy (1 Chron. 24–26). Other stories involving Levites appear in Judges 19–21 and Luke 10:32.

lex talionis The law of strict retaliation, the principle of retributive justice expressed in the Torah command to exact "eye for eye, life for life" (Exod. 21:23–25; Lev. 24:19–20; Deut. 19:21).

literary criticism A form of literary analysis that attempts to isolate and define literary types, the sources behind them, the stages of composition from oral to written form with their characteristic rhetorical features, and the stages and degree of redaction (editing) of a text.

liturgy A body of formal rites, including both actions and spoken words, used in public worship, such as the sacrifices, prayers, and other rituals performed at YHWH's Temple in Jerusalem.

Lot The nephew of Abraham, with whom he migrated from Ur to Haran and finally to Canaan (Gen. 11:31; 12:5). Lot was separated from his uncle, who rescued him from kidnappers (Gen. 13:1–14:16). Lot later entertained angels who had come to destroy Sodom (Gen. 19:1–29) and who directed his escape from the doomed city. He reputedly fathered the nations of Moab and Ammon by incest with his two daughters (Gen. 19:30–38).

Lucifer A term meaning "light bearer" and referring to the planet Venus when it is the morning star, the English name *Lucifer* translates the Hebrew word for "shining one" (Isa. 14:12). An epithet applied to the king of Babylon, it was later mistakenly taken as a name for Satan before his expulsion from heaven.

LXX A common abbreviation for the Septuagint, the Greek translation of the Hebrew Bible made in Alexandria, Egypt, during the last three centuries B.C.E.

Lydia A once-powerful kingdom of western Asia Minor with its capital at Sardis, Lydia (Lud) is mentioned in Jeremiah 46:9 and Ezekiel 30:5.

Maat An ancient Egyptian goddess of truth and justice.

Maccabees A name bestowed on the family that won religious and political independence for the Jews from their Greek-Syrian oppressors. Judas, called Maccabeus (meaning the "hammer"), son of the aged priest Mattathias, led his brothers and other faithful Jews against the armies of Antiochus IV (Epiphanes) (175–163 B.C.E.). The dynasty his brothers established was called Hasmonean (after an ancestor named Hashmon) and ruled Judea until 63 B.C.E., when the Romans occupied Palestine.

Magog *See* Gog.

Malachi The title of the last book of the Minor Prophets, the word means "my messenger" (Mal. 3:1) and may have been affixed by an editor (Mal. 1:1) who mistook it for a proper name.

Mamre A plain near what later became the city of Hebron in southern Palestine, where Abraham temporarily settled under its ancient oaks (Gen. 13:18) and where angels on the way to Sodom visited him (Gen. 18). From a Hittite, Abraham bought a cave near Mamre in which his wife Sarah (Gen. 23:17, 19) and then he himself (Gen. 50:13) were buried.

Manasseh **(1)** The elder son of Joseph and the Egyptian Asenath, daughter of a high priest at On, who received a lesser blessing from the dying Jacob than his full brother Ephraim (Gen. 48:1–20), reflecting the tribe of Ephraim's greater importance in the later history of Israel. **(2)** One of Israel's twelve tribes, divided into two sections and occupying land east and west of the Jordan River (Josh. 17:1–18). **(3)** A son of Hezekiah and Hephzibah who was king of Judah longer than any other Davidic monarch (c. 687–642 B.C.E.). Despite the Deuteronomistic condemnation of him as the most evil ruler of Judah for his encouragement of Baalism, astrology, and human sacrifice, he proved an effective king, maintaining his country's relative independence during troubled times (2 Kings 21:1–18; 2 Chron. 33:1–20). The historicity of his supposed deportation to and return from Babylon has been questioned. In 2 Kings 23:26–27, Judah's final destruction is attributed to Manasseh's wickedness.

manna The food miraculously supplied the Israelites during their wanderings in the Sinai wilderness (Exod. 16:1–36). Described in Numbers 11:7–9 and commonly referred to as "bread" from heaven (Deut. 8:3; Nah. 9:20; Ps. 78:24; Heb. 9:4), its appearances ceased when Israel entered Canaan (Josh. 5:12).

Manoah A pious member of the tribe of Dan and father of Samson, Israel's Herculean judge (Judg. 13:2–25; 14:2–10; 16:31).

Marduk The patron god of Babylon, hero of the Babylonian creation epic *Enuma Elish,* in which he defeats the monster Tiamat and creates the cosmos from her bifurcated corpse.

Mari An ancient Near Eastern city located on the Middle Euphrates River near the boundary of modern Syria and Iraq. Destroyed by Hammurabi of Babylon (c. 1738–1686 B.C.E.), Mari's royal palace has yielded thousands of clay tablets that preserve a rich array of information about the Mari period (c. 1750–1697 B.C.E.).

Masada A stronghold built by Herod the Great on a fortified plateau 800 feet above the Dead Sea, Masada was captured by Zealots during the revolt against Rome (66 C.E.). When the attacking Romans finally entered Masada (73 C.E.), they found only 7 women and children alive, 953 others having died in a suicide pact.

mashal The Hebrew term for "proverb" or "parable," it refers to a short, pithy observation that is most often expressed through the use of poetic parallelism.

masoretes From a Hebrew term meaning "transmitters," the name given to medieval Jewish scholars who copied, annotated, and added vowels to the text of the Hebrew Bible.

Masoretic Text (MT) The standard text of the Hebrew Bible as given final form by the Masoretes in the seventh through ninth centuries C.E.

Mattathias A Jewish priest who, with his sons John, Simon, Judas, Eleazar, and Jonathan, led a revolt against the oppressions of Antiochus IV (c. 168–167 B.C.E.) (1 Macc. 2:1–70).

Medes An ancient Ayrian (Iranian) Indo-European people occupying mountainous country south of the Caspian Sea who established a kingdom that by 600 B.C.E. extended from near the Persian Gulf to the Black Sea. In 612 B.C.E., they joined the Neo-Babylonians and Scythians to destroy Nineveh and terminate the Assyrian Empire. They were subdued by Cyrus the Great (549 B.C.E.), whose dominion was commonly known as the Medo-Persian Empire (Nah. 2:3–3:19; Esther 1:19; Dan. 5:28). The "law of the Medes and Persians" was traditionally immutable (Esther 1:19; Dan. 6:8, 15) and once given could not be rescinded, a factor that plays an important part in the Book of Esther (Esther 8:7–12).

Megiddo An old Palestinian city overlooking the Valley of Jezreel (Plain of Esdraelon), the site of numerous decisive battles in biblical history (Josh. 12:21; 2 Kings 9:27; 23:29–30; 2 Chron. 35:20–24; Zech. 12:11) and symbolic location of the climactic War of Armageddon (Rev. 16:16).

Megillot A Hebrew word meaning "scrolls"; the five Hebrew Bible books — Song of Songs, Ruth, Lamentations, Ecclesiastes, and Esther — each of which was read publicly at one of Israel's annual religious festivals.

Melchizedek The king-priest of Canaanite Salem (probably the site of Jerusalem) to whom Abraham paid a tenth of his spoils of war (Gen. 14:17–20); cited by the author of Psalm 110 as an eternal royal priest (Ps. 110:4).

Merneptah The Egyptian pharaoh, son and successor of Rameses II, who reigned circa 1224–1211 B.C.E. His stele commemorating the defeat of several Canaanite nations includes the earliest known reference to Israel, which Merneptah claimed he had totally eradicated.

Merodach A Hebrew form of the Akkadian Marduk (also called Bel), the chief Babylonian god, ridiculed by Second Isaiah (Isa. 46:1–4) and Jeremiah (Jer. 51:44–45).

Meshach The Babylonian name of Mishael, one of Daniel's three Hebrew companions whom Nebuchadnezzar unsuccessfully tried to incinerate in a furnace (Dan. 1–3).

Mesopotamia The territory between the Euphrates and Tigris rivers at the head of the Persian Gulf (modern Iraq); cradle of the Sumerian, Akkadian, Assyrian, and Neo-Babylonian civilizations (Gen. 24:10; Judg. 3:8–10; 1 Chron. 19:6).

messiah A Hebrew term meaning "anointed one," designating a king or priest of ancient Israel who had been consecrated by having his head rubbed with holy oil, marking him as set apart for a special role. King David is the model of YHWH's anointed ruler; all his descendants who ruled over Judah were YHWH's messiahs (2 Sam. 7:1–29; Ps. 89:3–45). After the end of the Davidic monarchy (587 B.C.E.), various Hebrew prophets applied the promises made to the Davidic dynasty to a future heir who would eventually restore the kingdom of David (Pss. 2, 110; Dan. 9:25–26).

metaphor A figure of speech in which one object is used to describe the quality of another, an implied comparison of one thing to another, inferring that the first has a hitherto unrecognized likeness to the second. Biblical poets, for example, call YHWH a "shepherd" because he guides and protects Israel, his "flock," and a "rock" because he is solid and reliable (cf. Ps. 23:1; Deut. 32:4).

Methuselah According to Genesis 5:21–27, an antediluvian patriarch descended from Seth and Enoch who attained an age of 969 years. He appears as Methushael in Genesis 4:18.

Micah A Judean prophet of the late eighth century B.C.E. and younger contemporary of Isaiah of Jerusalem (Isa. 2:2–4; Mic. 4:1–3). A rural figure who denounced the evils of urban life (Mic. 1:5) and predicted Jerusalem's fall (Mic. 3:12; cited in Jer. 26:18–19), his oracles form most of the present Book of Micah in the Minor Prophets. His name means "Who is like YHWH?"

Micaiah An eighth-century B.C.E. prophet who predicted Ahab's defeat and death at the Battle of Ramoth-gilead (1 Kings 22:8–28; 2 Chron. 18:6–27).

Michael The angel whom the Book of Daniel represents as being the spirit prince, guardian, and protector of Israel (Dan. 10:13, 21; 12:1). His name means "Who is like God?"

Michal A daughter of Saul (1 Sam. 14:49) who was offered to David as his wife for his exploits against the Philistines (1 Sam. 18:20–27). Michal helped David escape Saul's wrath (1 Sam. 19:11–17), only to be rejected when she criticized his dancing naked before the Ark (2 Sam. 6:14–23).

Midian An ancient tribal territory, the exact location and extent of which is unknown, that lay in the northwestern Arabian desert, east of the Gulf of 'Aqaba, opposite the Sinai Peninsula, and south of Moab. According to Exodus, Moses is in Midian when he first encounters YHWH. *See* Midianites.

Midianites A nomadic or seminomadic group of shepherds and traders that played a significant role in Israel's early history. According to Genesis 25:1–6, they were descended from Abraham and his wife Keturah and thus closely associated with Israel's forebears. In Exodus, Moses takes refuge with the Midianite priest Jethro (or Ruel), whose daughter he marries (Exod. 2:15–3:1; 18:1–15). Although the Moses tradition presents them in a favorable light, later biblical writers portray them negatively as encroaching on Israel's territory (Judg. 1:16; 4:1; 6–8; cf. Num. 22; 25:6–18, where an Israelite is executed for following Moses' example by taking a Midianite wife).

midrash From a Hebrew word meaning "to search out," midrash refers to a commentary on or interpretation of Scripture. Collections of such haggadic or halakic expositions of the significance of the biblical text are called Midrashim.

Minor Prophets Twelve prophetic books short enough to be recorded together on a single scroll: Hosea, Joel, Amos, Obadiah, Jonah, Micah, Nahum, Habakkuk, Zephaniah, Haggai, Zechariah, and Malachi.

Miriam The daughter of Amram and Jochebed, older sister of Aaron and Moses, who brought her mother to nurse the infant Moses after he was found and adopted by Pharaoh's daughter (Exod. 2:4–8; Num. 26:59; 1 Chron. 6:3). Miriam led the victory celebration after the crossing of the Sea of Reeds (Exod. 15:20–21). Although later stricken with leprosy for criticizing Moses, she was cured and readmitted to YHWH's favor after her brother interceded for her (Num. 12:2–15; cf. Mic. 6:4).

Mishnah From the Hebrew verb "to repeat," a collection of Pharisaic oral interpretations (Halakah) of the Torah compiled and edited by Rabbi Judah ha-Nasi about 200 C.E.

Mizpah The name of several Israelite sites, the most important of which was located in the territory of Benjamin (Josh. 18:26) near the border of Judah and Israel, perhaps a cult site (Judg. 20:1–11) on Samuel's prophetic circuit (1 Sam. 7:5–16; 10:17–24) and the temporary center of Jews remaining in Palestine after Nebuchadnezzar's deportations (2 Kings 25:23; Jer. 40–41).

Mizraim According to Genesis 10:6, a son of Noah's son Ham and the progenitor of the Hamitic nations of Lower Egypt, North Africa, and Canaan. It is also the Hebrew name of Egypt.

Moab An ancient neighbor-state of Israel located in the Jordan highlands east of the Dead Sea and north of Edom. Supposedly descended from Lot's incestuous union with his daughter (Gen. 19:30–38), the Moabites were Israel's traditional enemies (Num. 22:3; 24:17; Judg. 3:12–20; 11:15; 2 Kings 1:1; 3:4–27) and frequently denounced by the prophets (Isa. 15:16; 25:10; Jer. 9:26; 25:26; 48; Ezek. 28:8–11; Amos 2:12; Zech. 2:8–11; Ps. 60:8). Yet, David was descended from Ruth, a Moabite (Ruth 4:13–22). In extreme emergencies, the national god Chemosh was sometimes worshiped with human sacrifice (2 Kings 3:27; 13:20).

Molech (Moloch) The national god of Ammon whose worship characteristically involved human sacrifice, an act specifically forbidden the Hebrews (Lev. 18:21; 20:2; Amos 5:26) but allegedly introduced by King Manasseh (2 Kings 21:6; 2 Chron. 33), rooted out by Josiah (2 Kings 23:10), and denounced by the prophets Jeremiah (Jer. 7:29–34; 19:1–13) and Ezekiel (Ezek. 16:20–21; 20:26, 31).

money In early biblical times, before coins were first minted, value in business transactions was determined by weighing quantities of precious metals. In the early period, the term *shekel* refers not to a coin, but to a certain weight of silver. The use of coinage was first introduced into Palestine during the Persian era when the daric or dram, named for Darius I (521–486 B.C.E.), appeared. After Alexander's conquest of Persia, Greek coinage became the standard. The silver drachma, a coin of small value, was equivalent to the Roman denarius.

monism A theological term denoting belief in a single, universal principle, as in the view that only one divine beign exists, a concept that precludes the existence of lesser divinities, such as angels or demons.

monolatry The worship of one god while conceding the existence of others.

monotheism The belief in the existence of one god, a major theme of Second Isaiah (Isa. 40–55).

Mordecai His name derived from Marduk or Merodach (the chief Babylonian deity), Mordecai was the cousin and foster father of Esther who, according to the book bearing her name, was the Jew married to Ahasuerus, emperor of Persia. Representing the typically devout but politically ambitious Jew living in the Diaspora, Mordecai saved his sovereign's life (Esther 2:21–23) and outwitted Haman, who attempted to exterminate him and all Jews throughout the Persian domain (Esther 3:6–15), a plot he employed his beautiful cousin to foil so that, by his astuteness, he became second in power to the emperor (Esther 8–10).

Mosaic Covenant An agreement between God and the nation of Israel that was mediated by Moses. According to the terms of this pact, Israel swore to keep all of the laws enumerated in the Torah. Failure to do so would result in suffering all the curses contained in Leviticus and Deuteronomy.

Moses The great Hebrew lawgiver, religious reformer, founder of the Israelite nation, and central figure of the Pentateuch was the son of Amram (a Levite) and Jochebed, and brother to Aaron and Miriam (Exod. 2:1–4). Adopted by Pharaoh's daughter and raised at the Egyptian royal court (Exod. 2:5–10; Acts 7:22), he fled Egypt after killing an Egyptian bully and settled in Midian among the Kenites, where he married Jethro's daughter Zipporah (Exod. 2:11–22).

After an encounter with YHWH at the burning bush (Exod. 3:1–4:17), he returned to Egypt (Exod. 4:18–31), interceded with Pharaoh during the ten plagues (Exod. 5–11), led the Israelites across the Sea of Reeds (Exod. 14–15) to Sinai where he mediated the law covenant between YHWH and Israel (Exod. 19–31), pled for his people (Exod. 33–34; Num. 14), directed their migration through the Sinai wilderness (Num. 11–14; 20–25), appointed Joshua as his successor (Num. 27:18–23), and died in Moab (Deut. 34:1–7; Acts 7:20–44). He is also credited with building the Tabernacle (Exod. 35–40), organizing Israel (Exod. 18:13–26), restating Israel's law code shortly before his death (Deut. 1–31), and composing several hymns (Deut. 32–33; Ps. 90).

Although Moses' name became synonymous with the covenant concept and Israel's traditions (Pss. 77:20; 103:7; 105:26; 106:23; Isa. 63:12; Mic. 6:4), modern scholars have concluded that much of the material in the Pentateuch dates from post-Mosaic times. (*See* documentary hypothesis.)

myth From the Greek *mythos* (story), the term denotes a narrative expressing a profound psychological or religious truth that cannot be verified by historical inquiry or other scientific means. When scholars speak of the "myth of Eden," for example, it is not to denigrate the tale's significance but to emphasize the Eden story's archetypal expression of humanity's sense of alienation from its creator. Myths typically feature stories about divine beings and national heroes who represent natural or psychological forces that deeply influence humans but that they cannot control. The psychologist Carl Jung interpreted myth as humanity's inherited concept of primeval events that persists in the unconscious mind and finds expression through repeated reenactments in ritual worship and other cultic practices. Israel's covenant renewal ceremonies and retellings of YHWH's saving acts during the Exodus are examples of such cultic myths.

mythology A system or cycle of myths, such as those featuring the deities of ancient Greece or Rome. Once the embodiment of living religious beliefs, Greco-Roman and other mythologies are now seen as archetypal symbols that give philosophical meaning to universal human experiences. Mythologies are thus "falsehoods" only in the narrowest literal sense.

They are probably akin to dreams in revealing persistent images and attitudes derived from the human unconscious.

Naaman The Syrian commander-in-chief of Benhadad, king of Damascus and an enemy of Israel, whom the prophet Elisha bathes in the Jordan River to cure his leprosy (2 Kings 5:1–27).

Nabal An epithet meaning "fool," the name applied to the rich shepherd, husband of Abigail, who refused to feed David's band of outlaw guerillas (1 Sam. 25:2–42).

Nabonidus The son of Nabu-balatsuikbi, father of Belshazzar, and last ruler of the Neo-Babylonian Empire (556–539 B.C.E.).

Nabopolassar The name means "son of a nobody." Nabopolassar founded the Neo-Babylonian Empire by revolting against Assyria, a move that enabled King Josiah of Israel to carry out his religious reforms without Assyrian interference and to regain much of the old territory of the northern kingdom. Allied with the Medes, Nabopolassar destroyed Nineveh (612 B.C.E.) and was succeeded by his son Nebuchadnezzar II (Nah. 3:1–3; Zeph. 2:12–14; Jer. 46). *See also* Josiah.

Naboth A landowner in the city of Jezreel whose vineyard King Ahab coveted, Naboth was illegally executed through Queen Jezebel's machinations (1 Kings 21:1–16). This crime, denounced by the prophet Elijah, became the focal point of resistance to Ahab's royal dynasty and culminated in its extermination by Jehu (1 Kings 21:17–29; 2 Kings 9:1–10:11).

Nadab One of the sons of Aaron who, along with his brother Abihu, defies God by burning "unholy fire" (presumably an illicit form of incense) within the sanctuary and who is burned to death by a fire that "came out from the presence of the Lord" (Lev. 10:1–2). No further explanation is given, either of the nature of the offense or of the severity of the punishment. *See also* Abihu.

Nahor According to Genesis 11:27–30, the son of Terah, brother of Abraham and Haran. By Milcah (and a concubine), Nahor fathered twelve sons, eponymous ancestors of the north-Semitic Aramean tribes (Gen. 21:33; 24:24; 29:5–6).

Nahum A prophet from Elkosh (Nah. 1:1) who delivered poems rejoicing in Nineveh's fall and the destruction of the Assyrian Empire (612 B.C.E.).

Naomi The wife of Elimelech of Bethlehem (Ruth 1:2) and mother-in-law to Ruth, whose marriage she arranged to her Jewish kinsman Boaz (Ruth 3–4). Her name means "my pleasantness."

Naphtali (1) According to Genesis 30:7–8, Naphtali was the son of Jacob and Rachel's handmaid Bilhah, and was compared to a wild hind in his father's blessing (Gen. 49:21); the eponymous ancestor of one of the northern tribes of Israel (1 Chron. 7:13; Exod. 1:4; Num. 1:15, 42; 26:50). (2) The tribe of Naphtali was assigned territory north of Megiddo along the upper Jordan and western shores of the Sea of Galilee (Josh. 19:32–39; Judg. 1:33). It supported King David (1 Chron. 12:34–40) but became part of the northern kingdom after 922 B.C.E. (1 Kings 15:20) and was dispersed by the Assyrians in 722–721 B.C.E. (2 Kings 15:29).

Naram-Sin A grandson of Sargon I, creator of the world's first empire, Naram-Sin (c. 2260–2223 B.C.E.) was also a famed military leader who campaigned throughout Mesopotamia and Iran, conquering numerous cities, including Ebla, with its extensive cuneiform library.

narrative A literary composition that tells a story, arranging the characters and events in a sequential order. Most of the Bible's first eleven books are theologically oriented narratives constructed to illustrate the origin, nature, and consequences of Israel's covenant relationship with YHWH (Gen.–2 Kings).

Nathan (1) A son of David (2 Sam. 5:14; Zech. 12:12; Luke 3:31). (2) A prophet and political counselor at David's court who enunciated the concept of an everlasting Davidic dynasty (2 Sam. 7), denounced the king for his adultery with Bathsheba (2 Sam. 12:1–23), revealed Adonijah's plan to seize power (1 Kings 1:5–8), helped Solomon succeed to David's throne (1 Kings 1:8–45), and is credited with writing a history of David and Solomon's reigns (1 Chron. 29:29; 2 Chron. 9:29).

navi (nabi) The Hebrew word for "prophet," a spokesperson for YHWH who delivered God's judgments on contemporary society and expressed his intentions toward the world (Deut. 13:1–5; 18:9–22; Amos 3:7; etc.).

Nazirites From the Hebrew *nazar* (to dedicate), referring to a group in ancient Israel that rigorously observed ascetic principles, including refusing to drink wine, cut their hair, come in contact with the dead, or eat religiously "unclean" food (Num. 6:1–21). Samson, despite his ill-fated love affairs, belonged to this sect (Judg. 13–16).

Nebuchadnezzar (1) A Fourth Dynasty king of the Old Babylonian Empire (twelfth century B.C.E.). (2) The son of Nabopolassar and the most powerful ruler of the Neo-Babylonian Empire (605–562 B.C.E.), Nebuchadnezzar II defeated Pharaoh Necho at the Battle of Carchemish (605 B.C.E.) (2 Kings 24:1–7; Jer. 46:2) and brought much of the Near East under his control. He attacked Judah and deported many members of its upper classes in 598–597 B.C.E., besieged and destroyed Jerusalem in 587 B.C.E., and took much of its population captive to Babylon (2 Kings 24:10–25; 25:11–21; 2 Chron. 26:6–21; Jer. 39:1–10; 52:1–30). The portrait of him in Daniel is probably not historical (Dan. 2:1–13; 3:1–7; 4:4–37).

Nebuzaradan The commander of the Babylonian guard under Nebuchadnezzar who was sent to oversee the destruction of Jerusalem (587 B.C.E.) and the deportation to Babylon of Judah's ruling classes (2 Kings 25:8–20).

Necho Pharaoh Necho II, son of Psammetichus I (Psamtik), second king of the Twenty-Sixth Egyptian Dynasty (610–594 B.C.E.), defeated and killed King Josiah of Judah at Megiddo (609 B.C.E.), thus ending Josiah's religious reforms and Judah's political renaissance (2 Kings 23:29–35; 2 Chron. 35:20–24; 36:4). His plans to reassert Egyptian hegemony in the Near East were permanently thwarted when Nebuchadnezzar of Babylon defeated Egyptian forces at Carchemish (605 B.C.E.) (2 Kings 24:7; Jer. 46).

Negeb The largely desert territory south of Beersheba in Judah (Deut. 1:42–46; Josh. 10:40; 15:21–32; 19:1–9; Judg. 6:3; 1 Sam. 27:5–10; etc.).

Nehemiah A Jewish court official (cupbearer) living at the Persian capital in Susa who persuaded the emperor Artaxerxes I (465–423 B.C.E.) to commission him to go to Judea and rebuild Jerusalem's walls (Neh. 1:1–2:20). Although he encountered resistance from Judah's jealous neighbors, Nehemiah finished the rebuilding in record time (Neh. 3:33–6:19) and, with the priest Ezra, effected numerous social and religious reforms among the returned exiles (Neh. 8:1–9:3; 11:1–3; 12:27–13:3).

nephesh In biblical Hebrew, the term for "living being" or "animate creature" that applies to both humans and animals. A physical body infused with God's *ruach* ("breath" or "spirit"), the first human is created a *nephesh* (Gen. 2:7), a mortal unity of clay and spirit. In Greek translations of the Hebrew Bible, *nephesh* was commonly rendered as *psyche*, the Greek term for "soul" that had connotations of immortality absent in the Hebrew text.

Nergal-sharezer A high Babylonian official present at the capture of Jerusalem who, on King Nebuchadnezzar's orders, helped protect the prophet Jeremiah (Jer. 39:1–14). He later became king of Babylon (560–556 B.C.E.) after murdering Amel-Marduk (the Evil-merodach of 2 Kings 25:27).

Nethinim A group of Temple servants who performed such menial tasks as carrying wood and water (Ezra 7:7, 24; 8:20; Neh. 3:26–31; 10:28–31).

Nevi'im (Prophets) The Hebrew term designating the second major division of the tripartite Hebrew Bible (Tanak), the Prophets.

New Year Festival (Rosh Hashanah) Also called the Feast of Trumpets (Lev. 23:23–25), this was a time when work ceased and the Israelites assembled together (Num. 29:1–6). Before the exile (587–538 B.C.E.), the Jews observed the festival in the autumn, but afterward they adopted the Babylonian celebration held in the spring, the first day of the month of Nisan (March–April). With a new emphasis on atonement, it became the first of Ten Days of Penitence, a solemn introduction to the Day of Atonement (Yom Kippur) (Lev. 16). Ezekiel urged the keeping of both New Years (Ezek. 40–48).

Nicanor A general of Antiochus IV whom the Maccabees defeated (1 Macc. 3:38; 7:26–32).

Nimrod According to J, the great-grandson of Noah, grandson of Ham, son of Cush, and a legendary hunter and founder of cities in Mesopotamia (Gen. 9:19; 10:8–12). Several ruined sites in Iraq preserve his name.

Nineveh The last capital of the Assyrian Empire, located on the east bank of the Tigris River and supposedly founded by Nimrod (Gen. 10:11), Nineveh was one of the greatest cities in the ancient Near East (Jon. 1:2; 3:2–4; 4:11). Several Judean kings, including Hezekiah, sent tribute there (2 Kings 18:13–16). Its destruction was foretold by the prophets (2 Kings 19:5–37; Zeph. 2:13) and celebrated by Nahum (Nah. 1–3). Assyria's last major ruler, Ashurbanipal (668–627 B.C.E.), was an antiquarian who collected thousands of literary works on clay tablets—including the *Epic of Gilgamesh* and the *Enuma Elish*—for the royal library at Nineveh. After a three-month siege, the city was destroyed in 612 B.C.E. by a coalition of Medes, Babylonians, and Scythians.

Noachan Covenant The promises YHWH makes to Noah after the Flood, emphasizing the sacredness of all life, both human and animal, and a divine vow never again to drown the world. Universal in scope, its symbol is the rainbow.

Noah The son of Lamech (Gen. 5:28–30) and father of Ham, Shem, and Japheth (Gen. 4:32), whom YHWH chose to build a wooden houseboat containing pairs of all living creatures to survive the Flood (Gen. 6:13–8:19) and with whom YHWH made an "everlasting" covenant (Gen. 8:20–9:17). In another story (Gen. 5:29; 9:18–27), Noah is the first vine grower and a victim of excessive drinking. He is rarely mentioned elsewhere in the Hebrew Bible (Isa. 54:9; Ezek. 14:14).

Obadiah (1) One of Ahab's stewards, who hid 100 Yahwist prophets in caves during Jezebel's persecutions and who arranged the meeting between Ahab and Elijah (1 Kings 18:3–16) that resulted in a contest between YHWH and Baal on Mount Carmel (1 Kings 18:17–46). (2) Traditionally recognized as author of the Book of Obadiah, about whom nothing is known. His book is fourth and shortest among the Minor Prophets.

Obed The son of Ruth and Boaz, and father of Jesse, father of David (Ruth 4:17–22; 1 Chron. 2:12; 11:47).

Obed-edom (1) A citizen of Gath in whose house David placed the Ark of the Covenant before taking it to Jerusalem (2 Sam. 6:10–12; 1 Chron. 13:13–14). (2) The founder of a group of singers at the Second Temple (1 Chron. 15:21; 16:5).

Olives, Mount of (Olivet) A mile-long limestone ridge with several distinct summits paralleling the eastern section of Jerusalem, from which it is separated by the narrow Kidron Valley. Here David fled during Absalom's rebellion (2 Sam. 15:30–32), and, according to Zechariah 14:3–5, here YHWH will stand at the final eschatological battle, when the mountain will be torn asunder from east to west.

Omri The sixth ruler of the northern kingdom (876–869 B.C.E.) and founder of a dynasty that included his son Ahab (869–850 B.C.E.), his grandson Ahaziah (850–849 B.C.E.), and a younger son Jehoram (849–842 B.C.E.), whose important military, political, and economic successes are minimized by the Deuteronomistic historians (2 Kings 16:23–28). Omri's leadership raised Israel to a level of power and prestige considerably above that of Judah. Even a century after his death and the extinction of his dynasty, Assyrian records referred to Israel as the "land of the House of Omri."

oneiromancy   The form of divination that employs dream-visions as a way of discovering the future or the divine will. When Joseph interprets the dreams of the cupbearer, the baker, and finally the pharaoh in Genesis 40–41, he is engaged in something like oneiromancy.

Ophel   The southern end of Jerusalem's eastern or Temple hill, the site of David's city (2 Chron. 27:3; 33:14; Neh. 3:26–27; 11:31).

oracle   **(1)** A divine message or utterance. **(2)** The inner sanctum of the Jerusalem Temple (1 Kings 6:5–6; 7:49; 8:6–8; Ps. 28:2). **(3)** The supposedly inspired words of a priest or priestess at such shrines as Delphi in ancient Greece and Cumae in Italy.

Oral Torah   Refers to the rabbinic concept of a second or "oral" body of teachings and laws imparted by God to Moses at Sinai/Horeb and transmitted orally over many centuries until it was gathered together and written down by rabbinic scholars from the second through the sixth centuries C.E. in the form of the Talmud. The belief in the existence and legitimacy of this secondary tradition is one of those articles of faith that distinguish the Pharisees (who accept the Oral Torah) from the Sadducees (who reject it).

oral tradition   Material passed from generation to generation by word of mouth before finding written form. Scholars believe that much of Israel's early history, customs, and beliefs about its origins, such as the stories about the patriarchs and Moses in the Pentateuch, were so transmitted before J first committed them to writing about 950–850 B.C.E..

original sin   The theological concept of humanity's innate depravity and sinfulness, a doctrine holding that the entire human race has inherited from the first man (Adam) an irresistible tendency to sin, thereby incurring God's condemnation. Not part of the Jewish tradition, this pessimistic view of human nature was formulated by the early Christian theologian Augustine.

Osiris   The ancient Egyptian god of fertility and also of the Underworld.

P   *See* priestly document.

Palestine   A strip of land bordering the eastern Mediterranean Sea, lying south of Syria, north of the Sinai Peninsula, and west of the Arabian Desert. Dur-

ing the patriarchal period, it was known as Canaan (Gen. 12:6–7; 15:18–21). Named for the Philistines, it was first called Palestine by the Greek historian Herodotus about 450 B.C.E.

pantheon   The accepted list or roster of a people's chief gods, such as the Olympian family of gods worshiped in classical Greece. It is also the name of a famous temple in Rome, the house of "all the gods."

paradise   Literally, a "park" or walled garden, paradise is the name applied to Eden (Gen. 2:8–17) and in post–Hebrew Bible times to the abode of the righteous dead, of which the lower part housed souls awaiting the resurrection and the higher was the permanent home of the just.

parallelism   A structural feature typical of Hebrew poetry, consisting of the repetition of similar or antithetical thoughts in similar phrasing: "The wicked will not stand firm when Judgment comes nor sinners when the virtuous assemble" (Ps. 1:5).

Passover   An annual Jewish observance commemorating Israel's last night of bondage in Egypt when the Angel of Death "passed over" Israelite homes marked with the blood of a sacrificial lamb to destroy the firstborn of every Egyptian household (Exod. 12:1–51). Beginning the seven-day Feast of Unleavened Bread, it is a ritual meal eaten on Nisan 14 (March-April) that traditionally includes roast lamb, unleavened bread, and bitter herbs (Exod. 12:15–20; 13:3–10; Lev. 23:5; Num. 9:5; 28:16; Deut. 16:1). The Passover was scrupulously observed by Israel's great leaders, including Joshua (Josh. 5:10), Hezekiah (2 Chron. 30:1), Josiah (2 Kings 23:21–23; 2 Chron. 35:1–18), and the returned exiles (Ezra 6:19).

patriarch   The male head (father) of an ancient family line, a venerable tribal founder or leader; especially **(1)** the early ancestors of humanity listed in Genesis 4–5, known as the "antediluvian patriarchs"; **(2)** prominent "fathers" living after the Flood to the time of Abraham (Gen. 11); **(3)** the immediate progenitors of the Israelites: Abraham, Isaac, and Jacob (Gen. 12–50; Exod. 3:6; 6:2–8).

Peniel   A site on the Jabbok River in Jordan where Jacob wrestled with El (God) and thereby won a blessing (Gen. 33:22–33).

Pentateuch   From a Greek word meaning "five scrolls," the term denotes the first five books of the Hebrew Bible, the Torah.

Pentecost   Also known as the Feast of Weeks (Exod. 34:22; Deut. 16:10), the Feast of Harvest (Exod.

23:16), and the Day of the First Fruits (Num. 28:26), Pentecost was a one-day celebration held fifty days after Passover at the juncture of May and June.

Peor A mountain in Moab on which King Balak commanded the prophet Balaam to build seven altars (Num. 23:28–30), Peor may also have been the place where Israel sinned by worshiping Baal (Num. 25:1–18; Josh. 22:17).

Peraea (Perea) A name the historian Flavius Josephus gave the area that the Hebrew Bible called the land "beyond" or "across" (east of) the Jordan River (Gen. 50:10; Num. 22:1).

pericope A term used in form criticism to describe a literary unit (a saying, anecdote, parable, or brief narrative) that forms a complete entity in itself and is attached to its context by later editorial commentary.

Persepolis A capital of the Persian Empire established by Darius I (522–486 B.C.E.) and burned by Alexander the Great (330 B.C.E.) (2 Macc. 9:2).

Persia A large Asian territory southeast of Elam inhabited by Indo-European (Ayrian, hence "Iran") peoples, Persia became a world power under Cyrus the Great, who united Media and Persia (549 B.C.E.); conquered Lydia (546 B.C.E.) and Babylon (539 B.C.E.), including its former dominion, Palestine; then permitted the formerly captive Jews to return to their homeland (2 Chron. 36:20–22; Ezra 1). Under the emperor Darius I (522–486 B.C.E.), the Jerusalem Temple was rebuilt (Ezra 3–6). A son of Darius, Xerxes I (486–465 B.C.E.) was probably the Ahasuerus of the Book of Esther (Esther 1:2; 2:1; 3:1; 8:1). Artaxerxes I (465–423 B.C.E.) decreed the return of two other exile groups under Ezra and Nehemiah.

personification A literary term denoting the attribution of personal qualities to an object or abstraction, such as the biblical practice of portraying the divine attribute of Wisdom (Hebrew, *hochmah;* Greek, *sophia*) as a female companion of YHWH who assists the Deity at creation and acts as his mediator between divinity and humanity (Prov. 8:1–36; Ecclus. 24:1–21; Wisd. of Sol. 7:22–9:18).

pesher A Hebrew word denoting an analysis or interpretation of Scripture, it is applied to the commentaries (*pesharim*) found among the Dead Sea Scrolls.

pharaoh The title of Egypt's king, commonly used in place of a ruler's proper name in the Hebrew Bible. Thus, the pharaohs who confiscated Abraham's wife (Gen. 12:14–20), rewarded Joseph (Gen. 41:37–57), enslaved the Israelites (Exod. 1:8–22), and opposed Moses (Exod. 5:1–6:1; 6:27–15:19) are all anonymous, although many scholars believe that the pharaoh of the Exodus was Rameses II (c. 1290–1224 B.C.E.). Solomon later made Egyptian pharaohs his allies (1 Kings 3:1; 7:8). Pharaoh Shishak (Sheshonk I) sacked the Jerusalem Temple during King Rehoboam's time (c. 922–915 B.C.E.) (1 Kings 14:25–28; 2 Chron. 12:2–9). Pharaoh Necho killed King Josiah at Megiddo but was later defeated by Nebuchadnezzar at Carchemish (2 Kings 23:29–34; 24:7; 2 Chron. 35:20–36:4).

Pharisees A leading religious movement or sect in Judaism during the last two centuries B.C.E. and the two first centuries C.E., the Pharisees were probably descendants of the hasidim who opposed Antiochus IV's attempts to destroy the Mosaic faith. Their name may derive from the Hebrew *parush* (separated) because their rigorous observance of the law bred a separatist view toward common life. Although the New Testament typically presents them as Jesus' opponents, their views on resurrection and the afterlife anticipated Christian teachings.

Philistines A people from Aegean Sea islands (called Caphtor in Amos 9:7) who settled along the southern coast of Palestine during the twelfth century B.C.E. to become the Israelites' chief rivals during the period of the judges and early monarchy (c. 1200–1000 B.C.E.) (Josh. 13:2–4; Judg. 1:18–19; 13:1–16:31; 1 Sam. 4:2–7:14; 13:1–14:46; 17:1–54; 2 Sam. 5:17–25; 8:1–2; 21:15–18; see also Jer. 47:1–7; Zeph. 2:4–7).

Philo Judaeus The most influential philosopher of Hellenistic Judaism, Philo was a Greek-educated Jew living in Alexandria, Egypt (c. 20 B.C.E.–50 C.E.), who promoted a method of interpreting the Hebrew Bible allegorically.

Phinehas A grandson of Aaron, son of Eleazar, Israel's third High Priest (Num. 10:8–10; 25:6–13; Josh. 22:13, 30–32; 24:33).

Phoenicia A narrow coastal territory along the northeast Mediterranean, lying between the Lebanon range on the east and the sea on the west. It included the ports of Tyre and Sidon. Notable Hebrew Bible Phoenicians are Ethbaal, king of Tyre (1 Kings 16:21); his daughter Jezebel, wife of Ahab (1 Kings 18:19); Hiram, king of Tyre (2 Sam. 5:11; 1 Kings 5:1–12; 2 Chron. 2:3–16); and Hiram, the architect-decorator of Solomon's Temple (1 Kings 7:13–47; 2 Chron. 2:13).

phylactery One of the two small leather pouches containing copies of four scriptural passages (Exod. 13:1–10, 11–16; Deut. 6:4–9; 11:13–21), worn on the left arm and forehead by Jewish men during weekday prayers (Exod. 13:9, 16; Deut. 6:8; 11:18).

Plato The Greek philosopher (427–347 B.C.E.) who postulated the existence of a dualistic universe consisting of an invisible spiritual realm containing ideal forms of everything that exists and an inferior material realm composed of imperfect replicas of those forms. Plato's view of the immortal human soul and its posthumous destiny greatly influenced virtually all subsequent Western thought, including that of some Hellenized Jews.

policy law Also known as *apodictic,* or *absolute,* law, this term refers to laws stated unconditionally, such as the Ten Commandments (Decalogue). *See also* apodictic law.

polytheism The belief in more than one god, the most common form of religion in the ancient world.

Pompey A leading Roman general and rival of Julius Caesar, with whom he established a temporary political alliance known as the First Triumvirate, Pompey (106–49 B.C.E.) conquered much of the eastern Mediterranean region for Rome, including Syria and Judea (63 B.C.E.).

Potiphar The head of Pharaoh's bodyguard who placed Joseph in charge of his household but later threw him in prison when the Hebrew slave was accused of seducing Potiphar's wife (Gen. 37:36; 39:1).

priestly document The priestly composition, referred to as P. This is the final written addition to the Pentateuch, consisting largely of genealogical, statistical, and legal material compiled during and after the Babylonian exile (c. 550–450 B.C.E.). Major blocks of P occur in Exodus 25–31 and 35–40, Leviticus 1–27, and Numbers 1–10. P incorporated the earlier J and E sources and provided an editorial framework for the entire Torah. Some recent scholars believe that P is responsible for most of the Pentateuch.

prophet One who preaches or proclaims the word or will of his or her Deity (Amos 3:7–8; Deut. 18:9–22). A true prophet in Israel was regarded as divinely inspired. *See navi.*

Prophets (Nevi'im) The second major division of the Hebrew Bible, including Joshua through 2 Kings, Isaiah, Jeremiah, Ezekiel, and the twelve Minor Prophets.

proverb A brief saying that memorably expresses a familiar or useful bit of folk wisdom, usually of a practical or prudential nature.

Providence A quasi-religious concept in which God is viewed as the force sustaining and guiding human destiny. It assumes that events occur as part of a divine plan or purpose working for the ultimate triumph of Good.

psalm A sacred song or poem used in praise or worship of the Deity, particularly those in the Book of Psalms.

Pseudepigrapha **(1)** Literally, books falsely ascribed to eminent biblical figures of the past, such as Enoch, Noah, Moses, or Isaiah. **(2)** A collection of religious books outside the Hebrew Bible canon or Apocrypha that were composed in Hebrew, Aramaic, and Greek from about 300 B.C.E. to 200 C.E.

pseudonymity A literary practice, common among Jewish writers of the last two centuries B.C.E. and the first two centuries C.E, of writing or publishing a book in the name of a famous religious figure of the past. Thus, an anonymous author of about 168 B.C.E. ascribed his work to Daniel, who supposedly lived during the sixth century B.C.E.

psyche The Greek word for "soul," which such philosophers as Pythagoras, Socrates, and Plato taught was the invisible center of rational consciousness and personality that survived bodily death to experience rewards or penalties in the afterlife. Although biblical concepts of the soul do not presume its inherent immortality, the Greek philosophic position deeply influenced later Judeo-Christian teachings on the subject.

Ptolemy **(1)** Ptolemy I (323–285 B.C.E.) was a Macedonian general who assumed rulership of Egypt after the death of Alexander the Great. The Ptolemaic dynasty controlled Egypt and its dominions until 31 B.C.E., when the Romans came to power. **(2)** Ptolemy II (285–246 B.C.E.) supposedly authorized the translation of the Hebrew Bible into Greek (the Septuagint).

Purim A Jewish nationalistic festival held on the fourteenth and fifteenth days of Adar (February-March) and based on events in the Book of Esther.

Queen of Heaven A Semitic goddess of love and fertility worshiped in various forms throughout the ancient Near East. Known as Ishtar to the Babylonians, she was denounced by Jeremiah but worshiped by

Jewish refugees in Egypt after the fall of Jerusalem (Jer. 7:18; 44:17–19, 25).

Qumran   Ruins of an Essene monastic community located near the northwest corner of the Dead Sea, near which the Essene library (Dead Sea Scrolls) were hidden in caves. The Romans destroyed it in 68 C.E.

rabbi   A Jewish title (meaning "master" or "teacher") given to scholars learned in the Torah.

Rabbi Akiba   A second-century-C.E. rabbinic scholar who was instrumental in gathering together the comments and rulings of his predecessors in the form of the Mishnah; for a time he was an active supporter of bar Kochba's messianic candidacy, and was martyred by the Romans after the revolt failed.

Rachel   The daughter of Laban, second and favorite wife of Jacob, and mother of Joseph and Benjamin (Gen. 29:6–30; 30:1–24; 35:16–19). When Rachel fled her father's house with Jacob, she stole Laban's household gods (Gen. 31:32–35). Jeremiah prophesied that Rachel (Israel) would "weep for her children," fulfilled during Babylon's sack of Jerusalem (Jer. 31:15; see also Ruth 4:11).

Rahab   **(1)** A prostitute of Jericho, possibly a priestess in a Canaanite fertility cult, who hid Israelite spies and was spared her city's destruction (Josh. 2:1–24; 6:25; Ps. 87:4; Heb. 11:31). **(2)** A mythological sea monster, the dragon of chaos, whom YHWH subdued before his creation of the universe (Ps. 89:10); also a symbol of Egypt (Ps. 87:4; Isa. 30:7).

Rameses (Ramses)   One of the two "store cities" that the enslaved Israelites built for Pharaoh (probably Rameses II) (Exod. 1:11; 12:37; Num. 33:3–5).

Rameses II   The ruler of Egypt (c. 1290–1224 B.C.E.) whom many scholars think was the pharaoh of the Exodus.

Ramoth-Gilead   A town in Gilead, east of Jordan near the Syrian border, that was a city of refuge (Deut. 4:43; Josh. 20:8) and a Levitical center (Josh. 21:38; 1 Chron. 6:80) for the tribe of Gad. Ahab of Israel (869–850 B.C.E.) was killed trying to recapture it from Aram (Syria) (1 Kings 22:1–38; 2 Chron. 18:1–34), and the usurper Jehu was anointed there (2 Kings 9:1–21).

Ras Shamra   *See* Ugarit.

Rebekah (Rebecca)   The daughter of Milcah and Bethuel, son of Abraham's brother Nahor (Gen. 24:15, 47), and sister of Laban (Gen. 25:20), whom Abraham's representative found at Haran and brought back to Canaan as a bride for Isaac (Gen. 24). Of Esau and Jacob, the twin sons she bore Isaac, she preferred Jacob and helped him trick his dying husband into giving him the paternal blessing (Gen. 25:21–28; 27:5–30).

Rechab   The father of Jehonadab (Jonadab), who assisted Jehu in exterminating Ahab's entire household and associates (2 Kings 10:1–28). The Rechabites were a group of ascetics who abstained from wine, settled dwellings, and other aspects of what they considered urban corruption.

redaction criticism   A method of analyzing written texts that tries to define the purpose and literary procedures of redactors (editors) who compile and edit older documents, transforming shorter works into longer ones, as did the redactor who collected and ordered the words of the prophets into their present canonical form.

redactor   An editor. *See* redaction criticism.

Rehoboam   A son of Solomon and Naamah (an Ammonite princess), the last ruler of the united kingdom (922–915 B.C.E.), whose harsh policies resulted in the ten northern tribes' deserting the Davidic monarchy in Judah and forming the independent northern kingdom of Israel (922 B.C.E.) (1 Kings 11:43; 12:1–24; 14:21–31; 2 Chron. 9:31–12:16) and in Pharaoh Shishak's (Sheshonk I) despoiling the Jerusalem Temple (1 Kings 14:25–28).

rephaim   The Hebrew Bible's term for the shades of the dead, which, like the souls in Homer's portrayal of Hades (*Odyssey* XI), had a grim, joyless posthumous quasi-existence in the depths of Sheol (Ps. 88:10). The term is also applied to the pre-Israelite inhabitants of Transjordan (Gen. 14:5; Deut. 2:10–11) and to Philistine giants (2 Sam. 21:16, 18, 20; 1 Chron. 20:4, 6, 8). The connection between these diverse usages of *rephaim* is unknown.

resurrection   The returning of the dead to life, a late Hebrew Bible belief (Isa. 26:19; Dan. 12:2–3, 13) that first became prevalent in Judaism during the time of the Maccabees (after 168 B.C.E.) and became a part of the Pharisees' doctrine. The prophets Elijah and Elisha (1 Kings 17:17–24; 2 Kings 4:18–37) performed several resuscitations of the recently dead.

Reuben   **(1)** The son of Jacob and Leah, eldest of his father's twelve sons (Gen. 29:32; Num. 26:5), Reuben slept with his father's concubine (Gen. 35:22), which cost him a paternal blessing (Gen. 49:3–4), but he defended Joseph against his brothers (Gen. 37:21–30). **(2)** The northern Israelite tribe supposedly descended from Reuben (Num. 32:1–38) that along with Gad settled in the highlands east of the Jordan River.

rhetorical criticism   A method of textual analysis that studies not only the form and structure of a given literary work but the distinctive style of the author.

Roman Empire   The international, interracial government centered in Rome, Italy, that conquered and administered the entire Mediterranean region from Gaul (France and southern Germany) in the northwest to Egypt in the southeast and ruled the Jews of Palestine from 63 B.C.E. until Hadrian's destruction of Jerusalem during the second Jewish Revolt (132–135 C.E.).

Rosetta Stone   A granite block bearing the same message inscribed in both Greek and ancient Egyptian hieroglyphics, a bilingual inscription that enabled scholars to decipher the language of the pharaohs. Discovered in 1799 and translated by the French linguist Champollion, it records a proclamation by Ptolemy V (c. 203–181 B.C.E.).

Royal Covenant   *See* Davidic Covenant.

ruach   In biblical Hebrew, a word meaning "wind," "breath," or "spirit" (Gen. 1:2). It can be interpreted as the mysterious power or presence of God operating in nature and human society, implementing the divine will and inspiring individuals or communities to carry out the divine purpose.

Ruel   In J's account, a priest of Midian and the father-in-law of Moses, whom E calls Jethro (Exod. 2:15–22). *See* Jethro.

Ruth   A widow from Moab who married Boaz of Bethlehem and became an ancestor of King David (Ruth 4:17).

Saba (Sheba)   A Semitic kingdom in western Arabia noted for its merchants and luxury trade but best known for the visit of one of its queens to Solomon's court (1 Kings 10:1–13; 2 Chron. 9:1–12).

Sabbath   The seventh day of the Jewish week, sacred to YHWH and dedicated to rest and worship. Enjoined upon Israel as a sign of YHWH's covenant (Exod. 20:8–11; 23:12; 31:12–17; Lev. 23:3; 24:1–9; Deut. 5:12–15) and a memorial of YHWH's repose after six days of creation, the Sabbath was strictly observed by leaders of the returned exiles (Neh. 13:15–22; Isa. 56:2–6; Ezek. 46:1–7).

Sabbatical Year   According to the Torah, every seventh year was to be a Sabbath among years, a time when fields were left fallow, native-born slaves freed, and outstanding debts canceled (Exod. 21:2–6; 23:10–13; Lev. 25:1–19; Deut. 15:1–6).

sacrifice   In ancient religion, something precious—usually an unblemished animal, fruit, or grain—offered to a god and thereby made sacred. The Mosaic Law required the regular ritual slaughter of sacrificial animals and birds (Lev. 1:1–7:38; 16:1–17:14; Deut. 15:19–23; etc.).

Sadducees   A conservative Jewish sect of the first century B.C.E. and first century C.E. composed largely of wealthy and politically influential landowners. Unlike the Pharisees, the Sadducees recognized only the Torah as binding and rejected the Prophets and Writings, denying both resurrection and a judgment in the afterlife. An aristocracy controlling the priesthood and Temple, they cooperated with the Roman rulers of Palestine, a collusion that made them unpopular with the common people.

saints   Holy ones, persons of exceptional virtue and sanctity, believers outstandingly faithful despite persecution (Dan. 7:18–21; 8:13).

Salem   The Canaanite settlement ruled by the king-priest Melchizedek (Gen. 14:18), later identified with Jerusalem (Ps. 76:2).

Samaria   The capital of the northern kingdom (Israel), Samaria was founded by Omri (c. 876–869 B.C.E.) (1 Kings 16:24–25) and included a temple and altar of Baal (1 Kings 16:32). The Assyrians destroyed it in 721 B.C.E. (2 Kings 17), a fate the prophets warned awaited Jerusalem (Isa. 8:4; 10:9–11; Mic. 1:1–7).

Samaritans   Inhabitants of the city or territory of Samaria, the central region of Palestine lying west of the Jordan River. According to a probably biased account in 2 Kings 17, the Samaritans were regarded by orthodox Jews as descendants of foreigners who had intermarried with survivors of the northern kingdom's fall to Assyria (721 B.C.E.). Separated from the rest of Judaism after about 400 B.C.E., they had a Bible consisting of their own edition of the Pentateuch (Torah) and a temple on Mount Gerizim, which was later destroyed by John Hyrcanus (128 B.C.E.).

Samson   The son of Manoah of the tribe of Dan, Samson was a Nazirite judge of Israel famous for his supernatural strength, abortive love affair with Delilah, and spectacular destruction of the Philistine temple of Dagon (Judg. 13–16).

Samuel The son of Hannah and Elkanah, an Ephraimite (1 Sam. 1:1–2), Samuel was Israel's last judge (1 Sam. 7:15), a prophet and seer (1 Sam. 9:9) who also performed priestly functions (1 Sam. 2:18, 27, 35; 7:9–12). Trained by the High Priest Eli at Shiloh (1 Sam. 2:11–21; 3:1–10), he became the single greatest influence in Israel's transition from the tribal confederacy to monarchy under Saul, whom he anointed king (1 Sam. 8:1–10:27) but later rejected in favor of David (1 Sam. 13:8–15; 15:10–35).

sanctuary A holy place dedicated to the worship of a god and believed to confer personal security to those who took refuge in it. Solomon's Temple on Mount Zion in Jerusalem was such a sacred edifice, although Jeremiah denounced those who trusted in its power to save a disobedient people from punishment (Jer. 7, 26).

Sanhedrin The supreme judicial council of the Jews from about the third century B.C.E. until the Romans destroyed Jerusalem in 70 C.E., its deliberations were led by the High Priest (2 Chron. 19:5–11).

Sarah The wife and half-sister of Abraham (Gen. 11:29; 16:1; 20:12), Sarah traveled with him from Ur to Haran and ultimately to Canaan, and after a long period of barrenness bore him a single son, Isaac (Gen. 18:9–15; 21:1–21). She died in Hebron (Gen. 23:2) and was buried at Machpelah in Canaan (Gen. 23:19).

Sardis The capital of the kingdom of Lydia (modern Turkey), captured by Cyrus the Great (546 B.C.E.); later part of the Roman province of Asia and the site of a cult of Cybele, a pagan fertility goddess.

Sargon I The Semitic founder of a Mesopotamian Empire incorporating ancient Sumer and Akkad and stretching from Elam to the Mediterranean (about 2360 B.C.E.).

Sargon II The successor of Shalmaneser V and king of Assyria (722–705 B.C.E.) who completed his predecessor's three-year siege of Samaria and captured the city, bringing the northern kingdom (Israel) to an end in 721 B.C.E. (Isa. 20:1; 2 Kings 17).

Satan In the Hebrew Bible, the "Satan" appears as a prosecutor in the heavenly court among the "sons of God" (Job 1–2; Zech. 3:1–3) and only later as a tempter (1 Chron. 21:1; cf. 2 Sam. 24:1). Although the Hebrew Bible says virtually nothing about Satan's

origin, the pseudepigraphal writings contain much legendary material about his fall from heaven and the establishment of a hierarchy of demons and devils.

Saul The son of Kish, a Benjaminite, and the first king of Israel (c. 1020–1000 B.C.E.), Saul was anointed by Samuel to meet the Philistine crisis, which demanded a strong centralized leadership (1 Sam. 9:1–10:27). He defeated the Ammonites (1 Sam. 11:1–11) and Philistines at Geba and Michmash but rapidly lost support after antagonizing Samuel (1 Sam. 13:8–15) and refusing to kill the Amalekite king (1 Sam. 15:7–35). He was also upstaged by David, of whom he became intensely jealous (1 Sam. 18:6–24:23). Saul and his son Jonathan were killed by the Philistines at the Battle of Gilboa (1 Sam. 31) and commemorated by one of David's most beautiful psalms (2 Sam. 1:17–27).

Savior One who saves from danger or destruction, a term applied to YHWH in the Hebrew Bible (Ps. 106:21; Isa. 43:1–13; 63:7–9; Hos. 13:4).

scapegoat According to Leviticus 16, a sacrificial goat on whose head Israel's High Priest placed the people's collective sins on the Day of Atonement, after which the goat was sent out into the desert to Azazel (possibly a demon). The term has come to signify anyone who bears the blame for others (Isa. 53).

scribes Professional copyists who recorded commercial, royal, and religious texts and served as clerks, secretaries, and archivists at Israel's royal court and Temple (2 Kings 12:10; 19:2; Ezra 4:8; 2 Chron. 34:8; Jer. 36:18). After the Jews' return from exile, professional teachers or "wise men" preserved and interpreted the Mosaic Torah (Ezra 7:6; Neh. 7:73–8:18).

Scripture Writings that a religious community regards as sacred and authoritative in regulating their group's beliefs and behavior, such as the Hebrew Bible (Tanak), the Vedas, the Upanishads, the Bhagavad Gita, the New Testament, and the Qur'an (Koran).

scroll A roll of papyrus, leather, or parchment such as those on which the Hebrew Bible and New Testament were written. The rolls were made of sheets about 9–11 inches high and 5–6 inches wide, sewed together to make a strip up to 25–30 feet long, which was wound around a stick and unrolled when read (Isa. 34:4; Jer. 36).

Scythians A fierce nomadic people from north and east of the Black Sea who swept southward toward

Egypt and Judah about 626 B.C.E. Jeremiah prophesied that Judah would be devastated (Jer. 4:5–31; 5:15–17; 6:1–8, 22–26), and Zephaniah saw the invasion as a sign that the Day of YHWH had arrived (Zeph. 1:7–8, 14–18); but the Scythians were bribed by Pharaoh Psammetichus I (664–610 B.C.E.) and returned north by the coastal route without attacking Palestine.

Sea of Reeds   A body of water or swampland bordering the Red Sea that the Israelites miraculously crossed during their flight from Egypt (Exod. 14:5–15:21). The origin of the name is uncertain because there are no reeds in the Red Sea, which is more than 7200 feet deep.

Second Isaiah   Also known as Deutero-Isaiah, the name assigned to the anonymous prophet responsible for Chapters 40–55 of the Book of Isaiah and to the work itself.

Second Temple period   The span of Judean history from the rebuilding of the Jerusalem Temple in 515 B.C.E. to the Temple's destruction by the Romans in 70 C.E., a period in which Judea was consecutively occupied by Persians, Greeks, and Romans.

seer   A clairvoyant or diviner who experiences ecstatic visions (1 Sam. 9:9–11); forerunner of the prophets.

Seir   A mountain range running through Edom almost to the Gulf of 'Aqaba through which the Israelites passed during their desert wanderings (Deut. 2:1; 33:2). Seir was regarded as the home of the Esau tribes, rivals of Israel (Gen. 36:8, 20–21; Josh. 24:4), and was also an early name for Edom (Gen. 32:3; 35:20–21, 30; Num. 14:18).

Seleucids   The Macedonian Greek dynasty founded by Alexander's general Seleucus (ruled 312–280 B.C.E.), centered in Syria with Antioch as its capital. After defeating the Ptolemies of Egypt, it controlled Palestine from 198 to 165 B.C.E., after which the Maccabeans defeated the forces of Antiochus IV and eventually drove the Seleucids from Judea (142 B.C.E.) (1 and 2 Macc.)

Seleucus   *See* Seleucids.

Semites   According to Genesis 10:21–31, peoples descended from Noah's son Shem, whose progeny included Elam, Asshur, Arpacshad (Hebrews and Arabs), Lud (Lydians), and Aram (Syrians) (Gen. 10:22). In modern usage, the term applies to linguistic rather than to ethnic groups, such as those who employ one of a common family of inflectional languages, including Akkadian, Aramaic, Hebrew, and Arabic.

Sennacherib   The son of Sargon II and king of Assyria (704–681 B.C.E.). In 701 B.C.E., Sennacherib devastated Tyre and besieged Jerusalem, after which he levied heavy tribute upon King Hezekiah of Judah (2 Kings 18). A clay prism recording Sennacherib's version of the Judean campaign tallies well with 2 Kings 18:14–16 but strikingly diverges from the story of 185,000 Assyrian soldiers slain by YHWH's angel in a single night (2 Kings 19:10–35; Isa. 37:9–36).

Septuagint (LXX)   A Greek translation of the Hebrew Bible traditionally attributed to about seventy Palestinian scholars during the reign of Ptolemy II (285–246 B.C.E.), the Septuagint was actually the work of several generations of Alexandrine translators, begun about 250 B.C.E. and not complete until the first century C.E. The later additions to the Septuagint were deleted from the standard Hebrew Bible (Masoretic Text) but included in the Christian Scriptures as the Apocrypha.

seraphim   Heavenly beings, usually depicted with six wings (Isa. 6), who attended the throne of God; perhaps derived from Assyrian or Egyptian mythology.

serpent   A common symbol in Near Eastern fertility cults, a snake was the original tempter of humanity (Gen. 3–4) and a symbol of Assyria, Babylon (Isa. 27:1), and the Israelite tribe of Dan (Gen. 49:17). A bronze image of a snake that was used to heal the Israelites during a plague of snakes in the wilderness (Num. 21:4–9) was later destroyed by King Hezekiah (2 Kings 18:4).

Servant Songs   Four poems in Second Isaiah (Isa. 40–55) emphasizing the role of YHWH's chosen servant (42:1–9; 49:1–7; 50:4–11; 52:13–53:12). For identification of Israel as the servant, see Isaiah 41:8; 44:1–2, 21; 45:4; 49:5; cf. 43:1–12. The most controversial poem is that describing an unnamed "Suffering Servant" (Isa. 52:13–53:12).

Seth   The third son of Adam and Eve (Gen. 4:25–26; 5:2–8), cited as the first man to invoke YHWH's sacred name.

Shadrach   The name the leading eunuch of Babylon gave the Hebrew boy Hananiah (Dan. 1:7; 2:49). Along with Abednego and Meshach, he survived incarceration in a fiery furnace (Dan. 3:1–30).

Shalmaneser   The name of five Assyrian kings, two of whom appear in the Hebrew Bible. **(1)** Shalmaneser

III (859–824 B.C.E.), one of Assyria's most effective rulers, defeated a coalition of Syrian and Palestinian states led by Ben-hadad (Hadadezer) of Damascus and King Ahab of Israel, a defense league that disintegrated largely because of Elijah's and Elisha's interference in Israelite and Syrian politics (2 Kings 8:7–15, 9–10). Shalmaneser's Black Obelisk shows either Jehu, who overthrew Ahab's dynasty, or one of his representatives groveling at the Assyrian king's feet and paying him tribute. **(2)** Shalmaneser V (726–722 B.C.E.), successor to Tiglath-pileser III, extorted tribute from Hoshea, last ruler of the northern kingdom (732–724 B.C.E.). When Hoshea later refused payment, Shalmaneser captured him and laid siege to Israel's capital, Samaria, for three years but died before he could take the city (2 Kings 17:3–5; 18:9).

Shamash   The Babylonian sun god associated with justice and prophecy, the Akkadian counterpart to the Sumerian Utu.

Shaphan   The scribal secretary of state for King Josiah (640–609 B.C.E.), to whom Hilkiah the priest entrusted the "lost" Book of the Law (probably Deuteronomy) found during repairs on the Jerusalem Temple. After reading it to Josiah, Shaphan was sent to ask the prophetess Huldah what YHWH wished done with the book. He may have been instrumental in the subsequent religious reforms (2 Kings 22:3–20).

Sharon, Plain of   The most fertile part of the coastal plain of Palestine, stretching about fifty miles north to the headland of Mount Carmel, belonged to the northern kingdom after 922 B.C.E. Its desirable fields became an image of the messianic bounty (Isa. 35:2).

Sheba, queen of   *See* Saba.

Shechem   **(1)** The son of Hamor the Hivite from whom Jacob bought land in Canaan and who later raped and wished to marry Jacob's daughter Dinah (Gen. 33:18–20; 34:1–31). Despite Hamor's friendly wish to ally his clan with Jacob's, Simon and Levi led Jacob's sons in a murderous attack on Shechem's clan to avenge their sister's dishonor. **(2)** An ancient Canaanite city located about forty miles north of Jerusalem in the hill country later allocated to the tribe of Ephraim, Shechem was the first site in Canaan that Abraham visited (Gen. 12:6) and the first place where the Hebrews came in touch with Canaanite culture (Gen. 33:18–20; 34:1–31). Here Joshua held a covenant renewal ceremony uniting the Israelite tribes under YHWH and, according to some scholars, in-

cluding native tribes friendly to the Israelites. Abimelech attempted to make himself king here (Judg. 9), and here Rehoboam came to be crowned (1 Kings 12), only to be divested of his northern territories by Jeroboam I, who made Shechem his capital. Although the Deuteronomists mention its religious importance (Deut. 11:26–32; 17:1–26; Josh. 8:30–37), Shechem fell into obscurity until the mid-fourth century B.C.E. when the Samaritans built a temple on Mount Gerizim. The city was destroyed by John Hyrcanus in the late second century B.C.E. but rebuilt as Flavia Neapolis.

Shem   Noah's oldest son, brother of Ham and Japheth, the eponymous ancestor of the Semites, including the Arameans, Hebrews, Akkadians, and Arabs (Gen. 5:32; 9:21–27; 10:1).

Shema   Judaism's supreme declaration of covenant faith, expressed in the words of Deuteronomy 6:4–9 beginning "Listen [Hebrew *shema*, "hear"], Israel, YHWH our God is the one YHWH." It also includes Deuteronomy 11:13–21 and Numbers 14:37–41.

Sheol   According to the Hebrew Bible, the subterranean region to which the "shades" of all the dead descended, a place of intense gloom, hopelessness, and virtual unconsciousness for its inhabitants. The term was translated *Hades* in the Greek Septuagint and in later Hellenistic times was regarded as an abode of the dead awaiting resurrection (Gen. 42:38; 1 Sam. 2:6; Job 7:9; 14:13–14; 26:6; Pss. 6:5; 16:10; 55:15; 139:8; Prov. 27:20; Eccles. 9:10; Isa. 14:15; 28:15; 38:10, 18; Hos. 13:14; Jon. 2:2).

Sheshbazzar   A member of the royal house of Judah who is appointed by Cyrus to be the first governor of the province of Judah and who accompanies the first wave of returning Judahites in 538 B.C.E. (Ezra 1:8, 11; 5:14, 16). In addition to bringing back the sacred vessels of the first Temple that were taken away by Nebuchadnezzar, Sheshbazzar also lays the foundations of the new Temple and then mysteriously disappears from history. His name appears in 1 Chronicles 3:18 as Shenazzar, and some have speculated that his name may be an cryptogram for the Judahite prince Zerubbabel.

shewbread   The term the King James Version uses for the twelve loaves of consecrated unleavened bread placed in the Holy Place of the Tabernacle and Temple (Exod. 25:30; Lev. 24:5–9; 1 Sam. 21:2–6).

shibboleth   The password Jephthah used to determine whether fugitives from a battle between the

Ephraimites and his own Gileadites were his people or the enemy's. The Ephraimites pronounced *sh* as *s* (Judg. 12:4–6). In contemporary usage, the term refers to the slogans or distinctive values of a party or class.

Shiloh   A prominent town and religious center that the Israelites established in the highlands of Ephraim, where Joshua assigned the tribes of Israel their territorial allotments (Josh. 18). Apparently a headquarters for the tribal confederacy during the time of the judges (Josh. 21:2; 22:9; Judg. 21:15–24; 1 Sam. 2; 3:30; 12–17), the Ark of the Covenant was kept there until the Philistine war, when it was taken to a camp at Ebenezer, where the Philistines captured it (1 Sam. 4). Returned, it was not again placed in Shiloh (1 Sam. 6:21–7:2), possibly because the Philistines had devastated the site. Jeremiah predicted that YHWH would deal with Jerusalem as he had with Shiloh (Jer. 7:12–15; 26:6–9).

Shinar, Plain of   An alluvial lowland between the Tigris and Euphrates rivers at the head of the Persian Gulf. Settled by Sumerians about 4000 B.C.E., it was later known as Babylonia after the principal city in the area (Gen. 11:2; 14:1, 9). This region is the traditional homeland of Abraham, ancestor of the Israelites (Gen. 11:31; see also Isa. 11:11; Zech. 5:11; Dan. 1:2).

Shishak   An Egyptian pharaoh (Sheshonk or Sheshonq I) (935–914 B.C.E.), founder of the Twenty-Second Dynasty, who during Solomon's reign gave asylum to the rebellious Jeroboam (1 Kings 11:40) but later invaded Judah and stripped the Temple of many of its treasures (1 Kings 14:25–28; 2 Chron. 12:2–9).

Shittim   The site of the Israelites' encampment in Moab, opposite Jericho, prior to their crossing the Jordan River into Canaan (Num. 24–36).

shrine   A sacred place or altar at which a god is worshiped, usually with ritual sacrifices. The discovery of Deuteronomy (621 B.C.E.), which prohibited sacrifice at any but a designated central sanctuary (assumed to be the Jerusalem Temple), inspired Josiah's sweeping destruction of all rival shrines in Judah and Samaria (2 Kings 22–23; 2 Chron. 34–35).

Shunammite   The "Shulamite" bride who is praised in the Song of Solomon 6:13; the origin and meaning of the name are uncertain.

Sibyl   Title given Apollo's virgin prophetess, particularly the god's spokeswoman at Cumae near the Bay

of Naples in Italy. According to the pseudepigraphal collection known as the Sibylline Oracles, the Sibyl was a daughter-in-law of Noah (Sib. Or. 8:327).

Sibylline Oracles   A collection (c. 250 B.C.E.–550 C.E.) of futuristic visions written in imitation of Greco-Roman prophecies attributed to Apollo's oracle, the Sibyl. It incorporates Greco-Roman, Jewish, and Christian apocalyptic utterances.

Sicarii   Jewish revolutionaries who actively opposed Roman occupation of Judea during and immediately after the first Jewish Revolt. Josephus uses this obviously disparaging term (it means "dagger men") to describe what he perceives as a terrorist movement committed not only to driving the Roman army out of Judea but also to destroying the priestly and Sadducean leadership. After the fall of Jerusalem in 70 C.E., some of the Sicarii take refuge at Masada while others flee to Alexandria, where (according to Josephus) they incite violent conflict between Jews and Greeks.

Sidon   A wealthy Phoenician port city (Gen. 10:15, 19; 1 Chron. 1:13) that suffered repeated destructions during the Assyrian, Babylonian, and Persian periods (Jer. 25:22; 27:3; Ezek. 27:8; 28:21–23) but was rebuilt in Hellenistic times. *Siddonians* is a common biblical term for Phoenicians.

Simeon   The second son of Jacob and Leah (Gen. 29:33) who helped avenge his sister's rape upon the people of Shechem (Gen. 34). The tribal group named after him, the Simeonites, was probably absorbed by Judah and is seldom mentioned in the Hebrew Bible (Deut. 27:12).

simile   A comparison, usually to illustrate an unexpected resemblance between a familiar object and a novel idea.

Sin   An Akkadian deity known to the Sumerians as Nanna, the moon god.

Sin, Wilderness of   A desert plain on the Sinai Peninsula through which the Israelites passed on their way to Mount Sinai (Exod. 16:1; 17:1; Num. 33:11–12).

Sinai   (1) A peninsula at whose southern apex the Gulf of 'Aqaba joins the Gulf of Suez at the head of the Red Sea. Its 150-mile inverted base borders the Mediterranean, forming the boundary between Egypt and Palestine. (2) According to the J and P accounts, Mount Sinai, the sacred mountain in the wilderness where Moses experienced YHWH's call (Exod. 3, 6) and to which he led the Israelites from Egypt for YHWH's revelation of the Torah (Exod. 19–24,

34:4). This site, which has never been positively identified, is called Horeb by E and D (Exod. 3:1; 17:6; Deut. 1:6; 4:10).

Sisera The Canaanite leader whose forces Deborah and Barak defeated and whom Jael, wife of Heber the Kenite, murdered in her tent (Judg. 4–5).

Sitz-im-Leben A German term used in form criticism to denote the social and cultural environment out of which a particular biblical unit grew and developed.

Socrates The Athenian philosopher (c. 469–399 B.C.E.) and mentor of Plato who taught that life's purpose was to seek the good and prepare the soul for immortality in the afterlife. After being executed for questioning conventional ideas about the gods, he became the subject of his disciples' memoirs, including very different accounts by Plato and Xenophon.

Sodom Along with Gomorrah, Admah, Zebolim, and Zoar (Gen. 13:10–12; 14:2; Deut. 29:23), one of the "five cities of the plain" (near the south shore of the Dead Sea) destroyed by a great cataclysm attributed to YHWH (Gen. 19:1–29). Abraham, who had been royally welcomed by Sodom's king (Gen. 14:13–24), pleaded for it to be spared (Gen. 18:16–32). Contrary to legend, its sins were regarded as violence and inhospitality to strangers rather than homosexuality. Later biblical writers cite it as a symbol of divine judgment upon wickedness (Isa. 3:9; Lam. 4:6; Matt. 10:15; 2 Pet. 2:6)

Solomon The son of David and Bathsheba and Israel's third king (c. 961–922 B.C.E.) (2 Sam. 12:24–25), who inherited the throne through David's fondness and the intrigues of his mother and the prophet Nathan (1 Kings 1:9–2:25). He became famous for his wisdom (1 Kings 3:5–28); allied himself with Hiram of Tyre (1 Kings 5); built and dedicated YHWH's Temple in Jerusalem (1 Kings 6, 8); built a huge palace for himself (1 Kings 7:1–12); received YHWH's renewal of the Davidic Covenant (1 Kings 9:1–9); was visited by the queen of Sheba (1 Kings 10:1–13); worshiped other gods than YHWH, presumably because of his foreign wives' influence (1 Kings 11:1–40); and died leaving his people financially exhausted and politically discontented (1 Kings 11:41–12:25). An idealized account of his reign is given in 2 Chronicles 1–9.

Son of Man (1) A Hebrew Bible phrase used to denote a human being (Pss. 8:4; 80:17; 144:3; 146:3; Isa. 56:2; Jer. 51:43), including a plural usage (Pss. 31:19; 33:13; Prov. 8:4; Eccles. 3:18–19; 8:11;

9:12). The phrase is characteristic of the Book of Ezekiel, where it is commonly used to indicate the prophet himself (Ezek. 2:1). (2) In Daniel 7:12–14, "one like a son of man" refers to Israel itself or to a divinely appointed future ruler of Israel, although this figure is not given specific messianic significance. (3) In some pseudepigraphal writings, particularly the Similitudes of the Book of Enoch, he who serves as YHWH's agent in the coming Day of Judgment is variously called the "Elect One," the "Anointed One," and the "Son of Man."

Sopherim The name applied to Jewish scribes, from the time of Ezra and after, who copied and transmitted the manuscripts of the Hebrew Bible.

soul In Hebrew, *nephesh* (breath), applied to both humans and animals as living beings (Gen. 1:20; 2:7; 2:19; 9:4; Exod. 1:5; 1 Chron. 5:21). It was translated *psyche* in the Greek Septuagint, the same term used (commonly for "life" rather than the immortal personality) in the New Testament (Matt. 10:28; 16:26; Acts 2:27; 3:23; Phil. 1:27; Rev. 20:4).

source criticism Analysis of a biblical document to discover the sources, written or oral, that the author(s) incorporated into it. Close study of the Pentateuch has led scholars to conclude that at least four main literary units—J, E, D, and P—were blended in its composition.

stele (stela) An upright slab or pillar inscribed with a commemorative message, such as that bearing the Code of Hammurabi (early seventeenth century B.C.E.) or that of King Mesha of Moab (c. 835 B.C.E.), who commemorated his victory over Israel following Jehu's revolution.

Stoicism A Greek philosophy that became popular among the upper classes in Roman times, Stoicism emphasized duty, endurance, self-control, and service to gods, family, and state. Its adherents believed in the soul's immortality, in rewards and punishments after death, and in a divine force (providence) that directs human destiny. Stoic ideas appear in Ecclesiastes, Proverbs, and the Wisdom of Solomon.

Succession Narrative The account of David's rise to kingship and his succession by Solomon that underlies the narrative in 2 Samuel 9–24 and 1 Kings 1–2. *See* Court History.

Succoth A Hebrew Bible term meaning "booths." (1) A town east of the Jordan River in the area allotted to Gad (Josh. 13:27), where Jacob had erected booths (Gen. 33:17). (2) An Egyptian site in the Nile delta given as the first Israelite camp during the Exodus (Exod. 12:37; 13:20).

Sukkoth   *See* Booths, Feast of.

Sumer   The land at the head of the Persian Gulf between the Tigris and Euphrates rivers, site of the oldest high civilization in the ancient Near East, and traditional homeland of Abraham and his ancestors. Its cities include Erech (Uruk), Ur (Gen. 10:10; 11:10–27; 15:7), and Calah (Nimrod). Whereas Sumer occupied southernmost Mesopotamia, Akkad lay to the north (Gen. 10:11–12); the two regions together were later known as Babylonia.

Sumerians   The inhabitants of ancient Sumer, who first emerged as a distinctive people in the late fourth millennium B.C.E.

symbol   From the Greek *symbolon,* a "token" or "sign," and *symballein,* to "throw together" or "compare." In its broadest usage, it means anything that stands for something else, as the Star of David signifies Judaism and the cross represents Christianity. The use of symbols characterizes prophetic and apocalyptic writing. In Daniel, for example, wild beasts symbolize pagan nations; in Ezekiel, YHWH's presence is symbolized by his radiant "glory."

sympathetic magic   A symbolic or manipulative form of behavior based on the belief that it is possible to exert influence over (or even control) someone or something by possessing its name or some representation of that being or object. Something similar to this belief seems to lie behind the narrative in Genesis 32:29, when Jacob asks the mysterious being with whom he has wrestled for his name, only to have that request rejected.

synagogue   In Judaism, a gathering of no fewer than ten adult males assembled for worship, scriptural instruction, and administration of local Jewish affairs. Synagogues probably began forming during the Babylonian exile when the Jerusalem Temple no longer existed. Organization of such religious centers throughout the Diaspora played an important role in the faith's transmission and survival. The synagogue liturgy included lessons from the Torah, the Prophets, the Shema, Psalms, and eighteen prayers.

syncretism   The blending of different religions, a term biblical scholars typically apply to the mingling of Canaanite rites and customs (Baalism) with the Israelites' Mosaic faith. Although a practice repeatedly denounced by the prophets (Judg. 2:13; 3:7; 6:31; 8:33; 1 Kings 16:31; 18:26; 2 Kings 10:18; Jer. 2:8;

7:9; 19:5; 23:13; Hos. 2:8), Judaism borrowed many of its characteristic forms, psalms, concepts, and religious rituals from earlier Canaanite models.

Syria   **(1)** The territory extending from the upper Euphrates River to northern Palestine. **(2)** The kingdom of Aram, with its capital at Damascus (Isa. 7:8). As the creed in Deuteronomy 26:5 states, the Israelites regarded themselves as descended from Arameans (Syrians). Isaiah 7 refers to the Syro-Ephraimite coalition against Assyria.

Tabernacle   The portable tent-shrine, elaborately decorated, that housed the Ark of the Covenant (Exod. 25–31, 35–40; Num. 7–9) from the Exodus to the building of Solomon's Temple (1 Kings 6–8); used in the Hebrew Bible as a symbol of God's presence with humanity (Num. 9:5; Deut. 31:15; Pss. 15:1; 43:3; 61:4; 132:7; Isa. 4:6; 33:20; Hos. 12:9).

Tables (Tablets) of the Law   The stone slabs on which the Ten Commandments were inscribed (Exod. 24:12; 32:15–20).

Tabor   A prominent limestone hill in Galilee (Deut. 33:19; Josh. 19–22; Judg. 4:6; 5:15–21; Ps. 89:12–13; Jer. 46:18).

Talmud   A huge collection of Jewish religious traditions consisting of two parts: **(1)** the Mishnah (written editions of ancient oral interpretations of the Torah), published in Palestine by Judah ha-Nasi (died c. 220 C.E.) and his disciples; **(2)** the Gemara, extensive commentaries on the Mishnah. The Palestinian version of the Talmud, which is incomplete, was produced about 450 C.E.; the Babylonian Talmud, nearly four times as long, was finished about 500 C.E. Both Talmuds contain Mishnah and Gemara.

Tamar   **(1)** The wife of Er, son of Judah (Gen. 38:6), who, when widowed, posed as a prostitute to trick her father-in-law into begetting children (the twins Pharez and Zerah) by her (Gen. 38:6–30). **(2)** Absalom's sister who was raped by her half-brother Amnon, whom Absalom later killed (2 Sam. 13:1–32; 1 Chron. 3:9).

Tammuz   An ancient Near Eastern fertility god, a counterpart to the Semitic-Greek Adonis, at whose mythic death women ritually wept (Jer. 22:18; Amos 8:10; Ezek. 8:14).

Tanak   A comparatively modern name for the Hebrew Bible, an acronym consisting of the consonants that represent the three major divisions of the Bible;

the *T*orah (Law), the *N*evi'im (Prophets), and the *K*ethivim (Writings).

Targum Interpretative translations of the Hebrew Bible into Aramaic, such as that made by Ezra after the Jews' return from the Babylonian exile (Neh. 8:1–18). The practice may have begun in the postexilic synagogues, where Hebrew passages were read aloud and then translated into Aramaic with interpretative comments added.

Tarshish **(1)** A son of Javan (Aegean peoples) (Gen. 10:4; 1 Chron. 1:7). **(2)** A Hebrew Bible term used to designate ships and ports, particularly the Phoenician variety (1 Kings 10:22; 22:48; Jon. 1:3; 2 Chron. 20:36).

tel Flat-topped artifical mounds consisting of the ruins of ancient cities that dot the landscape of Mesopotamia, Syria, and Palestine.

Temple, the **(1)** The imposing structure built by King Solomon (using Phoenician architects and craftsmen) on Mount Zion in Jerusalem to house the Ark of the Covenant in its innermost room (the Holy of Holies) (1 Kings 5:15–9:25). Later recognized as the only authorized center for sacrifice and worship of YHWH, it was destroyed by Nebuchadnezzar's troops in 587 B.C.E. (2 Kings 25:8–17; 2 Chron. 36:18–19). **(2)** The Second Temple, rebuilt by Jews returned from the Babylonian exile under Governor Zerubbabel, was dedicated circa 515 B.C.E. (Ezra 1:1–11; 3:1–13; 4:24–6:22; Hag. 1–2; Zech. 1:1–8:13). **(3)** Herod's splendid Temple that replaced the inferior edifice of Zerubbabel's time, that took nearly a half-century to complete was destroyed by the Romans in 70 C.E.

Ten Commandments (Decalogue) The set of ten religious and moral laws that YHWH inscribed on stone tablets and gave Moses (Exod. 20:1–17; repeated in Deut. 5:6–21). Some scholars believe that a ritual Decalogue is contained in Exodus 34:1–16 and 22:29b–30; 23:12, 15–19 (see also Exod. 31:18–32:16).

Tent of Meeting *See* Tabernacle.

Terah A son of Nahor, father of Abraham, a younger Nahor, and Haran (Gen. 11:26; 1 Chron. 1:26–27), Terah migrated from the Sumerian city of Ur to Haran in northwest Mesopotamia (Gen. 11:27–32).

teraphim Household gods, probably in the form of human figurines, perhaps representing a family's guardian spirit or ancestors and thought to confer good luck on their possessor. When secretly absconding with her husband Jacob, Rachel stole and hid her father's teraphim (Gen. 31:30–35). Even as late as the monarchy, owning such domestic idols was not necessarily viewed as conflicting with YHWH's worship (Judg. 17:4–13; Hos. 3:4), although Samuel likened their use to idolatry (1 Sam. 15:23) and King Josiah outlawed them (2 Kings 23:24). They may have been used in fortune-telling.

testament From the Latin for "covenant," this is the term used for the two main divisions of the Bible — the Old Testament (canonical Hebrew Scriptures) and the New Testament (Christian-Greek Scriptures).

Tetragrammaton The four consonants (YHWH) composing the sacred name *Yahweh*, the God of Israel. Although the name appears nearly 7000 times in the canonical Hebrew Bible, some modern Bible translations continue the Jewish practice of inaccurately rendering it as "the Lord."

Tetrateuch A critical term for the first four books of the Bible. Genesis through Numbers are composed primarily of J, E, and P material, with little discernible contribution from the Deuteronomist (D), who is responsible for Deuteronomy, the fifth book of the Torah.

textual criticism The comparison and analysis of ancient manuscripts to discover copyists' errors and, if possible, to reconstruct the true or original form of the document; also known as *lower criticism*.

theocracy Literally, a "rule by God," typically a society or state in which priests or other religious authorities govern in the name of a deity, such as in ancient Israel. The Vatican and Iran are modern examples.

theodicy From a Greek term combining "god" and "justice," theodicy denotes a rational attempt to understand how an all-good, all-powerful God can permit the existence of Evil and undeserved suffering. Job, Habakkuk, and 2 Esdras contain notable theodicies.

theology The study and interpretation of concepts about God's nature, purpose, attributes, and relationship with humanity; from the Greek *theos* (god) and *logos* (rational discourse).

theomachy Any struggle in the upper world between divine beings. Daniel 10·13, for example, refers to heavenly conflict between the "guardian angel" of Persia and the angel Michael (who serves, among other unnamed angels, as Israel's "champion").

theomancy A type of divination that takes the form of a divine response rendered through oracles. One example of this approach to divine-human communication is to be found in 1 Samuel 30:7, where David asks the priest Abiathar to "inquire" of YHWH whether to pursue the Amalekite warriors who have kidnapped his wives and children. The response to this type of inquiry is normally a yes or a no.

theophany From the Greek, meaning an appearance of a god to a person, as when El wrestled with Jacob (Gen. 32:26–32) and YHWH appeared to Moses (Exod. 3:1–4:17; 6:2–13) and the elders of Israel (Exod. 24:9–11).

Third Isaiah *See* Isaiah.

Thummim *See* Urim and Thummim.

Tiglath-pileser III The emperor of Assyria (745–727 B.C.E.), and the biblical "Pul" (2 Kings 15:19) who captured Damascus in 732 B.C.E. and coerced tribute from kings Menahem of Israel and Ahaz of Judah (2 Kings 16:7–18; 2 Chron. 28:20–25). Ahaz's stripping of the Jerusalem Temple and sponsoring of pagan cults were probably done to placate Assyria's king.

Tigris River According to Genesis 2:14 (where it is called the Hiddekel), the Tigris was the third of four rivers that watered Eden (see Dan. 10:4). Approximately 1146 miles long, it forms the eastern boundary of Mesopotamia (the land between the Tigris and Euphrates). On its banks rose the ancient cities of Nineveh, Asshur, and Calah (Gen. 10:11), centers of the Assyrian Empire.

Tirzah A Canaanite city that Joshua captured (Josh. 12:24), later the home of King Jeroboam (1 Kings 14:17), and the northern kingdom's capital during the reigns of Baasha (c. 900–877 B.C.E.), Elah (877–876 B.C.E.), Zimri (seven days, c. 876 B.C.E.), and Omri (c. 876–869 B.C.E.), who took it by siege and ruled there for six years until he transferred the capital to Samaria (1 Kings 15:33–16:28).

Tishbite A term used to describe the prophet Elijah (1 Kings 17:1; 21:17; 2 Kings 1:3, 8; 9:36). Its origin and meaning are uncertain.

tithe Paying a tenth of one's income in money, crops, or animals to support a government (1 Sam. 8:15–17) or religion (Lev. 27:30–33; Num. 18:24–28; Deut. 12:17–19; 14:22–29; Neh. 10:36–38). In Israel, the High Priests, Levites, and Temple upkeep were supported by required levies. Abraham is reported to have paid Melchizedek tithes (Gen. 14:20).

Titus The son of and successor to Vespasian and emperor of Rome (79–81 C.E.), he directed the siege of Jerusalem, which culminated in the destruction of the city and Herodian Temple in 70 C.E. His carrying of the Temple treasures to Rome is commemorated in the triumphal Arch of Titus that still stands in the Roman Forum.

Tobiah A partly Jewish Ammonite who occupied a storeroom in the rebuilt Temple area after the exile and whom Nehemiah threw out of his lodgings (Neh. 13:6–9), Tobiah allied himself with Sanballat the Samaritan in opposing Nehemiah's reconstruction of Jerusalem's walls (Neh. 2:10; 4:3, 7; 6:1–19).

Torah A Hebrew term usually translated "law," "instruction," or "teaching," it refers primarily to the Pentateuch, the first five books of the Hebrew Bible, and in a general sense to all the canonical writings, which are traditionally regarded as a direct oracle or revelation from YHWH.

tradition (1) Collections of stories and interpretations transmitted orally from generation to generation and embodying the religious history and beliefs of a people or community. Traditions of the patriarchs were eventually included in the J and E sagas and finally incorporated into the first book of the Torah. (2) Oral explanations, interpretations, and applications of the written Torah (1 Chron. 4:22; Neh. 8:1–9), many of which were eventually compiled in the Mishnah.

tradition criticism The analysis of the origin and development of specific biblical themes—such as the Exodus motif in the Hebrew Bible and the eschatology of the kingdom of God in the New Testament—as presented by different biblical writers. In some cases, tradition criticism emphasizes the early and oral stages of development.

transcendence The quality of God expressing the Deity's inherent limitlessness and transcending of all physical and cosmic boundaries.

Transjordan The rugged plateau area east of the Jordan River, a region Joshua assigned to the tribes of Reuben, Gad, and half of Manasseh (Josh. 13) but which they failed to wrest from other Semites living there.

tree of life An ancient Mesopotamian symbol of rejuvenation or immortality (as in the *Epic of Gilgamesh*), the J (Yahwist) author places it in the Garden of Eden, humanity's original home, where its fruit would confer everlasting life on the eater (Gen. 2:9; 3:22–24). YHWH's express motive for expelling the first human couple from Eden was to prevent their rivaling him further by eating from the tree of life (Gen. 3:22–24).

It is often referred to in apocalyptic literature (En. 24:4; 25:4–6; Asmp. M. [Life of Adam and Eve] 19:2; 22:3; 28:2–4; XII P.: Levi 18:11), where it is usually reserved for the righteous to eat after the Day of Judgment (2 Esd. 8:52; cf. Rev. 2:7 and 22:2, 24).

Trumpets, Feast of   The Hebrew month began with a new moon. On the first day of the seventh (sabbatical) month, a festival, assembly, and sacrifice were to be held (Lev. 13:23–25; Num. 29:1–7).

Tubal-cain   According to J, the son of Lamech and Zillah and the ancestor of all metalworkers in bronze and iron (Gen. 4:19–26). He may have been regarded as the eponymous progenitor of the Kenites.

Twelve, Book of the   The twelve books of the Minor Prophets — Hosea to Malachi — originally compiled on a single scroll.

Twelve Tribes of Israel   In ancient Israel, tribes were confederations of clans, which, in turn, were composed of families related by blood, adoption, or long association, all forming a corporate community with a distinct social, religious, or ethnic identity. Traditionally believed to have descended from the twelve sons of Jacob (Israel) (Gen. 49:2–28; a parallel list, Moses' Blessing, mentions only eleven, omitting Simeon; Deut. 33:6–25), the tribes were Reuben, Simeon, Levi, Judah, Issachar, Zebulun (born of Jacob's wife Leah), Joseph (later divided into the tribes of Ephraim and Manasseh) and Benjamin (both born to Jacob's favorite wife, Rachel), Gad and Asher (by the handmaid Zilpah), and Dan and Naphtali (by another concubine, Bilhah).

The apportionment of tribal territories in Palestine is described in Joshua 13–19. Ezekiel foresaw an idealized tribal state in Israel (Ezek. 48). The so-called ten lost tribes were those of the northern kingdom assimilated into the Assyrian Empire after 721 B.C.E. (2 Kings 17).

Tyre   An ancient Phoenician seaport famous for its commerce and wealth, Tyre was originally built on a small offshore island about twenty-five miles south of Sidon. King Solomon made an alliance with its ruler, Hiram, whose architects and craftsmen he used in constructing the Jerusalem Temple (1 Kings 5:15–32; 7:13–51). Its power and luxury were later denounced by the prophets (Isa. 23; Ezek. 26–28; Amos 1:9–10; Zech. 9:3–4). Alexander the Great sacked the city in 332 B.C.E., although it was later rebuilt.

Ugarit   An ancient Canaanite city (Arabic Ras Shamra) in modern Syria where cuneiform archives were found that preserve prebiblical religious texts and myths about El and Baal, some of which anticipate traditions later associated with YHWH.

under the thigh   A euphemistic expression for the grasping of another's male organs during the conclusion of a vow, oath, or covenant (Gen. 24:2, 9; 47:29; see also Judg. 8:30).

Ur   One of the world's oldest cities, in Sumer, Ur was the ancestral homeland (Gen. 11:28–31) from which Abraham and his family migrated to Haran, although some scholars have suggested a northern location for the Abrahamic Ur. Archaeologically, the Sumerian Ur is notable for its well-preserved ziggurat and "royal cemetery," whose tombs have yielded a number of beautifully crafted artworks, furniture, jewelry, and other sophisticated artifacts (mid-third millennium B.C.E.).

Uriah   **(1)** A Hittite practicer of Yahwism and soldier of David whose wife, Bathsheba, the Israelite king seduced and wished to marry. David ordered him exposed in the front lines of battle so that he was inevitably killed, a crime the prophet Nathan denounced to the king's face (2 Sam. 11–12). **(2)** A priest whom King Ahaz of Judah (c. 735–716 B.C.E.) commissioned to remodel the Temple area and construct an altar modeled on that which Ahaz had seen in Assyrian-dominated Damascus (2 Kings 16:10–16). **(3)** A Judean prophet who predicted the Babylonian destruction of Jerusalem, fled to Egypt to escape King Jehoiakim's wrath, but was murdered. His body was returned to Judah, where it was buried in a common grave (Jer. 26:20–23).

Urim and **Thummim**   Undescribed objects (whose names may mean "oracle" and "truth") that were used by Israel's priests in casting lots to determine YHWH's will on a specific matter. They could apparently indicate only yes or no responses (Exod. 28:29–30; Num. 27:21; 1 Sam. 28:6; Ezra 2:63; Neh. 7:65).

Uruk   One of Mesopotamia's oldest cities, it was the capital of Gilgamesh.

Utnapishtim   The Babylonian Noah, the only man (with his wife and servants) to survive the Flood and the only mortal on whom the gods conferred immortality. When his descendant Gilgamesh visits him at his remote paradise home, Utnapishtim describes Enlil's plot to destroy humanity and Ea's role as humankind's savior.

Uz   Job's unidentified homeland, which various scholars have suggested to be Edom, Arabia, or a location east of the Jordan River.

Uzziah (Azariah)   The son of Amaziah, king of Judah (783–742 B.C.E.), and a contemporary of King Jeroboam II of Israel (786–746 B.C.E.) (2 Kings 14:22; 15:1–7; 2 Chron. 26:1–23), Uzziah fortified Jerusalem; defeated the Philistines, Ammonites, and Arabs; and greatly extended Judah's political jurisdiction. Both the Deuteronomist and the Chronicler rate him as "pleasing" YHWH, although the latter attributes the king's leprosy to his usurping priestly functions in the Temple.

Vashti   The empress of Persia (unknown to history) who refused to exhibit herself to the male friends of her husband, Ahasuerus (Xerxes I), and whom Esther replaced as queen (Esther 1:9–2:18).

veil   The elaborately decorated curtain separating the Holy Place from the Most Holy Place in the Tabernacle and Jerusalem Temple (Exod. 26:31–37).

Vespasian   The emperor of Rome (69–79 C.E.) who led Roman legions into Judea during the Jewish Revolt (66–73 C.E.), the siege of Jerusalem passing to his son Titus when Vespasian became emperor.

Vulgate   Jerome's Latin translation of the Bible (late fourth century C.E.), which became the official version of Roman Catholicism.

Wisdom   A personification of the divine attribute of creative intelligence, pictured in the form of a gracious woman (YHWH's daughter) who mediates between God and humanity (Prov. 1:20–33; 8:1–31; 9:1–6; Ecclus. 24; etc.).

wisdom literature   Biblical works dealing primarily with practical and ethical behavior and ultimate religious questions, such as divine justice and the problem of Evil. The books include Proverbs, Job, Ecclesiastes, Ecclesiasticus, and the Wisdom of Solomon. Habakkuk and 2 Esdras also have characteristics of wisdom writing.

Writings   *See* Kethuvim.

Xerxes I   Thought to be the biblical Ahasuerus, emperor of Persia (486–465 B.C.E.) (Esther; Ezra 4:6).

Yahweh   A translation of the sacred name of Israel's god, represented almost 7000 times in the canonical Hebrew Bible by the four consonants of the Tetragrammaton (YHWH). According to Exodus 6:2–4, it was revealed for the first time to Moses at the burning bush; according to J, it was used from the time of Enosh before the Flood (Gen. 4:26). Scholars have offered various interpretations of the origin and meaning of the divine name. According to one accepted theory, it is derived from the Hebrew verb "to be" and means "he is" or "he causes to be," implying that YHWH is the maker of events and shaper of history.

Yahwist (J)   The name scholars give the anonymous writer or compiler who produced the J document, the oldest stratum in the Pentateuch (c. 950–850 B.C.E.).

YHWH   English letters transliterating the four Hebrew consonants (the Tetragrammaton) denoting the sacred personal name of Israel's God, *Yahweh*.

Yom Kippur   *See* Day of Atonement.

Zadok   A priest officiating during the reigns of David and Solomon who supported the latter's claim to the throne and was rewarded by being made chief priest at the Temple (2 Sam. 15:24–29; 17:15; 19:11; 20:25; 1 Kings 1:7–8; 32–39; 45; 2 Kings 35; 1 Chron. 6:4–15, 50–52; 12:28). Ezekiel regarded Zadok's descendants as the only legitimate priests (Ezek. 40:46; 43:19; 44:15; 48:11). After the exile, they apparently enjoyed a monopoly in the Second Temple (1 Chron. 24:2–19; 27:17; 29:22).

Zaphenath-paneah   According to Genesis 41:45, the Egyptian name given Joseph, son of Jacob. It has been variously translated as "says the God: he will live," "revealer of secrets," and "minister of agriculture."

Zarephath   According to 1 Kings 17:8–24, a Phoenician town near Sidon where Elijah befriended a widow during a famine and resuscitated her son.

Zealots   An extremely nationalistic party in first-century-C.E. Judaism dedicated to freeing Judea from foreign domination, by armed revolt if necessary. Their militarism and fanatical patriotism generated several uprisings, culminating in the great rebellion against Rome (66–73 C.E.). According to Flavius Josephus's possibly biased account, their intransigence led to the destruction of Jerusalem and the Temple.

Zebulun   **(1)** The sixth son of Jacob and Leah, full brother of Reuben, Simeon, Levi, Judah, and Issachar (Gen. 30:20; 35:23). **(2)** The tribe of Zebulun, represented in Jacob's blessing (Gen. 49:13) as a seagoing group located near the Phoenician port of Sidon, actually settled in a landlocked farming area of northern Palestine (Josh. 19:10–16), although they were on a main trading route with coastal cities. Except for their failure to expel the Canaanites from their allotted territory and their joining Barak and Deborah against Sisera (Judg. 1:27–30; 4:10–16; 5:18), they are seldom mentioned in the Hebrew Bible.

Zechariah   **(1)** The son of Jehoiada the priest, Zechariah was stoned to death for denouncing Judah's idolatry (late ninth century B.C.E.) (2 Chron. 25:20–22; he is usually identified with Zacharias in Matt. 23:35 and Luke 11:51). **(2)** The son of Jeroboam II and the last king of Jehu's dynasty in Israel, who reigned only six months (c. 746–745 B.C.E.) before he was murdered (2 Kings 10:30). **(3)** The son of Berechiah or the priest Iddo (Zech. 1:1, 8; Ezra 5:1; Neh. 12:16), a Judean prophet whose message is contained in the book of the Minor Prophets bearing his name. A contemporary of Haggai (c. 520–515 B.C.E.), he urged the returned exiles to rebuild YHWH's Temple in Jerusalem. Although Judah was then part of the Persian Empire ruled by Darius, he apparently regarded the Jewish governor, Zerubbabel, a descendant of David, as a potential messianic king (Zech. 4:6–15; 6:9–14). His work is characterized by strange imagery and apocalyptic visions. Chapters 9–14 of the Book of Zechariah are thought to have been appended by a later author.

Zedekiah The last king of Judah (c. 597–587 B.C.E.), Zedekiah reigned as a tribute-paying vassal of Nebuchadnezzar (2 Chron. 36:13; Jer. 29:3–7; Ezek. 17:15–18). A weak ruler, he consulted the prophet Jeremiah (Jer. 21:1–7) but acceded to his advisors' pressures to seek help from Egypt in throwing off Babylon's yoke (Jer. 27:12–22; 37:6–21; 38:7–28). When he rebelled against Babylon, Nebuchadnezzar laid siege to and destroyed Jerusalem (587 B.C.E.). Zedekiah tried to escape but was captured, tried, and condemned to having his sons slain before his eyes and his own eyes put out, after which he was imprisoned in Babylon, where he died (2 Kings 24:17–25:7; 2 Chron. 36:10–21; Jer. 39:6–14; 52:1–27).

Zephaniah **(1)** Son of Maaseiah and second-ranking priest under King Zedekiah who acted as go-between for the king in his consultations with Jeremiah (2 Kings 25:18; Jer. 21:1; 29:25–32; 37:3–4; 52:24–27). After Jerusalem's fall, he was executed by the Babylonians. **(2)** A seventh-century-B.C.E. Judean prophet whose pronouncements of judgment are collected in the book bearing his name (Zeph. 1:1). Virtually nothing is known of his life.

Zerubbabel A son of Shealtiel or Salathiel (Ezra 3:2, 8; Hag. 1:1) or of Pedaiah (1 Chron. 3:19), Zerubbabel (meaning "begotten in Babylon") was a grandson of Jehoiachin, the king of Judah imprisoned in Babylon (1 Chron. 3:17), and therefore a legitimate heir to the Davidic throne. Appointed governor of the restored Jewish community in Jerusalem (Ezra 3; Hag. 1:1, 14), he returned from Babylon with the first group of exiles and, with Joshua, the High Priest, set up an altar to YHWH and made arrangements to rebuild the Temple. Between the time the work began and the Temple's dedication in 515 B.C.E. (Ezra 6), however, Zerubbabel disappeared from history. The prophets Haggai and Zechariah, who had urged the rebuilding, had both regarded him as a potential messianic king (Hag. 2:20–23; Zech. 4:6b–10a; 6:9–15 — the latter passage reworked by later scribes). When these political expectations failed to materialize, hopes were focused on a priestly hierarchy represented by Joshua (Zech. 3:1–4; 6:11–12).

Zeus In Greek mythology, the son of Cronus and Rhea, king of the Olympian gods, and patron of civic order. A personification of storms and other heavenly powers, he ruled by wielding the lightning bolt. The Romans identified him with Jupiter (Jove).

ziggurat A characteristic architectural form of Sumerian and Babylonian temples, the ziggurat was a multileveled tower resembling a stepped or recessed pyramid consisting of succeedingly smaller platforms built one atop the other. At its apex was a chapel dedicated to a major civic god. Broad ceremonial staircases used for liturgical processions led to the ziggurat's summit, to which it was believed the gods invisibly descended. The story of the Tower of Babel in Genesis 11:1–9 is probably based on a misunderstanding of the ziggurat's function.

Zilpah The handmaid of Leah by whom Jacob begot Gad and Asher (Gen. 29:24; 30:9–13, 35:26).

Zimri A chariot captain who murdered King Elah and seized Israel's throne, which he held for only seven days (876 B.C.E.). When Omri, leader of the military, attacked him at Tirzah, Zimri set the palace on fire and perished in the ruins, after which Omri became king (1 Kings 16:8–20).

Zion The name, probably meaning "citadel," for a hill in old Jerusalem, it was originally a Jebusite acropolis that David captured and on which he built his palace and housed the Ark of the Covenant (Judg. 19:11–12; 2 Sam. 5:6–12; 6:12–17; 1 Chron. 11:5–8). David purchased a threshing floor in Zion (2 Sam. 24:18–25) on which Solomon later built the Temple. In time, the term referred either to the hill on which the Temple stood or to the surrounding city of Jerusalem (Pss. 2:6; 9:11; 76:2; 127:3; Isa. 1:26–27;

10:24; 30:19; 64:10; Jer. 31:6; Amos 1:2; Mic. 3:12).

Zipporah   A daughter of Jethro, a Midianite shepherd and priest, Zipporah became Moses' wife (Exod. 2:11–22) and bore him at least two sons, Gershom (Exod. 2:22) and Eliezer (Exod. 18:3–4), saving the latter from YHWH's wrath by circumcising him with a flint stone (Exod. 4:18–26).

Zoar   One of the five "cities of the plain" on the eastern shore of the Dead Sea (Gen. 13:10; 14:2, 8) that Lot reached as Sodom was being destroyed (Gen. 19:20–23). Because it is referred to by the prophets, it may have survived the catastrophe (Isa. 15:5; Jer. 48:34).

Zophar   A Naamathite, one of Job's three companions (Job 2:11; 11:1; 20:1; 42:9).

Zoroastrianism   The official religion of imperial Persia, it was founded in about the sixth century B.C.E. by the east Iranian prophet Zoroaster. According to his followers, the universe is dualistic, composed of parallel worlds of matter and spirit in which legions of good and evil spirits contend. In a final cosmic battle, Ahura Mazda, god of light and righteousness, will totally defeat Ahriman, embodiment of darkness and chaos. Historians believe that many biblical concepts of angelology and demonology, including the character of Satan, ultimately derive from Zoroastrian influence.

Selected Bibliography

This bibliography provides a representative list of important scholarly works on the Hebrew Bible (Old Testament). Many additional references on specific topics and individual biblical books are included in the Recommended Reading at the end of each chapter.

Bible Commentaries, Dictionaries, and Hebrew Bible Introductions

Achtemeier, Paul J., ed. *Harper's Bible Dictionary,* San Francisco: HarperSanFrancisco, 1996. An excellent one-volume dictionary.

Ackroyd, P. R., et al., eds. *The Cambridge Bible Commentary,* Cambridge, England: Cambridge University Press, 1972–1979.

Anderson, Bernard. *Understanding the Old Testament.* 4th ed. Englewood Cliffs, N.J.: Prentice-Hall, 1986. An abridged edition was issued in 1998.

Black, Matthew, and Rowley, H. H., eds. *Peake's Commentary on the Bible,* rev. ed. New York: Nelson, 1962.

Brown, Raymond E.; Fitzmeyer, Joseph A.; and Murphy, Roland E. *The New Jerome Biblical Commentary,* 2nd ed. Englewood Cliffs, N.J.: Prentice-Hall, 1990.

Campbell, Antony F., and O'Brien, M. A. *Sources of the Pentateuch: Texts, Introductions, Annotations.* Minneapolis: Fortress Press, 1993. Prints separate narratives of J, E, and P with interpretive commentary; a major resource.

Dorsey, David A. *The Literary Structure of the Old Testament: A Commentary on Genesis–Malachi.* Grand Rapids, Mich.: Baker Books, 1999. Examines major themes of each biblical book.

Freedman, David Noel., ed, *The Anchor Bible Dictionary,* Vols. 1–6. New York: Doubleday, 1992. An indispensable resource.

———, ed. *Eerdmans Dictionary of the Bible.* Grand Rapids, Mich.: Eerdmans, 2000. A superb one-volume reference.

Gottwald, Norman K. *The Hebrew Bible: A Socio-Literary Introduction.* Philadelphia: Fortress Press, 1985.

Humphreys, W. Lee. *Crisis and Story: Introduction to the Old Testament,* 2nd ed. Mountain View, Calif.: Mayfield, 1990.

Keck, Leander E., ed. *The New Interpreter's Bible.* Nashville, Tenn.: Abingdon Press, 1994. The complete biblical text in twelve volumes with scholarly commentary (Vols. 1, 3, 5–9, and 12 currently available).

Lasor, William S., et al., *Old Testament Survey: The Message, Form, and Background of the Old Testament,* 2nd ed. Grand Rapids, Mich.: Eerdmans, 1996. A meticulously detailed, conservative approach.

Metzger, B. M., and Coogan, M. D., eds. *The Oxford Companion to the Bible.* New York: Oxford University Press, 1993.

Soggin, J. Alberto. *Introduction to the Old Testament,* 3rd ed. Translated by J. Bowden. Louisville: John Knox Press, 1989.

Suggs, M. J.; Sakenfeld, K. D.; and Mueller, J. R., eds. *The Oxford Study Bible.* New York: Oxford University Press, 1992.

Wigoder, Geoffrey, ed. *The Encyclopedia of Judaism.* New York: Macmillan, 1989.

Ancient Texts Relating to the Hebrew Bible (Tanak)

Beyerlin, Walter, ed. *Near Eastern Religious Texts Relating to the Old Testament.* Translated by J. Bowden. Philadelphia: Westminster Press, 1978.

Coogan, Michael David. *Stories from Ancient Canaan.* Philadelphia: Westminster Press, 1978. A paperback collection of Canaanite myths and their biblical parallels.

Cross, Frank M. *Canaanite Myth and Hebrew Epic, Essays in the History of the Religion of Israel.* Cambridge, Mass.: Harvard University Press, 1973.

Dalley, Stephanie. *Myths from Mesopotamia: Creation, the Flood, Gilgarmeds and Others.* New York: Oxford University Press, 1989.

Foster, Benjamin R. *Before the Muses: An Anthology of Akkadian Literature.* 2 vols. Bethesda, Md.: CDL Press, 1993. A valuable collection of Near Eastern texts.

Gardner, John, and Maier, John. *Gilgamesh.* New York: Knopf, 1984. A useful translation with scholarly annotations.

Halls, William W., ed. *The Context of Scripture.* Vol. 1, *Canonical Compositions from the Biblical World.* Leiden: Brill, 1997.

Lichtheim, Miriam. *Ancient Egyptian Literature: A Book of Readings.* 3 vols. Berkeley: University of California Press, 1973–1980.

Maier, John, ed. *Gilgamesh: A Reader.* Wauconda, Ill.: Bolohazy-Carducci, 1997.

Matthews, Victor H., and Benjamin, Don C. *Old Testament Parallels: Documents from the Ancient Near East.* Mahwah, N.J.: Paulist Press, 1991.

Parker, Simon B. *Stories in Scripture and Inscriptions: Comparative Studies on Northwest Semitic Inscriptions and the Hebrew Bible.* New York: Oxford University Press, 1997.

Pritchard, James B. *The Ancient Near East: An Anthology of Texts and Pictures.* Princeton, N.J.: Princeton University Press, 1965. A text that contains excerpts from the following two books:

———, ed. *Ancient Near Eastern Texts Relating to the Old Testament,* 3rd ed. supp. Princeton, N.J.: Princeton University Press, 1969. Translations of relevant Egyptian, Babylonian, Canaanite, and other ancient literatures — the standard work.

———. *The Ancient Near East in Pictures Relating to the Old Testament.* Princeton, NJ: Princton University Press, 1965.

Roth, Martha T. *Law Collections from Mesopotamia and Asia Minor.* Atlanta: Scholars Press, 1997.

Sanders, N. K. *The Epic of Gilgamesh.* Baltimore: Penguin Books, 1972. A readable paraphrase of the *Epic of Gilgamesh* with a scholarly introduction.

———. *Poems of Heaven and Hell from Ancient Mesopotamia.* London and New York: Penguin Books, 1971.

Biblical Archaeology

Aharoni, Yohanan, and Avi-Yonah, Michael. *The Macmillan Bible Atlas,* 3rd ed. New York: Macmillan, 1993. Oriented toward specific biblical texts.

Ahlström, Gösta W. *The History of Ancient Palestine.* Minneapolis: Fortress Press, 1993. A comprehensive study of the archaeological record in Canaan.

Báez-Camargo, Gonzalo. *Archaeological Commentary on the Bible.* Garden City, N.Y.: Doubleday, 1984. A book-by-book study of archaeology's contribution to understanding biblical literature.

Dever, William G. *What Did Biblical Writers Know and When Did They Know it? What Archaeology Can Tell Us about the Reality of Ancient Israel.* Grand Rapids, Mich.: Eerdmans, 2001. A valuable study.

Drinkard, Joel F., Jr., et al., eds. *Benchmarks in Time and Culture: An Introduction to the History and Methodology of Syro-Palestinian Archaeology.* Atlanta: Scholars Press, 1988.

Finkelstein, Israel, and Silberman, Neil A. *The Bible Unearthed: Archaeology's New Vision of Ancient Israel and the Origin of Its Sacred Texts.* New York: The Free Press, 2001. A lucid survey of what archaeology reveals about the history of Israel.

Harris, Roberta L. *The World of the Bible.* London: Thames & Hudson, 1995.

Isserlin, B. S. J. *The Israelites.* London: Thames and Hudson, 1998.

Magnusson, Magnus. *Archaeology of the Bible.* New York: Simon & Schuster, 1977.

Mazzar, Amihai. *Archaeology of the Land of the Bible, 10,000–586.* New York: Doubleday, 1990.

Moscati, Sabatino. *The Face of the Ancient Orient.* Garden City, N.Y.: Doubleday/Anchor Books, 1962.

Negev, Auraham, ed. *The Archaeological Encyclopedia of the Holy Land,* rev. ed. Nelson, 1986.

Pritchard, James B. *The Harper Atlas of the Bible.* New York and San Francisco: Harper & Row, 1987. Includes beautifully illustrated discussions of archaeological sites.

Stern, Ephraim, et al., eds. *The New Encyclopedia of Archaeological Excavations in the Holy Land.* 4 vols. Jerusalem: Israel Exploration Society, 1993.

Wright, George E. *Biblical Archaeology,* rev. ed. Philadelphia: Westminster Press, 1966.

Hebrew Bible History, Theology, and Interpretation

Ackroyd, Peter R. *Exile and Restoration: A Study of Hebrew Thought in the Sixth Century B.C.E.* Philadelphia: Westminster Press, 1968.

Ahlström, Gosta W. *Who Were the Israelites?* Winona Lake, Ind.: Eisenbrauns, 1986.

Albertz, Rainier. *A History of Israelite Religion in the Old Testament Period.* 2 vols. Translated by John Bowden. Louisville, Ky.: Westminster/John Knox Press, 1994. Analyzes the growth of the Hebrew Bible in its sociohistorical context.

Albrektson, Bertil. *History and the Gods.* Lund, Sweden: Gleerup, 1967.

Alt, Albrecht. *Essays on Old Testament History and Religion.* Translated by R. A. Wilson. New York: Doubleday, 1967.

Alter, Robert, and Kermode, Frank, eds. *The Literary Guide to the Bible.* Cambridge, Mass.: Harvard University Press, 1987. Scholarly essays on the critical interpretation of biblical literature.

Anderson, Bernhard W., ed. *Creation in the Old Testament.* Philadelphia: Fortress Press, 1984.

Anderson, G. W., ed. *Tradition and Interpretation.* Oxford, England: Clarendon Press, 1979.

Birch, Bruce, et al. *A Theological Introduction to the Old Testament.* Nashville, Tenn.: Abingdon Press, 1999. Thoughtful essays on evolving ideas in the biblical texts.

Bright, John. *A History of Israel,* 4th ed. Louisville, Ky.: Westminster/John Knox Press, 2000. A standard reference.

Brueggemann, Walter. *Theology of the Old Testament: Testimony, Dispute, Advocacy.* Minneapolis: Fortress Press, 1997. A superb study of the biblical God and his troubled relationship with Israel.

Coogan, Michael D., ed. *The Oxford History of the Biblical World.* New York: Oxford University Press, 1998. Provides up-to-date information on the cultural/historical environment in which the Bible originated.

Coote, Robert B., and Coote, Mary P. *Power, Politics and the Making of the Bible.* Minneapolis: Augsburg/Fortress Press, 1990.

Cross, Frank M. *The Ancient Library of Qumran and Modern Biblical Studies.* Garden City, N.Y.: Doubleday, 1961.

Crüsemann, Frank. *The Torah: Theology and Social History of Old Testament Law.* Minneapolis: Fortress Press, 1996.

Eichrodt, Walther. *Theology of the Old Testament,* Vol. 1. Translated by J. A. Baker. Philadelphia: Westminster Press, 1961.

———. *Theology of the Old Testament,* Vol. 2. Translated by J. A. Baker. Philadelphia: Westminster Press, 1967.

Eliade, Mircea. *Cosmos and History: The Myth of the Eternal Return.* New York: HarperTorch, 1954.

———. *The Sacred and the Profane: The Nature of Religion.* New York: HarperTorch, 1961.

Ellis, Peter. *The Yahwist: The Bible's First Theologian.* Notre Dame, Ind.: Fides, 1968.

Fohrer, Georg. *History of Israelite Religion.* Translated by D. Green. Nashville, Tenn.: Abingdon Press, 1972. Traces the development of Israel's characteristic religious concepts and traditions.

Friedman, Richard E. *Commentary on the Torah with a New English Translation.* San Francisco: HarperSanFrancisco, 2001.

———. *The Hidden Book in the Bible.* San Francisco: HarperSanFrancisco, 1998.

———. *Who Wrote the Bible?* San Francisco: Harper & Row, 1987. A superb analysis of theories about biblical authorship, including the suggestion that J (the Yahwist) was a woman.

Gabel, John B. *The Bible as Literature: An Introduction,* 3rd ed. New York: Oxford University Press, 1996.

Gaster, Theodor H. *The Dead Sea Scriptures in English Translation,* Garden City, N.Y.: Doubleday, 1976.

———. *Myth, Legend, and Custom in the Old Testament.* New York: Harper & Row, 1969.

———. *Thespis: Ritual, Myth, and Drama in the Ancient Near East.* New York: Abelard-Schuman, 1950.

Gordon, Cyrus H., and Rendsburg, G. A. *The Bible and the Ancient Near East,* 4th ed. New York: W. W. Norton & Co., 1998.

Gottwald, Norman K. *The Tribes of Yahweh: A Sociology of the Religion of Liberated Israel, 1250–1050 B.C.E.* Maryknoll, N.Y.: Orbis Books, 1979.

Gray, John. *Near Eastern Mythology.* New York: Peter Bedrick Books, 1982.

Halpern, Baruch. *The First Historians: The Hebrew Bible and History.* San Francisco: Harper & Row, 1988.

Hillers, Delbert R. *Covenant: The History of a Biblical Idea.* Baltimore: Johns Hopkins University Press, 1969.

Klein, Ralph W. *Textual Criticism of the Old Testament: The Septuagint After Qumran.* Philadelphia: Fortress Press, 1974.

Koch, Klaus. *The Growth of the Biblical Tradition: The Form-Critical Method.* Translated by S. M. Cupitt. New York: Scribner, 1969.

———. *The Prophets.* Vol. 1, *The Assyrian Age.* Translated by M. Kohl. Philadelphia: Fortress Press, 1982.

Kugel, James L. *The Bible As It Was.* Cambridge, Mass.: The Belknap Press of Harvard University Press, 1997. Examines the earliest extant interpretations of the biblical narratives.

Levenson, Jon D. *Creation and the Persistence of Evil.* San Francisco: Harper & Row, 1988.

————. *Sinai and Zion: An Entry into the Jewish Bible.* San Francisco: HarperSanFrancisco, 1985. A concise but incisive analysis of the sometimes conflicting covenants associated with Moses and David.

Mays, James L., ed. *Harper's Bible Commentary.* San Francisco: Harper & Row, 1988. Provides clear, scholarly discussions of each book in the Hebrew Bible and New Testament Aprocrypha.

McCurley, Foster R. *Ancient Myths and Biblical Faith: Scriptural Transformations.* Philadelphia: Fortress Press, 1983.

McKenzie, John L. *A Theology of the Old Testament.* Garden City, N.Y.: Doubleday, 1974.

Mendenhall, George. "Biblical History in Transition." In G. E. Wright, ed., *The Bible and the Ancient Near East.* New York: Doubleday/Anchor Books, 1965.

————. *Law and Covenant in Israel and the Ancient Near East.* Pittsburgh: Biblical Colloquium, 1955.

————. *The Tenth Generation: The Origins of the Biblical Tradition.* Baltimore: Johns Hopkins University Press, 1973.

Miller, Patrick D. *The Religion of Ancient Israel.* Louisville, Ky.: Westminster/John Knox Press, 2000. An important study of the biblical concept of God.

Niditch, Susan. *Ancient Israelite Religion.* New York: Oxford University Press, 1997. A helpful introductory survey.

Noth, Martin. *The History of Israel.* New York: Harper & Row, 1960.

————. *A History of Pentateuchal Traditions.* Englewood Cliffs, N.J.: Prentice-Hall, 1972.

Redford, Donald B. *Egypt, Canaan, and Israel in Ancient Times.* Princeton, N.J.: Princeton University Press, 1992.

Robertson, David. *The Old Testament and the Literary Critic.* Guides to Biblical Scholarship. Philadelphia: Fortress Press, 1977.

Sanders, James A. *Torah and Canon.* Philadelphia: Fortress Press, 1972. A concise and helpful introduction to canonical information.

Shanks, Hershel, ed. *Ancient Israel: A Short History from Abraham to the Roman Destruction of the Temple,* rev. ed. Washington, D.C.: Biblical Archives Society, 1999.

————, ed. *Understanding the Dead Sea Scrolls.* New York: Random House, 1992.

Smith, Morton, and Hoffman, R. Joseph, eds. *What the Bible Really Says.* Buffalo: Prometheus Books, 1989. A collection of essays on key biblical topics, for the nonspecialist.

Soulen, Richard N. *Handbook of Biblical Criticism.* Atlanta: John Knox Press, 1976.

Tucker, Gene M. *Form Criticism of the Old Testament.* Guides to Biblical Scholarship. Philadelphia: Fortress Press, 1971.

von Rad, Gerhard. *God at Work in Israel.* Translated by J. Marks. Nashville, Tenn.: Abingdon Press, 1980.

————. *Old Testament Theology.* Vol. 1, *The Theology of Israel's Historical Traditions.* Translated by M. G. Stalker. New York: Harper & Row, 1962.

————. *Old Testament Theology.* Vol. 2, *The Theology of Israel's Prophetic Traditions.* Translated by M. G. Stalker. New York: Harper & Row, 1965.

Westermann, Claus, ed. *Essays on Old Testament Hermeneutics.* Translated and edited by J. L. Mays. Richmond, Va.: John Knox Press, 1963.

————. *The Promises to the Fathers: Studies on the Patriarchal Narratives.* Translated by D. E. Green. Philadelphia: Fortress Press, 1980.

Wolff, Hans W. *Anthropology of the Old Testament.* Translated by M. Kohl. Philadelphia: Fortress Press, 1981.

————. *Confrontations with Prophets.* Philadelphia: Fortress Press, 1983.

Wright, G. Ernest. *The Old Testament and Theology.* New York: Harper & Row, 1969.

Zimmerli, Walther. *Man and His Hope in the Old Testament: Studies in Biblical Theology,* 2nd series. Naperville, Ill.: Allenson, 1968.

————. *Old Testament Theology in Outline.* Translated by D. E. Green. Atlanta: John Knox Press, 1978.

Old Testament Apocrypha, Pseudepigrapha, and Apocalyptic Writings

Becker, Joachim. *Messianic Expectation in the Old Testament.* Translated by D. E. Green. Philadelphia: Fortress Press, 1980.

Charles, R. H., ed. *The Apocrypha and Pseudepigrapha of the Old Testament in English,* Vols. 1 and 2. New York: Oxford University Press, 1963 (1913).

Charlesworth, J. H., ed. *The Old Testament Pseudepigrapha.* Vol. 1, *Apocalyptic Literature and Testaments.* Garden City, N.Y.: Doubleday/Anchor Books, 1983.

————, ed. *The Old Testament Pseudepigrapha.* Vol. 2, *Expansions of the "Old Testament" and Philosophical Literature, Prayers, Psalms, and Odes, Fragments of Lost Judeo-Hellenistic Works.* Garden City, N.Y.: Doubleday/Anchor Books, 1985.

Cohen, Shaye J. D. *From the Maccabees to the Mishnah.* Philadelphia: Westminster Press, 1987.

Collins, John C. *The Apocalyptic Imagination: An Introduction to Jewish Apocalyptic Literature.* Grand Rapids, Mich.: Eerdmans, 1998. An important study of this biblical eschatology.

————, ed. *The Encyclopedia of Apocalypticism.* Vol. 1, *The Origins of Apocalypticism in Judaism and Christianity.*

New York: Continuum, 2000. A collection of scholarly essays analyzing the ancient Near Eastern roots and later growth of Jewish eschatology.

Hanson, Paul D. *The Dawn of Apocalyptic: The Historical and Sociological Roots of Jewish Eschatology.* Philadelphia: Fortress Press, 1979.

Mowinckel, Sigmund. *He That Cometh.* Translated by G. W. Anderson. Nashville, Tenn.: Abingdon Press, 1956.

Nickelsburg, George W. E. *Jewish Literature Between the Bible and the Mishnah: A Historical and Literary Introduction.* Philadelphia: Fortress Press, 1981.

Ringgren, Helmer. *The Messiah in the Old Testament: Studies in Biblical Theology,* no. 18. Chicago: Allenson, 1956.

Rost, Leonard. *Judaism Outside the Hebrew Canon: An Introduction to the Documents.* Nashville, Tenn.: Abingdon Press, 1976.

Russell, D. S. *Apocalyptic: Ancient and Modern.* Philadelphia: Fortress Press, 1978.

———. *The Method and Message of Jewish Apocalyptic: 200 B.C.–A.D. 100.* Philadelphia: Westminster Press, 1964. A useful review of apocalyptic literature of the Greco-Roman period.

Credits

Chapter 2 2.1, © Hirmer Fotoarchiv; 2.2, Courtesy of the British Library, no. 43725 ƒ 260; 2.3, © British Museum; 2.4, © Jewish Museum, London; 2.5, © The Pierpont Morgan Library/Art Resource, NY Chapter 3 3.2, © The British Museum; 3.3, Courtesy of the University Museum, University of Pennsylvania, Neg. #S8-139343; 3.4, Courtesy of the Ashmolean Museum, Oxford; 3.5, Courtesy of the University Museum, University of Pennsylvania, Neg. #S5-23215; 3.6, © The British Museum; 3.7, © Réunion des Musées Nationaux/Art Resource, NY; 3.8, © Réunion des Musées Nationaux/Art Resource, NY; 3.9, © Réunion des Musées Nationaux/Art Resource, NY; 3.10, © Alinari/Art Resource, NY; 3.11, © Egyptian Museum/PhotoEdit; 3.13, Courtesy of NASA Chapter 4 4.1, © Erich Lessing/Art Resource, NY; 4.2, Courtesy Nicolas Wyatt/Edinburgh Ras Shamra Project/University of Edinburgh; 4.3, © R.Sheridan/ Ancient Art & Architecture Collection Ltd.; 4.4, © Ze'ev Meschel Chapter 7 7.2, Courtesy of the University Museum, University of Pennsylvania, Neg. #S4-142836 Chapter 8 8.1, Courtesy of the Asian and Middle Eastern Division, The New York Public Library, Astor, Lenox and Tilden Foundations; 8.2, © Erich Lessing/Art Resource, NY; 8.4, © Alan Oddie/PhotoEdit; 8.5, © Réunion des Musées Nationaux/Art Resource, NY Chapter 9 9.1, © Erich Lessing/Art Resource, NY Chapter 11 11.1, © The Israel Museum, Jerusalem; 11.2, © The British Museum Chapter 12 12.2, © PhotoEdit; 12.3, © Erich Less-

ing/Art Resource, NY Chapter 13 13.1, © Zev Radovan/PhotoEdit Chapter 15 15.4, © The British Museum; 15.5, © The British Museum; 15.6, © Réunion des Musées Nationaux/Art Resource, NY Chapter 18 18.2, © Oriental Institute Museum, University of Chicago; 18.3, © The British Museum Chapter 19 19.2, © Oriental Institute Museum, University of Chicago Chapter 20 20.1, © The British Museum; 20.2, © The British Museum; 20.3, Courtesy of Vorderasiatisches Museum, Berlin Chapter 23 23.2, Courtesy of Vorderasiatisches Museum, Berlin Chapter 25 25.1, © The British Museum; 25.2, Courtesy of the University Museum, University of Pennsylvania, Neg. #S8-68052b; 25.3, Courtesy of the Bible Lands Museum Jerusalem. Photo Credit: Dietrich Widmer Chapter 26 26.1, © Oriental Institute Museum, University of Chicago; 26.2, © Erich Lessing/Art Resource, NY Chapter 27 27.1, Courtesy of the Israel Antiquities Authority Chapter 28 28.3, © Alinari/Art Resource, NY; 28.4, © Foto Marburg/Art Resource, NY; 28.5, © Hirmer Fotoarchiv Chapter 29 29.1, © Alinari/Art Resource, NY; 29.2, © Israel Museum/PhotoEdit ; 29.4, © Erich Lessing/Art Resource, NY Chapter 30 30.1, © Richard T. Nowitz; 30.2, © Jacques Benbassat/eStock Photo, Inc. Chapter 31 31.2, © British Museum; 31.2, © The British Museum; 31.3, © Israel Museum, Jerusalem; 31.4, © Erich Lessing/PhotoEdit; 31.5, © Alinari/Art Resource, NY; 31.6, © British Museum; 31.7, © Zev Radovan, Jerusalem

Index